PERMANENT REVOLUTION IN LATIN AMERICA

John Peter Roberts &
Jorge Martín

Wellred Books
London

Permanent Revolution in Latin America
John Peter Roberts and Jorge Martin

First Edition
Wellred Books, October 2018

UK distribution: Wellred Books, wellredbooks.net
PO Box 50525
London
E14 6WG
books@wellredbooks.net

USA distribution: Marxist Books, marxistbooks.com
WR Books
250 44th Street #208
Brooklyn
New York
NY 11232
wrbooks17@gmail.com

DK distribution: Forlaget Marx, forlagetmarx.dk
Degnestavnen 19, st. tv.
2400 København NV
forlag@forlagetmarx.dk

Cover design by Daniel Morley

Layout by Jack Halinski-Fitzpatrick

Printed by Lightning Source, London, England

ISBN: 978 1 900 007 94 8

Louis de Saint-Just, the youngest deputy to the French revolutionary National Convention of 1792 said before he was guillotined by the counter-revolution: "*Those who make half a revolution dig their own graves*". The tragedy of the Bolivarian and Nicaraguan revolutions is that they were never completed. Now the popular masses are paying the price.

Acknowledgements
Thanks to Marie Frederiksen and Carlos Márquez,
comrades who have generously given their time
to contribute comments and suggestions.
Also a big thank you to my wife, Diane, for stimulating
discussions on the concepts and ideas contained in
this book, and undertaking the enormous task of
proofreading and correcting the manuscript – JR.

CONTENTS

INTRODUCTION

Most of today's major states originated in a revolution, the USA doubly so; first the Revolutionary War of Independence, 1775-83, and then the second American Revolution of 1861-65, which crushed the economic and political power of the slave oligarchy and secured the dictatorship of the bourgeoisie. Revolutions have been, and will continue to be facts of life because the structural contradictions that prevail both politically and economically due to the class nature of societies, do not simply fade away. The ruling classes resist the elimination of their privileges to the very end, with all the oppressive means at their disposal. Revolutions are the birth pains whereby the overthrow of the old relations is realised and a new, more democratic, less despotic, society emerges.

The world has entered a new global crisis of imperialism, similar in many ways to the impasse seen at the beginning of the twentieth century. The prospect is one of wars, revolutions and counter-revolutions; especially so with the relative weakening of the power base of US imperialism as shown by its inability to impose its chosen solution on the Middle East where it had long been the dominant force. The US is increasingly fragile both socially and economically, and while the raising of tariff barriers might bring a temporary lull, such actions can only make things worse in the longer run. Simultaneously, the numerical strength of the working class on a world scale has never been greater, and combined with the growing, and increasingly obvious abyss between a tiny and obscenely wealthy minority, and the impoverished, exploited masses, points to heightened class struggles.

Oppressed people feel weak before their oppressors despite their numerical superiority, because they are on their knees. Revolutions occur when that feeling of weakness and helplessness is overcome, when the mass of the people suddenly thinks "we won't take it any more", and acts accordingly.

A revolution is the combination of the sudden massive active intervention of huge numbers of ordinary people into political life and the overthrow of the ruling class. When the majority of the people refuse to be intimidated any longer; when they refuse to stay on their knees; when they recognise the fundamental weakness of their oppressors, they can become transformed overnight from seemingly subdued and helpless into performing exceptional acts of heroism, self-sacrifice, and endurance.

It is in just such situations that reformists of all hues attempt to restrain the revolutionary energies of the masses by taking political control and directing the insurrection into channels safe for the exploiters. In countries dominated by imperialism they do this by maintaining that the best way to achieve democracy and improve living conditions is to support the development of a national, bourgeois democracy. This capitalist path of development is particularly favoured by academics as the means of eliminating the repressive states that exist in Latin America. And this argument is often supported by the liberal wing of imperialism which appreciates that while such a perspective can lead to some reforms (usually temporary), it poses no serious, long-term threat to imperialist interests.

This line of argument is also championed by national Communist Parties which assert the opportunist argument that the priority in underdeveloped countries such as Cuba, Nicaragua and Venezuela is the bourgeois-democratic revolution, and this has priority over the struggle for socialism. This argument has its roots in the Stalinist degeneration of the Russian Revolution, when the 'theory of stages', together with 'socialism in one country', and 'peaceful co-existence', was developed not in response to the situations in the countries concerned, but to preserve the power and privileges of the Russian bureaucracy. Stalinist discipline was imposed on the international communist movement, and the national Communist Parties became little more than transmission belts for the international policies of the Russian bureaucracy. When applied to colonial and under-developed countries, this class-collaborationist perspective became the 'theory of stages', according to which the task of the Communist Parties is to enable the national bourgeoisie to take power in a revolution against imperialism. Since then, Communist Parties have consistently sought to identify an anti-imperialist wing within the national bourgeoisie with which to unite against the imperialists.

During World War II, this meant the national Communist Parties openly supported bourgeois dictators such as Batista in Cuba, and Somoza in Nicaragua, because they were formally fighting fascism. This was not the case, however, with the most able Communists who began their analyses of Latin American societies before the Stalinist degeneration. We show that the founders of the Communist movement in Latin America, revolutionary leaders such as Julio Mella in Cuba, and José Mariátegui in Peru, developed their own theories, and now that their writings are available it is clear they argued for a strategy that was strikingly close to that of Trotsky's theory of permanent revolution.

Theoretical distortions of Marxism were integral to the Stalinist degeneration, in particular, Marxism was perverted into economic determinism whereby human history became a rigid series: slavery, feudalism, capitalism and socialism, in that order, were the stages through which all societies passed. The feudal nature of Spanish colonialism, left important cultural legacies and Stalinist historians sought to justify a political liaison with the national bourgeoisie, by falsely claiming that the feudal nature of the *latifundia* persisted into the late twentieth century.

The history of Latin America gives a certain form to the class struggle. The great liberators, such as Simón Bolívar, correctly understood that Central and South America could tear themselves out of enslavement and backwardness only by uniting all their states into one powerful federation. This is an important reason why as American replaced Spanish imperialism, it imposed on Central America a patchwork of small states, each with a belated and already decaying capitalism, kept in power either by direct US military intervention or comprador strong men who imposed military dictatorships. The American bourgeoisie, during its historic rise, united the northern half of the American continent into a single country, but now uses its power to weaken and enslave the southern half. We show that the belated South American bourgeoisie, are thoroughly corrupt agents of a foreign power, and are quite unable to lead a struggle to achieve national independence. We show that the popular masses, led by a young proletariat, are capable and willing to carry through the national democratic revolution, against the bloody violence of the native compradors and world imperialism. We also show that the gains made in such a revolution can be safeguarded only by taking the first steps towards a socialist state. The natural slogan will be: the *Soviet United States of Central and South America*.

In practice, the theory of stages means handing economic authority to the capitalists. In Nicaragua and Venezuela this was most clearly seen in the refusal to implement a thorough land reform programme to end the *latifundia*. We argue that the theory of stages has proved a fatal trap for bourgeois democratic, anti-imperialist revolutions in the 'third world' and this book describes and analyses three cases in which this theory has been tested in practice: Cuba, Nicaragua, and Venezuela. These were chosen because, despite significant common features, the revolutions in the three countries have unfolded in quite different ways. We show how, in all three countries, the national bourgeois, when faced with a make-or-break choice, sided with imperialism against the democratic revolution.

In Cuba, the revolution has been to the benefit of the great majority of the population because it went all the way to abolish capitalism. In Nicaragua and Venezuela, the revolutionary masses initially made substantial gains but, gradually, those gains were subverted and now the great majority of the population are no better, and possibly worse off than before the revolutions. We explain the qualitative difference between the Cuban, and the Nicaraguan and Venezuelan revolutions in terms of the theory of permanent revolution, and the categorical failure of the reformist theory of stages. We show that, in the epoch of imperialism, to achieve the demands of the bourgeois democratic revolution: national independence, return of land seized by the *latifundios* to the peasants, a democratic state, greater social equality, and an end to the oppression of women, black people and national minorities, the revolution must take the first steps towards socialism. We demonstrate that the alternative theory, that claims these progressive, but still, bourgeois democratic measures will be achieved by developing a national capitalism, is a sure-fire way of ensuring the continued dominance of imperialism.

The theory of stages is prettified by being presented in terms of the coming together of the widest possible popular alliance against imperialism and its agents. The nation's bourgeoisie, urban petty-bourgeoisie, proletariat and peasantry will unite in a common struggle against a common foe. 'People's power' will seize only the enterprises and businesses of the imperialists, the compradors and the supposedly feudal landed estates. However, as Augusto Sandino found by his own experience as a fighter for national liberation, the national bourgeoisie of Latin America is too servile, too weak, too tied to imperialism to carry through such a struggle; "only the workers and peasants will take the struggle through to its ultimate conclusion". For Sandino (and later the Stalinists) this meant the popular masses would fight, guns in hands for the national bourgeois revolution, and then having won political power, would allow the bourgeoisie to retain economic power.

The Workers' and Peasants' Government formed as a result of the revolutionary upsurge would change social relationships in favour of working people. It would carry out important reforms for the benefit of the masses; education and health provision, improved working and living conditions, the growth of democracy, taking measures for a more equal distribution of wealth, etc. The stagist theory argues that, in a relatively economically backward country such as, say, Nicaragua, it will be the bourgeoisie jointly with the new government that will develop the productive forces, building an effective infrastructure for communications, electrical supply, transportation, water supply and sewage systems, etc. The socialist transition to a state-planned economy will take many years, possibly decades. The reformists invariably obfuscate that, during this period, the state is capitalist, using formulas such as 'broad popular alliance' or 'people's power' to disguise the fact that, in practice, economic power remains in the hands of the bourgeoisie.

The stagist perspective means that the government resulting from the revolutionary uprising voluntarily accepts to be constrained within the laws of capitalism, usually under the misnomer 'mixed economy'. The revolutionary democratic government would guarantee the property rights of the capitalists, subject to certain conditions, for instance, their refraining from economic sabotage. The new government would need the knowledge, expertise and skills of the middle and professional classes who would retain their managerial positions and be suitably rewarded.

We will show that there are fundamental problems that fatally undermine this schema. At a methodological level, the theory of stages fails to recognise that the roles of the relevant social classes are very different during the rise of capitalism and in the epoch of its decline. In the former, the bourgeoisie overthrew a decadent feudal system and was immensely progressive but, it must be remembered, only in Western Europe and the US. The American Civil War was the last great radical act of international capitalism; with it, the progressive role of the bourgeoisie came to an end. As capitalism extended across the world, it made use of all kinds of pre-capitalist relations in the underdeveloped countries, adapting them to its needs and, in doing so, stunting the growth of the national bourgeoisie.

Marxist analysis, confirmed by the examples described in this book, has shown the roles of the national bourgeoisie during the decline and decay of imperialism is very different from that in its progressive stages. The growth of imperialism and consequent dependence of both big and small native bourgeoisie in underdeveloped countries on it, meant they had neither the capacity nor the will to provide a lead for the masses to carry through a thorough-going democratic transformation of the existing regime. Capitalism in its imperialist phase was a world-wide system that largely eliminated pre-capitalist relations of production, and in doing so bound the emerging national bourgeoisie to it. Now, in the period of capitalism's decline the bourgeoisie desperately clings to power and is thoroughly reactionary, conservative, anti-democratic, and counter-revolutionary.

In order to justify the theory of stages the Stalinists searched for pre-capitalist formations against which they could unite with the national bourgeois. i.e., the great *latifundia*, which began as feudal estates, continued to be classified as such by the Stalinists even in the late 1970s when, in their majority, they had developed into capitalist agribusinesses and were fully integrated with the national bourgeoisie and imperialism. The national bourgeoisie may be variegated but it has common interests that far outweigh any sectional differences. Real life has shown that, in its great majority, the national bourgeoisie will, after the revolution, choose to side with imperialism against the popular masses. We show that the ties between the national bourgeoisie and the imperialists are far stronger than any ties between any significant section of the national bourgeoisie and the revolutionary masses.

The examples from Latin America presented here show that, in the twenty-first century, the national bourgeoisie is hostile to a bourgeois-democratic revolution; it is outraged at losing political power, it sees a more equal distribution of wealth as bare-faced robbery, price controls are an intolerable burden to be circumvented, campaigns to end injustice against women and black people are seen as unnatural, and education and healthcare are wastes of money. Egged on, and supported by US imperialism, it does not reconcile to the new regime but plots and plans to take back political power by any means necessary.

Because the stagist theory has as its goal the development of a strong national capitalism, the national bourgeoisie is able to hold the revolutionary-democratic government hostage and, as we show, unless its power is broken, it is only a matter of time before it re-asserts its political dominance, regains state power and re-establishes the control of the imperialist interests that the revolution was meant to break. While revolutionaries remain bound to the stagist theory, the bourgeoisie can and will run rings round them. For example, in both Nicaragua and Venezuela, the bourgeoisie was allowed to retain control of food processing and distribution, and was able to undermine the revolution by economic sabotage, creating artificial shortages of food, medicines and other necessities, deliberately stoking inflation, in a well-orchestrated campaign to wear down the masses and subvert the revolution. In all this they were actively supported by US imperialism.

Popular masses seeking to take control of their lives are a great attractor and a dangerous example. The US will confront and seek to overthrow any popular government that attempts to qualitatively better the living conditions of its people, because such moves are seen as a direct threat to US interests. In all three examples given here the US used military intervention, then trade and financial embargoes to economically paralyse the new regime. In Cuba the national bourgeoisie fled to America, and then with US support attempted a military invasion. In Nicaragua, the national bourgeoisie and US imperialism carried on a war of attrition against the government and the masses. In Venezuela, the national bourgeoisie launched a military coup. After the failure of the military adventures, the US Administration organised and supported prolonged wars of economic sabotage to depress the living standards of the masses and destabilise the regime.

Despite determined attempts by reformists to obfuscate the issue, what revolutions are all about is the class nature of state power. Either the overthrow of the bourgeois-oligarchic state, its army and its repressive apparatus, and the establishment of a workers' state with one foot in socialism, or the historical tasks of the national democratic revolution will not be completed.

This does not mean that no democratic goals can be achieved under bourgeois or petty-bourgeois governments. In Mexico, for example, a process of semi-industrialisation was accompanied by a degree of land reform greater than that carried out in Nicaragua or Venezuela, and was indispensable for mobilising mass support for the government. However, the dominance of US imperialism remains, and is seen in particularly stark terms with the descent of Mexico's northern states into war zones in obedience to US demands for a 'War on Drugs'. Under the unique conditions existing after World War II (1939-1945); world imperialism both as a whole and in its constituent parts was greatly weakened, the victory of the Chinese Revolution and the creation of workers' states in Eastern Europe, the upsurge in revolutionary struggles across the colonial world, and the refusal of the conscript armies to continue fighting, meant it was temporarily incapable of imposing its will. Under these conditions, many previously colonial countries did achieve political and national independence without overthrowing the capitalist order. In some cases at least, India being the most striking, this was not purely formal but also included a degree of economic autonomy from imperialism, which made an initial industrialisation under national bourgeois ownership possible. However, the ongoing oppression of, in particular, women, the peasantry, and minority religions demonstrates that the revolution is far from completed. The unique conditions are now long gone, and we have returned to the situation where imperialism will intervene directly to stop any national democratic revolution.

The theory of the permanent revolution does require the overthrow of the old state order and a radical agrarian revolution to achieve genuine independence from imperialism. But it does not call for the immediate and complete destruction of all capitalist private property relations. The crucial issue is whether the workers hold governmental and state power. Each country will make its own decisions. Genuine differences will arise when determining the border between expropriation and tolerance of medium-sized capitalists, with all consequential implications for economic growth, social equality and motivation of producers. The issue is whether the capitalist enterprises are allowed to retain so much economic power that they can subvert the policies and programme of the new regime.

Theory predicted, and experience has confirmed, that it is impossible to achieve genuine independence from imperialism and motivate the working class for the tasks of socialist reconstruction of the nation without expropriating big capital (international and national) in agriculture, banking, industrial production, wholesale trade, and transportation.

Events in Cuba, Nicaragua, and Venezuela, have confirmed these perspectives. Where there was a full break with the old ruling classes and with international capitalism, the historical tasks of the national-democratic revolution were realised. Where the revolution became locked into the stagist perspective, imperialism has re-asserted its dominance.

Of the three revolutions considered in this book, only the Cuban can be considered to have been part of a plan of action; guerrilla warfare preparing the ground for an urban insurrection and a successful general strike. In Nicaragua, a spontaneous general strike and urban insurrection played the decisive role. In Venezuela, it was the spontaneous response of the urban masses from the *barrios*, taking over the streets to defeat an attempted coup by the army. It is this entry of the broadest masses into political action that is the outstanding characteristic of revolutions.

But it cannot be supposed that the masses are conscious of the unfolding historical process of which they are so important a part. Long-term victory depends above all on the presence of a leadership that incorporates a practical knowledge and theoretical understanding of capitalist society. That leadership must consciously understand the tasks in hand, the need to weld together the oppressed classes and social movements into a force to overthrow the opposing classes which stand in the way of the Workers' and Peasants' Government transition to a socialist state (Nicaragua and Venezuela) or, in the case of Cuba, the need to introduce the necessary soviet democracy to protect the gains of the socialist revolution.

The absence of such leaderships in the cases of Cuba, Nicaragua, and Venezuela is characteristic of the epoch in which we live; correctly categorised as one of a "crisis of leadership". Obviously, this matter has a personal dimension, and comparison of Fidel Castro, Celia Sánchez and Che Guevara in Cuba with Humberto and Daniel Ortega in Nicaragua is living proof of this. But we will argue that, possibly more important, in all three cases what was missing and is desperately needed, is a collective leadership, a party able to correctly apply the theory of the permanent revolution in order to guide the revolutionary masses. The programme and constitution of the party are not determined by the immediate consciousness of the working class but on the basis of Marxist theory and international experience.

So long as the working class is not mobilised by such a party, its actions can rise to revolutionary peaks but its consciousness will remain determined by bourgeois culture. Without Marxist theory and a Marxist party the struggles of the masses will only temporarily and partially challenge bourgeois domination, and will tend to fall back and suffer defeats. Deep crises can arouse tremendous forces, and the task of the party is to maximise these forces and direct them, ensuring they are not dissipated.

Certainly, no workers' party will be successful if it is not responsive to changes in the moods of the working class. That response is a matter of tactics, of timing, of the form of propaganda, etc., and corresponds to the immediate consciousness of the masses. Of course, the party must have the correct action slogans, and Trotsky's *Transitional Programme* (subtitled: the mobilisation of the masses around transitional demands to prepare the conquest of power) provides a method by which these can be determined.

In each of Cuba, Nicaragua, and Venezuela the governmental parties originated in guerrilla and military organisations with top-down command, and subsequent links with the national Communist Parties strengthened the bureaucratic nature of the structures. In each case we show that these parties have little in common with a revolutionary party characterised by democracy and centralism; a combination which is not in the least contradictory. The revolutionary party is strictly defined in terms of who is a member, and party members have the right to define party policy. Once agreed, all members are then expected to carry out the decisions made. To obtain an objective assessment of the outcomes, to ensure party policy is best matched to objective conditions, internal democracy is essential.

It would be expected that the more experienced a revolutionary leadership, the more flexible it would be in assisting the ranks to understand the need for a democratic centralist party, to encourage an atmosphere in which differences of opinion can usefully develop the programme and policy of the Marxist movement to match the needs of the moment. Freedom of criticism and intellectual struggle is an irrevocable element in party democracy, and the right to form factions is essential for a healthy revolutionary party. It is a Stalinist distortion to say that factions have no place in the revolutionary party, and it reflects the fact that the Stalinists stand in opposition to the revolutionary process.

There are many Socialists who are repelled by the bureaucratic distortions of the Stalinist Parties, as well as by the shameful record of Social-Democracy on a world scale since 1917, and yet fail to free themselves from the theory of stages. It will be seen in the test cases presented here that a major contributing factor is that they perceive the state as neutral in the class struggle, able to assist in building a strong national bourgeoisie and at the same time better the conditions of the masses, and alleviate the exploitation and poverty caused by the operation of the capitalist market. They do not understand, or close their eyes to, the class nature of the state.

We also show that participatory democracy is essential for the masses to overcome such a collaborationist perspective which, certainly in the cases of Nicaragua and Venezuela, is endemic in the state and trade union bureaucracies, which act in collaboration with the bourgeoisie. We argue that direct, soviet-style democracy is a life-and-death requirement for any popular revolution. The bringing of direct democracy into society has been attempted by the masses since the Paris Commune of 1871, but the top-down structures of both Stalinist and guerrilla organisations are inherently non-democratic and bureaucratic. Social-Democratic parties appear less bureaucratic, but only until the leadership faces a serious challenge. The natural democratic form of the working masses is the Soviet which appeared in February 1917, on the basis of the experience of the 1905 Revolution, and was essential for the success of the October Revolution. Soviets are, in their essence, organs of class rule, and cannot be anything else. Bourgeois-democratic institutions of administration can be local councils, municipalities, counties, national parliaments, almost anything you like, but never Soviets.

In this book, the term Workers' and Peasants' Government is used to describe the transitional regime after the revolutions in Cuba and Nicaragua. In Cuba, the transition was to a workers' state, but not so in Nicaragua. In Nicaragua the regime leaders had a stagist perspective, of building a national capitalism via a mixed economy. As in all previous cases, this allowed US imperialism to re-assert its dominance. The lack of a direct, participatory democracy in Nicaragua was a major factor in the destruction of the Workers' and Peasants' Government. In Venezuela, the specific conditions; the lack of either a Marxist leadership or any real form of direct democracy, meant the revolutionary upsurge of the masses that could easily have overthrown the bourgeois state and established a Workers' and Peasants' Government, was reined in and, eventually, dissipated.

The effective participation in the running of society by the masses themselves is unthinkable without Soviet democracy. We see leadership as a two-way street in which the soviets exert control over the leaders through the election (and immediate recall when necessary) of their representatives. Soviet democracy gives the party the power to carry through both the democratic and socialist revolutions, while allowing the masses to exert control on the party. Democracy demands freedom of criticism and local initiatives, conditions incompatible with a bureaucratic regime which fears the masses with a perfectly bourgeois fear.

We explain that counter-revolutions are not simply natural reactions to revolutions, the product of some inevitable social yo-yo. They may originate from the same forces that gave rise to the revolution, but with a qualitative shift in the socio-political relations. A genuine popular revolution generally implies a qualitatively increased level of political activity by the masses, but this cannot be sustained indefinitely, for obvious material and psychological reasons. The great masses of people cannot live permanently at a high level of excitement and expenditure of nervous energy. In this book we describe and discuss the different factors at play in the three countries that led to the decline of mass political activity and, in Nicaragua and Venezuela, generated a deep economic crisis, high levels of unemployment, scarcity of food, and the impoverishment of the working masses.

The recent histories of Cuba, Nicaragua, and Venezuela are the latest episodes demonstrating the penalty the working masses pay for the absence of revolutionary Marxist parties. Contrary to the expectation of the leaders in the three countries, the national bourgeoisie did not welcome a democratic revolution, did not help develop the economy, did not support education and health provision, fought hard against increasing democratic rights, anti-racist legislation and any redistribution of wealth. In all three countries the national bourgeoisie joined forces with imperialism to reverse the progressive measures made and to re-introduce their own and US imperialism's stranglehold. In this they were quite prepared to use violent methods, and when these failed, to starve the masses into submission.

We have entered a decisive epoch in the world revolution but, as in Nicaragua and Venezuela, reformists are holding that revolution back. In the face of experience, their solution to social crises is that revolutionary activities must be curtailed; the goal of the revolution must be limited to a progressive, independent bourgeois state. This book is a contribution, intended to convince the exploited and oppressed to reject these false friends and avoid the mistakes made in Nicaragua and Venezuela, to learn from the lessons of the past, and by basing themselves on revolutionary Marxism achieve victory over exploitation and oppression.

August 2018

CHAPTER ONE
DYNAMICS OF THE CUBAN
REVOLUTION: WHERE
NOW?

1) INTRODUCTION

The Cuban Revolution of 1959 overthrew capitalist relations, blacked the eye of American imperialism and established the only workers' state in the Western hemisphere. This revolution was entirely novel in that it was led throughout by a group that considered itself radical bourgeois democrats. What was not new, and had to be re-discovered yet again, was that the demands for national independence, the liberation of the Cuban people, social equality, and a better life could not be realised in a capitalist Cuba subject to imperialist domination. To achieve these goals, it would be necessary for the Cuban Revolution to take the first steps towards socialism and create a workers' state.

The Cuban revolution booted out US-backed dictator, Fulgencio Batista in a victory for popular democracy, for the exploited masses of Cuba and the world. Its continuing existence is a daily reminder to US imperialism of its defeat and the triumph of the Cuban people. To follow and understand what happens in Cuba is a duty for every socialist, every revolutionary and every socially-aware person, because knowledge of what happens in Cuba is essential for understanding the social dynamics in all so-called Third World countries.

Cuba led the way forward, not only for Latin America, but the world, and how it has developed, and will develop, holds important lessons for hundreds of millions of people. In ex-colonies across the world, the local bourgeoisie and landlords are the ruling classes inherited from colonial times. But they have failed to accomplish the main tasks of the democratic revolution: truly national independence, land reform, creation of a democratic state, and equality for women and black people. In 1959 these tasks were still pending in Cuba, and throughout Latin America.

The nature of the Cuban leadership was key to the progress of the Cuban revolution. Farrell Dobbs led the historic Minneapolis truck-drivers' strike (and the accompanying street battles with police and vigilante gangs) that transformed the American mid-west from an open shop into a union stronghold, and knew a thing or two about the class struggle. He described the characteristics of those, initially left-wing reformists within the union, who under the pressure of events, adopted a revolutionary position. He listed their characteristics: they had to be committed to the cause of the working class, they had to be honest, they had to have the vision to see that victory was possible, they had to be prepared "to try new things", to have the foresight to see the potential gains of the struggle, but most importantly they had to have "guts".[1]

We will argue that the Cuban guerrilla leaders possessed these qualities and were prepared to transcend bourgeois limits when those limits became a barrier to bettering the conditions of the Cuban people. To achieve democratic goals, they were ready to transform the Cuban struggle into a struggle for socialism. The decisive element in the victory of the Cuban Revolution was unquestionably the leadership provided by Fidel Castro and his team, who succeeded in overcoming the long default in revolutionary leadership due to Stalinist domination of the world labour movement, by-passing the Cuban Stalinists from the left. Naturally, the masses responded, as did the overwhelming majority of young people throughout the world, who rallied to support what they hoped would be the opening of the democratic anti-imperialist revolution in all oppressed colonies. The appearance of a new leadership, generated in the very process of a revolution, largely untainted by Stalinism and imbued with revolutionary determination, was hailed with immense enthusiasm.

The background of the Cuban Revolution was, at least initially, propitious. The context was a highly unstable world situation: (1) with the end of World War II there had been a significant decline in the power of imperialism internationally, the US had been forced to take on the central responsibility for world capitalism, but it had recently been fought to a standstill in Korea; (2) the Soviet Union had risen in status to the second strongest power in the

---

1 Holt Labor Library, collection audio index, Farrell Dobbs, Lecture 3:07 Lecture 3/ Trotskyist leadership of 574.

world; (3) WWII had given rise to a tremendous groundswell of national liberation movements that challenged imperialism and served to weaken it further – China, the most populous nation on earth was now a workers' state. However, the growth of Stalinist parties as a result of the Soviet victory in Europe and the Chinese Revolution obscured Stalinism's essentially counter-revolutionary nature, and blocked the growth of mass Marxist parties that could challenge capitalism in the advanced capitalist countries.

2) SOME HISTORY

The history of Cuba can begin with the invasion of Cuba by Spaniards in the first years of the sixteenth century and the indigenous population who fought the conquistadors being driven to virtual extinction. Spain attempted to keep tight control of Cuba. However, a series of momentous events eventually freed the island from the grasp of the Spanish crown, but placed it in thrall to its neighbour, the imperialist giant, the United States of America.

To weaken England in the American Revolutionary War (1775-1783) in which the Thirteen English Colonies of North America declared their independence from the British crown, Spain suspended many of its economic restrictions and approved trade between Cuba and the colonists. The price of sugar shot up and, free to trade, the Cuban economy boomed. After the victory of the colonists, the Spanish crown re-imposed many of its tariff controls, and the Cuban economy temporarily declined, generating ill-feeling, especially amongst the merchants.

In 1789, in the Great French Revolution, the French populace rose in revolt against the crown and the church. Under the banner of Liberty, Equality and Fraternity they abolished feudalism and adopted the Declaration of the Rights of Man. These events reverberated throughout the French colonies and nowhere more than in Saint-Dominque (Haiti) where slaves and freed slaves comprised about ninety per cent of the island's population. Inspired by the Revolution and driven by the cruelties of a slave state, in August 1791 the historic slave revolt led by Toussaint L'Ouverture and Jean-Jacques Dessalines, began. Despite attempts by both British and French imperialism to quell the rebellion, by 1804, the sovereign state of Haiti had been established as the first colonial society to free itself, and explicitly reject race as the basis of social ranking.

Only sixty miles away, Cuba became the destination for some 30,000 French settler refugees who brought with them their knowledge of the most efficient sugar and tobacco production processes then in existence. These settlers soon transformed the Cuban economy from small-scale village-style farms to agribusiness. Simultaneously, they chaffed under the economic restrictions imposed on them by the Spanish crown, a state that was, at heart, feudal. However, their innovations demanded the use of slave labour on a previously unimaginable scale and by the mid-1800s black slaves comprised about forty-five per cent of the population, and freed slaves another thirteen per cent.[2]

With the victory of the national independence forces led by Simón Bolívar over the Spanish continental army at Ayacucho in Peru on 9 December, 1824, Spain was, to all intents and purposes, ejected from the Latin American mainland. The USA took the opportunity to stake its claim to economic dominance in the region and announced the Monroe Doctrine in December 1823. At this time, the USA contained some 4 million slaves, predominantly in the cotton-producing southern states. Naturally, after the events in Haiti, the US took great interest in the Caribbean islands, particularly Cuba because it was so close to the Florida coast and events there might inspire the slaves in the south to rebel.

In November 1843, Carlota, a female slave at the *Triumvirato* sugar mill in Matanzas Province, and fellow slaves, many of whom were women, organised and led the most important uprising prior to the first war of independence. "In terms of its vigour and bravery, Carlota's liberation struggle is part of the Cuban heritage of rebellion against oppression".[3] The uprising was quashed. A reign of terror was instituted, and all free black people not born in Cuba were expelled. A few days after the rebellion began, the *Vandalia*, a US Navy corvette, appeared in the port of Havana under the command of Rear-Admiral Chauncey who, accompanied by the US consul in Havana, officially notified the Spanish colonial governor that he could count on the aid of the US to crush the "Afro-Cuban" rebellion.

In 1845, the USA annexed the newly independent republic of Texas as the twenty-eighth state in the union. President Polk, who had campaigned on the slogan that the US should "extend from sea to sea," instigated a war with Mexico in 1846 by sending troops to occupy land then in dispute between the two countries. The Americans emerged victorious in 1848 and the Treaty of Guadalupe Hidalgo gave the US the vast northern provinces of the Mexican state that would become the states of California, Arizona, New Mexico, Nevada, and Utah.

By the mid-nineteenth century, the US had emerged as Cuba's largest trading partner, taking sugar, tobacco, and coffee in exchange for manufactured products. Cuba was producing about a third of the world's sugar, and between 1848 and 1854, the US made three offers to buy Cuba,

---

2 Ramiro Guerra y Sánchez, 'Sugar and Society in the Caribbean', Yale University Press, 1964.

3 Carlota, la rebelde, *Granma*, 11/05, de Marta Rojas.

which were welcomed by the majority of Cubans engaged in business or trade. Each time the Spanish crown refused and, to silence the voices of dissent, increased its despotic and unpopular hold on the island.

2.1) THE TEN YEAR WAR, THE END OF SLAVERY AND JOSÉ MARTÍ

Then, in 1867, in a move that seemed designed to provoke outrage and resistance by the sugar, tobacco, and coffee plantation owners, Spain imposed a new tax on land and increased taxes on incomes and trade. The result was the first War of Independence. In October 1868, Carlos de Céspedes, a forty-nine-year old lawyer and landowner called his friends, co-thinkers and slaves to hear him formally declare Cuba's independence on the grounds that the Spanish crown was no longer fit to rule Cuba on account of its excessive taxes, corruption, and deprivation of political and religious freedoms. He declared Cuba to be a republic based on universal suffrage, freed his own slaves, many of whom joined his volunteer army, and called for the indemnified emancipation of all slaves. Other local planters joined in, freed their slaves and, by November, the rebel army had grown to 12,000.

Certainly, the moment seemed propitious because Spain was riven by civil war, but both sides insisted on retaining Cuba as a Spanish colony. It was too valuable for either side to let go. To supplement the 22,000 ill-paid, ill-disciplined troops at his disposal, the Captain-General recruited a volunteer force of poor white immigrants. Most of these were from the Spanish mainland, had been granted land by the Spanish government and were loyal to the motherland. They were often deeply racist and the authorities played up the fear that the emancipation demands of the rebels would turn Cuba into another Haiti. A well-organised force of some 35,000 – the *voluntarios* – was formed, faithfully reflecting the views of the slave traders and most backward of the landowners against emancipation.

This was the Ten-Year War, ending on 11 February, 1878 when both sides signed the *Treaty of Zanjón*. The treaty contained face-saving clauses for the rebel leaders but neither independence nor emancipation were mentioned. The outstanding and leading rebel guerrilla fighter, Antonio Maceo Grajales, son of a free black Venezuelan farming couple, opposed the treaty and was exiled to Jamaica.

However, the victory of the North in the US Civil War (1865) and other factors had made the sugar barons reconsider their need for slaves. With eighty per cent of Cuba's overseas earnings coming from sugar, fluctuations in market conditions meant big risks for the sugar barons. It was becoming increasingly obvious that slavery was not as economically beneficial to the slave-owners as might be first thought. Sugar production in Cuba is highly seasonal, requiring intensive labour only a few months of the year. The summer months bring the rains, the so-called dead season; and sugar cane farmers, require few labourers. In October, the soil begins to dry and the cane farmers prepare the harvesting equipment. By January, the sugar mills are ready, and so begin the feverish activity that will last until about June. Coffee production followed much the same cycle. The sugar barons did their calculations. By the 1880s, sugar production in Cuba had been totally reorganised in a new economic system that de facto ended slavery. Seasonal labourers and field hands, the former slaves now working for wages, had to feed, clothe, and house themselves and their families from May/June to November/December with little or no paid work available. Capitalist emancipation meant, for many former slaves, worse living conditions!

American capitalism was brimming with aggressive self-confidence; in 1803 with the Louisiana Land Purchase, Thomas Jefferson had bought the French title to a swathe of land extending from the Gulf of Mexico to the Canadian border containing the present states of Arkansas, Iowa, Kansas, Missouri, Nebraska and Oklahoma; it had seized Texas at gunpoint, thrashed the Mexican army and taken the American mid-west (1845-48); it had carried through the last great bourgeois revolution and won the American Civil War (1861-65); it was rapidly clearing the native Americans from their homelands; and in 1893 US marines invaded and seized Hawaii. By 1894, most sugar mills in Cuba were in the hands of American companies, fewer than one in five mill owners were Cubans, and more than ninety per cent of all Cuban sugar exports went to the US. Most of the other key sectors of the economy (electricity, telephones, etc.) were American-owned. Essentially, Cuba was being reduced to a single-crop economy with a single customer.

José Martí embodies Cuba's struggle for independence from Spain. Soon after the commencement of the first War of Independence, at the age of sixteen, he was arrested and found guilty of treason for criticising Spain in a letter to a friend. His sentence of six years hard labour was commuted to exile in Spain. Martí returned to Cuba in 1878, and immediately took a leading role amongst those demanding Cuban independence, but fearing arrest he fled to New York in September 1879 where he lectured, wrote, raised funds, and worked to form the Cuban Revolutionary Party (PRC) a petty-bourgeois nationalist party with a revolutionary programme.

In March 1892, he launched *Patria*, a newspaper dedicated to building the newly-launched PRC on a programme of armed struggle to achieve independence and establish a bourgeois-democratic state. In January 1894, he denounced collusion between the Spanish and American commercial interests in an article, 'A Cuba!' Martí understood that the policy of the US, had been accurately expressed by the then-Secretary of State, James G. Blaine, "(Cuba) the key to the Gulf of Mexico … a part of the American commercial system… If ever ceasing to be Spanish, Cuba must necessarily become American." The US perspective was not one of an independent Cuba.

In Cuba, no less than in Algeria, Palestine, South Africa, Vietnam and elsewhere, unfolding anti-imperialist struggles intertwined with struggles by women to end their own brutal forms of oppression. August Bebel, in his seminal work, *Woman and Socialism*, wrote in 1879: "In Cuba, the women fought beside the men and enjoyed great independence" but was at pains to point out that only the road of the socialist revolution can open the way to a qualitative transformation in the lives of the masses of women, especially in the semi-colonial countries.

Parallel to the evolution of Cuban nationalism, was the growth of a bourgeois feminism, the one feeding the other. Despite social limitations imposed by church, state and custom, women made bold personal and anti-colonial statements. Participation of the men of a family in the anti-colonial struggle encouraged women to examine their own position and role within the family and society. In a dramatic shift of cultural attitudes, many women began to view themselves as equal partners with men. Disseminating leaflets, raising funds, speaking in public, and writing political pamphlets, opened their minds to expanding their rights not only as Cubans but also as women, and soon the slogan 'Votes for Women' was heard.

Its economic dominance of Cuba now assured, the US was determined that the country would be neither a Spanish colony nor fully independent. It decided to take control of Cuba while appearing to act within international law, and at minimal cost. Its method was devious, presenting an appearance that blatantly contradicted the reality. The Spanish empire was falling apart, everywhere its colonies were on the point of open rebellion. The American strategy was to publicly encourage the independence movements while working behind the scenes to ensure they would be so handicapped in terms of supplies that a quick victory was impossible. The US would strive to ensure the two sides would battle to a state of mutual exhaustion, at which time they would step in, on purely humanitarian grounds, to become the new colonial master.

Martí and his fellow Cuban rebels had planned to launch the war of independence in February 1895. But on 12 January, three or four ships full of armaments bound for the rebels were stopped at Fernandina port, Florida, by US authorities, their cargoes confiscated and the Spanish government alerted. Despite this terrible blow, Martí and Maceo (the latter representing continuity with the veterans of the first Cuban War of Independence) did return to Cuba in early February 1895 to renew the struggle, and were both killed in the battle of Dos Ríos on 19 May. On paper, the colonial forces looked impregnable, and robbed by the US of most of their armaments, the rebels had no choice but to adopt a guerrilla-style war. But the mood in Cuba had changed dramatically since the Ten-Year War. Now the rebels had the support of the overwhelming majority of the population.

The war did not go well for Spain, though neither the rebels nor the Spanish forces were able to win a decisive victory. The *mambises*, the independence fighters, despite being outnumbered and outgunned, were inflicting defeat after defeat on the Spanish forces. In January 1896, General Valeriano Weyler y Nicolau (nicknamed the 'butcher') took control. Weyler, recognising that the guerrillas had the support of the civilian population, attempted to break the link by introducing containment camps. Half a million peasants were crowded into squalid, unhealthy containment camps with little provision made for food, housing, clothing, sanitation or medical care. The local economy collapsed in areas where the camps were created, causing tens of thousands of Cubans to starve to death or die from disease.

Faced with these prospects, many families, including the women, joined the fight for national liberation. Coming from a wide variety of backgrounds, young and old, rural and urban, black and white, rich and poor, these women resolutely and ardently helped forge Cuba's new national identity. The majority of women who participated in the actual fighting were, as one would expect, poor black women. These *mambisas*[4] took on dangerous missions as couriers and carried military correspondence across enemy lines, served as nurses, fought in the rebel army, some as officers,[5] and established workshops in the rebel territory that produced war supplies of all sorts. Women also single-handedly ran field hospitals. Added to all these activities they also raised their families.

The best known *mambisa* is Mariana Grajales Coello, Maceo's mother. Mariana and her sons participated in all three wars of independence. Mariana was in charge of a hospital, responsible for tending the wounded and keeping it supplied. As for 'Votes for Women', Cuban women would have to wait until 1934 before they could vote, but the women's movement in the fight for an independent Cuba helped set the stage for the women's liberation movement in post-revolutionary Cuba.

---

4 The feminine form of the term *mambises*.
5 María Hidalgo Santana, who participated in the Battle of Jicarita, was promoted to Captain for outstanding bravery.

2.2) "REMEMBER THE MAINE!", CUBA BECOMES AN AMERICAN COLONY

Important US economic interests were being harmed by the prolonged conflict and deepening uncertainty about the future of Cuba. The US press, especially those newspapers that favoured a take-over of the country, informed their readers of the gross inhumanities taking place, presenting them as "a policy of extermination". The sub-text was that someone had to do something about it. That someone was the US, and that something was the invasion of Cuba.

In August 1896, the Philippine revolution began. Spain now had two wars of independence on its hands, presenting the US with the opportunity to strike at the Spanish empire as it fell apart and pick up the pieces. Wanting to retain Cuba, Spain decided to sacrifice the Philippines. To end the unwinnable war against the Cuban guerrillas, it offered an amnesty for political prisoners in Spanish gaols and a 'home rule' government for Cuba. To show good faith no further military offensive would take place. But the offer was too little, too late; the rebels who remained were determined to fight on for full independence.

On 25 January, 1898, the US battleship *USS Maine* arrived in Havana harbour in a show of strength to ensure American property and lives were not threatened. On 15 February, the *Maine* exploded. A naval court of inquiry was inconclusive, but the American yellow press laid the blame on a mine planted by the Spanish. On 19 April, the US passed an ultimatum: independence for Cuba or war with the US. President McKinley was given the authorisation to declare war if Spain did not yield.

On 21 April, the US severed diplomatic relations with Spain and the US Navy began a blockade of Cuba. Four days later, the US Congress declared a state of war existed between the US and Spain. On 1 July, 1898, US troops landed in Cuba. Superior fire-power and overwhelming numbers gave them victory in the one and only substantial battle in the war, the battle of San Juan Hill, for control of the harbour at Santiago. Within six weeks, the war with Spain was over with the US in control of Cuba, Guam, the Philippines, and Puerto Rico.

Supposedly, the US had intervened to support the Cuban independence fighters, but it ordered them to disarm immediately. A military government was established in January 1899, headed by US general John Rutter Brooke. At the treaty officially granting Cuba's independence, it was the US flag, not the Cuban, that was raised over Havana, and during the surrender ceremonies in Santiago, US General William Shafter refused to allow the rebel forces to participate.

The island of Cuba was transferred from one colonial master to another: for three years after 1898, Cuba was militarily occupied and ruled by the USA. During those three years the oath of loyalty sworn by Cuba's state officials was to the US, not Cuba. During this occupation, black people and mulattoes were generally kept out of government as America's systemic racism was imposed on Cuba. The American Governor created an all-white-Cuban artillery corps, just as after the Indian rebellion (1857-1859) the artillery units in the Indian Army were staffed with white British troops.

Afro-Cubans were greatly angered and concerned when Cuban history was re-written to suggest that black people had not made an equal contribution to the War of Independence when, in fact, over 80,000 Afro-Cubans had died in the war compared to fewer than 30,000 whites. Veterans of the war protested the blatant contradiction between the segregationist policy of the US Government of Occupation and the integrationist ideology of the Cuban nationalists.

A Bill containing the Platt Amendment, which reduced Cuba to a colony of the US was rushed through the US legislature and signed by the President on 2 March, 1901. On 3 March, 1901, the Cuban Convention was presented with a fait accompli; with US marines looking over their shoulders, and the US fleet occupying their harbours, it was told that until it signed up, Cuba was clearly unpacified and the American army of occupation would have to remain. The carrot offered was that, if they agreed to accept the Platt Amendment, the marines would go home and Cuban sugar would have preferential access to the US market. They were free to agree or disagree, they were free to secure a facade of independence under the Platt Amendment or continue under a US military administration. The Amendment, word for word, was voted into the Cuban constitution as an 'appendix' on 12 June.

The Amendment gave the US the right to intervene in Cuba if the US administration felt American property was threatened. It surrendered, "indefinitely", three important bays as military bases for the US; it also surrendered the right "to enter into any treaty or other compact" with any foreign power which the US did not approve. For Cuba, the period of the pseudo-republic had begun.

In December 1902, a Convention was signed in Havana, which gave US companies preferential treatment regarding import duties. From now on, US imports would pay between twenty-five per cent and forty per cent less than those from Western Europe, or elsewhere. In return, Cuban sugar (i.e. what would soon be United Fruit Company sugar) would be given a virtual monopoly in the US market. One year later the Platt Amendment was included in a permanent treaty between the two countries, and received the formal approval of two-thirds of the Senate. The US formally handed over power to the new Cuban government in May 1902. Guantánamo Bay and Bahía Honda were leased to the US as military bases in perpetuity. (Bahía Honda was given up in 1912, in return for the expansion of Guantánamo.)

Cuban politics for the next sixty years would be determined by the US, which sent in its troops no fewer than four times; 1906-1909, 1912, 1917-1920 and 1933; in each case (save 1912) to install a government of its choice.

The crushing domination of the US relied not only on overwhelming military force, but on an economic system whereby a few landowners owned most of the land while the great majority of peasants were landless labourers. The war for independence had seen the wholesale destruction of the smaller, more isolated sugar mills; of the 1,100 sugar mills registered in Cuba in 1894, only about 200 survived the war. The capital to buy up bankrupt estates, to rebuild and refurbish came, as expected, mostly from American sources. By 1905, nearly two-thirds of rural properties were owned by Americans. The United Fruit Company purchased nearly 200,000 acres (80,000 hectares) of land in Oriente at the give-away price of US$1 per acre. Soon, fewer than 0.1 per cent of farms occupied twenty per cent of the land while at the other end of the scale forty per cent of farms occupied only about four per cent of the land.

Where Cubans sought capital to invest and expand, it came from American banks, machinery for the mills came from American companies, increasingly senior managers and administrators were American. During and after the 1906 elections, there was considerable unrest and President Roosevelt, to protect US interests sent in the marines. Two thousand US marines landed near Havana in September 1906. The US established a new provisional government headed by a US judge, Charles Magoon, and US marines 'kept order' until 1909.

The Magoon administration attacked each and every political and social gain made in the struggle for independence. The remnants of the Liberation Army were demobilised, all the institutional expressions of a 'free Cuba' (*Cuba Libre*) in which Afro-Cubans had registered important gains disappeared, and with them political positions, military ranks, and public offices. In response, in 1908, Evaristo Estenoz and others founded the Partido Independiente de Color (PIC) to address these losses, but found itself facing the entrenched racism of the American and Cuban bourgeoisie. The Morúa Law of 1909 was passed, which effectively banned the PIC by banning political parties based on race or class, with no independent allowed to run for president. Simultaneously, a limit was placed on immigration of black Haitians and Jamaicans. In 1910, in an attempt at intimidation, the leaders of the PIC were arrested and charged with conspiracy against the Cuban government. After being found not guilty, the PIC held a mass, peaceful demonstration on 20 May, 1912 behind the slogan 'Down with the Morúa Law!'

Bourgeois newspapers presented the demonstration as the beginning of a race war, carrying exaggerated and lying reports of the demonstration; *El Día* on 26 May, 1912, portrayed the demonstration as an "uprising of blacks" and subsequently reported fictitious attacks by blacks on whites including murders and rapes. Former members of the *voluntarios* formed the backbone of white vigilante groups which sprang into existence all over the island, harassing, arresting and killing Afro-Cubans simply out of 'suspicion'. Those 'protecting civilisation' did so with impunity. Bodies of suspected rebels were left hanging outside the towns for 'moral reasons', and severed heads were placed on the side of railroad tracks for the edification of train passengers.

> This massacre achieved what Morúa's amendment and the trial against the party in 1910 had been unable to do; it put a definitive end to the PIC and made clear to all Afro-Cubans that any further attempt to challenge the social order would be crushed with bloodshed.[6]

The true reason for this concerted attack on black people soon became clear. In 1912, the Cuban government lifted the ban on importing black workers, and the United Fruit Company was granted special permission to bring in workers from Jamaica and elsewhere, who would be paid less than Cuban workers. United Fruit and other employers built villages on their properties for these new employees, who were kept separated from the rest of Cuban society.

US sugar tycoons increased their profits tremendously. Between 1912 and 1931, over a quarter of a million black workers from Barbados, Haiti, Jamaica and other Caribbean islands arrived in Cuba to work in the expanding sugar industry, mainly in the eastern provinces of Oriente and Camagüey, where the biggest and most modern estates on the island had been developed by US capital. Meanwhile, the living conditions of the Cuban masses were hard hit. In good years twenty-five per cent of the workforce was unemployed and the percentage went up to fifty per cent in bad years. Illiteracy was over ninety per cent in many rural areas where few dwellings had either running water or electricity.

World War I (1914-18) brought temporary prosperity as Cuban sugar replaced that lost due to the war: the price of sugar doubled and output increased by 175 per cent. Immigration from Spain had been encouraged,

---

6 Helg, A., *Our Rightful Share: The Afro-Cuban Struggle for Equality, 1886-1912,* University of N. Carolina, 1995.

but many of the immigrants were workers from areas where anarchism was a strong influence. A significant number had taken jobs in the sugar industry and now flexed their industrial muscle by organising what is commonly known as the first great sugar strike, demanding an eight-hour day and an increase in pay. The US sent in the marines to protect US property and 'keep the peace'.

The troops ensured US sugar plantations were safe against strikers and their efforts contributed substantially to a record sugar crop that year. The presence of the marines meant that, by mid-1918, the focus of the strikes had moved to the cities, targeting sugar exports and shipping. The American authorities presented these protests as political, which justified their continued intervention under the Platt Amendment. In December 1918, the US poured thousands more marines, fresh from the Western Front into Cuba to break the strike.

As the European sugar beet industry recovered after WWI, the Cuban sugar industry virtually collapsed, meaning many of the small Cuban-owned banks went bust with the resulting vacuum filled by US banks. Simultaneously, the Cuban bourgeoisie was increasingly being limited to those areas of production not dominated by US industry.

To stifle any likelihood of protest, in January 1921 Major-General Enoch Crowder, President Wilson's personal representative, arrived in Havana harbour aboard the American battleship *Minnesota*, with the job of re-writing Cuba's election laws. To ensure the Cubans had no ideas above their station, all discussions took place aboard the *Minnesota*. In May 1921, Alfredo Zayas ran unopposed for the Conservative Party.

Cuba was formally independent and democratic (although women could not vote) but these qualities were, to a large extent, fictitious as the US could veto or overturn any decision by the Cuban government. This situation was conducive to high levels of corruption in a political system where elected representatives openly accepted bribes in return for government contracts, pardons, jobs, etc.

The *Minnesota*, and Crowder remained in Havana and, on Crowder's advice, elections were called for 1 November, 1924. This time Crowder chose Gerardo Machado y Morales, a member of the Liberal Party, a farmer with business connections to several US companies, and who ran on a platform of the closest possible co-operation with the US.

2.3) MELLA AND THE FOUNDING OF THE CUBAN COMMUNIST PARTY

There were periodic outbreaks of protest and rebellion, most of which were crushed. But in 1922-23, protests by university students secured a victory. Across Latin America, students campaigned for the autonomy of the universities, in particular, against the influence of the Catholic Church and corrupt practices in the universities. In Cuba, Julio Antonio Mella (then about twenty years old) was secretary of the newly-formed University Students Federation (*Federación Estudiantil Universitaria*, FEU) which was successful in having more than a hundred corrupt 'professors', cronies of the president, who had been given fictitious jobs at the university, sacked. Further, a system of election of the rector by students, staff and ex-students was achieved. For its successes, the FEU was banned in 1924. Mella rapidly evolved in his revolutionary thinking. He soon understood that the struggle for university reform had to be part of the struggle for social emancipation which could only be achieved by the proletariat's seizure of power.

Initially, Machado had some successes, increasing investment in construction, mining, manufacturing, and tourism. But his manner was arrogant, his style dictatorial, and his methods increasingly brutal. As economic problems grew, a small trade union organisation, the National Confederation of Cuban Workers (*Confederación Nacional Obrera Cubana*, CNOC) was founded, and about the same time (August 1925) the Cuban Communist Party (*Partido Comunista de Cuba*, PCC) was launched by Carlos Baliño and Mella (who was elected to the Central Committee).

The government showed little or no interest in addressing the working or living condition of the workers, nor did private enterprise do much to alleviate the grievances of the working class. Struggles for better wages and improved working conditions were often led by 'Spanish radicals' who were more open to the ideas flowing from the Russian Revolution. Despite government suppression, the PCC survived and, by playing a leading role in these struggles, especially of sugar mill and railway workers, made significant headway in the labour unions. The Machado government responded by clamping down on all opposition groups, Mella and other party leaders were arrested, forcing the communists underground.

The government was rapidly becoming an authoritarian dictatorship, jailing, torturing and assassinating oppositionists. Those who dared to participate in strikes put themselves, literally, in the firing line. The repression extended to the middle classes, much to their surprise and consternation. Machado's response was more repression; he imprisoned Mella who, although released under the pressure of mass protests, feared for his life and went into exile in Mexico City, where he was assassinated in 1929.

Mella's untimely death was a serious blow against the development of revolutionary theory in Latin America. At the time of his death, Mella was already well-advanced in a developing a theory on how the revolutions in Latin America would develop, with strong similarities to Trotsky's theory of the permanent revolution:

> (T)he revolutionaries of the Americas who aspire to defeat the tyrannies of their respective countries (....) cannot live with the principles of 1789. Despite the mental backwardness of some, humanity has progressed and in making revolutions in this century one should count on a new factor: the ideas of socialism in general, which in one shade or another takes root in every corner of the globe.[7]

Mella, in his best-known work *¿Qué Es el APRA?*[8] contended that the *Apristas* made political concessions to the petty and national bourgeoisie, and gave a classical Trotskyist definition of the role of the national bourgeoisie:

> In their struggle against imperialism (the foreign thief), the bourgeoisies (the national thieves) unite with the proletariat, the good old cannon fodder. But they end up realising that it is better to form an alliance with imperialism, which at the end of the day pursues similar interests.

For statements such as these, the official Communist Parties damned him for "Trotskyist tendencies".[9]

At that time it was almost impossible for Mella and other Latin American Communists to acquire accurate factual information on parallel struggles elsewhere. China was the most important of these, but after the Shanghai massacre of April 1927 and the total disaster of the Canton Commune in the December, a dense smokescreen of outright lies was published in the international Communist press to protect Stalin. Thus, those Latin American Communists who argued against Stalin's theory of stages had the trebly difficult task of having to produce an accurate analysis of the relation between the class struggle and the anti-imperialist struggle in their own countries, of having to face down the criticisms of the official Communist International, and to explain why a policy which – allegedly – had produced such wonderful results in China, should not apply in Latin America.

7   Mella, J., *Imperialismo, Tiranía y Soviet, Venezuela Libre*, July 1925.
8   APRA – the Popular Revolutionary Alliance for the Americas, an anti-imperialist party.
9   Lowy, M., *Marxism in Latin America from 1909 to the Present*, Humanity Books, 1992.

The Machado government deported many Spanish radicals, but Cuban militants replaced them. The PCC organised illegally, forming 'revolutionary fractions' in the unions, particularly among railroad, tobacco, and sugar workers. Eventually, the PCC became one of the strongest parties in Latin America; succeeding in publishing an illegal weekly, *El Comunista*. Its core strength was urban labour, and by the late 1920s the PCC was strong enough to take control of the National Confederation of Cuban Workers. The Machado government responded by declaring the CNOC illegal but failed to suppress it. Kapcia gives the following membership numbers for the 'old' PCC; 1927 – 199, 1932 – over a thousand, 1935 – 2,480, 1958 – 15,000 and, after its reconstitution as the 'new' PCC, in 1965 – 45,000.[10]

The Wall Street crash of 1929 had severe repercussions for Cuba. The Communist Party gained in strength because of the depression, despite the repression. In 1930, 200,000 workers participated in a political strike against Machado, and the CNOC became increasingly important as a centre of opposition to the government. On 30 September, 1930, a demonstration led to a mass confrontation with the police in which the demonstrators, many of them students, successfully repelled the police attacks.

In the early 1930s the PCC led and supported many workers' strikes; textile, shoemakers, cigar, transportation, and sugar. On 27 July, 1933, bus drivers in Havana struck against a new tax imposed on urban transport. Tram drivers, inter-city truck drivers, dockworkers, teachers, and others joined the strike. Fearing US intervention, the PCC reluctantly supported the workers immediate demands but then, to everyone's surprise, added a call for an end to the Machado government. After bloody confrontations with the police and army on 1 August, the strike escalated to include sugar workers. There were reports of many strikes in the interior of the country, and the CNOC called for a general strike to begin on 5 August. As train drivers and tobacco workers joined in, army officers, faced with a situation outside their control, demanded that Machado quit. Machado tried to divide the opposition by making a deal with the CNOC; offering legal recognition as well as official government support if it ended the strike. CNOC leaders were in favour of the agreement as was the Central Committee of the PCC. The workers, however, rejected their leaders' agreement and remained on strike. The PCC's support for the return to work, seen by many militant workers as a betrayal, was a good indicator of the future role of the PCC.

Under pressure from the US ambassador, Sumner Welles, Machado resigned and fled the country on 12 August. Welles tried to organise a new openly pro-US government and arranged the mobilisation of the US marines

---

10 Kapcia, A., *Leadership in the Cuban Revolution*, Zed Books, 2014.

and for the American Atlantic Fleet to be stationed off the Cuban coast. Carlos Manuel de Céspedes y Quesada, a conservative diplomat, was declared President on 10 September.

De Céspedes, was a man of such political ineptitude that, despite American blessing, his presidency lasted less than one month. The rapid amputation of the de Céspedes regime occurred due to its complete failure to enlist any support from amongst the population or the armed forces. Although the Havana workers ended their strike, strikes continued on the sugar plantations, and soldiers sent to put down these strikes, for the most part, fraternised with the workers. The first mills were seized by their workers towards the end of August, and by the end of September, thirty-six mills were under workers' control, and revolutionary councils (proto-soviets) established. Of particular concern to authorities were the leading roles taken by black people and women in the mill seizures and mass demonstrations which challenged their deepest racist and patriarchal prejudices. On the revolutionary left, these events were seen as the formation of embryo soviets and a promise for the future.

3) BATISTA TAKES POWER: THE 1933 COUP

The de Céspedes regime made no secret of its pro-American sympathies and proceeded to infuriate the anti-imperialist elements amongst the petty-bourgeoisie by refusing to expel Machado's appointees from governmental posts. Then de Céspedes declared his intention to cut soldiers' pay, and that was the final straw. The soldiers rebelled and, on 4 September, soldiers of Camp Columbia, a giant military base on the outskirts of Havana, under the leadership of their sergeants (amongst whom Fulgencio Batista Zaldívar was a central figure) took to the radio and asked for the support of all enlisted men. The response was immediate: almost the entire army and navy joined them. Students from the University of Havana joined in, supporting the soldiers.

It is claimed that the sergeants sent out cars to collect all the well-known radicals they could find and bring them back to the camp to produce a 'Proclamation to the People of Cuba'. This was signed by eighteen prominent civilians and Batista – on his own authority raised to the rank of 'Revolutionary Chief Sergeant of all the Armed Forces of Cuba'. The resulting provisional Junta, headed by university professor, Ramón Grau San, in gratitude, promoted him to the rank of colonel, and would soon appoint him Head of the Army.

This petty-bourgeois Junta of four professors and a banker called for the immediate convocation of a Constituent Assembly. To progress, the national bourgeois revolution demanded, as priority, an end to a treaty which gave the

US the right to intervene at will in Cuba, but no such demand was made. These leaders were quite incapable of leading the Cuban national bourgeois revolution and, in a pitiable attempt to stave off further US intervention, they proclaimed: "Strict respect of the debts and obligations of the republic". The Chase National Bank and the House of Morgan were assured that their loans and the magnificent interest rates they charged had nothing to fear from that junta. But the other jaw of the vise pressing the junta were the class actions of the workers, the 'riots' and 'bloodshed'.

The demands of the proletariat were, at that time, democratic in character and appeared quite compatible with the continued existence of capitalist society. But there were clear signs, as Mella had foreseen, that the workers would not limit their demands to the economic: higher wages and better working conditions. In the interior, sugar plantations had been seized, managers were still being held prisoner and made to comply with the workers' demands. Such actions are the first step towards workers' control and soviets. Patrols of workers and local peasants (sometimes soldiers also) armed with clubs, with red armbands as uniform, kept order, which was an important step towards a workers' militia. Relief committees were formed to feed the strikers and their families.[11] Given that the vast majority of the plantations in Cuba were American owned, it followed that the majority of the plantations seized were owned by American interests.

Caught between these two opposing forces and with no sense of direction of its own, the junta could provide no way forward for the Cuban masses. It was doomed to early extinction, and on 10 September, the junta was dissolved and Grau San Martin, became the provisional president. Refused American recognition, the Grau government staggered on, basing itself on populist not socialist measures: all businesses had to ensure fifty per cent of their employees were Cuban born, tens of thousands of Haitians were deported, demands for academic freedom in the universities, the eight-hour day, paid holidays and better working conditions for urban workers were, nominally, introduced, Cuban Electric was nationalised and Batista was appointed Army Chief of Staff.[12] The only pro-worker and consistently anti-imperialist actions of Gran San Martín's short lived '100 days government' were introduced by Antonio Guiteras, minister of labour, a Cuban revolutionary who started from the position of armed struggle for national liberation and who had adopted socialist ideas. It was during this period that the PCC made significant headway, and most Cuban trade unions affiliated to the CNOC, with the result that CNOC membership was 300,000 by January 1934.

11 Foreign Policy Association, *Problems of the New Cuba*, New York 1935.
12 Frei Betto, *Fidel and Religion*, Ocean Press, 2006.

The army under Batista remained a repressive force. On 29 September, for example, it attacked a memorial rally for Julio Mella and sacked the headquarters of the National Labour Confederation. The US sent warships into Cuban waters but did not intervene, possibly because during the entire period of the Grau presidency, Batista was in secret talks with US ambassador Welles and had mutually agreed on a front man for interim president. Colonel Carlos Mendieta was duly installed in a coup organised by Batista, on 18 January, 1934.

Batista's coup marked a turn to the right, but it did not mean the immediate and total reversal of all the gains made under Grau. Batista still claimed to be a revolutionary. While he was willing to repress militant workers, he also wanted to win popular support, which required him to accept some progressive reforms. In some ways, Batista in his early years was comparable to other third-world bourgeois-nationalist leaders of military origin, such as Peron and Nasser. Within five days, the US recognised Cuba's new government. For the next six years, Batista ran the country from the background, using a series of puppet presidents; Carlos Mendieta (1934-35), José Barnet (1935-36), Miguel Gomes (1936), and Frederico Bru (1936-40).

Mendieta is the best remembered of this bunch because, in February 1934, a provisional constitution was approved, formally extending the vote to women; and on 9 June, 1934, the Platt Amendment was abrogated and the Reciprocity Tariff Act signed, giving Cuban sugar (United Fruit Company sugar) preferential access to the US, and US-manufactured goods preferential access to Cuba, seriously impeding Cuba's industrial development. The Platt Amendment had been a major source of hatred of the US in Cuba, and throughout Latin America. This concession was one of the results of the workers' upsurge which had been powerful enough to shake the rule of the exploiters to the very foundations. Renouncing the Platt Amendment and granting a few reforms were measures taken by the American imperialists, in conjunction with the native exploiters, to reinforce the position of Mendieta, to prevent any rekindling of the revolutionary fires and to protect the capitalists and landowners.

The years of colonial and semi-colonial domination, by Spain and then the US, restricted and distorted all aspects of Cuba's development, with women suffering the extreme oppression that is characteristic of countries dominated by imperialism. By the 1930s many Cuban women from the upper and middle classes considered themselves 'revolutionary feminists'. Given their social positions, these women assumed their voices would be heard and listened to, they were shocked when they weren't. Their activities began with charitable works and education of the less privileged, but their support of women's issues such as maternity rights meant that they were soon involved in the rights of domestic workers. These women wanted political representation not to challenge the social system, but to better the welfare of women.[13] However, even this limited goal could not be achieved without the women's movement attacking traditional norms, such as the Catholic Church, patriarchal privilege, and the social order embodied in the plantation-centred economy.

This was a society in which women were discouraged from taking part in public life, and in many families, women were not even allowed to venture out of the house without a chaperone. Fewer than ten per cent of urban women worked outside the domestic environment, primarily as nurses, secretaries, and teachers though a few found jobs in factories, mills or mines. Some peasant women found work in the sugar cane fields. However, the great majority of working women were employed as servants of the rich, so the centuries-old myth that women were not suited to work outside the family domain went largely unchallenged. Contraception was generally unavailable and abortion was illegal, which meant many women were forced into prostitution to survive and feed their families, a survival route that was encouraged by many in authority.[14]

This legacy of economic and social backwardness was the most serious obstacle to women's equality. Real changes could only occur with economic development and the incorporation of women into social production. Thus, changes in the situation of women in Cuba took place in step with the struggle against underdevelopment, against the Catholic hierarchy, and against the many who held to traditional Spanish customs and myths that denigrated women (*machismo*). Although the women's movement succeeded in inserting women's rights and laws against gender discrimination in the workplace into the Cuban Constitution of 1940, it was not until Cuba implemented the Family Code in 1975, that wives who worked were officially regarded as equal wage earners.

The 1933 coup had not fully extinguished the revolutionary mood, and more than 100 strikes occurred between 1934 and 1935. In late February 1935, teachers and students in Cuba's public schools staged a walkout, demanding increased government funding for public schools. By 25 February, 4,000 teachers and 100,000 students were on strike. They were joined by students and staff of the University of Havana, who appealed for a general strike to re-establish civilian government (as a colonel, Mendieta was widely regarded as representing the armed forces), the military to be subject

13 Stoner, L., *From the House to the Streets*, Duke University Press, 1997.
14 Hinze, M., *The Revolutionary Role of Women in Cuba*, liberationschool.org, 2007 and Stone, E., *Women and the Cuban Revolution*, Pathfinder. 1981.

to civil authority, withdrawal of all troops from educational institutions, and restoration of social and economic stability.

Initially, the CNOC and the PCC were reluctant to support a general strike, declaring it premature. In Latin America, the policies of the national communist parties followed the Stalinised Communist International, which had entered its ultra-left Third Period and viewed all governments, whether of a bourgeois-reformist or pro-imperialist hue, as fascist, and all non-communist workers' organisations as the moderate wing of fascism (and were accordingly denounced as 'social fascist'). Such a stance meant the CNOC leadership was divided, and it took until 10 March to issue a strike call. As the strike extended and deepened, the PCC hesitantly gave its support. Participation in the general strike numbered up to 500,000, walk-outs by civil servants paralysed ten of the twelve government departments, and crippled government functions. Banks, newspapers, the telephone services, and manufacturing industries were all seriously affected.

President Mendieta (and Batista) suspended the constitution, martial law was declared in Havana, prohibiting public meetings, striking unions were dissolved, and strike leaders were abducted and assassinated. The University of Havana, a centre of resistance, was occupied by the military and closed for over three years. There were mass arrests of strikers who were brought before special courts created for the sole purpose of convicting them of activities illegal under martial law. Indefinite detention was implemented, and for the first time civilians were executed by firing squad. Mendieta dismissed government employees on strike. Troops took over some public services and compelled reluctant employees to work, literally at gunpoint. Soldiers were sent to vandalise the union headquarters and ferry in strike-breakers to keep Havana running.

These actions succeeded in crushing the strike and driving all political opposition into exile or underground. The defeated strike was followed by a period of intense repression, in which all unions and free speech were banned. The government's actions, its treatment of strikers and students, had made Mendieta a figure of hate. Batista now made sure the press and other media gave Mendieta full responsibility for every unpopular measure, and forced him to resign in December 1935. Mendieta was replaced by another puppet president, José Barnet, and the oppression continued until toward the end of 1937, when the restrictions began to be eased.

By 1938, the Stalinist International had turned its previous policy upside down. Popular Frontism was now the order of the day and the PCC adapted its policy accordingly, resolving to "adopt a more positive attitude towards Colonel Batista", in the hope he would adopt "positively democratic attitudes".[15] The popular front strategy of cuddling up to the bourgeoisie was prettified by declaring it an 'anti-fascist alliance'. The PCC, in line with the Stalinist International had previously adopted the theory of the 'two-stages'. According to this, Communist Parties in, for example, Latin America, were supposed to form an alliance with the so-called progressive national bourgeoisie and support them in the 'anti-imperialist and democratic revolution', with the struggle for socialism postponed to some unspecified time in the future.

The Stalinists needed a national and progressive bourgeoisie with which local parties could ally themselves if the theory of stages was to be realised. Thus, in the early 1930s, Communist Party theoreticians, ignoring agribusinesses and the myriad of business and family links between the urban bourgeoisie and the owners of the vast ranches and farms (*latifundismo*), found the latter were inherited from the Spanish conquistadors and the Latin American form of feudalism. The national bourgeoisie was then presented as a progressive force who would be the natural allies of the peasants and workers. This view continued to be accepted by CP historians until the collapse of the Soviet Union.

In contrast were the two documents drawn up by the Communist International during Lenin's life time; *On the Revolution in America* (1921) and *To the Workers and Peasants of South America* (1923). These had posed the task before the Communist Parties of Latin America as forging an alliance between workers and peasants to break the power of the landowners, capitalists, and government. Neither mentioned feudalism as a characteristic of Latin American economies and certainly no suggestion of feudalism as a separate stage to be overcome. This permanentist perspective was developed separately by Mella, and taken up later and developed by Trotskyists and independent Marxists.

Mella had argued that the theory of stages was utterly divorced from the real class relationships existing in Latin American countries. The Cuban landowners and the tiny bourgeoisie were completely linked to, and dominated by, the US. They had no intention of carrying through the tasks of the bourgeois revolution because that would have meant dealing a mortal blow to themselves. The PCC searched hard for this progressive national bourgeoisie; all it found was Batista, so it determined to support him.[16]

---

15 Thomas, H., *Cuba*, Pan Books, 2002.
16 Martin, J., '40th Anniversary of the Cuban Revolution', www.marxist.com, 1999.

This perspective had been disproved by the experience of the Russian Revolution of 1917.[17] Lenin had quite the opposite view. In August 1917 in *From a Publicist's Diary* he wrote:

> You do not have to give these demands (confiscation and distribution of land) a lot of thought to see that it is absolutely impossible to realise them *in alliance* with the capitalists, without breaking completely with them, without waging the most determined and ruthless struggle against the capitalist class, without overthrowing its rule.

In practice, the stagist perspective, when practised by the Communist Parties in colonial countries restricted the actions of the workers and peasants to what was acceptable to the national bourgeoisie and that meant, as Mella had pointed out, to what was acceptable to the imperialists.

Although the Communist Party was still illegal, Batista permitted the formation of a Communist front party, the *Partido Unión Revolucionaria* (PUR), headed by Juan Marinello. By the summer of 1938 a compromise had been agreed between Batista and the CCP, and in May 1939, it was permitted to publish a party organ, *Noticias de Hoy* (always abbreviated to *Hoy*), edited by Anibal Escalante Dellundé. At its tenth Plenum, convened in June, the Party abandoned its former public antagonism toward the ex-sergeant, and agreed to support him as an anti-imperialist, as a 'man of the people'. Following a meeting between Batista and top Communist leaders a week later it appeared that, in return for Communist backing, he would allow the Communists to take formal control of the trade union movement. The CCP was granted legal status in September 1939.

This adoption of dictators and would-be dictators as good bourgeois democrats was a world-wide phenomenon. The same process had unfolded in China a decade earlier, Chiang Kai-sheck was lauded as an anti-imperialist, even elected to the Central Executive Committee of the Communist International, and his army trained and armed by the USSR. The pay-back; tens of thousands of Communists massacred.[18] Batista would be Chiang writ small. However, without this coalition, Batista could never have got into a position to secure his bloody dictatorship, which definitely involved two stages; in the first, the revolutionary forces supported a 'man of the people', who was supposed to carry through the bourgeois democratic stage of the revolution. In the second, on taking power, the 'man of the people' destroyed the revolutionary forces and consolidated his dictatorship.

17 Roberts, J., *Lenin, Trotsky and the Theory of the Permanent Revolution*, Wellred Books, 2007.

18 Roberts, J., *China: From Permanent Revolution to Counter-Revolution*, Wellred Books, 2016.

Now legal, the PCC immediately began to organise to take leadership positions within the labour movement. In January 1939, the Cuban Workers' Confederation (*Confederación de Trabajadores de Cuba*, CTC) was established under Lázaro Peña, Communist leader of the tobacco workers union. Soon, most of the urban labour unions had joined, with a total membership of some half a million. The CTC was given favoured status by the Ministry of Labor and significant advances and improvements in pay and working conditions of urban workers followed. The Communist Party and the PUR merged into the Unión Revolucionaria Comunista (URC) and, in the 1939 election for the Constitutional Convention, won six seats on the basis of an election campaign which included demonstrations to demand the inclusion of workers' rights in the proposed constitution. The Communists delivered their end of the deal by calling on the workers to support Batista in the 1940 presidential election.

Batista's deal with the PCC, which included giving them substantially enhanced authority within the trade unions, was a blow to revolutionaries who were also trade unionists. During the 1930's, the Cuban Trotskyists had a significant presence in the trade unions, controlling the Havana Workers' Federation (*Federación Obrera de la Habana*), the umbrella trade union body for the capital and whose general secretary was Gastón Medina. They were also strong in Oriente province (traditionally the revolutionary heart of Cuba), where their trade union work was through the Orient Workers' Union (*Unión Obrera de Oriente*). In particular they were strong in Guantánamo, forming the leadership in the local trade union federation (*Federación Obrera Local*), and also had strong bases in the railway workers and local Bakery Workers Union. The Guantánamo militants, specifically, Antonio 'Ñico' Torres, would join the Castroist guerrillas and provide the model for their industrial organisation.

With Batista's backing, the Cuban Constitution formulated in 1940 gave substantial benefits to labour, making it one of the most advanced in the capitalist world. Among the commitments in the new Constitution were: equal pay for equal work; provision for social insurance; eight-hour working day and forty-four-hour working week; prohibition of child labour; one month annual paid vacation; maternity benefits; right to organise and to strike. Amidst a great fanfare, Juan Marinello, and other PCC leaders took credit, claiming the gains made confirmed the correctness of Communist Party policy. Few of these provisions were even partially realised.

On the other hand, the proletariat paid a very high price for the small gains actually made; direct interference and *de facto* state control of the unions and the virtual destruction of legitimate, independent labour organisations such as the General Confederation of Workers (CGT). After the invasion of the Soviet Union by Nazi Germany in 1941, PCC members themselves policed the unions denouncing militants to the police as class traitors. These actions contributed to a hostility towards the PCC that continued for many years amongst both workers and peasants, including amongst many members of the radicalised petty-bourgeois youth.

Co-operation between Batista and the Communists continued through World War II, with the labour unions supporting the President. Batista's confidence in the PCC was demonstrated when it was allowed its own radio station, *Radio Mil Diez* (Radio 1010). Launched on 1 April, 1943, it broadcast from Havana under the slogan 'Voice of the People', and is still remembered today for its cutting-edge music programmes, particularly Cuban jazz. The number of registered Communist voters increased from 90,000 in 1940 to 150,000 by 1946, and several of their members, including CTC chief Lázaro Peña, were elected to the National Congress. Additionally, in March 1943, Juan Marinello and Carlos Rafael Rodriguez became the first Latin American Communists to hold cabinet posts. During the war, the Communists changed their party name to the *Partido Socialista Popular* (PSP).

During and after World War II, the degree to which the Communist Parties of both the USA and Latin America prostrated themselves before the US and local bourgeoisies is, today, almost unbelievable. By declaring the economies of Latin America feudal, the development of capitalism became a 'revolutionary objective'. The Cuban CP published a pamphlet lauding *Collaboration between Bosses and Workers*, the Mexican CP was wholeheartedly in favour of an *Historic Worker-Boss Pact*, both to be based on 'an alliance of the workers and capitalists', and other Communist Parties (most notably in Bolivia and Brazil) followed suit. All this was to be achieved with the active collaboration of US imperialism!

Later, Batista insisted that his co-operation with the PSP was necessary for the struggle against fascism and that he made an important distinction between 'international communism', represented by Lázaro Peña, and 'local communism', represented by Eusebio Mujal, who quit the PSP for the Cuban Revolutionary Party (also known as the *Auténticos*) whose main slogan was 'Cuba for Cubans' but which had a substantial base in the unions.

Batista, did not contest the 1944 presidential election; instead, he left office a very wealthy man as a result of corruption and a last-minute raid on the Cuban treasury, and migrated to Miami. In the election, the Communists supported the Batista candidate who was defeated by Grau San Martín of the *Auténticos*, but managed to get nine of their candidates elected to the

Chamber of Deputies, three to the Senate and more than a hundred posts in Municipal councils.

The growing strength of the *Auténticos*, demonstrated by the election of Grau, was reflected in their attempts, led by Mujal, to take control of the CTC. In July of 1944, Lázaro Peña met with the new president and it was agreed that Peña could remain as Secretary General of the CTC. In return, the PSP would support and co-operate with the *Auténtico* administration.

With the onset of the Cold War, and under pressure from the US, the Grau government launched an offensive against communists in the unions, leading to communist union leaders being murdered by government thugs. The formal break between the PSP and the *Auténticos* came at the Fifth Congress of the CTC held in May 1947, when the *Auténticos* tried to gain control. However, they over-estimated their strength and in July the Minister of Labour, Carlos Prio Socorrás, had the CTC headquarters seized by the police and handed over to union officials who were *Auténtico* supporters. Angel Cofiño of the Electrical Workers' Union was declared the new Secretary General and an Executive Council composed of *Auténticos* and independents imposed.

Later in 1947, there was a general purge of Communists. Lázaro Peña and over a hundred other Communists were arrested and communist newspapers suppressed. The following year, 1948, *Radio Mil Diez* was confiscated. Gradually, and accompanied by a good deal of violence, the chief unions went over to the *Auténticos*, especially after the government gave them official recognition. Communist membership declined steadily, and by the early 1950s it had been reduced to a shadow of its former self. Most PSP-led trade unions were dissolved or applied to join the *Auténtico*-led federation. The reforms agreed between the CP and Batista in 1940 were now only words on paper. After World War II, inflation had severely eroded the real wages of workers but the new leadership of the CTC was so tied to the *Auténticos* that its efforts were mainly to contain any protests, and it did little to make up the losses.

The Grau government turned out to be even more corrupt than Batista's. The issue of corruption led to a split in the *Auténticos*, with Eduardo Chibás establishing a new party, the bourgeois Cuban Peoples' Party (commonly known as the *Ortodoxos*), in 1947, on an anti-corruption platform. However, for the 1948 elections Carlos Prió Socarrás replaced Grau as a face-saving measure, and the *Auténticos* won an easy victory. Batista, from Miami, spent huge sums to get himself elected, in absentia, as Senator from Las Villas Province.

4) BATISTA RETURNS: THE 1952 COUP

Chibás regularly denounced corruption on his weekly radio programme, and won the *Ortodoxos* increasing support. The succession of corrupt governments and military coups with the real power in the island remaining firmly in the hands of the US and their local crooks, created widespread discontent amongst the population: small businessmen made bankrupt by the big monopolies, small landowners crushed by the big US landlords, poor people who were going hungry, students who resented the foreign domination of their country, all supported the opposition. It was then that a young Fidel Castro became active in politics as a supporter of the *Ortodoxos*. But in 1951, Chibás committed suicide, depriving the *Ortodoxos* of their most popular leader and candidate for the May 1952 presidential elections.

Batista had declared himself a candidate, but the opinion polls placed him a poor third. Although no longer an army commander, Batista still had support amongst army officers. He sounded out young officers and NCOs, who had gained nothing from the rampant political corruption and saw *gangsterismo* as an insult to national pride. On the night of 9-10 March, 1952, Havana's main army base, Camp Colombia, arrested the senior officers and sent tanks to surround the presidential palace.

The ambassadors for both the UK and USA welcomed the coup's timing and its leadership. They also noted the support given to the coup by Cuban business, commerce, and industry. They expected Batista to tackle the problem of low labour productivity with a stick rather than a carrot, to restrict the ability of the Cuban workers to defend their wages and working conditions, and to reduce the power of organised labour.

The most significant resistance to Batista's coup was on 10 March, when hundreds of students at Havana University staged a protest rally, but this had little support because Batista was in contact with CTC leader Mujal and promised that he would respect the existing labour laws and confirmed all existing trade union officials would remain in post. Mujal subsequently became one of Batista's closest collaborators, and helped suppress opposition to the dictatorship within the unions.

The leadership of the CTC around Mujal would become known as the *mujalistas*, an openly self-seeking group of trade union bureaucrats whose level of corruption fully reflected that in Cuban society generally. The arguments used by Mujal were the same as those used by class-collaborationist trade union officials everywhere; that any pay deal had to be within the limits the company could afford, that workers in employment should be prepared to sacrifice pay and conditions to create jobs for the unemployed and, when the price of sugar on the international market fell, workers had to accept pay cuts.

Batista worked closely with the US, so closely that US Ambassador Earl Smith claimed that the American Ambassador in Cuba held a position second only to the President "because of our vast business, cultural and social ties". To all intents and purposes, Cuba became a wholly owned subsidiary of North American businesses. As a neo-colony, Cuba was a dependent satellite of the US economy; a US plantation producing sugar and tobacco with cheap labour and a Mafia-dominated playground for Americans who came for the beaches, the gambling casinos and the prostitutes.

Cubans who opposed the Batista regime were taken into custody, beaten up, tortured or disappeared; over 20,000 people were murdered in the years leading to his overthrow. The North American Mafia owned and controlled every casino, most hotels, and the sex tourism industry in Havana, and was a law unto itself. The drug trade and child prostitution went unrestricted, thousands of children were kidnapped and sold into sex slavery. Batista looked the other way as the US raped Cuba of its riches: in addition to its land and sugar interests, US businesses owned ninety per cent of Cuba's mines, eighty per cent of its public utilities, fifty per cent of its railways, and twenty-five per cent of its bank deposits.

What little economic progress was made, was at the price of political suffocation, of state terrorism and intimidation, torture and reprisals. Efforts by Cubans to reform this system in the name of social justice and national dignity faltered in the face of the fundamental reality of any neo-colony, viz. while nominally independent, any serious effort to reform would inevitably court US hostility. Reform was not possible without real independence, and that required a revolution.

The PSP remained legal until November 1953, when it was banned. At first, the ban was not enforced strictly and the illegal Communist Party continued to maintain a base in the urban areas and trade unions, but not enough to challenge Mujal for leadership of the CTC. Its remaining support largely evaporated when, in 1957, the regime launched a wave of assassinations of PSP members and repression of the PSP.

Henry Gitano[19] has given a brief review of conditions in rural Cuba at this time: sixty per cent (of the peasants) lived in huts with thatched palm roofs and bare dirt floors without running water or sanitary facilities of any sort. Kerosene lighting was used by seventy per cent, with the remaining thirty per cent having no illumination at all. Basic foods consisted of rice, beans and vegetables, with only eleven per cent drinking milk, four per cent eating meat, and two per cent having eggs. The result was a caloric deficiency of 1,000 units daily. The Cuban government's own 1953 census confirmed

---

19 Gitano, H., *First Year of the Cuban Revolution*, Int. Soc. Rev., 21(2) 38-42, 1960.

that, in rural dwellings, eighty-five per cent had no inside or outside piped water.

Women suffered most from all the effects of under-development. It was women who did household chores without benefit of electricity and running water, walking to the nearest water source, loading up and carrying (often contaminated) water home, while caring for their children. The economic stagnation and low level of industrialisation – results of imperialist exploitation – meant they suffered from the highest levels of illiteracy so that, as in all Caribbean countries at this time, it was almost impossible for a woman to get a job except as someone's personal servant.

Accentuating the poverty was job insecurity. According to *Investment in Cuba*, a US Department of Commerce study of July 1956:

> The spectre of unemployment affects all thinking on labour … unemployment normally reaches a total of one million … in a country of 6,500,000 inhabitants.

The study notes:

> [D]istinct improvement has occurred in recent years, however, in the atmosphere of labour-management relations … declining economic activities have also had an influence in moderating excessive demands.

A starving people and a corrupt, puppet dictatorship provided an ideal environment for US investors.

5) REVOLUTIONARY STRUGGLE AGAINST BATISTA

Groups of activists began, independently, to make plans for the overthrow of Batista. Fidel and his brother Raúl were leaders of one such group, consisting of as many as fifty students from the University of Havana, sometimes referred to as the Youth of the Centenary (the centenary of José Martí's birth). In 1944, at the age of eighteen, Fidel had been acclaimed as Cuba's best all-round school athlete. At university, he demonstrated he was an exceptional student leader, outstanding public speaker, charismatic, with great self-assurance and a dominant physical presence (his height was 1.93 m [6ft 4 inch]). From university, Fidel became a lawyer in Havana, taking the cases of poor people, many of whom could not afford to pay him. His first-hand experience made him extremely critical of the great inequalities in wealth that existed in Cuba for which he blamed the American businessmen who controlled the country. Raúl, the youngest of the five Castro children, had joined the PSP youth group while at university and in 1953 attended a World Youth Congress where he met and befriended Soviet diplomat Nikolai Leonov, a KGB agent, who would be posted to Havana in 1960.[20]

In 1947, Fidel joined the newly formed *Ortodoxos*, attracted by its campaign against corruption and injustice. He was attracted to anti-imperialist policies, which included his participation in a failed military expedition to the Dominican Republic to overthrow the Trujillo dictatorship in 1947. Later, he was part of a delegation to a student congress in Colombia, where he witnessed the Bogotazo uprising, which followed the assassination of radical leader Jorge Eliécer Gaitán on 9 April, 1948. With his public speaking skills and charisma, he soon built a strong following amongst the young members of the party. In 1952, he was an *Ortodoxo* candidate for Congress and expected to win, but during the campaign Batista thwarted the election by staging his coup.

Fidel Castro concluded that revolution was the only way the Cuban People's Party would gain power, and with an armed group of about 130 men (this figure has appeared variously as 120, 123, 135 and 140) and two women, the overwhelming majority being *Ortodoxos*, attacked the Moncada Army Barracks on 26 July, 1953. The attack was planned in the smart Havana apartment rented by Abel, younger brother of Haydée Santamaría Cuadrado, both from the village of Encrucijada. After the Batista coup, Abel began inviting home those with radical ideas for social change, including Fidel Castro. The apartment became a meeting place for what would become the leadership of the 26 July Revolutionary Movement, and its organisational centre, housing a simple duplicator on which they produced the underground paper *El Acusador*. A small bookcase housed 'the library', reflecting the group's political orientation, Martí was prominent, Marx was missing.

The aim of the attack was to act as a spark that would detonate a nationwide insurrection, which would overthrow Batista's regime. Here we have a small group of petty-bourgeois, with no mass base, no links to the workers or peasants, hoping to spark a national insurrection by an heroic action. They may have been brave and bold but as with almost every such ultra-left endeavour, it was a disaster. The plan ended in tragedy and, although only eight were killed in the fighting, Batista ordered that ten prisoners should be shot for each dead soldier and eighty were murdered by the army after they were captured. Fidel was arrested and, as luck would have it, was not taken to the Moncada barracks, where he would have been killed, but to a police station.

---

20 Gott, R., *Cuba, A New History*, Yale University Press, 2004.

5.1) FIDEL CASTRO: HISTORY WILL ABSOLVE ME

Haydée with Melba Hernández Rodríguez del Rey were the only two women directly involved in the Moncada attack. Both were arrested and tortured using lighted cigarettes, but neither gave anything away, not even when:

> With a bleeding eye in their hands, a sergeant and several other men went to the cell where our comrades Melba Hernández and Haydée Santamaría were held. Addressing the latter, and showing her the eye, they said: "This eye belonged to your brother. If you will not tell us what he refused to say, we will tear out the other."[21]

The PSP, still clinging to legality and largely limiting itself to verbal criticisms of Batista, denounced the attack on the Moncada barracks as a 'putsch'. That did not save them, *Hoy* was closed down and the party banned.

In September, over 100 radicals, leftists and socialists, few of whom had anything to do with the Moncada attack, were charged with organising an armed uprising. As a qualified lawyer, Fidel Castro took charge of the defence proceedings so successfully that only twenty-six were convicted, though his brother Raúl received a fifteen-year prison sentence. Fidel was tried separately from the others in October. He was found guilty and also sentenced to fifteen years in prison. He used this opportunity to make an historic speech 'History Will Absolve Me', which became the manifesto of the Castroist current.

The attack, the subsequent trial, and the publication of the speech made Fidel Castro famous in Cuba. Most demands of the manifesto were reformist, but radical, an advanced democratic programme of national liberation and agrarian reform, with a strong social content: to reinstate the rights given in the 1940 constitution, including for the state to ensure gainful employment for all citizens. The programme of what would become the 26 July Revolutionary Movement, was summarised in the five revolutionary demands they had planned to broadcast:

- The reinstatement of the 1940 Cuban constitution.
- Agrarian reform: setting a maximum size to land holdings; all those peasants farming less than about seventy hectares (170 acres), including squatters, to receive title to the land and the owners compensated with ten years rent.
- The right of industrial workers to a thirty per cent share of company profits.
- The right of sugar workers to receive fifty-five per cent of company profits.

---

21 Castro, F., 'History will Absolve Me', www.marxists.org.

- The confiscation of holdings of those found guilty of fraud under previous administrations.

These demands would be the basis of a progressive, national democratic programme, intended to improve the conditions of the mass of the people. It was consistent with the ideological balance and social composition of the membership of the Movement but did not to go beyond the limits of the capitalist system, nor did it question private property. Such goals, which appeared reasonable to the petty-bourgeoisie, would, of course, prove quite unattainable in an economy dominated by US multi-nationals.

A veteran reporter for the *New York Times*, Herbert Mathews, described Fidel Castro at this time thus:

> The personality of the man is overpowering. It is easy to see that his men adore him and also to see why he has caught the imagination of the youth of Cuba all over the island. Here was an educated, dedicated fanatic, a man of ideals, of courage, and of remarkable qualities of leadership. ... the most remarkable and romantic figure ... in Cuban history since José Martí.

Fidel's attempt to start a revolution had considerable support in the country. After all, the party he represented would probably have won the election in 1952 had it been allowed to take place. Batista did stand for president in late 1954 and, having won handsomely, decreed an amnesty under which Fidel and Raúl were released in May 1955. However, Fidel's insurrectionary perspective was not welcomed by the *Ortodoxo* party and he and his brother soon left for Mexico where they began to plan another attempt to overthrow the Batista government.

Melba Hernández and Haydée Santamaría had both been sentenced to seven months in the women's prison in Guanajay. They were flung into cells with common criminals who were expected to abuse them, but instead protected them from the abuse of the guards.[22] After their release, these women were instrumental in assuring the publication of 'History Will Absolve Me'. Fidel had posted his speech in parts, in letters to different comrades with the text written in lemon juice between the lines written in ink. These were collected, collated and re-constructed, then printed and distributed as the political programme of the 26 July Movement.

Fidel was held in Isle of Pines off the coast of Cuba. On his release, he was met by Haydée and it was on their ferry trip back to the mainland that the name 26 July Movement (M-26J) was decided upon. Fidel and other amnestied prisoners, constituting the leadership of what was now the M-26J travelled to Mexico. Frank País, leader of the M-26J's urban underground,

---

22 Randall, M., *Haydée Santamaría*, Duke University Press 2015.

designated 'national director of action', and Fidel's equal in the Movement, would later request Haydée to join him in meetings with the US Consul, during the period before 1957, when the Movement still believed it could do a deal with US imperialism. She was also liaison with the *Ortodoxo* party and would succeed in winning the support of an important group of more radical members.

A Hidden History of the Cuban Revolution,[23] reports that the founding meeting of the M-26J was on 12 June, 1955, and that it agreed to establish a workers' section, (*sección obrera*) to co-ordinate activities amongst workers. The activities of this section have been largely ignored, official histories have concentrated on the activities of Fidel Castro and guerrilla warfare. However, Frank País was extending the M-26J into the working class and had some important initial successes. In September, a group of railway workers in Guantánamo led by Ñico Torres (a Cuban Trotskyist) affiliated, as did the entire workers' section of the *Ortodoxo* Party in Santiago. País took as his model the newly-formed M-26J cell in Guantánamo and this led to the formation of a nation-wide committee within M-26J to organise its industrial work.

Almost immediately on arriving in Mexico City in July 1955, Fidel and Raúl met Ernesto Che Guevara, with whom they had an immediate rapport, and Che signed up for the duration. Their time was spent mainly in fund-raising, isolated from events in Cuba where the FEU led by José Antonio Echeverria was making its presence felt, as were sugar workers led by Conrado Bécquer. Eventually, enough money flowed in to rent a local farm where guerrilla recruits could gather for training, for the purchase of weapons and a sixty-four foot (19.5 metres) diesel-powered motor yacht, the *Granma*, which would carry the core of the Rebel Army (*Ejército Rebelde*) to Cuba.

In March 1956, Fidel Castro formally broke with the *Ortodoxo* Party declaring the M-26J would be a movement "without sugar barons, without stock-market speculators, without magnates of industry and commerce, without lawyers for big interests, without the provincial political bosses..." Instead, the M-26J would be "the revolutionary movement of the ... Cuban working class, the hope of land for the peasants who live like pariahs in the country that their grandfathers liberated".[24]

In preparation for the landing of the *Granma* the M-26J formulated its (1956) Programme/Manifesto. As to be expected it was much the same as that drafted in 1953, defining itself as "guided by the ideals of democracy, nationalism and social justice ... of Jeffersonian democracy". It contained

23 Cushion, S., *A Hidden History of the Cuban Revolution*, Monthly Review Press, 2016.
24 Tabor, R., *M-26: The Biography of a Revolution*, Lyle Stuart, 1961.

the traditional aim of the petty-bourgeoisie, of marrying together for their mutual benefit the conflicting interests of capital and labour, of reaching a "state of solidarity and harmony between capital and workers to raise the country's productivity". However, the programme of the M-26J demanded the revolutionary overthrow of the dictatorship and its refusal to compromise on this would gain it mass popular support.

At this time the administration of the M-26J was under the supervision of Armando Hart, assisted by Haydée Santamaria, both located in Havana. Haydée later joined Frank País, to plan the M-26J attacks that would be launched in Santiago de Cuba to act as a cover for the landing of the *Granma*. In Cuba, support for the M-26J was growing, despite the dangers associated with joining such a movement, and at this time its membership was almost entirely urban.

Celia Sánchez, one of the earliest members of the M-26J and a leading militant, was given responsibility for ensuring the rebels on board the *Granma* were swiftly and efficiently transported to the Sierra Maestra mountains which was to be their base. Celia was receptionist, orderly, and nurse to her doctor father (who was famous for not charging his poorest patients while respecting all his patients equally), and was also well known for her charitable work of collecting and distributing toys to children on the Feast of the Epiphany. In these capacities she had access to almost everywhere, and almost everyone.

Villalobos describes how Celia, while supporting her father's provision of healthcare to his peasant workers became extremely attached to María Ochoa, a peasant girl who, it is said, she treated as her own. In 1953, Ochoa, at the age of ten, went missing and several days later one of Celia's closest friends, who worked in Havana at a high-end casino, found Ochoa's body in the basement. María Ochoa was one of many victims of Cuba's child sex industry. She had been "used up and thrown away" by a wealthy North American gambler who requested a young girl for the night. "Sánchez declared war on both Batista, who refused to make paedophilia illegal, and the US Mafia which organised the crimes."[25]

Celia's task was to establish a network of militants to act as spies and guides, and to do this quickly to meet the deadline of a landing planned for the end of November. Celia targeted women who had been raped by Rural Guards. As the doctor's daughter and nurse, she could genuinely offer comfort and assistance while discretely sounding out the likelihood of a family member being prepared to join her network. Unfortunately, rape was common and Celia soon had a numerous, well-organised and growing band

---

25 Villalobos, M., 'Revolution within a revolution', Eastern Washington University, Master's Thesis, 2014.

of activists. In rural Cuba at that time, recruiting one member of a family gave access to a clan network that spread for miles. In the last few days of 1955, Frank País travelled to the area where the *Granma*'s landing would take place. There he met with Celia, who had lived in that area all her life, and together they made the necessary plans.

5.2) CLASS STRUGGLES 1955-56

During and shortly after World War II the Cuban sugar industry boomed, but as the former producers came back on line, the price of sugar fell. Cuban sugar farmers attempted to maintain their profits by cutting wages. In one year, 1952 to 1953 the total wages fell by almost forty per cent. The price of sugar continued to fall through 1954 and into 1955, and then the US unilaterally declared it was cutting Cuban sugar imports by about 100,000 tons.

Batista waited until the 1954 elections were over before attempting to attack working conditions. In conjunction with Mujal it was decided to divide the Cuban workers and attack working conditions sector by sector. The state began with the railway workers, demanding a cut in both the workforce and pay. The attack was launched only after the sugar harvest was in store, robbing the rail workers of their strongest weapon. The superior forces of the state forced the workers to accept an eight per cent pay cut, 600 lay-offs, and a no-strike agreement.

The decisive struggle was, of course, with the half a million sugar cane workers. Strikes at different farms started at different times. Typically, the owners would announce job losses and this would be followed by a strike. By the end of December 1954, most of Cuba's 500,000 sugar workers were on strike. That most of the *centrales* were US-owned gave an anti-imperialist and populist dimension to the struggle and the *mujalista* union officials hurried to assume leadership of the strike, all the better to settle for some trivial offer. The normal trade union practices such as peaceful picketing were useless in the face of ferocious attacks by police and army. Soon the strikers were actively engaged in street battles, setting up barricades, occupying public buildings, derailing trains carrying troops, and burning bridges to hamper troop transports. However, at the end of 1955, the *mujalistas* signed a deal which surrendered all the sugar workers' demands.

Women's support groups were an important component of these struggles, particularly in stopping strike-breakers from going to work. In one case, some 200 women managed to stop police from taking arrested strikers to prison. Cuban students have a long history of supporting the struggles of the working class and these strikes were no exception. Students participated in demonstrations, occupied their colleges, and generally behaved in ways that won them respect and gratitude from the Cuban working class. José Antonio Echeverria, a self-professed revolutionary, had been elected president of the FEU. He had concluded that the violence of the regime was such that the traditional trade union tactics of strikes and demonstrations was no longer sufficient and formed the Revolutionary Directorate (*Directorio Revolucionario*, DR) composed largely of students of Havana University, and which would become an important component of the anti-Batista struggle.

The greatest support for the sugar workers came from dockers, who were themselves fighting their own battle against the bulk loading of sugar, whereby sugar was poured directly into the ship's hold rather than carried on board in jute bags. Mujal personally chaired a rigged meeting of union 'delegates' that approved bulk loading as the official union position, but in the ports themselves the dockers were refusing to implement the decision. So strong and effective was the opposition that the Batista government was forced to delay its implementation.

Similar confrontations over productivity measures and increased mechanisation were taking place across Cuban industry, from cigar production to textiles to banking. These events produced a strong reaction with a solid anti-US content amongst the workers of Cuba. The mass of workers were ready to support any movement that opposed the Batista regime and the US imperialists. During 1955, the Cuban working class had suffered a series of defeats and many militants drew the lesson that, to defend their interests, they had to move beyond traditional trade union methods. They were looking for new ways of fighting back and there was a growth of the M-26J amongst the working class.

The working class took stock of the situation and, as is typical after such defeats, turned to its base organisations, the trade unions. There was a general lull (though not a cessation) of strike activity, but, at grass roots level, substantial changes were evident. Within the union structures, three forces were competing for the workers' loyalty.

(i) The *mujalistas* were fighting a losing battle and increasingly relied on election fraud and heavy-handed armed interventions by troops to remove militants (many of them women) and any remaining independent officials.

(ii) The M-26J, from a small start, was making considerable headway amongst workers who saw the futility of the peaceful road to the overthrow of Batista. It was successfully establishing dozens of workplace cells, particularly in the east of the island, and was having a significant impact on the youth section of the PSP, the *Juventud Socialista*.

(iii) The PSP was calling for *la lucha de masas* (mass struggle) counterposing this to the M-26J, which it continued to condemn as 'putchist'. The main thrust of this initiative was the setting up of committees for the democratisation of the trade unions.

By the time that Fidel and the guerrillas set sail from the Mexican port of Tuxpan on 25 November, 1956, the M-26J, under Frank País' leadership, had successfully established a network of workers' cells in areas ranging from banking to railways. It was this success and the strength of the network that enabled the M-26J to launch a series of actions on the scheduled landing date of the *Granma* to divert attention. The most important started at 05:00 on 26 November, in Santiago, when Frank País aided by Haydée Santamaría, led an attack with some twenty fighters on the customs house. Simultaneously, and surprisingly, the PSP member and dockers' leader Juan Taquechel, called a strike in Santiago docks.

5.3) *GRANMA;* RURAL GUERRILLA WARFARE IN THE SIERRA MAESTRA

The landing of the *Granma* was planned to re-trace the route taken by José Martí in beginning Cuba's War of Independence in 1895. The target was a town called Niquero, in Oriente province where Celia Sánchez would be waiting with an assortment of trucks, jeeps, food, weapons and about fifty militants. They planned to establish a base in the Sierra Maestra mountains and from there launch a campaign to ignite an irresistible national uprising.

The *Granma*, overloaded with eighty-two guerrillas on board, leaking and delayed by bad weather, landed at Playa Las Coloradas, about fifteen miles south of the designated spot, two days late, on 2 December, 1956. The well-planned diversions that had taken place had alerted the local police and army that something was afoot. Forewarned, Batista's troops were waiting, killing many, and capturing twenty-two.

The trucks organised by Celia were long gone, and the remaining guerrillas had to walk the fifty kilometres to the Sierra Maestra. These remnants were harried by Batista's troops and, by the time they reached the Sierra Maestra, there were only sixteen left with twelve guns between them. Lost, hungry, and exhausted, it took ten days before contact was made with the local resistance, one Crescencio Pérez, an outlaw peasant leader who had been recruited by Celia and would play a central role in obtaining local support.

The Batista regime maintained that Fidel had been killed in the landing, and to refute this lie the M-26J decided to combine a national leadership meeting on 17 January with an interview with the renowned *New York Times* reporter Hubert Mathews. The task of making arrangements was given to

Celia. Armando and Haydée flew from Havana to Santiago and then drove with Frank and Vilma Espín Guillois over the mountains to the meeting. Che and Raúl came with Fidel. It was at this meeting that Fidel met Celia for the first time.

The first of Mathews' three articles appeared on the front page of the *Times* on 24 February, 1957, declaring Fidel was alive, and painting a picture of a young, vigorous and committed group of rebels who were running rings around Batista and his troops. This was a serious blow to Batista's prestige.

Soon after, differences arose between Frank País and Fidel: Fidel had requested that the M-26J supply him with more "men", to at least restore the guerilla army to eighty-two, the number that had been on the *Granma*. Frank argued that, so far, the guerillas had shown themselves unprepared for the situation in Cuba, and that Fidel should consider leaving the country. Frank decried the poor level of organisation shown thus far by the guerrillas.[26] The delay in the arrival of the *Granma* had cost lives needlessly, poor discipline was demonstrated by the lack of maintenance of the guerrillas' weapons (Frank had spent the afternoon going round the camp cleaning rifles that were, reportedly, filthy), and lax security that had allowed, in the short time since the landing, one, and possibly two, informers to infiltrate the camp.

A compromise was reached. Fidel would stay and the movement would supply the soldiers requested. But these fighters would be selected by Frank and undergo preparatory training by Celia. Frank and Celia decided that her organisation skills were desperately needed on the Sierra Maestra and on Tuesday, 23 April, 1957, Celia Sánchez became the first woman to become a member of the Rebel Army.

Fidel, Che and the majority of the Rebel Army were urban. Frank was sending those members of the urban underground whose cover had been blown and were in danger of being killed. The guerrillas needed to integrate themselves into the local communities, they did this by teaching the peasants to read and write and providing medical services – Che acted as doctor and, so it is said, was extremely proud of his skills at extracting teeth.[27] For the next few months the guerrillas raided isolated army garrisons and were gradually able to build up their stock of weapons, all the time their numbers growing with many of the additions being local peasants.

Frank País worked on widening the network of support for the M-26J with the priority of supporting and supplying the guerrillas in the Sierra Maestra. The M-26J had around it a number of front organisations, one of which was the Civic Resistance Movement (*Movimiento de Resistencia Cívica,*

---

26 Stout, N., *One Day in October*, Monthly Review Press, 2013.
27 Puebla, T., *Marianas in Combat*, Pathfinder, 2003.

MRC), composed mainly of local business owners and professionals who were sufficiently radical to give financial and other support to the M-26J. The representatives of the professional bodies (*Conjunto de Instituciones Cívicas*), representing the middle-class professional layers, were one of the first to sign up to the Manifesto of the Sierra Maestra, of 12 July, 1957, which promised free elections, a democratic regime, a constitutional government and a non-partisan provisional president.

The Manifesto was smuggled into Havana and published in the magazine *Bohemia* on 28 July. It is claimed that its appeal was so wide that even bourgeois garden parties declared in its favour. The US ambassador, Earl Smith, saw the writing was on the wall for Batista, and began looking for a transition of power that would safeguard American interests. On 14 March, 1958, he met with business leaders and jointly signed a letter calling on Batista to resign. To show that it meant business the US simultaneously announced it would stop selling arms to the Cuban government, signalling to the Cuban army that it was prepared to ditch Batista. Fidel denounced this 'pact' because: 1) it did not reject foreign intervention in Cuba's affairs; 2) it did not reject rule by military junta; 3) it declared that Batista's army and police would be an integral part of the bodies of armed men forming the power of any new state; and 4) it was only half-hearted in its intent to overthrow Batista.

From the start of 1957, the workers began to make demands for better wages and conditions. Havana bus drivers (one of the most militant groups of workers in Cuba) struck against the employers' refusal to pay the traditional Christmas bonus, and later against a reduction in services. Dockers in Caibarién went on strike against the employers' attempt to reduce the number of workers required to unload cargo. Cushion lists twenty-five industrial actions in the first half of 1957 but, as he admits, this was just a glimpse of what was happening nationally.

The response of the state was to intensify intimidation, force workers back to work, and to launch a reign of terror in which known opponents of the regime would be seized tortured, killed and their bodies dumped by the road. After the attack by the Revolutionary Directorate (DR) on the presidential palace on 13 March, 1957, the level of the terror increased with the Rural Guard, police, army and death squads killing almost at will.

The police were informed of Frank's whereabouts, arrested him, drove him to a quiet alley and shot him. The MRC called a general shut down and, by dusk, Santiago was a ghost town. 31 July was the day of Frank's funeral and some 60,000 marched behind the cortège – over one third of the population of Santiago. The strike is often described as spontaneous and, in the sense that it was sparked by Frank's murder, that is true, but the speed with which it spread is a strong indication that there was an underground grass-roots organisation in place to give form to the expression of popular emotion. The strike spread across Cuba, to Holguín, Camagüey and as far as Santa Clara, and showed the Cuban people were ready to overthrow Batista.

Frank had been considered Fidel's equal and, with Frank's death, Fidel was pre-eminent. He jumped-in to appoint one Faustino Pérez as Frank's successor, much to the dismay of Armando, Haydée, and Celia. Celia, as Fidel's intellectual equal, was given the task of persuading him to accept the national directorate's nominee, Rene Ramos Latour. Fidel agreed but used the occasion to demand: "a directive must be given to the movement right now: all weapons, all bullets, and all resources are for the Sierra".

By March 1958, the Rebel Army considered itself sufficiently numerous for Raúl Castro to lead a column to the Sierra Cristal near Guantánamo to form a second front, to begin co-ordinating activities with other guerrilla groups such as the DR who were already active in the area, but also with PSP militants. Soon, a third front was established closer to Santiago. By the time of the final assault on Batista, there were eight such fronts.

The Communists under Blas Roca's leadership, had denounced the M-26J as adventurers, putschists, and gangsters. But by late 1957, the PSP (under pressure from the *Juventud Socialista* and rank and file militants, and impressed by how successful the strike after Frank's death had been) was re-assessing whether the M-26J could be supported. Carlos Rafael Rodríguez, editor of *Hoy*, and a member of Batista's cabinet in 1942, contacted Haydée who arranged a meeting, in February 1958, with Fidel in the Sierra Maestra, one outcome of which was an agreement for a general strike on 9 April, 1958.

The August strike had not had a resonance in Havana, but to be considered successful, a general strike had to seriously affect the capital. Unfortunately, so great was the hostility of many of the supporters of M-26J towards the Communists that they refused to include them in the preparatory arrangements. This attitude was particularly prevalent in Havana, where the Communists were cold-shouldered and the support of the relatively large numbers of workers under their influence, lost. At the same time the M-26J approached the strike as if it were a guerrilla action with the emphasis on armed interventions by the M-26J urban underground rather than mobilising the masses. Fidel received numerous reports of these difficulties but decided to press ahead.

On 12 March, Fidel Castro made his statement, 'Total War Against Tyranny', in which he announced there would be a general strike. Preparations for a general strike are difficult to keep secret, extensive preparations must be made because large numbers of people are involved, and there are always turncoats, but this was different: the strike was announced to the world before winning the support of the workers! The M-26J did keep the date of the strike secret – from the workers. It was not until late in the morning of 9 April that the strike call was issued, certainly after 10:00, when most workers were already at work. This fitted with the M-26J's petty-bourgeois concept of a general strike as composed of armed actions accompanied by acts of sabotage, rather than the self-activity of masses of workers. The police and army were waiting, many of the poorly armed M-26J urban guerrillas (the best weapons had been sent to the Sierra Maestra) were stopped by the police before they even grouped to attack their targets and achieved very little. The strike was a disaster.

There were two major consequences of the failure of the strike. Fidel used it to increase the emphasis of the M-26J on a rural guerrilla strategy, insisting that the Cuban revolution had to be led from the countryside. Of course, the M-26J leaders did not discount the importance of the working class in the cities, but now they were clearly subordinated to the rural armed struggle. Activities in the cities were now limited to providing supplies, funds, intelligence and personnel for the guerrillas. Now, however, many individuals within the M-26J better appreciated the organisation's weak roots in organised labour and adopted a more friendly approach to the PSP.

Batista had, for some time, been planning an all-out assault on the guerrillas' strongholds. Celia had been placed in charge of stockpiling food and supplies, and establishing a robust communications network in case Batista achieved an effective blockade. The failure of the general strike gave Batista the confidence to launch his assault. In May, 12,000 soldiers set out to 'encircle and annihilate' the estimated 300 guerrillas. But Batista's troops never got as far as encircling the guerrillas, let alone annihilating them. Irving Horowitz in his book, *Cuban Communism*, gives part of the explanation when he describes the arrival of one army unit at a village.

> The soldiers hurriedly dismounted from their trucks, falling over themselves in a mad scramble to get to a nearby park where there was a grove of coconut trees. The desperate soldiers climbed those trees like monkeys and knocked down every coconut, which they opened with their bayonets and devoured as if someone were going to take them away. ... The frenzied enthusiasm that Colonel Sosa Blanco's soldiers demonstrated for coconuts had a very simple explanation: they were starving. Their scoundrelly colonel had sold their rations.

Led by officers such as this, lacking training and motivation, the bulk of Batista's soldiers were looking to surrender not fight. In a series of skirmishes, committed and determined, the guerrillas defeated the Cuban army. In the key Battle of La Plata, 11-21 July, the guerillas defeated a 500-strong battalion, capturing 240 men while losing just three of their own. Fidel Castro claimed a triumph that more than compensated for the failure of the general strike; that the time was right for a major extension of activities.

But Batista did not rely only on his army. Prior to troops arriving in a village, the village would be bombed, whether or not it contained rebel troops. Villages would be burned to the ground, wholesale massacres of men, women and children took place. One incident in particular had a determining effect on Fidel. On 5 June, 1958, Fidel observed the use of napalm supplied by the US, against civilians. He wrote to Celia:

> I swore to myself that the North Americans were going to pay dearly for what they are doing. When the war is over, a much wider and bigger war will commence for me: the war I am going to wage against them. I am aware that this is my true destiny.[28]

All the atrocities were to no avail, Batista's army, comprised mainly of peasants, had no stomach for fighting a courageous opponent who was voicing their own aspirations. Over the summer and autumn, all Cuba's focus of attention was on the war between the guerrillas and Batista's army. Strikes and demonstrations were few and far between.

To further undermine Batista's war effort, the Cuban economy was collapsing as factories closed due to a lack of supplies, lay-offs in the docks due to so few ships coming in to harbour, redundancies due to cuts in public services, and so on. Unable to find work elsewhere, thousands of homeless women with their children roamed the streets of Havana. Most were to be found begging on church steps. Out of necessity, young women sought sex work because vice dominated the cities and resort areas. By the end of the year, Batista could no longer ensure even basic commercial activity. He had lost control of the roads and railways to guerrilla road blocks and blown-up bridges. The city workers favoured the revolution and by the summer of 1958 the *mujalista* union bureaucracy, tied directly to the Batista dictatorship, was quietly fading away in order to protect its own skin.

In the first days of September, Che Guevara set off westwards for the central province of Las Villas. He was accompanied by Camilo Cienfuegos who would proceed to Pinar del Rio, the most westerly province. In the Sierra del Escambray of central Cuba, Guevara and Cienfuegos formed a united front with guerrillas from the DR, cutting road and rail links crossing the country. Guevara and Cienfuegos started with 230 guerrillas but, as they marched westward, recruits flooded in and by the time the two columns

---

28 In Stout, op cit.

arrived at their destinations they had grown tenfold. These forces were in place by November and ready for a combined assault on Batista's army. Supported by workers in the towns, the rebels now had an unstoppable momentum, which would culminate in their victory on 1 January, 1959.

Because it was a crime, meriting severe punishment, to treat wounded or sick members of the underground, many doctors fled to the Sierra Maestra for self-protection. It is said that the Rebel Army had the highest ratio of doctors to soldiers of any army on earth! This gave Che the opportunity to take military responsibilities and demonstrate his talent. Che was promoted to Comandante in July 1957 and moved to his own encampment managed by Lydia Doce. Lydia was later captured in Havana in September 1958 along with Clodomira Acosta, a woman courier for Fidel. Batista's police placed them in sand-filled bags, took them out to sea in a boat and, in order to make them talk, repeatedly dunked them. They drowned rather than betray, and their bodies were thrown into the sea.

During the offensive, the women on the Sierra Maestra did just about everything the men did, but were not allowed to fight Batista's troops. Fidel was under increasing pressure from the women to allow them to join the fighting. On 4 September, he announced to a meeting of his general staff the formation of what would become known as the Mariana Grajales Women's platoon. In reply to the criticism that, if there weren't enough weapons for the men how could women be given rifles, he is alleged to have replied, "because they are better soldiers than you, they are more disciplined, and I'm going to teach them how to shoot."[29] Fidel did teach the platoon to shoot and placed Isabel Rielo, the best shot, in command. The platoon's first combat was in the battle of Cerro Pelado, only three weeks after their formation. They acquitted themselves so well that every member was armed with the highly prized, M-1 semi-automatic carbine. By the victory of the Revolution it had grown from an initial membership of thirteen volunteers to company size.

5.4) THE FALL OF BATISTA

Fidel came down from the Sierra Maestra and won a series of engagements that meant he would soon have control of Santiago de Cuba. In a key battle, Guevara captured the central city of Santa Clara on 31 December, 1958. Faced with the rapid progress of the Rebel Army and a popular uprising, Batista cut and run, fleeing Cuba with his family and closest associates in three planes heading for Santo Domingo. The US did its best to appear to endorse a change of government while, in reality, keeping everything much the same by supporting the transfer of power from Batista to another army

---

29 Puebla, op cit.

officer. During the early hours of 1 January, 1959, General Eulogio Cantillo stepped into Batista's shoes and appointed Supreme Court Justice Carlos Piedra as provisional president. The M-26J replied by calling a nation-wide general strike, demanding unconditional surrender to the Rebel Army and pledging to continue the armed struggle. The message by Fidel, broadcast by Rebel Radio (*Radio Rebelde*), in the early hours of New Year's Day, was sharp and clear "Revolution yes, military coup no!"[30]

Speaking over the radio from Santiago, Fidel called on all workers to seize their union offices, bring all workplaces to a standstill and paralyse the country. Everything stopped. The strike was decisive in stopping the manoeuvres of US imperialism and the army chiefs; it delivered the island to the Revolution. Faced with such a display of popular support for the new regime, and the news of Batista's flight, army units throughout the island simply ceased to resist and surrendered their weapons. The apparatus of the dictatorship collapsed like a house of cards, with its henchmen fleeing as fast as they could. With its target met, Fidel called a halt to the strike. This completely successful strike ensured the consolidation of the new revolutionary power.

The dawn of 1959 brought forth a massive outpouring of popular joy over the fall of Batista and nearly unanimous support for M-26J. Cienfuegos took over the Camp Colombia base and Fidel marched into Santiago on 2 January, 1959. In his victory speech Fidel promised: "this time will not be like 1898, when the North Americans came and made themselves masters of our country". At this stage of the Revolution, it would be true to say that the vast majority of Cubans, the M-26J included, were motivated to get rid of the hated Batista, for national independence from US gangsters and hopes of a better society. This gave the Revolution a very wide base with support from all sections of Cuban society.

The guerrilla army was the mainstay of revolutionary power and authority throughout the country, in cities, towns, villages, and the countryside. It took over all military posts and police stations everywhere and became the revolutionary administrative apparatus throughout Cuba. Initially, summary executions of the worst of the military butchers and most hated secret policemen took place by firing squad. Then public trials were held before mass juries of the population. Evidence against each prisoner was presented and, if a guilty verdict was reached, executions were promptly carried out. A total of some 600 were executed, a small number compared to the tens of thousands jailed, tortured, and murdered by Batista's henchmen. However, great play was made by the more reactionary media in the US and Europe

---

30 Martin, J., 'Cuba 50 Years Later', www.marxist.com, 2009.

of the swift and exemplary justice handed out to Batista's policemen and torturers. Allen Dulles Head of the CIA at the time commented:

> When you have a revolution you kill your enemies. There were many instances of cruelty and repression by (Batista's) army ... now there will probably be a lot of justice.

The judiciary at this stage of the Revolution was left relatively untouched. Known Batista enthusiasts, and all Supreme Court judges, were removed, a new layer of magistrates appointed whose determining feature was that they had not been Batista supporters.

M-26J had launched a heroic three-year long guerrilla struggle, which won the overwhelming support of the Cuban people, with the exception of only a tiny handful of people directly linked to the regime, to the landlords, and to US imperialism. The main base of the movement during the initial period was the urban underground, but it rapidly became the peasants, workers, and small producers in the countryside. Both urban and rural groups were eager for an end to the terror and repression that was the Batista regime, were eager for democratic freedoms. But, in the countryside, the only way of solving the problem of poverty was the expropriation of the land.

The guerrillas of the Sierra Maestra did play the central role in overthrowing Batista, but they won only because of a broad underground support movement throughout Cuba as well as in Miami, New York, Mexico City, and Puerto Rico. The basic objectives of the movement were adherence to the democratic provisions of the constitution and national liberation. The M-26J adopted a more radical orientation after its experiences with the Sierra Maestra peasants, but it still adhered to bourgeois democracy and was willing to make programmatic compromises.

By its origin, aims, and social composition, the M-26J was a petty-bourgeois formation, but an extremely radical one. Other, similar groups committed to the overthrow of Batista were engaged in negotiations with the M-26J for united action. Most important was the Revolutionary Directorate that, during the revolutionary upheaval, had seized and still held both the Presidential Palace and Havana University.

What distinguished the Castro team, and which proved decisive, was that it made a principle of no compromise with the Batista dictatorship or its supporters. They were determined to carry the armed struggle through to the end, and to achieve this aim, they launched a peasant guerrilla movement that has been compared to Mao's. Better parallels can be found, however, in the revolutionary experiences of Latin America, including Cuba itself.[31]

---

31 Hansen, J., *Dynamics of the Cuban Revolution*, Pathfinder, 1978.

The guerrillas had the support of the peasantry, which shaded into a great mass of agricultural workers employed in the sugar industry, a dynamic section of the Cuban proletariat. These groups solidly backed the revolution. In a country like Cuba, where the sugar crop provided the main economic base, this was crucial to victory and the core slogan of 'land reform', which became the banner and spearhead of the movement, mobilised the oppressed Cuban masses to fight for the seizure of the land. As the military victories grew, support in the countryside broadened in massive waves.

There was a continuity in the political perspective of the M-26J. From Fidel's 'History Will Absolve Me' speech through to his 12 July, 1957 'Manifesto From the Sierra', there was no suggestion that the guerrillas would take steps in a socialist direction. In response to a question on his views at that time Fidel later stated, he considered himself a revolutionary but not a Marxist-Leninist.[32] Fidel proclaimed on 21 May, 1959:

> Our revolution is neither capitalist nor Communist! ... Our revolution is not red, but olive green, the colour of the rebel army.

6) REVOLUTIONARY STRUGGLE: FROM DUAL POWER TO A WORKERS' AND PEASANTS' GOVERNMENT

Soon after the seizure of power, Fidel went to the US on a goodwill tour, declaring in New York:

> I have clearly and definitely stated that we are not Communists... The gates are open for private investment that contributes to the development of Cuba.

As an aside here, note the similarity with Mao's comments made before the Korean War:

> China must industrialise. This can be done – in China – only by free enterprise and with the aid of foreign capital. Chinese and American interests are correlated and similar. They fit together, economically and politically...[33]

Fidel's initial moves were intended to be seen by the US as placatory. The first government was a coalition based on the 1940 constitution. On Fidel's initiative, meeting the promises given to the MRC, Dr Manuel Urrutia Lleó, a jurist who did not belong to any party, a leading figure in the civil resistance movement against Batista and known to be anti-Communist was made President. Dr José Miró Cardona, President of the Bar Association, another noted leader in the civil opposition to Batista, a liberal academic who

---

32 Lockwood, L., *Castro's Cuba*, Macmillan, 1967.
33 Service, J., *Lost Chance in China*, Random House, 1975.

had been Fidel's professor, and known to be an anti-Communist, was named prime minister. Fidel at first refused any government post, but eventually was appointed Military Commander-in-Chief. Only three of the twenty-five members of the new cabinet, a body without any unified programme or policy, came from the guerrilla army.

The official title of the January 1959 government of President Urrutia was *The Cuban Revolutionary Government*, though there was little revolutionary about Urrutia. In February, new ministries were created, including the enormously popular Ministry for the Recuperation of Misappropriated Goods, headed by Faustino Pérez Hernández which, it was widely believed, would seize and re-distribute the properties of Batista and his associates.

The M-26J had come to power as the result of a revolutionary mass insurrection that had destroyed the political power of the bourgeoisie and smashed the state apparatus. A petty-bourgeois group, the M-26J, was the effective force in the government, and the power of the state, the "special bodies of armed men" referred to by Lenin in *State and Revolution*, was in its hands, but it was generally welcoming to other groups such as the DR, which had proved themselves in the fight against Batista.

The main demands of the peasantry were an end to hunger, an end to Batista's savage killings, and agrarian reform. These demands had become the slogans of the M-26J. On taking power, the M-26J established a coalition government, the composition of which corresponded to the political aims of the revolution as they were then conceived by its leaders. It was not long before differences between the guerrilla fighters, the 'men of action' who wanted to get on with the job of land reform, and the others in the government became apparent. Fidel explained:

> In the hands of the ruling class at this moment were: all the financial resources, all the economic resources, the entire press... all the big radio and television stations... they were, to put it simply, still the owners of the country... the responsibility for making revolutionary laws was in their hands... we waited to see what would happen... The weeks went by and they had not passed a single revolutionary law.[34]

The Urrutia government stood in opposition to the demands of the insurgent masses and to the commitments of the M-26J. To satisfy these demands, the revolution urgently needed to make far-reaching inroads into private property, including imperialist holdings. As Fidel and his collaborators pushed for moves that fulfilled the promises of agrarian reform, they met resistance from their partners in the coalition. This was stiffened by the support of Wall

---

34 Castro, F., *Fidel Castro Speaks*, Penguin, 1972.

Street, which viewed them as the 'reasonable' elements in a regime packed with bearded 'wild men'.

It was during this period that Raúl Castro was formally and publicly presented as second only to Fidel in the senior leadership; on 22 January, Fidel named Raúl as second-in-command of M-26J, in February he was named Commander-in-Chief of Cuba's armed forces and on 15 October, 1959, as Minister of Defence. This approach was justified as necessary in the circumstances, but was a worrying sign of the lack of the democratic accountability of the leadership. In June 1960, Raúl personally visited Moscow to establish closer links with the Soviet military and obtain a steady supply of arms and munitions.

The contradiction between the masses' demands for radical measures and the government's determined inaction forced Cardona to offer his resignation on 17 January, 1959. It was accepted on 13 February along with those of other members of the cabinet. On 16 February, Fidel became prime minister on a twenty point programme that was still, in essence, reformist.[35] In March, and April, the government enacted many of the points contained in Fidel's programme. Intended to be popular, these laws and regulations included: reduction of rents by up to a half, reduction in mortgage rates, landlords forbidden to evict tenants, urban landowners to sell vacant sites at controlled prices to anyone with plans to build a house for their family. A minimum wage for cane cutters, pay rises for the poorest paid civil servants and pay cuts for the tops were also introduced. The cost of electricity was reduced by thirty per cent and public phone rates halved (these were largely US-owned). Dozens of new bridges were built giving access to previously isolated and excluded villages.

The guerrillas won huge public approval for not abandoning their fatigues for well-cut suits, their jeeps for chauffeured limousines, and backed this up with the death penalty for the misappropriation of public funds. The intention of the new Cuban government to honour its promises to the workers and peasants of Cuba took the US government by surprise; this was something new.

The wearing of the olive green guerrilla uniform had many purposes, the relative importance of which has changed with time and circumstances. It reminded the population of who had overthrown Batista, liberating the island, and so legitimised the regime, it reassured the population that the generation of guerrilla fighters remained true to their aims, it was a show of identity with guerrillas across the country who held posts in the administration, and it reinforced the top-down structure of party and state. Thus, for example,

---

35 Ibid.

when Raúl Castro appeared on television on 14 December, 2014 to announce negotiations with the USA, he wore his general's uniform.

In the old Cuba, racism had been particularly virulent. Batista may have been President, but he was not white and had been barred from the island's most select clubs. At this personal level, one aspect of the new regime was causing especial concern: epitomised in Fidel's speech on 21 March, 1959, to a workers' rally in Havana – 'Proclamation Against Discrimination', which ended 'whites-only' facilities in Cuba, and for which the old elite would not forgive him.

The New York Times (16 April, 1959) understood the major threat. If Cuba got rid of US economic exploitation its example might be copied throughout Latin America:

> If we didn't have Latin America on our side, our situation would be desperate. To be denied the products and markets of Latin America would reduce the US to being a second-rate nation and cause a devastating reduction in our standard of living… Latin American raw materials are essential to our existence as a world power.

By October, *The New York Times* (and Washington) would have deepened its criticisms, damning the new regime for vowing to end hunger and unemployment, for introducing economic planning, for organising co-operatives, financing and managing practically all the land on the island.

In the Sierra Maestra, during 1957-58, the guerrillas had implemented small-scale land distribution to tenant coffee-growers and subsistence farmers, and had confirmed at first hand the importance of agricultural reform for the peasants. The first major revolutionary legislation was the Agrarian Reform Law announced on 17 May, 1959 with the slogan: 'Those who work the land shall own it'. This Reform Law was, de facto, the first 'class issue' of the Revolution, the first issue to divide opinion along programmatic lines. On 11 June, four cabinet members resigned, including the Minister of Agriculture.[36] The National Institute of Agrarian Reform (INRA) was created to implement the new law. On 18 July, President Urrutia resigned and publicly attacked the 'communism' of the new order. Less than two per cent of the population owned half of all farmland and the new law was intended to abolish these *latifundia*. Privately-owned land over about 400 hectares (1,000 acres) or, in the case of the cattle ranches and sugar farms, over 1,300 hectares (3,200 acres), was 'intervened' (taken over) by the INRA – notionally headed by Fidel Castro but with Che Guevara and Raúl Castro in day-to-day charge.

---

36 Martin, J., 'Cuba 50 Years Later', www.marxist.com, 2009.

The property of Batista's henchmen was expropriated outright, but there were exceptions. Those farms that were highly productive, producing at least fifty per cent more per hectare than the national average, were exempt.[37] All land expropriated was to be run as co-operatives or distributed in parcels to peasants, free of charge. Henceforth, agricultural lands could only be inherited or sold directly to the state, eliminating any building-up of large estates. The turn to co-operatives was determined by Fidel's belief that large farms and plantations were more efficient than individually-owned plots; that the large landed estates had already trained a section of the Cuban peasantry in co-operative labour and that would make the transition to cooperative and state farms comparatively easy.

The Reform Law was intended to progress the interests of all social classes and groups interested in change (e.g., the rural and urban proletariat, the peasantry, and the middle classes, amongst others). The only ones adversely affected were the sugar bourgeoisie, the importing bourgeoisie, and the capitalist investors in agriculture, sugar, and foreign trade.

Land owners were to be indemnified with twenty-year bonds carrying four per cent interest, with the sting in the tail that this compensation was based on the owners' own valuation submitted to the authorities for tax purposes. United Fruit refused to accept the offer. Its resistance to the measures was backed by the US administration. These lands were finally expropriated in April 1960 and the US pulled the plug on the sugar quota. A popular revolution with a limited programme of progressive land reforms clashed head-on with the interests of the big landlords and the US multinationals. To carry through the programme of the democratic revolution in a backward country in the epoch of imperialism meant to challenge capitalism and imperialism itself, confirming the practical experience of the Russian Revolution in 1917, and China after 1949.

It is at this point, confronted by imperialism that, typically, the petty-bourgeois leaderships of national revolutions pull back, re-assess their programme, and drop the more radical demands. The Cuban leadership now demonstrated its unique character. It re-assessed its programme and decided to pursue its demands, even if it meant rupture with US imperialism. We must accept that part of the answer lies in the personal qualities of the leadership. The use of US napalm against Cuban civilians had given Fidel Castro the 'guts' to stand up to American imperialism, that he and his team were committed to the cause of the Cuban masses and had the vision to see that victory was possible. We have since learned that these are rare qualities.

---

37 O'Connor, J., *Agrarian Reforms in Cuba 1959-63*, Science & Society, 32(2)169-217, 1969.

The Cuban leadership appreciated the threat hanging over land reform. If they continued, it was only a matter of time before the US would stop importing sugar from Cuba. In June 1959, Guevara was sent on a tour of the Third World to see what deals could be done. In Cairo, he had his first meeting with Soviet officials who agreed, in principle, to an initial exchange of crude oil for sugar.

Although the Agrarian Reform Law had been signed by all the Cabinet, many were hostile to it and considered its provisions to be indicative of 'communism'. The infighting within the Cabinet was a reflection of the growing hostility of beneficiaries of the old system, to the actions being taken by the new government. On 17 July, 1959, Conrado Bécquer, a long-time, and respected leader of the sugar workers demanded Urrutia's resignation and Fidel Castro appeared on television to deliver a lengthy denouncement of Urrutia and his "fevered anti-Communism".

Fidel received widespread support, tens of thousands surrounded the presidential palace demanding Urrutia's resignation, which was duly received. On 23 July, 1959, Fidel appointed a staunch supporter, Osvaldo Dorticós (a leading member of the PSP), as the new president and took the opportunity to replace others.[38] The revolutionary government had clashed with the interests of the international telephone trust, the international mining trusts, and the interests of the United Fruit Company, it had clashed with the most powerful interests of the US and relations deteriorated rapidly. In Cuba, this conflict precipitated a political crisis, which was resolved by a categorical turn to the left and the implementation of sweeping agrarian reform.

Responsibility for land reform was given to the INRA, which was empowered to enforce its rulings. INRA contained many who had been active guerrillas, and who tended to follow their wartime practices of assuming whatever authority they felt necessary to achieve their objectives. Simultaneously, it used its powers to implement a broad social programme, including building new houses and schools, thereby ensuring the revolution had an immediate impact on the lives of the peasants. It would be a fair comment that the INRA was in effective control of the Cuban economy in the early years of the revolution.

The takeover of the land proceeded relatively peacefully. The landholders protested against the land reform, both individually and through their associations, and sabotaged its progress as much as they could without directly confronting the new regime. They increased their rate of cattle slaughter, reduced purchase of fertilisers, bought hardly any new equipment,

---

38 Chester, R., *Workers' and Farmers' Governments Since the Second World War*, Pathfinder, 1978.

and neglected ploughing, sowing and planting. Many attempted to convert their physical assets into cash and transfer it out of the country.

After the Revolution, the CTC changed its designation to CTC-R (CTC-Revolutionary), and at the first CTC-R Congress in September 1959, Fidel gave a speech to more than 3,200 delegates. He emphasised that, though the vast majority (possibly as high as ninety per cent) of delegates were M-26J activists and supporters, they had been freely elected by the grass roots. He commended them for "(January's) general strike that gave all the power to the Revolution". Three days later, after a series of acrimonious debates between anti-communists in the M-26J and those who were *unitarios*, thirteen delegates (including three communists) were elected to form a new executive committee. Fidel again addressed the Congress, criticising the way the discussions were held on the grounds that any divisions or quarrels at the Congress made the enemies of the Revolution happy. In his opinion, if the working class wished to become an army defending the Revolution, then the existence of political factions made that aim nonsensical. This authoritarian, top-down approach reflected his guerrilla background, but threatened to block soviet democracy within Cuba.

After the revolutionary seizure of power, reactionary gangs continued to make attacks on leading members of M-26J, committing criminal damage on a wide scale, disrupting communications by destroying telephone exchanges, burning warehouses, killing farm animals in the fields, and so on. All this was strongly supported by the CIA with money, weapons and training. The centre of these activities was the Escambray mountains of south-central Cuba. A local militia was launched to counter these attacks, which it did relatively successfully. Expecting an attack by the US, the militia was expanded and launched as a national organisation, the National Revolutionary Militia (MNR), in October 1959. The militia was one of the first activities to draw in large numbers of women. Counter-revolutionaries of all hues, cried out against the 'immorality' of women who wore trousers instead of skirts, and carried guns. But there were also supporters of the Revolution who questioned whether women should be in the militia. The performance of these women both against saboteurs and, later, during the Bay of Pigs (*Playa Girón*) invasion effectively silenced such criticisms.

The road from armed victory to planned economy was marked by ongoing conflict. On 25 November, 1959, in yet another cabinet shake-up, Che Guevara was named head of the National Bank (BNC), replacing Dr Felipe Pazos. Pazos tendered his resignation on 23 October, 1959, transferred the Presidency of the BNC to Che Guevara and left Cuba soon after. *The Times of Havana* reported, 26 November: "The replacement of Pazos by

Guevara came as a stunning blow to businessmen and bankers." At that time, the BNC was in a critical situation. Not yet nationalised and with few reserves (Batista had helped himself on leaving the country), the Cuban banking system lacked the conditions to promote the country's economic and social development. The revolutionary government needed to take control of the banking system and Guevara immediately enacted reforms that freed Cuba from American banking interests. Under his Presidency, between 1959 and 1961, all American banks were kicked out, allowing Cuba the freedom to control its own money through a state-run bank.[39] When Guevara assumed the Presidency of the BNC, he retained close links with the leading personnel at INRA.

6.1) THE WORKERS' AND PEASANTS' GOVERNMENT

Che's promotion to President of the BNC marked a clear turning point in the direction of the revolution. It symbolised an end to coalition government and a qualitative change in the banking system. The Cuban government declared its independence from the bourgeoisie. The army and police had been destroyed and replaced by forces loyal to the new regime. The existing legal system was being dismantled and replaced. There were comprehensive changes in governmental personnel and policies. Land reform was sweeping the country, imperialism was being faced down, and the masses were mobilising on an ever-broadening basis. Cuba now had a Workers' and Peasants' Government. This was a government in transition, its intervention in the economic sphere was still in its infancy; nationalisations had only just begun, there was no clear-cut programme or plan. The leadership operated empirically, trying to solve each problem as it arose, but there was a clear direction of travel.

The Ministers of Public Works and Recuperation of Misappropriated Goods were replaced, with the new Cabinet members expected to give full support to rapid agrarian reform. The new Minister of Public Works accelerated the pace of road building to speed up rural communication and transportation; and the Ministry for the Recuperation of Misappropriated Goods began to transfer the properties it seized to the INRA.

A shift of power was taking place; from those who believed in fighting dictatorship but not imperialism, to those who spoke for the workers and *campesinos* and were prepared to enact radical anti-imperialist measures. The M-26J was of diminishing importance. According to *The New York Times* 18 December, 1959, INRA had become Cuba's most important economic and political entity, supported by the army and the INRA militias. Fidel's base of support was swinging from the middle class to peasants, workers, and

---

39 Karol, K., *Guerillas in Power*, Hill and Wang, 1970.

soldiers. This shift resulted from the fact that the Cuban masses were being drawn into the revolutionary arena in ever greater numbers as a prelude to building a new type of society.

From 22 December, 1959, all possessions and property of persons convicted of counter-revolutionary activities, and of persons who conspired from abroad, were to be seized. The Cuban Workers' and Peasants' Government firmly resisted imperialism and its Cuban agents, resolutely proceeded with agrarian reform, disarmed the reaction, armed the people, and nationalised capitalist properties; all this was coupled with bold projects to meet the needs of the masses for employment, housing, education, recreation, and culture. During 1959, the Cuban Government effected a series of important expropriations (even if limited) of capitalist property and social prerogatives.

At this time, there were many articles in the US news media praising the achievements of the revolution; in improving the level and quality of food production, the provision of housing for those earning less than US$100 per month, the creativity of the new co-operatives in meeting their own needs, provision of schools and hospitals, etc.[40] But there were also reports of the Federation of Cuban Sugar Workers having trained and armed 55,000 sugar workers in the interior "to defend the sugar crop". In January 1960, the US threatened to cut the sugar quota unless US interests were protected, and the test case would be the interests of United Fruit.

Havana Radio, 5 February, 1960, carried Che Guevara's, defiance of the backers of 'free enterprise':

> During the past seven years Cuba has lost $450 million… we were paying… for the privilege of having a so-called free enterprise… This is why some time ago I said that we are not interested in free enterprise… We serve the Cuban people and profits are invested in works beneficial to the nation.[41]

The key leaders of the revolution (they often admitted it) began as petty-bourgeois. Why then, despite this background, did Fidel and his collaborators not hesitate to nationalise the land and industry, introduce a planned economy and take many measures for the immediate benefit of the workers and peasants? Why did a petty-bourgeois leadership with no intention of doing so, at least initially, lead a national-bourgeois revolution on to a socialist revolution in one continuous process? The answer lay in the way the new regime had come to power and the character of the leadership, the tasks it faced, and the constraints imperialism imposes on the development of neo-colonial countries. The objective reality of the situation facing Cuba was that

---

40 NBC-TV, *Castro's Year of Power*, 23 January, 1960.
41 Gitano, op cit.

the leadership could make good on its promises of a better life for workers and peasants only if it went beyond its original economic goals and took the first steps towards socialism.

Fidel and his comrades of the M-26J Movement were finding out by their own experience that the revolution had become a test of their strength of character. Having taken power at the head of the oppressed classes, to meet the promises given and ensure the survival of the revolution, the leadership of the Cuban Revolution had to proceed step-by-step to carry through the first tasks of the socialist revolution. The reason was simple, the basic reforms necessary to give Cuban workers and peasants an adequate standard of living as part of the national-democratic revolution challenged the interests of imperialism and its allies, the national bourgeoisie. As Farrell Dobbs might have put it, they had vision and they had guts. What gave the government its revolutionary vitality and dynamism was its responsiveness to the needs of the masses and its reliance on mass mobilisations – operating in effect by popular consensus. The masses became deeply loyal to this leadership and, at every critical stage, massive turnouts supported their actions.

It should be noted that, during the period 1960-1962, following the launch of the militia in October 1959, a number of mass organisations mobilised hundreds of thousands to take to the streets to voice their demands. Kapcia goes so far as to claim that in this period the Revolution was carried out by such organisations: the militia, the Revolutionary Defence Committees, the National Federation of Cuban Women, the University Students Federation (supported by high school students), and the Federation of Cuban Workers (under new leadership after the Revolution).[42]

7) REVOLUTIONARY STRUGGLE, CUBA BECOMES A WORKERS' STATE

The Cuban Revolution took place at the peak of the Cold War. By breaking with capitalism, the Cuban leadership was inexorably propelled in the direction of the USSR, but this process was not free of conflicts and difficulties.

The presence of the Soviet Union restrained the US State Department and Pentagon, who now had to consider the international repercussions of their actions vis-a-vis Cuba. The existence of the Soviet Union as a counterforce to imperialism and an example of a society that had successfully overthrown capitalism gave Cuba a degree of flexibility. Confronted by imperialist economic blockades, the leadership could turn to the Soviet Union for aid, trade, loans, military hardware, and technical assistance. While these relations helped the Soviet Union politically, they were vital to

---

42 Kapcia, op cit.

the Workers' and Peasants' Government. Foreign trade underwent a tectonic shift in February 1960, when Anastas Mikoyan arrived at the head of a trade mission. The Soviet Union would buy 5 million tons of sugar over a five-year period and give Cuba credit of US$100 million for the purchase of Soviet agricultural and industrial machinery. The agreement with the Soviet Union was supplemented with trade agreements with China and Eastern Europe.

Certainly, the material aid supplied was essential to the Cuban Revolution's survival but the USSR had another great attraction for all 'third-world' regimes seeking national independence. The Soviet Union had transformed the peasant Russia of the Bolshevik Revolution to the second greatest industrial power on the planet. The strength and superiority of the nationalised, planned economy had been doubly demonstrated by the victory of the USSR over fascist Germany in World War II, and the rebuilding of the Soviet economy. This was a model that might be worth emulating

On 20 February, 1960, all private enterprise was placed under the direct control of the revolutionary government with a central planning board to "supervise, coordinate (and) rebuild the general economy of the country". The army was mobilised to build houses for farm workers, construct roads, lay drainage systems, reforest denuded lands, help farm the co-operatives, build an entire school system in Oriente. With no need for military fortresses, Camp Columbia had become 'Liberty City' and, instead of housing 30,000 of Batista's soldiers, was converted into a technical school. All the larger army posts were transformed into educational centres.

INRA was a major force pushing the revolution to implement a programme of economic and social transformation for the industrial development and social advancement of the country. Strategically, it was pushing to break free of imperialist control its replacement with an economy based on national planning. Throughout Cuba, outside of the wealthy suburbs of Miramar and Varadero, the masses identified with this goal.

By mid-1959, before any Cuba-USSR deal, US President Eisenhower had decided in principle that the US would fund Cuban exiles to overthrow Castro. The plan proposed the invasion of Cuba and the military overthrow of the revolutionary government.[43] In preparation, sabotage attacks on Cuba were executed by Cuban exiles, their major targets being sugar mills, although blowing up the Belgian freighter, *La Coubre*, in Havana harbour on 4 March, 1960, killed over a hundred people and injured 300 more.

In April 1960, the first shipment of Russian crude oil arrived, 300,000 tons. Previously, Cuba had to pay for its oil with dollars, which meant the US had ultimate control over the Cuban economy. To attempt to retain its

---

43 Gleijeses, P., *Conflicting Missions*, Univ of North Carolina Press, 2011.

stranglehold, the US administration pressurised the three existing refineries in Cuba not to process the Soviet oil. Shell, Standard Oil and Texaco agreed. In a make-or-break situation, the Cuban government 'intervened', placing the refineries under government supervision.

This was a major blow to the US attempts to control Cuba's trade, and precipitated a chain of actions and reactions. On 7 July, Eisenhower cut the Cuban annual sugar quota by ninety-five per cent. This was a serious blow for the Cuban economy, and Cuba countered by nationalising American property. Fidel declared: "They may take away our quota pound by pound and we will take away their sugar mills one by one", and on 6 August, he announced the nationalisation of all US-owned properties; telephone, electric, railways, port facilities, and thirty-six sugar refineries. In September, the Cuban branches of American banks were nationalised. When the first steps were taken, the masses helped to accelerate them by joining huge demonstrations in support of the government's actions. The radical measures further undermined the possibility of coming to terms with the bourgeoisie. Instead, the bourgeoisie and the middle classes began to flee the country or engage in subversion that compelled the regime to take action against them. This increased the pressure on the leaders to organise the economy through nationalisations and planning to prevent the growth of social instability.

The workers were intimately involved in many of the nationalisations. Two examples given by Cushion are the nationalisation of the US-owned oil companies; when the managers fled, the battle between capitalism and the budding socialism in Cuba became a battle for maintaining oil production, which was achieved only because the refinery workers rallied to the revolution. The second example is the workers' take-over in June 1960, of the newspaper *Diario de la Marina*, the public face behind which the forces of reaction and counter-revolution were coalescing. After the workers had seized the presses and been supported by mass demonstrations in Havana, the paper was expropriated and the presses turned over to printing other material.

Cuba, now economically reliant on the Soviet states, took the decision in the summer of 1960 to create a government department to produce a general plan to enable the country to stand on its own two feet economically. The Junta Central de Planificacion (*Juceplan*) to be led by Guevara would be formally launched in early 1961, staffed by young volunteers who had some background in economics, mainly from Latin America but with a significant proportion from Eastern Europe. *Juceplan* was tasked to produce a state plan for Cuba's economy. Not surprisingly, given the presence of so many Eastern Europeans, the plan adopted closely followed that of the USSR with all its bureaucratic dead weight.

As a consequence of the objective conditions which Cuba faced, pressures towards bureaucratisation existed in all organisations to a greater or lesser extent. The unions were one example. With the fall of Batista, his most prominent supporters had fled, being replaced by anti-Batista activists, mainly from the M-26J, with PSP members also holding positions in some unions. However, some less prominent union officials switched sides, claimed to be supporters of democracy, and retained their posts. The Stalinists, combined with the left-overs from the Batista years and elements of the *unitarios* wing of the M-26J, began to harden into a bureaucratic layer, resulting in a deterioration in democracy within the union movement.

An effective argument used by the bureaucrats against having democratic discussions which, of course, posed a serious threat to their existence, was to argue that the US embargo was the cause of all Cuba's major problems. In a besieged fortress, it was necessary to stand shoulder-to-shoulder against the main enemy and not to dissipate energy in internal recriminations.

Shortly after the victory of the revolution, a small Trotskyist organisation in Cuba was re-established: the Workers Revolutionary Party (Trotskyist) (POR(T)). Its members were able to attend and intervene, with some success, in the July 1960 First Latin American Congress of Youth, in Havana.[44] The Stalinist apparatus was ready to resort to almost any means to silence the Trotskyists and, without the protection of the Cuban authorities, they would undoubtedly have been silenced physically. As it was, the Stalinist leadership decided to rob the Trotskyists of the right to speak at the Congress by challenging their mandate, naming them on the front pages of their newspapers as CIA agents.

The Trotskyist delegation, in the person of Juan León Ferrera, a sergeant in the Rebel Army, immediately distributed to all Congress delegates the manifesto they had brought to support their intended presentation. Copies were also sent to political, trade union, and popular organisations and was widely quoted in the Cuban press the following day. Ferrera had impeccable credentials. He had joined the Rebel Army with his father and fought so well he had been promoted to Sergeant; his mother had served as a nurse with the guerrillas.

To confront and defeat the Stalinists, the Trotskyists attended the first session of the Congress and demanded a revolutionary tribunal judge the truth of the accusations. The Trotskyist delegates were ready to submit their conduct to a review by such a tribunal and asked that if they were cleared of the Stalinist slanders, their accusers should be put on trial as defamers of revolutionaries, and expelled from the Congress.

---

44 Fanjul, A., *The Role of Trotskyists in the Cuban Revolution*, IP, 11 May, 1981.

When Fanjul requested to speak, and was handed a microphone, the Stalinist delegates and some others stood up and drowned him out with shouts of "Cuba sí, Yankees no!". The uproar went on for some ten minutes, but Fanjul stood his ground, and started to speak, over and over again, until finally he was able to make himself heard. He had been given five minutes to state his case but spoke for nearly half an hour to a completely silent audience.

The Congress president asked whether any delegates took responsibility for the accusations. If no-one did, the Congress could be considered to have confirmed that at no time had the Trotskyist delegation been attacked in word or in deed. No-one rose to take responsibility for the slanders. The POR(T) was allowed to participate in the Congress as a Trotskyist delegation, and have its amendments voted on, a real achievement given the vicious hostility and gagging moves of the Stalinists.

The Federation of Cuban Women (FMC) was launched in late summer 1960 with Vilma Espín its first president. With similar aims to Zhenotdel (Department for Work among Women Workers and Peasants, established by the Bolshevik Party in September 1919) the FMC used the Russian organisation as its model. Its main aims: Bringing women out of the home and into the economy, reorganising peasant households that kept women in subservient positions, developing communal services to alleviate domestic work and childcare, providing equal opportunities for women, mobilising women into political work and government administration, and providing adequate working conditions "to satisfy the particular needs of the female organism and the moral and spiritual needs of women as mothers".[45]

The FMC remains a powerful and influential organisation, making women's social liberation and their integration into the revolutionary process a reality. Initially, its activities were to help organise the masses of women, both urban and rural, into building the militias and the CDRs (see below), establishing a network of childcare centres enabling women to enter the workforce and spreading education on contraception and abortion. As with Zhenotdel, the FMC was an organisation intended for and composed of women; men were not excluded but the reality is that the vast majority of meetings – certainly at local levels – were (and remain) women only. Thus, women who had never previously participated in public activities could feel comfortable in its ranks. With both Zhenotdel and the FMC, the link with the PCC was/is at the top; in Russia the President of Zhenotdel reported personally to the Political Committee of the Party via the Orgburo, in Cuba

---

45 Harris, C., *Socialist Societies and the Emancipation of Women: The Case of Cuba*. Socialism and Democracy, 1995, 9(1)91-113.

the link is less direct, as the FMC is officially an NGO and Party control is ensured by having the President and FMC tops, as PCC members.

In late September 1960, the Revolutionary Defence Committees (*Comités de Defensa de la Revolución*, CDRs) were launched to combat CIA terrorism and sabotage that had mushroomed in the run-up to the Bay of Pigs. CDR units were established on each city block throughout all urban areas. Rural areas had their counterparts. The CDRs were intended to act as a 'neighbourhood watch' to protect public buildings, locate and identify terrorist activities and feed information to the police. Women soon provided over half the total membership.

The functions of the CDRs expanded over time and now include approval of proposed building works, change of address, and organisation of voluntary work such as the growing of fresh vegetables in gardens and upkeep of chickens in backyard plots. Current estimates give the CDRs a membership of as high as eight million. Despite their unquestionable social usefulness and mass membership, the pyramidal structure of the CDRs did not, and does not, encourage democratisation or horizontality.

In September/October 1960, all US-owned banks were nationalised, and the Law for Urban Reform, allowing nationalisation of the property of those who had left the country, was passed. Finally, the biggest Cuban companies were taken into public ownership. Cuban-owned factories and industry, generally, had no separate existence from the American firms that dominated the Cuban economy. Thus, the nationalisation of foreign-owned industry meant Cuban-owned factories found it difficult to operate privately when both their major suppliers and customers were government-operated. As a result, nationalisations soon encompassed not only railroads, port facilities and those enterprises engaged in foreign trade, but also Cuban-owned enterprises. In a very short period, Cuba made the transition from an overwhelmingly privately-owned economy to one that was eighty per cent nationalised. The state ran the banking system, and ninety per cent of industries that produced Cuba's exports, which meant that, by the end of 1960, foreign trade was fully under state control.

US administrations have made much of the number of Cubans who have fled from Cuba, but they forget their own history. At least 100,000 people left the British colonies in America during and after the American Revolution, a higher proportion of the population than fled Cuba after the Revolution. The high church Tories could not stomach the political and social changes which attend all revolutions worthy of the name – that those regarded as inferiors no longer know their place. The Tories fled to Canada carrying tales of barbaric, dissolute and godless American revolutionaries.

Those who remained and refused to take an oath of allegiance to the new state governments were denied their civil liberties. Many were jailed, forced into exile or even murdered.

Judges who had not been replaced immediately after the revolution were now being called on to enforce measures such as rent reductions and land seizures that hurt the interests of the bourgeoisie. Where they could not stop the individual cases being brought before them, they awarded excessively generous compensation to the previous land owners. Matters came to a head at the end of 1960 when the entire judiciary was purged of counter-revolutionaries and a new Supreme Court appointed. This time the process extended to the regional and provincial judges. Blas Roca, General Secretary of the PSP, was given the job of hurriedly drawing up a new judicial system in accord with the principles of the revolution. The new system was further modified in 1970 and 1975 to strengthen the position of the lay judges who serve for two months a year, for two-and-a-half years.

The cancellation of the sugar quota marked the beginning of the blockade of Cuba by America. The Soviet Union, followed by the People's Republic of China, was quick to buy up the surplus sugar. The US refused to trade with Cuba, and when the Soviet Union again stepped in, the US scolded Cuba for cuddling up to 'Communism'. In a very real sense, the US administration pushed Cuba into the arms of the Soviet Union. As the trade war with the US hotted up, additional treaties were agreed with the Soviet Union and China, so that the major portion of Cuban trade was with the workers' states. The US retaliated by placing an embargo on all exports to Cuba. Notionally, food and medicines were excluded but trade in these items declined rapidly.

In November 1960, the US announced the blockade of Cuba and, in January 1961, Eisenhower broke off diplomatic relations. By this time Cuba was a state with a government that had come to power by a popular revolution, which had smashed the bourgeois army and police force, and replaced them with a rebel army. It had a new police force recruited largely from the ranks of revolutionary fighters determined to defend the gains of the revolution. The new state was based on the monopoly of foreign trade, nationalisation of the land and every important sector of the economy, and the economy was subject to a national plan based on social need not private profit. When these measures were complete, Cuba had entered the transitional phase known as a workers' state (transitional between capitalism and socialism). However, it lacked any form of democratic proletarian rule.

The M-26J had smashed the old state structure in coming to power, but the initial failure of the new government to proclaim socialist aims demonstrated that the subjective factor in the revolution remained unclear.

This was a workers' state in which the working class did not hold power directly through, e.g. soviets, and in which there was no organised means to express their demands. Similar formations had occurred after World War II in, e.g., Yugoslavia and China. However, because the leadership of the regime in Cuba was not Stalinist, as were the leaders in Yugoslavia and China, there were those who argued that Cuba must be a healthy workers' state, despite the state not being under the democratic control of the workers and peasants.

Politically, the revolution was not keeping pace with the economic developments. The M-26J was not a Leninist party. Proletarian democratic forms, such as the soviets of the Russian Revolution, were not established. Control rested with Fidel Castro and a thin layer of leaders who set policies and saw to their execution. The leaders had the enthusiastic support of the workers and peasants, but the masses could not express their views through institutions which allowed for rank and file discussion and decision-making. For example, the Declarations of Havana (both one and two) were presented to mass rallies, read through by Fidel and carried by acclamation. That was not soviet democracy.

Of course, it was correct for revolutionaries to support the M-26J either as members or as allies, but it was also necessary to attempt to establish democratic structures, particularly in the factories and amongst the workers as no structure or mechanism for such discussions existed. A possible substitute might have been the unofficial structures that had organised strike actions within the individual factories and enterprises. The call would have been for the Castro-Guevara team to introduce mechanisms for workers' control and management of the economy and government. But the dynamism of the revolutionary process meant that the importance of such considerations was obscured.

In early 1961, the campaign to eradicate illiteracy was launched. Brigades composed of thousands of students went to the countryside to teach and live with the peasants. Allowed out of the home to freely associate with other young people for the first time meant that many of these activists look back on the literacy campaign as one of the highlights of their lives. It was a living demonstration that women could work alongside men on an equal basis. Following the literacy drive, women were very much involved in all areas; within a decade over half of medical students were women, the nationalised industries needed managers and in Cuba many women occupied those positions. Over 4,000 women were appointed workplace managers and, whilst *machismo* was not entirely absent, in the workplaces where women were managers, it went a long way in changing attitudes.

Simultaneously, the vast disparities between rich and poor, city and country were being rapidly narrowed. The mass support of the political and economic revolutionary measures was accompanied by a spontaneous growth of anti-imperialist sentiment among the Cuban people. During 1959 and 1960, the actions of the US helped the Cuban people to become more conscious of their country's previous subordination to American imperialism.

7.1) PERMANENT REVOLUTION OR REVOLUTION BY STAGES?

Leon Trotsky was the first to give a full theoretical explanation of the theory of the permanent revolution as applied to a 'backward' country. The revolution would have to be 'permanent' in two regards: it would start with the national democratic tasks, but these could be fully achieved only if the leaders of the revolution took the first steps towards socialism. The bourgeois democratic revolution could be successful only if it flowed into the socialist, and the socialist revolution, while beginning on a national scale is completed on the world arena; the "construction of an independent socialist society in any single country in the world is impossible".[46]

The alternative to the theory of the permanent revolution, was a revival of the class collaborationist theory of stages, promoted by Stalin to protect the rising bureaucracy within the Russian Communist Party. These bureaucrats were accumulating material privileges due to their position within the party and state, and wanted to be left in peace to enjoy them. They convinced themselves that only war with an advanced imperialist power could dislodge them and so were utterly opposed to the theory of permanent revolution, which argued that, for the Russian workers' state to survive, the proletarian revolution had to spread internationally, seeking the help of the mighty working classes in the advanced capitalist countries. Lenin's view, expressed many times, that the final victory of socialism in a single country was "impossible"[47] and "inconceivable"[48] was written out of history, as was his argument that the Russian revolution had to spread to Western Europe or it would eventually succumb to capitalist counter-revolution.

By 1959, the theory of the permanent revolution had, apparently, been buried by wholesale massacres in the Soviet Union, the murders of such Marxists as Trotsky and Mella, and an international campaign in which those opposing Stalin were labelled the running dogs of fascism, for whom a thorough beating was too good. Such gangster methods can never resolve a theoretical question because it will keep rearing its head in new guises.

---

46 Trotsky, L., *The Revolution Betrayed* www.marxists.org.
47 Lenin, V., *Third All-Russian Congress of Soviets*, 11 January, 1918, CW26:470.
48 Lenin, V., *Speech on the Anniversary of the Revolution*, 9 Nov., 1918, CW28:151.

The theory of stages would, apart from a sudden lurch to the left in the late 1920s, imposed by internal Russian considerations, flow into the People's Front, then Peaceful Co-existence, and finally the downfall of the Soviet Union. It was not war that overthrew the workers' states, but higher levels of productivity under capitalism, and better quality goods.

Stalin's approach was both schematic and formalistic, epitomised by the argument that, because the revolution in a 'backward' country had as its immediate objectives bourgeois democratic goals, the national bourgeoisie would not, could not, betray its 'own' revolution. Thus, there was a unity of interests between the national bourgeoisie, petty-bourgeoisie, workers and peasants (referred to in the Chinese Revolution as the 'bloc of four classes') against the common enemy, imperialism. Unfortunately, to keep the national bourgeoisie on side and preserve the unity of the Popular Front, it was necessary for the workers and peasants to restrict their demands to what was acceptable to the national bourgeoisie.

There was no historical justification for this argument, indeed the facts of the Russian Revolution, demonstrated just the opposite. The first application of the theory was in China during the 1925 revolutionary upsurge. Its application led to the defeat of the revolution and the deaths of tens of thousands of Chinese revolutionaries and Communists. The Chinese national bourgeoisie, faced with revolution, discovered they had more in common with the imperialists than Chinese workers and peasants. For factional reasons, to protect their interests, the Russian party bureaucracy stood reality on its head and hailed the defeat as proof of the correctness of the new theory, which was then enshrined in the programme of the Stalinised Communist International.[49]

In *The Permanent Revolution,* Trotsky wrote:

> With regard to countries with a belated bourgeois development, especially the colonial and semi-colonial countries, the theory of permanent revolution signifies that the complete and genuine solution of their tasks of achieving *democracy and emancipation* is conceivable only through the dictatorship of the proletariat as the leader of the subjugated nation, above all of its peasant masses.

The events which followed the seizure of power in Cuba are a striking confirmation of Trotsky's theory because the M-26J leaders were forced to act in the opposite way they had intended. The Cuban Revolution, starting out as a bourgeois democratic revolution, was forced to move against capitalism to achieve its bourgeois-democratic aims. The development of the Cuban

49 Roberts, J., *China: From Permanent Revolution to Counter-Revolution*, Wellred Books, 2016.

Revolution between 1959 and 1962 is a dramatic, practical confirmation of Trotsky's theory.

In Cuba, the national bourgeoisie in their majority followed the example of their counterparts in China and elsewhere, and played no revolutionary role. The most direct agents of international capital were thoroughly hostile to the mass upsurges and did what they could to sabotage them, before finally going into exile. The 'progressive' bourgeoisie, those that remained in Cuba, attempted to subvert the revolutionary process through their influence within the coalition governments. Most of these would finally go abroad. A few tried to insert themselves into the state apparatus, hoping for an eventual turn in their direction.

Initially, the government tried to set a moderate pace, endeavouring to collaborate with the remaining capitalists and with the upper layers of the peasantry. What upset their plans, and forced them to take drastic action, was the hostile reaction of the US imperialists. The reality was that it was not possible to implement an advanced national democratic programme for Cuba without clashing head-on with the interests of the US, which controlled the country's economy, and with the tightly-knit alliance of landlords and national bourgeoisie that were imperialism's local lackeys.

In an interview in August 1960, Armando Hart, Minister of Education, emphasised this aspect of the process:

> United States policy is forcing us to make our revolution much faster than we wanted to. It is a stupid policy, because the reaction is always the contrary of what the US wants. Communism was no problem here. If it is now, you (the US) created it by forcing us into policies for which we had no other choice.[50]

The Cubans were pushed into taking socialist measures to achieve their social goals, and the deepening of the social revolution dealt powerful shocks to the imperialists' control of the economy.

The Cuban Stalinists, such as Blas Roca and Carlos Rafael Rodríguez, often spoke of the need to avoid the 'super-revolutionary language' of socialism, preferring to advance the theory of stages. Roca and Rodríguez conveniently forgot to mention that their own attempts to achieve agrarian reform and national sovereignty in Cuba, by following a stagist strategy, had failed dismally.

In Cuba, Trotsky has been completely verified. Those national movements in countries like India and Indonesia that won independence remain dependent on imperialism in the form of the international banks and

---

50 Matthews, H., *Fidel Castro*, Simon and Schuster, 1970.

imperialist powers for credit and other financial aid, including imperialist investment in the form of new factories which exploit cheap labour. Key aspects that show formal independence has brought neither real national emancipation nor real democracy are the ongoing impoverishment of the peasants, and treatment of women.

8) BAY OF PIGS AND THE RISE OF THE CUBAN COMMUNIST PARTY

'Jack' Kennedy became President in January 1961 and approved the existing plan for the CIA to find, fund and train, supposedly in absolute secrecy but, in reality in full view of the world, a small army of dissident exiles to invade Cuba and overthrow the new government. The plan was based on the false belief that there was widespread anti-Castro feeling across Cuba. A trial run took place in the autumn of 1960 when anti-Castro forces infiltrated into the Escambray mountains, supplied by CIA air-drops. But local militia, informed in advance of the adventure, combed the area, taking possession of the air-drops and capturing most, if not all, of the 'bandits'. The CIA changed tack and proposed landing an 'advance guard' of 1,500, which would establish a bridgehead and trigger the expected popular anti-Castro revolt. On 17 April, 1961, the CIA launched the invasion at the Bay of Pigs (*Playa Girón*).

It was a disaster at every level. The Cuban army and local militia were prepared and waiting, the fighting was intense but lasted only two days. Of the 1,500 exiles who participated, over 100 were killed and nearly 1,200 were captured, the remnants fled back to the USA. The Cuban people rallied to their new government, which was now fully convinced that an alliance with the USSR, China, and Eastern Europe was the way forward. The youth of the world, and Latin America in particular, had witnessed the defeat of the US-backed invasion, had seen that US imperialism was not as powerful as it had once appeared. The new Cuba was there to stay.

Fidel made much of the social composition of the invaders: of those captured about 800 came from wealthy families who had owned, between them, two banks, five mines, ten sugar mills, seventy factories, nearly 10,000 houses and 370,000 hectares (almost a million acres) of land. Most of the officers were former soldiers of Batista. The class character of the invaders was presented as proof positive of the different class character of the new Cuba from the old.

Prior to the counter-revolutionary invasion at the Bay of Pigs the Cuban leaders generally had not described their actions as socialist, but on 16 April, 1961, at the funeral of the victims of a US-sponsored air-raid, Fidel and others openly proclaimed the revolution as socialist. At the May Day rally following the attempted invasion, Fidel declared to over a million Cubans; "This is a socialist regime, yes! Yes, this is a socialist regime".[51]

In a televised address on 2 December, 1961, Fidel for the first time declared:

> I am a Marxist-Leninist and shall be one until the end of my life… Marxism or scientific socialism has become the revolutionary movement of the working class

This was welcomed by revolutionaries world-wide as a proclamation of a socialist Cuba with a socialist government. In 1963, Fidel gave more details about his transition:

> It was a gradual process, a dynamic process in which the pressure of events forced me to accept Marxism as the answer to what I was seeking… So, as events developed, I gradually moved into a Marxist-Leninist position. I cannot tell you just when; the process was so gradual and so natural.[52]

There is a current within academia which promotes the line that Mao, Castro and others gained power by deception; that they hid their true goals behind popular demands, and that, if the populations of China and Cuba had known their real motives, they would have stuck with Uncle Sam's nominees. On one occasion Fidel was asked, "If you had announced that you were a Marxist and openly espoused a socialist program while you were still a guerrilla leader in the Sierra Maestra, do you think you still would have been able to come to power?" Fidel responded, "Possibly not. It would not have been intelligent to bring about such an open confrontation".

It cannot be denied that, in Cuba in 1957, proclaiming socialism would have been unpopular because of the enormous damage done to the reputation of socialism, of communism, by the record of Stalinism in the Soviet Union and in Cuba, where the PCC had supported Batista. However, what is a 'socialist programme'? Did Lenin's demands for 'Bread, Peace and Land' constitute a 'socialist programme'?

Fidel Castro was no Trotskyist, and had no concept of transitional demands, demands which solve the problems actually faced by the workers and peasants and lead naturally to a socialist transformation of society. In the reality of a Cuba dominated by United Fruit, had "Land to those that work it" not become a transitional demand? What these academics fail to grasp is that, in the era of imperialism, it is necessary to take the first steps towards socialism in order to fully carry out the democratic revolution. Failing to

---

51 Castro, F., May Day Speech 1 May, 1961, www.marxists.org.
52 Matthews, H., *Fidel Castro*, Simon and Schuster, 1970.

understand the theory of the permanent revolution, they cannot comprehend how a democratic revolution can end up as socialist, feeling that somehow they've been cheated. In their vanity, they cannot see the fault is their own lack of comprehension; instead they label Castro as a deceiver.

It was sensible of Fidel to avoid misunderstandings and, of course, he had been repelled by the record of the PCC. Ideological debates were not his strong point, he was a man of action and the revolution moved forward under the slogan: armed struggle to overthrow Batista. Some might argue this was a particular form of a single issue campaign, and on that basis the M-26J avoided programmatic debates that would have differentiated the anti-Batista groupings.

To protect the Cuban Revolution it was the right and duty of the Castro team to establish whatever economic and military agreements with the Soviet Union they deemed necessary. The problem was the extent of political subordination to the bureaucracy. When Fidel gave unqualified praise to the USSR and its leaders, he did a great disservice to the struggle of the worker and peasant masses. He undermined the struggle of revolutionists everywhere against the bureaucratic counter-revolution and Stalinism.

When the new regime broke with capitalism, the model it emulated was not that of Soviet Russia of 1917, but that of the Stalinist Russia of 1961 where all traces of soviet democracy and workers' control had long been eradicated. Cuba's top leaders claimed that they were the government of the workers, peasants and students and it was true that the strength of the masses had brought them to power. However, the guerrilla struggle gave a top-down form to the new government that fitted well with the Russian system, but contained no mechanism by which the masses were organised as the supreme and legal state power. If the masses were to hold power, a new style of state apparatus was needed. To match the soviet democracy of Lenin, it would be necessary to transfer authority to the revolutionary mass organisations, comprised of elected representatives.

The Stalinists of the PCC had organisational experience that was generally lacking, this together with the weight of the Soviet Union in Cuban affairs, meant they were being promoted within the state apparatus. The second CTC-R Congress was held in November 1961, two years after the first, and in that time a seasoned communist leader, Lazaro Peña, had been appointed as chairperson, and would remain in post until his death, in 1974.

The Bay of Pigs invasion brought a regime crack-down on all those seen as oppositionists or dissenters. At this time, the POR(T) was preparing to publish Trotsky's *Revolution Betrayed*. In May 1961, an issue of the POR(T) paper, *Voz Proletaria*, made a number of criticisms of the process by which the Cuban Communist Party was being formed. The paper was seized, then the printing presses were closed down and the plates for the book smashed. Those who produced and sold subsequent duplicated editions of the paper were arrested and imprisoned on the grounds that they were calling for a provocative march on the Guantánamo naval base to expel the imperialists, a claim that has been vigorously denied.[53]

While supporting the new regime, and limiting their criticisms to what they perceived to be distortions within the post-1959 revolutionary order, the POR(T) raised two important questions, both focused on the need for soviet democracy, and based on Lenin's argument that, in the initial phase of a workers' state, it was necessary to have trade unions separate from the state, "to protect the workers from their state".[54]

Stemming from the May Day declaration that Cuba was a socialist country, there was a common agreement amongst Trotskyist organisations that a constitution based on a government representing workers' organisations or councils was needed. Also stemming from the May Day declaration, was a general agreement that this representative workers' government must be led by a mass revolutionary party, open to the most class-conscious and active revolutionary fighters. The leadership of this party could be none other than the Castro team, but the new constitution should provide for a regime of genuine workers' democracy, in which all tendencies supporting the revolution had full freedom of expression and association. Trotskyists should be allowed to organise as a propaganda group because Trotskyism represented the continuation of revolutionary theory and practice and should be permitted to be a tendency within the new revolutionary party.

The POR(T) called for free elections within, e.g. the Cuban trade unions, and for the right of all tendencies supporting the regime to be allowed to stand for office. Such a demand is, of course, a necessity for soviet democracy. However, it is quite impossible for such a process to be effective without the right of those standing for office to organise. The POR(T) defended the right of all working-class parties and tendencies which supported the revolution and defended the workers' state to an open and legal existence. They argued that the masses should have the right to choose their representatives from among these revolutionary tendencies and positions.[55]

The round of arrests and imprisonment reflected the growing political weight of the pro-Moscow Stalinists, but Fidel had already expressed a similar attitude in response to the raising of different opinions at the September

53 Tennant, G., *Dissident Cuban Communism: The Case of Trotskyism, 1932-1965*, PhD Thesis, Bradford University, 1999.
54 Lenin, V., *On the Trade Unions*, 30 December, 1920, CW 32:15-42.
55 Tennant, op cit.

1959 CTC-R Congress. The difficulty facing the POR(T) or any other revolutionary group supporting the revolution, but wanting to correct its deficiencies by calling for soviet democracy, was that there was no party or other structure within which they could express their views.

8.1) THE 1962 MISSILE CRISIS

The Kennedy administration remained committed to the overthrow of the Castro regime, but the Bay of Pigs disaster had cured them of any intention of invading Cuba; instead, they put their efforts into diplomatic and economic sabotage. Nevertheless, after April 1961, the Cuban leadership welcomed the protection of the Soviet bureaucracy and, to strengthen the alliance, the Soviet Union was allowed to establish missile bases in Cuba as a deterrent to a US invasion. For the Soviet leadership, these bases were to balance the numerous US missile sites in countries such as Turkey and Italy aimed at the Soviet Union. This led to the so-called Cuban missile crisis of October 1962.

Initial discussions between Soviet and Cuban military leaders provisionally agreed a Soviet presence of: 42,000 soldiers; Mig fighters; Ilyushin bombers; fast, lightweight missile carrying boats; surface-to-air missile batteries; and a total of forty intermediate range missiles with nuclear warheads. The missile bases were detected by American U2 spy planes while under construction. In the face-off between President Kennedy and Premier Khrushchev that followed, the missiles were removed in exchange for the removal of US missiles from Turkey, and a verbal undertaking from Kennedy that he would not sanction a US invasion of the island – though pirate raids by exiles continued along Cuba's coast for more than a decade. The Cuban political leaders were not involved in the decision to remove the missiles. Indeed, some authors, such as Gott, insist they were not even involved in the original decision to site the missiles in Cuba.

Khrushchev handled the Missiles Crisis as a bilateral USSR-USA deal, with no reference to Havana. This gave the Castro leadership serious qualms over entrusting their future security exclusively to Moscow. In response, the early 1960s saw the Fidelistas seeking to establish and maintain a degree of political independence, both with regard to Latin American politics and within the 'world socialist movement'. But the Soviet Union's economic stranglehold on Cuba was overwhelming and, increasingly, Cuba was forced to agree that its foreign policy decisions be co-ordinated with the Soviet Union. The close working relationship between the Cuban and Soviet armed forces not only helped strengthen the Stalinist and bureaucratic currents within Cuba but there were parallel links between the Soviet KGB and the Cuban equivalent, the DGI. Finally, the process of bureaucratisation would have a serious and negative impact on the leaders of the Cuban Revolution, especially regarding the democratic movements that would arise in Eastern Europe.

8.2) CHE FAILS TO EXPORT THE REVOLUTION TO LATIN AMERICA

Khrushchev's deal with the US at the time of the 1962 missile crisis made the Cuban leaders deeply suspicious of the USSR. Pushed by Che Guevara, the Cubans attempted to spread the revolution to other countries in Latin America and beyond, something which clashed with the policy of 'peaceful coexistence' pursued by the Soviet Union as well as with the profoundly conservative outlook of most of the Latin American Communist Parties. Che announced:

> There are no frontiers in this struggle to the death. We cannot remain indifferent in the face of what occurs in any part of the world. A victory for any country against imperialism is our victory, just as any country's defeat is our defeat... The socialist countries have the moral duty of liquidating their tacit complicity with the exploiting countries of the West.[56]

The period between 1963 and 1971 was one of widespread ideological and political ferment in Cuba. The discussions and debates can – at the risk of doing damage to the reality – be divided into four:

- Extending the revolution to the rest of Latin America through guerrilla action, which ended with the death of Che in 1967.
- The introduction of soviet realism in art and culture generally, which generated widespread resistance especially in cinema and film.
- The struggle against Stalinism led by the Philosophy Department in Havana University, which ended with the closure of the department and the dispersal of its staff in 1971.
- Che's differences with Stalinists such as Carlos Rafael Rodríguez on whether it was possible to develop a socialist consciousness and industrial productivity simultaneously.

Che is best known for his "two, three, many Vietnams" message to the Tricontinental Conference in 1967 (made all the more significant by his death in the October), in which he appeared to have come to the same conclusions on the nature of the national bourgeoisie as Mella:

> [T]he indigenous bourgeoisies have lost all their capacity to oppose imperialism – if they ever had it – and they have become the last card in the

---

56 www.marxists.org/archive/guevara/1965/ 02/24.htm

pack. There are no other alternatives; either a socialist revolution or a make-believe revolution.[57]

During Che's life and until about a year after his death, Fidel showed a significant degree of independence from the Kremlin. During this time, he (and Che) still believed that rural guerrilla war on the Cuban model could be successful in other Latin American countries. Clearly, Fidel and Che saw the Cuban Revolution as part of the Latin American revolution and, more widely, as part of the struggle of the colonial peoples against imperialism. This concept clashed head-on with the foreign policy of the Soviet bureaucracy and led to a conflict in many Communist parties on the continent. However, the Cubans lacked an understanding of the need for a revolutionary party, and the emphasis on guerrilla action in opposition to the official Communist Parties, meant a continental-wide debate between those supporting the guerrilla line and the more orthodox communists.

This debate was carried on in the open. The issues were posed in terms of men of action leading rural guerrilla warfare having final command of the course of the struggle, which was the subordination of politics to the tactics of rural guerrilla warfare. Fidel made this the subject of a major speech: 'Those who are not revolutionary fighters cannot be called Communists', on 13 March, 1967, at the University of Havana.[58] The speech was immediately denounced by the Political Bureau of the *Partido Communista de Venezuela* (PCV), which, soon after, under strong pressure from Moscow, officially renounced armed struggle.[59] The Cubans affirmed the need for the masses to take the road of armed struggle and condemned the decision of the Venezuelan Communists to revert to electoral politics and peaceful coexistence.

The PCV advanced as their strongest arguments the need for a revolutionary party, and for the revolutionary vanguard to maintain its ties with the masses in the cities which, in his speech, Fidel had declared "an absurdity". The Cubans were inexperienced in this kind of debate and, by default, the Stalinists were able to obscure the essential question of whether a revolutionary struggle was necessary to achieve socialism or it could be achieved by peaceful co-existence. In this factional struggle, when the votes were counted, the supporters of the Cuban line ended up a small minority, not only in Venezuela, but throughout Latin America. Nowhere in Latin America did the Cubans succeed in grouping around themselves new forces

---

57 Ibid.

58 Castro, F., *Those who are not revolutionary fighters cannot be called Communists,* Merit Publishers, 1968.

59 *Text of Venezuelan CP Reply to Fidel Castro* in World Outlook, 14 April, 1967, 5(15)407-408.

of a size and quality capable of launching a struggle on the Cuban model. Once again, the Cubans showed their limitations; no attempt was made to draw a balance sheet of the political lessons of the struggle and of the political role of Stalinism – see Castro's attack on Trotskyism at the Tricontinental Conference in Havana in January 1966, and his support for Russian tanks to put down the Czech spring.

The top leaders of the PCV had moved towards an understanding with the Venezuelan government under which they would be released in exchange for stopping the guerrilla war. The rationale offered for this change of course was that conditions for guerrilla warfare had been proved absent in Venezuela, and that the correct policy was to build a mass party within the existing legal framework.

The PCV had signed a 'conciliatory document' on 7 November, 1965, but delayed announcing its retreat until the following year. The PCV view of guerrilla warfare in Venezuela was as a means to push forward a general politically reformist perspective. As a strategy for guerrilla warfare, such an approach was ineffective and bound to fail; and guerrilla leaders like Douglas Bravo, who bucked against it, were deprived of food, medical supplies, clothing and ammunition, and were even accused of being traitors to the revolution and provocateurs. It turned out that the PCV move in 1963 to support guerrilla war had been a cynical ploy to frighten the oligarchy into inviting the PCV to become part of the government. The Eighth Plenum of the PCV, held during the first two weeks in April 1967, formally agreed to end the guerrilla line and to participate in the coming 1968 elections under the slogan 'democratic peace' behind a candidate of 'national unification'. It was at this meeting that Bravo was expelled.

Fidel had led a successful revolution in 1959, so why was it that his current ended up in a small minority? The Cubans had made a socialist revolution, but the US and the local leaders had learned their lessons, as Che's death had tragically demonstrated. Now the objective situation in the countries of Latin America demanded mass mobilisations based on transitional demands. The Cuban leaders, the 'men of action', had scorned theory and were now doubly reluctant to draw a balance sheet of Stalinism, as they had to rely on aid from the Soviet Union for the survival of the revolution.

The attempts to export the revolution failed. US imperialism had learned a lesson in Cuba and had no intention of again being taken by surprise; it had invested heavily and had in place the necessary means to isolate and quickly defeat any small band of guerrillas. Che's attempt led to his death at the hands of US imperialism, and caused the Cubans to re-assess their guerrilla warfare line. The period from after Che's death in Bolivia in October 1967 to the failure of the ten-million ton sugar harvest in 1970 was one of transition for the Fidelista leadership at the end of which the Cubans had themselves ditched guerrilla warfare as a means of overthrowing the imperialist-backed regimes in Latin America.

The failure of Che's attempt to spread the revolution, and Russian pressure, had made the Cubans draw back from the guerrilla line and re-oriented their efforts; they no longer backed OLAS (Organisation for Latin American Solidarity launched by the Cubans as part of their guerrilla strategy). Fidel adopted a new line much more in accord with Moscow's strategy of peaceful coexistence: OLAS faded from the scene leaving those who were actively engaged in rural guerrilla warfare to bitterly decry the Cubans for letting slip what they saw as a historic opportunity.

However, there are none so blind as those that will not see, and a number of dedicated militants determinedly pursued the rural guerrilla line. One such was 'Inti' Peredo who, before he went into action declared: "We will build an armed force. We are not trying to build a political party". The September-October, 1968, *New Left Review* carried an article by Peredo: 'Guerrilla warfare in Bolivia is not dead: it has just begun'. Within a year Peredo and many of his supporters were dead, hundreds more were imprisoned and tortured. The guerrillas in Bolivia, far from being the motor force that would carry the revolution to victory, suffered a terrible defeat. Many cadres were killed needlessly in a hopeless venture.

Fidel Castro's new political line meant he dampened correct and necessary criticisms previously made of the Latin American Communist Parties, objectively helping to maintain illusions in those parties and their reformist and opportunist policies. Worse still, he took completely wrong positions toward certain bourgeois regimes in Latin America, staying silent about the repression of workers and revolutionists, creating confusion about the role to be played by bourgeois sectors in the Latin American revolution. Behind all this were the profoundly opportunistic conceptions of the Moscow bureaucracy of alliances with the 'national bourgeoisie'. Fidel's contributions in these areas were all the more harmful for being made by a leader who, to his credit, had the historic achievement of having established the first and only workers' state on the American continent.

Fidel was re-opening a question that his own revolution had answered very definitely. What is the nature of the revolutions now on the agenda in Latin American countries? To fall in line with official Soviet ideology the lessons of recent history were ignored. The reality of the Cuban Revolution had demonstrated that, in the era of imperialism, there would be no separate bourgeois-democratic stage, that to complete the bourgeois-democratic tasks the revolution had to take the first steps towards socialism. But Castro and the Cuban leaders were now accepting the contrary, stagist analysis of Blas Roca and Carlos Rafael Rodríguez.[60]

Despite his huge contribution at the level of practice, Fidel Castro made no contribution to the theory of Marxism. The M-26J programme was limited, an action programme, based on the experiences of the Cuban Revolution, i.e., rural guerrilla warfare. Fidel never understood some of the most important lessons and experiences of the world working-class movement, in particular the Bolshevik Revolution led by Lenin and Trotsky and the growth of counter-revolutionary Stalinism. This lack of understanding was expressed in Fidel's failure to establish any democratic-centralist party in Cuba, in the lack of a democratic government based upon workers' and peasants' soviets. While wholeheartedly supporting the Cuban workers' state against imperialism it is necessary to understand its political weaknesses: lack of workers' democracy, and acceptance of Stalinist organisation, methods and theory.

Without workers' democracy the question of who was to hold the government to account needed answering. The Cuban government functioned by decree and posts were filled by appointment rather than by elections and decisions of representative bodies. To the degree that Cuba remained constrained by its need for aid from the Soviet bureaucracy, it was inevitable that bureaucratic tendencies would develop and increase. What was needed was a form of proletarian democracy based on organs of a soviet type, councils elected by the workers and peasants with members subject to immediate recall and structured in such a way as to form the real backbone of the workers' state.

This was a fundamental deficiency that could not be compensated for by the prestige of Fidel Castro and the direct ties he and other leaders attempted to maintain with the masses, nor by the existence of other organs that played only a partial role. For instance, on May Day 1960 Fidel spoke to a packed *Plaza de la Revolución* praising the new militias and warning of an impending US invasion. He took the opportunity to declare that, if he died, his brother Raúl would take his place as prime minister. There was no need for any election since the people ruled Cuba already. The crowd cheered, repeating the slogan 'Cuba Sí! Yanqui No!' and adding, 'Revolución Sí! Elecciones No!'. Under threat from US imperialism, it was correct for the new government to take preventative measures, but this episode strikingly illustrates the lack of conscious collective control and management of government by the masses

---

60 Rodríguez, C., *Lenin and the Colonial Question*, New International, 1(1)93-144, 1983.

through their own democratic organisations. Instead, it demonstrated the plebiscitary character of the new government.

By 1962, the lack of involvement in decision-making had led to high levels of absenteeism in the workplaces. Che analysed the problem and declared:

> We have fallen behind in trying to get the workers involved... Who is guilty? They are clearly not guilty. We, the ministry, and the labour leaders are guilty... we have become perfect bureaucrats... Why did the massive tasks to be undertaken by the working class always appear as bureaucratic initiatives? ... What could we do in order to get the working class participating in their workplaces' leadership?[61]

But in the factories, as elsewhere, there was a hierarchical scale in the decision-making process. The workers had 'the last word', but only because they were the last to be consulted. What arrived at the workplaces were totally worked-out plans, already decided, to which the workers could only say yes. The factory managers might, or might not, take notice of their comments. At best, workers could suggest improvements, but there were no means by which they could question the premises of the plan or propose an alternative. This was a 'road to socialism' without basic democratic rights for the workers. The leadership had become self-selecting with virtually unlimited authority to make plans and enforce them, according to their own presumption of what was best for the people. The Soviet Union and Eastern Europe knew well enough that such a road generated nothing but apathy amongst the workers. For bureaucrats, perhaps, that was not such a bad thing.

Nor can it be claimed that the regime based itself *in practice* on democratic centralism as Lenin conceived it. For the first fifteen years of its formal existence, the Cuban Communist Party was almost completely inactive outside of the Politburo. The 100-person Central Committee rarely met, and it was ten years after its founding that the first regular Party Congress was held. During that time and still, the differences discussed in the leadership bodies are kept from the masses. Most damaging was that the USSR exported to an already chaotic, disorganised and backward Cuban economy, its own defective model of bureaucratic deformation and mismanagement. Despite tokens of 'workers' control' in planning decisions, Cuban workers (urban and rural) enjoyed less and less real control over the economy. The Cuban workers were becoming a part of a Stalinised economy, headed by a Stalinised party and state machine.

---

61 In Sobrino, F., *Essays on Interpretation of the Cuban Revolution*, www.marxists.org.

1967 was the last year in which many of the activists who had placed such hope in the Cuban revolution gave it unqualified support. The reason was the Cuban government's endorsement of the Warsaw Pact's invasion of Czechoslovakia in August 1968 to put down the revolutionary, democratic and anti-Stalinist upsurge that threatened to install Soviet democracy.

8.3) CREATION OF THE CUBAN COMMUNIST PARTY: THE ESCALANTE AFFAIR

The transition to a workers' state had, quite naturally, caused divisions within the M-26J, resulting in increasing collaboration of the left wing of the M-26J (essentially the military wing led by Fidel and Raúl Castro, Che Guevara, etc., fewer than 3,000 persons), the DR and the PSP (by far the most numerous of the three groups with as many as 15,000 members) on practical tasks such as building the militia. Subsequently, the three groups would merge into the PCC, a process that took several years. With time, the initial, occasional, meetings became more regular and, in the summer of 1961, the three groups fused to become the Integrated Revolutionary Organisations (*Organizaciones Revolucionarias Integradas* – ORI), then the United Party of the Socialist Revolution, and finally the Communist Party of Cuba on 3 October, 1965. To mark the occasion *Hoy* closed and *Granma* emerged as the new Party newspaper.

The PSP was very much the conservative wing of the new Party; in the discussions on how to progress the agrarian reforms, Castro and Guevara were for converting the sugar cane estates into state farms, but the PSP pushed for the sub-division of the land without collectivisation, strengthening the individualistic tendencies of the peasantry. Nor did the PSP favour the general nationalisation of business enterprises. On the very day Fidel was proclaiming the expropriation without indemnification of foreign industries, the leadership meeting of the PSP was discussing only moderate reforms.

However, the Castro leadership team badly needed a disciplined political body to support the government. The M-26J was a heterogeneous and amorphous collection of militants, and the leadership turned to the old Cuban communists, who had organisational skills and experience, but had been trained in Stalinist 'democratic centralism'. Their practice of blind trust in the top leaders, and their conviction that socialism must be built from above, were qualities that meshed well with the top-down practices of the guerrillas. It was noticed that Fidel had delayed the merger of the M-26J, the DR and the PSP until 1965, after all the major social and economic changes had already been implemented under his leadership and control.

During this period, there began a process of bureaucratisation. The task of setting up the ORI had been given to Anibal Escalante, Secretary the PSP who, in a sectarian and partisan manner, attempted to prepare the way for himself and the PSP to take control of the new party and, through it, the government of Cuba.

Using his authority within the ORI, Escalante began to remove from power revolutionaries who had gained their positions because of their activities during the revolution and thus had a degree of independence. His aim was to create an apparatus in which there would be minimal participation by those who were capable of independent thought or action. What was not on the agenda was a mass Marxist-Leninist party, one that was alive, dynamic, comprised of the most politically advanced workers, which would make democratic decisions and eliminate bureaucracy.

Escalante was intent on creating a structure that integrated the Fidelistas into a Stalinist-controlled party. In the provincial committees of the ORI and at lower levels too, Escalante appointed former PSP functionaries to leadership posts, and called for extending the party organisation inside the armed forces. *Escalantismo* grew in strength in the mass organisations such as in the CTC-R, where the Communist Party had a base. Escalante's clear objective was to have Stalinists as the key personnel of the new party so that they would be able to control the National Directorate despite having only ten of twenty-eight seats.

Escalantismo was an extreme form of the bureaucratic layer that was starting to emerge in Cuba. Grounds for bureaucratic growth were present in the objective situation – shortages of goods, relative economic backwardness, a capitalist world environment, the ongoing US blockade and, most important, Cuba's dependence on the bureaucratised Soviet Union.

The so-called Escalante Affair, was the response of the Fidelistas to the damage caused by Escalante and an attempt to avoid similar problems in the future. A policy of separating the party from day-to-day state administration was introduced, the right to free discussion was declared. But these attempts, welcome as they were, were made within the top-down structure that had been inherited from the guerrilla movement. A small group of people retained the power to say what was to be done and how to do it. Their intentions may have been the very best but methods such as these were counter-productive and eroded the only basis on which the transition to socialism can take place, the full, democratic and conscious participation of all Cuban workers and peasants.

The contradiction between a top-down and democratic approach was made clear in the attempts to draw workers into the party. The Fidelistas called mass meetings in factories to motivate workers to join the party. The declared intention was to recruit into the party many of those radicalised by the revolution, to recruit dedicated revolutionaries and to link the party more closely to the masses. What actually happened was that the names of selected 'model workers' were placed in a pool from which recruits to the party were drawn and, as with so much else in Cuba, the fact that this was a top-down process meant those selected were largely determined by local secretaries, who picked those most suited to their purposes.

Stalinist politics within the new party were not eliminated after Escalante was removed from his position, because former PSP and M-26J members, who were conscious supporters of Stalin and Stalinism, remained influential. Carlos Franqui, a participant in the M-26J and the Cuban Revolution alongside Fidel and Che, but who later fled Cuba, claims Raúl Castro was the leader of this current. He reports that at one meeting Raúl shouted: "Nobody offends Stalin when I'm around!" taking his jacket off and squaring up for a fight to stop any continued criticism of his hero.[62]

The way the revolution had triumphed, through the leadership of a guerrilla army, played a role in the bureaucratic nature of the state after the revolution. As Fidel explained: "a war is not led through collective, democratic methods, it is based on the responsibility of command".[63] Unfortunately, this attitude extended into the post-war period and was reinforced by the Bay of Pigs invasion and the undeclared war that is the blockade by the USA.

After the revolutionary victory, the leadership had huge authority and widespread support. However, there were no mechanisms of revolutionary democracy through which ideas could be debated and discussed and, above all, through which the masses of workers and peasants could exercise their own power and hold their leaders to account. The Castro-led forces came to power with a great deal of popular support, prestige, and credibility, but the M-26J was very far from a classical Marxist workers' movement engaged in self-emancipation. Fidel's radical policies were passed down to the masses, who could then express their support. This constituted a serious obstacle to raising the political consciousness of the Cuban people, reducing their understanding of the necessity of their active participation in all decision-making.

In February 1963, the ORI itself was dissolved and replaced by the United Party of the Socialist Revolution (*Partido Unido de la Revolución Socialista*, PURS). The National Directorate of the new party was the same as for the ORI, with the exception of Escalante. But now, the Fidelistas were aware of

---

62 Franqui, C., *Family Portrait with Fidel*, Random House, 1984.
63 In Martin, J., www.marxist.com, 26 November 2016.

the importance of retaining the organisational reins in their hands and only one of the six members of the Secretariat was from the PSP. It is claimed that, as a result of this struggle during 1962-63, the ORI expelled about half its membership in a succession of purges to eliminate Escalante's influence.[64]

In 1964, to drive home the lesson of who was in charge, the Fidelistas placed a prominent Stalinist, one 'Marquitos' Rodriguez, on trial for crimes against the revolution committed under Batista. In the mid-1950s the PSP had assigned informers and provocateurs to disrupt the activities of the student DR. In the summer of 1957, Marquitos had supplied the police with the whereabouts of four leading DR members, who were then immediately gunned down. Marquitos was brought to trial, found guilty and sentenced to death. Veteran PSP leader Joaquín Ordoqui, member of the ORI Directorate, was arrested and expelled from the party for his role in concealing the affair. Ordoqui later died in jail.

Rejection of Stalinism was very strong among a generation of revolutionaries who had come to Marxism through their own experience in the Cuban Revolution. The team of the Philosophy Department at Havana University, for instance, rejected the Soviet manuals of 'Marxism-Leninism', and worked out their own curriculum based on the study of the original texts of Marx, Engels, Lenin and the classical philosophers. The same group of revolutionaries (most of them young) began publishing a magazine, *Critical Thought* (*Pensamiento Crítico*), in which they debated, in an open and critical manner, different versions of Marxism, trying to break with the ossified, distorted and anti-Marxist version they were getting from the Soviet Union. In the field of arts, culture and cinema there were sharp public polemics against the attempt of the Stalinists to impose 'Soviet realism' and censorship of anything that deviated from it.

In 1964, Cuba and the USSR signed a new trade agreement. The Soviets were committed to purchase 2.1 million tons of sugar in 1965 at the preferential price of US$287 million. For the next five years, it would increase annually the amount of Cuban sugar it purchased. The sugar was now expected to provide adequate foreign exchange earnings to enable the purchase and importation of modern machinery and equipment. The obverse was a return by Cuba to a one-crop economy.

There was a minor hiccup in 1968 when Escalante, having returned from diplomatic service in the Cuban embassy in Czechoslovakia, raised his head again to found a 'micro-faction', which made wide-ranging criticisms of the party and its functioning: that no-one listened to the members, and too much

---

64 Domínguez, J., *Leadership Changes, Factionalism, and Organisational Politics in Cuba since 1960*, Unwin Hyman, 1989.

depended upon Fidel's personal views; in the economy, there was too much emphasis on 'moral' incentives and 'voluntary' labour, and not enough on material incentives. Escalante and eight others were purged from the party, accused of organising a faction, which was treated as a crime. This was a clear warning that organised opposition, criticism or disagreement with the official political line was not going to be tolerated. To many, this was an attack on Stalinism. That was the appearance, but not the content; this was an attack on party democracy, a demonstration by Fidel that he intended to maintain his personal pre-eminence and a degree of independence from the USSR.

The Cuban leadership perceived the family as, primarily, an economic institution, appreciating that, with it (and private property), the oppression of women came into being. They believed that it is necessary to see the family as an economic unit if one wants to end the oppression of women. Engels in *The Origin of the Family, Private Property, and the State*, argued that, to free women, it was necessary to: 1) end their economic dependence on their husbands; 2) get women out of the isolation of the home and into the workforce; 3) socialise traditional household chores done by women through the provision of childcare, public laundries, cafeterias, and other services; and 4) break the *economic* chains that bind family members together, so that relationships between people are based on affection and not economic necessity.

Starting in 1964, to help overcome the effects of the US blockade, the FMC began a campaign for women, on an unpaid and voluntary basis, to assist in the provision of health care and education systems, and to re-build agriculture by going into the countryside at weekends to pick crops. The response was generally good, and by 1968, the state had initiated a mass campaign under the slogan; 'Women, the Revolution in the Revolution' to get women either into the workforce, or to enrol on education programmes. The state was keen to increase the number of women in the workforce and, to that end, it carried out an extensive survey of the reasons for the lack of women applying for shop floor jobs in Cuban industry. Three reasons predominated: the first was that the pressures of housework, due to a lack of access to modern consumer goods, especially washing machines, made housework arduous and time-consuming; the other two showed the effect of the revolution – a much higher proportion of women entered the workforce as doctors, engineers, lawyers and technicians than, for example, in the USA because there was (and is) substantially more open access, and that women's pay in Cuba does not suffer from the discriminatory practices experienced elsewhere so jobs in industry did not pay women substantially more than jobs elsewhere.

8.4) THE TEN MILLION-TON SUGAR HARVEST

Economic dependence on the USSR inevitably meant a gradual adoption of the norms of the Soviet Union, both economic and political. This turn went through various stages, slowly at first with Fidel Castro's public alignment with the Soviet Union in the Sino-Soviet dispute in early 1966, and accelerated rapidly after the 'Ten Million-Ton' sugar harvest in 1970, with the Cuban leadership openly adopting Moscow-inspired internal policies and structures.

Historically, Cuba had been the world's major sugar producing country, but after 1959 the new government had adopted a policy of agricultural diversification and industrial renovation, which led to serious neglect of the sugar industry and would have exactly the opposite effect to that which was intended. The investment required for these new developments led to a serious trade deficit and economic pressures that could not be ignored. The only Cuban product the Russians wanted was sugar and, though they may have been relatively generous in the terms agreed and the price paid, there were two consequences unpalatable to the Cuban leaders: pressure to return to monoculture and increasing political control over their actions.

A large increase in sugar production became increasingly necessary if Cuba was to supply the Russians with the amounts agreed, and to have a surplus for sale on the global market to obtain the funds to buy urgently-needed western imports. In 1966, the leadership decided to turn Cuba once again into a sugar-exporting giant. The emphasis was to be on producing as much sugar as possible for sale on the world market, and to produce ten million tons a year by 1970. This latter aim might have seemed possible, given that in 1952 the harvest was more than 7 million tons, but the reforms of the intervening years, aimed at doing away with monoculture as the cause of poverty, had been taking Cuba in the opposite direction.

Thousands of hectares of planted sugar cane had been run down; the maintenance and repair of many sugar mills and associated sugarcane railroads had been neglected; over 200,000 experienced cane cutters had retired or been transferred to non-sugar activities between 1959 and 1964. These policies had caused a steady annual decrease in sugar production to 4.8 million tons in 1969.[65]

To meet the ten million-ton target required bringing back into production, not only all the sugar plantations that had been neglected, but placing substantial new acreage under sugar cultivation. Even then, the target was achievable only if modern agricultural techniques were used: irrigation expanded; increasing application of fertilisers and insecticides; replacing of

65 Fraginals, M., and Moreno, T., *The Ten Million Ton Sugar Harvest*, faculty.mdc. edu, Miami-Dade College.

the traditional sugarcane with varieties with higher yields; and mechanisation of harvesting. Unused railroads and sugar mills had to be reinstated and upgraded, and hundreds of thousands of cane cutters had to be found.

To prepare the population for the major mobilisation needed to harvest ten million tons of sugar, Fidel announced on 13 March, 1968, what he called the 'The Great Revolutionary Offensive', a measure intended to eliminate small private businesses and carry Cuba upwards onto the plane of economic self-sufficiency. This had strong similarities with the 'high tide of socialist transformation' in China, launched in October 1953, when private traders of all kinds, from street-hawkers to small retail shops, were merged into co-operative teams, and private markets in rural areas were banned. In Cuba in 1968, some 58,000 small businesses – including individual craftsmen, stalls and shops – were nationalised! Such wholesale measures, unless there are exceptional circumstances, are not part of Marxist economic thinking. This was a forced march to reach targets arbitrarily determined by the government.

The 'Ten Million-Ton Harvest' was a local version of the Maoist "great leap forward", an adventure in the Stalinist tradition, attempting to overcome the limitations imposed by backwardness through the forced mobilisation of millions of ordinary Cubans. It was believed that enthusiasm and hard work would be sufficient to overcome the technical, engineering, economic, social and political problems faced by Cuban society. And, like Mao, who sacked Central Committee members who pointed out that the great leap forward was an inherently flawed project, Gott records how Fidel sacked Orlando Borrego, the sugar minister, for "faint-heartedness" for suggesting the target would be "almost impossible to reach". Seasoned managers, administrators and technicians who had left the industry were hurriedly replaced with loyal and politically trustworthy, but inexperienced personnel.

The ten million-ton harvest was officially inaugurated in December 1969, but the technical difficulties in achieving the target, as in China, proved to be greater than could be overcome by exhorting the masses to undertake extra work. Some of these technical difficulties bordered on the ludicrous and demonstrated the inherent failings of top-down control – modern machines from the Soviet Union replaced the now antiquated mill machinery from North America and/or Western Europe, but were significantly larger and there was not enough space within the mills for the workers to operate them.

Other failings were more obvious; the total area planted was insufficient to produce ten million tons; there were insufficient supplies of fertilisers; mechanisation of sugar cane collection was inadequate; the shortfall in professional cane cutters was addressed by using industrial workers, students, housewives, professionals and about 100,000 members of the armed forces

(FAR). These may have been committed revolutionaries but mostly they were ignorant of cane cutting and caused immense damage to the harvest. In some areas, the harvested sugar was of such a poor quality due to contamination with leaves and the ends of stalks that cane collection centres had to be established to eliminate the debris before transferring the cut cane to the mills.

Workers were pushed to participate through a massive propaganda campaign in the government-controlled media, in the mass organisations, in schools, and work centres, all devoted to: *Los Diez Millones Van*. But bureaucratic miscalculation, mismanagement and lack of sober planning undermined this heroic effort. By the end of the 1970 harvest, more than one million people had worked in the cutting, loading and transporting of the sugar cane.[66]

The concentration of all resources and energies into achieving a 10 million-ton sugar harvest had adverse effects on production in many other sectors of the economy, and economic dependence upon the Soviet Union increased. Personnel and transport were taken from key sectors in order to cut cane. Farmers were forced to change from raising cattle to producing sugar cane. Meat, milk and even cement supplies were about twenty-five per cent less than in 1968, and supplies of construction steel fell by thirty-eight per cent. The mismatch between promises made by the government and the actual harvest meant that, in 1971, domestic consumption of sugar per capita was rationed to one kilo (two pounds) a month in order to meet export obligations.

Turning the harvest into the sole objective of every agency and mass organisation promoted the disorganisation of society more than the organisation of the harvest. The 1970 harvest achieved, at most, 8,500,000 tons and occupied the lives of the Cuban people for an entire year; the total social and economic cost of the 1970 harvest will never be fully known. In September 1970, the failure to meet the ten million-ton target had to be faced. Fidel, in a surprise admission, declared that democratisation of party and trade union bodies was necessary to stop such a mistake happening again. It was a dramatic admission. It came to nothing. By 1975, the sugar harvest had returned to more normal levels – 5.4 million tons.

Having failed to achieve the ten million-ton sugar harvest, the regime pulled back from its more radical domestic and international policies. The leadership adopted a new, Soviet-like economic policy, abandoning the primacy of moral incentives as 'idealist mistakes', and publicly acknowledged and defended pay differentials (which are quite acceptable in a workers' state)

---

66 Fraginals and Moreno, op cit.

into which category they placed the privileges that accrued to elite office-holders in the Party and state hierarchy (which are quite unacceptable in a workers' state).

However, Fidel's reputation did not suffer in the way that Mao's did after the collapse of the Great Leap Forward, for two reasons; he frankly and honestly admitted that mistakes had been made, and there was no mass famine as in China. Nor did Cuba's reputation suffer internationally – if anything, it was enhanced by the efforts of the Cuban people to rise to the challenges facing them. However, it was the undeniable failure of the ten million-ton harvest, which gave the USSR and its supporters the specific weight to pull Castro into line and place its own adherents into positions of power.

9) THE 'GREY YEARS' – RESTRUCTURING CUBA IN THE RUSSIAN IMAGE

The failure of the harvest meant the domination of Moscow escalated. Increasingly, Russian technicians, economists, academics and diplomats flooded into Cuba. By the summer of 1972, it was estimated that there were ten thousand Russians in Havana alone.[67] English, the traditional business language of Cuba was replaced by Russian. Kosygin, the Russian premier came, and toured factories being built with Russian aid. In July, Cuba formally joined COMECON, accepting full integration of the Cuban economy with the Soviet Union and Eastern Europe. In December, a fifteen-year deal was signed in which the Russians agreed to pay an increased price for sugar, provide US$350 million in credit spread over three years, and allow debts to be repaid over twenty-five years, interest free.

The economic and political changes were accompanied on the cultural level by ideological subjugation. These were the dreadful Five Grey Years (*Quinquenio Gris*; 1971-1975). It was at this time that homophobia, discrimination and harassment of gay men became institutionalised. The Philosophy Department of Havana University and the journal *Pensamiento Critico* were closed, social sciences were practically banned. In the field of arts and culture, there was repression and censorship to impose Stalinist thinking. Any difference of opinion with official thinking was suppressed, and self-censorship became the norm, laying the base for future indifference or aversion to official ideology.

On 27 April, in the evening, at the headquarters of the Cuban Writers and Artists Association (UNEAC), the poet, Heberto Padilla and his wife (the poet Cuza Malé), surrounded by members of the security forces, were made

---

67 Quirke, R., *Fidel Castro*, Norton, 1995.

to publicly humiliate themselves, in a scene that was all too reminiscent of the Moscow show trials. Padilla, repented his recent book *Out of the Game* (*Fuera del juego*) declaring himself a "bourgeois writer, unworthy of being read by the workers". He implicated other artists and writers, who then had to criticise themselves for their poor relationships with the "historical moment that the country was living through." As a result, many leading intellectuals who had supported the revolution, including Nobel laureates in literature Jean Paul Sartre, Octavio Paz, and Mario Vargas Llosa, and distinguished writers Jorge Luis Borges and Carlos Fuentes, angrily and publicly condemned the actions of the Cuban government. This obscene event marked the beginning of a new policy of state control of the island's artists.

The Grey Years brought into the open the bureaucratic tendencies of a layer of cadres and leaders who, thanks to their posts in the structures of the state, army and party, benefited from social privileges. Structures and mechanisms which favoured bureaucratisation were endorsed and amplified, reflecting the practices in the USSR.

In strictly economic terms, Cuba benefited, with a growth rate of about four per cent per annum for the next decade. But the Soviet 'advisors' had the parallel task of creating new political institutions, the most important of which was – naturally – an invigorated and enlarged PCC, and a Russian-style constitution. The first change was to streamline the Council of Ministers and concentrate power in a new, eight-member Executive Committee. Of these eight, three (Raúl Castro, Osvaldo Dorticós, and Carlos Rafael Rodríguez) had strong and direct links with Moscow, and it was generally accepted that they were spokespersons for the Russians.

The second change was the introduction of a new (1976) constitution, which closely resembled the pyramidal structure of the USSR and was promoted as 'Popular Power', supposedly providing a means of ventilating grievances against bureaucracy. According to Fidel, the People's Power Assemblies (also called Organs of People's Power) would:

> [G]ive the masses decision making power in many problems… genuinely democratic principles replacing the administrative work habits of the first years of the Revolution. We must begin to substitute democratic methods for the administrative methods that run the risk of becoming bureaucratic methods.[68]

However, in Cuba, it was well understood that this new structure placed power firmly in the hands of the new Communist Party.

---

68 Sobrino, F., *Essays on Interpretation of the Cuban Revolution,* isj.org.uk.

Experimental municipal elections to assemblies of Popular Power were held in Matanzas province during August 1974, with as many as eight candidates standing against each other for particular seats. The candidates were elected by secret ballot, at neighbourhood meetings organised by the CDRs. The local PCC did not officially nominate candidates, but the reality of the process was that all successful candidates were PCC members, or one of its constituent organisations such as the Young Communist League.

In the Matanzas elections only 7.6 per cent of the candidates nominated were women and less than half of those were elected. In a follow-up speech, Fidel drew attention to this and condemned the fact that more women had not been elected. A survey found that prejudice was a significant factor and the PCC declared it would address this at its forthcoming First Congress.

At the local level, there appeared to be a genuine decentralisation of Popular Power, in sharp contrast to the centralisation in the upper levels. The members of the decision-making Provincial and National Assemblies were not directly elected but were, instead, elected by those candidates who had been successful in the municipal elections. The latter could vote for one of a list of candidates pre-selected by party functionaries and the 'Mass Organisations' controlled by the party, which were listed in Article 7 of the new constitution: "the Committees for the Defence of the Revolution, the Cuban Women's Federation, the National Association of Small Farmers, the University Students' Federation, the High School Students' Federation and the Union of Cuban Pioneers".

Hierarchical voting had been introduced by the Stalinist party apparatus in the faction struggles in the Russian party in the 1920s, to sieve out the Opposition. In Moscow, for example, the supporters of the Opposition claimed they were in a majority in the party cells, but they attained only thirty-six per cent of the vote in the district conferences, which was further reduced to sixty-one votes against 325 in the provincial conference.[69] The structure was intended to superimpose the PCC on the new state edifice. Subsequent analysis of election results showed that three-quarters of the municipal delegates were party members and almost all 614 national deputies were members of the party or the Communist Youth. However, in Cuba, there was an additional safeguard; forty-five per cent of the National Assembly deputies, including Fidel and the whole central government team, were not subject to popular election.

At the time of writing, the local People's Power delegates did not receive salaries, they had day a week off work without loss of pay for their duties, they lived in and among their constituents and so have close personal contact with

---

69 Murphy, K. *Class Struggle in a Moscow Metal Factory*, Berghan Books, 2005.

them. They represent very small districts, typically between 1,000 to 1,500 voters and must report back to their constituents every six months at open public meetings. They are subject to recall if twenty per cent or more of their constituents petition for it. Only local delegates can be recalled by popular demand. The elected provincial and national representatives are subject to recall only by the delegates of the municipality they represent. Given that the great majority of delegates and representatives are PCC members the matter is, de facto, a Party, not a popular decision. Only if the relevant body determines that a recall is justified, is the matter referred to the electorate.

Naturally, some people took the declaration that Popular Power was the highest authority in Cuba at face value, and presented their problems and complaints (predominantly concerning housing) to their local municipalities. They were then confronted by the obvious fact that there was no real control over the central state, which defined its priorities with little or no reference to the rank and file. The Cuban people soon understood the deficiencies in what was called "the most democratic system in the world". (There was a sense of *déjà vu* here, this being the very same description used by Stalin for the USSR's 1936 constitution.)

Fidel's justifications for a new constitution were dressed up in radical rhetoric and spelled out in November 1973. The core of his argument had been developed nearly forty years previously by Joseph Stalin when launching the 1936 Soviet Constitution: "The principle (is) 'From each according to his ability, to each according to his work'".[70] In the USSR, this formula was intended to justify the inequalities existing. "From each according to his ability" meant the extraction of the maximum labour by any means possible, including the whip of police intimidation; and "to each according to his work" meant the majority of the working population living in general want and on near starvation wages while preserving privileges and luxuries for the tops.

Fidel put it thus:

> Logically, every worker's remuneration should be linked to the quality and quantity of the work he does. If he is in a responsible job, an important job, he should be paid more... (the wages of) personnel in charge of directing production must compare favourably with those of tractor drivers and operators of other equipment.[71]

About this time, there was a distribution of refrigerators, electrical appliances and 100,000 TV sets to those workers recommended by union and party

70 Stalin, J. *Constitution (Fundamental law) of the Union of Soviet Socialist Republics* Dec. 5, 1936, www.marxists.org.
71 In Castro, F., *Our Power is that of the Working People*, Pathfinder, 1983.

organisers. The criteria for distribution should have been open to public scrutiny, but the organisers had their own criteria, and while these may have been quite correct and proper, they were not subject to democratic control.

The moves towards material rewards were not only due to pressure from the Russians. The expected improvements in productivity were not happening (in 1979 it was expected to be four per cent when, in fact, it was 0.8 per cent) and the response was to link wages more closely to productivity through a bonus system paid by the individual enterprise in money or consumer goods. In parallel, wage differentials were allowed to increase; the number of administrative and managerial staff rose rapidly, and the bonuses they paid themselves reduced the profitability of the enterprises, while increasing wage inequality between workers and management.

In any such system, egalitarianism can be left far behind. This, of course, is not to deny that post-revolutionary Cuba had largely wiped out pre-revolutionary social inequalities, for example, life expectancy has risen by twenty years – from fifty-three years in 1959 to seventy-three in 1984. Despite this and other important gains, the US embargo had imposed a system of generalised want on Cuba, a condition that invariably sows the seed for a self-seeking bureaucracy, which places its own interests above those of society generally. Control of the distribution of consumer goods is an important stage in the development of such a bureaucracy as had been demonstrated forty years earlier in the USSR.

The third change was to re-configure the PCC along the lines of the Russian Party. This was a necessary preparation for the 1976 constitution because, in Article 5, the Cuban CP was defined as "the superior leading force of society and the state, in charge of organizing the common effort towards the goals of building socialism and advancing towards a communist society". The fourth change was to legitimise certain small-scale craft activities on payment of a license fee. This was recognition that the public sector was failing to supply certain essential services such as repair of domestic appliances: fridges, washing machines, and so on. About 50,000 workers took out these licenses, as plumbers, mechanics, joiners, dressmakers, etc.

The PCC had been established in 1965 but there was a ten-year delay before its First Congress in 1975. Both the Fidelistas and PSP had a policy of top-down decision-making, where differences in the leadership were covered up, where decisions already made were presented to the membership for approval, not discussion. The long delay was a sure sign that there were serious differences within the Cuban leadership that were proving difficult to resolve.

A recruitment drive preceding the Congress had more than doubled the CP's membership from about 100,000 in 1970 to just over 200,000 in 1975, and would rise to over 400,000 in 1980.[72] The PSP leaders were now old men, of diminishing importance with no prospect of making a come-back. They were handed a few posts of lesser importance. The Fidelistas dominated the new Political Bureau, Secretariat and Central Committee that were unveiled to the membership. The reformed party was warmly welcomed by the Soviet bureaucracy and acclaimed by Brezhnev as evidence of the 'growing maturity' of the Cuban Revolution. No doubt the almost complete elimination of any reference to Che was a factor in this. A very important decision at the Congress was to incorporate a ban on factions into the Party statutes. Such a ban is a defining character of a Stalinist party, it acts as and is intended to be, a barrier to both internal party, and soviet, democracy.

Even Fidel's staunchest supporters had to admit:

> The Cuban Communist Party is not a Leninist party. It allows no democratic internal life in the Bolshevik sense. There are no organised tendencies and factions around programmatic points that could advance the clarity of discussion and contribute to solving the problems facing the Cuban Revolution... Moreover, to a certain degree the Cuban Communist Party is not a political party as we think of one, so much as a part of the administrative apparatus. It suffers from the same bureaucratic degenerations as the rest of the governmental apparatus.[73]

These factors notwithstanding, the First Congress took time to discuss how to advance women's equality. Their proposal was in two parts, the first was to reduce the burden of domestic housework by, amongst other things, greatly expanding child care (e.g. providing crèches in workplaces), more laundries, more workplace cafeterias, and setting up '*plan jaba*' (literally, plan shopping-bag, drop your shopping list at the store and come back later to pay and collect your shopping). The second part was to launch a wide-ranging ideological debate across the island on women's rights. This was centred around proposed changes to the Family Code, Articles 24-28, that men and women were equal in marriage; that men should share in housework and raising children; that both members of a couple should have an equal right to pursue an education or have a job; and that the couple should co-operate with each other to make that possible.

One of the most revolutionary aspects of Cuban society was the diverse and creative manner in which Cubans had socialised the responsibilities previously assumed by the family. At their peak, these gains of the revolution

72 Kapcia, op cit.
73 Seigle, L., *Revolutionary Cuba Today*, Pathfinder, 2000.

included: free medical care; free dental care; free child care; rents which are a maximum of ten per cent of a family's income; free meals in schools; supervised after-school activities; inexpensive lunches in workplaces; socialised care for the elderly, including day-centres, meals and pensions; free amateur sports programmes; free museums and cultural activities; state support for amateur poets, artists, musicians and writers.

Before the revolution, marriage was a matter of economic survival for women and divorce was not easy. Millions of women remained married to husbands they may have hated, because they had no economic alternative. Many women of the older generation believe the right to freely choose a marriage partner and leave one with whom they did not want to live, was one of the most important gains of the Revolution.[74] It was at this time that the PCC, in its theses on women's equality, pointed out that views inherited from capitalism on women as sexual, decorative and passive objects whose highest aspiration was marriage, were a major obstacle to the realisation of equality between men and women. Beauty contests, in particular, were seen as encouraging objectification and sexist attitudes in society and were singled out as "negative and absurd", "vulgar and grotesque" hangovers from capitalism not in keeping with revolutionary Cuba's view of women. With direct, mass interventions by the FMC, beauty contests were soon banned.

The Family Code, in its entirety was endorsed by the majority of the population and passed into law on International Women's Day, 8 March, 1975. The document around which the debate took place was titled: 'On the Full Exercise of Women's Equality'.[75] This document says many fine things that all progressive people will applaud, but it was silent on the central question of a woman's right to control her own body, i.e. to decide whether or not to have an abortion.

In all major countries in 1917, women were enmeshed in a thick web of discriminatory laws and sexist oppression. The Soviet government of October 1917 took swift action and women in Soviet Russia achieved full legal and political rights, including the right to abortion. But, with the growth of the bureaucracy, the marriage and family laws established by the October Revolution were re-written. The clock was turned backwards; in 1934, homosexuality was made a criminal offence, punishable with up to eight years of imprisonment. In 1936, legal abortion was abolished, except where life or health was endangered.

It is possible to detect the dead hand of Stalinism reaching out to corrupt the present, in the influence of the PCC on abortion law in Cuba. Before the

---

74 Stone, op cit, 1981.
75 Ibid.

revolution, abortion was illegal under the Civil Defence Code except "to save the life of the mother, when the pregnancy was the result of rape, and to avoid birth defects due to hereditary sickness or contagious disease". This aspect of the Code remained in force during the first five years of the revolution, and for reasons that have never been explained, the Castro government opposed changes in the abortion law during this period. In form, the law was highly restrictive, but the reality was that most middle- and upper-class women were able to afford private abortions when necessary, outside of the law. With the revolution, the number of private abortions climbed, but so did the mortality rate, and in 1965 the Ministry of Public Health (*Ministerio de Salud Pública*, MINSAP) stepped in to 'institutionalise' abortion, extending the scope of legal abortion, no longer restricting it to extreme cases, and agreeing that abortions should be carried out by public doctors free of charge rather than by private practitioners. After 1965, despite the formal restrictions, Cuban women were largely free to exercise their right to choose.

It took until December 1979, when Article 267 was inserted into Cuba's Penal Code, before abortion became legal. Or, to be more precise, ceased to be illegal, since Article 267 did not legalise a woman's right to choose, but instead it defined what constituted an illegal abortion and set down prohibitions and punishments. In December 1987, Cuba updated its Penal Code but made no substantive changes to the section on abortion: if gestation is less than five weeks the woman concerned (including minors) need show no proof of pregnancy and menstrual regulation is used; for gestation of ten to twelve weeks, abortion requires confirmation of pregnancy (women under eighteen must have parental approval and women under sixteen must have approval of a medical committee); abortions after week twelve require the authorisation of a committee comprising doctors and a social worker.

Stone has observed how, after the 1975 Congress, the position of women in Cuba did improve, reporting that between 1975 and 1981, in terms of per 100 households the number of refrigerators rose from fifteen to thirty-eight, the number of washing machines from six to thirty-four, the number of childcare places almost doubled, and the percentage of women in the workforce rose from twenty-five per cent to over thirty per cent. Today, that figure is forty-two per cent, a high figure for an underdeveloped country, but it also means that a large proportion of Cuban women are primarily housewives. Cuban women also benefit from a level of maternity care that has reduced infant mortality to four per 1,000, lower than the six per 1,000 of the USA. Contraception is available to all women, who also have the de facto right to abortion free of charge, as are all medical services. Black women, poor women, and peasant women have benefited most from these processes.

In terms of representation, in 2013, Cuban women comprised just under fifty per cent of the members of the National Assembly (ranked third in the world), while, in the USA, the senate and congress had just twenty per cent women (ranked 101 in the world).

Trade with COMECON, where Cuba was the sugar and tropical fruits provider, inevitably brought with it further adoption of Soviet economic norms, material incentives and growing autonomy for managers. In the same way that Russian had become the new business language to facilitate trade, so a new Soviet style 'Management and Planning System' was adopted. In all the productive branches, there was a general mood of discontent. This showed itself as high levels of absenteeism from work, and other 'unrevolutionary' attitudes such as slovenly work, bad time-keeping, high levels of waste, and lack of care of expensive machines. Dr Jorge Risquest, Minister of Labour, gave an inkling of the real causes of this malaise. He attributed "the country's economic problems to widespread passive resistance by the workers", admitting that "there was no proper rapport between workers on the one hand and the state administration, the officials of the Communist Party and the trade unions on the other".[76]

Party pronouncements began to reverse the theory proposed by Che Guevara, regarding the sources of the revolution's bureaucratisation. Che had argued that the institution should reflect the changes in society, not society reflect the new bureaucratic structures; that the state bureaucracy could, in itself, be a source of bureaucratisation. This theory was turned inside out. Now it was an insufficiency of bureaucrats that was the source of bureaucratisation. What was needed was more bureaucrats, more dead-end bureaucratic channels where individuals with problems would be passed from one branch of the bureaucracy to another until so exhausted by the process, they gave up. Without Soviet democracy there was no forum where these workers could be heard.

In an attempt to increase productivity, in 1980 the government passed law number thirty-two, limiting the authority of the workers' councils (set up by Che) and gave greater authority to the managers to increase workplace discipline. In a single decree the government eliminated twenty years of workers' power, even if of a very limited form. By 1984, the CTC itself was moved to protest that the new law was being used arbitrarily and excessively, sometimes as a cover for bonus payments which increased inequalities. However, the Cuban government justified its measures by pointing to the

---

76 In Taaffe, P., *Cuba: Socialism and Democracy*, Fortress, 2000.

fivefold increase in the incomes of the poorest section of the population between 1960 and 1982.[77]

Workers in agriculture, the lowest paid sector, left in their thousands, reducing the production of food just when it was needed. In 1980, the government experimented with private farmers by allowing the sale of surplus produce at free farmers' markets according to the laws of supply and demand. The experiment was short-lived because, just as in Russia under the New Economic Policy (NEP), a layer of 'kulaks' allied to wealthy 'middle-men' soon emerged to dominate the market. With agricultural prices rising not falling, the experiment was terminated in 1986, and land re-allocated to the co-operatives.[78]

10) CUBA AND AFRICA

Today, Fidel Castro is revered throughout Africa because he did so much to assist the overthrow of the white, racist regime in South Africa. In 1961, Cuba sent a shipment of weapons to the Algerian National Liberation Front during its war for independence against French imperialism, and for nearly three decades afterwards, Cuba was active in Africa supporting national liberation struggles; Algeria in 1961-63, Congo in 1965, Ethiopia in 1974 and, most important, Angola 1975-89. By 1975, Cuba had provided more than 30,000 doctors to work in over forty countries, providing humanitarian aid. But the sending of tens of thousands of 'internationalist volunteers', from 1975 onwards, to Angola is considered by many an even greater achievement. In Angola, Cuban troops fought the invading South African apartheid army and, for the first time, inflicted a military defeat on it. Cuban forces were crucial in freeing Angola from South African rule and, in doing so, helped inspire the youth of Soweto to rise in rebellion, hastening the fall of the apartheid regime.

The collapse of the Portuguese empire in Africa placed guerrilla leaderships in power, particularly in Angola. Cuba swiftly offered aid. Such an intervention had strong resonances amongst the Cuban people, many of whom could trace their roots back to Africa. There were no complex issues involved in the initial intervention. The MPLA, which had been supported by the Cubans in its battles against Portuguese colonial rule for over ten years, was in de-facto control of most of Angola including the capital, Luanda, and had expected to officially take over the government when the Portuguese left. Now they were challenged by armed resistance from rightist forces;

---

77 Vilas, C., *Transition from Under development*, Editorial Nueva Sociedad, Venezuela, 1989.

78 Habel, J., *Cuba*, Verso, 1991.

the National Front for the Liberation of Angola (FNLA) led by Holden Roberto, who was on the CIA payroll,[79] and the National Union for the Total Independence of Angola (UNITA) led by Jonas Savimbi, who was well known for his collaboration with the Portuguese colonialists during the civil war.

The situation in Angola was complicated by the role played by China. At that time, China's foreign policy in Africa was dominated by its determination to oppose 'Russian imperialism', even if that meant supporting openly counter-revolutionary forces. As the MPLA developed ties with Moscow, so Peking supported the FNLA. In May 1974, 200 Chinese instructors arrived in Zaire to start training FNLA guerrillas, despite the FNLA being firmly under the thumb of Mobutu and, behind him, US imperialism. There is some evidence that the Chinese flirted with the idea of supporting Savimbi, but his links with racist South Africa were too much for them to swallow.[80]

The independence movement in Angola had a profound effect within South Africa itself, as would soon be shown by the Soweto uprising of 1976. South African imperialism, therefore, had every reason to want a client regime in Angola, to be obtained by supporting UNITA. It decided in 1975 to intervene to assist in the military overthrow of the MPLA. This had the tacit support of the major world imperialist power, the US, but a defeat for the MPLA would have represented a severe humiliation for the diplomatic, military, and strategic interests of the Russian bureaucracy.

The strategy behind the interventions (orchestrated by the US) had the intention of dividing Angola between Zaire and South Africa. The first intervention was from Zaire to the north by the FNLA, supported by the CIA. Zaire's pro-imperialist dictator, Mobutu Sese Seko, was to annex the oil-rich province of Cabinda (and whatever other Angolan territory he could) so that US oil companies would have control of the largest oil and gas reserves on the African continent. The second, and of more immediate danger to the MPLA, was by UNITA in the south, where Savimbi was being used as a front for the South African Defence Force (SADF).

Gott has claimed that, in July 1975, President Gerald Ford authorised covert assistance of US$24 million to Roberto and Savimbi. In August, South African troops moved into southern Angola under the pretext of protecting its investment in the massive Cunene hydro-electric project. Fidel phoned the Kremlin and announced Cuba was going to send help to the MPLA, but Brezhnev was more concerned with peaceful coexistence and refused to assist. That Fidel went ahead can be taken as an indication, both of his personal

---

79 Gleijeses, op cit.
80 Guimarães, F., *Origins of the Angolan Civil War*, Palgrave, 2001.

commitment to the African liberation struggle, and that Brezhnev did not categorically veto the enterprise. In early October, 480 Cuban instructors arrived in Angola and quickly dispersed to four training camps.

On 14 October, the SADF went onto the offensive and, with about 1,000 UNITA guerrillas, moved deeper into Angola. They soon reached Benguela, a coastal town half way to Luanda and the road to Luanda looked open. Fidel chose not to consult the Russians (using the excuse there was no time), and sent Cuban troops to defend Luanda. *Operation Carlota* was launched. The Cuban effort inspired Gabriel Garcia Marquez, Nobel Prize-winning author, to write *Operation Carlota*,[81] which provides details of the mechanics of the operation. In it, 250 Cuban troops were flown to Angola in planes so antiquated that their brakes were completely shot. The first 100 troops arrived just in time to play a key role in the successful defence of Luanda against an attack by the FNLA, and British and American mercenaries paid for by the CIA. The Cuban troops now moved south to help block the SADF/UNITA advance, and together with MPLA forces made their stand just outside Sumbe (then known as Novo Redondo), halting the apparently inexorable advance on 13 November, 1975.

At the same time, some 3,500 Cuban civilian volunteers travelled to Angola and played a major role in repairing destroyed bridges and restoring road and rail links. In fact, most new construction was undertaken by Cubans or under Cuban supervision.

President Ford's administration in the USA was still shaking from the Watergate scandal, which had forced the resignation of President Nixon, and was well aware that the Vietnam syndrome made it impossible to give more than logistical support to the FNLA, UNITA and South Africa. The US media and its allies launched a barrage of propaganda accusing Cuban and Soviet Russia of 'expansionism' in Africa. But the involvement of South Africa was enough to unite the leaders of the Organisation of African Unity in support of Cuba's actions. Nigeria, the most pro-Western of the black African states, praised the role played by Cuba. Worldwide, sympathy for the struggle against the South African apartheid regime spilled over into support for the Cuban intervention: "The only non-African country that fought and spilled its blood for Africa and against the odious apartheid regime".

The political benefits of Cuba's intervention were too obvious to be missed, and the Kremlin was soon providing extensive economic and military support. The sending of combat troops to Angola in 1975 was a Cuban *initiative*, but its extent, both in terms of the numbers of personnel (some 50,000 troops) and duration (about fifteen years) was possible only

---

81 Available at www.rhodesia.nl/marquez.htm.

because of large-scale Soviet logistical support and Soviet subsidies; cut-price petroleum and free supplies of weapons. This would not have been the case had Cuba been violating the Kremlin's wishes.

By early 1976, the emphasis was on stamping out the counter-revolutionaries in the North, driving the FNLA back across the border into Zaire. However, from bases in occupied Namibia, South African-backed UNITA forces and regular troops of the SADF maintained a programme of sabotage, rural guerrilla warfare and economic disruption, which cost billions of dollars. Instead of being swiftly withdrawn, Cuban troops became an integral part of the defences of the Angolan regime.

If Cuba (and the Soviet Union) had not supported Angola, it would have been partitioned between South Africa and Zaire. It was, then, no surprise that, after independence, Angola declared itself a 'People's Republic' and officially adopted 'Marxism-Leninism' of the Russian Stalinist variety, as state ideology. The MPLA was modelled on the Soviet bureaucracy; it had adopted the theory of stages, and was hostile to taking the first steps towards socialism that were needed to ensure the victory of the bourgeois democratic revolution. However, the only viable way of preventing total economic collapse in Angola was wholesale nationalisation, rationing, subsidies and price controls. Under the pressure of events, the MPLA was forced to take emergency measures to prevent the complete breakdown of society. When the Chinese Communist Party had taken similar measures, it had led to the formation of the Chinese workers' state, but such an outcome was not the only one.

The Angolan authorities had responded to the flight of the settlers by seizing their assets, along with the property of those who had collaborated with the South Africans. Portuguese farms were nationalised, as were the manganese, steel, sugar, textile, and timber industries, and most of the coffee, cotton, sisal, and tobacco plantations. Steps were also taken to bring wholesale trade under state control. Transport became a state enterprise. With the destruction of the bourgeois state in Angola and the "bodies of armed men" being the guerrilla forces of the MPLA, many argued that, at this time, Angola had a Workers' and Peasants' Government. The Cubans had moved forward to a workers' state through the determination of the Castro team to solve the problems that the great majority of their fellow citizens faced, irrespective of any personal gain. This would not be the direction taken by the MPLA leaders.

There were already worrying signs of what the future might hold. In 1976, after the wave of nationalisations had begun, the MPLA's Political Bureau pointed out that, while state enterprises were projected to play a leading role in the economy, "this does not mean that capitalist private property is finished, nor is an immediate end being put to the development of capitalist production". The all-important oil industry, bigger than the rest of the economy combined, remained under imperialist ownership.

The exports from Gulf Oil's Cabinda fields accounted for three-quarters of the value of all Angolan exports. The Angolan government did talk about eventually nationalising oil and transferring its assets to SONANGOL, the state oil company, but stressed that this was not a short-term possibility as it had neither the finance to pay compensation nor the trained personnel to oversee production. The MPLA urged Gulf Oil to continue its operations in Cabinda province and guaranteed the safety of American staff and property while the fighting was ongoing. IP of 24 May, 1982, reported how the oil industry was shielded from the political changes taking place in the country.

By 1987, the MPLA decided to drop any pretence of Angola being a Workers' and Peasants' Government when it joined the International Monetary Fund and the World Bank. Without the perspective of moving towards a workers' state, without a planned economy prioritising production for need not profit, the country was soon reduced to an economic shambles, in which the multinational oil and mineral companies coined in the cash, with kick-backs to the families of MPLA leaders. Today, the daughter of Angolan President José Eduardo dos Santos, is named by Forbes magazine as the "richest woman in Africa", with a fortune of some US$3 billion. The MPLA government of Angola, runs the country as if it were a family business.

The military situation climaxed in 1988, when 18,000 troops of the Angolan armed forces, supported by 3,000 Cuban regulars, moved to take control of the important military airfield of Cuito Cuanavale and occupy UNITA's primary operating bases. They faced over 60,000 UNITA regulars and irregulars supported by 3,000 SADF troops. This was the largest battle on African soil since World War II. Both sides claimed victory, but the SADF quit Angola, retreating into Namibia, leaving the UNITA forces within Angola to disintegrate under the MPLA/Cuban offensive.

This battle had a major impact on politics throughout Southern Africa, greatly boosting the confidence of South Africa's black majority. Three years later, on 26 July, 1991, Nelson Mandela, in a speech made in Matanzas, a centre of Black culture in Cuba, thanked the people of Cuba for their "unparalleled" contribution, and explained the defeat of the South African army at Cuito Cuanavale was "a victory for all of Africa... a turning point in the struggle to free the continent and our country from the scourge of apartheid!"

After 1988, differences appeared between the MPLA and the Cubans over what policy to adopt towards UNITA. The Cuban forces had joined with SWAPO (the South West Africa People's Organisation), which was fighting a guerilla war for the liberation of Namibia, to attack and inflict significant defeats on UNITA without the consent of the Angolan leadership. By this time, the MPLA leaders were pocketing US financial support and it was only a matter of time before they struck a deal with UNITA.

With the SADF ejected from Angola, the US offered to broker a deal between the MPLA, the remnants of UNITA and South Africa. The offer was for Namibia to become a notionally independent country on condition the Cuban troops withdrew. The Soviet Union informed Fidel that arms supplies for the Angolan war were to be discontinued. The tripartite deal was signed in December 1988 and, as part of the deal, SWAPO would be kept north of the sixteenth parallel, well away from Namibia.

It would have been quite wrong for the Cubans to have attempted to use their military presence to attempt to impose a workers' state on Angola. But the Cuban leadership could have, and should have, made political criticisms of the MPLA's policies. Instead, the Cubans restricted their advice to within the constraints set by the Stalinist theory of stages. In the national liberation struggles in Africa and the successful revolutions in Latin America, such as that of Nicaragua in 1979, the Cubans offered invaluable practical and material support and solidarity, but the political advice given by the Cuban leadership was *not to follow* the same path as the Cuban Revolution in abolishing capitalism. This advice not only had a negative impact on the Nicaraguan and Venezuelan revolutions, it also compounded the problem of the isolation of the Cuban Revolution.

11) THE FALL OF THE USSR, CUBA AND THE WORLD MARKET

However, despite the process of Stalinisation, the Cuban Revolution was not dead, and its vitality and roots amongst the masses came back to the surface at the end of the 1980s, with the collapse of the USSR. For nearly two decades, the Cuban economy, blockaded by the US, had become completely dependent on that of the USSR and the Eastern European countries. The collapse of the Stalinist regimes was catastrophic for the Cuban economy.

The first sign of the trouble ahead was when Raúl Castro was summoned to Moscow in March 1983 and informed that the USSR would no longer commit ground forces to the defence of Cuba, with the added warning that Russia now had a "new strategic reality". Sensing trouble ahead, the National Assembly passed a law enabling tenants to become house-owners and encouraging the people themselves to become active in building their own homes. There were at least three targets here: to reduce the financial burden on the state by placing greater responsibility on individuals to both provide and maintain their own accommodation, to solve the housing shortage, and to revive the mass mobilisations of the early 1960s, which had been successful in tackling many entrenched problems. In immediate terms, this initiative was a great success, over 100,000 dwellings were constructed in 1984-85, most by private initiative. But Cuba was a poor country and, almost immediately, large quantities of construction materials began to be stolen. This was followed by private construction for sale, and a consequent growth in corruption.[82] The construction boom spotlighted the differences in income that existed, with luxury apartments being built for top earners. The experiment was brought to an end in 1987.

At a Conference, 'Foreign Debt of Latin America and the Caribbean', in Havana on 3 August, 1985, Fidel announced that Cuba's debt was unpayable, and that Cuba would have to re-orient its economy. In February 1986, at the Third Congress of the PCC, Fidel announced a new economic plan to reduce reliance on imports (which included more centralised control of foreign trade and an austerity programme), to deal with the balance of payments deficit (servicing foreign debts was suspended), and to reduce reliance on material incentives (place greater emphasis on exhortation).

The crisis in the Cuban economy led, of course, to a political crisis. The Third Congress was held in two parts; Part one in February, and Part two in November-December 1986. The Party responded to the new situation with wholesale changes in the personnel holding Party posts; those who had played any leading role in steering the Cuban economy into the whirlpool of the Russian economic collapse were unceremoniously sacked. In an effort to prepare the Party for the coming economic shocks, one third of the Central Committee were replaced and, later, so too were nearly half of municipal Party secretaries.

The economy had never really recovered from the rupture with the US, made worse by the chaos of the ten million-ton harvest, and now there was the coming break with the Soviet Union. On 11 January, 1987, the first round of austerity measures were announced, including: an end to free meals in works' canteens, increased fares on public transport, replacement of the evening meal served at playschools by a snack, and the elimination of the traditional work breaks at 10 am and 4 pm, which took about two hours out of the working day. To offset these unpopular moves, the lowest wage rates were increased and a brake put on increases at the top. The bureaucrats had their expenses cut by fifteen per cent, and the provision of official vehicles substantially reduced but, despite Fidel's personal intervention these latter measures were largely a dead letter.

---

82 Habel, op cit.

Mikhail Gorbachev visited Cuba in April 1989, when he warned that Russian subsidies to Cuba would soon be phased out. Those in positions of authority such as enterprise managers or local party secretaries could and did use their positions to overcome the shortages, to acquire scarce goods and food.[83] The level of corruption was small beer compared to the Stalinist states, but it was an affront to the sense of equality that had been a bulwark of Cuban society against US imperialism.

Symbolic of the turbulence of these times were a number of high profile anti-corruption cases, in particular the Arnaldo Ochoa affair. General Ochoa, one of the best known and most decorated soldiers in the Cuban army, had commanded Cuban forces in Angola and had imported Cuban sugar and sold it on the local black market to raise funds to feed his troops. Part of the payment was in diamonds, some of which stuck to Ochoa's fingers.

Angolan diamonds began to be sold in Panama. Very rapidly this illicit enterprise escalated into the extremely lucrative field of drug smuggling. The first shipment, in April 1987, was 300 kg of cocaine bound for Florida. The consignment was intercepted by US coastguards and the subsequent arrests netted Reinaldo Ruiz, a petty criminal who was party to the Cuban end of the deal and turned informer in exchange for a lighter sentence. On 25 June, 1989, Ochoa, and fifteen others stood trial in Cuba. All were found guilty and Ochoa was sentenced to death and executed on 13 July. The Minister in charge was dismissed, tried, found guilty of negligence and sentenced to twenty years in prison where he died in 1991.

Naturally, the US and European media built the story as a major scandal: Ochoa was about to launch a popular coup and unseat Castro; this was a purge of those supporting a Russian course for Cuba; that Castro had personally approved the drug smuggling. But the scandal was short-lived and came to nothing, drowned out by the political tsunami caused by the collapse of the Stalinist regimes in Eastern Europe and Russia.

In Panama, General Noriega's drug dealing activities had made him unacceptable to a US administration launching an international war on drugs. The May 1989 elections in Panama appeared to give the US-sponsored candidate three quarters of the votes cast. Noriega simply declared the results null and void, and continued in office. In December 1989, the US instructed its large garrison stationed throughout the Canal Zone to begin manoeuvres and military exercises with the express purpose of provoking Panamanian troops, in which they succeeded. Protection of the lives of US citizens in Panama then required the take-over of Panama with the installation of a more compliant regime. This US intervention was a clear warning to revolutionary

---

83 Kapcia, op cit.

forces throughout Latin America that Uncle Sam believed direct, limited actions by US troops would now be acceptable to the American people.

In the February 1990 elections, the Sandinista government in Nicaragua was defeated by a US-sponsored coalition and Cuba lost an ally. This was a double blow, bringing not just the loss of economic and political support but also coming at a time when Russian sponsorship would soon end.

After eight months of negotiation on 19 January, 1991, Cuba and Russia signed a trade deal. Unlike previous accords, the Soviet side insisted that the prices of Russian goods should be based on world market prices and, very significantly, after 31 March, 1991 payments would have to be in US dollars. There was to be a one year stay of execution during which a preferential rate for sugar would be maintained. In September 1991, Gorbachev announced to the Cubans that they were militarily on their own. The remaining Soviet troops stationed there were being withdrawn.

The new trade accords came at a time when supplies of goods and food from the Soviet Union and Eastern European governments were already faltering. Cuba was now deprived of trade on favourable terms, access to finance for industrial development and the purchase of products on the world market was cut off. Immediately prior to the collapse of the USSR, eighty per cent of Cuba's trade took place with the USSR and the Eastern European block, sixty-three per cent of Cuba's imports of food came from the USSR and eighty per cent of imported machinery. All of this vanished almost overnight. This led to a collapse of Cuban GDP between 1989 and 1993 of forty per cent (comparable to the 1929 crash in the US), the fall in exports was seventy-nine per cent, the fall in imports seventy-five per cent, and the fall in gross investment was sixty-one per cent.[84]

The human cost of the collapse of the economy was horrendous: lack of food, lack of fuel for power generation (with accompanying blackouts) and almost complete lack of transport. To these must be added the political impact, the collapse of a system which had been a point of reference for Cuba for twenty years, and of which no serious criticism had been made. There was also the colossal campaign of the ruling classes worldwide to the effect that socialism had failed. And yet, despite everything, Cuba survived what became known as the 'special period in peace time'.

To help lessen the impact of the shortages, the Cuban government took a series of steps including a food programme to encourage local production of foodstuffs to replace food that could no longer be afforded, a big reduction in the number of state employees, a recycling campaign, increased rationing of basic food items and other goods, a reduction in the printing of newspapers,

84 Martin, J., 'Cuba After 50 Years', www.marxist.com, 2009.

and energy conservation measures. An American, Margaret Randall, in Havana at the time, reported an adult food ration of one quarter of a kilo of meat (1/2 lb) a week, three eggs per week, one tin of condensed milk per month, fruit and vegetables that varied with the season, but were adequate.[85] Children under twelve had, in addition, one litre of milk every day but children were also fed at school, and Randall claims they "ate well". Other sources, however, tell a different story, of villages where food was so scarce that there were outbreaks of optical neuropathy.

In the USSR, the leadership of the misnamed Communist Party led the restoration of capitalism, attempting to become capitalists themselves, through the theft, looting and plundering of state property. In Cuba, the revolution resisted and rejected the restoration of capitalism, despite all the hardships. It was a time in which the spirit of struggle of the Cuban Revolution was reborn.

Russian oil supplies to Cuba dropped from 13.1 million tons in 1985 to 8.1 million tons in 1991 to 5.5 million tons in 1993. The cause of this was not Cuba's failure to pay its bills on time. With privatisation, the Russian oil industry suffered its steepest decline in crude oil production since World War II. Russian shipments were delayed or failed to materialise altogether, with severe disruption of the Cuban economy. In fact, the period of transition back to capitalism was the most catastrophic peacetime economic collapse in history. In only six years the Russian economic production fell by over fifty per cent as 'uneconomic' enterprises were shut down.

But the collapse of the USSR should not have been a shock to the politically aware. Lenin and Trotsky, the leaders of the Russian (1917) Revolution, had both warned that the Soviet Union could not survive without a socialist revolution in the advanced capitalist countries. Before Lenin's death, Lenin and Trotsky had united in a struggle against the bureaucracy that was forming within the Party and the state machine. The analysis of the Stalinist bureaucracy was one of Trotsky's greatest achievements. As early as 1936 Trotsky's analysis foresaw the direction the bureaucracy was heading and the eventual outcome:

> One may argue that the big bureaucrat cares little what the prevailing forms of property are, provided only they guarantee him the necessary income. This argument ignores … the question of his descendants. … Privileges have only half their worth, if they cannot be transmitted to one's children. But the right of testament is inseparable from the right of property. It is not

---

85 Randall, op cit.

enough to be the director of a trust; it is necessary to be a stockholder ... a new possessing class.[86]

In the end, the Russian and Chinese Revolutions were defeated not by external enemies but by the pro-capitalist wings of their own bureaucracies.

In May 1992, a new Russian government led by Boris Yeltsin made clear the new relationship with Cuba: work on a Russian nuclear power plant in Cuba would continue only after Cuba agreed to assume all hard currency expenses associated with the project. The plant, when fully operational, would have replaced over a million tons a year of imported oil. Work ended in September, when the Cuban government announced it could no longer afford to meet the demands of the Russian government to finish the plant.

The heroic resistance of the Cuban Revolution after the collapse of the USSR is truly impressive; it was the will of a people who had conquered freedom and were determined not to be enslaved again that carried the country forward. Fidel and the Cuban leadership defended the gains of the revolution. A generation was alive which still remembered what life was like before the revolution and many others who had served abroad could compare their own living standards with those of neighbouring countries under capitalism. The Cuban people collectively found ways and means of overcoming the economic hardship.

The Castro team fully appreciated that the 'special period in time of peace' would be one in which Cuba's economy suffered severe contraction. To minimise disruption and de-fuse opposition it was decided to launch 'Workers' Parliaments' (*Parlamentos Obreras*) sponsored by the CTC-R in which workers were invited to receive reports on the situation, discuss them and present their own measures to help solve the problems faced. These took place over three months between January and March 1994, eighty-five per cent of the workforce participated – about three million workers in 80,000 workplaces. Summaries of the workers' suggestions which, of course, contained many comments about their specific work situations, were forwarded to municipal and provincial meetings of the CTC at which delegates from the municipal, provincial, and national assemblies were present.

While it is obviously true that the general public was being asked to make proposals to ease an already agreed policy, it is also true that this was a national census without precedence anywhere in the world, and helped provide the basis for the discussions at the special session of the National Assembly held on 1 and 2 May, 1994, and the regular session held on 3 and 4 August, 1994. In some factories the workers expressed considerable scepticism at the start of the process, since they had raised similar issues at

---

86 Trotsky, L, *The Revolution Betrayed*, www.marxists.org

workers' meetings for years. But it was soon clear that this was a serious attempt to gather information that would be acted upon. Roman claims that by mid-February these 'Workers' Parliaments' had the support of about eighty per cent of the workers.[87]

Generally the issues discussed fell into four categories:

The venting of grievances such as the poor quality food served in the factory canteen, or wanting the authority to reject defective raw materials. Occasionally these issues took up the majority of the meetings. A recurring theme was bad management and mismanagement; the covering up of theft from the factory, allowing those faking illness to receive their wages and engage in other jobs. In this context about half of workers wanted collective or individual productivity bonuses, and for managers to stop letting slackers 'get away with it', which pulled average productivity down.

Considerable anger was expressed against the small private sector, because private vendors such as stall owners were seen to pay no taxes, despite earning much more than those who worked for a wage. Again and again, there were calls for action against the thieves who stole products, speculators and *macetas* – those who amassed fortunes through illicit activities. State employees who closed their eyes to what was going on (police officers and inspectors) received strong criticism.

There was little willingness to shoulder higher income tax while the relatively wealthy got away with paying nothing or next to nothing. Nearly three-quarters of the workers favoured eliminating subsidies for other than basic items and it was generally agreed that cigarettes and rum should be removed from the ration books and sold at higher prices. Throughout the meetings a clear thread was protection of the basic gains of the Revolution; free education and healthcare, and an opposition to any growth in economic inequalities. Great concern was shown for the fate of 'surplus workers', the effects of the proposals on low-income workers and their families.

In some meetings, workers raised the demand for more openness and honesty in the news and media on the problems being faced. Often it was said that the official news reports were not believed, that people were turning to the Miami radio stations for their information.

As expected, the National Assembly was unanimous in its resolutions and, obviously, made its decisions sound as though they were derived from the consultation process. There were many references made to the Workers' Parliaments during the debates and Roman goes so far as to claim that the

---

87 Roman, P., *Workers' Parliaments in Cuba*, Latin American Perspectives 22(4)43-58, 1995.

most frequent demands made by the workers were met, with the exception of no income tax on workers' salaries.

On 4 May, 1994, the Council of State passed Decree 149 for "confiscation of goods and earnings obtained by unjustified enrichment", including theft, speculation, diversion of state resources, and black market activities. In July, the Council of State increased penalties for crimes related to the national economy and empowered the state to seize goods stolen from the state. US and Western observers greeted these measures as a witch hunt, though later, the UK and USA did much the same thing when they respectively introduced the Proceeds of Crime Act, and Asset Forfeiture.

On 20 May, 1994, the prices of cigarettes and cigars, beer, rum, brandy, gasoline, electricity, inter-city public transportation, water and sewage services, postage and telegrams, and lunch in workers' cafeterias were all increased. On 7 July, 1994, many items that had formerly been free, including lunch for boarding students, language schools, sports and cultural events, and higher education now charged a fee. The resolution did, however, provide for extra assistance for low-income families.

It is undeniable that workers were consulted, and it is notable that this consultation occurred in the depths of a serious economic crisis. Much of what the workers requested and suggested was adopted, mostly because they fell within an expected framework. While consultations with workers regarding problems had long been a regular part of union activity in the workplace, the suggestions made in the Workers' Parliaments were given much more weight and publicity, and were taken up by the National Assembly. The whole exercise was judged a magnificent success. It would be used again at the time of the Sixth PCC Congress in 2011.

There were also changes to the political structures to help retain popular loyalty, including: in July 1992, the (1976) Constitution was amended to allow direct election of delegates to the National Assembly, making it more responsive to the electorate (though the list of candidates had to be approved by the PCC); rewording of the Constitution to make it more explicitly 'Cuban' and less 'Soviet'; dropping the ban on Christians joining the party and reinstating Christmas as a national holiday (there had been three priests with the guerrillas in the Sierra Maestra who performed, marriages, baptisms, confirmations, and burials); and military assistance from Cuba was a thing of the past, Cuba's military capacity was to be dramatically reduced.

People's Councils (between the street-level CDRs and the *municipios*) were introduced to assist in generating a new grass roots-based spontaneity, returning to the days immediately following the revolution. This was a *comunitario* movement, which encouraged the development of all positive activities from growing your own vegetables to the reconstruction of buildings in Old Havana which, Kapacia argues, made as great a contribution to 'saving' the system as any of the economic reforms.

11.1) THE CUBAN ECONOMY IN THE WORLD MARKET

The Castro leadership had before it the history of the Chinese communes, a disaster that led to the deaths of some 20 million people. But they also had the example of the Beijing leadership introducing a New Economic Policy in 1978 in which there was de facto restoration of personal responsibility for land and livestock followed by a huge expansion in food production. This had been achieved by allocating land to individual households that were then free to sell produce over and above their assigned quotas, as they wished. This was accompanied by a revival of individual enterprises in the form of handicrafts, which had virtually disappeared.

Constitutionally in China, urban land was state-owned and rural land owned by collectives, but the 1978 measures allowed land to be treated as private property under the slogan of 'collective land ownership but individual land use'. This was accompanied by the removal of state control of prices to help ensure the profitability of the more efficient farms. These moves were eminently successful in increasing production of agricultural produce. The Cubans thought they could learn from this experience.

Isolated by the US blockade, the actions taken had proved insufficient and further liberalising measures were agreed: legalising small businesses such as cafés, bars and restaurants that had emerged to service the tourist trade; allowing private farmers, small peasant cooperatives, and state farms to sell above-quota produce at free market prices at non-state agricultural markets. As in China, small scale agricultural production flourished and soon every city block in Havana had its own market stall selling fruit, salads, vegetables, and even meat.

Virgilio Díaz, a co-operative beneficial owner growing garlic, maize, sweet potato, papaya and sorghum on a twenty-two-acre plot leased to him for twenty years, claimed his income rose by over seventy per cent: he was able to build a new house and request a lease on more land. Díaz claimed he and his five fellow co-operative workers would, between them with favourable weather, produce 200 tonnes of food a year.[88] Such initiatives were welcome after the straight-jacket of bureaucratic control, which feared any sign of independence. But bureaucratic mismanagement continued to obstruct private agricultural producers who still had to negotiate with a bureaucratic

---

88 González, I., Inter-Press Service, News Agency, June 2017.

state system to determine their quotas and purchase their produce, with delays in payments and problems in accessing fertilisers and seeds.

It is quite acceptable within a workers' state for individual peasant families to farm state-owned land and sell anything produced above their quotas on the free market. This was the New Economic Policy introduced by Lenin into the Soviet Union. In China, however, the acceptance that land could be treated as private property while formally remaining state-owned became the first step in the return to capitalism. The Chinese bureaucracy was blinded by the increased production achieved, and became convinced that if privatisation worked for the peasants it should be extended to industrial enterprises.

The Cuban leadership also introduced a series of measures to enable the economy to participate in the world market, inevitably meaning important concessions to capitalism. These were unavoidable, determined by the immediate need to survive, but at the same time were a source of dangers for the planned economy. Among the measures was the acceptance of foreign investment in, and promotion of, tourism as a source of hard currency (with all the contradictions it brought, such as decriminalising possession of dollars).

After the fall of the Soviet Union, with the Cuban economy on the ropes the US administration went on the attack. First, the so-called Cuban Democracy Act of 1992 sought to give the USA the right to decide the form of 'democracy' to be introduced in Cuba. Then the Helms-Burton Act of 1996, ruled that any person who bought or used confiscated property in any way, could be tried in an American court for 'trafficking in property'. This was to scare off Canadian and European companies from trading with Cuba. The Cubans rightly replied that the property of those Cubans who chose to emigrate could not be included in any negotiations, and negotiations on nationalised North American properties must include the costs imposed on the Cuban economy by the US embargo.

Tourism became a major source of income, but an important negative effect of this was the reinforcement of a layer of relatively better-off Cubans, such as managers of the new tourist hotels, many of whom now look to capitalism as the solution to Cuba's problems. Tourism, especially, was used to launch joint ventures with overseas partners who were given permission to take their profits out of the country as hard currency. The *Havana Times*, at the end of October, 2013, reported that, while a foreign investor was limited to owning forty-nine per cent of the venture, this constraint was more apparent than real. The foreign investors always supplied the finance and often supplied the know-how so, for the most part, the final decisions were left in their hands.

The participation of Cuba in the world market was taking place on very unequal terms. Based predominantly on raw materials and services, the Cuban economy needed to import almost all manufactured goods. The role of industry in the Cuban economy was, and remains, extremely weak and oriented to service tourism. The economic measures taken at the time meant the inevitable penetration by the world market and threatened to unleash an unstoppable movement towards capitalism. The decisive factor was the weakness of the Cuban economy, which was then based on the export of services (mainly doctors, nurses and teachers), income from tourism, and the export of nickel, cigars, and sugar. Cuba's nickel reserves are fifth largest in the world and production volumes are tenth largest; nickel became Cuba's largest merchandise export with the collapse of sugar in 2002.

Dependency on tourism generated contradictions and unevenness within Cuban society; a large part of the limited agricultural production had to be channelled towards this sector, to the detriment of the needs of the Cuban population in general. Those in contact with the tourist industry have access to dollars with which to supplement their monthly budget. But these supplementary payments could be relatively huge; a taxi driver paid in US$, a hotel doorman tipped in US$ or someone renting out a room for US$, could get in one day more than the monthly wage of, say, a health care worker or a teacher. This not only reduces the relative value of the wages for essential jobs but also creates a situation in which an important section of the population earn their living through *lucharla*, semi-legal or openly illegal methods, promoting the idea of individual solutions to social problems as opposed to collective ones.

By 1994, the Cuban economy was picking itself up by its bootstraps, the GDP had stopped sliding downwards and started to edge upwards. The military were given economic responsibilities. For example, the *Havana Times* of 16 June, 2017 carried the headline 'Cuba's Largest Company: The Revolutionary Armed Forces'. It appears that *Grupo de Administración Empresarial* SA (GAESA), a holding company of the Revolutionary Armed Forces chaired by Brigadier-General Luis Alberto Rodríguez López-Callejas, ex-son in law of President Raúl Castro, owns a forty per cent share of the tourism market, many of its activities are partnerships with foreign companies such as the US Marriott chain. Possibly more important, the sending of remittances to Cuba is monopolised by GAESA's *Financiera Cimex* (Fincimex), which also controls the processing of Visa and Mastercard on the island.

At the same time, we find the children and other relatives of the Cuban leadership being allocated important roles in many different areas. It has now been made public that Raúl's son, Colonel Alejandro Castro Espín, was the official representative of Cuba in the secret negotiations with the US that ended with the decision on 17 December, 2014, to open a new stage of bilateral relations. As part of these secret negotiations, the Cubans, to show their good intentions, released a number of so-called political prisoners. The Americans were deaf, however, to demands for the closure of the only prison on Cuba that systematically degrades, tortures and dehumanises its inmates – Guantánamo.

In 1993, the Cuban government launched the convertible peso (CUC) in parallel to the peso in common use. The CUC was pegged equal to the dollar and to twenty-four ordinary pesos. In joint ventures, foreign firms pay a government agency in CUCs for the services of Cuban staff. The agency then pays the workers in Cuban pesos at the rate of one-for-one, making a gain of ninety-five per cent on the deal. This currency system is economically corrosive, because in some government transactions, the two kinds of peso are valued equally, which means that dishonest officials can manipulate the system to fraudulently acquire huge sums of money. More seriously, it made many Governmental accounts nonsensical, with the state unable to accurately identify which of its initiatives were efficient and which were not.

In economic terms, it would be true to say that Cuba limped through the 1990s, but it did not collapse nor did its revolutionary spirit disappear. Tourism and joint ventures halted the decline in GDP, but distorted the economy with an accompanying black market, which increased the division in wealth between those with access to dollars and those without. Exacerbating the problem for the government was that by 2002, overseas investment in Cuba was drying up.

Faced with yet one more crisis, the Cuban leadership launched the 'Battle of Ideas'. The launch pad was the Elián González case and the resulting mass nationwide campaign. Six-year-old Elián González was taken by his mother on a boat across the Florida Straits (without his father's consent). He and his mother were shipwrecked, his mother died but he was rescued by the US Coastguard. Since he was found at sea, US regulations required he be returned to Cuba. However, his relatives in the US took legal measures to prevent this, which generated a mass, sustained campaign of marches and rallies in Cuba for Elián to be returned. Elián's return was seen as a political success, not least because, after years of demoralisation, it reminded Cubans of the power of mass action.

The government seized the opportunity and presented its Battle of Ideas, a multi-faceted social, ideological and cultural campaign, as a continuation of the Elián mobilisations. The form was to challenge the corrosive effects of capitalist penetration of Cuba; with the influx of foreign tourists and US dollars there had been a noticeable rise in petty crime and prostitution, a weakening in the sense of collective solidarity and a worrying increase in levels of inequality. The campaign also sought to revive the energy of the early 1960s, when mass mobilisations had successfully tackled many deep-seated problems. Additionally, the campaign was used to justify the previous economic policy of austerity and the proposed reforms, including the creation of a new layer of petty traders and artisans (in many respects the genesis of a new petty-bourgeoisie).

It was during the Battle of Ideas that individuals on the left of the PCC took the opportunity to publish their own analysis of the fall of the Soviet Union. Ariel Dacal and Francisco Brown Infante, two outspoken intellectuals, began publishing articles such as: 'The USSR, The Thwarted Transition'[89] in which they introduced the idea that Stalinism was a "rupture of the Bolshevik project"; that the Russian Communist Party, despite claims to the contrary was, in reality, a block on the road to socialism. Their ideas were systematised in a book, *Russia: From Real Socialism to Real Capitalism*, published by *Editorial Ciencias Sociales*. This book explained the why and how of the development of the Russian bureaucracy, its accumulation of privileges and perks, and the growing difference in the standard of living between the *nomenklatura* and the workers. Because what had happened in Russia had obvious lessons for Cuba, the book was influential in introducing into the Battle of Ideas the notion that the major danger to the Cuban Revolution came not from the American blockade but from internal contradictions.

Hugo Chávez, President of Venezuela, offered Cuba an economic lifeline via an exchange of Cuban doctors, nurses and teachers for Venezuelan oil. This rekindled the enthusiasm of the Cuban masses, seeing a new revolutionary upsurge of the masses in Latin America. Economic difficulties and the exhaustion of the revolution in Venezuela (precisely because it did not go all the way and expropriate the property of the oligarchs and imperialists as Cuba had done) means that this assistance is now coming to an end.

With the support of Venezuelan oil, the Cuban government felt more confident and turned towards re-centralising the economy: foreign trade was brought more under central control with the resulting closure of around 200 joint venture companies and a drop in the inflow of capital. The circulation of the dollar was banned; concessions to the self-employed and small businesses were limited. The emphasis moved towards prioritising investment from the Venezuelan and Chinese governments to prepare Cuba for a more independent role in the world market.

---

89 Available at www.marxist.com.

When Fidel fell gravely ill in July 2006, he provisionally delegated his dual posts – President of the Council of State and First Secretary of the Communist Party of Cuba – to his younger brother, Raúl, head of the Revolutionary Armed Forces and Second Secretary of the Communist Party. As Fidel's health further deteriorated, the National Assembly declared Raúl President in February 2008.

By this time, the Cubans had experienced how the petty-bourgeois regimes of the Angolan MPLA and Nicaraguan FSLN had failed to carry their revolutions through to a workers' state and degenerated. So it is all the more astounding that, given the experience of their own revolution, the Cuban leadership did not advise Chávez to deepen the Venezuelan revolution. Instead, Fidel, Raúl and the other Cuban leaders followed the Stalinist path: the theory of stages internationally and bureaucratic control at home.

In contrast, the political sensitivity of Cuba's intellectuals and left-wing activists can be demonstrated by an incident at the start of 2007. On 5 January, 2007, an elderly poet, Luis Pavón appeared on Cuban television celebrating the achievements of artists and intellectuals. Pavón had been head of the National Cultural Council (*Consejo nacional de cultura*) where he had acted as censor on behalf of the regime during the five grey years, and oversaw a cultural policy in which gay or otherwise 'problematic' artists were fired from their jobs, when long-haired young men were picked up off the streets and brutally subjected to forced hair-cuts, and so on. The following morning, the writer Jorge Pérez emailed friends and acquaintances denouncing the re-appearance of this Stalinist hard-man, and expressing his fears that this could be a signal of a return to a more repressive cultural policy. The email went viral and an intense debate (the 'war of the emails', so-called because, for the first, time such a debate had been carried out on the Internet) ensued. That ended on 30 November, with a statement by the Minister of Culture, Abel Pietro, that neo-Stalinist censorship had no place in Cuba.

How much genuine freedom of expression and actual power the Cuban working class and the population as a whole can exercise is a vital matter for the survival of the workers' state and its development towards socialism. This was, and is, a question openly discussed by university students, academics, professionals and revolutionaries. Ever since the revolution, the PCC and government have had a policy of unity around the top leaders. That Cuba had resisted the attempts by the US to smash it apparently confirmed the correctness of the top-down party structure. Cuba could not afford the luxury of any significant level of divergence in deciding the direction of the country's politics and economy. The leadership maintained that any meaningful broadening of freedom of expression in the political sphere could place the nation's sovereignty in peril. But voices on the left observed this was the same argument used to justify the Stalinist regimes in Eastern Europe and Russia, right up to their collapse.

Workers' democracy is not a luxury which one can choose or not; it is an essential pre-condition for a socialist economy. Without workers' democracy any workers' state is deformed and will, ultimately, perish. In Cuba, strict government control of the channels of information and debate cripple the ability of the common man and woman to obtain the information and ideas necessary for them to become politically empowered. Leftists, including students from the University of Havana and Cujae University, began to hold regular workshops to discuss the future of socialism in Cuba and other questions. So far, the government has allowed these discussions to continue, and its opposition has been of the 'soft' kind: confining the meetings to indoor locations, meeting rooms being double-booked, failure to deliver resources to produce leaflets, events with big name speakers organised to clash with the student meetings, etc.

The state closely monitors those who raise criticisms, but discussions about the future of the Cuban revolution are taking place at all levels. There is a growing interest in Trotsky, his books have been sold at the Havana Book Fair where *The Revolution Betrayed* was officially presented, Trotskyist speakers have been officially invited to conferences, there is open criticism of Stalin, etc. In this context, those who advocated the need for workers' democracy and proletarian internationalism as the best way to defend the Cuban revolution express their viewpoint openly as members of the PCC, University Students Federation, supplemented by meetings and the use of the internet.

Possibly the most important event was a workshop in 2007 to celebrate the ninetieth anniversary of the Russian revolution and to discuss its trajectory and collapse, organised by a group of students in the FEU. Twice the expected number turned up (some 500 people) to celebrate the October Revolution and hold a vigil for 'Ninety Years of the Silenced Revolution'. Speakers included Ariel Dacal, who addressed the question of Stalinism as a counter-revolutionary force, and Fernando Rojas of the FEU, who argued that a new interpretation of the past was necessary for participants to be ideologically equipped to deal with the coming discussions on change in Cuba.

The meeting launched a website, www.cuba-urss.cult.cu, which now has several hundred articles and essays submitted by activists and such authorities as: Lenin, Trotsky, Gramsci, Luxemburg, and Guevara. Since then, this current has met monthly at the Ministry of Culture's, Juan Marinello Centre in a meeting hall with a capacity of just under 100 people. The hall was packed at the end of January, 2009, for the initial workshop: 'The significance and meaning of the revolution in our lives'. Other workshops followed, one being of particular note: 'The political system of the revolution: participation, popular subject and citizenship', which focused on how citizens participated in the political system and how they made the revolution their own. On one wall were posted words by Paulo Freire: "If the structure does not permit dialogue the structure must be changed".

At the time of writing, the last such meeting was in February 2017; a seminar attended by some 200 people to celebrate fifty years since the founding of *Pensamiento Critico*. At that meeting, punningly entitled, 'Critical Thinking and the transition to socialism', Frank Josué Solar Cabrales, a Cuban communist and lecturer at the Universidad de Oriente, Santiago de Cuba, made a presentation, stating:

> [T]he only way to increase productivity and generate economic growth by socialist means, is through consciousness, education, the formation of new men and women, with new social relations of production among them. In this sense, genuine workers' control over politics and the economy is not secondary, but the necessary condition for the transition, and the only way it can develop the productive forces in a socialist sense.[90]

After describing essential similarities between the Cuban and Russian Revolutions; particularly the release of the creative energy of the masses, and the freedom of discussion that occurred, he explained how the gains of the Cuban Revolution could not have been achieved under capitalism, that a socialist revolution was necessary. Cabrales explained that the reason why almost nobody talks about the transition to socialism in Cuba is due to:

> ...a widespread misconception ... socialism is very fair and works wonders to secure cultural and social rights, but economically it is a disaster, it is inefficient and does not create wealth, nor does it stimulate production and growth. Therefore, it seems clear that the solution should be to combine the best of both systems ... capitalist economic mechanisms to produce wealth, and the socialist political model to distribute it as fairly as possible ... (but) socialism is not a mere system of more or less fair distribution of wealth, but rather is the creation of a new culture, with new social relations, new human beings – along with the material basis necessary to satisfy people's needs. This purpose cannot be served by just any kind of economic development, much less one that is based on the exploitation of the labour of others, which

---

90 Available at www.marxist.com.

engenders selfishness, inequality, and poverty ... We cannot use the old whips of capitalism if we wish to achieve true emancipation.[91]

Cabrales presented his alternative to the official views:

> ... genuine workers' control over politics and the economy is not secondary, but the necessary condition for the transition (to socialism) ... Left criticism ... is not dangerous to the Revolution, but to the bureaucracy. ... Today, this left criticism is more necessary than ever to avoid capitalist restoration in Cuba. The unity of all revolutionaries is a precondition for the strengthening and defence of the Revolution from attacks by imperialists and the right wing. ... but unity alone is not enough to further its development and prevent its defeat. Revolution must come with popular control over the bureaucracy, that is, as an effective exercise of popular power and a purposeful act of critical left thought.

He explained the kind of socialism that Cuba should aim for:

> ... most of the regimes that called themselves socialist in the 20th century had nothing to do with real socialism. Mistaking the Stalinist model ... for true socialism is like mistaking the Inquisition for primitive Christianity – which was revolutionary, collectivist, and tied to the popular masses. The socialism that we strive for here and around the world is in favour of freedom and equality; the kind of socialism which points to a society of free associated workers, where the free development of the individual is the condition for the development of all, and where power and property belong to all. A new world, with no Caesars and no bourgeois. A revolutionary cannot settle for less.

12) THE SIXTH AND SEVENTH PARTY CONGRESSES, OBAMA AND TRUMP

The long-delayed Sixth Congress of the PCC was held in April 2011, on the fiftieth anniversary of the victory at the Bay of Pigs. Despite party rules requiring a Congress every five years, the previous party Congress had been in 1997. The reason for the delay was obvious. Cuba had faced a sequence of serious problems, each one requiring the state taking action, and which had required the party tops to thrash out disagreements and make decisions. Such discussions took place behind closed doors with the masses excluded.

The central document, 'Draft Guidelines for the Economic and Social Policy', which contained 291 proposals for consolidating or amending social and economic policy, was published earlier to allow for public discussion.

---

91 Available at www.marxist.com.

The Congress itself was expected to be limited to endorsing and legitimising the policies proposed and, indeed, when Venezuelan President Hugo Chávez visited in December of 2010, he was presented with a large bound volume containing the resolutions and decisions of the 2011 Congress.

The thirty-two-page document, although focused on economic restructuring, mentioned neither the workers nor their unions; there was no mention of bureaucracy; popular, democratic organisms of control and planning, were noticeable by their absence. Rather than democratisation there was to be an increase in the powers of the state, an admission of increasing divisions within Cuban society. Missing from the document was any self-criticism by the party of its actions, neither since its foundation nor between the Fifth and Sixth Congresses. Cuba had made mistakes but the lack of any self-criticism underlined the bureaucratic and undemocratic nature of the document and the Congress. Nor was there any assessment of the likely dangers from strengthening the bourgeois sectors and capitalist values, of the likely impact of the world economy on Cuban society, or of the social and political dangers of opening Cuba to the world market.

The introduction affirmed that only socialism was capable of overcoming the difficulties facing Cuba and preserving the conquests of the Revolution. "Socialism" the document stated meant "equality of rights and opportunities … Work is both a right and a duty; the personal responsibility of every citizen, and must be remunerated according to its quantity and quality".

The package as presented by Raúl Castro was a Cuban version of the 'Four Modernisations' announced by Deng Xiaoping after his election as Vice Premier in January 1975. Both Deng and Raúl had the same goal, to introduce economic reforms to save their revolutions. Raúl, aged 79, appeared a Cuban version of the geriatric Chinese Stalinist as he announced:

- The incomes of workers in the state sector will depend on the profitability of their business (Point 19). Shedding workers was one way of increasing profitability, increased pay would be a means to persuade staff to accept the deal.
- Each enterprise to be empowered to set the prices for its products and services (Point 23), the market to decide the price of goods, i.e. supply and demand (Point 177). A strengthening of market forces within the country.
- Control of production to be decentralised and administered by local municipal councils (Point 35), weakening the state plan.
- To expand the services provided by the self-employed, and the granting of credits to individual, self-employed workers (Point 158).

- Investments will be concentrated "on the most efficient producers", i.e., not on the most socially useful sectors (Point 184).
- To continue the programme whereby land declared 'idle' is transferred as a rent-free loan to those agricultural producers with outstanding results. Between 2008 and 2014, over 1.5 million hectares (nearly 4 million acres) would be transferred in this way, nearly a quarter of Cuba's total arable land.

These measures were, objectively, a significant step towards the restoration of capitalism. To divert attention and channel the discussion, the leadership included a series of proposals that were deliberately provocative. The cost of the proposed economic changes would be shouldered largely by the Cuban workers by such measures as the "orderly elimination" of the ration book (Point 162), removal of subsidies from workers' canteens (Point 164), and an increase in the price of electricity (Point 230). As would be expected, it was these points, which had an immediate and direct effect on people's lives, that generated most heat and gained most attention in the Congress discussions.

Despite the enormous difficulties Cuba faced, there were important social compensations that improved the living standards of every Cuban, in particular, access to education. Minister of Culture, Abel Prieto, explained that Cuba, a blockaded Third World country with one-thirteenth of the per capita GDP of the US, could still guarantee conditions for a decent life, rich in spiritual and cultural terms. He was convinced "that culture could be an antidote against consumerism and against the oft-repeated idea that only buying can create happiness in this world". There were two problems here: such a perspective can only work if inequality is limited and not allowed to flourish, and Raúl had just announced the removal of grants and subsidies for workers wishing to enter Higher Education, which would still be open to them, but only on a self-financing basis.

The Guidelines were widely discussed amongst the population, every Cuban having access to the document and invited to participate in open debates on its content. People were genuinely interested in what they regarded as a crucial discussion on Cuba's future. The questions of capitalism, private property, personal property, self-employment, etc., were all included in this discussion. *Granma* reported that between 1 December, 2010, and 28 February, 2011, 163,000 meetings, were organised by work or study centres, political and residential groups, so that every Cuban regardless of political or organisational affiliation, was able to attend. It is claimed that, of a total population of 11.2 million, nearly 9 million people participated, and over 3 million comments were received.[92]

92 http://en.granma.cu/cuba/2016-03-28

However, while the discussion was genuine, no democratic mechanism existed for processing the proposals and comments so they could be voted and acted upon. These proposals were sent 'up' to a bureaucratically-appointed committee which analysed, classified and modified them, placing a bureaucratic lid on the process.

The Sixth Congress was attended by almost 1,000 delegates, who approved the Guidelines and passed them to the National Assembly of Peoples' Power for legislative ratification with only minimal changes. The Congress also acknowledged that the existing full employment was based on systematic overstaffing of government enterprises and endorsed the decision to cut more than a million government jobs. This was coupled with the approval of a series of policies intended to promote co-operatives and self-employment. The measures resulted in a decrease of government employees, down from four and a quarter million in 2009 to just over three and a half million in 2012 with a consequent peak of 3.5 per cent in unemployment.[93]

Raúl also announced an increase in the proportion of women, black and mixed-race people in leadership positions; women were to be forty-two per cent of the new Central committee, up from fourteen per cent; black and mixed race people were increased from ten per cent to thirty per cent (around one-third of the Cuban population are black or mixed race). Breaking with accepted practice, Raúl recommended to the Congress that public officials be limited to a maximum of two five-year terms, and the unstated requirement that only a PCC member could hold public office be eliminated.

As part of the discussions around the Sixth Congress, Frank Josué Solar Cabrales presented an article entitled, 'Cuba, the traps on the road', declaring:

> The socialist solution (to Cuba's problems, requires) workers' democracy in the party and the state structures and government; the democratic participation of the workers in the planning of the economy and an internationalist policy promoting the extension of the socialist revolution throughout Latin America and the world.[94]

Another current within the PCC raised the important question of workers' self-management; the participation of workers in the management of the economy and the decision-making processes at all levels. The suggestion was that ownership of companies was to be handed to their workers who would receive their wages as a share of the profits made. These proposals were parallel to the Chinese government's measures for small and medium-

93 González-Corzo, M., and Justo, O. *Self-employment in Cuba*, CUNY Academic Works, 2014.
94 www.marxist.com/cuba-pcc-conferencia.htm, April 2012.

sized enterprises introduced in 1982. Experience showed that, whatever the intentions of the proposers, such measures accelerated a return to capitalism.

The system proposed also had strong similarities to the 'socialist self-management' implemented in Yugoslavia and which was a significant factor in the economic collapse of that country. This type of ownership did increase productivity at a local level but, because of its unplanned nature, also created unemployment, sharp trade cycles and regional disparities that played a substantial role in the break-up of the country and its reversion to capitalism. Experience has taught that, within a capitalist world market, self-management for profit within an unplanned economy, may improve production, but inevitably leads back to capitalism, and in a very short time.

In the discussions, those who proposed moving Cuba towards capitalism emphasised the practicality of their schemes: obtaining foreign investment, developing small and medium-sized enterprises, decentralising economic activity, and emphasising market forces in the economy, and so on. Omar Everleny Perez, the most renowned of the academics favouring pro-capitalist economic reforms, an economist with the influential Centre for the Study of the Cuban Economy (CEEC) at Havana University, wrote:

> Of course, there are people who will lose as a result of these reforms. Of course, some people are going to be unemployed. Of course, inequalities will increase … what we have today is false egalitarianism. What is at stake is who really deserves to be *on top*.[95] (Emphasis in original.)

These people can claim one success: the Cuban government is moving away from the system whereby products are subsidised, and moving towards a system which provides subsidies to the poorest and most disadvantaged. This will reduce government expenditure but at the cost of introducing means-testing. All experience shows that, over time, this will result in the stigmatisation of the poor with a consequent loss of social cohesion.

The Sixth Congress opened the door to procuring from countries that received solidarity aid from Cuba *at least* the equivalent of the cost of this aid, a proposal which transformed solidarity into service provision. Also announced was the first Special Development Zone to be created in port Mariel, forty-five kilometres west of Havana. Here, as in China's Special Economic Zones, foreign companies would be able to transfer their profits abroad without paying the usual taxes or tariffs for ten years. The initiative, backed by US$900 million of Brazilian capital, would cover more than 465 square kilometres, and be managed by a Singapore-based firm, PSA.

---

95 *Le Monde Diplomatique*, No. 142, 2011.

The international capitalist media speculate about whether Raúl Castro is proposing a 'Chinese way' for Cuba, that is, the progressive introduction of market measures that will ultimately lead to the restoration of capitalism. Obviously, this would be the preferred option for the capitalists internationally, but the official Cuban media insists that Cuba is not China, that conditions are different and models cannot be copied. However, Cuban economists are indeed proposing exactly the same kinds of market reforms which in China led to the restoration of capitalism.

Raúl Castro's challenge over the past decade has been to place the Cuban economy on what he believes are firm foundations. The question of economic performance is clearly central to that task. Raúl claims to see 'market socialism' as a way to strengthen Cuba's economy without abandoning its Castro-era ideals. But it remains to be seen how long – and if – this ideological limit will survive. In this Raúl, stands shoulder to shoulder with Deng Xiaoping who, intending to preserve a bureaucratic system based on a nationalised, planned economy, actually began the march back to capitalism.

After being elected president in February 2008, Raúl accelerated the economic reforms and began to re-structure the cabinet he had inherited to head off opposition and smooth the process. A number of ministers, including the two (Carlos Lage and Felipe Pérez Roque) seen as likely to cause problems, were replaced by younger, more docile, more efficient and reform-minded 'specialists'.[96] It was this new cabinet which approved the plan to shed a million public sector jobs and is likely to approve future changes necessary to commit Cuba to something like the Chinese economic model.

The income from export of medical services, based on about 37,000 Cuban doctors and nurses serving abroad, is possibly as high as US$5 billion annually, much more than the income from tourism. For example, in 2013, the Brazilian Ministry of Health signed a deal for the services of 4,000 Cuban doctors, for which it pays US$270 million a year to the Cuban government.[97] The programme, *Mais Medicos* (More Doctors – also known as Castrocare), was to redress the shortage of doctors in communities in Brazil's interior and in the poorer districts on the outskirts of major cities. The deal was extended for three years commencing September 2016 and, up to the date of renewal, 11,429 Cuban health professionals had participated. Those they had treated were overwhelmingly (eighty-one per cent) low-income and ninety-five per cent of those said they were satisfied with the treatment they had received. Brazil pays Cuba about US$4,000 per month for each doctor. The doctors get US$400 per month while in Brazil, and – as an inducement to return

---

96 Kapcia, op cit.
97 *Forbes Magazine*, 8 June, 2015.

home – a lump sum at a rate of US$600 per month for the time served abroad when they return to Cuba. The money earned while working abroad is, relative to the salaries of those remaining in Cuba, a huge amount.

Remittances from Cubans abroad are worth US$3 billion annually, with over half of all Cuban families receiving this benefit. While these payments are an important source of revenue, they do not reach all sections of society equally, increasing social inequality and reducing the status of wages as the main source of income.

12.1) OBAMA, TRUMP, US-CUBA RAPPROCHEMENT AND FOREIGN DEBT

The resumption of diplomatic relations between the USA and Cuba was a victory for the Cuban people. Obama recognised the failure of fifty years of US attempts to destroy the Cuban Revolution. Military intervention in 1961 at the Bay of Pigs, terrorism and economic sabotage, conspiracies to assassinate Cuban leaders, an economic embargo to strangle the life of the island, everything has been tried to break Cuba. But Cuba held fast, not without difficulty, not without suffering. Cuba held on to become the anti-imperialist reference for the entire Latin American left.

Cuba's resistance has successfully withstood the politico-military confrontation with US imperialism, but has not been so successful resisting the pressures of the capitalist world market. Once more, it is confirmed that socialism cannot be built in one country. But Obama did not lift the US embargo, and no-one should be fooled that the US administration was changing its goals; its aim remains the destruction of the Cuban Revolution because, while it exists, it is a serious threat to US interests in Latin America. The US was simply changing its tactics, using the possibility of rapprochement to launch a three-pronged attack. The most obvious was the call for economic changes within Cuba in return for lifting the blockade. The second was to dangle the carrot of US investment in, particularly, tourism, agribusiness, pharmaceuticals and telecommunications to draw Cuba back into its zone of influence. Thirdly, it wielded the big stick by repealing the US policy of giving Cuban migrants favoured immigration status and thus eliminating an escape route for dissatisfied citizens, hoping they will generate additional pressure on the regime, and pose an additional financial burden.

Obama made his first overtures at the end of 2009, when he announced measures that ended restrictions on the amounts that American citizens could send to family members in Cuba. This move was intended to complement Cuban government measures taken in September 2010 relaxing its control of the economy. Many of the three-quarters of a million public sector workers who lost their jobs were expected to become self-employed. Obama's measures were intended to help finance a petty-bourgeois layer friendly to the US.[98] In 2007, eighty per cent of Cuban workers were state employees, by 2015 this had fallen to seventy-one per cent, as reported by Cuba's National Office of Statistics. The number of (mostly urban) self-employed workers has grown from 141,600 in 2008 to about one-third of a total workforce of five million by 2017.

Secret negotiations were held between the Cuban leadership and the Obama administration on several issues. Raúl and Obama used their influence and political authority on the warring sides in Colombia to bring about the end of the FARC's armed struggle, leading eventually to a peace agreement. The Colombian deal was key in the re-establishment of diplomatic relations between Cuba and the US. After spending thirty-three years listed as a state sponsor of terrorism by the US State Department, Cuba was formally, and silently, removed in May 2015. In July the same year, the USA allowed the Cubans to re-open their embassy in Washington DC. During the two years of secret negotiations, Cuba increased its cooperation with the US on anti-narcotics efforts, and now forms an integral part of the US defensive wall against drug smuggling.

In May 2013, Cuba amended its Penal Code and Proceedings to make its treatment of foreigners more 'flexible'. The courts are instructed to pay "special attention … where the accused are foreigners or individuals with permanent residence abroad", to guarantee they receive "essential" consular assistance. Those arrested for a crime should be held in jail ("preventive, temporary imprisonment") prior to their trial "only in such cases where it is absolutely necessary", "the least number of individuals should be imprisoned" and then "only in highly serious cases". The "policy of granting early prison release" will be applied whenever possible. Cynics might say Cuba was preparing for an influx of capitalist entrepreneurs.

In early 2014, the Cuban government passed Law 118 enacting the key points agreed at the Sixth Congress. In certain important areas, this new law was an extension of the Congress decisions; foreign investment was to be allowed in all economic sectors, including: utilities, real estate (including houses), hotel management and professional services. There will be an initial eight-year exemption on taxes after which tax on profits will be half the current rate (fifteen per cent compared to thirty per cent), tax exemption when profits are re-invested in Cuba, and 100 per cent foreign ownership permitted. Health, education, and the armed forces are excluded. These

98 Sullivan, M., *Cuba: U.S. Restrictions on Travel and Remittances,* Congressional Research Service, Feb., 2017.

moves parallel the changes introduced in China in 1983 when, to boost the performance of the Special Economic Zones, wholly foreign-owned companies were freed to operate in the country. This was followed by actively encouraging foreign owned enterprises to set up in China and, within two years, it had abandoned the monopoly of foreign trade.

In Cuba, all investment must be authorised by the Ministry of Foreign Trade and it remains the case that no foreign investor may hire labour directly. That continues to be done (as in China) by a government employment agency which both charges a fee for its services and insists the employees are paid in US dollars. This is such a lucrative activity that doubtless it will continue as a state monopoly.

Cuba is a country in which environmental issues are taken seriously and the new legislation does provide for strict environmental controls with any environmental damage having to be made good. This has been cited by some on the left as a mechanism which will control the degree of capitalist exploitation that can take place. However, as China found, to maximise profits, many firms decamp overnight, leaving an empty factory, unpaid employees and without redressing environmental damage. How Cuba deals with such situations remains to be seen.

For ordinary Cubans, a major change will be the ability to buy and sell their homes on an open market, classified by the *Wall Street Journal* (3 April, 2015) as a "real-estate revolution". Here, it was noted that the asking price for luxury apartments in Havana is as high as US$1.2 million and, using Air BnB, the daily rental rate for a room in a family house is between US$16 and US$50 per day, the latter being about the average monthly wage in Cuba. If anything can deal the CDRs their coup de grace, it is this new dawn of private property. Cuba is seeing the division between those who use their own homes for some commercial purpose – as a restaurant, or workshop or simply to rent out – and those who do not. These divisions will deepen, bringing the danger of the polarisation of the cities into well-to-do neighbourhoods and shanties. Already in wealthy neighbourhoods, private forms of security are becoming the norm.

In August, 1985, Fidel had announced that Cuba's debt had become unpayable. Some thirty years later, in December 2015, there was an historic agreement between Cuba and the Major Creditors of Cuba (also known as the Paris Club) including Canada, France, Italy, Spain, and the United Kingdom to restructure its debt following its default in 1986. The terms of the agreement provided that the Paris Club wrote off the penalties that had accumulated, totalling some US$8.5 billion, and Cuba would pay US$2.6 billion (corresponding to the original principal) by 2033. There is a moratorium on interest levied until 2020, after which there will be an interest rate of 1.5 per cent per annum until the debt is fully repaid. But all is not as charitable as it might seem.

Creditors are using debt as a vehicle to obtain trade and investment advantages. The possibility of re-establishing diplomatic relations with the US and of a gradual weakening of the blockade, created a race between international investors to obtain the best conditions for accessing Cuba's high growth sectors of tourism, mining, and pharmaceuticals. It is in this context that Cuba concluded agreements with China, Japan and Mexico to write off billions of dollars of debt, and to restructure the remaining debts over ten to twenty years on much easier terms. With Russia, ninety per cent of Cuba's debt, estimated at US$35.2 billion was written off and in return, Cuba will pay the remaining US$3.2 billion over a ten-year period. The settlement of Cuba's debts is central for attracting foreign capital, for the country's re-inclusion in international financial markets, and will greatly reduce obstacles to capitalist investment.

In each of these agreements trade concessions were central in obtaining debt cancellation. For example, both the Canadian and the Spanish are active in the tourism sector and wish to protect their position in the face of possible increased competition from US companies. Canada heads the countries sending tourists to Cuba, with 1.2 million visitors in 2016, while Spain is expected to be the major holiday destination for the Cuban *nouveau riche*. Another example of the kind of deals being struck was seen in May 2017, when the South Korean technology giant, Samsung, opened a store in co-operation with the Cuban retail chain, Caribbean TRD, owned by the Cuban Armed Forces, and which has over fifty per cent of the Cuban electronics market. On sale will be Samsung products, including smartphones, TVs and fridges.

However, the surprise election of Donald Trump in November 2016, has created a situation of considerable uncertainty for the Cuban leadership. They had a deal with Obama which they thought would lead towards the lifting of the US embargo at a time when the crisis in the Venezuelan revolution had already started to cut off what had been Cuba's oil lifeline for ten years. In July 2016, for example, a twenty per cent cut in promised Venezuelan oil shipments meant blackouts and short-time working in offices and factories.

It is not yet clear to the Cuban leadership what policy Trump will follow. On the one hand, he is a businessman and the change in policy by Obama was based on the pressure of a substantial sector of US capitalists who did not want to lose investment opportunities to Canada, China, and the EU.

That sector still exists and will attempt to push Trump to maintain the same policy as Obama.

On the other hand, there are powerful interests within the Republican party, many in the Trump camp, that remain ideologically committed to banging the anti-Communism drum. On 16 June, 2017, before a cheering crowd of Cuban émigrés at the Manuel Artime Theatre (named after the leader of the Bay of Pigs fiasco) in Miami's Little Havana, Trump vowed that he would not be silent in the face of "Communist aggression", and "cancelled" Obama's initiative.

However, behind the scenes, the actions of the Trump camp are not as anti-Cuba as they appear in front of the cameras. Deliberately giving the appearance of reinstating a ban on Americans going to Cuba as tourists, what Trump actually did was to demand US tourists avoid hotels and villas, and tour companies owned by the Cuban military. For the moment, key parts of the Obama initiative remain intact, in particular the ability to remit money to the island, and commercial deals in the pipe-line can continue as planned (even those with GAESA). Cuba has some of the best and most inventive biotech and medical research in the world, and trials of the Cuban lung cancer drug Cimavax, the success of which would mean big bucks for the Cuban government, have been underway in the US since 2015. Roswell Park Cancer Institute has an agreement with Cuba's Centre for Molecular Immunology to begin clinical trials in the US for approval by the Food and Drug Administration.

However, the National Security Presidential Memorandum on Cuba signed by Trump on 16 June, 2017, could deprive millions of Cubans of remittances from their US relatives. By the end of his presidency, Obama had reduced the restrictions on remittances to a narrow layer of state officials and senior officers of the Cuban armed forces. Trump has potentially extended the ban to hundreds of senior officials in every government agency, Cubans who act as leaders of their local CDR, and every one of the 60,000 employees of the Ministry of the Interior. If employees of the two big holding companies, GAESA and CIMEX, are included, then as many as a quarter of the Cuban labour force will no longer be eligible for remittances. Hidden in the small print of an obscure piece of legislation, because of their undoubted unpopularity in the Cuban-American community, these measures could deny clerks, truck drivers, and privates doing national service in the Cuban army help from family members in the USA. Now it is the Treasury Department's Office of Foreign Assets Control that will interpret and enact the new regulations. But people are very resourceful and unofficial remittances have jumped in value by a factor of five. That said, even without any change to remittances,

Trump's actions will mean a drop in Cuban GDP and a small but significant drop in family consumption.

Whether Cuba's leaders can balance the incentives offered to foreign capital, and the consequent impact within Cuba, with protecting the social gains made in the revolution remains to be seen. There are grounds for optimism: there is Cuba's high level of educational attainment, there is a real anti-imperialist sentiment amongst the people, there is a high level of technological development in sectors such as mining, medical services and pharmaceuticals, and tourism. To discard these special characteristics in the pursuit of a form of development dictated from abroad would be the worst course of action.

12.2) SEVENTH PARTY CONGRESS, APRIL 2017

In contrast to previous congresses, PCC members were kept in the dark about the key programmatic and strategic documents to be placed before the Seventh Congress. On 23 February, *Granma*, had reported the Central Committee Plenum announcement of "a popular consultation" on the Congress documents. But with just weeks to go, only the 800 or so delegates, the 280 guests, National Assembly deputies, high-level PCC cadres and some academics and consultants had been given access to the drafts. From many parts of the country rank and file members asked: Did the PCC leadership not have sufficient confidence in them to allow them to help decide the destiny of their country? If not, what was the point of them being Party activists? This questioning was a welcome sign of life within the PCC.

The response of the PCC leadership, an editorial in *Granma* on 27 March, was, frankly, an embarrassment to all those who defend the Cuban state against imperialist aggression. The paper informed its readers that the Seventh Congress on 16-19 April, 2017 was being held only to fulfil the Party Statute that a Congress should be held every five years. Party-wide consultation on the Congress documents was unnecessary, because such consultation had occurred five years previously for the Sixth Congress, and the decisions of that Congress were still being implemented. The unanswered questions: Were the measures agreed those being implemented? Were the measures being implemented taking Cuba towards a more democratic form of socialism or to a Chinese-style capitalist restoration? That the leadership did not consider it worthwhile to bring these issues into the open was a clear warning of the degree of differences among PCC tops on where Cuba might be heading.

A sprightly, eighty-four year-old Raúl Castro presented the main report to the Congress and hinted strongly that divisions within the leadership made free and open debate an impossibility in a party which forbade factions. In the code so often used in the Russian and Chinese Communist Parties, Raúl stated that the "great technical complexity" of the main document to be presented to Congress meant it had yet to be completed. He confirmed the "sanctity" of the socialist basis of the Cuban state while declaring that capitalist reforms would proceed.

A number of apparently secondary events confirmed Raúl as a firm supporter of the capitalist initiatives. His re-affirmation that the PCC would remain the only party allowed in Cuba is, while factions are banned within the PCC, a serious block to party democracy. Such a declaration is an attempt to stifle democratic debate just when it is essential. Other changes show that he is determined to reduce the number of guerrilla fighters on the Central and Political Committees. In his opening address he stated: "We propose establishing 60 as the maximum age for joining the party's Central Committee … and 70 for leadership jobs in the party", adding that the goal was the systematic rejuvenation of all party posts so that "we are never surprised by developments" and succession "flows naturally".

Such moves would, normally, be welcomed by socialists but here we see an attempt to remove from the Party leadership those most opposed to pro-capitalist policies. The Political Committee, came to the Congress with a membership of fourteen, two members were dropped and five new members elected. All the new members are too young to have been directly involved in the revolution and, generally, are technocrats such as Miriam Nicado García, age fifty-four, Director of the University of Information Sciences, and Marta Ayala Avila, age fifty, Deputy Director General of the Engineering Centre for Genetics and Biotechnology.

Raúl called for Congress to accept the Central Committee document in principle, take it back to their local areas and continue the discussion, saying that in this way it could be the basis of a wide, deep and democratic process that would extend to society at large, and the results of the discussions would then be submitted for final approval by the Central Committee. This would not be on the scale of the discussions around the Sixth Congress because matters had already been decided in principle. The proposal was, most likely, a device to defuse a situation where there could have been extensive criticism of Party policy. Despite the appearance of continued and extended democratic discussion – in the Party, in the Communist Youth, in the mass organisations, etc., the reality was that, in the end, there would be a myriad of suggestions and comments, far too many to consider, and nobody would hear of them again. The Central Committee would then be free to make its own policy decisions, claiming the support of the Cuban people, present them to the National Assembly, formally the highest institution of state power, which would then gave them legal status.

The Seventh Party Congress appointed Raúl to be First Secretary, a post that he can legitimately hold until 2021 when he will be ninety years of age. In 2018, Raúl was replaced as President and, for the first time, the PCC top and President is not the same person. At his advanced age, Raúl could not expect to hold two demanding jobs.

13) BUREAUCRACY AND CORRUPTION: WHAT WAY FORWARD FOR CUBA?

Currently, the market is a junior partner in Cuba's central planning. The Seventh Party Congress approved continued controlled liberalisation, accepting market socialism as PCC doctrine, stating that "the State recognises and integrates the market into the functioning of the system of planned direction of the economy." The similarities with China are too obvious to ignore.

The Deng wing of the CCP coined the phrase 'market socialism' in which the main levers of the economy remained under state control guided by a state plan including a monopoly of foreign trade. Deng and his co-thinkers knew that bureaucratic attempts to achieve economic self-sufficiency had failed and recognised that China could not develop in isolation from the world market. 'Socialism in One Country', previously basic Stalinist dogma, while remaining official ideology, was finally, though quietly, buried.

When Deng and the other leaders of the CP in China began their programme of reforms, they had no inkling that they were preparing the way for capitalist restoration. But the incremental introduction of market measures (in the name of efficiency) led to the restoration of capitalism, with a massive increase in inequality, the destruction of the social welfare system, etc. At each stage of the process, the bureaucracy considered how to proceed, convinced it was doing the best for the country. In fact, the bureaucracy took those decisions which benefited itself, the CCP, state bureaucrats and hangers-on, because it falsely identified its own interests as those of China. It is no surprise, therefore, that sections of the bureaucracy in Cuba are looking to China as a model. These people point to the growth in China's GDP and the continued rule of the CCP, and are blind to, or choose to ignore, the massive accompanying social contradictions.

Aid from Venezuela, the delivery of oil at below world market prices, is coming to an end and hence a worsening of the Cuban economic situation is anticipated. Cuba cannot wait around. China is making Latin America, especially Cuba, a priority area for investment and shipped US$1.8 billion of exports to Cuba in 2016. Plans are in place for projects encompassing tourism (US$460 million in golf resorts), telecommunications (a computer assembly plant funded by Haier with capacity for 120,000 laptops and tablets annually), and infrastructure (Shanghai Electric is funding development of bioelectricity plants).[99] China is selling its products on 'soft credit', making Cuba China's largest creditor. But capitalist China does not have the same priorities as the former Soviet Union and, sooner rather than later, it will be asking Cuba to settle its debts.

There is a strong current amongst Cuban economists, supporting measures that, taken as a whole, can be called the 'Chinese way', with the aim of developing the economy but which will inevitably end up with the restoration of capitalism. Because of the strong criticism of China from left-wing intellectuals, the term preferred by the rightists is the 'Vietnamese model'. Recent proposals include emulating the Chinese example by changing the basis of Cuban law to expand reliance on the private sector, to enlarge the free trade zone around the port of Mariel, and offer even greater tax exemptions to new business.

Everleny argued the Cuban economy's urgent need for deep structural transformation, emphasising decentralisation and the necessity for non-state forms of property, not only in agriculture but also in the manufacturing and service sectors. He insisted that time would show that reform of the economic system must include the rise of the market. But Everleny was moving too fast, and in April 2016 was fired from his University post for sharing information with Americans without authorisation.

In the same month, Julio Antonio Fernandez Estrada, Professor in the Faculty of Law at Havana University, wrote an article for the online magazine *OnCuba*, which was posted on 16 April, 2016. The article contained calls for greater democracy in Cuba:

> Our people want to talk about and feel the emotions of socialist Cuban politics; which means democratically, intensely, with no holds barred and without any taboos – the only way to lay the first stone in the walkway to true popular sovereignty.

The article raised demands for opening the books on the personal wealth of Party tops:

> [T]he Cuban people want to know what our politicians eat. If they ever go to a 'paladar', we want to know how many CUC they have and what tastes they have.

---

99 Ritte, A., Reuters, 14 Feb., 2017.

To cap it all the article ended by challenging Raúl's perspective of a mixed-economy:

> Obama will not give us happiness, nor will those who want to divide the country up among big businesses, nor the bureaucracy which does not understand the people ...

A few months later, Estrada's contract with the university was not renewed. He was told that this was because of what he wrote in *OnCuba*. He replied:

> [M]y fault has been telling the truth, being trustworthy and honest, to defend socialism and criticise the opportunists and the impudent ones. These are my crimes and I will continue to commit them.

The introduction of market mechanisms in the Cuban economy has been encouraged by the growth in self-employment, which has increased with the layoffs of public sector employees. Inequalities in society have been strengthened between those with access to privilege, such as elements of the state apparatus linked to the military hierarchy, often in business with big capitalist companies and multinationals, and those with access to the dollar (those who have relatives abroad, or work abroad, or work in the tourism industry), and the rest of the Cuban people. Inequality was the determining factor in the development of the Soviet bureaucracy, and its growth in Cuba would strengthen the evolution of a Chinese-type state capitalism with an authoritarian, bureaucratic Communist Party, with specific Cuban characteristics, in charge.

However, the concrete conditions in Cuba today are completely different from those in China under Deng. China is a huge country with over a billion inhabitants to provide capitalist enterprises with a vast reserve of cheap labour, where one factory can employ over a quarter of a million workers most in the age range seventeen to twenty-five years. Such measures cannot be adopted in Cuba, with or without the restoration of capitalism. Cuba might attempt to emulate China, but there can be no comparable economies of scale. In a world beset by a crisis of overproduction, a capitalist Cuba would resemble neither China nor Vietnam, but rather Nicaragua after the victory of the counter-revolution. It would soon revert to a similar situation that existed before 1959, one of misery, degradation, and semi-colonial dependence.

There is much advice being offered on how to remedy Cuba's economic problems; within Cuba there are those from the Centre for the Study of the Cuban Economy, Havana University, who argue for a free market economy, those who argue for legalising all forms of self-employment excluding only the military, those who argue for workers' control over their individual workplaces, those who call for an alliance of PCC activists with fundamentalist Christians to launch agricultural co-operatives outside of any government control, those who call for constraints on government subsidies and the introduction of means-testing. All these views can be read in official and semi-official publications. One line of argument, now gaining support in Cuba is the call for Soviet democracy.

In his brilliant analysis of the USSR, Leon Trotsky insisted that "the planned economy needs workers' democracy as much as the human body needs oxygen". The workers should be, and really feel themselves to be, owners of the means of production and the state, and participate directly and effectively, in the running of the economy and the administration of public affairs. The programme, which faithfully reflects these needs, is the programme of workers' democracy and democratic planning of the means of production, the programme of Lenin and Trotsky.

The Internet's arrival in Cuba has considerably opened political discussion and weakened the hold of the censors. The process used by Esteban Morales[100] for raising and publicising his arguments on the reasons behind the collapse of the Soviet Union and possible parallels in Cuba, was to first discuss the issue within his local branch of the PCC, then informally with others using emails and other means of communication, and finally to publish his articles on websites inside and outside Cuba. Today in Cuba, websites and blogs are accessible and are a means by which those with positive criticisms of the regime are able to spread their ideas. In parallel is the publication of the printed word, such as: *From Real Socialism to Real Capitalism* by Ariel Dacal and Francisco Brown.

Early in 2016, Cuban journalists received verbal instructions prohibiting them from publishing in non-government media. The authorities deemed the matter so sensitive that they would not put their instructions in writing, and provoked a hornet's nest. In July 2016, Esteban Morales, in his widely-read blog, alerted his readers to a serious struggle against this and other forms of censorship taking place within *Granma* itself, led by the deputy editor Karina Marron. At a closed meeting of the Congress of the Cuban Journalists' Union, Marron made a biting criticism of the censorship that existed in Cuba. Her intervention was briefly mentioned in the official reports of the Congress, but her more incendiary comments, including criticism of the leadership of the PCC, were airbrushed out. However, a full report of Marron's comments was uploaded onto the personal blog of one José Pantoja, a journalist working for Radio Holguin (who was sacked almost immediately). This went viral and resulted in a storm of controversy.

---

100 Honorary Director of the Centre for US Studies at the University of Havana.

Because Raúl Castro has a much less interventionist style than his brother, preferring to work behind the scenes, *Granma* has assumed greater importance. Many in Cuba, such as Marron, believe a greater role for the media now exists, and this has brought into the open the differences between those in the leadership who favour rigid subordination to the Party and those who argue that policy must be the result of discussion and democratic agreement.

Marron's comments were explosive, not only because of her position, but because they were demonstrative of the politicisation of a layer of Cuban youth and the issues concerning them. Since Obama's visit, the Young Communist League (*Union de Jovenes Comunistas*, UJC) has experienced a steep growth in membership as more and more young people become interested in politics, and the ideas of communism. In July 2017, the UJC announced its membership had risen to over 300,000, reversing the trend of previous years. Many of these young people have been drawn into activity in order to participate in determining the future of their country, and are a receptive audience for ideas on soviet democracy.

For example, on 26 September, 2014, forty-three college students disappeared in the Mexican town of Iguala. University students in Cuba were determined to show their solidarity with and support for the Mexican students, and on 1 October, 2015 a group of about thirty youth marched from Havana University to the Presidents' Avenue in Havana in solidarity with the Mexican students. This was a left-wing demonstration in Cuba, which had not been organised, nor sanctioned, by any official organisation, and the University authorities used this to try to prevent them from gathering on the institution's steps, an historical gathering point for revolutionary marches in Cuba before 1959.

Amongst those who organised the protest were a group of students who had been following a course on Marxism at the Juan Marinello Institute. In November 2015, they, and students from Santiago and other universities, formed the Anti-Capitalist Youth Network, aiming to combat the "growing de-politicisation of wide layers of the population" and increase the "participation of the people in controlling" economic policies. They want to "stimulate the critical appropriation of Marxism" and insist that it is necessary to "relaunch socialism and anti-capitalism". This is a welcome sign that there are those amongst the young generation who are worried about the possible restoration of capitalism in Cuba, want to fight against it, and are looking towards Marxist theory to give them the tools to wage this struggle.

13.1) BUREAUCRACY AND CORRUPTION

The superiority of a nationalised planned economy was demonstrated by the colossal successes of the early USSR and its rapid recovery after the devastation it suffered during WWII. But the Stalinist bureaucracy, from its earliest stages, retarded economic development and, as industry and commerce advanced technologically, the bureaucracy became an unqualified and absolute brake on economic development. The bureaucrats' protection of their own interests had higher priority than the performance of soviet industry, so they never considered introducing the most effective measure for solving the problems of the Soviet economy – workers' democracy. The only kind of state-owned industries they could imagine were those that existed under a Stalinist state bureaucracy, with all the mismanagement involved. They could not envisage efficient state-owned industries under workers' control. Soviet democracy is the death knell of bureaucracy, the Soviet bureaucrats had more to lose from workers' control than a return to capitalism; with the latter, they were more likely to retain their privileges.

A centralised bureaucracy cannot determine every aspect of production, and terrible distortions and inefficiencies are inevitable. A centrally-planned economy can work efficiently only if there are checks at every level by the workers involved. Workers' democracy, workers' control, and workers' management are essential for determining the optimum goals and the efficient functioning of any proletarian regime. The workers, who are also the consumers, have a material interest in ensuring that the plan works efficiently at all levels. Bureaucrats are only interested in meeting their quotas, regardless of quality of output, so that they will get their bonuses and retain their privileged positions.

In 1967, Guevara had cause to comment on the problem of absenteeism, today the problem is low productivity (particularly in agriculture) which, generally, lags well below the rest of Latin America. The reason for both failings was, and is, a bureaucratic system that systematically generates disorganisation and disorder, that fails to motivate workers by providing them with either a say and/or control over what they do, or with material incentives. How can moral exhortations work when the worker sees a regime of corruption, back-handers, and privileges? Such appeals are seen as a way of getting the workers to take responsibility for improving the operation of the system while denying them the power to take the decisions necessary, and to work harder without getting any material benefits.

Mismanagement, corruption and swindling are the inevitable consequence of a bureaucratic regime. By the 1980s, the workers in Eastern Europe and the USSR no longer had any memory of the revolutionary upsurge that established the first workers' state. Their experience was of a self-serving, incompetent, oppressive regime that was mismanaging the economy to a state of collapse. In Cuba today, the situation is not yet the same; there is economic mismanagement, there are serious constraints on freedom of speech, there is no internal party democracy, but there have been no mass purges as in Russia and China, PCC members who criticise are not killed but expelled from the Party, and even then are often re-admitted, and the US embargo has generated a strong sense of a country determined to be free of imperialism. The leadership must tread carefully, the Cuban people have shown no great desire for increased inequality and strongly oppose corruption – both of which are integral to any attempts to restore capitalism.

All those in Cuba who consider themselves revolutionary or communist are duty bound to actively protect the gains of the revolution, and to do so must study the lessons of the degeneration of the Russian revolution. It was the parasitic excrescence that was the bureaucracy, itself a consequence of the isolation of the revolution in a backward country, which finally led to the restoration of capitalism and the catastrophic social collapse which accompanied it.

Trotsky warned that, as the bureaucracy developed, the more senior the bureaucrats, the more they would want to pass their privileges on to their children and grandchildren. And this was best done through private ownership. He predicted that the bureaucracy could and would adapt very easily to capitalist restoration. Transforming the workers' state into a bourgeois regime would be realised largely by the bureaucrats themselves, who would become the captains of capitalist industry or its favoured servants. Few bureaucrats would have to be purged. On the other hand, a political revolution would impose on those bureaucrats a worker's wage and remove their privileges. For most bureaucrats there was, and is, a bigger conflict with workers' democracy than capitalism. Trotsky's prognosis of capitalist restoration was almost a blueprint for the actions of the Chinese Stalinists and a warning to Cuban socialists:

> … The chief task of the new (bourgeois) power would be to restore private property in the means of production. First of all, it would be necessary to create conditions for the development of strong farmers from the weak collective farms … In the sphere of industry, denationalization would begin with the light industries and those producing food. The planning principle would be converted for the transitional period into a series of compromises between state power and individual 'corporations' – potential proprietors, that is, among the Soviet captains of industry … and foreign capitalists.[101]

---

101 Trotsky, L. Revolution Betrayed, Ch9, 1936, www.marxists.org.

The dynamism of the Chinese economy and the chaotic collapse of the Soviet Union are very powerful factors in the thinking of Raúl and the other PCC leaders. There is every likelihood that at least a section of the PCC has concluded that the Chinese route should be followed, especially the retention of tight party control. The steps already taken are in this direction. Will the PCC, like the Chinese Communist Party, stagger from one empiric measure to the next, thinking it is avoiding the collapse that occurred in Russia, only to end up with a capitalist Cuba? One major factor stands in their way: fear of how the masses will respond.

The problem of corruption and bureaucracy in Cuba was denounced by Fidel himself, in an important speech to staff and students of Havana University on 17 November, 2005. More recently, the matter was taken up in a sharp way by Esteban Morales. In an article published on the UNEAC website, he clearly identified the main counter-revolutionary threat in Cuba today:

> We can have no doubt that the counter-revolution, little by little, is taking positions at certain levels of the state and government. Without a doubt, it is becoming evident that there are people in positions of government and state who are preparing themselves financially for when the Revolution falls, and others may have everything almost ready to transfer state-owned assets to private hands, as happened in the old USSR.

Yes, the black market and corruption exists but it is not the individuals standing outside shopping centres selling small amounts of black-market goods who are the real criminals, rather, it is those in the state bureaucracy who are supplying goods wholesale from government warehouses. Morales is keen to demonstrate that corruption at all levels of the bureaucracy is more dangerous to Cuba than so-called dissidents, who are being scapegoated.

Morales is a Communist with more than fifty years of struggle behind him, but shortly after publishing an article, entitled 'Corruption: The true counter-revolution?' (April 2010) he was expelled from the PCC, despite protests from his local branch. His article was removed from the UNEAC website, prompting Morales to write a further article denouncing these methods and continuing to insist on linking the problem of corruption to the question of bureaucracy. He appealed to the rank and file members of the party to wage a campaign against both, arguing that the rank and file of the party should not limit their actions and discussions to purely local issues, but consider problems in their totality. The current situation, he said, prevented the rank and file of the party from effective criticisms of the tops, something necessary for democratic control of the activities of the higher bodies, and which cost the working masses in the USSR very dear. Clearly,

Morales is addressing a central problem facing the Cuban revolution. In 1930's Russia, Morales would have been summarily shot, in China today, he would be in prison, but in Cuba the situation is more contradictory and fluid. Morales was expelled from the PCC, but has since been re-admitted. Freedom of speech is certain to feature prominently once leftists begin to build an audience of workers.

The lack of genuine workers' democracy, in which ordinary working people participate directly in managing the state and the economy, is one of the main threats to the revolution. It breeds demoralisation, scepticism, cynicism and generally undermines the revolutionary morale of the people. If it is combined with a situation where everyone is aware of corruption and theft going on at the top of the state while basic needs are not met and the purchasing power of wages decreases, then it becomes a counter-revolutionary danger of the first order. There are now many amongst the members of the PCC who share the concerns of Esteban Morales fearing that sections of the bureaucracy will use people's dissatisfaction to lead the restoration of capitalism, as happened in the USSR.

Those on the left must convince the masses that they have a practical answer to the critical question of how a socialist and democratic Cuba could emerge from poverty and economic stagnation, that the mobilisation of the people and the constitution of a genuine socialist democracy is the best way to protect Cubans from US capitalist pressure. To do this, it is necessary to create the conditions of democratic debate in all the popular organisations in Cuba. This requires the acceptance of forms of pluralism in the PCC and in the popular movement (with limitations on pro-capitalist parties).

For most Cubans, the chance to improve their material conditions is a necessary condition for supporting political change. Much could be achieved simply by removing the dead hand of the bureaucracy, for example, allowing local organisations such as the branches of the CDR to use their ingenuity to solve immediate problems. All over the island old, antiquated and poorly-serviced water pipes are leaking but not repaired, leading not only to a massive loss of scarce, clean water, but the larger water spills (ponds) provide breeding grounds for mosquitos which transmit fever. Given the authority to use their natural inventiveness this is a problem that could be readily solved by local people with minimum need for additional resources.

This loss of potable water is occurring while Cuba is experiencing the worst drought of the past 115 years. There is no quick fix for the problem of Cuba's declining rainfall, and drought will continue to impact negatively on the island, but a mass mobilisation tackling a real problem and achieving meaningful results will greatly boost morale and social cohesion. The limits of bureaucracy are exposed but, dialectically, the opportunity for demonstrating the power of state planning is demonstrated. Just as the Soviet planned economy was able to re-organise and quickly move giant factories from one part of Russia to another to avoid destruction by the advancing German armies, so the Cuban workers' government can provide a national response to the drought it faces. State planning can develop an integrated strategy to ensure the water remaining in the reservoirs is monitored and rationed to maintain an adequate supply to people and crops. Likewise, it can enact emergency measures such as installing new water distribution systems redirecting water to the worst hit zones (e.g., in Santiago); initiating more efficient irrigation systems to reduce the impact of the drought on agriculture, replacing sprinklers (the most inefficient means of irrigation), and substituting more efficient drip systems; introducing water-saving technology in the tourism sector for use in local irrigation and toilets.

13.2) THE WAY FORWARD – A NEW ECONOMIC POLICY FOR CUBA?

In the very early stages of the transition to capitalism in China, it was customary to refer to Lenin and the NEP to justify the changes being made. As a general proposition, it is undoubtedly correct that sometimes a tactical retreat is necessary, and when the Russian Revolution became isolated in conditions of frightful backwardness, a retreat was inevitable. Lenin clearly presented the NEP as a setback necessary because of the delay in the world revolution, not as the way forward. He pointed out many times that, to consolidate the gains of the revolution and advance to socialism, the victory of the socialist revolution in one or more advanced countries was necessary. That would have happened in the years after World War I, had it not been for the betrayal of the leaders of European Social Democracy.

Lenin and Trotsky continued to stress the need for international revolution to come to the aid of Soviet Russia and fought against the creeping bureaucratisation of the state institutions, and for the preservation of workers' democracy. All their hopes were based on the perspectives of the international socialist revolution, which is why they paid so much attention to building the Third (Communist) International. In the same way, Che Guevara understood that, in the last analysis, the only way to save the Cuban Revolution was to spread the revolution to Latin America, a cause for which he sacrificed his life.

Today in Cuba we are faced not with a temporary retreat, but the very real danger of the subversion of the workers' state. The changes being proposed for the Cuban economy pose a threat to the continued existence of the workers' state. To defend the revolutionary gains it is necessary that (i) the key sectors of the economy (banks, heavy industry [e.g. mining], tourism, pharmaceuticals and the wholesale distribution of food and goods) remain in the hands of the state, (ii) the state and industry remain in the hands of the working class (e.g., national economic plan based on production for need not profit, and state control of foreign trade), and (iii) the problem of bureaucracy and corruption is addressed (e.g., an end to social differentiation and special privileges) through the introduction of workers' control and soviet democracy. Within that context, a relatively small private sector that meets designated needs could and should be allowed. The key is the bureaucracy, since it is the drive to protect its privileges that led the bureaucracies in Russia, China, and Eastern Europe to return to capitalism. Cuba desperately needs soviet democracy, whether rank and file committees, organisations of worker's councils or revitalised CDRs, to effectively combat the growth of corruption and privilege and halt the slide back to capitalism.

At the Twelfth Congress of the CCP in September 1982, Deng Xiaoping announced the building of socialism with Chinese characteristics; of a so-called 'planned commodity economy'. To increase productivity, managers of small (and medium) state businesses were given much greater autonomy, encouraged to produce goods outside the state plan for sale on the market, and permitted to introduce individual bonuses. From that time on the planning element of the economy was restricted to only major projects. However, the official position of the Party was that the state sector of the economy was, and would remain, dominant. In Cuba we have Points Nineteen and Thirty-Five in the Guidelines presented to the Sixth Congress which, when enacted, will empower each enterprise to set its own prices and give control of production to local municipal councils.

The discussions on updating Cuba's economic and social goals, launched for the Sixth Congress and then continued after the Seventh Congress, were brought to a conclusion at the National Assembly of People's Power on 1 June, 2017. Three documents were approved: the 'Guidelines of the Social and Economic Policy of the Party', the 'Conceptualisation of the Economic and Social Model of Cuban Social Development', and the 'Basis of the Plan of Economic and Social Development up to 2030'. The time taken to produce these documents was, according to President Raúl Castro, due to their being "the most studied, discussed and rediscussed documents in the history of the revolution". He might also have added that this reflected both their importance and the depth of the disagreements within the top layers of the Party on the direction the Cuban economy was heading, and the speed of that development. That this was the last gasp of the historic generation that carried out the revolution, made the infighting all the more intense.

The three documents define where Cuban socialism is going and how it will get there, updating the Cuban model to improve economic efficiency and productive capacity within a socialist framework. Helen Yaffe in her analysis[102] lists three core elements to the updated economic model:

- The primacy of a planned economy which takes into account the functioning of the market.
- The introduction of diverse forms of non-state management and ownership.
- Consolidation of the socialist nature of the Cuban state through its socialist welfare and cohesion policies, its political structures which contain organs of people's power and workers' representation, and economically through communal ownership via the state.

Yaffe emphasises that no details are given about the policies to be adopted to achieve these goals, nor how they might be implemented:

> The real test, however, will emerge in the practice of formulating, implementing and enforcing the policies required to achieve their aims. In practice, how can market forces be both encouraged, as a means of increasing employment and enterprise, and constrained, which is imperative to maintain the dominance of non-exploitative social-relations? These are the difficult challenges facing Cuban socialism

We know that the Deng and his allies had the same goal as Raúl, and they too felt that they could control the processes they introduced. The Chinese government allowed small and medium state businesses to pay a tax on their profits and retain the balance for reinvestment and distribution as bonuses. Here we had the bureaucracy of a deformed workers' state, using capitalistic methods to revitalise part of the state sector but, in so doing, took a significant step in downgrading the importance of the national economic plan. Determined to increase the number of private companies in China, the government encouraged management buy-outs with the managers urged to rationalise their companies to make them more profitable. This has strong similarities with Point Nineteen of the Guidelines, whereby the incomes of workers in the state sector will depend on the profitability of their business. If China is the example that is being followed, we must recognise that Deng's reforms were a first decisive step towards capitalism. The main threat to the planned economy did not come from taxi drivers and hairdressers, but from

---

102 Yaffe, H., *Conceptualising Cuban Socialism*, June 17, 2017.

those elements in the Party and state bureaucracy who favoured the market as opposed to a socialist planned economy, and used the successes of small businesses to promote more extensive privatisation measures.

The decisions made by the National Assembly on 1 June, sparked considerable comment and discussion in the Cuban media. The *Havana Times*, for example, carried a number of articles on the theme that legalising private ownership of modes of production threatened that the national economy will no longer be regulated by 'socialist laws'; that wealth will become concentrated in the hands of a few, and social inequality similar to that in the rest of Latin America will result.

Others claim that the legislation only recognises what already exists. The new measures will allow a better distribution of wealth because the government will be able to charge taxes on people who have never previously paid them. That inequality won't be a result of 'updating the system', because it already exists and has been growing since the 1990s due to factors such as family remittances, opening the national economy to foreign investment, tourism, and the children of the elite reaching adulthood and inheriting their parents' privileges. The claim is that the meritocracy – those who have gained positions of trust and authority for their dedication to, and work for, the revolution – are acting as though their privileges are hereditary, to ensure their children enjoy those same privileges, even though they have no record of making any contribution of their own. It is claimed that, with the new changes, the national economy will bring this world into the open, which has been operating clandestinely for years.

Some economists claim that if you don't allow the self-employed to accumulate wealth, they will never be able to become business people; that, without accumulation of capital, the only people who can become owners of small and medium-sized companies are those who receive money from abroad or those who are corrupt and/or criminals. These commentators accept that, in one way or another, the concentration of wealth will lead to deepening social differences between Cubans and this can lead to a few people taking so much of the national cake for themselves, that they leave others without even a taste.

The guidelines offer little or no protection to the economic base of the workers' state. The Chinese bureaucracy claimed to uphold the primacy of the planned economy even as it introduced diverse forms of non-state management and ownership. As for people's power and workers' representation, they noticeably lack any real substance. However, the truth is that there is still much to be determined: What are the limits on the accumulation of capital? What government mechanisms will redistribute wealth? How many employees can a medium-sized company employ? How will the government ensure that there are equal opportunities for all Cubans in this kind of society?

In both Russia and China, with the growth of capitalist enterprises, the rules on foreign travel were relaxed and the newly wealthy were able to holiday abroad. On 3 August, 2017, the *Havana Times* reported on how the newly-accumulated wealth of a section of Cuban society was showing itself in the same way. For summer 2017, Spain was the international holiday destination for those Cubans who enjoyed greatest purchasing power. Holidays were offered at about 2,500 Euros and the package included: a Schengen visa so they could enter Europe, the plane ticket, four days in Madrid and two in Barcelona, four-star hotels, visits to the Royal Palace in Madrid, the Real Madrid stadium, and Gaudí's Crypt at Colonia Guell.

Cubans who travel abroad are the tip of an iceberg. There are now many more (though still only a small part of the population) who can afford the forty Euros per night per person to stay at Cuban tourist hotels. These are predominantly members of business cooperatives, employees of foreign companies or 'independent labourers'. Prior to Raúl Castro's reforms, especially opening the economy to independent labour, nobody would have believed there would be people on the island able to pay to stay at five-star hotels in Varadero, much less that there would be thousands of people travelling to Europe as tourists.

The Chinese Communist Party was (and is) renowned for its corruption, and local CCP officials seized the opportunities offered by Deng's initiatives and used the authority given to them by their Party status to launch their own private businesses. All too often these had sweetheart deals with local authorities and were officially described as state run, but the profits went into private pockets. These moves weakened state planning but simultaneously, and, more importantly, generated a layer within the CPP of active capitalists, the so-called 'red capitalists'; a layer that grew with each subsequent reform, helped by generous state loans and economic decentralisation, all of which downgraded the importance of the national economic plan.

Historic comparisons can be useful but what is needed is a concrete analysis of Cuba today. The first problem we see immediately is that Cuba still has a serious level of debt and a weak economic base, which has been weakened further by years of bureaucratic mismanagement. More importantly, the workers have no sense of controlling the industries in which they work and thus little interest in productivity and efficiency. In fact, in the face of the government's policy of shedding jobs, the workers' immediate interests are in reducing productivity to maintain staffing levels. There is a general and growing sense of malaise and discontent which generates alienation, a serious danger to the future of the revolution, as was found in the USSR. Everybody agrees that the present situation cannot continue, that something must change and something must be done. The question of questions is: *what is to be done?*

In many ways, the Cuban economy is typical of a Third World country, heavily dependent on the export of raw materials and the provision of services. Its exports of, e.g. nickel and sugar are subject to the volatility of the market. In 2007, nickel peaked at US$50 per kilogram, by 2016 the price had dropped to below US$10 per kilogram, while the sugar crop in 2014 was twenty per cent below expectations due to disastrous weather. These are the sources of hard currency to purchase on the world market all the goods Cuba needs and which it does not produce (from food to buses for public transport). The need for hard currency is periodically increased by hurricanes which destroy crops, infrastructure, and houses. For example, 2008 was a particularly bad year and Cuba was hit by three hurricanes: Gustav, Ike and Paloma, collectively causing damage worth US$10 billion (twenty per cent of GDP).

Believing that the problems of the Cuban economy can be solved by pushing state employees into starting their own businesses is an error posing serious dangers for the future of the revolution. However, the leadership appears determined to move in that direction. Cuba's 2014 Labour Code specifies a maximum forty-four hour working week and a minimum of seven days paid holiday but, importantly, removes previous restrictions on the number of employees that a self-employed individual can hire. This will create a sizeable layer of tens of thousands of small capitalists and will open the door to the creation of larger capitalist enterprises; this step was extremely important in China's return to capitalism.

Deng and his fellow Stalinist bureaucrats staggered towards capitalism, pushed by the 'red capitalists', opposed by the section of the bureaucracy representing the old, capital-intensive, loss-making industries. In Cuba, there is little heavy industry so there will be a smaller proportion of the PCC with vested interests in opposing moves towards capitalism and the rate of change could be very rapid. Ariel Dacal claims that the US is confident that, with a free hand, it would take just *15 days* to carry through the economic changes it wants.[103]

No doubt sections of the Cuban bureaucracy are taking measures and positioning themselves to take advantage of any loosening of state controls. Some will already be eyeing up the foreign multinationals from Brazil,

---

103 *vimeo.com/144157407*, October 2015.

Canada, China, Mexico, Spain and others already operating in Cuba, preparing to act as compradors in the re-colonisation of the island. But there is no certainty that the "Chinese way" would lead to economic growth for Cuba, far from it. Given the size of the Cuban economy, it is far more likely to lead to a rapid and catastrophic collapse. The restoration of capitalism in Cuba is more likely to throw the island back to the 1930s, dominated by foreign capital, a playground for tourists rather than an industrial dynamo. The first signs of this can be seen in the new capitalist enterprises. These often promote themselves on their pay rates being higher than in the state sector, but the extra money comes from the abolition of maternity and paternity benefits, ending equal pay for equal work, the use of the equivalent of zero hours contracts, and black market activities.

It is clear that the status quo cannot be maintained indefinitely. Within Cuba there are many who do not see a solution to Cuba's economic problems along market lines. A clear alternative based on revolutionary internationalism and workers' democracy could rally thousands of honest communists, intellectuals, youth and workers, who are not prepared to let the revolution be destroyed. Before making concessions to capitalist tendencies, the Cuban Revolution should be setting an example of soviet democracy and workers' control.

At a political, theoretical level, Cuba needs to dump the false, Stalinist theory of stages, and argue clearly on the basis of its own experience that the democratic revolution can be carried through to completion only if the revolution takes the first steps towards socialism: the expropriation of the oligarchs, the major capitalists and imperialists (but without the bureaucratic extreme of nationalising every bootblack and hairdresser). The real way forward for the Cuban Revolution is workers' democracy and revolutionary internationalism. The fate of the Cuban Revolution is intimately linked to the fate of the Latin American revolution in the first instance, and to the world revolution more generally. The objective conditions for the victory of the socialist revolution in Latin America are a thousand times more advanced today than in 1967. Cuba can provide a rallying point for revolution across the continent.

In Cuba, the island's economic heavyweights (banks, etc.,) must remain in the state sector under workers' control and subject to a national plan based on need as determined by a soviet democracy. This is doubly necessary because, as the Cubans themselves admit, most of the public sector is inefficient and functions badly. This can be corrected only if the problems are brought into the open, responsibility allocated and remedial measures taken. This is an essential condition for improving the lives of most Cubans. An essential part of this struggle must be a fight against Cuba's growing inequality. Such a scenario is only possible with independent trade unions and workers' control.

Starting from the rejection of any possibility that socialism can be developed in one country, and accepting the present integration of Cuba into the world market as a Third World economy, the task becomes one of protecting the workers' state that presently exists. It will be necessary to combine a revolutionary internationalist policy with specific measures to solve the present economic problems in Cuba, but how? Class-conscious workers and peasants will welcome reforms if they appreciate they are in their interests. Labour productivity will improve once the workers feel that they are the ones in charge, that is, by introducing the widest measures of workers' democracy into industry, society and the state.

The Cuban people have shown repeatedly that they are prepared to make sacrifices to defend the revolution. But it is essential that the sacrifices should be made by everybody. There must be a serious and effective campaign against privilege. Cuba must return to the simple rules of Soviet democracy that Lenin proposed in *State and Revolution*, not for communism or socialism but for the day after the revolution: that all officials be elected and subject to recall, that no official should have a wage higher than that of a skilled worker. However, we know from the history of Stalinism that the privileges of the bureaucrats came not from their salaries but the perks of the job (luxury accommodation, chauffeur-driven limousines, access to exclusive restaurants, etc.) This emphasises the importance of the ability to recall representatives, for workers' control and collective decision-making, for accountability of officials, and so on. The workers themselves will determine what measures are required, because no mechanism can substitute for the vigilance of the masses themselves, there is no bureaucratic solution to bureaucracy. It should be remembered, Stalin built his personal base within both party and state when Commissar in charge of Rabkrin (the Workers' and Peasants' Inspectorate) which was set up in 1919 to eliminate bureaucracy.

The Cuban people have repeatedly shown an indomitable spirit, they have been heroes for fifty years, but for how much longer? Cubans draw much of their strength from two sources: winning national sovereignty, and with it national dignity; and the ending of hunger and poverty, and the provision of healthcare and education for all. Any programme for the survival of the Cuban workers' state must emphasise these features.

However, never-ending adversity under a regime over which they feel they have no control will lead to a decline in consciousness. Che Guevara insisted on the importance of the moral element in socialism. That is obviously true, but it can only be sustained in a regime when all workers feel that they are equally responsible for taking the decisions that affect production and every aspect of life. Because the worker's state is a transitional regime between capitalism and socialism, for some time the principle applied will be "From each according to his ability, to each according to his work". This is a capitalist principle that implies the existence of wage differentials, as was the case in Russia immediately after the revolution. But the levels of the differentials between skilled and unskilled labour, between a nurse and a doctor, should be democratically determined by the workforce through whatever bodies are in place exercising soviet democracy, not by bureaucratic diktat. The goal would be the gradual reduction of differentials, to the degree that production increased and with it, the wealth and well-being of society.

But the biggest incentive is clearly when the workers feel that the country, the economy and the state belongs to them, and that can only be achieved if the workers themselves take control of the decision-making process and all elected officials are accountable to them. Only on this basis, of popular power, can the socialist base of the Cuban Revolution be defended and the capitalist counter-revolution defeated.

14) THE QUESTION OF REVOLUTIONARY LEADERSHIP IN CUBA TODAY

What are the tasks of Marxists and revolutionaries in this situation? Obviously, the immediate one is to continue to analyse what is happening, to present an explanation of events that corresponds to the real situation in order to enter into a meaningful dialogue with workers, peasants, students, and honest Communist Party members. It would be a serious error to try to deal with complex, contradictory and unprecedented processes on the basis of ready-made formulae which do not accurately correspond to what the Cuban people are living through.

The PCC, being both the party of government and state apparatus, will be subject to all the centrifugal forces that in Western democracies are represented by a whole range of parties and other organisations. Depending on the relative strengths of those forces there could be serious divisions between the party tops. It is to be expected that many rank and file Party members, delegates directly elected to People's Power Assemblies or union officials, and thus closest to the workers' struggles, will look with horror on the transition to capitalism and the inequalities it is bringing. These currents are confirmed by letters and articles that have appeared in the Cuban press and internet. Many hark back to Fidel's Cuba but as they find themselves forced to confront the question of workers' power and Soviet democracy it is to be expected that they will build on his positive contributions to the establishment of a workers' state in Cuba.

When the working class begins to move, it invariably expresses itself through its traditional mass organisations, although these can be in surprising and unanticipated ways. The first step taken by many workers who find themselves in conflict with management, is to visit the local union branch office for advice and support. It is absolutely necessary for Marxists to find a way to engage with the rank and file of the Cuban trade union movement.

As Russia returned to capitalism the CP fractured, but that did not happen in China; instead the CCP has remained in control and successfully transformed itself into a mass bourgeois party. It is clear that the Party tops in Cuba will attempt to follow the Chinese path. However, the PCC has not been as repressive as the CCP and as the class war in Cuba heats up we can expect it to be reflected in the PCC. To what degree and to what extent cannot be predicted. However, in the event of an open struggle between a wing of the PCC and the restorationist tendency, Marxists would fight for the defeat of the main enemy, the restorationists, while patiently explaining that only Soviet democracy can solve the problems facing Cuba.

While struggling in a united front with those who oppose capitalist restoration, the aim would be to mobilise the masses, but not to defend the privileged positions of bureaucrats. Marxists would explain to the workers the need to take power into their own hands through, for example, workers' councils or factory committees, initially as organs of struggle and then as Soviet organs of workers' power. It should never be forgotten that Soviets were not an invention of the Bolsheviks or any other party, but rather the spontaneous invention of the working class.

An important consideration is that, in Cuba, there has never been any real Bolshevik party, but there is a very real desire amongst many Party activists and young people to discover the true ideas of Marxism. The great weakness of these Cuban leftists is that their struggles tend to be isolated, but this is gradually being overcome as they network using the internet. There is a sense amongst many that the left is on the verge of a leap forward, but this will only occur if workers, peasants and intellectuals find issues that unite the different forces of opposition to capitalist restoration. Socialists should, of course, fight for immediate demands but pose them in a way that links day-to-day problems to the socialist transformation of society. Such demands, transitional demands as Trotsky referred to them, act as a bridge between actions taken in the struggle for bettering the condition of the masses and the idea of the socialist revolution.

The 'partial', 'minimal' demands of the masses must be supported, as every successful struggle raises the combativity of the workers involved. It might be necessary to start with small demands that are relatively easy to win in order to build up a dynamic, because when workers are in struggle events tend to unfold fast. As the international capitalist system becomes ever more degrading and decadent the most advanced workers should propose a platform of transitional demands, the essence of which is that they are directed to protect the foundations of the workers' state and the planned economy. In their totality, these transitional demands would seek to systematically mobilise the masses for a political revolution.

In their struggles, the workers need mass organisations and these will be, in the early stages, trade unions. It is necessary for revolutionaries in Cuba to be active in the Cuban Confederation of Workers, because in Cuba it is in the CTC-R that class relations are expressed most directly and immediately. Every attempt to subordinate the union to a capitalist enterprise must be opposed: instead workers must demand it supports their claims. Initially, at least, it will not be possible to replace the leadership of the CTC-R at the top or regional level because of the way these leaders are chosen. However, it is quite possible to militate in local union branches for the election of shop stewards, to argue that the good practice of co-opting strike leaders onto local branch committees be universally adopted, and to form local, even if unofficial, committees to represent the workers in individual enterprises.

A campaign for transitional/democratic demands could provide the basis for a powerful mobilisation of workers and peasants. The precise demands, the way they are posed and the means by which they are realised are extremely important so they must be determined by those directly involved. But, in the context of a bureaucratic regime and the threat of capitalist restoration, such demands would likely be based on the workers' right to organise and almost certainly would include:

- For the defence of all the conquests of the revolution (health care, housing, education, etc.);
- Democratic workers' control of production through elected and recallable representatives;
- No privileges for the bureaucracy, for the election and right of recall of all public officials, no public official to receive a wage higher than that of a skilled worker;
- Freedom of expression and association for all those who defend the gains of the revolution;
- Freedom to bargain collectively and to take industrial action on such issues as unemployment, low pay, health and safety.

Such a programme would rekindle the enthusiasm amongst the masses because it would start to address the key problems of the economic crisis. It would have to be supported by the self-organisation of the people in the working class and poor neighbourhoods, their armed self-defence, and close fraternisation between the armed workers and peasants and rank and file soldiers, especially army reservists. Clearly, a governmental slogan will be required to bind these demands into a coherent programme. In Russia this was given substance in 'All Power to the Soviets', and this may be one path for Cuban revolutionaries. Such a slogan would have to be built on freedom to form action committees in every factory, workplace, college, street, army barracks, and village, and for aggregates of such committees to form the cores of a new generation of democratic Soviets.

15) POSTSCRIPT

In April 2018, on the day before his fifty-eighth birthday, Miguel Díaz-Canel Bermúdez, replaced Raúl Castro as President of Cuba, while Raúl remains General-Secretary of the PCC and head of the armed forces. The President is not elected by the Cuban people, but by the Council of State, and is responsible to the Council of State. Díaz-Canel was the youngest ever member of the Political Bureau of the Cuban Communist Party and had been senior Vice-President of the Council for five years before his promotion to president.

Díaz-Canel came to the fore as part of Raúl's reformation of Cuba's economic model; opening the doors to foreign investment, allowing Cubans to open small-scale private businesses and decentralising decision-making. He has shown himself to be fully committed to the reform wing of the party and is seen as a safe pair of hands providing continuity of leadership. He was and remains Raúl's protégée, and is expected to continue implementing the 'Guidelines for Economic and Social Policy' under Raúl's guidance, with no ideological changes expected.

As the *New York Times* (19 April, 2018) put it:

> After opening up the economy to private investment and entrepreneurialism, expanding travel in and out of the country and re-establishing ties with the great enemy, the US, Raúl Castro has selected Mr. Díaz-Canel to fill his shoes.

He faces the same challenges as when the 'Guidelines' were first introduced: to increase productivity and efficiency in state enterprises, to bring in foreign investment, to oversee privatisation while limiting displays of inequality, but with the additional problem of how to handle Trump.

The debate which is taking place on the reform of the Cuban Constitution gives very clear indications of the direction the leadership wants to go to. As Ariel Dacal has pointed out in a very sharp criticism (*¿A dónde van las palabras que no se quedaron? Ariel Dacal, La Tizza,* https://medium.com/la-tiza), a number of very significant words and formulations have been deleted from the new draft, including: the aim of "building a communist society", as well as the commitment that "in Cuba capitalism will never be restored". Of course, the wording of the Constitution does not determine the character of the regime, but the fact that these sentences are to be removed tells us a lot about the socio-economic direction in which those who propose the changes wish to go.

CHAPTER TWO
NICARAGUA: A COUNTRY
THAT DID NOT FINISH ITS
REVOLUTION

1) INTRODUCTION

The insurrection of July 1979 overthrew the inhuman and despotic Somoza regime in Nicaragua in the most thorough-going democratic revolution in Latin America since the victory of the 26 July Movement in Cuba twenty years previously. All sections of Nicaragua's 3 million population participated: young, old, men, women, workers and peasants and the middle class. It was an event of enormous and worldwide importance, offsetting both the defeat suffered in Chile six years earlier when US-sponsored generals overthrew the Social-Democratic government of Salvador Allende and unleashed a regime of vicious repression against workers and peasants, and the 1976 coup in Argentina which replaced Isabel Perón with a military junta that 'disappeared' some 30,000 Argentinians.

The Nicaraguan revolution triumphed as part of a rising wave of revolutionary victories from which it drew strength and to which it contributed. As 1979 began, the Shah of Iran was overthrown, and in March a Workers' and Peasants' Government, the New Jewel Movement took power on the Caribbean island of Grenada. These advances followed the overthrow of Portuguese colonialism in Mozambique and Angola (1974-75), the defeat of both US imperialism in Vietnam (1975) and the South African invasion of Angola (1976), and the Soweto uprising (1976), which marked the political emergence of a new generation of revolutionary-minded youth in South

Africa. Victory in Nicaragua, spurred on the urban and rural revolutionary struggles, particularly in El Salvador and Guatemala.

It was an inspiring revolution, raising the hopes, sympathies and support of workers and youth around the world. Very few people can remember a more inspirational revolution than the Sandinista. In 1979, the people of the poorest Latin American country rose up and overthrew one of the most bloodthirsty and hated tyrants in the world, Anastasio Somoza, capturing the imagination of young people and workers in a way not seen since the victory of the Cuban guerrillas led by Fidel Castro and Che Guevara.

But the experience of Cuba had created high expectations, so that when, a decade later, a reactionary government regained control of Nicaragua the disappointment was all the greater. Today, Nicaragua is again the poorest country in Latin America and the second poorest country in the Western Hemisphere, after Haiti. But how did the reaction triumph in Nicaragua? By what process did it regain governmental and state power? Was the revolution doomed from the start? What lessons can we draw for today? What should have been the course of action of revolutionaries to maximise the chances of success?

Notwithstanding criticisms of the Sandinista National Liberation Front (*Frente Sandinista de Liberación Nacional*, FSLN), its structure, programme and policies, the Nicaraguan revolution was a great advance, demonstrating how the seemingly invincible military dictator supported by US imperialism could be defeated. It was, correctly, common ground among both socialists and democrats that imperialism's attempts to crush the Nicaraguan revolution had to be resisted at every level.

2) SOME HISTORY

Like all of Latin America and the Caribbean, Nicaragua was invaded, looted and exploited by imperialism, first by Spain and Britain, and then by the USA. Having achieved independence from the Mexican Empire, the United Provinces of Central America (now Costa Rica, Guatemala, Panama, Honduras, Nicaragua, and El Salvador) under the leadership of Francisco Morazán, attempted to establish a Federal Republic of Central America in 1824 as a single, progressive bourgeois nation. There were two major obstacles, the medieval privileges of the church and the interests of the ultra-conservative *caudillos*, the wealthy landowners.

The Republic began a programme of building schools and roads, enacted free trade policies, abolished slavery, invited foreign capital and immigrants, separated church from state, proclaimed religious liberties such as secular marriage and divorce, confiscated church property and removed education from church control. These measures both downgraded the authority of the oligarchs and scandalised them. It was the Nicaraguan oligarchs who launched the civil war that began the Balkanisation of the region, its division into mini-states none of which were economically viable. The common history of the region presented these countries with common problems both economically and socially, and what happens in any one is strongly echoed in the others.

The USA saw this division of Central America as very much in its own interest, particularly in controlling trade routes between the Pacific and Atlantic Oceans. In 1882, Ferdinand de Lesseps had started work on a canal, but the effort ended in bankruptcy. The US Congress agreed to take over the project in 1902. However, at that time Panama was not a separate country, but the base of the Colombian Liberals, who were fighting a civil war against a US-backed Conservative government. Philippe Banau-Varilla, closely linked with the US Administration, arranged for a small revolt in favour of Panamanian independence in Panama City. Simultaneously, President Roosevelt dispatched the USS *Nashville* to ensure that no Colombian troops could reach Panama City. On 3 November, 1903, after some sixty years of supporting the government in Bogotá, the US switched sides and the Republic of Panama was born. Banau-Varilla was immediately appointed Panama's ambassador to Washington and within a fortnight had signed a treaty allowing for perpetual US sovereignty over the 'Canal zone', a strip of land sixteen kilometres wide and eighty kilometres long, with permission for the US Army Corps of Engineers to build a canal.

Prior to the opening of the Panama Canal in 1914, Nicaragua had been considered strategically essential by the US bourgeoisie because it offered an alternative route between the Atlantic and Pacific Oceans. Between 1896 and 1912, US marines invaded Nicaragua four times to ensure US control over any canal built across the Central American isthmus. After the 1912 invasion, the US marines provided Nicaragua with 'internal stability' in return for not competing with the Panama Canal. They stayed for over two decades.

Until the last third of the nineteenth century, when coffee production was introduced, Nicaragua's economy was based largely on great cattle *latifundios* dominated by an oligarchy centred in the cities of Granada and León. The introduction of coffee brought wealth and power to a new 'coffee bourgeoisie', which was soon translated into control of the government which enacted laws facilitating the appropriation of Church, communal and public land by private individuals anxious to extend their estates. The dispossessed, with increasing numbers of immigrants, formed a free labour force working for minimum wages.

Suppression of civil liberties was acceptable to the US, but opening negotiations with European companies on the possible construction of a second canal was too much. In 1909, the traditional landed oligarchy, in a feudal-imperialist alliance backed the US overthrow of the government. Henceforward, American private banks had almost complete financial control of the Nicaraguan economy, and direct control over the collection of customs duties, taxes and the National Bank.

For fifty years this Conservative government preserved and encouraged the most backward forms of surplus extraction and, under its rule, the *latifundios* were generally characterised by stagnant production, primitive cultivation, lack of soil conservation, and labourers bound to the estate by their debts. By 1950, as a result of lack of innovation, of economic and social stagnation, Nicaragua's coffee producers had the lowest average yields per hectare in Central America (half those in El Salvador and Costa Rica).

The first to organise a nationalist struggle for freedom from imperialism was Augusto Cesar Sandino, the illegitimate son of a landowner and an Indian woman employed by the Sandino family. By seventeen, he had been radicalised by his mother's suffering and the actions of General Benjamín Zeledón who, in 1912, unsuccessfully fought the invasion of Nicaragua by US marines. At twenty-five, Sandino was forced to flee Nicaragua and for three years (1923-1926) worked in the Mexican oil fields, becoming acquainted with the organised workers' movement then dominated by the anarcho-syndicalist Industrial Workers of the World (the 'Wobblies') and the Mexican Communist Party, and experiencing first-hand the results of the Mexican Revolution that lasted from 1910 to 1920.[1]

Sandino began a struggle for national independence in 1927, with just twenty-nine rebels, building a fighting force of 3,000 guerrillas coming predominantly from among the *campesinos* and urban poor but also, and importantly, including a significant group of miners from the San Albino gold mines. Sandino offered the vision of a capitalist Nicaragua based on co-operatives of small landowners, free from imperialist domination. This was, of course, an impossible goal in a world dominated by imperialism but, based on practical experience, Sandino did contribute to the understanding that the national bourgeoisie of Nicaragua were too servile, too weak, too tied to imperialism to carry through the struggle for national liberation; that "only the workers and peasants will take the struggle through to its ultimate conclusion". Essentially this echoed the view of Georgy Valentinovitch Plekhanov, father of Russian Marxism, that the Russian (bourgeois-

---

1 Vanden, H., and Prevost, G., *Democracy and Socialism in Nicaragua*, Rienner 1993.

democratic) Revolution "will triumph only as a working-class movement or else it will never triumph".[2]

In its initial stages, Sandino's guerrilla war gained substantial support from the Communist Parties of Central America, particularly Mexico and Cuba. At that time the Communist International was led by Nikolai Bukharin and its policy was stagist – the national bourgeoisie would lead their own revolutions for national independence from imperialism, and Communists should limit themselves to assisting that struggle. The 'Hands Off Nicaragua' campaign run by the Mexican Communist Party was a major part of the international support for Sandino's struggle. Simultaneously, he was joined in his fight against US occupation by Salvadoran Farabundo Martí, who was one of his closest collaborators until he returned to El Salvador in 1930 to help launch the Salvadoran Communist Party.[3]

A sharp turn to the left by the stalinised Communist International meant that for six years, 1927-1933, social-democrats and national revolutionaries were considered as great a danger to a socialist revolution as fascists. In such a scenario, co-operation between national Communist Parties and local national liberation fighters was, at best, lukewarm. This policy precipitated the nonsensical accusation by the Mexican CP that Sandino was an agent of US imperialism, and the demand that the Nicaraguan struggle for national independence should wait for the formation of a Nicaraguan Communist Party. Sandino was left puzzled and angry by these accusations and demands, he accused Martí of spying for the Communist International and severed relations with him.

The puppet regimes of, first Adolfo Diaz and then José Moncada, were unable to smash the Sandino movement, even with the direct support of US marines, regular troops and air attacks. As part of the fight against Sandino the US created, organised and trained a National Guard (*Guardia Nacional*) that combined many of the functions of the army, police and secret police. The Guards were trained in the use of terror tactics against the *campesinos* and urban population, conducting mass executions and systematic torture described by Fonseca as:

> [T]he ferocious National Guard maintains the cruel practices inculcated by its creator, the United States Marines. The bombarding of villages, the butchering of children, the raping of women, the burning of huts with peasants still inside, mutilation as a form of torture: these were the subjects that the North American professors of civilisation taught the Guards

2 In Roberts, J., *Lenin, Trotsky and the Theory of the Permanent Revolution*, Wellred Books, 2007.

3 *Sandino: Testimony of a Nicaraguan Patriot, 1921–1934,* Princeton Legacy.

during the epoch of the guerrilla resistance (1927-32) led by Augusto Cesar Sandino.[4]

Nicaragua was a test-bed for US shock tactics that would later be used world-wide. From 1950 to 1979, nearly 5,000 Nicaraguan soldiers would be sent to the US to receive counter-insurgency training. Nicaragua would become the strategic base of the imperialists in Central America, from where the CIA-sponsored invasion of Guatemala in 1954 and the Bay of Pigs invasion against the Cuban revolution, in April 1961, were launched.

Despite Sandino's heroic struggle he was not victorious. A fundamental and fatal flaw existed in his analysis that was to reappear in the programme of the *Frente Sandinista de Liberación Nacional* (FSLN) fifty years later. Sandino believed it was possible to free Nicaragua from US domination with the collaboration of the 'national-colonial bourgeoisie'. In 1932, Sandino naively agreed to lay down arms in exchange for the withdrawal of US marines from Nicaragua, and the promise that the lives of his guerrillas would be spared. The following year, General Anastasio Somoza Garcia, the son of a wealthy coffee grower, was appointed commander of the National Guard.

On 21 February, 1934 after a dinner with President Bautista Sacasa, the 'liberal' puppet of Washington, Sandino and two of his generals were arrested by National Guard officers, executed, and buried in unmarked graves in the rural village of Waslala. Somoza was later to say:

> I went to the US embassy where I had a chat with Ambassador Arthur Bliss who confirmed that the Washington government recommended the elimination of Augusto Sandino because they considered him a threat to peace in the country.

After Sandino's murder, in less than a month, the National Guard had slaughtered the former guerrillas.

Sandino's assassination prepared the way for the coup d'etat by Somoza, who took power as President on 1 January, 1937, and established a forty-two-year dictatorship of the Somoza family. As head of the National Guard, Somoza was more the direct agent of US imperialism than a representative of the Nicaraguan bourgeoisie. The fact that the US Embassy in Nicaragua stood next door to Somoza's palace was, most Nicaraguans believed, symbolic of who actually ruled.

Within Nicaragua, Somoza promoted the production of agricultural produce for export, primarily to the United States. His policy for maintaining profits for himself, his family and US accomplices was simple: falls in the world market price for, e.g. coffee, meant *campesinos* were dispossessed of

---

4 Fonseca, C., 'Nicaragua: Zero Hour', in *Sandinistas Speak*, Pathfinder, 1982.

their land to increase the area under cultivation. The National Guard stifled any resistance and, naturally, no *campesinos* ever had their land returned.

After the death of Sandino, the two decades from 1934 to 1956 saw a sharp decline in the national liberation struggle. However, despite the repression and the general downturn, not all opposition was smashed. In Managua for instance, the Managuan Workers' Confederation (CTM) managed to organise 3,000 workers in underground conditions. The party most involved in the unions was the clandestine Communist Party, which faithfully followed the line of the Stalinised Communist International.

After the Nazi attack on the Soviet Union in 1941, the policy of the Communist International underwent a complete reversal. On 3 July, 1944, the Nicaraguan Socialist Party (*Partido Socialista Nicaragüense*, (PSN) the Nicaraguan Communist Party) called a public meeting in the Managua Gymnasium in which it proclaimed its support for Somoza as an anti-fascist. It was legalised and allowed to campaign for increased production as part of the war effort. To secure social peace, Somoza offered a Labour Code guaranteeing wages and a minimum level of social services and, to win over the *campesinos*, promised to divide the idle lands of the *latifundios* between small farmers. When, on 5 March, 1946, Winston Churchill announced the start of the Cold War with his now famous 'Iron Curtain' speech, Somoza began the repression of the PSN and the de-facto end of the Labour Code.

Despite a boom in prices and demand during the Second World War, Nicaragua emerged from the war with a very backward economy and extremely low productivity of land and labour. The cotton boom, which began in 1949, was a turning point for Nicaraguan agriculture. After 1949, Nicaragua's real GDP increased at nearly ten per cent per annum. Despite sharp cyclical swings in both demand and prices, this period was, generally, the most economically dynamic in Nicaraguan history and, unsurprisingly, one consequence of this was a sharp increase in union membership.

The most noticeable features of cotton production (a highly capital-intensive crop on large farms) were accelerated mechanisation and increased use of agrochemicals. Credit and tariff policies were introduced to encourage investment in labour-saving machinery, to the benefit of large, export-oriented, capitalist producers. In 1950 there were fewer than 500 tractors in Nicaragua, by 1955 there were more than 2,500. Labour was no longer needed on a year-round basis, and fewer than one in ten agricultural workers had permanent employment. However, the harvest itself remained labour intensive, and increases in production required parallel increases in the seasonal labour force.

The state also contributed by providing additional port capacity and extensive road construction. The latter facilitated access to land previously used for subsistence farming, and the 1950s to the 1970s saw a massive expansion of cattle raising and cotton production. By 1955, the area planted with cotton was more than five times what it had been in 1950. By the 1970s, seasonal cotton workers numbered some 200,000, over half of the economically active population in agriculture. With cotton came herbicides, pesticides and toxins, the careless spraying of which contaminated the meagre fare of the agricultural workers giving Nicaraguans the highest levels of DDT in their bodies of any country on earth.[5]

In the late 1950s exports of chilled, boneless beef to the United States began, to feed the US hunger for burgers. Beef exports rose from a negligible level before 1958 to $6.7 million in 1965, and then increased rapidly to $26.6 million in 1970. Most of Nicaragua's cattle production continued to be based on traditional, extensive grazing practices. The expansion of cattle production meant a doubling of the land area used for pasture. Soon the largest cattle ranchers (two per cent of the total number) controlled more than half of the total area under pasture. The Somozas were not left out, by the late 1970s, they controlled, directly or indirectly, most of the seven export slaughter-houses in Nicaragua.

These developments meant the wholesale displacement of *campesinos* (small food producers) to farm in increasingly remote areas where they engaged in slash and burn agriculture,[6] or became semi-proletarian or proletarian rural labourers. Sub-family farms (those unable to provide for an average family) tripled between 1952 and 1963 (from nearly 18,000 to nearly 52,000). These farms, sixty-four per cent of the total, covered just one per cent of the arable land, while just two per cent of farms covered eighty-six per cent. However, having cleared a forested area and cultivated food for a year or two, the newly-cleared land would be seized by cattle ranchers for pasture and the *campesinos* expelled to repeat the process elsewhere, compounding the problems of rural hunger and poverty, with increasing numbers forced to migrate to the towns and swell the semi-proletarian population.

In 1959 the urban population had been about one third the total, but by 1977 it had grown to about half, most of the increase occurring in Managua, which grew from about 100,000 to 400,000. The widespread expropriation of the peasantry and rapid differentiation of classes in the countryside was the result of a growth in capitalist agriculture. Dispossession and lack of stable employment led to pervasive rural poverty and considerable discontent

5   Faber, D., *Imperialism, Revolution and the Ecological Crisis in Central America*, Latin American Perspectives 19(1)17-44, 1992.
6   International Fund for Agricultural Development FIDA, 1980.

expressed in violent landlord-tenant confrontations and organised land invasions by the dispossessed.

It is estimated that, at the end of the 1970s, as much as one third of the economically active agricultural population was completely dependent on wage labour – three months of harvest after which they transferred from agricultural work to other types of labour, often in the towns. Another third owned plots of land too small to survive on, and had to sell their labour.[7]

On 21 September, 1956 Anastasio Somoza was assassinated by Rigoberto López a Nicaraguan poet, artist and composer. López had infiltrated a party attended by the President and shot him in the chest. López died instantly in a hail of bullets, and Somoza followed a few days later. Somoza's son, Luis Somoza Debayle, replaced his father as president and inaugurated his period in office with brutal repressions and extensive reprisals.

Within three years, the Cuban revolution had overthrown the dictatorship of Fulgencio Batista, a powder flash that sparked workers' strikes, the creation of trade unions, student demonstrations, land seizures, and the creation of peasant federations across Latin America. These spontaneous actions confirmed the revolutionary potential of the Nicaraguan people, and the need for a revolutionary organisation.

Nicaraguan industry was small, accounting for twenty-three per cent of the GDP in 1970. It was highly capital intensive and geared to exports rather than to developing an industrial infrastructure for Nicaragua. This made the country highly dependent on imports of machinery and spare parts, especially agricultural machinery. The industrial proletariat was therefore small, about 113,000. In the 1970s a much larger number of city workers was involved in petty commerce or artisan production – street vendors, shoe-shiners, fruit sellers, etc. The factory workers tended to be concentrated in large plants, seventy-five per cent working in factories of over 170 workers. There was also, as elsewhere in Latin America, a large and expanding white collar 'salariat' – technicians, professionals, administrators and managers, and a growing and radical student population.

State support continued and, as previously, the largest cotton growers benefited disproportionately. These activities were highly concentrated. Five exporters, most owned by or associated with foreign firms, controlled over half the trade. As the land devoted to beef and cotton rose sharply, domestic food crops fell dramatically as small producers of corn, beans and rice were dispossessed. There was an increasing polarisation and a sharpening of the

---

7 Villa, C., *The Sandinista Revolution*, 1986, see Chapter 2 for the rural class structure.

struggle between exploiters and exploited, a process continually denied from the pulpit and at the banqueting tables of the bourgeoisie.[8]

The short-lived Central American Common Market launched in 1960, was a US initiative to counteract the impact of the Cuban revolution. IP (Intercontinental Press, 12 December, 1983) reported how Nicaragua and other Central American countries were supposed to industrialise and improve living conditions, but not enough to significantly change relations between Central America and the USA. It was, at best, a half-hearted measure. Semi-obsolete plants were brought from the USA to process American supplied materials, to the extent that Nicaraguan factories received Colgate toothpaste to package and label, 'Made in Nicaragua'.

During the 1960s, sugar and tobacco production expanded, stimulated by the Cuban Revolution, with Somoza and associates controlling five of the six enterprises that dominated the sugar industry. They were also heavily involved in tobacco production, in plantations that were characterised by permanent labour forces as well as a high level of development of the productive forces.

Numerous loans from private sources at high interest rates were obtained by the Nicaraguan state for vague and undefined purposes. As much as half of these went into the Somoza family coffers, but the repayments took an ever-increasing proportion of annual export revenues (thirty-eight per cent in 1978) leading to a serious balance of payment crisis.

In the 1960s and early 1970s, some two-thirds of rural families had an income which was incapable of providing minimum nutritional requirements, seventy per cent of the population suffered from malnutrition and ninety per cent lived below the poverty line. Diets were so bad that entire villages suffered from dementia and there were schools where every single pupil had tuberculosis. In some villages, most of the population would die of hunger, giving Nicaragua the lowest life expectancy (between fifty-three and fifty-five years) of any Central American country.[9]

While the general conditions experienced by the people of Nicaragua were awful, the burdens fell heaviest on women. Some forty per cent of the population was literate but the illiterates were predominantly women. In some rural areas, not a single woman could read or write. In the poorer areas, lack of any kind of medical care meant two babies died for every three that lived. Women's unemployment was much higher than men's, forcing them to take the worst paid jobs, so they made up the majority of seasonal labourers harvesting the cotton and coffee.

8 Borge, T., *"A Nose for Power"*, Second National Seminar of Political Education in Nicaragua, 20 May, 1983.

9 World Bank, *World Development Report*, 1980.

This work pattern, and the *machismo* attitude prevailing amongst men, massively disrupted family life due to abandonment by fathers and husbands. Hence, a large proportion of mothers had to raise their families alone, bearing the full brunt of the brutal and inhuman conditions. By 1978, despite the patriarchal propaganda in the teachings of the Catholic Church, an estimated one-third of all families in Nicaragua were headed by women, and two-thirds in Managua.[10] Of single mothers, eighty per cent were wage earners. Because of the extreme oppression they faced, and the lack of perspective for improving their lives under capitalism, women in the colonial and semi-colonial countries were thrust into the vanguard of the struggle for social change.

The Somoza state continued to preferentially assist its own supporters amongst the capitalist farmers via subsidies and infrastructure investment, subsidised construction of cotton gins and slaughterhouses, etc. However, the process was uneven in geographic, social, and sectoral terms. Capitalism was most advanced in the Pacific coastal region, where most of the export-oriented activities were concentrated, and considerably less advanced in the central or interior region, where small food producers and subsistence farmers predominated. Economic activity in the Atlantic Coast region was relatively low, limited to subsistence farming, mining (largely owned by the Somoza family, but with significant US investment), and timber.

The expansion of capitalist production brought vast wealth to a few and increased dependence on the US market, giving imperialism a tighter political and economic grip, and increasing cultural subjugation to Coca-Cola and Hollywood. The rural workers, the poor and middle peasants, and the urban poor were all experiencing hunger, impoverishment, degradation, and facing the brutality of the National Guard, arbitrary arrest and torture. They were all subject to a system of police spies and provocateurs but would be the force that smashed the Somoza state.

3) FOUNDING, DEVELOPMENT AND DIFFERENCES WITHIN THE FSLN

In 1957, Carlos Fonseca Amador (with Tomás Borge) established the first all-student branch of the PSN in Léon. He subsequently travelled to the Soviet Union as a PSN delegate to the Sixth World Festival of Youth and Students.[11] In late 1960, Fonseca, still officially a law student, travelled to Cuba to see the revolution first hand. There, he met Che Guevara, was inspired and sought

---

10 Viterna, J., *Pushed, Pulled and Persuaded, Women's Mobilisation*, American Journal of Sociology, 112(1)1-45, 2006.

11 Fonseca, C., *A Nicaraguan in Moscow,* 1981, available on the internet.

aid and training for the struggle in Nicaragua. He began to host meetings in his apartment which were frequented by people, many of whom would become leaders in the liberation struggle.

On his return, he gathered like-minded young people (mostly students) around him and walked out of the PSN in disgust at its acceptance of the Somoza regime. In 1961 he founded (again with Tomás Borge) the *Frente de Liberación Nacional*, which changed its name in 1963 to *Frente Sandinista de Liberación Nacional*. That became the nucleus of the Sandinista guerrillas. The name change was because Fonseca understood his struggle was the continuation of Sandino's, and accepted the Cuban strategy that any serious struggle against imperialism would be in the form of guerrilla warfare based on the workers and peasants.

The Historic Programme of the FSLN, written by Fonseca in 1969, talked of "agrarian revolution", and of a "revolutionary government" that would "create a Nicaragua that is free from exploitation, oppression (and) backwardness".[12] But its actual economic demands were limited: the expropriation of "landed estates, factories, companies, buildings, means of transportation" would be restricted to those of the Somoza family and their closest associates. There would be nationalisation of foreign companies that exploited natural resources, but not enough to control foreign trade or to develop a planned economy. The programme contained the promise of workers' control, that the banking system would be nationalised, that there would be a degree of state control over foreign trade, and a national economic plan for a mixed economy containing elements of workers' control. Whilst a very radical programme it was, at heart, reformist.

Actually, the public face of the FSLN was not Fonseca's Historic Programme. The adoption of the programme was completely overshadowed by a gun battle in Managua on 15 July, 1969, in which Comandante Julio Buitrago was killed by the Guard. Buitrago, twenty-five years old, holed up in a small house in the *barrio de Las Delicias del Volga*, armed only with a sub-machine gun, held off some 300 Guards, two tanks, two helicopters and an aeroplane. The regime televised the entire event, believing that the population would be further intimidated by seeing a top FSLN militant gunned down. However, events didn't work out that way: the lessons the young people of Nicaragua learned was that heavily armed Guards ran in fear of their lives when Buitrago opened fire. The Guards were not invulnerable, they could be wounded and killed, and they were certainly not heroic. Young people were inspired, not terrified.[13]

---

12 In *Sandinistas Speak*, Pathfinder, 1982.
13 Cabezas, O., *Fire in the Mountain*, Cape, 1985.

However, the details of the Programme, at that stage, were not decisive. The FSLN, like the 26-J Movement could, faced with reality, take the actual revolution beyond what was written in its programme. That said, what did not bode well, and what separated the FSLN from the 26-J Movement was the Stalinist theory and experiences of many of its key leaders. The rigidity imposed by this framework could mean the flexibility exhibited by the Cuban leadership might be missing from the FSLN.

The Stalinist political education to which Fonseca had been subject within the PSN was now endorsed by the Cuban leadership (Che had been killed two years previously in 1967) who raised little or no objection when the FSLN adopted the Stalinist/reformist theory of a two-stage revolution: first the national democratic to bring the country to an acceptable level of capitalist development, later, at some indeterminate time, the fight for socialism. For example, although Fonseca was a great supporter of Sandino, he never defended him against the political attacks by the Central American Communist Parties resulting from the ultra-left policies of the Communist International, policies originating with Joseph Stalin. This reflected an important theoretical weakness in Fonseca's writings.

By the 1960s, Nicaragua had a small newly-created, hereditary working class. A constant theme throughout the history of capitalism is that self-awareness by the working class usually occurs in the second and third generations of those who migrate to work in industrial centres. This new generation of Nicaraguan workers had a much greater awareness of workers' rights, of ways to protest and a sense of self-worth. For Marxists, these workers had an importance out of all proportion to their numbers because they would be expected to take the lead in the coming struggle, determining the programme and character of the revolution for national independence. To be successful this struggle would require a close alliance between workers and peasants, invariably based on the demand: 'Land to those who work it.'

When the FSLN launched its first offensive in 1963 it already had a clearly-defined 'guerrilla-ist' organisation; Guevara's 'foco' strategy, whereby a small group of guerrillas with support of the *campesinos*, would wear down and eventually defeat the superior armed forces of the state. Later, Comandante Henry Ruiz summarised the FSLN attitude to the proletarian struggle during this period as: "A (single) worker who transfers to the mountains becomes a far greater danger to the Somocista regime than an economic strike carried out by hundreds of workers".[14] The FSLN at this time regarded workers' fighting for their own interests as 'Economism', an attitude that would be alive and well when it was in government.

---

14 Gonzalez, M., *Nicaragua: Revolution under Siege*, Bookmarks, 1985.

The conditions of life under the Somoza tyranny meant any revolutionary organisation had to work clandestinely, which meant it could not become a mass organisation. In the cities an FSLN cadre would not know other members of the FSLN, or their activities. A major problem with such an organisation is the absence of the participation of the members in decision-making processes regarding policy and the election (and possible recall) of leaders. A clandestine meeting on a street corner would whisper instructions to be implemented without question. Such organisations are very dependent on the quality of the individual top leaders. Those that were sloppy and inefficient did tend to be removed quite quickly by the National Guard, but they could compromise many others in the process. Too often cadres only discovered who other members of the FSLN were when their names were broadcast after the Guard had killed them. Another severe drawback with such an organisation was that membership was small: Cabezas in his book *Fire in the Mountain* claims that, during his activities in León, the membership in that city was six, of whom four or five were students.

The FSLN received a bloody nose in its first major guerrilla sortie at Río Coco in 1963, and for a while the FSLN barely existed. The entire national membership was estimated at less than thirty.[15] Coincident with the attack at Río Coco, US President Kennedy announced the so-called Alliance for Progress. In response to the Cuban Revolution, the US changed its tactics and strategy for defending the economic interests of US imperialists in Central America. The dictatorships in such countries as Nicaragua were to be given a liberal facade. In response, the Somoza family engineered the election of a lawyer, René Schick to the Presidency. He substituted for Luis Somoza Debayle, who had ruled since his father's assassination in 1956. Despite a certain relaxation of oppression during 1963-67, the Somoza apparatus remained firmly in place under the watchful eye of Luis' brother, Anastasio Somoza Debayle (educated at West Point), Chief of the National Guard.

On 29 June, 1964, Fonseca was arrested for the eighth time. The government refused to confirm his detention and there was serious concern that he might be murdered. The Sandinista-led Revolutionary Student Front (*Frente Estudiantil Revolucionario*, FER), the youth group of the Independent Liberal Party, and even the youth group of the Conservative Party launched a series of petitions, strikes, marches and sit-ins which probably saved Fonseca's life. On 9 July, 1963, he was put on trial and, following Castro's 'History Will Absolve Me' speech, made his own statement, 'From Jail I Accuse the Dictatorship'. In late January 1965 he was secretly deported to Guatemala

---

15 Zimmerman, M., *Sandinista: Carlos Fonseca and the Nicaraguan Revolution*, Duke University Press, 2000.

(his family is rumoured to have paid a ransom) and from there travelled to Cuba where he stayed until the end of 1966.

During this period of Schick liberalisation, and with Fonseca in jail or Cuba, the FSLN stepped back temporarily from the foco strategy and worked to consolidate and expand the FER in high schools and colleges, to collaborate with the PSN and the bourgeois Republican Party, in a broad electoral organisation called Republican Mobilisation.

For the latter half of 1964 through to 1970 the FSLN cadres were heavily engaged in legal political work, and began to attract significant support as they extended their activities to campaigns for, e.g., safe drinking water (out of a population of about 3 million only about 350,000 had running water[16]). However, the main purpose of the so-called 'intermediate organisations', the most important of which was the FER, was to provide support for, and recruit members to the FSLN guerrilla force.

Strangely, the Somoza regime gave the universities and students considerable leeway (relatively) to protest and agitate; university students became the spearhead of nationalistic and anti-Somoza movements. The official student union was the CUUN (The University of Nicaragua Student Council, *Consejo Universitario de la Universidad Nicaragua*) and was allowed offices on university premises, to openly recruit, to have its own financial resources and, even hold processions and demonstrations. The FER, founded in 1961, was the FSLN student organisation and was, at best, semi-legal. Naturally, the FER militants worked within the CUUN, campaigning for office and seeking to win the student body to its points of view.

As part of its successful campaign to gain control of the CUUN (and its facilities) the FER organised campaigns on issues such as the relevance of the university curriculum. This included mass demonstrations of students around the university grounds and even into León. The demonstrations were made entertaining for participants and onlookers. The Somozistas were colloquially called toads. On one demonstration the call went out "If you don't jump you're a toad": soon everyone took up the chant "El que no brinque es sapo, el que no brinque es sapo" and jumped up and down as they marched.

Cabezas has described the level of activity amongst the students at León University over the period up to 1971. The FER had seven study circles amongst the students, each with three or so members and each meeting weekly with Cabezas as facilitator. These concentrated on theoretical discussions using the *Communist Manifesto* and Marta Harnecker's *Elementary Principles of Historical Materialism*. From then until the insurrection and civil war the

---

16 *Las condiciones de salud en las Américas*: 1971-1973, *Organisación Panamericana de la Salud.*

student milieu was of major importance for revolutionaries. FER militants did achieve important successes, winning elections at León and Managua universities, e.g. as editor of *El Estudiante* a national student journal. However, there were two major factors hampering their activities, they were very small numerically, and the PSN did all it could to isolate them.

A natural extension of student activities in the *barrios*, on such questions as the provision of electricity and drinking water, was organising study circles and the FER soon had a real presence. Many of these circles would later be foci for the local Civil Defence Committees formed during the uprising of 1979. In all of this, the FSLN had one huge advantage, they had the field to themselves, there was no other group calling for getting rid of Somoza lock, stock and barrel, either in the universities, in the *barrios* or amongst the peasants. By claiming to be Sandino's heirs they accessed a generation of older *campesinos*.

On 3 August, 1966, President René Schick died of a heart attack, and within a month Anastasio Somoza announced his candidacy for President. The pro-Moscow PSN formed an electoral alliance (the Democratic Union for Liberation, UDEL) with dissident capitalists including bankers, exporters and landlords, who had broken with Somoza because his economic stranglehold prevented them from receiving their fair share of surplus value. The PSN also tied its trade union federation (CGT-I) to the UDEL. In this the stalinist PSN was, of course, acting quite the opposite of Lenin who, during the Russian Revolution, argued that it was precisely the task of revolutionary leaders to "clarify proletarian minds by emancipating them from the influence of the bourgeoisie".[17]

The UDEL organised a mass anti-Somoza demonstration for 22 January, 1967, mobilising their support in preparation for the presidential election scheduled for 1 May. At 5 p.m., as the 50,000-strong demonstration made its way down Avenida Roosevelt toward the National Palace, soldiers of the National Guard blocked the way. On the pretext that the demonstration was the cover for an armed coup, the National Guard opened fire on the crowd with automatic weapons, gunning down hundreds. The FSLN took this as confirmation that the guerrilla approach was the only one likely to get results.

Anastasio Somoza, running on a Nationalist Liberal Party (PLN) ticket, won the election on 1 May, 1967, with some seventy per cent of the votes cast and was duly elected President. His views were summed up when asked about education and training: "I don't want an educated population; I want oxen".[18] The same election gave the PLN an absolute majority in both Senate

---

17 Lenin, V., *The Dual Power*, CW24:40, 1917.
18 Holloway, T., *A Companion to Latin American History*. Blackwell, Ltd., 2011.

and Chamber of Deputies. The interlude of relative liberality was quickly ended, and the Somoza family returned to accumulating wealth. By the time of the revolution in 1979, they personally owned twenty-five per cent of Nicaraguan industry (150 factories), twenty per cent of all workable land, the national airline, a TV channel, and numerous other enterprises such as the Nicaraguan branch of Mercedes Benz.[19]

During the election campaign, and with Fonseca's return, the FSLN assessed itself as strong enough to relaunch the guerrilla struggle and follow the Cuban example of having the base for its armed actions not in neighbouring Honduras, but within Nicaragua's central mountains. Wheelock described the organisation and leadership of the FSLN during this time to Marta Harnecker for the Mexican journal *Punto Final*, available in English in IP, 14 November, 1983. Because the interview was for public consumption Wheelock was at pains to play down the very sharp differences existing within the FSLN at that time.

His description of the day-to-day activities of the FSLN during this guerrilla period revealed the fluidity and unstructured nature of the leadership, not least because active guerrillas tended to have short lives. It was also necessary for leading figures to flee Nicaragua for quite lengthy periods, during which times they could well be out of contact with the active cadres within the country who would, consequently, form their own leaderships. It was, thus, extremely difficult to maintain any coherent structure.

True, the FSLN had a democratic constitution that allowed its members to express themselves freely and to participate in the political life of the FSLN, to be elected and to elect who they wished to the leadership bodies; but the promises were constrained by the reality of a dispersed membership, where communications were difficult and membership meetings almost impossible. Democratic discussion, debate and decision-making gave way to the more robust, top-down, military-political, hierarchical chain of command.

As in Cuba, the guerrilla foci were to be sustained by a network of supporters, the backbone of which were women who established safe houses, clothed and fed the guerrillas, organised first aid and medical supplies, carried messages and ammunition, and rallied support for political prisoners.

Starting with Gladys Baez, a twenty-six-year old, factory worker from a working-class family who had been active in the PSN for ten years before joining the FSLN, the FSLN began integrating women into their guerrilla forces. Unlike other left-wing guerrilla groups in the region, the FSLN championed progressive views on gender equality because they believed that

---

19 All police vehicles were Mercedes, as were the cars of the top brass of the National Guard, the top politicians, even the country's refuse trucks.

winning women's support and their participation in the revolutionary process
was essential for the success of the guerrilla struggle. At the time there were
very few women members of the FSLN, perhaps no more than five or six,
about ten per cent of the membership, mostly student activists.[20]

Fonseca's second attempt to reopen the foco campaign was in the remote
Pancasán region. The guerrillas were also better prepared but fewer (forty as
compared to sixty) than they had been in 1963. Several leaders including
Fonseca, entered the region and began locating *campesino* families who would
provide shelter and food. However, now for the first time, a woman, Gladys
Baez, fought in the guerrilla ranks.[21]

As the guerrilla struggle progressed, women's participation in the FSLN
came to represent a new stage in Latin American revolutionary history.
Women participated more massively and more significantly than in any
other twentieth century revolution. They were integrated into the FSLN's
actual fighting forces, even in combat and positions of command, something
unprecedented in Latin American history. 'Exceptional' women had been part
of the guerrilla organisations in the Mexican and Cuban revolutions. Never,
however, had there been so many women in combat in such high positions
of responsibility, with men as well as women under their command. One
such was Dora Maria Tellez who was second in command at the seizure of
the National Palace in 1978 and would command one of the most important
fronts during the insurrection. Chinchilla estimated that, by 1979, women
comprised thirty per cent of the guerrilla armies in Nicaragua and were
active at every level of Nicaraguan society where opposition to the Somoza
dictatorship existed – neighbourhoods, farms, factories, offices, universities
and schools (even the private schools of the rich).

3.1) GROWTH OF DIFFERENCES WITHIN THE FSLN

The Pancasán foco was crushed in August 1967, with thirteen senior members
of the organisation killed. The defeat raised profound questions. October
1967 saw the capture and murder of Che Guevara in Bolivia. In country
after country in Latin America, government armies crushed rural guerrilla
movements, some of them much larger than the FSLN. A discussion began
at the very centre of the FSLN. Was the FSLN a party? An armed group? A
foco? Members were interpreting the lessons of Pancasán in sharply divergent
ways. Some wanted to maintain the focus on rural guerrilla warfare, but

---

20 Chinchilla, N., *Women in Revolutionary Movements: the Case of Nicaragua*,
    Stanford University, 1983.
21 Zimmerman, op cit.

others favoured abandoning guerrilla warfare and concentrating on political work in the student movement and urban *barrios*.

Cabezas claims that after Pancasán the FSLN existed in only Managua, Esteli and León. By 1970, it had been reduced to "only a dozen militants" in Managua and had ceased all armed actions, although a small number of combatants with a long-term guerrilla perspective did remain in the mountains. Differences developed within the FSLN through 1971 and 1972 and, by 1973 the organisation had splintered into three tendencies and, "for some time the practical work for armed struggle was interrupted".[22] Over the next two years the differences deepened until the tendencies worked in virtual isolation from each other.

The first tendency, which was closest to the 'orthodox' FSLN position, saw a protracted guerrilla war in the countryside as the only possible strategy for the overthrow of the Somoza dictatorship. This Prolonged People's War Tendency (GPP) was led by Tomás Borge, Henry Ruiz and Bayardo Arce and believed the 'political backwardness' of the masses necessitated a long, armed struggle, which would educate those masses and develop a socialist consciousness. The orientation was rural guerrilla warfare for an extended period, outside the cities amongst the peasants. This was a perspective similar to the Chinese Communist Party (CCP) of the early 1930s; revolutionaries should leave the cities and move to the guerrilla bases. The GPP along with the CCP falsely believed that moving a proletarian militant into a petty-bourgeois milieu proletarianised the milieu when, in reality, it gave the militant a petty-bourgeois perspective.[23]

A second tendency around Jaime Wheelock, Luis Carrión, and Carlos Nuñez drew the conclusion that there had to be a greater orientation to the working class in the cities. This 'Proletarian Tendency' (TP), as it came to be called, spoke of the need for a 'Marxist-Leninist Party' and saw itself as an "embryo of the future revolutionary party of the working class".[24] The TP called for the 'liquidation' of the large landowners and the redistribution of idle land to the poor and landless peasants, for the nationalisation of the banks, a state monopoly of foreign trade, and the nationalisation of foreign firms and basic industry. The TP was the smallest of the three tendencies within the FSLN but, nonetheless, Marxist revolutionaries would have had considerable interest in encouraging the development of this Tendency as a possible nucleus of a Leninist Party.

---

22 Fonseca, C., *Nicaragua: Zero Hour*, in Sandinistas Speak, Pathfinder Press, 1982.

23 Roberts, J., *China: From Permanent Revolution to Counter Revolution*, Wellred Books, 2016.

24 Black, G., *Triumph of the People*, Lawrence Hill & Co., 1981.

The third tendency, the *Terceristas* or 'Insurrectionary Tendency', developed a short time after the other two. Its analysis was that the growing alienation of sections of the bourgeoisie and the supposed 'floating' nature of Nicaragua's middle classes indicated insurrection in the short term. For the *Terceristas* it followed that the insurrection would be the work of a broad multi-class alliance. The leading figures in the *Terceristas* were the brothers Humberto and Daniel Ortega, and the Mexican Victor Tirado Lopez.

The *Terceristas* had close links with international social-democracy, especially, the Spanish Socialist Party (PSOE). Contacts made with Christian Democratic Parties of Venezuela, Costa Rica, and Mexico resulted in promises of aid. These connections with international social-democracy and 'progressive' regimes and parties in the rest of Latin America gave the *Terceristas* a respectability amongst bourgeois sectors that the other two tendencies lacked, and the Ortega brothers soon become the leading figures in the FSLN. They had grown up in Managua where their parents, both of whom had been imprisoned for anti-Somoza activities, ran a small import-export business. Both brothers studied at private and church schools, and joined the JPN, youth arm of the PSN, where they received their political education. They were active guerrillas from at least 1966, were both captured, imprisoned and tortured under Somoza. Humberto was freed in 1970 in exchange for four kidnapped United Fruit Company officials, and Daniel was freed by an FSLN commando group in 1974 after seven years in jail.

Prior to the revolutionary upsurge, the divisions between the Tendencies were acrimonious, the one Tendency expelling members of another from 'the FSLN'. The Tendencies operated virtually independent of each other, the *Terceristas* were the most active guerrillas, though the GPP was also active in ambushing National Guard units. The TP was the only one of the three that never fielded its own guerrilla units and was criticised by Fonseca for that. Both the GPP and the TP were active in the student milieu, each with its own groups of students though the GPP had the formal leadership of the FER. This meant that the FER, despite the good response to its literacy campaigns and projects demanding neighbourhood improvements, was held back by having as its major goal providing personnel for the guerrillas.

Latin America at this time experienced an upsurge in humanitarian socialism, expressed most widely as Liberation Theology. The call was for an improvement of the lives of workers and *campesinos* by placing legal restraints on unacceptable behaviour by individual capitalists. But the capitalist system would not be challenged. In January 1969, the Catholic Bishops in Nicaragua held a Pastoral Conference which dared to criticise the Somoza government by calling for the democratisation of the regime.

By the early 1970s, Catholic priests had well-established grassroots Christian Base Communities in poor neighbourhoods, using the Bible to question and criticise the Somoza regime's repression, lack of democracy, and the country's backward economic and social situation. This movement led protests against higher bus fares, increases in food prices, etc. Many paid for their commitment with jail and torture. The FSLN reached out to the leading Christian radicals and recruited as many as it could. This was reflected in the Historic Programme of the FSLN, which included the statement that it would "support the work of priests and other religious figures that defend working people". There were so many active Christian members of the FSLN that they were referred to as the revolutionary Christian current or the revolutionary Christian wing. While they did not coalesce into an actual Tendency, they did vote as a bloc on occasions. For example, five of the twelve FSLN delegates on the constitutional commission combined to insert into the preamble of the constitution "(to) those Christians who inspired by their belief in God have joined and committed themselves to the struggle for the liberation of the oppressed…"

The Popular Church in Nicaragua, especially, wanted to play a part in the revolutionary changes affecting the masses, and Fernando Cardenal, a Jesuit priest, played an important role when, in 1976, he testified in Washington before a congressional committee investigating human rights abuses by the Somoza regime. However, such activities were distrusted by the Catholic hierarchy who opposed both the Popular Church and the Sandinistas.

The exploited masses suffered terribly between 1969 and 1974 due to an economic slump worsened by a severe earthquake that destroyed the entire downtown section of Managua (1972), killing up to 20,000 of the city's 400,000 residents, leaving 50,000 homeless and causing the temporary closure of thirty-seven per cent of industry. Somoza took direct charge of the reconstruction activities, pocketing the relief funds that flowed into Nicaragua. His scheme was to purchase, at knock down prices, the real estate on which the former commercial and light industrial centre of the country had stood, re-develop it and sell it back to the previous owners at a massive profit. The result – seven years later, at the time of the revolution, an area of some 500 hectares (about two square miles) remained gutted, empty and overgrown with weeds.

It was this action in particular, that alienated many of the national bourgeoisie. Not because of Somoza's cold-blooded selfishness, but because they saw themselves as being robbed twice, of their property and of what they considered their fair share of the profits that would come from redevelopment. It was also the final insult to many of the urban salaried population, who faced unprecedented housing, transport and food problems. By 1974, the middle and petty-bourgeoisie were flocking to UDEL and it grew considerably. It was led by Pedro Joaquín Chamorro, a Conservative Party dissident, and editor of the leading bourgeois daily, *La Prensa*. While supported by the PSN, UDEL was condemned by the FSLN as "Somoza-ism without Somoza", politically tied to the US, the very force which had generated Somoza in the first place.

The massive corruption and incompetence revealed by the earthquake had a radicalising effect on the masses, deepening the socio-political crisis and further radicalising many Christian activists working in poor *barrios*. The *Terceristas* were considerably influenced by this, and internal FSLN documents now available show that by mid-1973, the *Terceristas* were already arguing for a more relaxed approach to ideological questions, for loosening restrictions on recruitment, and for building a wider base for the popular armed uprising by proposing strategic alliances with other sectors of society, including Conservatives and Liberals.[25]

As the economic and political crisis developed in the late 1970s, the *Terceristas* grew rapidly, and soon overtook the other two tendencies numerically. Because the FSLN saw itself as an armed revolutionary army, not a political party, it found it quite acceptable to recruit "very diverse sectors of national life". Wheelock, as part of his Harnecker interview, explained in IP (28 Nov, 1983) that the FSLN (that is the *Terceristas*) incorporated "in an organised way, young people who had come together around a Christian movement that was active at a student and neighbourhood level and included a few progressive priests... to link up with as combatants".

It was the PSN, not the Sandinistas, that led the industrial struggles, which followed the 1972 earthquake, and in 1973 did what many had believed impossible – led 3,000 construction workers in a victorious strike over Social Security registration and unpaid wages.

Despite having severe internal differences, the FSLN still managed to launch spectacular actions, epitomised in 24 Dec, 1974, when a *Tercerista* team of ten men and three women seized the house of an associate of Somoza and held party-goers hostage until eighteen political prisoners were released, US$1 million paid as ransom, and a lengthy FSLN communique published. This action was followed by Somoza declaring a 'state of siege', with massive military repression against the Sandinistas and other oppositionists. As many as 3,000 people, mostly peasants, were murdered during the three years of the emergency. Nevertheless, the FSLN took hold of the mass consciousness as the only real alternative to Somoza.

---

25 Foroohar, M., *The Catholic Church and Social Change in Nicaragua*. N.Y. Press, 1989.

Fonseca had returned to Nicaragua from Cuba to unite the three tendencies. Betrayed, he was ambushed in the mountains of Zinica by the National Guard and wounded. He was shot dead the following day, 8 Nov, 1976, at the age of forty. The military initiative was now firmly in the hands of the *Terceristas*, whose actions were much bolder than the other two tendencies and whose numbers were relatively much larger, though objectively still very small.

Displaced and unemployed peasants continued to leave the land for the cities, by 1977 the agrarian population had fallen to forty-four per cent of the total, light industry was expanding and workers numbered nearly twenty per cent of the total population (estimated at over 60,000 industrial workers by the Economic Commission for Latin America and the Caribbean, 1979). In 1977 the building workers, the most militant sector, went on strike at the same time as the *Tercerista* Tendency staged a guerrilla offensive in the countryside and in some smaller towns in the provinces on the border with Costa Rica. These developments occurred virtually simultaneously but they were uncoordinated because the FSLN had no established roots amongst the workers and because any such joint action would have been opposed by the PSN. In an interview with Marta Harnecker, in *Granma*, 27 January, 1980, Humberto Ortega described how, by 1977, most of the FSLN's leaders had been killed during the emergency, and the remaining guerrillas launched a limited offensive "to make their presence felt" and demonstrate their continuing existence. Estimates put the strength of the FSLN at no more than 200 active members at that time.[26]

Increasingly, the regime was called into question by all sectors of Nicaraguan society, from sections of big business, which saw Somoza as a threat to their economic well-being, through layers of the middle and small bourgeoisie (many of whose children had been targets for National Guard brutality) to the *campesinos*, semi-proletarians, and proletarians. The *Terceristas* now approached twelve well-known and respected Nicaraguans comprising industrialists, businessmen, priests, lawyers and academics; these would be known as The Twelve (*Los Doce*). This was an attempt to form a bridge to establish a popular front with important sections of the bourgeoisie on what the *Terceristas* were convinced was the eve of the insurrection.

The question remains as to whether it was correct to form a 'multi-class alliance' in the struggle against the brutal Somoza dictatorship. When sections of the bourgeois and petty-bourgeois take concrete actions against an imperialist-backed regime, communists and socialists should participate. This would be correct even if some of the parties or mass formations are

---

26 Zimmerman. op. cit.

under openly bourgeois leadership. The litmus test is the willingness to fight. Such a united front is not a new concept; it was present in Lenin's writings as early as February 1905.[27]

Lenin called for a united front of all revolutionary forces to participate in an uprising against the Tsar, on the basis of the slogan "march separately and strike together" but, as always, he emphasised the absolute necessity of maintaining the complete political independence of the working class. A pre-condition of unity in action is that the revolutionary socialists maintain their own objectives in the struggle, always fighting to strengthen the workers' organisations, 'striking together' in demonstrations, general strikes and armed actions, but never confusing their banner with that of the bourgeoisie. Above all, revolutionary socialists, even whilst whole-heartedly supporting democratic slogans such as the rights of assembly and free speech, and the right to strike, should never forget they are fighting to win the workers and peasants to the goal of an anti-capitalist government in which all the revolutionary petty-bourgeois elements, especially the *campesinos*, are welcome but in which the proletarian party is the determining factor.

The perspectives of the *Terceristas* and the PSN, had nothing in common with this method. Rather, they pursued the policy of a class collaborationist People's Front, tying the workers and peasants to the programme of the bourgeoisie, guaranteeing the bourgeoisie that there would be no expropriations after the revolution, nor the establishment of a workers' state.

In May 1977, the *Terceristas*, in the name of the FSLN, issued its own *General Political-Military Platform of the FSLN*, a sixty-page document written by Humberto Ortega.[28] Surprisingly, for the time, the document made no mention of the Cuban revolution, and Fonseca was demoted to a single mention, as contributing to the FSLN's Historic Programme. Zimmerman quotes Humberto as defining the *Terceristas*' perspective as a "revolutionary democratic popular government", which had all the hall marks of Stalin's theory of stages. A theory which, amongst many other things, had laid the basis for the defeat of the Chinese revolution in 1925 and the military coup in Chile in 1973.

In fact, the *Tercerista* Tendency demonstrated its commitment to limit the FSLN to a secondary role in the post-revolution government by dropping 'Revolutionary' from its description of the 'Democratic and Popular Government'. It stressed that nationalisation of property should be limited to that belonging to the Somoza family; the land reform proposal was limited and vague. Previous FSLN demands for the immediate abolition of

---

27 Lenin, V., *A Militant Agreement for the Uprising*, 1905, CW8:158-166.
28 Ortega, H., Journal Latin American Perspectives 6(1)108-113, 1978.

the National Guard and formation of a 'Revolutionary, Patriotic and Popular Army' and armed popular militias disappeared. The *Terceristas* now accepted a call for a new army that would include elements of the National Guard. The Historic Programme had pledged solidarity with those struggling against US imperialism, for the withdrawal of US military bases from around the world, and championed the struggles of North American black people against racism. The new *Tercerista* programme omitted mention of US imperialism, stating that post-revolution Nicaragua should "have relations with all the nations in the world". The Historic Programme's references to the "odious discrimination" suffered by Miskito and Sumo Indians and black people of the Atlantic Coast was omitted.[29]

In the Pancasán guerrilla foco it is claimed there were just ten books to read, one of which was Margaret Randall's, *Cuban Women Today* [*La Mujer Cuban de Hoy*]. Building on the experiences of Cuba, but in contrast to Cuba which did not establish the Cuban Women's Federation until one year after the revolution (1960), the FSLN decided to launch and to channel significant energies and resources into establishing a mass women's organisation at an early stage of the struggle. In 1977, the FSLN launched the Association of Women Confronting the Nation's Problems, (AMPRONAC) and in doing so, declared it had broken with the concept that women's organisations should be totally subordinate to the parent organisation.

There is no doubt that AMPRONAC, one of the few mass organisations allowed by the Somoza regime, generated considerable support for the FSLN and this was attributed to its being an organisation in which the masses of women could participate, obtain political education, raise their questions, voice their opinions openly and without fear, and learn leadership skills. Molyneux claims that, by the summer of 1978, AMPRONAC, with some 8,000 members, was stimulating and coordinating "a large part of women's grass roots involvement in the revolution."[30]

On the women's question, the practice of the FSLN was ground-breaking but the content of its programme was limited. The 1969 Historic Programme as it appears in *Sandanistas Speak* had:

> Emancipation of women: The Sandinista people's revolution will abolish the odious discrimination that women have been subjected to compared to men, it will establish economic, political, and cultural equality between woman and man. A. It will pay special attention to the mother and child, B. It will eliminate prostitution and other social vices through which the

---

29 Zimmerman. op. cit.

30 Molyneux, M., *Mobilisation without emancipation?* Feminist Studies, 11(2)227-254, 1985.

dignity of women will be raised, C. It will put an end to the system of servitude which is reflected in the tragedy of the abandoned working mother, D. It will establish for children born out of wedlock equal protection by the revolutionary institutions, E. It will establish day-care centres for the care of children of working women, F. It will establish a two-month maternity leave before and after birth for women who work, and G. It will raise women's political, cultural, and levels through their participation in the revolutionary process.

The programme, as re-written in 1977, by Humberto Ortega stated:

> We Will Struggle to End Discrimination Against Women: Women will be treated equally with men. We will struggle to end prostitution and servitude. Mothers will receive the complete protection of the state and all women shall be encouraged to organise in defense of their rights.

When this latter version was published, there were world-wide mass demonstrations demanding the right for every woman to control her own body. A woman's right to choose was a major concern for any political activist. This omission from the FSLN programme was especially worrying because of the toll in human misery due to the Somoza regime's ban on abortion. Molyneux had shown that poverty meant that many pregnant women sought illegal, back-street or self-induced abortions, so many that botched abortions accounted for nearly two-thirds of admissions to the main women's hospital in Managua.

By the end of 1977, revolution was in the air and the *Terceristas* responded by showing that the petty-bourgeois could be revolutionary, launching a series of attacks on National Guard barracks, which were claimed successful because they demonstrated that the FSLN was still in existence and active as a fighting force, and when the dust settled, found its numbers had increased from about 150 to nearly 500.[31] Interestingly, many of the guerrillas captured during these attacks identified themselves as 'Radical Christians'.

4) REVOLUTION: THE FSLN COMES TO POWER

Pedro Joaquin Chamorro, the well-known editor of *La Prensa*, and popular journalist had gained the respect and sympathy of broad sectors of the population, and had become the major spokesperson of the national bourgeoisie opposed to the Somoza family. On 10 January, 1978, the Somozas made a grave error in celebrating the New Year by having Chamorro murdered on his way to work. Over 120,000 mourners, predominantly workers and lower middle-class people participated in the funeral.

---

31 Ortega, H., *Nicaragua - Strategy for Victory*, *Granma* 27 January, 1980.

There followed an explosion of popular protest. The trade unions and the UDEL called a general strike on 23-24 January, which, according to the US Embassy, successfully shut down eighty per cent of businesses not only in Managua but also in the provincial capitals of Granada, León, and Matagalpa. However, the big capitalists of the Banamérica Group (representing interests in sugar, cattle, coffee, and retailing) and the BANIC Group (with interests in cotton, coffee, beer, lumber, and construction) did not participate.

The Somoza dictatorship had created the conditions for a 'national revolution'. As in tsarist Russia, and in Iran under the tyranny of the Shah, the bourgeoisie, petty-bourgeoisie, peasantry, salaried and proletariat shared a common interest in the overthrow of the autocracy. The crucial question was which class would give the political leadership to that revolution and determine its class content. The opposition forces, from the *Partido Conservador* (the traditional bourgeois opposition party) across the political spectrum to the PSN and FSLN, organised themselves into a bloc, the child of UDEL, called the Broad Opposition Front (*Frente Amplio Opositor*, FAO).

The small employers launched a shut-down with the slogans: 'peaceful resistance', and 'don't leave your homes' to dampen popular mobilisation. The shut-down lasted twelve days. Under pressure from the US embassy to end its actions, the FAO capitulated, and thereby demonstrated what hopeless and treacherous allies they were. In a country like Nicaragua, with a weak bourgeoisie closely tied to the apron strings of imperialism, any popular front deals could only be episodic and partial. Events in Nicaragua fully confirmed the Trotskyist perspective that the national bourgeoisie in semi-colonial countries will never carry the democratic and anti-imperialist struggle to completion because the independent mobilisation of the workers and peasants threatens their material interests, especially their profitable links with US imperialism.

Many of Somoza's businesses and factories were burned to the ground. The first to be torched was Somoza's plasma business, known to the Managuans as the 'House of Dracula'. This was where blood was taken from Managuan drunks and down-and-outs brought there by the Guard. The blood was then sold on the international market. But Somoza felt reassured, major sectors of the bourgeoisie were not supporting the action and he believed he could ride out the storm.

On 26 February, 1978, in Monimbó, a community on the outskirts of Masaya the country's fourth largest city, a protest march against the murder of Chamorro was brutally dispersed by the Guards. Monimbó exploded with rage, releasing decades of pent-up bitterness. The inhabitants held off the National Guard for a week, rocks against bullets, handguns against tanks.

The fighting continued until some 200 people were dead and the Guards triumphant.[32] Members of the *Tercerista* Tendency arrived soon after and awarded the Monimbó leaders the status of FSLN militants, with rank of military commanders in the guerrilla organisation. In this way they were recruited to the FSLN. During the rest of 1978 and increasingly in the early months of 1979, growing numbers of popular urban insurrections against the Somoza regime occurred. Sometimes they were spontaneous, as in Monimbó, sometimes they were part of a planned offensive by the FSLN.

It was during the spring of 1978 that the FSLN began organising coffee and cotton workers into Nicaragua's first rural trade union, the Association of Agricultural Workers (*Asociación de Trabajadores del Campo* – ATC). Because of the nature of the FSLN as a guerrilla organisation, its work within the ATC was, at first, sporadic and often ill-sustained, waxing and waning as the guerrilla struggle required.

On 22 August, 1978, the FSLN staged the most daring and spectacular guerrilla action in Latin American history. Led by Edén Pastora,[33] a group of FSLN guerrillas dressed in National Guard uniforms infiltrated and seized the National Palace while both the Senate and Chamber of Deputies were in session. The action was seen by the FSLN as hugely successful. After two days, the government agreed to release about fifty FSLN members held in Somoza's prisons.[34] On the very same day, 12,000 hospital workers (on a national strike for a month) were joined by the Union of Carpenters, Fitters, Bricklayers and Allied Trades (*Sindicato de la Construcción*, SCAAS) and workers at the University of León.

The FAO called for another nationwide lockout, but with no pay for the workers, and by 4 September, eighty per cent of all economic life was again paralysed. Simultaneously, the FSLN launched a series of actions across the country, intending to occupy a number of towns and cities and proclaim a provisional government. One major battle was in the city of Matagalpa, in which about 500 students played an important role. This action was not organised by the FSLN, but red and black flags and bandanas flooded the city while the uprising lasted. The events in Matagalpa demonstrated two things: that events and the masses were ahead of the FSLN leadership and that, by default, the FSLN was popularly accepted as the leadership of the revolution.

Before the revolution, the situation in which the FSLN had placed itself, with a guerrilla-ist structure, meant it could not be a mass organisation. Nevertheless, the revolutionary upsurge was, itself, placing the FSLN in

---

32 Benjamin, A., *Nicaragua: Dynamics of an unfinished Revolution*, Walnut, 1989.

33 '*Comandante Cero*', of the *Tercerista* Tendency, an ex-member of the Nicaraguan Conservative Party who would later desert to the counter-revolution.

34 Borge, op. cit., 1983.

the leadership. In every student demonstration, in every strike, in every confrontation, even where the FSLN was entirely absent, the masses were raising the Sandinista flag and the dead were being buried wrapped in Sandinista colours. Cabezas claims three factors played a major role in this popularity: the FSLN was the only organisation that was seen as prepared to go all the way to get rid of Somoza, the example of the Cuban revolution, and the glamour of guerrillaism.

However, the FSLN forces allocated to taking the cities were ridiculously small, the bulk of their cadres being retained in the rural areas along the frontiers with Honduras and Costa Rica. FSLN commandos reportedly occupied Masaya, León, Jinotepe, Diriamba, and Estelí but soon retreated before National Guard and army units supported by air attacks. Estelí was the last to be retaken and was made an example of. Only torrential rains saved Estelí being razed to the ground by a blizzard of phosphorus bombs. This fierce repression, including attacks on the middle classes, led to the complete and total political isolation of the Somoza regime.

On 13 September, 1978, Somoza suspended all constitutional rights for a period of thirty days throughout the country. Previously he had suspended constitutional rights in only the Departments of Managua and Estelí. On 12 October, the suspension of rights was extended for a further six months. It became clear that Somoza's strategy was to affect the greatest slaughter possible under the cover of the armed actions to break the will of the people. Thousands of homes were destroyed, the harvesting of cotton and coffee crops seriously disrupted, and over 5,000 people killed, with ten times that number injured or wounded. During these operations Somoza took pains to ensure all army officers (even those in nominally administrative positions) bloodied their hands, so that a coalition between officers with 'clean hands' and the FAO was not possible.

It became clear that, while the actions of the FSLN were widely welcomed by the local populations, at least initially, there was an almost complete lack of organised support. A serious weakness of the armed offensive was that it was made according the FSLN's timetable and not by the level of activity of the masses. The activities of the FSLN commandos – mainly collecting arms and ambushing National Guardsmen – left little room for the locals to participate. Such an approach revealed a serious lack of appreciation or historical knowledge of the ways in which masses mobilise to overthrow oppressive regimes. In Cuba it was quite clear that there was a general uprising against Batista. This was not yet the situation in Nicaragua, the actions of the FSLN were separate from, and to a certain extent, counterproductive for the mass movement.

The result of the September actions was that Somoza's reign of terror was imposed with increased ferocity; the violence was terrible, disappearances and murders were widespread, carried out by paramilitary gangs acting with total impunity. The National Guard was given a free hand and killed indiscriminately. After the September events a sharp downturn in mass struggles occurred, but it was only three months before the workers dared to come out on the streets in a demonstration.

Internationally, the atrocities being committed by the National Guard had become an embarrassment to President Carter and the US Administration. In November, the Organisation of American States published a report charging the National Guard with many gross violations of human rights. The United Nations passed a resolution condemning the actions of the Somoza regime.

At this moment, the PSN and Nicaraguan Communist Party (PCN – a small breakaway from the PSN favouring armed struggle) and fellow travellers formed the United People's Movement (MPU) and launched themselves as a working-class organisation independent of the bourgeoisie, calling for the establishment of Workers' Defence Committees and Civil Defence Committees. However, in early December 1978, the MPU revealed its Stalinist nature when it called for a government of Democratic Unity of all anti-Somoza forces, with a political platform determined by the national bourgeoisie.

The surge in revolutionary actions had its effect on the FSLN. In circumstances where the movement is going forward, it is usual for differences between tendencies and factions to be reined in, and this is what happened in the FSLN. With the help of Cuban intermediaries, the three tendencies re-unified at the end of 1978, with a nine-member National Directorate, with three representatives from each of the three tendencies.

It is claimed that Castro himself was party to the discussions and pushed strongly for unification. In January 1979, representatives of the three tendencies of the FSLN visited Cuba. The visit was not made public and all those who travelled did so with false identity papers. Fidel Castro, the only person with sufficient authority to do so, explained that Cuban help was conditional on a re-united FSLN.

> Fidel Castro… made unification of the tendencies a condition of his help… Castro told the FLSN leaders to stop messing around, to unite because (otherwise) they would be destroyed.[35]

At the organisational level, Castro's action was entirely correct, but at the political level he advised a class-collaborationist perspective, for a mixed

---

35 Blanco, F., and Dolores, M., *La Nicaragua de los Somoza*: 1936-1979, 2012.

NICARAGUA: A COUNTRY THAT DID NOT FINISH ITS REVOLUTION   193

economy that would encourage private industrialists and capitalist farmers, for a bourgeois democratic regime. These views would be publicly expressed in two speeches, both made on the anniversary of the 1953 attack on the Moncada barracks. The first was only days after the victory of the Sandinistas, the second, a year later on 27 July, 1980.

A communiqué from the nine-member Joint National Directorate (*Dirección Nacional Conjunta* – DNC), the new ruling body of the FSLN, made no suggestion that the struggle in which they were engaged was to establish a workers' state. It has been suggested that the FSLN was being duplicitous, that it had a 'secret' policy document, 'The Seventy-Two-Hour Document', in which it defined itself as a Marxist-Leninist Party committed to the Dictatorship of the Proletariat.[36] In La Botz' book the phrase 'Dictatorship of the Proletariat' was placed within single quotation marks, suggesting it to be a quote when, in fact, the phrase does not occur in the document. There was nothing in the Seventy-Two-Hour Document that contradicted the public statements of the FSLN.

The *Terceristas* had been responsible for initiating the discussions with bourgeois parties and for the August/September offensive. Despite the serious political and military errors that had been made, the GPP came out in support of the *Terceristas*, as did the TP after a short delay. The TP, the most left-leaning of the three tendencies, in complete opposition to everything Lenin wrote, stated (emphasis added):

> For us the (Somoza) dictatorship was and still is the main obstacle ... For this reason we have appealed for the unity not only of the democratic and progressive forces, but of the people as a whole without excluding the bourgeoisie itself... the *proletariat is never sectarian, and always seeks the general interest of the nation, without having separate intentions of its own or putting its own interests first.*[37]

By the end of 1978 there appeared to be no fundamental differences within the FSLN. Unification of the three tendencies had been on the acceptable basis that unity with elements of the national-bourgeoisie was a means of getting rid of the Somoza dictatorship, but also on the totally unreal expectation that national independence could be obtained with a bourgeois-democratic state.

1978 had seen a general upsurge of protests across the country; student demonstrations, workers on strike, rallies, factory closures, spontaneous urban uprisings, and even condemnatory sermons from the pulpits. The anti-Somoza bourgeoisie, together with the Roman Catholic Church, recognised

36 La Botz, D., *The Nicaraguan Revolution*, 2018, Haymarket.
37 *Revista Dialogo Social*, interview with Jaime Wheelock Roman, 1 November, 1978.

the highly explosive state of the class struggle in Nicaragua. Seeking to avert the threat of a revolution by the workers and peasants, these elements turned for support to the Carter administration in the US and European Social Democracy. They hoped to establish a bourgeois democracy which would limit or eliminate Somoza's power before there was a revolution, leaving them free to develop the exploitation of the workers and peasants for their own profit.

The Nicaraguan national-bourgeoisie desperately pressed the US to insist Somoza resign and prevent the 'Marxist' FSLN seizing power at the head of a popular rebellion. Their hopes had been raised by President Jimmy Carter and his 'human rights' policy. The US ruling class was, however, far from willing to dump its trusted stooge, though arms supplies were suspended (because they could quickly be replaced by supplies from Israel and Argentina), and Somoza was urged to reach a deal with the bourgeois opposition. Unfortunately for US policy, Somoza, was intransigent, having no intention of allowing democratic elections, and refusing to resign, believing that sheer repression would crush the opposition.

But by the end of 1978 many Nicaraguan businessmen, and the international banks, were re-assessing the security of their investments. Capital to the value of US$220 million flew abroad, while investment dropped like a stone. Military expenditure rose sharply, the balance of payments deficit rocketed, and, with it, came inflation. The GNP fell sharply (by about twenty-five per cent), real wages decreased by as much as ten per cent, while unemployment rose; employers responded by requiring those still employed do the work of those they had just sacked.

4.1) THE FALL OF SOMOZA

Alfonso Robelo Callejas, a key bourgeois figure, an industrialist and President of the Nicaraguan Development Institute (INDE) with close links to BANIC, warned the US Administration in a newspaper interview, that "if Somoza continues in power, giving the people no option but armed insurrection, the country will be in danger of falling under communist rule". In March, Robelo would establish the Nicaraguan Democratic Movement (*Movimiento Democrático Nicaragüense*, MDN) and soon after would be a major figure in the FSLN's 'Government of National Reconstruction'.

The Somoza dictatorship in Nicaragua was now so brutal and inefficient that, by the start of 1979, the US Administration understood his remaining in power would spark a revolution. President Carter moved to replace the Somoza family with a bourgeois regime with a broader base. No-one was expecting the mass upsurge of late May to early July 1979. Carter would be in the process of ditching Somoza even as the revolution began.

On 1 February, 1979, on the initiative of the *Tercerista* Tendency, the FSLN established the National Patriotic Front (*Frente Patriótico Nacional*, FPN) in partnership with the Group of Twelve, the Independent Liberal Party (*Partido Liberal Independiente*, PLI[38]), the Popular Social Christian Party (*Partido Popular Social Cristiano*, PPSC[39]), the Maoist Workers' Front (*Frente Obrero*, FO[40]), and the MPU.[41] The FPN had a multi-class appeal, including political support from elements of the FAO and the private sector. For the FSLN, this approach was a natural consequence of its perspective that, in the national struggle, the contradiction between 'the people' and Somoza was primary, and class contradictions within 'the people' were secondary.[42]

The three tendencies were now working together with formal unification in March 1979. Soon after, heavy fighting broke out throughout the country. By then the FSLN was better equipped with weapons flowing in from Venezuela, Panama, and Cuba, mostly through Costa Rica.

By this time, women within the FSLN were officially participating in all aspects of combat and civilian life equally with men. They were obliged to carry the same twenty-kilogram backpacks as men; and men, likewise, were required to engage in traditional 'female tasks' such as food preparation. Men heavily outnumbered women in leadership positions within the FSLN but a feature was made of women-only battalions which marched in rallies organised by the FSLN, such as the one held in 1979 in the town of Carazo where walls were adorned with the slogan: 'No revolution without women's emancipation; no emancipation without revolution'. Being equal within the ranks of the organisation was extremely important to the morale of the women of the FSLN:

> Women here participated in the revolution not at the level of the kitchen but at the level of combatant and at the level of political leadership. ... In fact, women acquired a tremendous moral authority ... It would be difficult for any woman combatant to allow some man to raise his hand to hit her, to mistreat her. Because there is an authority to her, a moral authority (that is) reflected even in intimate relations. The conception of the relationship has changed...[43]

---

38 A small formation claiming to represent patriotic professionals.
39 Break-away from the Social Christian Party.
40 A splinter group with its own militia, MILPAS.
41 Amador, F., and Santiago, S., *Where is Nicaragua Going?*, IP 11 June, 1979.
42 Chinchilla, *Women* ... op cit.
43 Dora Maria Tellez, quoted in Chinchilla, op. cit.

At the end of May 1979, as the 15,000-strong National Guard began to crumble and lose control of many areas of the country in the face of spontaneous mass actions, the FSLN decided to launch a final offensive. On 4 June, the FSLN, as part of its insurrectionary strategy and to show its strength, called a general strike which was massively supported by both workers and peasants. By 8 June, as many as twenty-five towns and villages in the north-west of the country were fully under Sandinista control.

FSLN leaders Daniel Ortega, Jaime Wheelock, and Tomás Borge, called for a general mobilisation, and for a final offensive. The masses in Managua and the main cities had been self-mobilising since May, so the FSLN guerrilla columns often arrived after the main fighting was over. It was the speed with which the workers' mobilisations took place, "the sudden and abrupt increase in the number of 'ordinary citizens' who began to participate actively, independently and effectively in political life" as Lenin had put it, that showed Nicaragua was experiencing a 'real revolution'.[44]

On 9 June, fierce battles broke out in the working-class districts of Managua as part of the general strike; attacks were made on the National Guard HQ, the very heart of Somoza's regime. Barricades were built with whatever materials were available. Thousands of people demonstrated in their own areas, with the middle-class districts joining in. The National Guard patrols remained active on the streets, but their morale was cracking and Guards soon began to desert in their hundreds, if not thousands.

Local barracks fell to the demonstrators who proceeded to arm themselves as local militias under the control of local Civil Defence Committees (CDCs) which arose spontaneously on a block-by-block basis, becoming the basic unit of self-organisation of the rank and file of the urban masses. Despite their membership being overwhelmingly the young and very young, they assumed such vital tasks as defence against National Guard patrols, provision of first aid, and soon many took over city administrative tasks such as food distribution. In the early days of the revolution, the militias and the CDCs were hardly separable, both in terms of personnel and in tasks undertaken. CDC militias dispensed justice to Somoza's National Guard and kept public order. At this moment, the CDCs were the armed bodies of men and women who held state power.

On 17 June, 1979, the FSLN agreed to the formation of a five-person Junta of the Nicaraguan Government of National Reconstruction, a provisional government in exile. The five members met in Costa Rica; Daniel Ortega for the FSLN Directorate, Moisés Hassan of the FPN, and Sergio Ramírez Mercado of The Twelve, (both members of the FSLN). The two

---

44 Lenin, V., *The Tasks of the Proletariat in Our Revolution*, CW 24 61-62, 1917.

business representatives were Violeta Barrios de Chamorro (the widow of *La Prensa's* editor), and Alfonso Robelo Callejas. This body reached an agreement known as the 'Puntarenas Pact', which called for the establishment of a mixed economy, political pluralism, and a non-aligned foreign policy. Free elections were to be held at a later date.

The proposed Junta and the Puntarenas Pact were endorsed by the FAO and the Superior Council of Private Enterprise (COSEP), the largest employers' grouping. On 22 June, 1979, the Junta agreed that the Constituent Assembly, which had been part of the FSLN's programme, should be dropped in favour of a non-elected consultative, Council of State which would represent "all political, economic and social forces who contributed to the overthrow of the Somoza dictatorship" and would share legislative powers with the Junta. The thirty-three appointees to the Council were to be divided amongst about twenty organisations, on the understanding that the bourgeois elements would have a clear majority.

The Junta agreed to incorporate 'patriotic' elements of the National Guard into a new non-partisan army. The programme guaranteed the rights of private property, apart from that belonging to Somoza, which was to be nationalised. The Council could approve laws submitted to it by the Junta or initiate its own legislation. However, it would require a two-thirds majority for the Council to veto Junta-initiated legislation. A separate Supreme Court was appointed by the Junta and approved by the Council. The combination of Junta and Council of State – with the undertaking to preserve capitalism in the form of a mixed economy, to preserve elements of the National Guard as the basis for a new army and with the masses effectively excluded – was undoubtedly a Stalin-style, Popular Front. But this was all decided in the unreal, secluded atmosphere of the Costa Rican capital, begging the question of which direction the FSLN would travel when the masses intervened.

The *New York Times*[45] explained that a seventeen-person advisory group, composed overwhelmingly of bourgeois figures, had been established to guide the proposed government's economic thinking. Figures such as Arturo Cruz, a former economist with the Inter-American Development Bank in Washington was appointed President of the Central Bank, Roberto Mayorga ex-secretary of the US-inspired Central American Common Market was appointed Minister of Economic Planning, Joaquín Cuadra Chamorro, with his close connections with Banamérica, was in charge of finance, and the Minister of Defence was Bernardino Larios, an ex-colonel in the National Guard who had deserted only in 1978. Only four ministries: Agricultural

---

45 10 July, 1979

Reform, Culture, Interior, and Social Welfare were allocated to known FSLN members.

The FAO, with such eminent persons as Miguel Obando y Bravo, Catholic Archbishop of Managua, met to endorse Carter's plan to remove Somoza from office, but their proposals included no governmental role for the FSLN, which was asked to surrender its weapons.[46] Ortega had been prepared to be part of a coalition regime with a majority of bourgeois elements, even accepting the incorporation of National Guard units into the new army, but not prepared to be excluded and disarmed. The FSLN representatives walked out of the meeting and, before any further discussion, the revolutionary upsurge blew any agreement out of the water.

Isolated, Somoza attempted to retain power through a series of bloody actions by the National Guard. But without US support, his regime rapidly disintegrated and the mass killings of women and children triggered a national uprising centred on the towns, so that when the guerrilla forces arrived they found them already liberated by the urban populations.[47] The USA desperately tried to salvage something from the wreckage, calling for the Organisation of American States (OAS) to send a so-called 'peace-keeping force' and prevent a Sandinista take-over. But, so great was the enthusiasm generated by the overthrow of Somoza, that not one Latin American regime agreed. When Estelí was liberated by a guerrilla column, Somoza knew the situation was hopeless and handed his resignation to the US ambassador. He fled to Miami on 17 July, leaving behind a national debt of US$1.6 billion. A report by John Pilger claims that most of this had been stolen by the Somoza-ists and never actually arrived in Nicaragua.[48] But there was also US$80 million material damage to the infrastructure – water, electricity, housing, etc., – and reserves of only US$3.5 million.

On 13 July, the Junta made a number of ceasefire proposals, including agreeing to the USA's last desperate attempt to retain some direct control in Nicaragua by the integration of 'healthy' elements of the National Guard into any new army. On the same day, President Carter ordered two amphibious assault ships to assume positions off the Nicaraguan coast. But this was an empty threat: neither the Carter nor, subsequently, the Reagan administrations were capable of moving directly against the Nicaraguan revolution. The revolution occurred too soon after the defeat of the US army in Vietnam, largely due to opposition to the war by millions of youth, workers and the soldiers themselves.

---

46 Pastor, R., *Condemned to Repetition. The US and Nicaragua*, Princeton UP, 1987.
47 Roberts, op cit. 2016.
48 Pilger, J., July 19, 1979: *Nicaragua's Sandinista Revolution Remembered*. Video.

The numbers spontaneously demonstrating on the streets were many orders of magnitude greater than those that could have been mobilised by the FSLN, who had fewer than 500 lightly-armed guerrillas. Mostly, small columns of guerrillas, often as few as twelve, entered already-liberated cities although there was a real battle for Léon, where the National Guard rallied and put up a fight, to be defeated by a guerrilla column in which four of the seven commanders were women.[49]

Humberto Ortega, the main military strategist of the FSLN later described the situation:

> [W]e always took the masses into account, but more in terms of supporting the guerrillas, so that the guerrillas could defeat the National Guard. What actually happened... was that it was the guerrillas who provided the support for the masses... It was not a mass movement responding to a call by the Sandinistas; it was a response to a situation nobody had foreseen... thousands of people fought with machetes, picks and shovels and home-made bombs.[50]

When the FSLN columns reached Managua on the afternoon of 19 July, the city was already in the hands of the popular militias formed during the insurrectionary general strike and under whose onslaught the National Guard had disintegrated. The remnants surrendered to the Sandinistas or fled to the provinces and into Honduras. The Bunker, the National Guard HQ in the heart of Managua and symbol of the Somoza regime, was captured by the urban masses who distributed the thousands of weapons they found there amongst themselves. The self-mobilisation of the working class, the peasants and the petty bourgeoisie was decisive in bringing about the collapse of the Somozista state. The last US hope of engineering a 'controlled' hand-over of power was gone.

Virtually all studies of the revolution note two things: that the revolutionary masses were, by and large, concentrated in the urban slums and consisted of casual labourers, artisans, and petty merchants; and that the 'revolutionary vanguard' of the FSLN followed rather than led the insurrection. The entry of the masses pushed the FSLN to the left, not only in terms of accelerating the war against Somoza but also in terms of the radicalisation of the FSLN and the revolution's goals.

By the spring of 1979, committed FSLN militants recently recruited from CDCs, often only a month or so previously, were leading the day-to-day activity of the revolution, distributing the weapons available, organising community support, food supplies, and care of wounded, deciding when and where to strike, and, in the process, recruiting and training new cadres.

49 Flynn, P, *Women Challenge the Myth*, Stanford, 1983.
50 Ortega, H., *Nicaragua - Strategy for Victory*, Granma, 27 January, 1980.

The Junta of National Reconstruction arrived in Managua on 20 July, 1979. Almost all of the twenty organisations that were to have been allocated seats on the Council of State, had been by-passed by the revolution. It was obvious that the composition of the Council, as decided in Costa Rica, did not reflect the reality of mass action on the streets, and the balance of forces within Nicaragua. It had been agreed that the FSLN would name only a minority of the thirty-three appointees on the Council, but with the change in the relationship of forces, the FSLN Directorate proposed (and the Junta agreed) that the Council be increased to forty-seven; fourteen new organisations formed during and since the revolution needed representation, eight organisations were dropped.

The Junta allocated nine seats to the Sandinista Defence Committees (*Comités de Defensa Sandinista* – CDSs), three to the Sandinista Workers' Federation, and two to the Agricultural Workers' Association. Two seats were given to the National Union of Agriculturalists and Cattlemen (UNAG), and one seat each to the Sandinista Women's Organisation (AMNLAE), the teachers' union, the health workers' union, the Sandinista youth organisation, and the armed forces, even though these were still in the process of formation. To give the FSLN a majority, six seats were allocated to the FSLN itself. Two seats went to the CGT-I, and one to the PCN-led Confederation of Trades Union Action and Unification (CAUS). The remaining seats were allocated to big business, right-wing political parties and the two right-wing union federations.

This action, together with the FSLN having control of the "coercive instruments of the state apparatus" – the Sandinista People's Army (*Ejército Popular Sandinista*, EPS) and the new police force – was seen as an event similar to that in the Cuban Revolution when the bourgeois ministers began to quit the government.[51]

Opponents of the FSLN cried 'foul', viewing the addition of the new members as a power grab. A recurring theme in *La Prensa* from then on was for the immediate convocation of the Council with its original composition, for the FSLN to respect the Puntarenas accords and behave 'democratically'. This call was echoed by all bourgeois organisations; but the Junta assumed power in a very different situation than had been originally envisaged. The effects of the civil war in 1978 and 1979 were far more devastating for the country than the Cubans had faced. The National Guard had left the economy in ruins, the cities were in ruins, many factories, stores and shops were in ruins, much of the housing in the poor districts had been razed. The first and

---

51 *New Advance in the Nicaraguan Revolution*, USec Fourth International, Sept. 28, 1980.

immediate problem for the new regime was organising the collection and distribution of food and water. The next would be to reactivate the economy.

The Frente's influence among the young was overwhelming and the Sandinista Youth (JS-19) had the very important job of organising those young people who had made up the bulk of the anti-Somoza fighting forces, and tying them in a more permanent way to the FSLN.

The US Administration was fearful that the Nicaraguan Revolution would spread throughout Central America. The Nicaraguan masses had shown, above everything else, that when the workers and the poor peasants united in struggle, the might of US imperialism could not stop them. The overthrow of Somoza had sparked sit-ins, strikes, land occupations and marches in sympathy, especially in El Salvador where the US hurriedly organised a preventative coup against General Carlos Humberto Romero. US policy focussed on how best to contain the revolution and 'promote stability' in the region.

US policy flew in the face of reality: the revolution meant a rapid and substantial improvement in living conditions, an increase in employment and many fewer people going hungry. Poor peasants and farm labourers, backed by militia, launched their own land reforms. Workers formed defence committees and took over and managed factories owned by those who had openly supported Somoza. Rationing improved nutritional standards and protected the value of workers' wages.

5) THE JUNTA OF NATIONAL RECONSTRUCTION (JULY-DECEMBER 1979)

The Junta of National Reconstruction was a governing body comprised of the petty-bourgeois FSLN in alliance with the bourgeoisie, whether the latter liked it or not. On 22 August, 1979, the Junta issued the 'Fundamental Statute' abolishing the constitution, Presidency and Congress. The Junta would rule by unappealable decree under emergency powers. Policy came from the nine-member Directorate, the ruling body of the FSLN, transmitted by Daniel Ortega for the Junta's discussion and approval.

It was clear that the Directorate expected a degree of hostility, at least initially, from Nicaraguan capitalists, and the Statute contained clear statements to the effect that the trade unions should be integral to the drawing up, operation, control and assessment of production on both farm and factory. This was an important mechanism by which the FSLN hoped to overcome the 'arrogance', 'excessive centralism' and 'hierarchical methods' of the Nicaraguan capitalists and their managers, and so increase production and modernise the Nicaraguan economy.

Much space was given in the columns of *Barricada* (the central organ of the FSLN) to union representatives' attempts to persuade companies to form production councils to ensure they were following government guidelines on pay but also, and more importantly, to ensure that production targets were met and there was no industrial or economic sabotage. Economic sabotage included withholding of investment, disinvestment through allowing plant and machinery to run down, illegal sale of plant and machinery for dollars, which were then sent to banks abroad, pocketing of government credits and low interest loans and even direct sabotage of machinery.[52]

The CGT-I raised the question of how workers' representatives could be expected to detect economic sabotage without having direct access to all aspects of management and investment decisions, but the Ministry of Labour was entirely unsympathetic to such a common-sense approach. These gentlemen were reformists who, like so many before them, stopped short before the threshold of the business enterprise and its 'commercial confidences'. Their accounts remained the capitalists' secrets. The principle of 'non-interference' dominated but, of course, only by opening the books of all Nicaraguan businesses, and not just those going bust, could the FSLN hope to end economic sabotage. Such a move would prove impossible within the constraints of the mixed economy.

Union representatives on the factory floor exerted real pressure on the owners and managers to increase production and better workers' conditions, but by no stretch of the imagination was it workers' control. It soon became clear that the prime purpose of this style of 'workers' control' was to establish greater labour discipline and increase production. The workers quickly found they had very little input to the process, apart from working harder and/or longer.

While the workers did gain many benefits initially, the system was essentially a means of increasing the rate of exploitation, and in a so-called mixed economy, that meant capitalist exploitation. The FSLN were relying on a layer of managers and technocrats from the Somoza era and a new layer of party members and trade union officials to extract more surplus value from the workers. In a society where there is generalised want no better way could be found for the generation of a bureaucracy separated from the masses of people.

But the scheme was not effective even by its own goals. Economic sabotage, referred to as 'decapitalisation' was too weighty a problem to be overcome by pressurising individual workers to increase their output,

---

52 Harris, R., *Evaluating Nicaragua's Agrarian Reform*, Latin American Perspectives, 14(1)101-114, 1987.

because decapitalisation meant that the workers had no machines and no raw materials to work with. Nor did the scheme have any means whereby the workers could inspect financial records such as invoices and delivery notes, so there was no way of checking where company funds or products were going – Miami bank accounts or the black market. Such a mechanism was essential to combat the most common form of decapitalisation – over-billing imports and under-billing exports with the difference being paid into a Miami bank account. Nor was there any vehicle whereby the workers could take control of an enterprise if they found corruption and industrial sabotage. The FSLN version of 'workers' control' had a fundamental flaw – it was geared to increase capitalist production and profit, not to rationally plan production for the needs of the Nicaraguan workers and peasants. The *Christian Science Monitor* estimated that between 1979 and 1988 nearly US$2 billion was lost to Nicaragua through decapitalisation.

The new government inherited a country in ruins, with an estimated two per cent of the population (50,000) killed in the civil war, 120,000 in exile in neighbouring countries, 600,000 homeless and 40,000 orphans to be cared for. Food and fuel supplies were exhausted yet the attitude of the vast majority of Nicaraguans toward the revolution was decidedly optimistic. Most Nicaraguans saw the Sandinista victory as an opportunity to create a system free of the political, social, and economic inequalities of the universally-hated Somoza regime.

The first phase was taking into public ownership (under the now-famous Decrees No. Three and No. Thirty-Eight) of all rural properties owned by the Somoza family and its associates, a total of 1 million hectares, 2,000 farms, representing just less than one quarter of Nicaragua's cultivable land. These were generally amongst the most modern farms, more accurately agro-industrial plantations, and so were usually retained intact with the farm workers encouraged to organise as state farms, worked as profitable enterprises. Contrary to popular opinion, the FSLN did not have 'Land to the Tiller' as a priority; its goal was to increase production, so very little of this land went to individual peasants, possibly as little as one per cent. Generally, large agro-export farms not owned by the Somozas were not affected by the agrarian reform. Other interests of the Somoza family which were expropriated totalled a quarter of all manufacturing.

Prior to 1979, Nicaragua's banking system consisted of the Central Bank of Nicaragua and several domestic and foreign-owned commercial banks. The three national banks, Banco America, Banco Centroamerica, and Banco Nicaraguense had been bankrupted by Somoza's economic policies, and were nationalised for the same reasons the UK government nationalised sections of the UK banking industry – to save it from the bankers.

Barricada, of 26 July, 1979, boasted Somoza's debts to Israel and Argentina for weaponry were abrogated, but failed to make clear that the Nicaraguan state had assumed bank debts of over US$200 million, repayment of which, with interest, would effectively bankrupt the country. In addition, shareholders were given very generous compensation, to assure the private sector, both abroad and at home, that the FSLN were 'good guys', people you could trust and work with. The class-collaborationist (mixed economy) perspective of the Sandinista leadership meant that even as they introduced much-needed reforms, they simultaneously implemented economic measures to appease imperialism, such as transferring private bank debts to the Nicaraguan people. The FSLN was locking Nicaragua into the international money market. By 1983, there would be a net outflow of half a billion US$ paid to overseas private banks.

To stop the haemorrhage of funds, foreign banks were prevented from receiving deposits from the public. However, in 1985, a decree loosened state control of foreign exchange by allowing the establishment of privately-owned local exchange houses. Insurance companies were nationalised and a National Insurance Institution established to take future payments and fulfil the terms of policies already held. That was done because the insurance companies were foreign, which meant an outflow of capital.

The new government nationalised all foreign trade in the principal agricultural products and established a state monopoly, greatly benefiting small and medium producers because the prices they had received previously were very much less than those on the international market. State monopoly of trade, a measure used in Russia, China and Cuba as part of establishing a workers' state would, however, in Nicaragua's mixed economy, become a means whereby the big landowners manipulated the government to extract fortunes.

The largest denomination notes, C$500 (500 Córdobas) and C$1,000 were withdrawn from circulation, to hit the pockets of those who had fled abroad taking with them suitcases of banknotes. Estimates put the loss to Somoza supporters at nearly C$200 million (US$20 million).

On 7 August, 1979, the Junta announced that all land and property seized during the revolution that had not belonged to the Somoza family had been taken 'illegally' and must be handed back to its owners. 'Land to the Tiller' was ended before it had properly begun. The FSLN was prepared to use the police to restore these lands to anti-Somoza bourgeois. National Guards who had fled to Honduras, frightened peasants in the border regions with no title to the land they worked, by saying that the FSLN was taking the peasant's land from them. This was the only time when the Contras made even the slightest headway amongst the peasants. These gains were soon reversed by changes in the land laws and the slogan of the Sandinistas in the border zones did become 'Land to whoever works it'.

To alleviate the disappointment of the landless, the government enacted a series of popular measures: laws were passed which forced landlords to rent underused or unused land at low rents which benefited thousands of peasants and squatters, a new credit policy was introduced which greatly increased available loans to peasants and small farmers. For peasants a moratorium was declared on debt interest repayments for bank loans.

The judicial system was left largely unaffected. While numerous court officials were dismissed, the basic court structure remained, with many openly bourgeois figures in positions of authority. The Supreme Court's authority was re-established with FSLN approval, and the appointment of a number of bourgeois figures including members of the Liberal Party and PPSC.[53] A special Agrarian Tribunal was created to deal with land seizures and rural property and, in several well-publicised cases, land seized from people other than the Somoza family was returned to its former owners.

In December 1979, the Directorate decided to shuffle Ministerial appointments to reflect the strength of the FSLN in the country. The Junta placed all nine Directorate members in charge of one or other Ministry. Including Humberto Ortega to Defence and Commander of the EPS, Henry Ruiz to Economic Planning, others continued in their posts, e.g. Jaime Wheelock as Agrarian Reform Minister.[54] This, together with the Junta's decision the previous October to put off the convening of the Council of State in order to increase its membership to forty-seven and alter its composition, sparked off a period of struggle with COSEP, which would result in the resignations of Violeta Chamorro and Robelo. This important consolidation of power in the hands of the FSLN was made under pressure of the masses, and appeared to be a deepening of the revolutionary process.

The establishment of an FSLN government gave a big impulse to the struggle of Nicaraguan women for equality and against oppression. The Fundamental Statute gave women legal equality with men, enacted stronger child-support laws; gave women the right to own land and join co-operative farms; and required wages to be paid to the woman worker not her husband. Attempts were made to implement these decisions, but the available resources

53 Benjamin, op. cit.

54 See Gorman, S., 'Power and Consolidation in the Nicaraguan Revolution', Journal of Latin American Studies Vol 13, No 1 for details of government changes in this period.

were not always sufficient. For example, the Statute required the provision of child-care facilities in larger factories and state farms; Borge, at the time, observed that it was easy to legislate that factories and farms should have day care centres but, due to the cost of construction, equipment, maintenance and staffing, few had actually been built.[55]

Divorce procedures were changed to the benefit of women, but there were delays. It was 1988 before restrictions such as a woman having to wait 300 days after a divorce before being allowed to remarry, or a woman convicted of adultery facing a two-year jail sentence and never being allowed to remarry, were removed from the statute book.

Marx explained that, even though a petty-bourgeois party was a contradictory phenomenon, it could still be revolutionary, but the contradictory nature of its goals (to harmonise the interests of capital and labour) meant that it is pulled in opposite directions.[56] Any resulting regime is highly contradictory in character and its course of action will depend on the character of the leadership, and the degree of involvement of the masses. Many welcome and progressive reforms were implemented after the seizure of power, but the tragedy of Nicaragua was the inability of the FSLN leadership to break decisively with its political roots, take the revolution forward and overthrow capitalism. All the efforts, courage and sacrifices of the Nicaraguan masses would not be enough to overcome this missing subjective element.

5.1) THE ROLE OF MOSCOW AND HAVANA

Leading figures on the left were enthusiastic about the Nicaraguan Revolution, drawing parallels between what was happening in Nicaragua with what had happened in Cuba twenty years previously. Both revolutions were correctly described as beginning under the leadership of a radical petty-bourgeois current, the J-26 and the FSLN. Both were distinguished by having ejected a military dictatorship by revolutionary means and having carried that struggle through to the end. In the process, the armed forces and the police had been smashed and replaced by a people's militia.

The Stalinist bureaucracy, itself in the last stages of decay and soon to collapse, made no effort to encourage a radical programme in Nicaragua, not only because it did not want problems with US imperialism, but also because it feared a successful revolution in any part of the world would open the question of workers' democracy in the USSR and threaten its position and privileges. The Moscow bureaucracy had, in reality, detested the Cuba revolution and it was two years after Castro's coming to power that it had been

---

55 Borge, T., *Women and the Nicaraguan Revolution*, Pathfinder, 1982.
56 Marx, K., *The Civil War in France*, Part III, 1871.

forced to accept the eradication of capitalism in Cuba as an accomplished fact. With Nicaragua, Moscow did its best to curtail the revolution and prevent its extension to the rest of the continent.

In a dialectical irony, as the Soviet bureaucracy collapsed, the Stalinist theory of revolution by stages was being played out by the FSLN. Stalinism had taught that only the fight for democracy was on the agenda in colonial and semi-colonial countries. The national liberation struggle had to be carried through to completion by the workers and peasants in alliance with the progressive elements of the national bourgeoisie. However, to maintain the alliance the oppressed layers had to curb their demands so as not to alienate the capitalists and landlords.

The Cubans needed allies in Latin America and had themselves only recently overthrown capitalism, but simultaneously, they saw the aid they received from the Soviet Union as their lifeline. This latter consideration combined with the realisation that they had failed to export guerrilla warfare to the rest of Latin America, would dominate their advice to the FSLN.

The initial aim of the Castro leadership had been to preserve capitalism, but this goal rapidly evaporated under the pressure of events. Cuba had carried out a sweeping and thorough-going agricultural reform; dividing the land between the peasants and co-operatives, expropriating foreign holdings and establishing a monopoly of foreign trade. On 17 May, 1959, the Cuban government enacted the Agrarian Reform Law which gave over 200,000 Cuban families their own land for the first time in their lives. Any holdings over 400 hectares (1,000 acres) were expropriated by the government and, crucially, foreign ownership of land was prohibited, incurring the undying hatred of the US sugar and fruit plantation owners, who had owned three-quarters of Cuba's most fertile land.

For the Cuban leaders, their priority was the needs of poor Cubans not rich Americans, to stand by the promises they had made and not bow to 'reality'. They chose to carry through the tasks of the bourgeois democratic revolution, which in the twentieth Century meant facing up to imperialism and its allies within Cuba. The Cuban leaders were truly committed to ending the social injustices inherent in imperialist domination and had faced each new challenge by taking the revolution forward. They broke with the programme on which they had taken power and, in confrontation with US imperialism, took steps which left them with one foot in socialism. This did not happen with the revolutionary leaders in Nicaragua and, as a consequence, the masses in Nicaragua – despite important gains – have been thrown back into misery.

Marxists should, of course, go by the facts. Unfortunately, all too often the events in Nicaragua were analysed not as they applied to Nicaragua but

presented as parallels to Cuba. Well-known figures overstated the seizure
of the Somoza holdings, gave too much importance to the resignations of,
for example, Violeta Chamorro and Alfonso Robelo from the Junta, and
presented the perspective as – "the 'Cuban Road' is undoubtedly taking
shape".[57] Others, such as the SWP(USA), were so enamoured of the FSLN
that they accepted the mixed economy perspective as the correct path for
Nicaragua and ditched Trotsky's theory of permanent revolution as no longer
valid. An infamous edition of their theoretical journal gave fifty pages to
Carlos Rafael Rodríguez (long-time Cuban Stalinist and CP member of
Batista's cabinet in 1942) to justify Stalin's theory of stages.[58]

In 1979 and 1980, the Cuban government called for an international
campaign of solidarity with Nicaragua. On 19 July, 1980, President Fidel
Castro spoke in Managua to half a million participants celebrating the first
anniversary of the Nicaraguan revolution. He likened Cuba, Grenada, and
Nicaragua to "three giants rising up to defend their right to independence,
sovereignty and justice, on the very threshold of imperialism".[59] At the
time, the actions of the FSLN government had given a powerful impetus
to the revolution in Grenada and the guerrilla struggles in El Salvador and
Guatemala, and inspired many young people in the imperialist heartlands
of America and Europe, who greeted the Nicaraguan victory enthusiastically
and gave it unqualified support.

But the Cuban leadership without Che had, what for the Nicaraguans
would turn out to be, a fatal flaw. Central to the defeat of the Nicaraguan
revolution would be the FSLN's lack of understanding of the nature of the
bourgeoisie. The theory which guided Sandinista practice was a peculiar and
eclectic mix of the Stalinist theory of stages and the Social Democratic mixed
economy, enhanced by ideas gained from co-operation with Catholic priests
in the Liberation Church. These found their way into the FSLN via the
dominant *Tercerista* Tendency.

The view of the Soviet bureaucracy – opposition to a socialist revolution
in Nicaragua – was reflected by the leaders of the Cuban Communist Party.
In an interview with the San Francisco Chronicle, 11 January, 1984, the Vice
President of Cuba, Carlos Rafael Rodríguez, endorsed the stagist perspective
of the FSLN, saying:

> [T]hey will have private enterprise in agriculture, industry and trade. They
> are not going to socialism, least of all to the Cuban model. We don't believe

57 Maitan, L., IP, 30 June, 1980.
58 Rodríguez, C., *Lenin and the Colonial Question*, New International, 1(1)93-144,
   1983.
59 In Stone, E., *Women and the Cuban Revolution*, Pathfinder, 1980.

that the Cuban model is to be exported either to Central America or to the rest of the world.

In December 1975, Castro, in his speech to the First Congress of the Cuban Communist Party, had said of the Cuban revolution:

[I]n the conditions of a country like Cuba, could the revolution limit itself simply to national liberation while maintaining a regime of capitalist exploitation? Or was it not necessary to move forward toward full social liberation as well?

Imperialism could not even tolerate a revolution of national liberation in Cuba. From the time of the first Agrarian Reform Law, the United States began to organise a military operation against Cuba. They were even less disposed to tolerate socialism in our country. The simple idea that a victorious revolution in Cuba could provide an example for all Latin America frightened the Yankee ruling circles. But the Cuban nation had no other alternative. The people could not be stopped.

Our national and our social liberation were inextricably bound up. Moving forward became a historic necessity. Standing still would have been an act of treason and cowardice that would have transformed us once again into a Yankee colony and wage slaves.

The Cubans had prioritised education and healthcare, making them the envy of most nations of the world. Cuba had launched a vast literacy crusade, an example the Nicaraguans followed and which helped convince many that Nicaragua was a Cuba in the making. A vast national network of Committees for the Defence of the Revolution (the Nicaraguan CDSs were very similar) was organised against counter-revolution. But the final steps taken by Cuba were what was missing in Nicaragua: the implementation of the agricultural transformation, introduction of central planning, and state ownership of the means of production.

Ten years later, on 11 January, 1985, Fidel Castro declared in *Barricada*:

Daniel Ortega… has been serious and responsible… the aims of the Sandinista Front (are)… a mixed economy, political pluralism and legislated foreign investment… You can have a capitalist economy. What you are not, without any doubt, going to have is a government serving the interests of the capitalists.

This is a good demonstration of why the Cuban leaders were described as men of action and not theoreticians.

The views expressed by the Cuban leadership, from the moment the FSLN came to power in July 1979, served to obstruct the course toward socialist revolution in Nicaragua. They approved the Sandinistas' preservation of the capitalist mixed economy; the lessons articulated in 1975, that a government cannot serve the interests of the working class and at the same time grant capitalism a free hand in the national economy, were reversed. The Cuban revolution, of course, had clearly shown it was impossible to satisfy the demands of the workers and *campesinos*, and the national bourgeoisie, and that it was impossible to develop the economy in any meaningful way, within the framework of capitalist property relations.

One area Castro steered well clear of was Nicaragua's need for a Leninist Party with internal democracy, and a society organised to give the working people a decisive say through Soviets. Not only were (and are) these missing from Cuba, but the support Cuba received at that time from the Soviet bloc would have ended overnight had Castro made such a statement.

Nicaragua is an economically-backward, dependent country, and its level of development at the time of the 1979 revolution was lower than Cuba's in 1959. Its resources, moreover, were heavily drained by the wars forced on it, first by Somoza and then by the Contras. It was both illusory and dangerous to act on the belief that Nicaragua, in an imperialist dominated world, could develop economically within its national borders on the basis of a regulated capitalist economy. Attempting such a strategy required major and ongoing political and economic concessions by the workers and peasants to the capitalist class, which could only undermine the revolution and pave the way for defeat. However, the notion that a poor and isolated country like Nicaragua could achieve socialism is ludicrous. All that Nicaragua could do was to take the first steps towards socialism by following the Cuban example and establishing a workers' state. That would have permitted the Sandinista government to respond to the economic sabotage of the national bourgeoisie and to eliminate the deformations inherent in the mixed economy.

However, to cite Cuba as an example for Nicaragua must allow for the exceptional circumstances under which the Cuban revolution developed and which may never be repeated. But one thing we can be absolutely sure of, the road to a workers' state and the dictatorship of the proletariat could not have had any worse consequences for the workers and peasants of Nicaragua than the mixed economy. At the very least, it would have bound the government and the working masses together in common cause. Such actions would have helped extend revolution to the rest of Central and Latin America. This was particularly the case in El Salvador and Guatemala where there were revolutionary movements which developed almost in parallel with and were heavily influenced by the Sandinista Revolution.

6) HOW FSLN GAINED AND RETAINED LEADERSHIP OF THE REVOLUTION

The speed at which the mass upsurge developed, and with which the Somoza regime was overthrown meant the FSLN, even if it had wanted to, was unable to recruit widely before the revolution had succeeded. It rode to power with a structure suited to guerrilla activities that did not allow for the participation of either FSLN members or the masses in decision-making processes regarding policy and the election (and possible recall) of leaders. The FSLN did not use the revolutionary period from September 1978 to July 1979 (when those active on the streets were genuine anti-Somoza-ists) to transform the FSLN into a political party with a mass membership.

Instead, the FSLN preserved an organisational form suited to the foco strategy, but which could not provide a structure by which workers and peasants could genuinely control either the party or the state apparatus. The structure of the FSLN remained one of command; the mass organisations were expected to implement the decisions of the Directorate, not to debate them. In line with this, one of the most common slogans at street demonstrations and meetings was 'National Directorate, we await your command'.

The FSLN membership was small, possibly only about 500, so there was an acute lack of personnel with either political or administrative experience. Moreover, the FSLN had to rely on middle-class professionals and technocrats, self-proclaimed Sandinistas, to administer the post-revolutionary state. Experience of every revolution from Russia onwards has shown the careerists are first in the queue for jobs, declaring their undying commitment to the regime.

True, the FSLN did recruit selected workers and peasants, but it did not open its doors to the masses, not least because, within the organisation, no structure existed to accommodate such numbers. Nor did the Directorate envisage introducing any organisational mechanism by which the masses could change governmental policy. But it appeared to have very well understood the actions required to preserve its unchallenged position as leader of the revolution.

Immediately after the revolution, the FSLN leadership adopted a strategy of bureaucratising the organs formed by the workers and peasants during the revolution and its immediate aftermath, and incorporating these into the reconstructed state apparatus. Five major mass representative organisations, with government support, enabled both a much greater degree of self-help for the people while allowing the FSLN to better exercise control over society. By the end of 1980, these mass organisations embraced a quarter of a million

Nicaraguans and were key in consolidating Sandinista governmental and state power.

6.1) THE LOCAL CIVIL DEFENCE COMMITTEES AND THE POPULAR MILITIA

The social and political demands of the urban elements were more radical and far-reaching than those of the FSLN, and challenged the bourgeois social and economic order. The relatively high level of self-organisation of the urban masses and their combativity meant that the FSLN, to maintain its undisputed leadership of the revolution, had to simultaneously assume a more radical and anti-bourgeois face than had been originally intended, and to take quick action to curb the activities of the masses. FSLN militants took the lead, the better to channel demands in safe directions.

First, the FSLN had to maintain a monopoly of military power. That meant immediately taking control of the urban CDCs that had been established, mostly spontaneously and independently of the FSLN. These were the core of the local militias, which had armed themselves by confronting and defeating the National Guards. The essence of the technique was simple and direct: visit the CDC, introduce yourselves as the FSLN, applaud their efforts and appoint one or more of the leading activists as FSLN militants subject to FSLN discipline. This was possible because, for the masses, there was no alternative to the FSLN.

In this way the local CDCs were taken under the wing of the FSLN, centralised, co-ordinated and transformed into mechanisms to implement orders from the top. To make their point the FSLN changed the name of the Civil Defence Committees to Sandinista Defence Committees and brought them within FSLN discipline. Encouraged by the FSLN, the CDSs became a symbol of the new regime.

However, by about mid-1985 the CDSs were in a profound crisis. *El Nuevo Diario*,[60] published a lengthy article on a stagnating membership due, primarily, to a lack of democracy. Orders from the top were issued in a heavy-handed manner; the quality of the leadership was poor, being those prepared to accept the authority of the Directorate without too many questions; and there was a lack of internal democracy, the CDSs couldn't decide their own response to local issues they had to deliver what the FSLN had already decided, and so on. Despite their heroic beginnings, the CDCs/CDSs would, within a decade, degenerate into little more than a means of providing jobs for corrupt state officials, though they were feared by the bourgeoisie up to and after the 1990 election.

---

60 11 November, 1985

Based in their localities, the urban militia were important armed forces that were not part of the guerrilla army. These militia were much more numerous and just as well equipped as the guerrillas, but totally uncoordinated and without a political programme. The most important elements within the armed militias were those units that had been established in factories and urban workplaces. The FSLN acted swiftly. On 27 July, 1979, a week after the taking of Managua, army chief Humberto Ortega announced that the popular militias would be re-grouped and integrated into a conventional army framework, the EPS.

The EPS was under the command of Humberto Ortega with Cuban military personnel as advisors. The FSLN was not prepared to make any compromises or concessions regarding its control over the military apparatus. Even during the revolutionary period itself, the FSLN was concerned to strengthen its military base, to strengthen and professionalise the army that emerged from the revolutionary war. This is why the CDC militias were disbanded and disarmed so quickly; they represented a major threat to the FSLN's military monopoly, and hence to its political monopoly. The new army was constructed incredibly rapidly. It was already holding parades through Managua by 1 September, 1980. It could be said that the revolutionary army and its associated militia, which enjoyed tremendous popular prestige, substituted for the FSLN's lack of organisational links with the working class.

On 28 September, the General Command of the EPS issued an order for all weapons and military equipment to be turned in. The militias were to be disarmed with sections of them integrated into the EPS. The militia were to be maintained with regular training sessions etc., but their weapons would be in the hands of the EPS. The Sandinista National Police (PNS) was created, with one of its immediate and important tasks being to remove responsibility for public order from the CDCs/CDSs. This was doubly necessary because, generally, new members and activists within the FSLN were supporting the demands of workers and peasants, and spoke openly of their determination to carry the revolution through to the end.

The militias handing their weapons over to the EPS was significant because it marked a qualitative change in their function. These moves curtailed any possibility of a Marxist opposition developing, that could have advanced the struggle for democratic workers' power and derailed the popular frontist project of the FSLN leaders. A crucial task for socialist revolutionaries in this period would have been to campaign to defend the CDCs and turn them into real Soviet-type bodies, democratically representing the workers, and the *barrios* and drawing in the small and poor peasants. These would have been linked, as in Russia in 1917, by a national Congress. And, let us not forget, the Russian Revolution was launched on the basis of defence of such a Congress.

At their height, during the Contra War, the militia was about 250,000 strong, based on communities and workplaces. But this militia was very different from the militias existing in the first months of the uprising.

6.2) LUISA AMANDA ESPINOSA NICARAGUAN WOMEN'S ASSOCIATION (AMNLAE)

Strictly, the first of the FSLN mass organisations was the AMNLAE (Luisa Amanda Espinosa Nicaraguan Women's Association, named after the first woman cadre to be killed in action). This was the successor to AMPRONAC which had been launched in 1977 and had a track record of successfully mobilising women in support of the FSLN. AMNLAE was notionally autonomous, its leadership acquired its legitimacy from its ability to lead and win the confidence of others. However, there was always a substantial overlap between the officers of AMNLAE and the FSLN. Its top leaders were always relatively high-ranking FSLN cadres ensuring that AMPRONAC carried the party line on all important questions, such as when the majority Tendency (*Tercerista*) supported the class collaborationist MPU, AMPRONAC was on board. There were open debates within AMNLAE on questions of key importance to women, such as the abortion issue but the FSLN leadership never changed its mind on the basis of AMNLAE recommendations. AMNLAE unfailingly mobilised its forces, possibly 50,000 card-carrying members, behind the Directorate's proposals.

With government support, women peasants and workers began taking up the fight for their right to participate on an equal basis in all aspects of economic and social life, seeking to win the unions and mass organisations to this cause. The fight was led and organised at the national level by AMNLAE, which gave support to those women who began to participate in the government-sponsored unions in their work-places. Particularly active were women members of the ATC, building on the work done by AMPRONAC.

Several of the provisions contained in the Statute were designed to protect and strengthen the family as the basic unit of society, promoting greater family cohesion and reducing gender inequalities. They were intended to strengthen the institution of marriage by making it more of a partnership; ending the feudal father-right law (giving the father total parental rights), requiring the father to support his children whether born in or out of wedlock, and giving courts the power to garnish his wages. All these provisions reduced the likelihood of the father absconding. In 1982 legislation stating that the relationship of all family members must be reciprocal and supportive, including the sharing of domestic labour strengthened this initiative.[61]

With the support of the government and AMNLAE, women activists made use of the 1979 decree, ensuring the courts enforced the changes in divorce procedures to the benefit of women, and carried out the stronger child-support laws. They also obtained a ruling to outlaw the exploitation of women in advertising. They fought and won the right for women to join the militias and armed forces, including some combat units; the creation of women's producers' and sellers' co-operatives. But, arguably, their most magnificent achievement was the advancement of literacy among women during the literacy campaign in 1980.

With the advance of the fight for greater women's equality came greater participation of women in many aspects of political life, particularly in the unions and the CDSs where the majority of members were women. However, while women formed a substantial part of the CDSs, militia, and were strong in the unions, there were – at that time – almost no women leaders at the national level; for example, in the summer 1981 elections to the national committee of the National Union of Nicaraguan Students not a single woman was endorsed.

6.3) THE WORKER'S ORGANISATIONS

Instead of basing the new regime on genuine workers' democracy, the FSLN leadership retained a model that did not permit democratic control of the state apparatus. Quite the opposite, the trade unions, movements and associations formed before and during the revolution were transformed into mechanisms for implementing decisions made at the top. True to its Stalinist roots, the Sandinista regime, far from counteracting bureaucratisation, actively bureaucratised the workers' and peasants' representative organisations.

The Directorate understood the need to exert control over the workers and established the Sandinista Workers' Federation (*Central Sandinista de Trabajadores* – CST). It had launched the ATC for the peasants and small land farmers the previous year. The primary task of both bodies was to increase the surplus value produced. Neither organisation existed to politically mobilise working people to actively participate in, and advance the social goals of the revolution in a way to benefit themselves.

---

61 Harris, H., *Nicaraguan Women in Struggle*, Third World Quarterly, 5(4)899-908, 1983.

6.4) THE ASSOCIATION OF AGRICULTURAL WORKERS

The ATC had been launched in the spring of 1978 as Nicaragua's first rural trade union and, within two years of the victory of the revolution, it had mushroomed to include over a quarter of all rural workers.

Cabezas, who spent years amongst the *campesinos* later wrote:

> The landowners, or the fathers or grandfathers of the landowners, had over a period of years gradually been stripping the campesinos of their land. So, the generation of campesinos we knew would tell us about how their great-grandfathers had owned land. And the story of what happened was passed down from great-grandfather to grandfather to father to son... The landowners had appropriated the land through a process of violent evictions, or through legal means... They had been corralled... working the landowner's land and tending his cattle... growing their crops on land lent them by the local landowners...

> We invited them to fight for the land, which was too great a temptation for a campesino to resist! How could they stand by and not fight for what was for them a mother, a wife, a way of living, affection, feeling, secret rapport? It would be very hard for the campesino to refuse to fight, particularly when we were awakening in him the feeling and the idea of class struggle.

The Sandinista government enacted several subsidiary regulations applicable to, amongst other things, land rents and wages, and the extension of government credit to agricultural producers. The ATC was very active in ensuring that workers were paid the correct minimum wage, that peasants were not charged too much rent for their properties, and that co-operatives were able to access their full credit entitlement, and in this way built for itself a solid base amongst the *campesinos*.

However, a central task of the ATC was not to take forward the peasants' demands for land, but to contain those demands within the economic perspective of a mixed economy. During the period immediately following the revolution, between 1979 and 1981, the seizure of the lands of the Somoza family and the creation of state farms, and co-operatives of poor *campesinos*, temporarily kept the peasant demand for land in check as the peasants waited to see what would happen. However, they soon acted and occupied land, breaking through the limits imposed by the Sandinistas. The government was forced to enact a series of limited reforms that it hoped would defuse the situation. In July 1980, on the first anniversary of the revolution, the FSLN announced that all fallow lands or lands not adequately cultivated could be expropriated.

But land occupations continued, and in July 1981 the government was forced to enact a moderate Land Reform Programme which extended expropriation to de-capitalised farms. The bourgeois revolution in Mexico, which had so inspired Sandino, had accepted the seizure of the landed estates by the peasantry and their distribution amongst the peasants. The bourgeois land reforms in Chile and Peru had been more radical in the expropriation of landholdings over a certain size. The truth was, as the Sandinistas themselves admitted, their agrarian reforms were "most conservative and most respectful of the private agricultural sector".[62]

Any land redistribution had to be sufficiently constrained not to challenge the alliance with the major agrarian capitalists who dominated the country's export sector and were the organised in COSEP. These supposedly anti-Somoza landlords were now transformed into so-called 'patriotic producers', required only to use their land productively. Indeed, with most agricultural production in capitalist hands, government measures to provide cheap credit and farm supplies tended to boost the profits of wealthy landowners without increasing agricultural production nor improving the lot of toiling peasants.

As with so many petty-bourgeois politicians, the FSLN leaders would increasingly use language as a smokescreen, obscuring political realities. Here, to better maintain a social pact with capitalist landowners and manufacturers, the FSLN leaders transformed the term 'producers' from a scientific one meaning exploited working people to one that included wealthy capitalist farmers and ranchers. For the toilers to advance their historic class interests, political clarity is essential, but the FSLN wanted to avoid such clarity; it did not want the operations of its social system to be laid bare, but rather to hide the ongoing class conflict inherent in the exploitation of working people.

6.5) THE SANDINISTA WORKERS' FEDERATION

The CST was formed shortly after the insurrection on the initiative of the FSLN Directorate to give leadership and direction to the factory workers, and to take the initiative away from the Workers' Defence Committees and other factory committees which had emerged during and after the revolution. Unlike the ATC, which could legitimately claim to have roots among the rural proletariat and poor peasants, the CST was artificial, as demonstrated by the fact that the CST had to wait to 1983, three-and-a-half years after it was formed, to hold its First Congress. Early 1980 saw a determined push by the FSLN to bring the workers' (and peasants') organisations under its unchallenged control; to have a FSLN-dominated workers' movement. This was especially the case with the workers in the factories, where, unlike the

---

62 *Barricada International*, Dec. 5, 1985

campesinos, established trade unions existed with organisations and traditions of their own, and often affiliated to political parties opposed to the FSLN.

Working-class men and women took advantage of the victory of the revolution to immediately demand better pay and conditions and also payment of wages lost during the revolutionary strikes called by the FSLN. During its first days, the CST was forced to support these actions, but as it grew into the largest of the unions it began to openly oppose any activities that hindered production. *Barricada*[63] explained: "The role of the union is not the same as previously, it is now to be the controller of production in the workplace… to increase production".

From its foundation, the CST's assigned role was to undertake the organisation of workers within the overall context of support for the FSLN's programme. It emphasised the necessity of increasing production and improving productivity not only in the new state sector but especially in the private sector where workers often gave priority to settling accounts with employers who had frequently used Somoza's laws and police against them. The FSLN showed no favour to workers in the private sector even during this early stage of the revolution, and both factory and agricultural workers were often thwarted in their attempts to gain wage increases. Its actions soon led the FSLN into a series of clashes with workers' organisations, first with the PSN trade union organisation, the General Confederation of Workers – Independent (CGT-I) founded in 1963, which included the construction union, SCAAS, one of the largest and historically most militant unions in Nicaragua.

While the FSLN was carried forward on the tidal wave of the revolutionary upsurge and doing much to better the working and living conditions of the masses, its actions with respect to most advanced workers gave worrying indications of less than democratic views amongst the leadership. It used government power to ensure the CST would become the major industrial union in the country and split established unions to achieve this. For example, it engineered a split-off from the SCAAS and then ensured its group obtained official recognition. This led to a wild-cat strike by SCAAS construction workers and the arrest of the union leader, a PSN member. A demonstration by striking workers to the Ministry of Labour successfully obtained his release. Soon after there was a successful strike by over 4,000 construction workers on a large government project in Managua against an arbitrary reduction in wages by the government.

---

63 19 October, 1980

Inevitably, this strategy involved suppression of the activities of forces to the left of the FSLN. *Barricada*[64] excused the FSLN campaign, launched under the slogan 'Sandino Lives – Death to the Counter-Revolution', as against those who were fomenting industrial unrest, and who were bracketed with Somoza-ism as enemies of the revolution. Included in this amalgam was the *Frente Obrero*, which considered the new Sandinista regime bourgeois nationalist, and thus it was right and proper that trade unions should pursue a higher standard of living for their members. Also included was the Revolutionary Marxist League (*Liga Marxista Revolucionaria*, LMR), a very small Trotskyist organisation associated with the United Secretariat of the Fourth International, which had fought alongside the FSLN. This now called for peasants to occupy the lands of the large landowners, for independent unions, for back-payment of lost wages, against the disarming of the militias and bureaucratisation of the CDCs. These attacks on the so-called ultra-lefts became an integral part of CST activities, so much so that any new branch seeking to join the CST had first to denounce the FO and the LMR.

Clashes with the FO became more serious, not least because the FO had played an active role in the struggle against Somoza and was to have had a seat on the Council of State. *El Pueblo*, the paper of the FO denounced the FSLN mixed-economy strategy as giving "great opportunities to the bourgeoisie and businessmen and few to the exploited masses".[65] From October 1979 through to January 1980, the FO led a series of strikes for higher wages and better working conditions, most importantly at the Amalia and San Antonio Sugar Mills (the largest in the country).

In response, the EPS occupied the FO offices and arrested the editor and leading members, who were given two-year prison sentences. *El Pueblo*'s printing works were handed over to the 'literacy crusade'. This action was combined with the suppression of the MILPAS. The response of the workers at the San Antonio Sugar Mills was to strike again, this time one of their demands being for the release of the FO members. Daniel Ortega, Jaime Wheelock, and Tomás Borge intervened to condemn the workers' actions, and on 1 February, 1980, *Barricada* carried a report that Borge had threatened to send in troops. This was a very worrying development, but fortunately, the FSLN drew back and the FO leaders were released early in May 1980.

The campaign was not a sledge-hammer to crack a nut, because the real targets were not two tiny left groups, but rather, the rising militancy in the factories for increased pay and greater workers' control. The measures against the FO and LMR were deemed necessary to consolidate the dominant position

----

64 9 October, 1979
65 Black, op cit,

in the CST in the workers' movement as part of the project of integrating the unions into the state apparatus. At the same time, the CST and FSLN were anxious to identify those owners who were deliberately running down their enterprises in order to take corrective measures, which could include nationalisation. Thus, the CST could present itself as militant and left wing by leading strikes and occupations, such as at the El Caracol food processing factory, against owners who were de-capitalising the enterprise demanding nationalisation of the factory.

6.6) NATIONAL UNION OF AGRICULTURALISTS AND CATTLEMEN

The last of the mass organisations launched by the FSLN was the National Union of Farmers and Ranchers (UNAG). In the battles to oust Somoza, agricultural workers, poor peasants, and middle peasants, fought side-by-side, and jointly carried out land seizures.

Immediately after the revolution, all these different groups joined the ATC, but it soon became clear that the peasants (both small and middle) needed a different kind of organisation from the agricultural workers. The one was concerned with, for example, obtaining cheap loans while the other called for better working conditions and pay. The FSLN was keen to retain the support of all peasants because they were seen as forming a solid base of support in the countryside. At its commencement, the UNAG was intended for co-operative farms and small and medium-sized peasant holdings, and the best way of organising that was for these peasants to have their own co-ordinating organisation.

UNAG was launched by the FSLN in 1981 in tandem with the First Agrarian Reform Law. The name had been carefully chosen to make it clear the organisation was open to all landholders. However, in the prevailing circumstances it was, de-facto, an organisation for small and medium peasants, many hundreds of whom attended its first national gathering and actively participated in the proceedings. In 1981/82, the main thrust of UNAG was to obtain land for landless peasants and adequate supplies of credit on reasonable terms for the small and middle farmers. At first the membership (and a section of the full-time officials, those who considered themselves socialist) blocked capitalist landowners from joining, preferring to see them in COSEP.

Over the next two years UNAG continued to press for land for landless peasants, cancellation of debts for small and middle farmers, increased production by all farmers, and organising militias to counter the Contra threat. However, there was a growing outcry from the larger landowners that the FSLN was 'dividing the producers'. The public face of Jaime Wheelock, the Minister for Agrarian Reform was that the interests of the small producers were different from those who had all kinds of facilities to hand:

> How can there be equality between the barefoot son of a peasant and the son of a big producer who is studying in the United States? It is the barefoot ones we have to think about.

The strategy of the FSLN to develop the agricultural sector was clear and repeated many times in speeches and documents. It aimed for a mixed economy which would be more just and equal than under Somoza in its redistribution of land and resources, while maintaining an alliance with the major agrarian capitalists who dominated the country's export sector and were the leading force within COSEP.

This was the heart of the popular front strategy of the Junta in 1979. The FSLN quickly discovered that the dominance of the state sector in agriculture was much less than it thought, believing that the nationalisation of Somoza's holdings would give it control of up to sixty per cent of the country's agricultural production. In fact, that control extended just over twenty per cent.[66] The discrepancy was serious: the difference between being able to satisfy the demands of the peasants for land, or not. And lest we forget, the distribution of land is key to the success of all national democratic revolutions. With their perspective of a mixed economy, the FSLN tops were soon backing the landlords not the tenants and, in so doing, gave the first concrete indication that this revolution would not follow Cuba's example. The FSLN now recommended that all but the largest landowners in COSEP should join UNAG to obtain the benefits on offer.

6.7) THE BOURGEOISIE MAKE THEIR FIRST DEMANDS

The first rifts in the broad array of social forces that toppled Somoza appeared soon after his overthrow. Faced with a steep growth in union membership and a deepening radicalisation, many of the capitalists who had opposed Somoza, doubtless looking over their shoulders at Cuba, were refusing to resume production and holding back on investment. Some were selling whatever possessions they could and leaving the country, others were trying to take their machinery with them. The premier bourgeois paper, *La Prensa*, began a campaign, declaring that the willing participation of the 'progressive bourgeoisie' was essential for the successful reconstruction of Nicaragua.

There was a regrouping of bourgeois politicians, and the simultaneous launch in late September 1979 of four bourgeois parties, all of which made

---

66 Collins, J., *Nicaragua: what difference could a revolution make*, 1986.

public statements claiming to support the revolution while emphasising the need for 'authentic democracy'. Vestiges of the old Conservative Party, the most openly anti-FLSN re-appeared as the Sandinista Social Democratic Party (PSDS). This cheeky adoption of 'Sandinista' for the name of the party sparked a storm of protest. The result was a governmental decree reserving the title 'Sandinista' for the FSLN and its organisations, resulting in the change of the name to the Social Democratic Party (PSD).

The PSD was launched on 23 September, with calls for the revolution to be limited to a bourgeois democracy, for the consolidation of capitalism, and bitter complaints against attacks being made on private property. These were not complaints about the FSLN leadership, whose declared and actual policy was that of no restrictions on capitalists running their businesses. What the PSD speakers were complaining about were the actions of workers in occupying factories and enterprises in support of demands for increased pay and better working conditions, and against decapitalisation.

The bourgeoisie was also regrouping in its employers' associations (such as, for example, Chambers of Commerce, Association of Cotton Producers, etc.) delaying re-opening their businesses or investing in the economy as a way of applying pressure on the government to meet their demands. *La Prensa*, which had a circulation more than twice that of *Barricada*, and the radio stations in capitalist hands campaigned for a Council of State as set out in the Puntarenas Pact without any 'unfair' change of rules by the FSLN. Ignoring the revolution, they demanded that all bourgeois parties be given guaranteed representation. In parallel were demands for curtailing the power and authority of the militia and CDCs/CSDs, and their replacement with normal bourgeois institutions.

These demands had the support of the Minister of Finance (Joaquin Cuadra Chamorro), Minister of Planning (Roberto Yorga Cortes) and the Governor of the Central Bank (Arturo Cruz), all appointed by the Junta. The Junta had appointed individuals from the private sector to head the government's economic team. These people were responsible for renegotiating the foreign debt and channelling foreign economic aid through the state-owned International Reconstruction Fund (*Fondo Internacional de Reconstrucción* - FIR) – which might be a partial answer to why the new government assumed responsibility for Somoza's debts instead of repudiating them.

On the one side stood the movement of workers, *campesinos* and urban poor, eager to throw off years of exploitation and oppression. On the other stood the bourgeoisie, backed by imperialism but deprived of its crucial weapon, its direct control of the repressive apparatus of the bourgeois state, the army and police. The old bourgeoisie was in no sense powerless, they had control of the great majority of the economy, the radio stations, the major daily paper (*La Prensa*), had great political influence over the middle classes and professionals, and at their disposal (even if indirectly) the hierarchy of the Catholic Church.

The masses were demanding thoroughgoing land reform, greater control over production, working conditions and wages, and the settling of outstanding scores with their employers. The anti-Somoza bourgeoisie, represented by Chamorro and Robelo, were pressing the FSLN to re-build the structures of the bourgeois state and to halt any radical anti-capitalist measures. Leaders of the European Social-Democratic parties hurried to Managua to urge the FSLN to maintain the block with the anti-Somoza bourgeoisie and, of course, made it clear that international aid would be dependent on this. The PSN added its small voice: that the FSLN "be sensitive to the interests and demands of its capitalist class allies".

7) A NICARAGUAN WORKERS' AND PEASANTS' GOVERNMENT?

In Nicaragua, in July 1979, the FSLN had come to power as the result of a revolutionary mass insurrection that had destroyed the political power of the bourgeoisie and smashed the state apparatus. As the only organised anti-Somoza force prepared to carry the revolution through to the end, the FSLN were the main beneficiaries of the insurrection. A petty-bourgeois group, the FSLN was the sole effective force in the government, and the power of the state was in its hands. During 1979 and 1980, the opening years of the revolution, the FSLN government responded to mass mobilisations of the toilers, carried out a series of expropriations (even if limited), and other measures against capitalist property and social prerogatives. It was anti-imperialist and responded with practical measures to the needs of the workers and peasants.

In total, its actions justified its characterisation as a Workers' and Peasants' Government, but its direction of travel was unclear. The hope world-wide was that Nicaragua would follow the Cuban example, that a revolutionary petty-bourgeois leadership would show itself to be dedicated to improving the conditions of all Nicaraguans and would take the necessary anti-capitalist measures: shed the bourgeois elements in the government and establish a workers state (even if deformed). It was hoped that the FSLN would continue to respond positively to the mass mobilisations, which both carried and pushed it to take the initiatives challenging capitalist prerogatives, and expropriated capitalist property.

With no democratic revolutionary party to give a voice to the masses, the new government called instead for an ongoing alliance with the national bourgeoisie, giving it a social and economic weight it did not deserve. Despite the leadership of the FSLN having the perspective, not of a workers' state, but of a capitalist mixed economy, despite the dangers of possible US intervention, despite the presence of large blocks of private property and independent bourgeois political parties, at that stage, matters still hung in the balance. The situation was not very different from Cuba in 1959, so the possibility that the FSLN regime would follow a parallel trajectory, towards a Nicaraguan workers' state could not be ruled out. The key step would be the expropriation of the landed estates. It was this that marked the qualitative stage of the Cuban revolution because it took back the lands snatched by the American corporations.

Instead, and with no dissenting voice, the FSLN Directorate declared that the maintenance of a mixed economy with more than sixty per cent remaining in private hands was an essential feature of the Nicaraguan revolution.[67] In Nicaragua, where the number of employees in enterprises with five or fewer workers was nearly 15,000, and only 120 plants employed more than fifty workers each,[68] small-scale commodity production by peasants, farmers, artisans and light industry was acceptable as part of a planned economy if the key sectors were nationalised with a state monopoly of foreign trade.

In 1979 it remained to be seen whether the FSLN, or even a section of it, would evolve to a socialist consciousness. As a petty-bourgeois formation it was unstable and, while its evolutionary direction (at least of the *Terceristas*) had not been encouraging, insofar as it took practical measures against the bourgeoisie and stood against imperialism, it had to be supported unconditionally.

Any theoretical analysis would do well to start with the 1922 World Congress of the Communist International. The *Thesis on Tactics* agreed at the Congress accepted the possibility that, as the result of class struggles, the power of the state could pass into the hands of a Workers' and Peasants' Government, but declared that such a government did not represent a workers' state – the dictatorship of the proletariat – but could become an important launch pad for the fight for that dictatorship.

That is where matters rested until the *Transitional Programme*, the founding document of the Fourth International, was published. That document is key to understanding the processes that occurred in China and Cuba, and is relevant to the FSLN in Nicaragua:

---

67 Molyneux, op cit., 1985.
68 IP 12 December, 1983.

> [O]ne cannot categorically deny in advance the theoretical possibility that, under the influence of completely exceptional circumstances (war, defeat, financial crash, mass revolutionary pressure, etc.), the petty-bourgeois parties, including the Stalinists, may go further than they wish along the road to a break with the bourgeoisie. In any case one thing is not to be doubted: even if this highly improbable variant somewhere at some time becomes a reality and the 'workers' and farmers' government' in the above-mentioned sense is established in fact, it would represent merely a short episode on the road to the actual dictatorship of the proletariat.[69]

By 1979, history had demonstrated that such regimes could progress to a workers' state (such as in China and Cuba), though some could regress (like Algeria). As all real processes take time, there is an interval between the overthrow of bourgeois military and political power, and the decisive expropriation of bourgeois economic power. This period in China had lasted for many months, during which the regime was not the dictatorship of the proletariat, but rather a transitional regime: A Workers' and Peasants' Government.

Lenin and Trotsky had both emphasised the necessity of the mobilisation of the masses to break the power of the bourgeoisie.[70] The mass mobilisations can, in exceptional circumstances such as occurred at the end of World War II, force even petty-bourgeois leaderships to accomplish the transition to a workers' state. The creation of a deformed workers' state in Cuba, where a leadership was determined to better the conditions of the working masses, showed that real life rarely conforms to the ideal; rather, distortions and variants are the norm.[71]

The first consideration, that a revolutionary mass mobilisation had destroyed the power of the bourgeoisie and established a Workers' and Peasants' Government, was a clear and striking confirmation of the theory of the permanent revolution, that in colonial and semi-colonial countries there is a natural tendency to transcend the bourgeois democratic phase and progress more or less directly to a workers' state, even if deformed.

However, the FSLN government did not accept such an analysis, stood in the way of this development, and called instead for an ongoing alliance with the national bourgeoisie in a mixed economy. The FSLN, riding on the mass upsurge that overthrew Somoza, believed it could use the carrot of economic concessions and stick of the mass movement to force the

---

69 Trotsky, L., *The Transitional Programme,* www.marxist.org, 1938.
70 Trotsky, L., *History of the Russian Revolution, Preface,* www.marxists.org.
71 Woods, A., *The Chinese Revolution of 1949,* 1 October, 2009. www.marxist.com.

Nicaraguan bourgeoisie, against its wishes, to carry through the bourgeois democratic revolution.

From the Marxist perspective, it is not possible to have a two-class state – though it is possible to have a two-class government, and in Nicaragua the Junta and Council of State was just such. The FSLN Directorate had clearly stated its aim of preserving a mixed economy, in a similar way to both the Chinese Communist Party and the J-26 Movement. But in the highly turbulent and contradictory conditions of post-revolutionary Nicaragua, what was in question was the outcome of the conflict between the stated programme of the FSLN and the natural progression of events which everywhere demanded actions that exceeded the limits of a mixed economy. Would these pressures push the FSLN to take measures which were socialist in principle, in the direction of developing a state with one foot firmly in socialism?

7.1) THE REGIME CONSOLIDATES

After the revolution and into 1980, the problem of mass hunger having been temporarily solved, the problem of unemployment was by far the most serious facing the FSLN. It had two basic causes. The first and the more important was the disruption of the planting of coffee and cotton due to the revolution. An emergency plan was needed in which public works would play the major role; for example, rebuilding the centre of Managua. But that would not be enough; the revival of production by the capitalist sector was needed, but the capitalists were using just that to blackmail the government. Their demands were carried in the columns of *La Prensa*: for the government to formally make them full partners in economic planning, to restrict the growing power of the unions, CDSs, AMNLAE and other mass organisations. They had to be guaranteed their investments would be sufficiently profitable, and that the FSLN would implement the original version of the Puntarenas Pact and give them control of the Council of State and the Supreme Court.

The agrarian reforms had been enough to raise the expectations of the *campesinos* but not enough to satisfy their land hunger nor, in the short term, significantly improve the working and living conditions of agricultural labourers and poor peasants. Thus, there was a swathe of occupations and seizures of land not approved by the FSLN and in some cases troops were brought in to restore the land to its 'rightful' owners.

The economic perspective of the FSLN government as articulated in its 1980 economic plan was for a mixed economy, one in which all sectors would be subject to the laws of the market, that is, the laws of capitalism. Nor was any debate allowed amongst peasants and workers on the economic direction of the revolution. Imperialism breathed a sigh of relief as an immediate danger appeared to have been removed. Many well-respected Social-Democratic leaders from Europe flew to Managua Airport to offer their services and assist in raising loans to help Nicaragua service its foreign debt. This was a prime example of reformist internationalism, because the beneficiaries were the big banks who had loaned Somoza the money to maintain his regime. Soon the Organisation of American States officially recognised the regime and after this came money from Costa Rica, Panama, and Venezuela. And on 25 October, 1979, the UN pitched in with a resolution appealing for economic assistance to be given to Nicaragua.

The Nicaraguan Revolution was being feted because, unlike in Cuba, a large part of the economy was left in the hands of multinational companies and the Nicaraguan bourgeoisie. The Sandinistas did not, and at the time, due to the pressure of the masses, could not hand political power to the anti-Somoza bourgeoisie, but they left in their hands decisive economic weapons that would allow them to take it in due course.

The narrowness of the productive base of a country as small as Nicaragua with only about 3,000,000 inhabitants meant that, to stimulate genuine economic development a truly revolutionary initiative was required such as establishing a Federation with Cuba, which in the long run would have strengthened both countries. However, FSLN leaders considered there was no need to take control of production, but only to direct investment and take a share of the surplus value generated. The reality, however, was the bulk of production remained in the private sector which demanded guaranteed rates of profit, in effect, determining what surplus would be left for the state.

The FSLN was the subsidiary partner, subject to all kinds of blackmail, one being the demand to provide the private sector with loans at very low interest rates. When the balance sheet was drawn up it was found that the private industrial sector had taken the loans but failed to mobilise even the production capacity available. By the end of 1980, foreign debt had risen to US$2 billion with nearly two-thirds of foreign earnings spent on debt repayment and oil imports.

Because the tasks of rebuilding Nicaragua were so great, the economy required a considerable inflow of resources, estimated by the World Bank at about US$300 million annually. Nevertheless, at first, the economy experienced positive growth, largely because of foreign aid and re-reconstruction after the revolution. Carter and the US Administration favoured financial pressure, and aid was forthcoming only after the revolution had proved it posed no threat to US interests in the region. Loans totalling over US$110 million from US sources for making good the infrastructure and re-vitalising the private sector were vetoed. A scenario repeated in all financial organisations in which the Americans were represented.

FSLN propaganda talked about class struggle and socialism sometime in the future, but to convince capitalists to invest, the FSLN had to control and discipline the workers. Consequently, it carried through a developmental programme for the immediate benefit of the poorest: provision of educational and health services, water supply and drainage schemes, subsidised food and transport, all of which greatly improved the lives of working people, ensuring CDS loyalty to the FSLN, all which frightened the US imperialists. The costs incurred were largely met by foreign aid and loans, which was not available after 1981 with Reagan in the White House.

Borge listed other major gains of the Nicaraguan revolution that benefited the workers, poor peasants and unemployed. The consumption of wheat rose by thirty-three per cent, rice thirty per cent and beans forty per cent; over 300,000 houses and building plots were handed to the masses. House rents were fixed at no more than five per cent of the declared value of the property, which meant rents were generally cut in half. Later, by the end of the decade, with rampant inflation, the rent paid by many tenants had reduced to negligible amounts. The infant mortality rate was already falling and a further substantial drop was expected. It is clear that the majority of poor families hugely benefited by the government's redistribution policies and provision of food subsidies.[72]

To counteract the attacks in the bourgeois media that it had reneged on the Puntarenas accords, the FSLN confirmed its intention of working within a multi-class bloc, and in February 1980 launched the Popular Patriotic Bloc (*Bloque Popular Patriótico*, BPP) which in addition to the FSLN, contained the MDN, PLI, PSN and PCN, and the PPSC. In July, the FSLN relaunched the BPP as the Revolutionary Patriotic Front (FPR) without the PCN, which was dropped because of its opposition to FSLN industrial policy, and without the MDN which had walked away, to the plaudits of *La Prensa*.

At home, the national bourgeoisie responded to the appeals of the FSLN, not by repatriating the capital it had sent out of the country, but by further 'de-capitalising', usually in preparation for the owners themselves running off. This was a serious problem, and the FSLN mobilised the workers to curb such behaviour, a strategy which gave the bourgeoisie another reason to fear the trade unions.

At the El Caracol food processing factory, the workers, the majority of whom were women, took over the plant on 19 February, 1980, locking out the owners. The workers were convinced that the owners were deliberately

---

72 Borge, T., *Latinamerica Press*, May and June 1981.

bankrupting the company by reducing production. Supported by union officials, the workers claimed that the necessary raw materials had not been purchased, no repairs or maintenance had been carried out on the fleet of delivery trucks, and that factory machinery was kept running only because the workers themselves were undertaking makeshift repairs. The workers were particularly outraged that vitamin supplements normally added to foods for children had been cut as they reduced profits. Matters had come to a head when twenty-eight women workers were fired. After opening the books, the workers found that the owners had received a US$400,000 government loan to help the company get back on its feet, but none of the money had reached the factory. Naturally, trade union action extended to landed estates and factories where the owners refused to pay the new government minimum wage or introduce the new standards of working conditions.

This initial period after the revolution was a time when the interests of workers, peasants and the FSLN government were most closely aligned. But even at this time, when the FSLN was most radical, there was no suggestion that the FSLN would progress the revolution to a workers' state. *Barricada*,[73] carried the statement 'The Workers Will Put an End to Inequality and Exploitation', which sounded revolutionary when it spoke about the creativity of workers and peasants and 'workers' control', but any suggestion of taking ownership of the means of production was absent.

The 24 February, 1980, issue of *Barricada* declared a new period was beginning for the popular militia. Having disarmed the militia in the weeks after the revolution, the government re-launched the militias as "the highest expression of the people in arms". The article called for all Nicaraguans to join and play their part in defending the nation. But now the militia was under the control of the Ministry of Defence and, as reported in IP[74] that this militia would only carry those arms supplied by the EPS at times determined by the EPS. Co-incidentally, the same issue of IP in which this news was reported carried an item on how seven leaders of the Maoist FO and its trade union wing were facing up to ten years imprisonment for "having a large cache of arms".

An outstanding success of the revolution, and one that resonated around the world, was the National Literacy Crusade for which Nicaragua, in the person of Fr. Fernando Cardenal, the organiser of the campaign, was awarded the UNESCO Nadezhda K. Krupskaya Literary Award for 1980, and the UNESCO Hassin Habif Literary Award. The literacy campaign was modelled on what was done in Cuba after the 1959 revolution, which re-assured those

---

73 14 March, 1980
74 10 March, 1980

on the left who wanted to see the Nicaraguan Revolution as a second Cuban Revolution.

Before the revolution three-quarters of the population had never opened a book and only forty per cent were literate. On 24 March, 1980, a mass literacy campaign was launched. Over 52,000 high-school and university students and teachers (well over half female) organised the People's Literacy Army. They travelled from towns and cities into the mountain areas and countryside where they spent five months living with the families whom they taught to read and write. In the towns, nearly 26,000 workers and housewives taught in their workplaces and community centres. There was a revolutionary transformation in education not least because these young people could do no less than explain the political motivation that made them give up five months to help end the conditions that had kept the *campesinos* in a state of poverty, illiteracy and degradation. These teachers were roundly condemned for 'indoctrination' in the pages of *La Prensa*, by people who all their lives had refused to lift a finger or spend a cent to aid the peasants!

It was quite true, of course, that the very existence of the crusade was, in and of itself, a massive boost for the FSLN, had a major impact in winning the support of broad layers of peasants, but further frightened the US Administration.

This highly successful campaign was planned like a military operation. After a 150-day campaign against centuries of ignorance, it was claimed that 406,000 Nicaraguans had learned to read. By 1987, the Sandinista regime had built 1,200 new schools and the literacy rate had jumped to eighty-six per cent. The mobilisation of women's, peasants' and workers' mass organisations was the reason for the success of the literacy campaign. However, it was not without cost, as sixty-three teachers and students were killed by Contra commandos.

Stories were common of women, who travelled for hours every day in order to learn to read:

> Everything that we did was for our children so that they could learn to read, so they could have a better life and participate in the Revolution. With the idea that they were going to learn to read, that they were going to learn many things that they didn't know, with this we integrated in the process of the Revolution.[75]

The membership of the Junta changed when Violeta Chamorro resigned on 18 April, 1980, ostensibly for health reasons, though she later claimed that she had become dissatisfied with increased FSLN dominance in the government.

---

75 *Being a Mother in Nicaragua* AMNLAE, Editorial Nueva Nicaragua, 1984.

Overnight, *La Prensa* became much more critical of the FSLN. Two days later, the managing editor (Xavier Chamorro Cardenal) resigned in protest; the papers' workers declared their support for Xavier and went on strike. The strike was portrayed by the bourgeoisie as a blow against freedom of the press. Faced with the intransigence of the owners, on 26 April, the workers and progressive journalists resigned on mass and followed the old editor to launch a new paper *El Nuevo Diario*. From then on, *La Prensa* was the voice of the most determined opposition to the revolution. These views were often expressed in the letters' column, where false reports and exaggerations could be passed off as personal opinions which needed no denial by the paper. Violeta's place on the Junta was taken by Arturo Cruz, Governor of the Central Bank.

Alfonso Robelo resigned from the Junta on 22 April, 1980 to protest the expansion of the Council of State, pointing out that the FSLN now had such a degree of control that the Council had been reduced to a false front. He was replaced by Rafael Córdova Rivas a rancher and leader of the Democratic Conservative Party representing business interests. The new appointment was promotion of the 'patriotic bourgeoisie' and Cruz in *La Prensa* of 28 May, 1980 presented his appointment as: "part of the government's firm decision (to) put a system of mixed economy into effect..."

The FSLN had re-scheduled the convocation of the re-structured Council of State to May 1980. In the meantime, the Supreme Court's jurisdiction was limited to routine matters of little or no political significance. However, the problem of what to do with captured ex-National Guards charged with murder, rape, arson and other crimes had led to the creation of tribunals independent of the regular court system: often dubbed 'Peoples' Tribunals', these operated from November 1979 to February 1981. Nine three-judge panels and three appeals panels were all appointed by the Junta and included lay members. Of the 6,310 cases presented to these Tribunals 1,760 prisoners were freed for lack of evidence and 1,229 were acquitted, giving an acquittal rate of forty-seven per cent, far higher than the average US court. The 3,331 who were convicted – many for murder – received sentences ranging from zero to thirty years, the maximum allowed under post-Somoza Nicaraguan law. *La Prensa* campaigned for these National Guards to receive a fair trial! Pyle, having investigated what happened wrote:

> (O)ne does not hear calls from the former Guards that they would have preferred a jury trial... they fared far better under the Special Tribunals than if their fate had been left to juries composed of their former victims.[76]

---

76 Pyle, J., *Seeing Justice Done*, Envio, No 17, 1988.

The FSLN in its Historic Programme had promised to "support the work of priests and other religious figures who defend the working people", and is one of the few revolutionary movements to have taken power and appointed priests to senior government posts: Miguel d'Escoto Brockman, Foreign Minister; Ernesto Cardenal Martínez, Minister of Culture; Edgardo Parrales Castillo, Minister of Social Welfare and, most prominent, Fernando Cardenal (Ernesto's brother), who had headed the literacy campaign before becoming Minister of Education. At the time, over 200 priests and nuns held lesser-governmental positions.[77] In May 1980, the Catholic Church hierarchy made its first move against the FSLN-dominated government. An Episcopal Conference in that month called for the resignation from the government of the four priests with ministerial positions. They refused.

Growing worker dissatisfaction led to a series of strikes, the most serious of which was in the country's only cement plant, situated on the outskirts of Managua. The strike was organised by CAUS (Confederation of Trades Union Action and Unification) which was gaining ground against the CST because of the latter's lack of militancy. Such strikes forced the government to introduce, on 11 June, 1980, an across-the-board wage increase in the minimum wage of C\$125 per month, but many employers did not pay it. This meant that, for example, one third of workers in Managua received less than the recommended minimum wage. Inflation made matters worse.

With government approval, the ATC continued to press landowners to pay the new national minimum rate, and to improve health and safety for agricultural labourers on both private and state-owned farms. In line with the FSLN priority of increasing food production, the ATC launched a campaign for landowners to rent underused or unused land to poor peasants with a rent ceiling established by law. On 7 July, 1980, *Barricada* denounced landowners who refused to rent as counter-revolutionaries who intended to starve the country. However, the Minister responsible for food production, Wilberto Lara, kept the demands of the government and the ATC well within bourgeois limits. He explained the FSLN position as one of ensuring maximum crop production, and made it clear that "once utilised we will hand it back to its owners".

The 3 October, 1980, issue of *Barricada* carried a decree that the Junta would no longer tolerate factory occupations or other illegal activities such as strikes that disrupted production. The CAUS, CGT-I and FO all increased their membership by taking up work-related issues discounted by the CST.

---

77 Close, D., Nicaragua, *Politics, Economics and Society*, Continuum International Publishing, 1988.

The 7 October, 1980, issue of *Barricada* carried a statement by the Directorate: 'The Role of Religion in the New Nicaragua', giving its official position on religion. Welcoming all those who were prepared to actively struggle against Somoza-ism, the document stated: "Some authors have asserted that religion is a mechanism for spreading false consciousness among people, which serves to justify the exploitation of one class by another". Some authors? Marx, Engels, Lenin, Trotsky and Guevara all fall into that category, and their theoretical and practical arguments become mere – 'assertions'. The mixed economy applied to religion!

The bourgeoisie were beginning to find their feet. MDN, probably the most influential bourgeois party called a public rally for Sunday 9 November, 1980, under the slogan 'March Against Totalitarianism'. Borge and others attempted to dissuade Robelo, citing the need for calm after an armed attack on Santa Maria by ex-National Guards, but Robelo was adamant. The government stepped in and invoked Decree 513, which banned all party-political campaigning until the election promised for 1984. However, the dominant sectors of the bourgeoisie felt now was the time to pressure the FSLN and at its 12 November, 1980, meeting walked out of the Council of State. In response, the FSLN brought out 100,000 supporters to a mass rally.

By the end of 1980, the state sectors in Nicaragua (also known as Areas of Peoples' Property – APP) contributed forty-one per cent to the GDP, a figure which would remain roughly static. At the same time, seventy per cent of the production of export items, the crucial area in the Nicaraguan economy, remained in private hands, mainly the big cotton and coffee farmers. The 1980 plan had been partially successful in making up the losses in agricultural production that occurred during the revolution but, being a primary producer, Nicaragua was at the mercy of world prices and these had fallen in the key areas of coffee and cotton. The matter was exacerbated because the foreign debt inherited from Somoza meant that, for every US$100 earned from exports, US$55 would go in repayments. Nicaragua imports all its oil and, while oil prices fell between 1980 and 1981, they fell much less than the price of coffee and cotton, leaving Nicaragua worse off. With the withdrawal of the bourgeoisie from the Council of State, the US giant Standard Fruit quit its operations in Nicaragua, its land was nationalised, the US Administration believed its worst fears were being realised, and US economic assistance was suspended indefinitely.

The call by the FSLN to develop the agricultural sector was clear and repeated many times. The aim was a mixed economy that relied on maintaining an alliance with the major agrarian capitalists who dominated the country's export sector and were the leading force within COSEP. The

FSLN was attempting what the national-bourgeoisie had failed to do – to achieve independent national development. For the near future the FSLN model envisaged the country continuing to be an exporter of agricultural produce, giving the private farmers and ranchers who produced the majority of crops for export the whip hand. The problem was accumulating sufficient surplus for planned investments, which implied minimising those costs which subtracted from that surplus – such as the standard of living of the working class and peasants.

With the active assistance of the US media, the US Administration set in motion a programme of increasing the level and number of (untrue) 'horror' stories about the Sandinista government; it was totalitarian, the centre for arms smuggling in the Caribbean, it was receiving masses of Soviet weapons, all with the aim of justifying planned actions against Nicaragua.

8) AUSTERITY, THE CONTRA WAR AND THE NATIONAL QUESTION

With his speech of 13 January, 1981 to the CST, the FSLN Planning Minister (Henry Ruiz) launched a national discussion on the 1981 Economic Plan, which was called 'Austerity and Economic Efficiency'. The aims were the creation of 60,000 jobs (giving Nicaragua its lowest ever unemployment rate), and increasing investment in industrial production by 43.5 per cent with an expected boost in exports of twenty-two per cent. Consumption of food by the workers was planned to rise by twelve per cent. Ruiz explained that the 'privileged sector' would have to make sacrifices for the common good and might find it difficult to continue eating caviar. The key to success was increasing productivity by nine per cent through a higher degree of organisation and mobilisation of the workers themselves.

The two problems at the core of this mixed economy approach were that those who eat caviar invariably see what they want as essential for the good of the country, while the surplus needed for investment comes from increased exploitation of labour. The government policy would thus have to obtain investment as surplus value from domestic sources with the emphasis on the private sector, since that owned the lion's share of the economy.

The priorities were much the same as in the 1980 plan but now Reagan, the new hard-line US President (in office from 20 January, 1981 to 20 January, 1989), would terminate foreign aid and loans and initiate a programme of economic destabilisation in the hope that hunger would weaken the loyalty of the population to the FSLN. Reagan and his Secretary of State, Haig, claimed the revolution in Nicaragua was a serious threat to the stability of the US-backed regimes in El Salvador and Guatemala. The US administration was determined to organise the overthrow of the FSLN government by force on the pretext that the Nicaraguans were aiding the guerrillas in El Salvador and elsewhere. The political colour of the Nicaraguan regime was not important, rather, simply by attempting to take control of its own destiny it shattered the classic model by which the US dominated Latin America, and it threatened the profits of the US capitalists.

Reagan and Haig saw the situation in Nicaragua as particularly dangerous because it was in the heart of what US imperialism considered its own backyard. The Vietnam War remained fresh in their memories and this seriously constrained US options, so it was decided to fund the re-organisation and expansion of the National Guard remnants, the Contras, as a counter-revolutionary army 'advised' by US Army and CIA personnel. This mercenary force would be based in Honduras on the Nicaraguan border and, for more than six years, would wage a war of terror against the Nicaraguan people.

The government plan had considerable impact on the workers who expressed their response through their trade unions, which in Nicaragua are generally organised on a workplace not a trade basis. Thus, when figures were published on the increase in trade unions after July 1979,[78] what was referred to was the unionisation of individual enterprises where the number of workers might be as few as ten or as many as 300. What is not in doubt is that urban workers were flocking to join trade unions and individual plants were raising demands that were outside the FSLN programme.

The PCN-dominated CAUS led a series of strikes in Managua in January/February 1981, some for 100 per cent wage increases, some against 'de-capitalising' employers and for nationalisation. A major strike was at Fabritex, a high technology textile factory. In response, the CST organised demonstrations, which seized the CAUS offices in León and Managua, and handed them over to the literacy crusade. Throughout the strikes the PCN, CAUS and FO were denounced as 'somozista agents', 'agents of the counter-revolution' and 'CIA agents'.

In February 1981, Jaime Wheelock laid out the expectations of the government.[79] The bourgeoisie and the middle classes would join the workers in the task of building a new homeland. The mutual benefits from such an approach would more than offset any class differences. In a rational plan for the economy there would be no need to expropriate the means of production;

---

78 "Between August 1979 and December 1980, there was an average monthly increase of 26 new unions. From January to June 1981, the average was 63 and from July to December 1981, the monthly average was 31 new unions" (www.envio.org.ni/ articulo/3291, 1983.)

79 IP, 2 March, 1981

all the government had to do was determine how to allocate the surpluses. The difference between 'expropriation of the surpluses' and 'expropriation of the means of production' was the Achilles heel of the FSLN economic plan, it was the difference between production for profit and production for use, the difference between dream and reality.

The CST and ATC were not immune from the pressures driving workers to strike and were forced to make demands that were, objectively, against government policy. On 17 February, the ACT led a demonstration of some 50,000 peasants demanding that all land occupations be legalised. Poor peasants and farm labourers were not waiting, they were pressing their demands for land through land occupations and other direct actions. The ATC officers attempted to defend their reputations by pointing out how they had won the support of the government for individual cases where the land had stood idle for some time, even years.

To remove the heat from the situation, families were encouraged to join co-operatives where each family had title to its own land. These 'agrarian reform' titles could be inherited, but neither the title nor any part of the land could be sold. The co-operatives came in two types, the first where the land was owned individually but everyone worked on centrally-allocated tasks and then received a share proportional to their land area and effort put in; and the second where the peasants worked their own lands individually but combined in making applications for loans, grants, feed and seed grain, etc.

A new Junta was announced on 4 March, 1981, with Daniel Ortega clearly playing the lead role as 'Co-ordinator'. Arturo Cruz went to Washington as Nicaragua's ambassador, but resigned in November 1981. By April the following year, Cruz had been joined by Pastora and Robelo with the aim of launching an armed struggle against the FSLN from Costa Rica. Years later the *New York Times*[80] leaked that Cruz had been on the payroll of the CIA at US$6,000 a month. Moisés Hassan now acted as liaison between the Council of Ministers and the Junta, and would serve as Minister of Construction and Deputy Interior Minister before being named Mayor of Managua in 1985. He opposed the rightward direction taken by the FSLN and was removed from his remaining posts of responsibility in 1988. The February demonstration was followed on 11 March by a demonstration of more than 10,000 factory workers demanding that the government confiscate those factories where it had been forced to intervene.

In May 1981, Tomás Borge, gave an interview to *Latinamerica Press*, reported in IP[81] in which he described the FSLN goal as the achievement of

80 8 January, 1988
81 19 September, 1981

a mixed economy and political pluralism. He claimed that the FSLN leaders had accepted that the bourgeoisie were necessary to maintain production levels. He made it clear: "we are not going to become another Cuba", and repeated his vision to a visiting delegation of Canadian trade unionists stating: "There is a mixed economy within the revolution, a mixed economy at the service of the workers, (not) a mixed economy at the service of the bourgeoisie". The problem with such a perspective is that in an imperialist world, notwithstanding personal intentions, a mixed economy, especially as in Nicaragua, with such a high proportion of private companies with imperialist connections, will always end by serving the capitalist element.

The CST was starting to make real progress in recruiting workers. It was seen as the government's preferred union and able to improve health and safety in the workplace, which often spilled over into protecting the environment of those living close to factories. One spectacularly awful case was the *Electroquimica Pennwalt* chemical processing plant which produced and supplied corrosive and dangerous chemicals for more than fifty local factories. An important component of the production process was mercury, yet health and safety in the plant was practically non-existent, with workers standing in pools of highly toxic liquid mercury which had leaked onto the floor.

In May 1981, health tests of the 150 workers revealed that fifty-six had serious nervous damage. But, even worse, the plant had dumped forty tons of mercury into lake Xolotlán from which many of the inhabitants of Managua drew their drinking water. It turned out that the plant's owners were 'de-capitalising' the plant using a scam whereby the company ran up debts importing raw materials from abroad while payments for finished products ended up in US$ in their Miami bank account, a process which would soon have bankrupted the business.

The government was forced to step in and nationalise the plant, pay for the clean-up, maintain production and install protective measures for the workers. It was later revealed that the plant manager was Jaime Montealegre, a Vice-President of the Council of State. One result was an article in the *New York Times*,[82] which placed the blame for the pollution and resulting health problems on the Nicaraguan government because it had nationalised the plant.

In June 1981, the Conference of Bishops, which had never objected to the presence of priests in the Somoza government, even as officers in the National Guard, found it impossible to accept Catholic priests should engage in activities that promoted the physical well-being of Nicaraguans.

---

82 1 August, 1981

Cardenal and his colleagues were again instructed to surrender their posts. One particularly petty and spiteful act by anti-Sandinistas within the church was against Sister Maria del Pilar Castellano, a nun from the Ciudad Sandino area, which had been a revolutionary stronghold. She had given first aid to those who fought on the streets against Somoza and had been instrumental in establishing the Roberto Clemente school and pioneering the literacy campaign. In 1981, she visited her parents in Spain and, while there, was informed that she would not be returning to Nicaragua. Borge used this incident to explain how religious persecution in Nicaragua was not by the state against the church but by the conservative elements of the church against those within the church supporting liberation theology.

Daniel Ortega and Jaime Wheelock were at a complete loss to understand why the bourgeoisie could not appreciate the logic of a mixed economy, how everyone would benefit. Why couldn't the capitalists see it was in their own interests to increase production, why were they deliberately continuing to polarise the situation and stimulate the class struggle? What reformist hasn't had the same thoughts? It was this failure to appreciate the class nature of the struggle that doomed the FSLN to lead the revolution to defeat.

The actions of the capitalists were placing union officials in a very difficult position. Notwithstanding official policy, the local and national officials of the CST were faced with the grubby reality of bourgeois deception. The trade union leaders were becoming frustrated with having to face one de-capitalising capitalist after another under conditions where the law as it stood invited the capitalists to run their enterprises into the ground.

Both CST and ATC officers had responsibility for identifying owners who were de-capitalising, and taking preventative action to stop them. However, their personal experiences demonstrated that the mass occupations essential to stop decapitalisation led inevitably to other demands by the workforce which they then had to curtail. At a workers' assembly held in July 1981, entitled 'Against De-capitalisation We Demand Confiscation', the General Secretary of the CST, Lucio Jiménez said:

> The workers could not remain on the defensive (...) we had to go over immediately onto the offensive in a clear struggle, not against an individual or one or two bourgeois administrators, or one or two bosses, but to go on to the struggle immediately and strike sharp blows against the bourgeoisie as a class.[83]

However, no measures were included for the workers' and peasants' democratic control of production – the only sure way to defeat decapitalisation.

---

83 In Vilas, C., *Perfiles de la Revolución Sandinista*, Casa de las Américas, 1984.

Under pressure from the rank and file, and failing to get the expected increases in production, Daniel Ortega announced the Agrarian Reform Law on 19 July, 1981, on behalf of the new Junta. Despite strong resistance from landowning capitalists, it was again promised that land that was underdeveloped, left fallow or abandoned for at least six months would be compulsorily purchased from its owners at a price set by the government. Additionally, the land of those who had taken up arms against the revolution could be seized. IP reported[84] that these lands (approximately 600,000 hectares) were to be made available to agricultural labourers, and the poorest *campesinos*, the 64,000 who owned less than 1 hectare of land. The government now owned the banks and, in a popular move, declared a moratorium on debt interest repayments for loans made to small and medium peasants.

Homesteaders were given free title to land they had occupied. Bank foreclosure in the event of default on a bank loan was prohibited. These moves had three goals: to increase government popularity and mobilise the *campesinos* behind the FSLN; to make Nicaragua self-sufficient in food production by 1983; and to increase the production of food and agricultural crops for export. These remained the dominant themes of FSLN agricultural policy until well after the 1984 elections.

Importantly, the new Agrarian Reform Law established the legal right of women to hold the title deeds for land; neither kinship nor gender barred a person from benefiting from land redistribution. Previously, the vast majority of women members of the co-operatives had been landless labourers, now they could be land-holders and full members.

According to Jaime Wheelock, these actions were at the heart of the FSLN's programme of a mixed economy with private, co-operative, and public ownership of production. They would improve Nicaragua's economy and thereby lay the groundwork for democracy by providing Nicaragua's population with the means to develop itself economically, politically and culturally. Wheelock later generously estimated that by mid-1986, almost one hundred thousand *campesino* families had benefited from the reform's land redistribution programme, with two million hectares having been affected.

La Prensa voiced the concerns of the bourgeoisie, stepping up its campaign of false allegations, COSEP denounced the government, Contra raids escalated. In response, the FSLN decreed a state of economic and social emergency (9 September, 1981), banned land seizures, strikes, threats to continued production and any actions which could lead to demands for workers' control of production. The penalties included jail terms of up to three years. As a gesture, twenty-four members of the PCN were arrested.

---

84 12 December, 1983

From September 1981 through to 1987, the right to strike was denied except for a short period around the elections, from 1984 to 1985.

The CAUS survived the attacks of the CST, but clashed again with the FSLN in October 1981 when its leaders were sentenced to several years in jail (later commuted) for violating the emergency decree. Once again, the PCN-led union CAUS and FO were denounced by the CST and *Barricada* as agents of Somoza, or the CIA or the counter-revolution.

By October 1981, AMNLAE's membership was 25,000. It was successfully mobilising women for the coffee and cotton harvests and when those were complete, recruited women students as teachers for the Literacy Crusade after which it organised preventative medicine brigades to undertake vaccinations, and gave advice on nutrition and personal hygiene. As if that weren't enough, it then undertook to mobilise women for the Popular Militia against the Contras.

Glenda Monterrey, "a central leader of AMNLAE"[85] explained that AMNLAE was not intended to organise around issues pertaining only to women. Its purpose was to organise around the practical tasks of the moment; e.g. its biggest campaign in 1981 was to recruit women to the militia reserve battalions – to spend two or three weeks a year on military exercises in the mountains, away from the family. However, the image of an organisation which simply enacted government decisions rather than its own initiatives grew and, by 1982, its effectiveness was noticeably declining.[86]

Under Somoza's dictatorship, easily curable diseases led to the death of over thirty per cent of the children in the countryside. A health awareness campaign similar to the literacy campaign was launched. Of the 78,000 health brigadistas, three quarters were women. Mothers and children were the priority, with over a million people vaccinated, and hygiene and nutrition education provided with the immediate result that infant mortality dropped to nine per cent. An essential element was the provision of clean water. Under the FSLN government, 500 doctors graduated annually and the healthcare system guaranteed doctors' visits for some 3,000,000 people. The government also launched housing construction programmes, especially in the countryside.

8.1) THE REVOLUTIONARY PATRIOTIC WAR HOTS UP (1982-83)

The decision to launch the Contra War was made in the White House no later than 1981, and, by 1983, had grown into a full-scale mercenary war

---

85 In an interview with IP 26 October, 1981.
86 Chichilla, *Women ...* op. cit.

that dominated all life and politics in Nicaragua. Because of its perspective of a mixed economy, the FSLN leadership decided 'national unity' was essential in the face of the Contras and declared a social pact (*concertación*) with the national bourgeoisie, in an effort to get them to back the war. The capitalists, certainly those that looked to *La Prensa* for leadership, had no intention of supporting an FSLN victory. But the FSLN saw *concertación* as possible, and to achieve it was quite prepared to slow down and, in some cases, curtail the more radical measures being taken to improve the living standards of working people.

Nicaragua, meanwhile was peacefully engaged in attempting to increase its exports in the face of the opposition of its own capitalists. These people had been robbed (as they saw it) of governmental and state power by a gang of terrorists in whom they had no confidence either politically or economically. They were terrified of revolutionary activities within the factories: sit-ins, strikes, and even the imprisonment of managers. As they saw it, the FSLN, despite all its statements and pleas, was gradually robbing them of their authority on their farms and in their factories by encouraging the workers to act against decapitalisation. They were only too anxious to be rid of the FSLN. For many, it meant covert support for a Contra victory by economic sabotage.

In February 1982, new financial incentives were announced for capitalists who increased their exports. The government would ensure profitability by paying a significant proportion of the cost of imports and guaranteeing a preferential exchange rate for exports. This scheme directed almost two-thirds of government financial assistance to the big farms. The thanks the government got? Private investment fell to an all-time low! But even worse, the loopholes in the scheme meant even greater decapitalisation, weakening the export sector further, the opposite of what was intended. The FSLN practically encouraged decapitalisation when, as an incentive to the capitalists to produce more, it gave them access to hard currency "for useful purposes, including recreation".[87]

As the Contra war was getting underway in May-June 1982, Nicaragua suffered devastation due to torrential rain. 800 mm of rain (thirty-four inches) in six days threatened to reverse the gains made since Somoza's overthrow, a third of basic food crops (beans, corn and rice) and ninety per cent of the cotton crop was destroyed, sixty factories partially or totally paralysed, hundreds dead, 40,000 homeless and US$200 million in damage. The national network of roads, bridges and drainage systems, inadequate even for normal conditions collapsed. Naturally, the Contras made every effort

---

87 IP, 14 November, 1983.

to exacerbate the situation. This was a major material disaster, but it was minimised by the spirit of self-confidence and creative self-help that prevailed in the country.

The war took a terrible toll on the Nicaraguan people, some 500 had been killed by early 1983. Given the level of medical support, severe wounds, particularly those due to land mines, meant amputees became a common sight in most towns. The economic impact was severe with shortages of everyday basic necessities such as cooking oil. The Contras made a special effort to target those engaged in education (fifteen schools destroyed) and health initiatives (seventeen healthcare centres destroyed), killing doctors, nurses, technicians, teachers, and children. Food production was another target, with regular attacks on *campesinos* in their fields, and warehouses storing coffee, cotton and tobacco.

Nicaragua was being forced to spend a quarter of its GDP to protect its citizens which meant increased inflation. As a result of the war, in 1983 inflation was nearly thirty per cent (rising to forty per cent in 1984) and, consequently, the real take-home pay of workers fell substantially. The government attempted to cushion these effects by introducing food subsidies. The effect on the factory workers was a surge of volunteers to fight the Contras, coupled with a tightening of belts in order to contribute even more to the war effort. Taking care of and resettling 114,000 refugees slowed the expansion of healthcare provision, schools and social housing. The destruction of resources meant the state had to impose greater control over the distribution of food and necessities.

Conflict within the Roman Catholic Church surfaced again when Pope John Paul II, a noted reactionary, visited Nicaragua in March 1983. The government provided free transport for some half a million Nicaraguans to attend the highlight of the visit, an outdoor mass in Managua at which the Pope refused to offer a prayer for the government or for the souls of deceased soldiers. Anti-government demonstrators began chanting, "We love the Pope". Pro-government supporters responded with chants of "We want peace", which soon drowned out the anti-government claque. The mass was interrupted, and the Pope angrily asked the crowd for silence several times. Edited highlights were broadcast worldwide as a deliberate attempt by the Sandinistas to disrupt the mass.

Outside of Nicaragua it was difficult to appreciate the scale of this war. Washington, using verbal camouflage, described the Contra war as 'low-intensity', but there was nothing 'low intensity' as far as Nicaragua was concerned. As an indication of the disruption caused by the war, the 43,000 Nicaraguans killed plus the 25,000 killed fighting against the National Guard during the revolution constituted some two per cent of the total population, equivalent in the USA to more than seven million people, not to mention the wounded, the war refugees, the orphaned and the massive destruction of the country's productive resources.

The destruction wreaked by the Contra armies came on top of the US trade embargo; the devastation caused by large-scale natural disasters, and failure to obtain sufficient aid from overseas. The Contra War was a war on two fronts, the battles against the Contras and the economic war being waged by the bourgeoisie within Nicaragua against the Sandinista regime. The refusal of the large producers to co-operate with the government did not stem from a lack of incentives or a reaction to the regime's more revolutionary rhetoric. Rather, it was a determined and conscious attempt to assist in the overthrow of the government. They were doing all they could to prevent a revolutionary regime from surviving, including not only economic sabotage but also running a campaign of lies and deceit aimed at undermining support for the regime both at home and abroad.

The FSLN should have followed the example set by the ex-colonists in the US after the American War of Independence when many states passed 'confiscation laws' which allowed the state to seize the property of those loyal to the British crown, selling it off on behalf of the state treasury.[88] The response of the FSLN was to cut back or abandon many of its social programmes and development projects: land reform, the fight for women's rights (legalisation of abortion, equal rights in hiring and on the job, and ending violence against women), and how to plan the economy so that production met social need not private profit.

Facing continuing attacks by US-sponsored Contras along both its northern and southern borders, on 10 August, 1983, Humberto Ortega, with overall command of the EPS, announced compulsory military service for the first time in Nicaragua's history. Conscription would begin in January 1984 with each conscript serving for a minimum of two years. Initially, women were not mentioned, but the AMNLAE argued that since women had proved themselves as effective fighters in the war against Somoza there was no reason to exclude them from the draft. Many women active in AMNLAE argued that this omission reflected a *machismo* view of women held by senior members of the FSLN (especially President Daniel Ortega and his brother Humberto). A compromise was reached whereby women were not required to register, but could do so on a voluntary basis.[89]

88 Boonshoft, M., *Dispossessing Loyalists ... in Revolutionary New York*, www.nypl. org.

89 Molyneux, M., *Women's role in the Nicaraguan revolutionary process*, Journal of Women in Culture and Society, 9(2)379-384, 1993.

AMNLAE re-focused its attention on the collection of materials for recycling, campaigning to save energy, convincing women to back the war effort when they were subject to frozen wages, inflation, shortages, black-market speculation, and lack of either child or maternity care. An important aspect of AMNLAE's work was the campaign to increase food production that relied heavily on women activists in the ACT. The AMNLAE leadership was doubly taken aback when women agricultural workers responded by challenging the thrust of the war effort, demanding a more anti-capitalist emphasis.

Catholics make up about half Nicaragua's population. The Catholic Church in Nicaragua was led by Obando, Archbishop of Managua, a vocal opponent of Liberation Theology, which condemned capitalism, in Latin America especially, as an unjust and iniquitous system and thus a form of structural sin. The Catholic hierarchy in Nicaragua threw itself behind the Contra leadership, leading to a de facto split with the so-called 'church of the poor' which supported the Sandinistas. Naturally, the bourgeois news media around the world emphasised the views of the hierarchy.

Obando would become the leading 'legal' Contra mouthpiece in Nicaragua. So eager was the Church hierarchy to undermine the FSLN government that it altered Canonical Law – the fundamental law of the Roman Catholic Church. On 27 November, 1983, Article 285 was introduced prohibiting priests from accepting "those public positions entailing participation in the exercise of civil authority". Obando personally saw to it that Fernando Cardenal, a Jesuit priest who refused to resign from his position in the Sandinista government, was expelled from his order. With the approval of Pope John II, all four priests with ministerial positions were suspended from their orders by 1985.

Obando was made a cardinal on 25 May, 1985. Fresh from the Vatican, he travelled to Miami to brief, and be briefed by, Contra leaders. The first Mass Obando celebrated after being made a cardinal was in Miami before the Contra leadership; after which he was claimed by the Contras in Honduras as their 'spiritual guide'. In January 1986, Obando travelled to the United States where he declared his support for the Contras and encouraged the US administration to provide them with military aid. Tomás Borge, in an interview published in the Mexican paper *El Día* (January 1986), argued that Obando was made a cardinal for political reasons that fully coincided with those of the US administration.

8.2 THE NATIONAL QUESTION IN NICARAGUA

The national question became an explosive issue in Nicaragua when it led to substantial numbers of Miskito Indians joining the Contras and fighting against the revolution.

The Spanish colonised the Pacific coast of Nicaragua and the British the Atlantic coast. This meant there were significant differences in the composition of the two populations with the 'Coast' a separate entity historically, religiously, culturally, linguistically, and ethnically. The term 'Atlantic Coast' is somewhat of a misnomer since it comprises just over half the land area of Nicaragua. The approximate make-up of the population of the Atlantic Coast was, at the time of the revolution, 120,000 Mestizos (of mixed Spanish and indigenous descent, as are the great majority of Nicaraguans), 80,000 Miskito Indians and 30,000 Creoles, with three other racial groups totalling about 10,000.

Under the Somoza regime the Atlantic Coast was isolated financially and socially. When the revolution triumphed in 1979 the peoples of the Atlantic coast, even though they suffered severe discrimination under the Somoza regime were, except for the mining areas which saw intense fighting between National Guards and FSLN guerrillas, by and large, not involved.

Later, Tomás Borge in an interview with *El Nuevo Diario*, on 15 January, 1986, explained that the Sandinistas accepted their treatment of the peoples of the Atlantic Coast had been high-handed. He described how young enthusiastic revolutionaries from Managua, speaking only Spanish, arrived on the Atlantic Coast and, although they introduced some reforms, they disappointed by promising far more than could be delivered by the new regime.

The local population had been used to the presence of only relatively few National Guards, but after the revolution, and in the fight against the Contras, large numbers of Sandinista militia speaking neither Miskito nor English arrived, in a virtual invasion. That, and the failure in the first stage of the revolution to give security of land tenure to the local peasants generated considerable mistrust and opposition.

Initially, the FSLN was insensitive to the demands of black people and indians for racial equality, greater autonomy and an end to economic subordination. The FSLN failed to appreciate the existence of ethnic dimensions and sought to integrate the Atlantic Coast within Nicaragua by purely economic means, ignoring demands for participation in decisions on matters affecting their lives, such as the use of their own languages in official documents and schools. These errors did not flow from the FSLN's Historic Programme as written by Fonseca. That programme had called for land to the peasants and for self-determination for the Atlantic Coast, both key democratic demands omitted from the Humberto Ortega version.

The result was the Atlantic Coast became an area where the local population provided substantial support for the Contras. Local chiefs, who had worked with the Somoza security services now made deals with the CIA, which supplied them with money and munitions. The FSLN appointed Steadman Fagoth Mueller, a Miskito, to the Council of State, only to arrest him in February 1981 on charges of fostering counter-revolution. He was also identified as an informer for the National Guard. The FSLN militants were astounded when the Miskitos remained loyal to their former leader and protested his arrest. Finally, the government freed him on the condition that he went abroad. Fagoth crossed into Honduras where he openly collaborated with the Contras.

The FSLN then made the disastrous decision to move the Miskitos from their traditional lands near the Rio Coco river, to Puerto Cabezas, away from the fighting. This caused some ten thousand Miskitos to flee to Honduras where, funded by the US and under the influence of Fagoth, they joined the Contra forces. It was not until the FSLN, having realised its mistakes, agreed the Miskitos should return home with security of land tenure, that the Miskitos drifted back and relinquished support for their former leaders and the Contras. Tomás Borge was given responsibility for developing government policy on National Autonomy which would incorporate the principles contained in the Historic Programme.

9) THE 4 NOVEMBER, 1984, ELECTION – A REFORMIST ORIENTATION

An alleged lack of political pluralism was one of the Reagan administration's frequently-used arguments to attack the Sandinistas. In early 1982, the USA began to demand the FSLN government hold free elections, despite knowing that elections were already scheduled for 1985. Bringing the elections forward became an ongoing demand of the bourgeois opposition within Nicaragua. Faced with the Contra War, and to enhance its legitimacy in the eyes of the world, the FSLN opened a discussion on the holding of a governmental election. In May 1983, Jaime Wheelock was interviewed extensively on the question of an election and explained why one could not be held immediately. A delay was necessary to give the election credibility by having a census of those over the age of sixteen and register them to vote.[90]

By mid-July 1983, it had been decided that certain constraints were necessary and some parties would be excluded, these were: Somoza-ist

---

90 Harnecker, M., *Interview with Jaime Wheelock*, jaimewheelock.com.

parties which did not respect the political and social gains conquered by the Nicaraguan people, parties which did not defend national sovereignty and self-determination of the Nicaraguan people, and parties that sought to impose a regime of oppression and exploitation on the Nicaraguan people. Within these constraints, to which all the bourgeois parties paid lip-service, any party could run in the elections, criticise the government, publicise their views through public meetings, newspapers, radio, TV and other mass media, raise funds, and establish and maintain a national network of offices.

The FSLN leadership openly declared in its election platform that the elimination of private enterprise and the socialisation of the means of production were not objectives of the Sandinista Revolution. Commandant Jaime Wheelock, formerly leader of the Proletarian Tendency and a major architect of economic strategy, openly embraced the Stalinist theory of stages:

> It is important to understand that the socialist model is a solution for contradictions that exist only in developed capitalist countries… socialising all the means of production… would not lead to socialism, rather, on the contrary, it could lead to the destruction and dis-articulation of our society.[91]

This was nothing less than a political disaster.

Although the FSLN leaders had formally broken organisationally with the PSN, they brought with them its reformist policy of socialism by stages. During the re-unification in 1978-79, all three tendencies publicly accepted there would, first, be a democratic revolution to bring the country to an acceptable level of capitalist development then, later, at some unknown time in the future, a second, socialist revolution. This false theory does not flow from a scientific analysis of reality and the actual history of revolutions, instead it is based on the bogus belief that the interests of the national bourgeoisie are qualitatively different from the interests of their imperialist masters.

This is the kind of reformism that Marx, Engels, Lenin, Trotsky, Luxemburg and Guevara fought against. Today, no country in the world can develop its own capitalism in the same way that the advanced capitalist countries did in the past, because the bourgeoisie in the advanced countries will fight to preserve their dominance. They have over two hundred years' experience of doing so in the bloodiest manner, including two world wars. Of course, the bourgeois in the advanced countries favour peaceful means of dominating the weak and cowardly national-colonial bourgeoisie in Latin America, Asia and Africa. The IMF, the World Bank, the Central European Bank, and so on are preferred because such methods allow the multinational companies to maximise their profits through looting raw materials, exploiting

---

91 Wheelock, J., *The Great Challenge*. Managua: Nueva Nicaragua No 101: 1983.

cheap labour and charging interest on loans to crooked despots which the
people of the country then repay in taxes.

The 'national' bourgeoisie in Latin and Central America had already
shown themselves unable and unwilling to carry through their own bourgeois-
national revolutions, to effect land reform by abolishing the big landed
estates, to seize full sovereignty, to provide social and economic development
independent of imperialism. The so-called 'national' bourgeoisie in Nicaragua,
in which the FSLN leaders had so much faith were, and remain, proxies of
the imperialists, rich thanks to their positions as agents for the imperialists
with whom they jointly exploited the poor, working, indigenous masses.

Pandering to the national bourgeoisie in an attempt to win their support,
the FSLN leaders further demoralised and demobilised the Nicaraguan
workers and peasants, who were increasingly less convinced that making
ever-greater sacrifices was a strategy which would advance the revolution.
The FSLN used numerous arguments to convince the vanguard: the only
realistic road forward for Nicaragua was to strengthen the mixed economy
(i.e. capitalist production and capitalist profits), that only by maintaining
a social pact with 'patriotic' capitalists (freezing the class struggle) would
give an improvement in living standards and lead toward socialism at some
unspecified time in the future.

It would be insufficient to say the FSLN bent under the pressure of
the national and international bourgeoisie because, right from the start, its
own ideology led it in this direction. Believing in the myth of a 'progressive
national bourgeoisie', the Sandinistas were left little room for manoeuvre,
particularly in the economic field. The hey-day of the mixed economy was in
the period following World War II when it was the official policy of European
Social Democracy. In the UK, it meant the nationalisation of basic industries
and their modernisation at public expense to enable British capitalists to
better compete in international markets. As a final irony these industries,
made profitable by public investment, were returned to the very same class
that had run them into the ground.

FSLN leaders insisted that state property and a planned economy were
incompatible with political liberties, that only a mixed economy could
guarantee political pluralism. We can all agree that extending and deepening
bourgeois-democratic rights in Nicaragua was a progressive development
that increased the opportunities for the exploited to organise and become
involved in politics. Such a struggle has a revolutionary dynamic if linked
to a deepening of workers' democracy, which will inevitably conflict
with capitalist exploitation. Limiting the struggle to one for bourgeois

parliamentary democracy and electoralism inevitably means the restriction, if not destruction, of any democratic freedoms gained.

The Transitional Programme explained:

> [T]he slogan of the 'workers' and peasants' government' in the bourgeois democratic version… when the party of the proletariat refuses to step beyond bourgeois democratic limits, its alliance with the peasantry is simply turned into support for capital, as was the case with the Mensheviks and Social Revolutionaries in 1917, with the Chinese Communist Party in 1925-27, and as is now the case with the peoples' front in Spain, France and other countries.[92]

On 21 February, 1984, the Council of State set the election date for 4 November, two days before the US presidential elections. Internationally, the announcement was well received – except by the United States. The Kissinger Commission had released its report on Central America on 10 January, calling on the FSLN to allow the Contras to run candidates in the election. Without the FSLN meeting this condition, Kissinger (fresh from the Vietnam conflict) advised that the US should consider the direct use of force.

From the second half of 1981 to the end of 1983, some land redistribution occurred, but much less and much more slowly than the peasants wanted. With the Contra war and the suffering of the population the government was anxious to maximise *campesino* support, particularly in the border regions and some parts of the Atlantic Coast, where the Contras had been able to recruit poor peasants who had received nothing from the land reform programme. The government accelerated the pace of confiscations of underused capitalist holdings and its distribution. It also ended the policy limiting land distribution to those who agreed to establish co-operatives. Naturally, this new tranche of land distribution was met by howls of protest from the bourgeoisie who saw it as a bribe to influence the outcome of the forthcoming election.

On 22 October, 1984, *El Nuevo Diario*, reported Commandante Víctor Tirado's announcement to an assembly of peasants; "In the framework of the mixed economy … expropriation of large farms came to an end with the expropriation of Somoza's land". But the FSLN could still be swept off-course; the peasants of Masaya (an impoverished area), fed up with their poor standard of living, took the law into their own hands and, en masse, in May 1985 took over large local landed estates refusing to leave despite the entreaties and threats of the local FSLN tops. In the end, the government agreed a deal with the landowners who accepted equivalent farms in areas of

---

92 Trotsky, L., *The Transitional Programme* www.marxist.org, 1938.

less militancy. The exception was Enrique Bolaños, President of COSEP, who engineered a political campaign out of the incident.

Despite Tirado's statement, the government distributed over half a million hectares in 1984, compared to 350,000 in 1983 and less than 100,000 in total in the two years 1981-82. The growth was because of the Contra threat, some two-thirds of the peasants in the border areas were allocated land and were photographed, filmed and televised being presented by Daniel Ortega or Jaime Wheelock with the title deed of their land and a gun to defend it. And it did make a big difference – support for the Contras fell away. Giving the people something concrete to defend was the most effective way to fight the war, and for the *campesino*, the best thing was land.

The primary source of the new land was from those landowners with more than 350 hectares (850 acres) neither used productively, nor rented to tenants. This, it was hoped, would strengthen government support in the countryside and produce more food.

The FSLN believed its policy for food production would be more effective if all producers were members of the organisation which the government controlled, and not in the opposition COSEP. In August 1984, UNAG took its first positive step towards actively recruiting 'patriotic producers' by calling on the government to guarantee the land of capitalist farmers would not be confiscated if they continued to produce efficiently. This change was symbolised by the election of Daniel Nuñez as President of UNAG. Nuñez, previously Head of the Ministry of Agrarian Development and Reform (MIDINRA), was a long-time FSLN stalwart. Beginning his political activities with a Catholic Church group, he joined the FSLN in 1972 and had his ranch of over 1,200 hectares confiscated when he was arrested by the Somoza regime in 1974.

Increasingly, the 'patriotic producers' and their class interests dominated UNAG and effectively ended its role as an organisation based on the peasantry. Increasingly, the voice of the 'agricultural producers' became that of capitalist farmers, the exploiters of agricultural workers. This turn had the effect of undermining the self-confidence and politicisation of the poor peasants, leaving them vulnerable to the demagogy of the capitalists.

According to objective observers, Nicaragua was one of the most democratic states in Central America. On 4 November, 1984, more than eighty per cent of the eligible population voted. *Barricada* announced the results, seats were allocated in proportion to the votes cast: FSLN sixty-seven per cent of votes cast (sixty-one seats); PCD fourteen per cent (thirteen seats), PLI ten per cent (eight seats), PPSC six per cent (five seats), the PSN, PCN and the People's Action Movement each got one seat but only about three per cent of the votes cast. Daniel Ortega was elected president and Sergio Ramirez vice-president. The election results showed the huge support of the masses for the FSLN. The US imperialists damned the election as repressive because the Contras were not allowed to run candidates, and because Ortega received a higher percentage of the popular vote than Reagan!

The 1984 election was, in a democratic sense, a real political advance for Nicaragua. Quite rightly, it was applauded, because it was held in the middle of a full-scale civil war, instigated and funded by the US. The election demonstrated that the conquest of power by workers and peasants is in no way a restriction on democratic freedoms. Compared to previous Nicaraguan elections, this was a huge increase in the right to assembly, free expression of ideas and association, freedom of the press, and casting one's vote without a guard looking over one's shoulder.

The FSLN's election programme was reprinted in *Intercontinental Press* of 1 October, 1984, and can be read with the benefit of hindsight. It contains much that is admirable and would have been supported by revolutionaries: right to a job, to organise and mobilise, to housing, equal pay for equal work, the provision of healthcare and educational services for all Nicaraguans, the provision of water, electricity, communication and transportation to even the most remote areas, particularly the Atlantic Coast. One of the first tasks of the new Assembly would be to draft a new constitution.

These undoubted positive aspects dazzled many on the left who exaggerated such statements as "Weapons will remain in the hands of the people" as proof that the FSLN still represented a Workers' and Peasants' Government on the way to a workers' state. That the weapons were under the control of the army, that the FSLN remained committed to the development of a mixed economy, that the promised land reform did not fundamentally challenge private ownership were ignored.

The FSLN promised to "deepen the popular anti-imperialist character of the Nicaraguan state". This was done by setting up a government department: 'the Comptroller-General of the Republic' to monitor the conduct of civil servants and improve their 'levels of efficiency'. What was not mentioned, because it cut across the priority of the mixed economy, was any kind of popular or Soviet control of government.

Most revealing was the policy proposed for 'Women'. This commenced with the statement: "The family laws adopted by the revolutionary government are aimed at protecting women as mothers and providing them the dignity due them within the family" and continues "The Sandinista Front will go on defending the nuclear family and the integrity of the home..." Such statements were a clear warning that this was a government of retrenchment, not one that would take the revolution forward. The bureaucratisation of both the Russian and Chinese Communist Parties was accompanied by just such statements.[93]

Hidden in the small print was the transformation of the Council of State into the Nicaraguan National Assembly. The FSLN leadership changed the governmental structure to that of the traditional bourgeois parliament. With hindsight, this was a clear indication that the FSLN regime could no longer be classified as a Workers' and Peasants' Government. However, this was not the response of the majority on the left. Three factors acted to obscure the change. Firstly, the new government had a sizeable FSLN majority and so, it was argued, could continue as before. Secondly, because Nicaragua was subject to imperialist attack, it was necessary to continue to defend the Sandinista government unconditionally (and to some that meant uncritically). Thirdly, there was a subjective element: having defended the revolutionary government for five years, it was very hard to acknowledge it had taken a qualitative step backwards.

Leading leftists now argued that it is not the form of a parliament that makes it bourgeois; because as the FSLN had come to power on a revolutionary wave and had control of the state apparatus, the parliament resulting from the election could not be bourgeois. However, to cover themselves against possible future criticisms, these commentators simultaneously and correctly called for the creation of Soviets on the grounds that such organs were more effective in consolidating workers' power, suggesting the possibility of some kind of job share between parliament and Soviets.[94] This having your cake and eating it approach, was strikingly similar to the counter-revolutionary argument proposed in 1917 by Kamenev and Zinoviev – and damned by Lenin – for the establishment of a dual-power in Russia, a Constituent Assembly and Soviets.

As the economic and social crisis deepened, the FSLN resisted the demands of working people in city and countryside to extend workers' control over capitalist production and distribution. Such moves were necessary to protect the living standards of workers and peasants, let alone enhance them, but would have challenged the rights of private ownership. As supplies of essential foodstuffs and other basic items decreased, prices spiralled upwards. The only way to guarantee fair access to necessities was to ration them and place their distribution in the hands of democratically-controlled local committees. During 1984, it was self-help initiatives by working women, creating communal soup kitchens, arranging for water

93 Trotsky, L., 'Thermidor in the Family', in *The Revolution Betrayed*, 1936, www. marxists.org and Roberts, op cit. 2007.

94 Mandel, E., *Road to Socialist Democracy*, La Gauche, 16 November, 1984.

distribution, establishing child healthcare centres and organising transport that kept many urban areas from social collapse.[95] The shortages in the early years of Soviet Russia had been even more severe: between 1919 and 1920, ninety per cent of Petrograd was fed communally, and in May 1920 nearly 315,000 working class families in Russia were eating in state canteens.

10) REVOLUTION UNDER SIEGE (1985)

When the newly elected Nicaraguan government took office in early 1985, it was clear that those leaders least attracted to a socialist course were dominant. Nevertheless, the government responded to pressure from the masses and advanced important anti-imperialist initiatives. First and foremost, the FSLN led the mobilisation of the toilers of Nicaragua to defeat the imperialist-organised and financed Contra War.

The FSLN government could no more guide a capitalist economy toward recovery and expansion than could any government of a poverty-stricken capitalist country in the semi-colonial world. To ease the crisis in production it was necessary to take steps towards a planned economy. Without that, no amount of government effort to reverse the economic decline could be successful. The top Sandinistas, however, still dreamed of collaborating with a 'national progressive bourgeoisie'.

On 3 August, 1985, Daniel Ortega called for the re-organisation of the FSLN, pointing out that the existing structure was suited to guerrilla groups and underground cells, not an open mass organisation governing a country. Defence of Nicaragua from merciless attack by the greatest military power on earth required improving the quality of the FSLN cadres, increasing the number of cadres, and strengthening the organisation.

The FSLN had a leadership, the National Directorate, the nine Commandants, who made decisions and policy, but no formal membership, even as late as 1978. Its only democratic element was a consultative 'Sandinista Assembly', whose members were appointed by the Directorate. Astounding though it may seem, the FSLN did not have its first party congress until 1991, one year after the disastrous election of 1990 and eleven years after the triumph over Somoza. The largest mass organisation supporting the FSLN was the CDSs, but the head of the CDSs was appointed by the Directorate and the CDSs themselves 'elected' their leaders from a pre-selected list compiled by the Directorate with no opportunity for democratic discussion on the policies and programmes of different candidates.

Obviously, changes were necessary, but those recommended by Daniel Ortega would not give the membership greater involvement in decision-

95 Stevens, K., *Women's Role in the Sandinista Revolution*, Stanford University, 2013.

making. Rather, they gave him greater personal control of the government and party. Ortega's rise within the FSLN had been steady and continuous. He was a guerrilla leader, a member of the first revolutionary Junta in 1979, then as Junta Co-ordinator in 1984, he was the FSLN Presidential candidate and won a decisive victory. His ambitions were revealed when he successfully proposed within the Directorate that the President be allowed to run for re-election. Despite an official news black-out, it was soon leaked that Interior Minister Tomás Borge had opposed the proposal.

Ortega moved quickly and his opponents were soon demoted. Borge was too senior and popular to be openly sacked, so Borge's allies became the targets. Henry Ruiz Hernandez was downgraded from Planning Minister to Minister of Foreign Co-operation; the Directorate's Political Commission, with Bayardo Arce Castano as head, was abolished and replaced with an Executive Committee which Ortega, himself, headed. Agriculture Minister Jaime Wheelock, notionally the country's top economic planner and another possible rival, was systematically undermined by Ortega's public apologies for failings in, for example, the government's agricultural planning, that brought shortages of beef and dairy products.

By November 1986, FSLN recruitment meetings for the new 'aspiring members' were being held throughout Nicaragua. One such meeting was at the University of Managua:

> A thousand people came to celebrate the admission to the FSLN of some 50 new members, the majority of them women… It was my impression that the FSLN is a young and dedicated party with the great bulk of its members in their twenties.[96]

Despite these jamborees, the FSLN had fewer than 10,000 militants at the end of 1986.

Membership turnover was high; by 1988 there were as many ex-members as there were current members, the reason being that although the great majority of leavers remained loyal to the revolution they found the undemocratic practices within the FSLN unacceptable. The internal structure and organisation made it impossible to have a political discussion in which honest differences were expressed.[97] Moisés Hassan, in an interview carried in the *Los Angeles Times* of 3 July, 1988, criticising the *Tercerista* Tendency for damaging the revolutionary quality of the Front, gave his reason for quitting the FSLN as its lack of internal democracy: that it still bore the stamp of its guerrilla origins with a military emphasis on discipline and duty, requiring

96 Benjamin, op. cit.
97 Ibid.

instructions from the top be obeyed immediately and without question – expressed in the slogan 'National Directorate – we await your command'.

Without internal democracy, a party has no in-built mechanisms to discuss, identify and correct mistakes. Political policy is inevitably settled more and more at the top, increasingly by an ever-smaller cabal and, in the end, by the Napoleon of the party – Stalin in Russia, Mao in China, and Daniel Ortega in Nicaragua. Lacking a party modelled on Lenin's Bolshevik Party, where there was maximum freedom of discussion within the party, but a firm discipline when enacting the decisions of the majority, the party inevitably becomes dictatorial. With chronic shortages the order of the day, it was no wonder that, by the time of the 1990 election, top party and state officials were supplied with free housing, free household goods, coupons for the 'dollar stores' and for the very tops, Toyota cars.[98]

Subsequent events confirm that the changes recommended by Ortega in 1985, and subsequently, were made to consolidate his personal base. The Directorate still met regularly and, formally, had the final word on policy matters. But increasingly Ortega became its principal figure with the firm backing of his brother Humberto, Minister of Defence, and Leticia Herrera, who was then in charge of the CDSs and a Vice-President of the National Assembly, described in *La Prensa*[99] as a former close personal companion of Mr Ortega and mother of his son Camilo. The more insightful of American commentators as in the *New York Times*,[100] looked positively on what was happening, and praised Ortega as "among the least dogmatic members of the National Directorate".

It appears there were no dissenting members of the Directorate regarding the need to preserve the mixed economy, and for the regime to defend capitalist property relations. The FSLN leaders repeated ad nauseum their commitment to preserving the mixed economy. As Tomás Borge said in an interview with *New Left Review*: "In Nicaragua… the bourgeoisie is… not eliminated, nor do we plan to eliminate it; quite the contrary, we have made substantial efforts to keep it in existence".[101]

In the same interview Borge explained that, to win the bourgeoisie to the revolution, it had to be given many economic incentives, "more even than the workers". "We have sacrificed the working class in favour of the economy as part of a strategic plan". By the time of this interview, the FSLN had eight years' experience of the machinations of the bourgeoisie, and one would have thought the Directorate would have realised this was a relationship going

98 Larmer, B., *Christian Science Monitor*, 25 January, 1989.
99 11 May, 2014
100 2 March, 1987
101 Interview with Borge, T., *New Left Review* 164, July/August 1987.

nowhere. It was crystal clear that the national bourgeoisie was waging an economic war against the revolution and the FSLN government and refusing to accept its designated role of partner in ending the country's dependency and under-development.

But the FSLN held firm in its commitment to an obviously failed partnership because its Stalinist, stagist perspective blinded it to what was really happening. It saw only what it wanted to see. Humberto Ortego confirmed: "We cannot resolve at the same time, the problems of national liberation and those of social liberation. We must first complete the stage of national independence and national liberation".[102] However, it was becoming painfully obvious to unbiased observers that, after the jolt of the revolution, the mixed economy experiment had not qualitatively changed the capitalist economic structures in Nicaragua.

By the late summer, the Contras had stepped up their attacks on bus stations and other acts of sabotage, and made their single largest incursion when about 2,500 contras advanced across the Honduran border into the Estelí region. The Directorate responded by re-instating the state of emergency, suspended one year previously. Quite correctly, the state of emergency banned any publicity for those advocating dialogue with the Contras, but it also included a ban on the right to strike, a measure deemed necessary by the Directorate because the government's austerity package had resulted in strikes and demonstrations demanding higher wages. The Directorate's thinking was made clear by Daniel Ortega's address to the United Nations on 21 October, 1985, when he equated those who sabotaged the economy by de-capitalising with those who encouraged strikes and labour 'indiscipline'.

The Directorate could not totally ignore the mass protests. In 1985, nearly 100,000 hectares of land was distributed to the peasantry, with a fourfold purpose: to strengthen its base amongst the peasants, to increase food supplies for the cities, to enable the government to end food subsidies, and to boost Ortega's personal prestige. About 7,500 families had received land under the First Agrarian Reform Programme in 1982; in both 1984 and 1983 about 12,000; and in 1985 nearly 15,500: totalling 47,000 families. Official figures claim a more optimistic 86,000. The land allocated per family, however, had halved, from over thirteen hectares per family in 1982 to about six hectares per family in 1985.

In 1985, poor and middle peasants still comprised the bulk of the UNAG members and its banners and flags were seen on demonstrations demanding land. However, Nuñez was remarkably successful in recruiting capitalist farmers to the UNAG, some of whom became FSLN candidates

---

102 Benjamin, op. cit.

in the 1984 and 1990 elections. These 'patriotic producers', of whom Samuel Amador, Nicaragua's largest rice producer and FSLN member in the Constituent Assembly was one, could have up to 200 permanent employees, increasing to 500 during the harvest. In line with government policy, there was a change in UNAG policy during 1985/86 – the call for redistributed land to be given exclusively to co-operatives was dropped and replaced by the demand for land titles to be given to individual *campesinos*, subject to their farming it productively. This had the additional benefit of reducing the costs to the government because it could no longer afford the machinery, seed, and technical help that was given to co-operatives.

The urban population had received a minimum of basic foodstuffs at subsidised prices. Within a mixed economy these subsidies fuelled budget deficits and increased inflation. The expectation was that increased food production from the new farms would compensate for the ending of food subsidies. However, many of the new, small farms were engaged in subsistence farming so that what actually occurred was a sharp increase in the price of the now unsubsidised food. The underlying cause of high food price remained: the shortage of supply exacerbated by Contra attacks on food producers. Marketplace food prices became the harsh reality. Managua housewives were outraged as hunger and malnutrition grew rapidly among the poorest city-dwellers.

Food shortages bore down most heavily on women, and at the same time, the revolutionary upsurge had given women a greater sense of self-worth. Thus, for some time members of the AMNLAE had been raising the question of a woman's right to choose. They had remained silent during the election campaign, but now increasingly raised the charge that, without the right to control one's own body, which is not possible if abortion is neither legal nor accessible, the road to full equality for women, whether peasants, workers, unemployed or middle class, was blocked. The FSLN government, however, made no change to the law as it existed under Somoza.

A case for abortion on medical grounds (the only grounds permitted) could be brought only by the woman's nearest male relative and would be heard by an all-male panel of three doctors. Given that many peasant women were lucky to live in a region with even one doctor, securing the approval of three was impossible. Back street or self-induced abortions, unlawful and often bungled, were killing and injuring thousands of women a year. Jon Hillson, a respected socialist and Nicaraguan solidarity activist, had – during a visit to Managua – investigated the major causes of injury and premature death for Nicaraguan women.[103] Hillson came to the shocking conclusion

---

103 Hillson, J., *Central American Reporter*, February 1989.

that between 1985 and 1988 the single greatest cause of death and injuries to women in Nicaragua was complications due to botched abortions, a greater number than the female casualties in the Contra War. How could a revolutionary and self-proclaimed socialist government tolerate such a situation?

In September 1985, AMNLAE convened a national conference on the actual progress made by women compared to the stated goals of the revolution. The Contra War was blamed for the slow progress, but six years after the revolution, women were serving in the armed forces, working as equals on the production line and were running the CDSs, all of which highlighted the gap between promise and reality. The AMNLAE conference emphasised that the failure to give a woman the right to determine for herself whether and when to have children limited her ability to determine all other aspects of her life. The question of abortion went right to the heart of women's rights.

The debate brought into the open a central obstacle holding women back from full participation in a self-proclaimed revolutionary society, but the FSLN leaders declared abortion too explosive an issue on which to adopt a public position given the strength of the opposition of the Catholic Church and conservative opposition parties. No member of the Council of Ministers or any of the nine members of the FSLN Directorate declared themselves for legal abortion. Consequently, thousands of women continued to die or suffer serious injuries each year. Botched, illegal abortions were, and would remain, the leading cause of maternal death.

The Sandinista paper *Barricada* reported on 19 November, 1985, the findings of a study by doctors at one Managua Women's Hospital: forty-five per cent of all admissions were due to complications from illegal abortions, of which about ten per cent died and a quarter required hysterectomies. Over eight-and-a-half thousand women presented themselves at the hospital in the fifteen months of the study. The pain, suffering and anguish of these women led the doctors and social workers concerned to make two recommendations: The Ministry of Health should implement family planning education programmes and remove restrictions on birth control devices; and the anti-abortion law should be revised.

One FSLN veteran, however, did make her position clear. In the 9 November, 1985 issue of *Barricada*, Commander Doris Tijerino, Chief of Nicaragua's police stated she was in favour of sex education in schools and that contraceptives should be cheaper and more easily available. She criticised the law whereby a woman seeking sterilisation needed the written approval of her husband, and explained, with obvious approval, that there was de-facto non-enforcement of the anti-abortion law. AMNLAE made no official statement, but María Lourdes Balaños, AMNLAE's legal officer stated:

> [T]he laws of the past were class-biased in favour of the bourgeoisie... (the current law) says that a woman who has an abortion can be sentenced to one to four years in prison. But if a man beats his wife so badly she has a miscarriage he faces only six months (in prison).

The Atlantic Coast autonomy process had been set in motion in late 1984. In October, 1985, Tomás Borge, Minister of the Interior, produced a report entitled 'Principles and Policies for the Exercise of the Rights to Autonomy by the Indigenous People and Communities of the Atlantic Coast', generally referred to as 'The Autonomy Plan'. This was the basis for the Autonomy Law that would be passed in 1987.

Borge's report, while emphasising Nicaraguan national unity, recognised:

> [T]hat the indigenous peoples and communities of the Atlantic Coast have the full right to preserve their own cultures and historical and religious heritages: the right to free use and development of their languages; the right to receive education in their own language and in Spanish; the right to organise their social and economic activity in accordance with their values and traditions... The rights of autonomy of the indigenous peoples and communities of the Atlantic Coast will be exercised in the geographic area they have traditionally occupied.

This reversed the earlier policy of the FSLN against autonomy on the Atlantic Coast, the FSLN was now pledged to protect local customs and languages while wiping out 'odious discrimination'.

On the first anniversary of the Autonomy Law, 2 September, 1988, Borge welcomed units of the Miskito militia to the celebration, many of whose members had, prior to the agreement on autonomy, fought alongside the Contras.

The fight against the Contras had forced the government to introduce conscription in August 1983. This was seen as a chink in the FSLN armour and *Radio Catolica*, broadcast from Managua, kept up a constant barrage of propaganda against the draft, appealing to young men to be draft dodgers. This illegal and highly provocative campaign forced the FSLN to start 1986 by closing the radio station to howls of protest by the international bourgeois media. Soon after, in an attempt to assuage the criticism, Daniel Ortega gave an interview to *TIME Magazine*. The 31 March, 1986 edition has him declaring firmly:

Now is not the time to establish socialism… We are convinced that our model should not be the countries of Eastern Europe or Cuba… The proper example for Nicaragua (is) the Scandinavian countries.

11) THE CONTRA WAR, THE ECONOMY AND THE ARIAS PLAN (1986-87)

The *Terceristas* in the leadership were consolidating their positions, developing a party 'apparatus', turning the CDSs into carefully controlled organs of 'popular power', establishing a regular army with direct control over the militias. At this juncture, the FSLN leaders still had to mobilise the masses and arm them against the counter-revolution in the form of the Contras backed by US imperialism. During 1986, working conditions in the factories deteriorated significantly. The Contra war brought a severe lack of replacement machine parts and shortages of raw materials. Skilled personnel were often transferred to the front to be replaced by enthusiastic, but inexperienced staff sent to administer and manage the factories. Some attempted to cut costs by not adhering to government pay scales, accelerating the development of currents in the unions that favoured strike action. Unfortunately, all too often, the new managers resorted to needless sackings, which only exacerbated the situation as the workers responded with strikes and picket lines. The managers then called in the police because the workers were violating the state of emergency.

In response, the FSLN launched an educational campaign explaining how industrial action played into the hands of the Contras. It moved to integrate selected union representatives into management structures. On 19 June, 1986, the government made great play of its taking temporary control of the country's largest car importers and repairers, the Julio Martínez group, in response to calls from the company's 400 workers alleging the company was union-busting, black marketeering and sabotaging the economy. The FSLN stressed that the company would be returned to the owners "when conditions improved".[104]

In June 1986 the FSLN opened public discussion on the proposed constitution to be enacted the following year. As Daniel Ortega had previously indicated, the constitution was based on the Swedish (bourgeois) parliamentary system and, as a bourgeois democratic constitution, it had no structures that gave the mass organisations representing workers any direct role. Marxists have long been aware that the working class cannot rule using a bourgeois state structure since its ideological, legal, parliamentary and military institutions are fine-tuned for the dictatorship of the bourgeoisie;

---

104 *Barricada*, 20 June, 1986.

it is not possible to exercise 'popular power' by these means because they are designed precisely to stop any genuine popular participation. The draft constitution with its bourgeois parliament demonstrated unequivocally that the FSLN government was now a radical, reformist government with a popular front strategy based on a mixed economy. It was clear that the FSLN leadership was consciously determined not to step outside capitalist limits economically, socially or politically.

Certain of the proposals, the more progressive democratic clauses such as those requiring equal pay for men and women doing the same work, the right of women to own land and join co-operative farms, the right of female agricultural workers (rather than their husbands) to receive their wages were, of course, to be welcomed. Across the country there were eighty-four public meetings to discuss the proposals, one in Managua on 10 June, 1986, as reported by IP[105] was attended by more than 800 women and chaired by Carlos Nuñez, National Assembly Member. According to the IP report only one person, an FO militant, Sara Marina Rodriguez, raised the question of direct representation through decision-making mass meetings.

On 25 June, 1986, the US Congress approved US$100 million in 'aid' for the Contras which marked a decisive turn from 1984 and 1985 when funds were restricted to so-called humanitarian assistance. The first Contra attacks were targeted on those Miskitos along the Nicaraguan-Honduran border who had gained land and a title, and who wanted an end to the war; some 4,500 had already returned from Honduras substantially weakening the Contra forces on the Atlantic Coast.

The Congressional vote sparked the most serious rift between Catholic Church and state in Nicaragua because a section of the clergy clearly endorsed the US action. In response, the FSLN suspended publication of *La Prensa* and denied a Catholic priest, Bismark Carballo confidant of Cardinal Obando the right to return to Nicaragua on the grounds that both *La Prensa* and Carballo were promoting the mercenary war and breaking Nicaraguan law. The government warned that similar actions would be taken against anyone else who aided and abetted Contra aggression.

On 2 July, 1986, Catholic Bishop Pablo Antonio Vega, Vice-President of the Nicaraguan Episcopal Conference, held a news conference in Managua. In his trips to the United States he had stated that armed struggle against the Nicaraguan government was justified because the FSLN was violating human rights, discriminating against the Catholic Church and had murdered three priests. But each time he returned to Nicaragua, he claimed he had been misquoted. However, at his Managua news conference he challenged

---

105 28 July, 1986

the World Court ruling that Washington systematically violated the human rights of Nicaragua, claiming that the real aggression Nicaragua faced was from Soviet 'imperialism'. Two days later, the Nicaraguan President's Office announced the decision to suspend indefinitely the right of Bishop Vega to reside in Nicaragua on the grounds that he had met with top Contra commanders, had justified US military intervention in Nicaragua, and had supported Congressional allocation of 'aid' for the Contras.

In the run up to the harvest season (December 1986-January 1987), the ATC launched a campaign with two goals: to increase coffee production and to recruit new members and improve working conditions. At this time, coffee provided about forty per cent of Nicaragua's exports, but in the countryside, many of the big landowners were de-capitalising by taking government subsidies for the harvest but then neglecting their farms. Working conditions declined, the neglected coffee trees deteriorated, and production fell. The ATC announced an important goal of the campaign was to win for the union some control in order to increase production on behalf of the owner! Despite gains in working conditions on the state farms and co-operatives, in the private sector they were often the same as before 1979. The ATC's list of demands, aimed at increasing both membership and production, included the employer providing first aid stations, childcare and, importantly, improved health and safety procedures in the use of pesticides and agrochemicals.

The philosophy of the FSLN was that a producer was a producer, whether s/he produced five kilograms of rice or 500 tons of rice. The only class division was whether the landlords were absentee or not, whether they remained on the farm or had moved to the city. By the time of its National Congress of January 1986, UNAG had recruited as many as one third of all large landowners.[106]

The Contra war was devastating, not only in terms of lives lost but also in terms of productive capacity destroyed, loss of trade, sabotage of ports and transport, and disruption of agricultural production. But the international situation was becoming even darker. By the mid-1980's, the guerrilla forces in El Salvador and Guatemala had been defeated, and US marines had invaded Grenada and overthrown the Workers' and Peasants' Government there. By 1987, the CST was the dominant urban trade union and, like the ACT, was actively implementing state policies. At its June 1987 Congress, the appointed leaders passed resolutions to the effect that ATC members would contribute to the war effort by forgoing wage increases and campaign

---

106 Nuñez, D., *The Farmers' View*, Envio, No 96, 1989; Núñez, D., *Making the Economy Our Own*, Envio, No 116, 1991.

for the suspension of the Labour Code as it limited the maximum number of hours in the working day.

The failure of the mixed economy meant the FSLN was heavily dependent on outside assistance. From July 1979 to December 1987, it received almost $6 billion in credits and donations. Soviet aid (usually in the form of tractors and oil) increased steadily from 1979 to 1985 when it was US$ 1 billion, it dropped to about US$ 400 million in 1986 and less in 1987. In total, Soviet aid amounted to $3.3 billion. However, the Stalinist regimes in Eastern Europe and Russia were collapsing. The combined economic and military assault from US imperialism left Nicaragua battered and exhausted at precisely the time the USSR was undergoing a counter-revolution and quite willing to wash its hands of Nicaragua, Cuba, Angola, and anything that stood in the way of a rapprochement with imperialism. The FSLN leaders, pointedly did not ask for closer economic collaboration with Cuba.

The US administration was also pressurising European and Latin American governments to stop the little remaining aid they were supplying to Nicaragua and demanding the Nicaraguan government agree to negotiate peace terms directly with the Contras, as though the latter really represented a body of opinion within the country. In this they were supported by the PSN and PCN, no doubt reflecting the views of Gorbachev, but going one step further and demanding the release of captured Contras.

Mass protests in the US over military aid for the Contras continued. Then, in November 1986, the policy of the Reagan administration toward Nicaragua was shaken by the Iran-Contra scandal (Irangate). Senior members of Reagan's staff secretly facilitated the illegal sale of arms to Iran and used the money obtained to, again secretly, fund the Contras, thumbing their noses at the authority of Congress. Israel acted as intermediary. The Iranians purchased arms from Israel. The Israelis then ordered replacement weapons from the US and paid for them with the money received from Iran. A portion of this money was siphoned off into Contra pockets.[107]

The result was that the US Congress stopped all overt military support to the Contras in 1987, but agreed to continue to indefinitely supply US$4.5 million a month in 'non-lethal' and 'humanitarian aid' to the estimated 10,000 Contra rebels and their dependents living in Honduras, with additional top-ups as required. Lacking any popular support in Nicaragua, the Contras were forced to cut back on their activities.

---

107 *The Contras, Cocaine, and Covert Operations*, National Security Archive, nsarchive.gwu.edu/NSAEBB/ NSAEBB2/index.html.

11.1) THE ARIAS PLAN

Many on the left claimed the Arias Plan reflected the weakened position of the Reagan administration due to the Iran-Contra affair. But the Arias Plan was not a defence against the Contra War, it complemented and extended it. The Arias Plan was designed to shore up the US-backed regimes in Central America by undermining the Nicaraguan revolution. The Plan was a tool to force concession after concession, giving nothing in return, until at last the FSLN government was replaced by the direct representatives of the national bourgeoisie.

An essential requirement for the Plan to succeed was for Nicaragua to be in an absolutely desperate economic situation. This had been achieved by the Contra War, and the US economic and financial blockade. The first step was for a US stooge, the President of Costa Rica, Oscar Arias Sánchez, to offer a deal to Daniel Ortega that gave all the appearances of ending the Contra War: five Central American states (Panama was not included) would cease aid and support to all 'irregular' military forces. Nicaragua would have to make concessions but would retain its principled positions, for example, that the Contras were a catspaw of the US, and thus no direct negotiations would take place between the FSLN and the Contras.

Gorbachev was desperately trying to rescue an economy strangled by bureaucracy, but the USSR and Eastern Europe was inexorably sliding back into capitalism. Anxious to ensure that no little local difficulties would compromise the general strategy of peaceful co-existence, Gorbachev had no intention of letting Nicaragua sour relations between Russia and the USA, and put considerable pressure on the FSLN government to sign up to the Arias Plan. In early 1987, Russian oil supplies to Nicaragua were temporarily suspended to pressure the FSLN to accept the Arias Plan, which was duly signed by the Presidents of the five Central American republics (Guatemala, Honduras, El Salvador, Nicaragua, and Costa Rica) on 7 August, 1987.

The signing up of the Arias Plan was the logical conclusion of the refusal of the FSLN to pursue a policy of breaking with capitalism at home and appealing for international revolution abroad. Lenin and the Bolsheviks had signed a much worse peace deal with Germany to save the fledgling workers' state. The big difference between the peace deal signed by Lenin in 1917 and that signed by the Sandinistas in 1987 was that the first gave the Bolshevik regime in Russia a breathing space in which to consolidate, whereas the Arias Plan was only a first step in overthrowing the Sandinista government. Instead of making an appeal for international support from the working masses, Ortega looked for capitalist sponsorship of Nicaragua's mixed economy. False friends of Nicaragua, such as Reverend Jesse Jackson, had howled for the FSLN to agree. Once the deal was agreed, the US and the Nicaraguan capitalists denounced it as being too soft on the Sandinistas, demanding a range of additional concessions before the Contras laid down their weapons.

Arias received the Nobel Peace Prize in October 1987 and, using the prestige he gained, immediately demanded the FSLN conduct direct negotiations with the Contras, and release those National Guards still in prison. The Nicaraguan bourgeoisie now launched a series of demands, including the requirement that the elected government step aside in favour of a non-elected 'Government of National Salvation', and that the Contra forces be integrated into the EPS.

On 15 January, 1988, at a summit of Central American presidents, President Ortega agreed to hold direct talks with the Contras. The *New York Times*,[108] ascribed this about-face as due to pressure from Gorbachev, who threatened to stop all aid to the FSLN. Some informed sources claim that refusal of the former Soviet Union to supply aid in sufficient quantities damaged the Sandinistas more than the presence of the Contras.[109] In March, the FSLN government met with representatives of the Contras and signed a cease-fire agreement. The Sandinistas granted a general amnesty to all Contra members who surrendered their weapons and, as goodwill gestures, freed former members of the National Guard who were still imprisoned, allowed the Catholic radio station to return to the air, and permitted the re-opening of *La Prensa*.

The economy was in free-fall. On 14 February, 1988, the government announced as series of economic measures intended to reduce inflation: the introduction of a new currency which represented a devaluation of 500 per cent; over 50,000 government employees to be laid off; the end of government subsidies on thirty basic foods. What could the FSLN have done if it had the workers' and peasants' interests at heart? The Chinese Workers' and Peasants' Government, in 1951-52, had been faced with hyper-inflation. It protected real wages by insisting workers and peasants were paid not with paper money but in kind, imposed a monopoly of foreign trade and nationalised the banks to control credit and foreign currency exchange.[110] Instead, the FSLN government had imposed a dramatic devaluation of the Córdoba, cutting real wages in half overnight.

The private producers, 'the most inefficient producers in all Central America' were treated very differently. The big cattle ranchers demanded the government pay a price for their beef five times that of the international market. The government agreed to pay them one and a half times. The rice

108 18 December, 1987
109 Harsch. J., *Christian Science Monitor*, 6 February, 1988.
110 Roberts, op cit. 2016.

growers were paid a price which gave them a 'mere' seventy per cent profit, when the government could have imported the same rice much cheaper. Given its chosen political and economic direction, the FSLN made concession after concession, including ending the state of emergency. Finally, *La Prensa* was sufficiently confident to demand seventeen constitutional reforms that would have reversed the revolution: including the return of the National Guard and its integration into the army, the return of all property seized by the government, dissolution of CDSs, and a 'private' TV channel.

The FSLN appeared to have learned nothing. Continuing with its mixed economy policy, it began to return nationalised properties to their owners. One of the first was the Julio Martinez auto group. In the teeth of the workers' opposition, five plants were returned to the Martinez family.

The government continued to meet its expenditures by printing money and so exacerbated inflation, which hit wage earners hardest. The degrading of wage rates and living standards led to an increasing number of strikes against government policies, the two most bitter originating with government reductions in pay. The first was by auto mechanics, who were protesting being transferred from piece work rates to a weekly wage that halved their take-home pay. The total number on strike was about 400. Most were members of the CST but sixty were members of CAUS. Because the CST opposed the strike, CAUS took the leadership by default.

The second was the result of the government announcement made on 29 February, 1988, of a new wage scale for construction workers. So poor were the proposed wages that a trainee would receive C$29 a day but be charged C$30 for lunch. As one trainee put it, "starve on strike, or starve on the job". For skilled workers the weekly pay fell by two-thirds, from about C$1,100 to about C$310. Over 4,500 workers on fifty-six building sites came out on strike, answering the call of their union, the SCAAS, demanding the new decree be lifted and workers be awarded a 200 per cent wage increase.

CAUS was a PCN union and SCAAS was a PSN union, both of which were pursuing even more obsequious deals with the bourgeoisie than the FSLN, and so were political dead ends.

The CST again attacked the strikes as the work of counter-revolutionaries, ignoring the fact that the economic demands of the workers were entirely legitimate, that they had sacrificed much for the revolution but were drawing the line at hand-outs for the capitalists and starvation wages for themselves. On 2 June, 1988, *Barricada International* carried an interview with Commandante Víctor Tirado, a leading *Tercerista*. Tirado did not beat about the bush. When asked if it wasn't time to spread the economic burdens more evenly he replied:

What is the thinking behind that proposal? That it is necessary to attack the bourgeoisie, those who are benefiting from some dollar incentives? ... The workers have to be clear about alliances, about the project of national unity, the strategic policy of the mixed economy. This is a revolution of the workers and campesinos and obviously the burden – primarily the problems and hardships – will fall on them.

On 4 June, 1988, wage and price controls were lifted and the currency again devalued. Daniel Ortega appeared on television and announced that wages and prices would be determined by market conditions. This was an open acknowledgement that the February measures and the whole mixed economy project had failed utterly. Prices soared but wages remained desperately low. COSEP jumped for joy and *La Prensa*'s headline was 'Returning to Capitalism'. Nearly all of the economic gains of the revolution were gone. Between 1980 and 1988 real wages fell by ninety per cent.

On 9 June, in discussions with the Sandinistas, differences between Contra factions burst into the open and sank the talks. With the Contras split, even with US\$ millions in their pockets, the military war was effectively over, but this was a Pyrrhic victory for the Sandinistas, because the Contras had achieved the major goal of their US paymasters. They had crippled the Nicaraguan economy. The battle was now one of economics and politics.

In one more step away from any kind of central planning, Ortega announced that state and private companies would be free to apply a more flexible wage policy, meaning that despite there being a notional legal minimum wage, employers had no obligation to pay it. On 14 June, 1988, another devaluation was announced. Prices immediately rose by over 1,000 per cent. On 31 August, President Ortega appeared on state-run radio to announce yet another currency devaluation to shore up the economy. The *New York Times*[111] gleefully reported that state agricultural workers were twenty per cent worse off while urban government workers would, in real terms, lose a third of their wages.

Ortega's proposals also included the concession that designated 'patriotic producers' no longer had to sell their produce to the state and were entitled to export their products directly. This marked the end of any pretence of state monopoly on the export of agricultural produce. The owners of the San Antonio sugar mills and those major cattle barons associated with UNAG were amongst the first to benefit from these moves.

In the same speech, Ortega placed yet more austerity measures on the shoulders of the workers and peasants. These entailed across-the-board government spending cuts, including healthcare and education; 23,000

---

111 1 September, 1988

members of the armed forced to be demobilised; 12,000 civil service jobs to be lost; an end to enforcement of the minimum wage.

In October 1988, Hurricane Joan, the final storm of the 1988 hurricane season, struck Nicaragua, killing hundreds, severely damaging or destroying 30,000 homes, leaving a quarter of a million people homeless, washing away 1,000 kilometres of power lines and 650 kilometres of road. There was extensive destruction of farms, with tens of thousands of livestock killed. A severe drought followed in 1989, ruining agricultural production for 1990. Total damage was estimated at nearly US$1 billion, with the resulting inflationary pressure cancelling out any financial benefits of the previous devaluations. The US sent no aid and pressured its allies to send none. Hurricane Joan could be said to be the event that caused the final collapse of the Nicaraguan economy.

The *Christian Science Monitor* of 25 January, 1989, described the situation:

> Even as the poor get squeezed, the government is bestowing privileges and incentives on large agricultural exporters and trained professionals in the sprawling state bureaucracy. Some bureaucrats now receive free housing, household goods, coupons for the 'dollar' store, even Toyota Cressidas – Nicaragua's new symbol of success. Such favoritism, with 50% cuts in most social programmes, has embittered pro-government unions and long-time Sandinista supporters.

The attempts by CST officials to support government policy meant that workers were increasingly turning to more militant alternatives. The FSLN and the CST responded in very much the same way as the Stalinists in the Soviet Union during the faction fights with the United Opposition. Elected union officers were refused entry to their workplaces, union meetings were broken up by strong-arm gangs of CST loyalists, secret ballots denied, FO and CAUS speakers were barracked, jeered, and shouted down. Strike leaders were slandered and sacked.

Ortega agreed to lift the state of emergency and call national elections. In January 1989, as the economy slid into an ever-deeper crisis, with hyperinflation destroying the living standards of the masses, the government launched an austerity plan which was a series of attacks on the living conditions of the masses including laying off one-third of public-sector workers and freezing wages.

12) WOMEN, WORKERS, AND LAND REFORM (1987-89)

12.1) WOMEN

On 8 March, 1987, International Women's Day, the FSLN published its long-awaited 'Proclamation on Women', the first programmatic statement on the relation of women's struggles to the Nicaraguan revolution. The statement highlighted women's historically unprecedented level of political participation in the new government and political organisations – comprising nearly one-third of positions in government, two-thirds of DCSs, and a quarter of FSLN membership. These reflections of participation in the revolutionary process, while unprecedented, were declared insufficient. The stated goal was to create conditions that would make women equal partners in decision-making in the revolution. However, the Proclamation did not mention the right to abortion or birth control and, in effect, marked a decision by the FSLN leadership to end the discussion on these questions. Despite its strong words against *machismo*, the Proclamation sounded a retreat on the fight for women's rights.

On 26 September, 1987, at a meeting to celebrate the founding of the AMNLAE, Daniel Ortega, in his role as President, made his first major public statement on abortion:

> The ones fighting in the front lines against this aggression (Contra terrorists) are young men. One way of depleting our youth is to promote the sterilisation of women in Nicaragua – just imagine what would happen then – or to promote a policy of abortion. The problem is that the woman is the one who reproduces. The man can't play that role ... some women, aspiring to be liberated, decide not to bear children. A woman who does so negates her own continuity and the continuity of the human species.[112]

Using such reactionary rationalisations to oppose a woman's right to choose was a clear demonstration of the political consequences of Ortega moving towards the Catholic Church, and may have had a lot to do with his statement that "the family is the basic unit of society and guarantees social reproduction not only from the biological point of view, but also the principles and values of society". In the same speech, Ortega declared that indians and black people had never suffered racial discrimination in Nicaragua, either under the Somoza regime or afterwards.

By retaining the current status on abortion, birth control and sex education, the statement offered an olive branch to those advocating a more traditional role for women. The lack of any subsequent public statements by, for example, AMNLAE, offering a pro-woman, pro-choice position reflected

---

112 Chinchilla, N., Gender and Society, 4(3)370-397, 1990.

the bureaucratic discipline of the FSLN rather than a measure of the opinions of its members. Earlier gains, such as childcare centres and the entry of women into jobs that were previously men-only, were being eroded under the impact of budget cuts and large-scale layoffs. This political retreat continued in 1988, symbolised by the newly-elected national leadership of the Sandinista Youth, which did not include a single woman, a clear statement on how seriously the FSLN viewed its 'Proclamation'.

In July 1988, a columnist in *El Nuevo Diario* wrote approvingly of the Miss Moscow contest and argued that Nicaragua should follow suit. Some hotels, restaurants, airlines and the Nicaraguan Institute of Tourism launched 'Miss Elegance', which was held on 12 August. This was followed by a competition for Miss Juventud sponsored by the Sandinista Youth, the EPS and the Sandinista Television System, to be held on 26 November. There was, naturally, considerable discussion and much public criticism. *Barricada* balanced its obvious editorial enthusiasm for the events with articles about the contestants, stressing their service to the revolution. *Ventana*, the cultural supplement to *Barricada*, was less discrete, boasting the display had challenged the prejudice of leftist dogmatists.

In early 1989, AMNLAE leaders announced plans calling for legislation by the summer to legalise abortion, outlaw wife beating, and stiffen legal penalties against rape. By the middle of the year, however, AMNLAE had bowed to pressure from the FSLN leadership, which argued that raising such issues would "only create confusion" and hurt the FSLN's candidates in the 1990 pre-election period. Those AMNLAE figures who now sat silent were cadres who, earlier, were outspoken about violence against women and strong defenders of abortion rights.

Women's share of the labour force had risen from fourteen per cent in 1950, to twenty-nine per cent in 1977 and to forty-five per cent in 1989. In the clothing, textiles, leather, shoes, food, and pharmaceutical industries, women constituted up to eighty per cent, of the workforce (though in the lowest paid jobs), in cotton, coffee and tobacco over half the workers were women, and forty per cent of the members of the ACT. However, defending the jobs of women in the face of cut-backs was becoming more and more difficult. AMNLAE convened a conference to receive reports from across Nicaragua and found that women were twice as likely to be laid off as men. Two members of the FSLN National Directorate, Victor Tirado and Bayardo Arce, spoke at the conference, their message: everything would get better if the FSLN were elected, and that women workers should put their efforts into winning the election on 25 February.

The reduction in the revolutionary content of the FSLN programme reflected its adherence to the theory of stages with the FSLN pushed inescapably to the right. To protect and extend its reformist perspective, the FSLN leadership, represented by Daniel Ortega, were abandoning progressive policies in virtually every sphere, and for women, this included reviving and fortifying the family system. Daniel Ortega would be elected President of Nicaragua in 2007, by which time he would be so strongly opposed to abortion that so-called therapeutic abortions (where the pregnancy endangers the mother's life) would be made illegal. Amnesty International documented how Ortega's anti-abortion laws decreed that a pregnancy – anencephalic or ectopic – that could not possibly result in a viable baby had to be carried to its limits; that women who became pregnant through acts of rape or incest had to have the babies; that a pregnant woman with cancer had to have the baby first, then treatment for the cancer, no matter what the risk to her chances of survival.

The situation of women in society, of course, reflects the progress of that society. As Charles Fourier said: "Social progress… takes place in proportion to the advance of women toward liberty, and social decline occurs as a result of the diminution of the liberty of women". This was demonstrated in a negative way in the former Soviet Union in the official attitude towards women and the family. Trotsky explained:

> The forty million Soviet families remain in their overwhelming majority nests of medievalism, female slavery and hysteria, daily humiliation of children, feminine and childish superstition… best of all characterise… the evolution of its ruling stratum.[113]

Much the same process was occurring in Nicaragua.

12.2) WORKERS

As the FSLN became increasingly enmeshed in *concertación*, efforts by unionised workers to gain a measure of control over decisions concerning investment, production, and conditions of work were, at best, hindered but more likely rejected. The FSLN's policy was to convince workers that it was in their interests to revive the economy (the theme of all Social Democratic Parties), and to this end they should accept increased exploitation and worse working conditions.

During 1988, the Nicaraguan government implemented a series of measures in response to the economic crisis it was facing. It devalued the C$ four times – 14 February, 4 June, 14 June and 31 August – each one of

---

113 Trotsky, *The Revolution Betrayed*, www.marxists.org, 1936.

which hit wage earners hard. It reduced subsidies to peasants, it stepped back from regulation of prices and wages in favour of a 'free market' approach to improving productivity. The burdens of a declining economy were placed overwhelmingly on wage earners, both urban and rural, the small producers and artisans, precisely those people who gave the government its popular character. Simultaneously, the top-down style of leadership exercised by the FSLN meant the lack of any serious public debate on the measures to be taken, with a consequent decline in popular support.

President Daniel Ortega denounced striking construction workers protesting against worsening work conditions and lower wages as in the pay of the CIA. Elaborating on his theme, Ortega, in a speech broadcast over Radio Sandino, referred to the strikers as "small groups of disoriented and confused workers who are being directed by people who are conscious elements of US and counter-revolutionary policy", and "ignorant workers – some of whom claim they are revolutionaries – [who] do not know who the enemy is". Despite Ortega's outrage, the FSLN's economic and political course strengthened those Nicaraguan unions which sought to defend their members from the effects of government policies.

Feeling ever more confident, individual capitalists were flagrantly breaking the law on de-capitalising, so enraging their workforces, that the workers occupied the factory or warehouse, which was then expropriated. These punitive actions were taken from time to time but did not constitute any change in the government's general course. Such nationalisations were ad-hoc measures implemented without political preparation, aimed at pressuring the capitalists to support the government's social pact policy. Some workers did welcome these measures, hoping their conditions would improve and they would have increased control over production, but these nationalisations did little or nothing to increase the class-consciousness and self-confidence of the working class generally or give workers increased decision-making powers in the workplace.

In July 1988, the government found itself in the position where it had to confiscate Nicaragua's largest private business and symbol of capitalism, the sprawling San Antonio sugar plantation and sugar mills. Since 1982, the mill workers had been accusing the mill owners of accepting government grants in US$ to buy replacement parts, but pocketing the money and blaming faulty machinery and poor-quality work for the shortfall in production. In 1987 alone, about US$30 million was put into American bank accounts.

Minister of Agriculture, Jaime Wheelock, who announced the confiscation, emphasised it was not a political measure, explaining that production was falling because the owners were deliberately not investing sufficiently to maintain the refinery. Production had fallen from 150,000 tons to just 55,000 tons in 1987-88. Previously, the FSLN government had refused to nationalise this particular mill on the grounds that Nicaragua needed a mixed economy and that 'patriotic producers' should have no problems with the government.

The owners of the San Antonio sugar mill had encouraged its workers to join the Federation of Trade Union Unity (CUS), an affiliate of the American AFL-CIO and as such, anti-FSLN. Preferential treatment, such as prioritised access to company housing, promotion, free sugar to sell on the black market, etc., had encouraged strong support amongst this section of the mill workers, some 200 out of a total of 800, who opposed the nationalisation.

The economic policies were meant to make companies more profitable but, as an article spread across two issues of *Barricada*[114] made clear, all too often this was achieved at the expense of the conditions of the workers. The article ended with a call for greater rank and file participation in determining policies, including workers' control and community control.

In the two years following the peace accords and victory over the Contras, the influence of the FSLN-led unions and mass organisations on government policy declined, membership participation diminished, and their political level consequently reduced. Leaders of the pro-FSLN trade unions tried to convince doubting workers that it was in their interests and of the revolution, to sacrifice more so the capitalists could gain a bigger share of Nicaragua's wealth. As the government placed an ever-increasing burden on the shoulders of working people, the leaders of the pro-FSLN unions were increasingly required to curtail efforts to advance workers' interests, meaning favoured candidates for union posts were the bootlickers. The promotion of the best union members, those experienced in organising and mobilising workers and peasants – for pay and conditions, for land reform, against *machismo* and for women's rights, and to advance Nicaragua toward socialism – was blocked.

12.3) LAND REFORM

The land question is central for any oppressed nation seeking independence, especially where the peasantry forms the majority of the population. In such a situation 'Land to the Tiller' is a vital slogan for winning the support of the majority of the population. This was proved beyond doubt in the Russian, Chinese, and Cuban revolutions where the resulting peasant-worker alliance enabled essential bourgeois-democratic tasks (national independence, formal equality for women, overcoming hunger and famine, control of inflation,

---

114 24 and 25 November, 1998

planning to overcome natural and man-made disasters, etc.) to be carried through successfully.

Even during the revolution itself, the FSLN had protected the estates and *latifundios* of those claiming to be part of the anti-Somoza bourgeoisie, but the FSLN criteria for differentiating between pro- and anti-Somoza landowners are still not clear. The strategy of the FSLN towards the agricultural sector, and repeated many times in speeches and documents was a mixed economy which would be more just and equal than under Somoza in its distribution of land and resources. But two factors seriously complicated the situation: the US-backed Contras displaced some 50,000 families, increasing peasant demands for land, and there was an exodus of peasants from countryside generally to the towns, especially Managua.

On 11 January, 1986, a revised Agrarian Reform Law was adopted. Formally, the new law extended the possibility of compulsory purchase of the larger farms where 'public necessity' required it, in particular where lands had lain idle. On 29 June, 1986, the law was further amended to allow the government to confiscate the land of any person who spent more than six months continuously outside the country. It was claimed that these and other measures resulted in over 80,000 hectares being distributed amongst 16,000 peasant families. In fact, the government continued to protect the large private farms, giving them (and medium and small private producers) priority over state farms and co-operatives and, increasingly, the land distributed came not from the private sector but from state farms and co-operatives.

How was the government repaid for its support of the private farmers? Taking the average over the years 1974-78 as 100 per cent, then between 1979 and 1988 the big landowners decreased agro-export production: coffee to seventy-five per cent, beef livestock to seventy per cent, and cotton to twenty-seven per cent, with similar figures for bananas, sesame, tobacco, sugar cane, and milk. The peasant smallholdings, except for beans, increased production for the domestic market: sorghum by seventy-six per cent, corn by thirty-five per cent, rice by twenty-four per cent, and both poultry and pork production more than doubled.[115]

As the threat from the Contras faded, land distribution slowed sharply and, in 1987, the number of peasant families benefiting from land distribution was at its lowest level since 1982. Under pressure from the biggest landlords, the government confirmed that there was no limit on the area of land that could be held by the largest farmers, provided they maintained production. The new 1987 constitution forbade the seizure of land by peasants and

---

115 Zalkin, M., *Sandinista Agrarian Reform*, Int. J. of Political Economy, 20(3)46-69, 1990.

promised "cash payment of fair compensation" for those whose uncultivated land was expropriated; there was a sharp fall in land distributed – *Barricada*[116] informed its readers that only about 9,000 families had been provided with land. The land bordering Honduras is particularly fertile and eminently suitable for beans, corn and rice and peasants moving back into these areas were demanding land. However, a necessary pre-condition was the clearing of land mines with priority given to displaced and demobilised soldiers. By December 1988, the process had begun and in the Jalapa area, for example, about 100 hectares was cleared of mines and allocated to about seventy landless families.

The government retreated by further weakening the degree of state control over foreign trade, and relaxing currency controls. It lifted many restrictions on imported goods and widened the range of products that could be exported directly by capitalists. This further reduced the resources available to the government for social programmes and undermined efforts to control inflation and establish a stable currency, without which effective economic planning was impossible. At this time, the sum total of the imbalance for the country was a deficit of between US$400 and US$500 million annually.

Capitalist domination of manufacturing industries inevitably meant that the prices paid by the peasants for manufactured goods rose faster than the prices they received for their crops. It was estimated that, between February and December 1988, the costs of producing corn, rice and beans rose twice as fast as the price for which these crops were sold. Hence, the peasants suffered a substantial drop in real net income.

A major problem now facing the peasants was that the government was restricting bank loans with the peasants expected to meet the shortfall from the sale of the previous year's crop. Thus, the Arlen Siú collective farm had agreed a bank loan of C$800 to prepare the soil for planting, but in mid-June, the government ended fixed rate loans and introduced interest rates linked to an inflation rate of more than 1,000 per cent, rendering the interest unpayable.

On 30 January, 1989, the government announced a halt to any further confiscations and re-distributions of land from capitalist farmers, President Daniel Ortega declared to the National Assembly "Sufficient land has already been distributed… there is no reason to take an inch of land from anyone". Later, the Minister for Agrarian Reform made things crystal clear when he confirmed that this was not a short-term measure. *The Militant*,[117] reported him as saying: "We want to make a long-term strategic arrangement with the

---

116 18 December, 1987
117 17 March, 1989

private owners, which is to say that the expropriations have finished". Violeta Chamorra would, after her election as President, go further. By granting amnesty and immunity to National Guards and Contras who surrendered, she opened the door for them to reclaim the lands and homes seized during the revolution.

The ATC was now playing a more openly class-collaborationist role. One 'patriotic producer' in Matagalpa Province stubbornly refused to allow a union to be organised. Firing the organiser of each attempt and hiring new workers. Exasperated, the workers occupied the farm and demanded support from the ATC. The union officer dealing with the matter is reported to have said, "Look, I know the workers are right... If I were in their shoes I would be doing exactly what they are doing. But we can't look at things just from the standpoint of this one struggle... We need to buy some time under peaceful conditions to allow us to get the economy back on its feet". Trapped within *concertación*, his response was that of any class-collaborationist union official. Alienation with the FSLN and *concertación* was spreading beyond militant workers and peasants, into the masses who saw increased workloads lining the pockets of the bosses while their own families went hungry.

Larry Seigle, in the *Militant*,[118] reported on the situation on a coffee farm owned by one of the richest families in Nicaragua. Workers were in dispute over the family's practice of firing older workers because, after a certain length of service, workers were supposed to receive a higher wage, be provided with housing, and be paid a pension when they retired. But the ATC would not organise a strike against the FSLN-sponsored *concertación*, instead it recommended workers refuse their pay when it was offered!

After the 1990 election, during 1991, the FSLN began revising its opinion of the agrarian policy of 1979-1986, questioning whether it had been correct to distribute land to landless peasants and agrarian workers. Luis Carrión, a member of the FSLN Directorate, made the astounding suggestion in the 20 June, 1991, issue of *Barricada*, that distribution of land had resulted in net loss of support amongst the peasantry. Carrión named three groups that had opposed land re-distribution: The first group were peasants who preferred to operate on the black market and not sell produce to the government for re-sale at fixed prices; the second group were peasants who had the goal of becoming big property owners and felt land distribution thwarted their ambitions; the third and last group consisted of the Contras who, it now turned out, were not a military force created and funded by the US, but an indigenous peasant movement.

---

118 22 December, 1989

13) DEMOBILISATION, ECONOMIC COLLAPSE AND THE 1990 ELECTION

The end of the Contra war should have been a huge step forward for the Nicaraguan people, and could have offered the opportunity to extend and deepen the revolution. Would the FSLN repeal the emergency measures constraining the actions of the workers, revoke the ban on public protests such as strikes, return to land re-distribution, end *concertación*, introduce a planned economy, and so on?

Over the period 1988-1989, thousands of returning workers and *campesinos*, youth and women, who had fought in the war, had gained leadership experience and self-confidence, came increasingly into conflict with the owners of the *latifundios*, large commercial enterprises and factories.

With the end of the war many thousands of young, experienced and disciplined cadres were available to assume leadership responsibilities. The military victory over the Contras had instilled the majority of Nicaraguans with a new confidence and a preparedness to deepen and advance the anti-imperialist and anti-capitalist characteristics of the revolution. It must be admitted that many of these returnees lacked both the training and the experience to immediately administer public affairs. Being a good soldier does not mean that you can be a good administrator, but post-civil war Russia had shown that, while it might be a rough ride, it was possible.

With the correct leadership, these cadres were capable of rapidly, effectively and consciously moving Nicaragua in an anti-capitalist direction. But just the opposite happened. Having won the war, these cadres were politically demobbed, dispersed, sent home or, if retained in the army, kept largely idle and not used in any significant way to progress social projects.

One example that exemplifies the attitude of the FSLN leaders was the battle the veterans fought with the Ministry of Transportation. On demob, veterans were given a bus pass that should have enabled them to free travel, but the owner-operators of the buses refused to honour these passes on the grounds they were not profitable. Neither the FSLN nor any of its mass organisations made any moves to support the veterans. With each clash such as this, the FSLN leadership made it ever clearer they had rejected an anti-capitalist direction. At the end of the Contra war, seventy-eight per cent of industry, seventy-six per cent of commercial agriculture, and sixty per cent of commerce was privately owned, but to pay for the economic crisis resulting from the war, wage controls and severe austerity measures were imposed on the workers.[119]

---

119 Molyneux, op cit., 1985.

Despite all the evidence of growing inequality, Ortega was still claiming to be convinced that his mixed economy approach with the dominance of market mechanisms would lead to a system in which wealth was fairly distributed. 'Now is not the time to establish socialism' became his catchphrase and the FSLN's stagist view for revolutions in less developed countries was spelled out in detail in *El Nuevo Diario* (29 and 30 January, 1989). Despite, or because of, FSLN class-collaborationist policies, production in 1988 fell by a third. The great surprise to socialists outside Nicaragua was the lack of any response from either the FSLN or trade union leaders. Quite the reverse. In factories, the local union officials collaborated with management in deciding who to lay off, a process made even more punitive because, in contrast to previous years, those made redundant received no severance pay. The leaders of the CST and ATC responded by calling for the newly laid-off workers to take up Ortega's offer, move to the countryside and take farm jobs to help raise food production.

On 4 January, 1989, the government devalued the Córdobas to C$2,000 to the United States dollar, up from eighty a year earlier. Simultaneously, it cut subsidies on food, spending on education, health, transport, and sacked 35,000 government workers. More than one-third of the work force was unemployed, there was widespread hunger, factories were closing for lack of power, tens of thousands of Nicaraguans, those with skills or a profession, were leaving the country – many to the US. The government's response: yet more sweeping austerity measures.

In March 1989, Tomás Borge gave a major interview in *Barricada* in which he attempted a theoretical justification for FSLN policy. His essential argument was that market mechanisms stand above capitalism and socialism, and could be used to serve the interests of the working class.[120] In an attempt to give weight to his argument, Borge cited the example of Lenin's New Economic Policy (NEP) adopted in the Soviet Republic in the early 1920's. The NEP was a necessary, but temporary, retreat in the face of starvation and hunger caused by imperialist military intervention and a civil war. Lenin insisted that the indispensable preconditions for the NEP were the state ownership of industry, nationalisation of the land and the state monopoly of foreign trade. The course being followed by the FSLN was very different from the NEP, which was implemented after, not before these tasks were accomplished; that is, after the establishment of a workers state.[121]

In mid-March 1989, Daniel Ortega, accompanied by the Minister of Agriculture (Jaime Wheelock), attended a fair supported by COSEP, the

120 *Barricada International*, March 25, 1989.
121 Lenin, V., *Political Report*, CW33:267, 1922.

organisation representing the openly capitalist landlords and ranchers. Wheelock chose this venue to announce the availability of large, low interest loans in support of the government's policy of making the beef industry the spearhead for the country's economic recovery. Ortega again emphasised there was no upper limit to the amount of land a rancher could own, subject to the sole condition that it was used profitably.

One month later, on 20 April, 1989, Daniel Ortega used a UNAG conference to formally announce a series of concessions to private farmers. The first was a fifty per cent reduction in the debts to the state bank for farmers who chose to grow basic food crops. In addition, the remaining debt was spread over five years at much lower interest rates than paid by the banks' other customers. Cotton farmers received an even better deal if they could increase production, effectively their debts would be written off. Cotton, of course, is farmed mostly on the big, capitalist farms. At the conference, the ATC representatives pressed Ortega on what he would do to help those *campesinos* still justly demanding some land for themselves and their families. Ortega responded that peasants who had seized land outside the new law would be dispossessed, but the government would allocate them scrub land in the interior, away from the arable coastal regions.

In May 1989, Matilde Zimmermann, an on-the-spot observer, writing in the *Militant*,[122] reported how every three months a Cuban ship arrived with food and other basic supplies sufficient to feed and clothe a quarter of the population of the North Atlantic coastal region. The supplies represented a great sacrifice by the Cuban people, who expected they would be distributed under a form of rationing, but such a strategy was at odds with the policies the FSLN was now promoting. Under its new policy, the FSLN sold these supplies on the free market. Wealthy residents bought what they wanted and merchants grabbed the rest, resold it at inflated prices, and little, if any, of the Cuban shipments reached the masses.

Zimmermann went on to explain that one expression of the political retreat since the end of the Contra war was the growing emphasis on the uniqueness and originality of the Nicaraguan revolution; that this was simply a ploy to conceal the real issue: whether the Nicaraguan revolution should move towards socialism. The 'defenders of the Nicaraguan revolution' in stressing how different they were from the Cubans, argued against following the path of the Cuban revolution on the grounds that the Nicaraguan revolution was unique and original. Naturally, every revolution has its unique and original features, but all too often the intention of those who highlight these, is to drown the essential, common socialist content in endless debate,

---

122 12 May, 1989

always putting off action until the discussion has been resolved – which they ensure never happens.

On 12 June 1989, the government announced yet another devaluation and, once again, the arithmetic meant workers were up to about thirty-three per cent worse off. The government promised to supply small, privately owned shops with basic necessities for sale at government set prices, but that did not stop a stampede that left all shops with empty shelves. Inflation was destroying any remaining economic stability. This was followed by a series of economic measures: finally abandoning any pretence of a minimum wage and other benefits for the lowest-paid sector of the workforce, cutting government subsidies to farmers to maintain staple food at prices affordable for the masses, cutting government subsidies of basic foods sold in local stores, but expanding concessions to capitalist growers of export commodities.

In June 1989, the EPS issued a new regulation, stipulating that all firearms (except those peasants in areas under attack from Contra remnants) were to be surrendered. Two reasons were given: Sandinistas with rifles slung over their shoulders would alarm the international observers monitoring the election promised for 1990 and, it was claimed, a large number of hand guns had fallen into the possession of criminals, though whether the latter would obey the new regulation was not mentioned. What was certain was that those peasants who had seized land and were squatting on it, or were defending their right to join a union, would now be at the mercy of the landowners.

These and other concessions by the FSLN leaders gave the national bourgeoisie the confidence to increase their opposition to the regime. In early July 1989, at a COSEP meeting, three leading coffee growers called on their fellows to reduce production, and to blackmail the government into making even more concessions. Few responded, but the government was forced to act in the face of this declaration of economic war, and expropriated the lands of all three. Jaime Wheelock, in the columns of *Barricada* (11 July, 1989), rushed to re-assure other large landowners that they remained 'absolutely necessary' for the new mixed economy society.

The promises of Ortega and Wheelock to the large landowners had in the small print some most unwelcome news for those working on state-owned farms. In July 1989, the workers on *La Gloria*, a state farm growing coffee, were visited by one Sergio Torres, who declared that their picking of bunches of bananas from trees growing on the farm would stop when he became the farm's owner. The astonished workers were told, by an army officer sent from Managua, that Torres was getting their farm in compensation for a farm he had had expropriated in 1979.

Luis Carrión, FSLN Minister for the Economy attempted to explain government policy:

> We're making an effort to bring together all the sectors of the nation, including the private sector, in order to deal with the economic crisis. This could lead to a qualitatively new style of government in the economic aspect, a style that would assure that the points of view and interests of all sectors are taken into account when it comes to formulating economic policy... we no longer talk of a planned economy... A planned economy becomes less and less possible to the extent that the policy we have been following grants more and more weight to market forces in the functioning of the economy.[123]

In July 1989, the ground rules for the February 1990 elections were agreed, one of which was that private property would not be subject to confiscation or expropriation for political reasons. Twenty opposition parties had been declared eligible to run against the FSLN. Published surveys showed that if the opposition parties could agree on a presidential candidate and form a bloc, then they could defeat the FSLN.

The FSLN's new and openly pro-capitalist course was too sudden to allay Washington's fears. George Bush (US President, 20 January, 1989 – 20 January, 1993) agreed to fund an electoral alliance and, after much horse-trading, a coalition of fourteen opposition parties agreed to form the National Opposition Union (*Unión Nacional Opositora*, UNO) and run Violeta Barrios de Chamorro for President with Virgilio Reyes Godoy (a former FSLN Minister of Labour who had moved steadily rightwards to eventually lead the PLI) for Vice-President. The UNO contained Contra leaders, conservatives and liberals, the Social Christian Party, and the Stalinist PSN.

A most significant event occurred over the summer of 1989 – private wards were re-introduced into state hospitals. The first hospital to do this was the Bertha Calderón Women's Hospital in Managua. As a pilot project, the hospital converted four rooms into two singles and two doubles with all the facilities a private patient could expect. The initiative was soon being copied by other hospitals, though prior to the election there was neither any public announcement nor news coverage. Doctor Maritza Quant, Director of the Women's Hospital, commented that the project would be extended to a separate annex for private patients and "as for the new private system, I don't see how it can be stopped". Of course, the privatisation of healthcare in Nicaragua has not solved the problem of lack of access to medication. Today, there is one physician for every 1,400 Nicaraguans, and in Cuba one for every 300 Cubans. At its best, the health service provided by the FSLN government

123 Seigle, L., *A Historic Opportunity is Being Lost*, New International, No 9, pp248-249, 1994.

reduced infant mortality from 120 per 1,000 live births to sixty-two. Cuba has a much lower figure, four. But as Ortega had made clear, Nicaragua's model was not going to be Cuba.

13.1) THE 25 FEBRUARY, 1990 ELECTION AND ITS AFTERMATH

These elections took place under conditions of unbearable blackmail by imperialism and were extremely polarised. Ninety percent of those over sixteen years of age and resident in Nicaragua registered to vote, and eighty-six per cent of those actually voted (Nicaragua, Parliamentary Report on 1990 elections). Hundreds of bourgeois observers, including ex-President Carter, searched in vain for reasons to declare the elections biased and unfair if it did not produce the result they wanted.

Significant numbers of National Guards, who had been allowed to return home after the Arias Accord, found their property occupied. In Managua, where there was a serious shortage of accommodation, they took legal steps to regain their property and, to everyone's surprise, were able to obtain court orders for eviction. One such case that received considerable publicity concerned a property that was in use as a health centre in a working-class neighbourhood. The local community rallied to protect it, confronting the authorities. Ultimately, Managua Council declared the building to be a public necessity. Across Managua there were hundreds of such instances, and in the majority, the tenants were evicted. This was no good for the FSLN in the run-up to the election so, at the end of August 1989, the National Assembly passed a bill to suspend all legal proceedings for repossession of urban dwellings for 180 days, just long enough to quieten things for the election, but not so long that the landlords were seriously inconvenienced.

The FSLN candidates in the 1990 election were Daniel Ortega for President and Sergio Ramirez for Vice-president. Their election programme was, officially, determined at a one-day convention of 1,200 selected FSLN delegates on 24 September, 1989. The programme was to be "realistic", "responsible", guaranteed "to maintain... private property" and to protect "ownership of the land", while promising land for 25,000 peasant families. Specific proposals were limited to mildly reformist demands: to build 500 kilometres of new road, to build 6,000 new homes annually and to double the number of telephone lines in Managua. The section on women promised to struggle for the stability and unity of the family and, within that framework, to provide sex education and family planning. AMNLAE had been expected to raise the question of the right to abortion, but behind-the-scenes manoeuvres meant it was not brought to the floor of the convention.

On 12 December, 1989, Daniel Ortega, jointly with the presidents of Costa Rica, Guatemala, Honduras, and El Salvador, issued a statement in support of the El Salvador regime, calling for the Farabundo Marti National Liberation Front (FMLN) to immediately and effectively cease hostilities and take steps towards immediate demobilisation. The FMLN was the parallel organisation to the FSLN when it was a guerrilla force. The regime in El Salvador, backed by the US, and to preserve its position, had killed more than 70,000 Salvadorans and driven a million more into refugee camps. The FMLN indignantly rejected the declaration on the grounds it was in flagrant contradiction to the wishes of all democratic forces in El Salvador and in support of those guilty of crimes against humanity. Ortega defended his actions in the columns of *Barricada* (21 December, 1989), on the grounds that the FSLN's support for people fighting for their freedom and independence had to be "within the norms of co-existence with other governments".

The FSLN leadership used the 1990 election to steer the revolution of 1979 into a capitalist straight-jacket. The more the FSLN leadership presented the election as bolstering the gains of the revolution, the more it miseducated an entire generation. For the 1990 election the leadership transformed the FSLN into an electoral machine with a party organisation modelled on that of a radical bourgeois electoral party, with a mass following, but with no political accountability of the leadership.

Up for election were the President, Vice President, ninety members of the National Assembly, hundreds of local councillors and, on the Atlantic Coast, local autonomous regional councils. The FSLN shared its election platforms with capitalist ranchers and farmers, called for the continuation of *concertación*, and instructed the CST and ACT to avoid confrontations with management during the election campaign. The FSLN election slogan was: "Daniel for President – With me everything will be better". Large glossy posters showed Daniel Ortega holding a suitably photogenic child, but in village meeting halls there were also posters of Marx, Engels, Lenin, and Sandino.

The Sandinistas lost the elections in a vote against hunger and misery, a protest vote against the FSLN because it offered no perspective. A substantial factor in undermining the FSLN support was that the masses could see that the suffering brought by the Contra War was not equally shared. Walking in the streets of Managua it was obvious that there were those that were doing well out of the situation. These privateers, the 'patriotic bourgeoisie', the owners of factories and large farms, made enormous sums out of state-subsidised credit. Borrowing at a fixed rate meant that, with inflation rates of 1,000 per cent or more, they paid back only a tiny fraction of the value of the sum lent. Wanting to be on good terms with these 'patriotic producers', the state bought their produce at fixed prices, higher than they would have paid on the international market.[124] This meant a layer of society was able to visit the 'dollar shops' selling jeans costing a month's wage of a teacher.

The 25 February, 1990, election saw the Sandinistas beaten by Violeta Chamorro – the candidate of the old oligarchy. The US Congress had intervened directly in the election through the National Endowment for Democracy (NED), a body established and funded by the US Congress, and the CIA. The NED spent some US$48 million on the election in favour of the UNO candidate, who gained fifty-five per cent of the votes cast. Chamorro and her supporters pushed the line that a vote for her was a vote that would ensure peace and prosperity. This was the natural outcome of a mixed economy policy, and the exclusion of the masses from government. With the UNO victory, Ortega declared the election "the consolidation of democracy".

But the most important factor, by far, was the lack of leadership from the FSLN Directorate. As living conditions fell, the FSLN turned increasingly to a market system, demanding ever higher production levels from workers in factories with no raw materials, where machines went unrepaired, and where the real value of wages fell by the week. When some workers fought back, the FSLN declared a state of emergency, banned the right to strike and cut social spending to rock bottom, climaxing in 1990, the crucial election year. Social differentiation increased as bourgeois values were promoted, children and families were again seen scavenging through rubbish piles to find the means to stay alive. By 1989, the average person's real income was less than half of what it had been in 1977. Morale among the Nicaraguan people was falling rapidly and scepticism towards the FSLN was widespread.

The 1989/90 electoral programme of the FSLN, the bourgeois form of the elected assembly and the constitution, which turned its back on any form of Soviet democracy, brought to a head simmering differences on the revolutionary left internationally concerning the class nature of the FSLN regime. The essential difference was whether the FSLN would "quickly reactivate itself, affirming its decision not to give up control of the army and to defend the social gains, relying on popular mobilisations",[125] or whether Humberto Ortega was retained in his post as Head of the ESP in order to ensure no such mass mobilisations occurred.

On 26 February, 1990, top government officials met with UNO leaders in the presence of high-ranking US diplomats, to discuss the hand-over. The next

---

124 Sagali, S., *Report from Managua*, Bookmarks, 1989.
125 1991 World Congress the USec Fourth International, International viewpoint.

day, *La Prensa* carried a large front-page photo of Chamorro and Humberto Ortega in an embrace under the headline: 'First step towards reconciliation'. On 27 February, Daniel Ortega addressed a crowd of thousands of FSLN party members and supporters urging them to accept the election results, leading them in the chant 'We will govern from below!' Perhaps he half-remembered the similar slogan used by third period Stalinism: an approach that resulted in the Nazis taking power in Germany.

The labour law existing in Nicaragua in 1990 had been adopted in 1945, drawn up by the PSN when it was in partnership with Somoza, and designed to ensure workers toiled flat-out for the war effort without any disruptions such as strikes. Between 1979 and 1990, there had been calls for change, but the FSLN had never felt it necessary to take remedial action. Now, however, the workers were faced with a legislature that would be dominated by the pro-US bloc led by Chamorro. After the election and before the new government took office, workers across Managua were taking advantage of the hand-over period to engage in industrial action in expectation of a much harsher regime. But the workers were not only demanding wage increases, they were demanding the ATC and CST get the FSLN to change the labour law before the UNO took over government. At the time, the total labour force consisted of approximately 1,300,000 persons. About one-third of these were female, and about one-third of all working-age women held jobs, but half of Nicaragua's work force was under- or unemployed.

Militants argued that workers would be faced with an openly capitalist regime and should have stronger legal protection. However, the FSLN leadership argued that such a course of action would be a declaration of war on the new government, 'the road of violence'. The FSLN had to take 'the road of peace', which both bosses and workers would be urged to follow. The union members were having other thoughts.

During the pre-inauguration discussions, the fifty-one UNO assembly delegates, an unstable and opportunist grouping, split into a majority faction supporting Violeta Chamorro and a smaller group supporting the Vice President, Virgilio Godoy. The differences centred on the speed at which the reforms and services (e.g. health and education) introduced by the FSLN would be dismantled. On its own, neither UNO grouping had a majority, and on 24 April, Chamorro and Daniel Ortega did a deal for the FSLN to support Chamorro's group and become part of the governing block. In her inaugural speech, Chamorro announced Humberto Ortega would be retained as army chief. Humberto, for his part, pronounced Violeta to be a Sandinista!

This deal was the natural extension of the *concertación* policy of the FSLN, a de-facto coalition government, a popular front government. That is not to say the Ortega brothers did not use the militancy of the workers to bolster their position in the negotiations with Chamorro. Leading militants had stopped listening to the FSLN and, beginning on 11 May, and for two weeks, over a hundred strikes, predominantly in the public sector, swept across the country in the final week of the hand-over. The National Federation of Workers (FNT, a coalition of pro-FSLN unions), in fear of losing members to PSN unions, demanded a 200 per cent pay increase, an end to lay-offs, for greater state support of nationalised industries, and an end to the return of state farms to private owners. About 60,000 Government workers staged sit-in strikes.

Cynically, Daniel Ortega came out publicly in support of the strikers, a manoeuvre that had the additional benefit of heading off opposition within the FSLN to the deal with Chamorro. Ortega's support was, however, heavily qualified: emphasising the need for the re-establishment of calm, rejection of provocations, rejection of physical violence. The overall outcome was a sizeable victory for the FNT, with wage rises of over sixty per cent, but while many of the strikes were victorious, others were not.

In the same way, the FSLN leaders called a mass May Day demonstration with the demand 'Disarm the Contras' – a real issue that needed to be raised and acted upon; vigilante groups, Contras who had not been disarmed, had attacked strikers and at least one picket had been killed. But here the demonstration was primarily to show Chamorro that the FSLN still had mass support and would make a better partner in government than either Godoy or the Contras.

Factors such as prices continued to shoot up, public splits in the FNT and the threat that state-owned enterprises would be returned to their private owners were wearing down the resistance of the workers. Many of the less class-conscious saw it as a choice between having a job, any job, rather than being out of work. However, it was not economic hardships that disoriented and demobilised Nicaraguan toilers, it was the leadership default of the FSLN in failing to project any course for working people to act collectively against the exploiters and by their own efforts to change the course of their lives.

Almost everyone sought some means to augment their inflation-ruined wages and salaries. A fixed pay-rate had become increasingly meaningless in the late 1980s due to inflation and high annual turnover, as much as 100 per cent for urban industrial workers, was also typical of the Nicaraguan labour force as workers continually sought a better deal. Many Nicaraguan workers took to black marketeering, street vending, driving taxicabs, with some earning their livings on the streets – all non-productive labour. By inauguration day, 1990, it was not unusual for members of the salariat to earn as little as the equivalent of US$10 per month (not enough to pay for the food necessary to feed a family) while black marketeers made over ten times as much. A direct result of the mixed economy.

The continuing class-collaborationist perspective of the FSLN was explained by Humberto Ortega in an interview for state-run television four months after the election, on 27 June, 1990. The army (of which Humberto was head) paid for the interview to be published as a supplement in both *La Prensa* and *El Nuevo Diario*. Humberto described the recent elections as decisive in achieving peace in Nicaragua, saying: "Elections equal peace, peace equals economic recovery equals a firm foundation to begin to overcome underdevelopment".

After the election, the FSLN, with an occasional squeal, supported the austerity measures of the Chamorro government accepting falling real wages and a return to unemployment and underemployment levels of fifty per cent, on the grounds that "we cannot return to the 80s".[126]

The extreme nature of the neo-liberal measures taken by Chamorro and her successor (Arnoldo Alemán) meant the privatisation of everything that could be privatised, with those lucky enough to find work labouring twelve hours a day, six days a week for less than US$1 an hour. This was accompanied by the return of the wealthy families which had supported Somoza, flaunting their riches and regained social positions.

The economic course of the Chamorro government after 1990, supported by the FSLN leadership, was to place an increasing burden of indebtedness and material want on the mass of toiling peasants such that many of them went bankrupt. Under the Chamorro government, large farms would, once again, swallow up the land-holdings of smaller peasants.

As these events were developing, the majority of the FSLN National Assembly delegates, led by the leader of the parliamentary group (Sergio Ramirez) and the editor of *Barricada*, formed a faction in the run-up to the FSLN's 1994 First Congress' Extraordinary Session. This group would split from the FSLN and would ensure the neo-liberals had the full backing of the National Assembly. In the run-up to the Congress, Daniel Ortega, again putting on a left face, toured the country vigorously, calling for mass actions against the Chamorro government, voicing undying opposition to imperialism and supporting strike actions. At the Congress he was elected by acclamation, after which it was business as usual. Once back in charge Daniel

---

126 FSLN Commander Bayardo Arce, *El Semanario*, September 1993.

Ortega imposed an even more rigid top-down structure than before, turning the FSLN into his personal election machine.

In 1996, the FSLN (with Daniel Ortega once again their candidate) would lose to Arnoldo Alemán of the Liberal Alliance. However, in 2006, Daniel Ortega would be elected President of the poorest country in Central America and the second poorest in the Western Hemisphere, with widespread unemployment, under-employment, poverty and hunger, and an income distribution that was one of the most unequal in the world. That was the price the Nicaraguan masses paid for the lack of political perspective of the leaders of the FSLN.

Ortega now sought to neutralise the opposition of the Catholic hierarchy. The neo-liberal economic policies had hit women hardest: they were the first to lose their jobs; they and their families suffered most from the cutbacks in health and education; patriarchal attitudes reasserted themselves, reducing women to second-class status. Ortega now chose to align himself with Archbishop Miguel Obando y Bravo, and the 2006 Presidential election was noticeable for the FSLN candidate's attacks on the women's movement, in particular his all-out attack on women's reproductive rights. Before Ortega's election, the FSLN voted to abolish the right to even therapeutic abortion. For women, Nicaragua is one of the most oppressive regimes in the world.

After Ortega and the FSLN lost the 1990 election, the FSLN women's organisation AMNLAE broke asunder. A Women's Movement had grown outside AMNLAE, largely independent of the FSLN, and outside the control of the Ortegas. It is the major voice protecting women's rights, both factory workers and *campesinos*. The focus has become 'A Woman's Right to Choose', and the Movement is under constant attack for, allegedly, serving the interests of the country's oligarchy, being upper-class intellectuals, out of touch with ordinary women and criminals. The severity of the onslaught demonstrates that this is a real issue in Nicaragua with the potential for becoming a mass movement.

The case of Nicaragua shows how important revolutionary leadership is. A petty-bourgeois guerrilla organisation was swept to power on a mass, urban uprising. With no perspective of overthrowing capitalism, they moved ever further to the right, protecting capitalism from the righteous demands of workers and peasants. There was no revolutionary party to correct this stagist perspective, no means by which the masses could impose their will on the FSLN tops. The self-sacrifice and heroism of the masses in their battles with the National Guard showed there was excellent human material from which to recruit a Marxist Party. But without workers' democracy, the anti-Marxist policies of the FSLN leadership, systematically miseducated sections of the youth, women, *campesinos*, and workers. There is, however, no way to bypass the challenge of building such a party, there are no short cuts around it.

14) CONCLUSIONS: WHAT COULD HAVE BEEN DONE?

Before Nicaragua, Workers' and Peasants' Governments had, within a couple of years, either progressed to a workers' state (e.g. China, Cuba, Russia and Yugoslavia) or been overthrown by a counter-revolutionary coup (e.g. Algeria and Grenada). What was unique about Nicaragua was that, after a successful revolution, the entire leadership united to take the revolution in an openly capitalist direction. The Nicaraguan revolution decayed from the head down. Nicaragua was a demonstration that in the real world, a world dominated by imperialism, a revolution, even with heroic and massively popular support, will, without revolutionary theory, revert to capitalist oppression.

With the 1990 elections, the FSLN could be seen for what it had become: a radical bourgeois electoral party representing an obstacle to the development and political education of Nicaragua's working classes. Its political roots were a mix of Social Democracy, Liberation Theology, remnants of Stalinism, and some liberal bourgeois ideas, that combined to promote the myths that revolutions all end with the capitalists back in control, that lasting victories are not possible, and that minor reforms are all that can be hoped for.

During the initial stages of the revolution, class-struggle alternatives to the FSLN did make a brief appearance, but in conditions of retreat and even defeat, it would not be expected that a class-struggle alternative to the FSLN would emerge. What would be expected and what happened is that workers and peasants engaged in local defensive actions. For example, in the spring of 1999, striking transport workers forced President Arnoldo Alemán's government to give in to nearly all their demands. Alemán promised to reverse the price of diesel fuel from $1.41 to $1.28 and abandon plans to deregulate the country's bus lines. Nor have all the revolutionary-democratic gains been lost. Students are no longer being dragged from their beds in the middle of the night by cops, taken to the outskirts of town, badly beaten and then shot. These gains will remain for some time, although they will inevitably weaken.

Where peasants benefited from land reform by taking over capitalist holdings, so long as capitalism exists, class differentiation will sharpen and the *campesinos* will gradually be driven off the land. The 1990 election accelerated that process, pardoned Contras were legally entitled to the return of their lands and properties. Banks now regularly foreclose on impoverished peasants, and the big landlords can find a thousand reasons for taking a peasant's land. Small farmers increasingly sink into the landless semi-proletarian and proletarian layers.

The character of the Sandinista regime, radical, petty-bourgeois and hierarchical, contained the basis for its own defeat. Its contradictory character and utopian perspectives played into the hands of the national bourgeoisie and imperialism. Mass mobilisation ousted Somoza, but that did not stop the remaining national bourgeoisie, with enormous help from US imperialism, European Social Democracy, the Catholic Church, and FSLN leaders, from making a comeback.

For the revolution, the two most serious problem were the lack of a Leninist party and no independent organs of workers' power, no Soviets, in either the cities or the countryside. These omissions were quickly and consciously filled by the FSLN, with a radical but reformist programme.

14.1) WHAT COULD HAVE BEEN DONE? PRE-REVOLUTION

Despite the setbacks experienced by the Nicaraguan workers, we expect a new generation of working-class fighters will eventually emerge and follow Carlos Fonseca in his determination to 'go all the way' but, with the experience of the class-collaboration of the FSLN, they will adopt the practice of permanent revolution conceptualised by Marx, Engels, Lenin, Trotsky and Mella.

There were many on the revolutionary left who, after the victory of the Cuban revolution, concluded that a Marxist, democratic centralist party was no longer necessary for a workers' victory over capitalism. The failure of the FSLN in Nicaragua to successfully carry through even the bourgeois-democratic tasks such as Land to the Tiller, gaining national independence, and equal rights for women, let alone taking the revolution forward to social equality, should have buried that particular fallacy. A petty-bourgeois, guerrilla organisation has been shown to be an insufficient instrument for the overthrow of capitalism.

The first task of revolutionary socialists in Nicaragua was, and is, to contribute to the building of a democratic, disciplined, and centralised Leninist party of committed cadres dedicated to the overthrow of capitalism. Such a party is suited both to lead a successful mass uprising and continue the revolution through to the creation of a workers' state. As part of building such a party, it is necessary to achieve ideological and strategic clarity: to provide an explanation of events that corresponds to the actual situation in order to enter into a meaningful dialogue with workers, students, women, *campesinos*, and honest FSLN members. It was a fatal error for the FSLN to try to deal with a complex and contradictory situation on the basis of an out-of-date schema.

Discipline in the FSLN was military-bureaucratic, orders from the top were to be obeyed, and policy was made with little or no input from the members. Lenin's democratic centralism was very different. Policy was determined by the membership by majority vote after free and thorough discussion. Once policy was determined, the minority was required to accept and implement the decisions of the majority and then allow the test of events to determine who was right. After the FSLN came to power in Nicaragua, such a process would not have been tolerated, because the leadership was determined to implement a class-collaborationist policy that protected the bourgeoisie. Indeed, a programme best matching reality would have meant the immediate end of *concertación* and the Directorate.

A Marxist cadre party was essential because the toilers in Nicaragua needed to take more than just defensive actions, more even than overthrow the Somoza regime. History has demonstrated that a democratic revolution, especially one beginning with demands such as land to the peasant, cannot be carried through to a successful conclusion without taking the first steps towards socialism. Living positive proof is the Cuban Revolution, living negative proof is the recent history of Nicaragua.

Building the Leninist combat party as the number one goal may be the objective, but how to do it with limited resources under the watchful eyes of the National Guard? What would have been its programme? In particular, what strategy/tactics would a revolutionary socialist organisation have adopted in the pre-revolution period, during the 1979-80 revolution, during the restructuring of the FSLN and constitutional change in 1987, and the 1990 election?

During the period after the Chinese Communist Party had adopted the strategy of rural guerrilla warfare it withdrew its cadres from the factories to fight in the rural areas. Trotsky advised that the situation in China was not then revolutionary, that the correct strategy should be to draw the masses into action with democratic demands, including the eight-hour-day. Such slogans were intended to bring broad masses into activity and prepare the ground for raising revolutionary slogans and establishing Soviets.[127] Later, Liu Shaoqi, when making an overall assessment of the work of the CCP during that period, admitted that democratic slogans were what had been required. He explained that the CCP had condemned the use of democratic slogans as 'rightist' ... "the losses we have suffered on this account are countless".[128] The possibility of organising and unionising workers in China in 1937 under Japanese occupation was less propitious than in Nicaragua in the 1970s as evidenced in the successful PSN-led strikes during the Somoza dictatorship.

---

127 Chen Duxiu, *Appeal to all the Comrades in the CCP*, 1929, www.marxist.org.
128 Liu Shaoqi, *Letter to the Party Centre... 1937*, in Saich, T., *The Rise to Power of the CCP*, Sharp, 1994.

Would revolutionary socialists have carried out their political work as part of the FSLN? This is not easy to answer. At first sight it appears obvious that the masses rallied to the guerrillas and swept them to victory. But the charisma and attraction of the guerrillas came almost entirely because they had demonstrated they were the only ones prepared to take the fight against Somoza to the end. They were also glamourised because they were seen as the Nicaraguan equivalent of the 'bearded ones' of the Cuban revolution. Yet it was urban, not rural uprisings, that swept Somoza from power. Guerrillas who had made their main focus the rural and border areas, often arrived after the urban uprisings had routed the National Guard. An experienced and tested urban insurrectionary leadership may well, in those early days of the uprisings, have taken power based on a Soviet-style network of local Civil Defence Committees.

14.2) WHAT COULD HAVE BEEN DONE? THE REVOLUTIONARY UPSURGE

In Nicaragua there was no better time to form Soviets than from the summer of 1979 to the spring of 1980. Lenin emphasised that the concept of the Soviet was simple and applicable to peasants and factory workers alike,[129] and Soviets would have meant the democratisation of the revolution. In the urban centres CDCs existed and the workers were demanding political rights such as freedom of assembly, association, speech, and to strike. In the countryside Soviets could have been based around actions taken on the basis of destruction of the system of *latifundios*, in particular, 'Land to the Tiller', and 'End Debt Repayment'. The Russian experience had shown that, given a firm lead, middle peasants would support the revolution if the revolutionary regime approved the seizure of the landed estates and their distribution to the peasants by the peasants. Though, of course, there had to be a minimum level of organisation in existence to pose such a programme.

In times of revolutionary upheavals, Soviets emerge organically from the mass movement: from strike committees, action committees, peasant leagues, and other representative bodies. In Nicaragua the CDCs were the basis for the self-activities of the masses, bringing into action broad sections and directly expressing their will. Soviet power could have been fought for through the convening of Soviets both locally and nationally. For CDCs and peasants' committees to take the lead and control the revolution through a national congress of delegates which would determine policy for the revolutionary government. Revolutionaries would have fought within those organisations

---

129 Lenin, V., CW31:243, July 1920.

for a programme of transitional demands leading to a Workers' and Peasants' Government.

The CDCs gave a structure to the mass opposition to the Somoza regime and would have done the same for the expropriation of the big bourgeoisie. These committees formed the embryo of a genuinely revolutionary force based on the actual movement unfolding in the cities. Free, democratic workers' Soviets are the mechanism by which the masses assess and impose their will on the parties that claim to represent them, and it was to avoid such a process that the FSLN took control of the CDCs so quickly. In this the FSLN followed the example of one of their mentors, the Chinese Communist Party, which was also terrified of genuine Soviets, to the extent that it developed the novel argument that the Bolsheviks had come to power against the Soviets and that any other interpretation was 'Trotskyist'.[130] The CDCs could have carried the revolution to the capture of governmental and state power, but such a concept was alien to the FSLN.

In the second half of 1979 Nicaragua was in the process of a revolution and the transitional demands made by revolutionary socialists would have led from the actual situation to the goal of a workers' state, and very likely have included:

- The CDCs to be transformed into workers' and peasants' councils (Soviets), into organs of power. The CDCs throughout Nicaragua to send delegates to a central congress in Managua.

- Complete destruction of Somoza's National Guard, police force, and judicial system.

- All major enterprises, factories, TV and radio stations, etc., to be nationalised and put under the control of the workers employed in them.

- All land to be nationalised and the large estates to be shared as decided by the peasants themselves.

- Control of the militia to be retained by the CDCs. Militia to retain their weapons.

- State monopoly of foreign trade.

- A national economic plan drawn up on the basis of production for need not for profit.

- Renunciation of all foreign debt pilfered by the Somoza family and its entourage.

---

130 Wales, N., *Why the Chinese Communists Support the United Front: An Interview with Lo Fu*, Pacific Affairs, 1938, 11(3)311-322.

- A woman's right to choose must be incorporated in the constitution, as must the rights of the indigenous, the Black Nicaraguans of the Atlantic coast, and all other groups.

- A socialist federation of Central America, beginning with Nicaragua and Cuba.

The Nicaraguan masses had armed and organised themselves to take and defend revolutionary power. Popular militias had been formed in localities, in factories and workplaces, and had demonstrated their effectiveness by smashing the Somoza regime and destroying the National Guard. One of the first actions of the FSLN was to regularise these militias. Neighbourhood and village CDCs were adopted by the FSLN in such a way that they retained the dual role of political mobilisation and active involvement of working people in the revolution, and yet keeping those activities within the bounds set by the FSLN. The FSLN showed great skill in rapidly transforming the CDCs into CDSs and quickly mobilising them for hugely popular campaigns such as the literacy drive, the child immunisation programme, and ensuring that food rationing was fair and effective. Instead of the CDCs becoming the organisations of revolutionary power, they were co-opted into the mixed economy as CDSs under FSLN control.

Revolutionary popular militias always terrify the bourgeoisie, for whom the disarming of the people is a priority. Such a goal was quite in accord with the *Programa Sandinista*, the only surprising aspect being the speed with which the FSLN moved to disarm the CDCs. Within two months of the revolutionary upsurge, on 28 September, 1979, the order was given: all weapons and military equipment to be turned in. Revolutionary Marxists would have called for the retention and strengthening of the armed militias based on the CDCs, not their demobilisation.

Nevertheless, during and following the revolution it was necessary to be cautious in proposing any course of action that challenged the FSLN leadership. It was hugely popular and had a dedicated following in the *barrios* and amongst the poor peasants because the first, most immediate and very important gain of the revolution was the end of the reign of terror and this was popularly ascribed to the FSLN. Tomás Borge in the May and June, 1981, issues of *Latinamerica Press* confirmed that the Directorate understood this and had used this popularity to control the direction of the revolution.

In such a situation, from 1979 to at least 1985, regardless of the leadership and/or programme and/or alliances of the FSLN, revolutionists had to place themselves within the current represented by the FSLN. The struggles for an independent working-class party, for independence from the bourgeoisie, for a Workers' and Peasants' Government and progression to socialism all had to take place as part of the FSLN's mass organisations. Revolutionaries would have been loyal militants but fought for the political and organisational independence of the working class, attempting to lead those struggles that posed the question of power and democracy, both urban and rural, as a focal point of democratic and transitional demands.

Party building after the revolution would have included working within the mass organisations: in AMPRONAC on a woman's right to choose; as militants within trade unions demanding free speech, the right to assembly, the right to strike, and nationalisation under workers' control; within the ATC, raising the demand for nationalisation of the land and its sharing out by the peasants themselves; within the student and youth movements calling for free speech and the right to assemble, for free education and/or training up to and including university level. Whether these activities would have been via an independent organisation such as the LMR, or from within the FSLN was a matter of practicalities, not principle.

14.3) WHAT COULD HAVE BEEN DONE? THE MIXED ECONOMY

The right of workers to representation and collective bargaining was generating confrontations with employers. Demands for wage rises or improvements in working conditions were supported by strikes and occupations, most importantly by health and construction workers. In towns and cities, workers were spontaneously confronting employers who used authoritarian methods and/or laid off workers who took industrial action.

These actions were opposed by the FSLN, ACT and (at the time, the embryonic) CST. *Barricada*[131] reported that workers' strikes and occupations were being met not only by sackings by the bosses, but also arrests by the new Sandinista police, and even threats to send in troops. It is claimed that often heard on the demonstrations at this time were the slogans 'Workers and Peasants to Power!' and 'Down with the Bourgeoisie!' These demands may well have originated with the FO, but needed to be made concrete to avoid the workers' anger being dissipated. Revolutionary socialists would have included specific and appropriate ways for the workers and peasants to actually take the power.

Simultaneously, workers were also mobilising to occupy enterprises where they believed the employers were attempting to liquidate their companies and take their monies abroad (to Miami, usually), or were sabotaging production in one way or another. The FSLN faced both ways on this question, supporting workers' action in one factory and opposing it in an

---

131 1 February, 1980

adjacent one. The more advanced layers of workers understood the need to open the capitalists' account books and to place the factories and enterprises under workers' control to end decapitalisation. At the same time, the peasants were for the immediate seizure of the landed estates and their division by the peasants to the peasants. But for the FSLN, carrying through the agrarian revolution to completion was unthinkable because that would have violated the existing property relations; a complete land reform would have affected the properties of allies like Violeta Chamorro and Alfonso Robelo.

Democratic control by the masses would have meant stepping beyond *concertación*, taking measures that could not be contained within the bourgeois democratic revolution, taking the first steps towards socialism. In Nicaragua, any scenario in which the workers and peasants determined policy would have meant a break with the mixed economy and the concept of a revolution by stages. Workers' democracy is the mechanism to counteract bureaucratisation, to ensure that party policy and all major economic decisions are in the interests of those who work for a living. It was thus studiously avoided by the Directorate.

Workers and peasants were brought into the FSLN after the revolution, but they had no control over its political course, or the selection of its leaders. As Trotsky wrote about the Popular Front government in France:

> In order to lead the revolutionary struggles for power, it is necessary to clearly see the class from which the power must be wrested. The workers did not recognise the enemy because he was disguised as a friend. In order to struggle for power, it is necessary, moreover, to have the instruments of struggle: the party, trade unions, and Soviets. The workers were deprived of these instruments because the leaders of the workers' organisations formed a wall around the bourgeois power in order to disguise it, to render it unrecognisable and invulnerable. Thus, the revolution that began found itself braked, arrested, demoralised.[132]

A governmental slogan is required to bind workers' demands into a coherent programme. The demand for a revolutionary Workers' and Peasants' Government based on Soviets (by any name) was vital to counterpose the popular front direction of the FSLN. Revolutionaries would have been demanding that the FSLN break with the bourgeoisie, by not only ejecting the capitalist ministers, although this was a crucial demand, but politically by renouncing the project of a capitalist Nicaragua.

The tactics used by revolutionaries would have had to start by accepting the immense respect and status the FSLN held amongst the masses as the leader of the popular insurrection. But neither the FSLN nor the bourgeoisie

132 Trotsky, L., *Whither France?* www.marxists.org, 1936.

wanted to place their policies before the masses for discussion and approval. The bourgeoisie initially pinned its hopes on the Junta and Council of State appointed by the FSLN, and attempted to use those bodies to protect its interests. But at that stage the pressure of the masses for radical change could not be fully contained and the bourgeois representatives quit.

The attempt to reconcile the revolution with capitalism is what led to its defeat. Successful revolutions cannot be achieved with half-measures. It is necessary to either break the power of the oligarchy and establish workers' power, or the ruling class will regain the initiative, sabotage the economy, create chaos and re-take power in a counter-revolution.

The state of the internal democracy within the FSLN can be better appreciated when we remember that in 1987 the organisation underwent a complete transformation and changed Nicaragua's constitution without any real involvement of its members; that the membership at large had no effective say in the election programme, strategy or even tactics of 1990. The very first FSLN Congress was held 19-21 July 1991.[133] In the run-up to the Congress there were calls for democratisation of the FSLN, to give workers and *campesinos* the right to have their voices heard. Revolutionary socialists would have whole-heartedly supported such calls and helped organise the rank and file meetings to formulate their own analyses of what had happened, to question the role played by the FSLN and, particularly, its leaders. Revolutionary socialists would have taken into all the Sandinista mass organisations the demands – suitably posed – to break the rank and file from the dangerous and non-revolutionary policies of the FSLN leadership. These would have included defence of every strike, every factory occupation and every land seizure, raising the need for democratic control of the militias. To oppose every attempt to use the police or EPS against such mobilisations, to call for rank and file committees within the EPS that would defend not attack the peasants.

Of course, the specific and concrete demands would have to be determined by those on the spot but would have been based on the workers' rights to act in their own interests and would almost certainly included, in addition to those above:

- Freedom of assembly, the right to make one's voice heard through public demonstrations, leaflets, newspapers.
- Freedom of association, whether trade union or political party, with the exception of those who supported the Contras, those who were intent on undermining the revolution.

---

133 *Envio* No 122, *The Sandinista Congress ... Inconclusive*, September 1991.

- Freedom to bargain collectively and to take industrial action on such issues as unemployment, low pay, health and safety.
- Freedom to elect local officers of the FSLN, ACT, CST, CDS, AMNLAE and the youth organisation, subject to recall at any time.
- Freedom to strike, to form picket lines and self-defence squads to protect them.
- Freedom for the peasants to seize the estates and plantations of the Nicaraguan bourgeoisie without compensation and to divide them between themselves.
- No official to get wages higher than the average skilled worker.

In the months before the Congress there was a structured discussion, and some 47,000 Sandinistas participated in these 'assemblies'. Over 3,000 locally-elected delegates met to elect 501 of their number to represent their department in the National Congress. This indirect method of election is the tradition in top-down parties to weed out oppositionists. The Congress, with nearly 600 delegates (only eighteen per cent were women) divided into two currents, the one led by the Directorate, convinced that the FSLN should move more openly in a Social-Democratic direction and put 'national interest' before class interests. This group proposed purely parliamentary means of struggle even, if necessary, dissociating from grassroots and trade union actions. The outcome of the Congress was symbolised by this group succeeding in having the FSLN establish formal links with the Social-Democratic International.

The counter-current was rooted in the trade unions' rejection of the "petty-bourgeois utopia of class-conciliation and non-antagonism between the interests of the exploited and exploiters, which only serves to undermine the struggle of the exploited". They described *concertación* as an "error", and called for deepening internal democracy, rejecting a top-down style of organisation; for defence of the living standards of the poor, and rejected the neo-liberal policies of the government.

The Congress was rigged from the start with the seating of eighty 'historic cadres' as voting delegates, and by manipulation of the agenda and careful selection of what was to be voted on, the main documents being released only hours before Congress began, and so on. The only unexpected aspect was the pre-Congress role of Daniel Ortega, who toured the country tub-thumping in favour of supporting strike actions, for undying opposition to imperialism, for no more deals behind the backs of the trade unions, and calling for mass actions against the Chamorro government. He defended 'the right to rebellion'. At the Congress he was elected by acclamation after which it was business as usual, with the same Directorate save for the replacement of Humberto who resigned in order to remain Minister of Defence. The Directorate was elected as a slate to ensure that those most identified with unpopular policies retained their places.

15) POSTSCRIPT

On 18 April, 2018, Ortega announced new pension regulations that would have increased the contributions of both employers and workers while, at the same time, reducing resulting benefits by introducing a new tax on pensions. Immediately after the announcement of the reform package, students took to the streets in impromptu demonstrations, which sparked spontaneous solidarity actions in the *barrios* when hundreds, then thousands, came out onto the streets to join the students and protect them from government repression. Barricades were erected, in particular in areas with strong Sandinista traditions, such as Masaya, León, Jinoteque, etc. This popular rebellion was met with violent repression.[134]

After four months of clashes, protests, mass demonstrations and repression the Ortega-Murillo government seems to have recovered control of the situation at the cost of over 300 people being killed.

Though the protests started over the issue of the reform of the pensions system, the scale and virulence of the movement reflected widespread opposition to the model of government introduced by the ruling couple (Ortega and Murillo are man and wife), when the FSLN returned to power in 2006, after sixteen years of openly right-wing governments. The Ortega-led FSLN, which won the election had little or nothing in common with the traditions of the Sandinista Revolution.

Ortega had made a deal with the reactionary hierarchy of the Catholic Church, through which FLSN deputies (in opposition) voted with the right wing for, especially, the banning of all abortion rights. This was part of a series of agreements between Ortega and the main representative of the right wing, Alemán, one of which was the lowering the threshold for election victory in the first round, in exchange for a legal reform which would benefit Alemán who was in jail on corruption charges.

Ortega's campaign in 2006 no longer used the red and black colours of the FSLN but yellow and pink, claiming to stand for 'Christian socialism' with emphasis on Christian (which here meant traditional, reactionary, Catholic values) and ditched the Sandinista anthem for a version of John Lennon's 'Give Peace a Chance'. *Reconciliation* was the main FSLN slogan.

---

134 The Postscript is based on De La Cruz. J., *The crisis of the regime in Nicaragua and the necessity of revolutionary leadership*, July 4, 2018, www.marxist.com

Once back in power, the presidential couple's only concern was to remain in power, with the ensuing perks, privileges and wealth. This meant establishing a pact with the capitalist class and clamping down on democratic rights. Ortega would guarantee social stability so that the employers would be able to make profits and they, in exchange, would stay out of politics. That agreement was hugely beneficial for the ruling class and particularly for those capitalists involved in the Free Trade Zones, which benefited from low taxes, cheap labour, and absence of trade unions.

Ortega enjoyed good relations with the US to the extent that Nicaragua was singled out for preferential status. There was close collaboration with Washington on migration, the war on drugs, security, etc. US agencies were allowed to operate freely in the country. Ortega's government enforced all the necessary conditions for the extraction and looting of wealth by US multinational corporations. In return, Nicaragua received substantial sums from USAID.

As a result of the Ortegas' policies the living standards of Nicaraguans is the lowest in Latin America. This was the background to why wide layers of the Nicaraguan people rose up in April.

Cunningly, Ortega combined these policies with an alliance with Venezuela. This was very convenient as it gave him access to cheap oil and, for a time, subsidies for social programmes. It also allowed him to indulge in a certain degree of left-wing rhetoric, which was used as a smokescreen to cover his pursuit of openly pro-business policies. Simultaneously, he tried to balance his trade and security links with the US with similar links with China and Russia. But here Ortega blotted his book, he established trade relations with China, including the idea of constructing an alternative to the Panama Canal, which is anathema to any US administration.

The US is always on the look-out for more compliant and openly pro-US regimes, and at the same time is anxious that if there is to be regime-change, it should be peaceful and not harm US interests. The US Ambassador, Carlos Trujillo, called for elections. Several senior US officials have visited Nicaragua in recent weeks to hold closed-door meetings with Ortega. What they want is some kind of early election that will deactivate the movement, and maintain 'peace and order' to continuing with the smooth running of their businesses.

The bourgeoisie prefer a quiet life, but they also prefer a government of their own kind no matter how servile and useful the Ortega-Murillo government may have been. In Nicaragua, a section of the capitalist class saw the protests as a means of getting rid of Ortega and replacing him with a 'safer pair of hands'. Quickly, the bosses' federation, COSEP, which had collaborated closely with Ortega for sixteen years, moved to take over the leadership of the protests in order to steer them towards the safe channels of negotiations and talks. The American Chamber of Commerce (AMCHAM) also jumped in.

The students, who took the lead in street protests, used social media in an attempt to form a national student council to provide organisation and leadership. Lacking experience and with no clear left-wing alternative being presented, the students' movement was also co-opted by right-wing organisations.

The only alternative to the ruling party, other than openly right-wing parties, is the Movement for Sandinista Renewal (MRS). However, the MRS is not a socialist organisation. Its criticism of the Ortega government is purely liberal, and it offers no real alternative to collaboration with the capitalists. In fact, on several occasions, the MRS has stood jointly in elections with bourgeois Liberals.

Self-appointed 'student leaders' travelled to the US to meet with the Republican right and then to El Salvador to meet with the leaders of the right wing and reactionary ARENA. Instead of advancing an independent strategy based on the unity of students and working people creating their own organisations of struggle, the student movement appealed to the bosses' organisations to call a 'civic strike'. In their communiques they fully accepted the idea of a 'necessary' alliance with the capitalists.

This, in turn, gave ammunition to the government to present the movement as a "US imperialist plot against the Sandinista Revolution", and this played a role in enabling it to crush the protests.

The protest movement, which started in April and acquired, at times, insurrectionary proportions was a genuine movement of opposition to a government carrying out capitalist policies. Due to the lack of any left-wing leadership, it was captured by right-wing bourgeois elements and crushed through repression.

In this situation, the great absentee has been the organised workers. Although there were some who came out to demonstrate individually, the bulk of the working class did not participate fully – a situation that is largely due to the domination of the unions by the Ortega government. In Nicaragua, the unions have long been a tool for putting a brake on class struggles. The most urgent task is to develop an independent class programme that confronts the repressive bourgeois government of Ortega, the capitalists, the right-wing parties and imperialism. The immediate challenge facing Nicaraguan revolutionaries is the elaboration of transitional demands, which will include calls for political democracy and social justice in very concrete terms.

The recent history of Nicaragua confirms the inability of the so-called progressive bourgeoisie to solve the problems of the masses. In the Revolution of 1979, it was the general strike and the popular urban insurrection that swept away the old regime and opened the door for social transformation. The bourgeoisie did not play any role; on the contrary it betrayed the revolution. The 1979 Revolution could have destroyed capitalism; however, the FSLN leaders, all of them, accepted the poisonous class-collaborationist schema of stages, instead of maintaining class independence as Carlos Fonseca Amador always advocated. Instead of taking the necessary steps to ensure the gains of the bourgeois-democratic revolution, which necessitated taking the first steps towards socialism, they combined the public sector with the private in a 'mixed economy', to the benefit of the latter.

It is necessary to rescue the true history of Nicaragua that shows the heroism of the workers, peasants and students, demonstrates the despicable role of the politics of class collaboration, and the treacherous role of the bourgeoisie. The real revolutionary traditions of Nicaragua must be saved in order to build an independent class leadership and genuine socialist programme based on the traditions of workers' democracy.

For the moment, the fight in Nicaragua has the form of a struggle for democracy and for social justice, but these are important and can be the basis for rallying the masses. Such a programme could inspire, unite, and advance the movement and would have strong similarities to the transitional demands applicable after the 1990 election (see Section 14.2). The demands would include legitimising the right to fight for decent wages, union rights and safe working conditions, especially in the Free Trade Zones; for decent pensions with costs borne by the capitalists out of their multi-billion-dollar profits; against repression; and identification and punishment of those responsible for the killings of demonstrators.

There must also be protection of the *campesinos'* and indigenous peoples' land, and new agricultural programs to raise the standard of living in the countryside. Women's rights, children's rights, and the rights of the indigenous, the Black Nicaraguans of the Atlantic coast, and all other groups must be protected and enhanced.

CHAPTER 3
VENEZUELA: THE ALMOST REVOLUTION

1) INTRODUCTION

Venezuela has been on the front line of the struggle against capitalism for two decades; every step forward by the masses has met ferocious opposition from the Venezuelan bourgeoisie backed by US imperialism. The Bolivarian Revolution – in the name of 'Socialism for the Twenty-First Century' – has restricted itself to the demands of the bourgeois-democratic revolution: national independence, land reform, a more equal distribution of wealth, and a democratic state. But in the twenty-first century, even these limited demands cannot be achieved without ending the looting of Venezuela by the imperialists and their allies. In this sense the Bolivarian Revolution is an integral part of the world crisis of capitalism, and a link in the world socialist revolution.

This chapter traces the history of the Bolivarian Revolution made in the interests of the poor and the oppressed, but where the gains are being taken back by the Venezuelan oligarchs, a tight-knit coalition of land-owners, bankers, capitalists, and the tops of the state bureaucracy.

The Venezuelan Revolution, from the time of the attempted coup in April 2002 to overthrow President Chávez by military and anti-democratic means, is unique in several important ways, not least that it was effected in full view of TV cameras. The bourgeois mass media was actively involved in plotting the coup, it deliberately misrepresented events in order to justify the actions of the military, it deliberately misreported the actions of Chávez, it gave widespread publicity to the plotters and amplified their limited successes, it silenced the voices of those opposed to the coup and, when the coup had failed, rather than report the success of the masses, it closed itself down for a day. Events in Venezuela in 2002, and later, have proved beyond any doubt that 'freedom of the press' under private ownership is freedom for the bourgeoisie to feed lies to the people.

But the most important factor by far, is that a spontaneous uprising of the popular masses defeated the coup. This was the first time in history such an event had occurred and undeniable proof of the extent and depth of the popular support for the Chávez government. However, the emphasis placed on Chávez by the mass media, and even academics, has tended to divert attention away from the actual process of the Revolution and the gains of the poor and dispossessed, the great majority of the Venezuelan people.

At its height, the Bolivarian Revolution had: largely abolished illiteracy; increased the proportion of children enrolling at secondary schools from just under half to three-quarters of the school age population; provided free university education, and increased student numbers from 800,000 to 2.6 million; had built over two million furnished new homes; provided access to free healthcare in community centres for most of the population; increased the number of persons receiving a pension from 380,000 to over 2 million, and increased the level of the pension; reduced the proportion of Venezuelans living in poverty from forty-eight per cent to twenty-seven per cent of the population; reduced malnourishment from twenty-one per cent to five per cent, introduced low-cost, state-run food stores, and increased the calorie intake of poor Venezuelans by fifty per cent.[1] These facts have been consistently downplayed and even ignored by the popular media in the West and it is these gains that gave Chávez his mass base, and the reason why Nicolás Maduro can still win elections.

Chávez gave the popular masses of Venezuela a sense of their own worth and in doing so made a bitter enemy of US imperialism. The gains made by Venezuela's masses pose a serious threat to imperialism, not only to its interests in Venezuela, but across Latin America.

2) SOME HISTORY

Venezuela, officially the Bolivarian Republic of Venezuela (*República Bolivariana de Venezuela*), is a federal republic located on the northern coast of South America. It is bordered by Colombia on the west, Brazil on the south, Guyana on the east, and the islands of Trinidad and Tobago to the north-east. Venezuela covers 916,400 km² (353,800 sq miles), one-and-a-half times the area of France but with only about 32 million people. Venezuela has

---

1 Wilpert, G., *Chávez' Legacy of Land Reform*, Review of Agrarian Studies, 3(2).

the world's largest proven reserves of oil, freshwater and gold, and the world's second largest gas reserves. The abundance of oil has shaped practically every aspect of the country's history, economy, politics, and culture.

The European bourgeoisie had built a world economic system, and the self-confidence it felt enabled it to make temporary and partial concessions to absorb upsurges in workers' militancy. However, the Venezuelan oligarchy, about 100 families with grand sounding surnames – are a product of colonialism and imperialism, and are particularly parasitical in nature. They enriched themselves by filching from state revenues, the mechanisms for which resulted in an all-pervasive culture of corruption. This gang of robbers and cut-throats has always been especially reactionary and obtuse, never willing to make any compromise that meant surrendering even the smallest part of their power or privileges.

Given Venezuela's vast areas of arable land, benign climate and relatively small population, it was astounding that it imported about two-thirds of the foodstuffs it consumed, the cause of the co-called 'food crisis'. Venezuelan agriculture was (and is) one of the most extreme expressions of the backwardness and parasitical character of the Venezuelan oligarchy. Tied to the big land-owners by a thousand links and wholly dependent on the imperialists, the national bourgeoisie never had any interest in leading a bourgeois democratic revolution, supporting the peasants' seizure of the *latifundia*, and breaking the control of the *caudillos*. For the oligarchy, it is preferable, i.e., more profitable, to invest their money abroad, milk the state's oil revenues, and produce beef for the international market, than it is to develop food production to feed Venezuelans. Without land reform there will be no farmers producing food to feed Venezuela's own population. But, in the twentieth and twenty-first centuries, seizing the *latifundia* means challenging imperialist domination root and branch, and this the national bourgeoisie will not do.

In 1908, General Juan Vicente Gómez, a military strongman, seized control of Venezuela and launched a dictatorial regime. Under his rule the first Venezuelan commercial oilfield was discovered in the Lake Maracaibo Basin (in Zulia state in western Venezuela), and, by the end of 1917, oil was a significant proportion of exports. Gómez granted concessions at bargain basement rates to foreign oil companies such as Royal Dutch Shell to exploit the oil. By 1928, Venezuela was the world's leading oil exporter with US companies the major players in the Venezuelan oil industry.

By 1935, oil dominated all aspects of the economy, and accounted for over ninety per cent of exports, with large numbers of Venezuelans employed in the oil fields. However, the profitability of this sector of the economy, in accord with the laws of a capitalist economy, sucked in the investment that could have been used to create other industries, and actually robbed Venezuela of its ability to generate new industries or to modernise existing ones. In 1920, the agricultural sector dominated the country; by 1941, the economy was totally dominated by the extraction of raw materials. Agriculture declined dramatically causing a significant fall in the living standards of the already poverty stricken *campesinos*.

Venezuelan democracy was a racket to further enrich the fabulously wealthy. The state bureaucracy, already corrupt, now had as its main purpose, the funnelling of state oil revenues into private pockets while avoiding any public backlash. Oil money was used to bribe the middle classes through the growth of a state bureaucracy until it employed nearly half the working population.[2] By 1998, Venezuela would rank as one of the ten most corrupt countries in the world with an interlocking system of graft and privileges feeding off the oil industry at the expense of the people. Of course, a small part of the oil revenues was spent on providing some social housing and the most basic of education, but these rose and fell with the price of oil on the world market.

By the start of World War II there were, in the cities and oil fields, large numbers of professional managers, technicians and literate wage-earners who wanted an end to the ultra-conservative rule of the *caudillos*. The World War 'for democracy' accelerated social and economic development, and different political parties were permitted, which allowed Rómulo Betancourt a well-known activist and, at that time, communist sympathiser, to tap into the widespread dissent and rapidly create what was, in effect, a mass party of the *pardo*, the non-white, impoverished overwhelming majority of the population, *Acción Democrática* (AD).[3] AD was a reformist party: it called for universal suffrage, an end to political rule by the military, genuine representative government, industrialisation of the country not just the oil industry, agrarian reform, more public health facilities and better educational provision.

The Allies' need for a secure source of oil, allowed the Venezuelan National Congress to pass the Hydrocarbons Law of 1943, imposing taxes and royalties amounting to about forty-three per cent of oil profits, and limiting concessions to a maximum of forty years. This law remained basically unchanged until 1976, the year of nationalisation. The Hydrocarbons Law brought in extra income but tied it to taxes on oil sales. Increasing oil

2   Ellner, S., *Rethinking Venezuelan Politics*, 2008, Lynne Reiner.
3   Ellner, S., *Factionalism... 1937-1948*, Science and Society 1981, 45(1)52-70.

production increased income, but meant an ever-greater reliance by the state on this one source of revenue.

General Isaías Medina Angarita, military dictator from 1941, in a bid to strengthen his regime, called elections at the end of 1945 but his manoeuvring angered Betancourt to such an extent that Betancourt pledged the support of the strongest political party in Venezuela to a group of military conspirators, creating the conditions for the 18 October, 1945 coup d'etat. Medina was quickly overthrown by a combination of a military rebellion and a popular movement led by AD. Betancourt, now the most popular politician in the country was called to chair the junta of government.

The three-year period from 1945 to 1948 saw the first free democratic elections in Venezuelan history, which AD won by a landslide on a radical programme of universal suffrage and an increase in tax on oil revenues from forty-three per cent to fifty per cent. The USA offered no serious opposition to the hike in oil taxes in return for a secure and plentiful supply close to home. However, AD also promised land reform. The landed oligarchy comprised less than two per cent of the population, but owned seventy-five per cent of the country's arable land. So powerful was this group that no government in Venezuela's history had succeeded in imposing any kind of land tax. The AD government proposed that idle and under-utilised land should be compulsorily purchased and distributed to landless peasants. The land-owners fought tooth and nail, and on 24 November, 1948, between the bill being passed and its implementation, Colonel Marcos Pérez Jiménez and Minister of Defence, Lt. Colonel Carlos Delgado Chalbaud (both coup organisers in 1945) staged another coup. In all class societies there have been strong links between the armed forces and the landed gentry, Venezuela was no exception.

Political parties were suppressed and all prominent members of AD and the Communist Party (PCV) were exiled or jailed. Then the Junta decided to legitimise its position by holding an election for president. The 30 November, 1952 election was a notorious travesty, which demonstrated just how much hostility there was towards the military. However, ignoring the popular vote, Pérez assumed the presidency on 19 April, 1953, and enacted a new constitution allowing him to rule openly as a military dictator. The limited reforms introduced by AD were reversed, but a temporary rise in the price of oil meant Pérez was able to buy a degree of support by launching a number of public works programmes such as social housing and building the Central University of Venezuela. His main expenditure, however, was modernising the military and expanding the secret police (*National Security, Seguridad*

Nacional), which ruthlessly hunted down, imprisoned, tortured and killed those who voiced opposition to his rule.

From the mid-1950s, Middle Eastern countries contributed significant amounts of oil to the world petroleum market and the over-supply meant Venezuela experienced a sharp drop in state income. This resulted in government spending on education, health and public housing being slashed, while the spending on lavish, costly and unnecessary construction projects such as the world's most expensive officers' club overlooking Caracas was maintained.

A referendum, on 15 December, 1957, to extend Pérez' mandate had exactly the opposite effect. Officially, eighty-seven per cent of voters favoured he stay in office for another five years, but so unanimous had been the opposition that the regime began to fragment immediately. On 1 January, 1958, a failed coup by air force officers provoked a popular rebellion. Street demonstrations mobilised by students, opposition political parties and some business leaders, culminated in a general strike on 21 January, with overwhelming mass support. A navy revolt led by Admiral Wolfgang Larrazábal followed, and in the early hours of 23 January, Pérez fled to the Dominican Republic.

At news of the overthrow, the people took to the streets, destroying the headquarters of the government newspaper, *El Heraldo*, attacking the headquarters of the security forces and dispensing quick justice to those they caught. A Provisional Government led by Larrazábal called elections, and released political prisoners.[4] Betancourt won the 7 December, 1958 presidential election handsomely; AD holding seventy-three of 133 seats in the Chamber of Deputies and thirty-two of fifty-one seats in the Senate.

Prior to the elections, AD, with the other two main political parties – COPEI (*Comité Popular Electoral Independiente*[5]) and URD (*Unión Republicana Democrática*[6]), signed the Punto Fijo Pact. This was a formal arrangement between the three main parties, under the pretext of protecting democracy, to share power whatever the election results. The Pact guaranteed the three parties access to power in proportion to the votes cast. In other words, whichever party won the presidential and legislative elections, it would be obliged to share the spoils of Venezuela's oil economy with the other two parties. This way, each of the main parties was guaranteed access to jobs, contracts, ministerial posts, etc. In accordance with the Pact, Betancourt

---

4 YouTube *FALN Venezuela*, 1965.
5 A Christian Democratic Party founded in early 1946, by Rafael Caldera and other
   prominent Catholic laypersons
6 A centre-left liberal party

invited members of COPEI and URD to join his cabinet. Radical socialist parties and the PCV were, naturally, excluded.

The agreement grew into an ongoing arrangement between AD and COPEI to share power and its accompanying perks, to the exclusion of all others, made all the more easy because there were no substantial ideological differences between them.[7] For the next thirty-five years AD and COPEI would play ping-pong with the presidency and government. The Punto Fijo pact began falling apart with the decline in oil rents in the mid 1980's. Its days were over when Hugo Chávez was elected president in 1998.

The main trade union federation, the Confederation of Venezuelan Workers (*Confederación de Trabajadores de Venezuela*, CTV), was similarly divided, although AD, as its founder, always retained final control. The overthrow of Pérez had raised expectations but Betancourt's response was soon seen as a betrayal. Elected on a left-wing programme and personal image, he rapidly reconciled himself with the interests of the dominant classes, convinced that no leftist government could face down US imperialism.[8] With the perspective of the US as invincible, Betancourt was little more than a pawn of the oil companies and the military who allowed him considerable leeway conditional upon their share of the oil monies remaining stable and their continued existence as virtually autonomous institutions. The Cuban revolution of January 1959 was a stinging refutation of his analysis.

3) LAND REFORM, GUERRILLA WARFARE

The uprising and street fighting against the Pérez dictatorship had been led by students and the members of the youth movements of both AD and COPEI and there was considerable impatience with the mismatch between Betancourt's pre-election promises and his actual programme. Dissent against the regime grew rapidly and, increasingly, protesting students, peasants and workers were assaulted, tortured and killed by the secret police.

Under the influence of the Cuban Revolution and the world-wide upsurge it inspired, the AD youth, in particular, moved rapidly leftwards, increasingly in opposition to Betancourt's leadership. Its youth movement split from the AD in April 1960 to form its own party, *Leftist Democratic Action*, but this name was soon changed to Movement of the Revolutionary Left (*Movimiento de Izquierda Revolucionaria*, MIR). The MIR rapidly concluded that the oppression was so intense that meaningful change within the system was impossible and in 1962 turned to guerrilla actions. Simultaneously, large

---

7 Derham, M., *Undemocratic Democracy*, Bulletin of Latin American Research, 2002, 21(2)270-289.

8 Diago, E., *Venezuela: when two worlds collide*, Int. Viewpoint V353, Sept. 2003.

numbers of young activists entered the PCV buoyed up by Castro's victory in Cuba, and pressed the Stalinist leadership to commence guerrilla warfare.

In response, Betancourt closed the premises of the MIR and PCV, closed opposition newspapers, suspended constitutional rights and civil liberties and arrested the MIR and PCV members of Congress. Against the background of the Cuban Revolution, this drive against leftists and the closure of democratic means of protests was interpreted by the PCV as obliging it to turn to armed struggle, and its Third Congress (1962) reluctantly approved the road of guerrilla warfare. A sector of the PCV under the leadership of Comandante Douglas Bravo was given responsibility for military work.[9]

The PCV and the MIR guerrillas were co-ordinated through the FALN (*Fuerzas Armadas de Liberación Nacional*, Armed Forces of National Liberation) launched on 20 February, 1963. However, the MIR and PCV differed over strategy: the MIR saw a long war stretching over many years while the PCV view of guerrilla warfare was one in which the CP tops in the city ordered attacks on such-and-such a place at such-and-such a time, in support of a reformist perspective,[10] a strategy doomed to failure.

The launch of the peasant guerrilla war could hardly have been less well-timed. Betancourt was proclaiming widely and loudly that there would be a thorough-going agrarian reform. Land reform bills were passed: unused, underused, and the least productive land was to be taken for the landless, though the compensation paid was higher than the best land would have fetched on the open market.[11] The US, fearful that the Cuban revolution might spread, endorsed these modest measures. Betancourt made a great show of visiting the countryside every week to hand over to poor peasants and rural labourers the deeds to their own land. The distribution of these small pieces of land succeeded, for the moment, in maintaining *campesino* support for the AD. Without the sincere support of a significant proportion of the *campesinos* it is impossible to think of successful guerrilla activity, but the guerrilla bands were getting a cold, even hostile, reception.[12]

In all, more than 90,000, almost a quarter of all, *campesino* families were given deeds. However, the corruption and disorganisation was such that peasants could be allocated land but not told where it was; certainly no equipment was supplied to the peasants to bring the land to a state where it could be farmed, no access to fertilisers, no loans to buy seed, and in many cases no access to the land itself. Land reform was being implemented but nothing was being achieved. A 1998 census revealed that ninety per cent of

9 Ibid.

10 Castro, F., *Those who are not revolutionary fighters... Granma*, 19 March, 1967.

11 YouTube *FALN Venezuela*, 1965.

12 Martz, op cit.

farmland given to the poor under the 1960 agrarian reform programme had since been sold back to the *caudillos* at ten per cent of the price they had been paid.

For the guerrillas, matters came to a head very rapidly when the FALN denounced the December 1963 elections and showed its amateurism, inexperience, and overwhelmingly petty-bourgeois nature by unequivocally promising they would not take place. Over ninety per cent of eligible voters cast their votes, the FALN failed to rally even the students, let alone the rural or urban poor. The result was a serious split within the PCV guerrilla cadres: Bravo now advocated a protracted guerrilla war, while Teodoro Petkoff accepted the peaceful road and went on to play a key role in founding and leading the Movement for Socialism (*Movimiento al Socialismo*, MAS).

Indicative of the attitudes of the urban poor to the guerrillas were the responses of *barrio* women who, generally steered clear of the guerrillas and concentrated their struggles on the provision of, for example, improved facilities for local schools, drinkable water, and so on. Not that these struggles were peaceful, all too often they incurred beatings from police clubs and imprisonment.[13] The reality was that the guerrilla struggles were isolated; they increased the political domination of the AD and COPEI, who used the guerrillas to defame the political left generally.

At the January 1966 Tricontinental Conference in Havana, the long-simmering differences between the Cubans and those adopting a class-collaborationist policy towards, particularly, the Betancourt and Leoni regimes in Venezuela (Raúl Leoni Otero succeeded as AD President on 13 March, 1964) burst into the open. The Cubans launched a broadside against those who opposed armed struggle as the necessary road to power in Latin America but were caught on the back foot when, to their surprise, the leadership of the PCV broke publicly with the FALN, declaring the tactic of guerrilla warfare "erroneous and harmful".

The Political Committee of the PCV furiously denounced Castro. The Eighth Plenum of the PCV, held in early April, 1967, formally agreed to end guerrilla activities and Bravo was expelled. The PCV then agreed to participate in the upcoming 1968 elections under the slogan 'democratic peace' behind a candidate of 'national unification'. Teodoro Petkoff accepted the new line and remained on the Central Committee of the PCV, but his experiences had led him to a more independent and critical position regarding the history of the PCV and the Soviet Union.[14]

---

13 Fernandes, S., *Barrio Women and Popular Politics*, Latin American Politics and Society, 2007, 49(3)97-127.

14 Ewell, J., *The History of the MAS*, Latin American Perspectives, 1991, 18(4)113-117.

President Caldera (1969-74) won the 1968 election for COPEI, finalised a ceasefire with the FALN, legalised the PCV, and reformed the 1961 Constitution to allow ex-guerrillas to be elected to public office. In autumn 1969, Petkoff published *Czechoslovakia – Socialism as a Problem*, which opened the door to a re-evaluation of Stalinism by defending Dubcek's liberalising measures against the slander that they were leading back to capitalism. It also, in the teeth of PCV criticisms, defended the Cuban Revolution. This book won him solid support amongst Young Communists, sufficient to retain his position on the Central Committee.

Petkoff now openly questioned whether the Venezuelan bourgeoisie could be progressive, since it relied for its existence on the USA and, in June 1970, he published *Socialism for Venezuela*, a book that challenged the core of the PCV programme, the theory of stages:[15]

> One of the sacred myths of Stalinism was the existence of a 'national bourgeoisie'… a section of the national bourgeoisie had developed with so little connection with imperialism that, under the colossal pressure of competition from imported goods and faced with the combined power of the imperialist economies and the local big bourgeoisie, it possessed an anti-imperialist capacity that meant it could collaborate in a meaningful way in a grand, multi-class front for national liberation…

> To this end, the party programmes made important concessions, including the fundamental one of limiting the objectives of the revolutionary transformation of the country to a bourgeois-democratic phase, offering the perspective of the expansion of national capitalisms once imperialist domination was broken and the internal market enlarged by agrarian reform…

> Conflicts between this social layer and imperialism do exist, and revolutionaries should intervene to foment and support them. But the Communist Parties in their attempts to win over or neutralize this sector inserted into their general political line concessions that lessened the revolutionary content of their own programmes, promoted bourgeois-democratic illusions, and created a general debilitating belief in the possibility of the independent development of Latin America by a capitalist road.

> The examples of the bourgeois democratic revolutions in Mexico nearly two hundred years ago, and in Bolivia and Cuba after World War II, should have demonstrated in practice the inability of the national bourgeoisie to lead the democratic revolution. But there are none so blind as those that won't see… Up to now 'operation national bourgeoisie' has not enabled

---

15 In Lowy, M., *Marxism in Latin America from 1909 to the Present*, Humanity Books, 1992.

us to win either this bourgeoisie... or the working class... What does this conception of 'national unity', of which the leadership of our party was the most outspoken champion... have to do with Marxism? ...it is nothing but a new formulation of the policy of class collaboration.

When Petkoff condemned the Soviet invasion of Czechoslovakia and reliance on the national bourgeoisie, the PCV – as a Stalinist party – disavowed both his argument and his right to organise support within the party. At the same time, the PCV, in line with its theory of stages, endorsed the presidential candidacy of an AD dissident, Luís Beltrán Prieto Figueroa.

Moscow intervened to close down discussion by vigorously denouncing Petkoff in the pages of *Pravda* as an anti-Leninist and anti-socialist. So crass were these manoeuvres that a combination of the youth section, a tendency around Pompeyo Márquez that had been calling for greater internal party democracy, and trade union leaders who opposed the setting up of rival unions to those of the AD, quit the party to found the MAS.[16]

The MAS held its first congress in January, 1971, and adopted a reformist perspective – democratic liberties would gradually expand until society achieved socialism. At its first major public rally (15 February, 1971) the MAS openly stated that it was seeking an accord with those bourgeois parties excluded from the AD/COPEI accord.

The overthrow of the Popular Unity government in Chile and the killing of Salvador Allende in September 1973 had a traumatic effect on all the left parties in Latin America. The leadership of the MAS moved decisively away from its socialist roots, dropping the labels 'Communist' and 'Leninist'.[17] The MIR and MAS were on the same trajectory, and in 1982 they began a process of alliance and merger which ended with the MIR disbanding, and most of its members joining the MAS. In the run-up to the 1983 election the MAS stopped calling itself 'Marxist', and symbolically refused to include a 'Woman's Right to Choose' in its election programme.[18] It would, however, never win more than about five per cent of votes.

Actually, the PCV fractured into three, a small group of militants rejected the rightward evolution of both the MAS and the PCV and launched Radical Cause (*La Causa Radical*, LCR) under the leadership of Alfredo Maneiro, an intellectual and one-time PCV guerrilla fighter. This was by far the smallest of the three groups, but had the largest proportion of workers in its ranks. Claiming to be Marxist, the LCR maintained a small but important base

---

16 Ellner, S., *The MAS Party...* Latin American Perspectives, 1986, 13(2)81-107.

17 Vallejo, A., *What Kind of Revolution for Venezuela?* IP Dec. 17, 1973.

18 Ellner, S., *Venezuela's MAS: From Guerrilla Defeat to Innovative Politics*, 1988, Duke UP.

in the trade unions, primarily amongst the steel workers in the Guayana Region, winning leadership positions in the steel workers' union (SUTISS) against the opposition of the AD.[19]

The Second World War had created a conjuncture of specific conditions: the entire capitalist world was in a state of unparalleled debility and disarray, of which the rise of the Chinese workers' state was the most extreme manifestation. The emergence of a rising nationalism and an end of formal colonial domination meant the 'Third World', especially the oil-exporters, saw an opportunity to flex their muscles and demand a greater share of oil revenues. The formation of the Organisation of Petroleum Exporting Countries (OPEC) – now a price-fixing cartel – represented an attempt by semi-colonial and colonial countries to gain national sovereignty over natural resources. Venezuela created the Venezuelan Oil Corporation, which would form the basis for the nationalisation of its oil industry. Then, in August 1971, President Caldera nationalised the country's natural gas industry and stipulated that all exploration, production, refining, and sales programmes of the oil companies required prior Ministerial approval.[20]

In 1973, the oil producers of the Persian Gulf countries decided to boycott those nations which had supported Israel during the Yom Kippur War against Egypt. Within a year, the price of oil had quadrupled. Venezuela experienced a flood of oil monies, and the newly-elected President Carlos Andrés Pérez Rodríguez (1974-79), a self-professed social-democrat, announced an ambitious economic plan, 'La Gran Venezuela', which called for the nationalisation of the oil industry and for the revenues gained to fund Venezuela's transformation into a developed country within a few years, fighting poverty by increasing incomes and diversifying the country's economy by import substitution.

On 1 January, 1976, the country officially nationalised its oil industry (paying the foreign companies US$1 billion), and created Venezuelan Oil (Petróleos de Venezuela SA, PDVSA). The fourteen transnational corporations became the Venezuelan state-owned petroleum company, but continued to operate as fourteen distinct and separate Venezuelan companies in competition with each other. Since all managers were Venezuelan, there was no change in management personnel, practices or culture on nationalisation. For example, Shell Venezuela became Maraven, the name changed but the president, management and ethos remained the same. At the top, Venezuela's oil industry maintained an anti-statist culture, placing its own interests

19 Ewell, J., *The History of the MAS*, Latin American Perspectives, 1991, 18(4)113-117.

20 Kobrin, S., *Diffusion as an Explanation of Oil Nationalization*, Journal of Conflict Resolution. 1985, 29(3) 3–32.

and those of the international oil industry above those of the Venezuelan government. The ties to the former owners were maintained through commercial deals, which seriously discounted the price of oil, and contracts to pay over-the-top fees for technical advice and assistance.[21]

The bourgeois politicians of the AD and COPEI were convinced that Venezuela's soaring oil revenues could be used to industrialise the country via huge infrastructure and public projects, spending on which was vastly in excess of the additional oil income, with the shortfall funded by external debt. The government's expectation was that high oil revenues were here to stay. These grand schemes caused the cost of living to rise significantly, leaving millions of Venezuelans even more mired in poverty.

For the next ten years, both COPEI and AD presidents used monies borrowed at high interest rates to generously fund selected agricultural and industrial projects. In 1980, as oil prices peaked, it was decided that PDVSA would aggressively expand, and it bought refineries in USA and Europe, and the American gas station network Citgo. In doing so, it catapulted itself into the third-largest oil company worldwide. However, oil prices began to fall, gradually at first and then more steeply, and with falling revenues, poverty increased. OPEC members, under pressure from the US, were violating production quotas, and oil prices fell drastically. Oil income was declining, but reducing government spending was not as easy as it had been to increase it. The result was a government getting deeper and deeper into debt, crippling the Venezuelan economy. Only through AD control of the major trade union federation, the CTV, did the regime manage to keep a lid on worker protests.

The crisis broke in January 1989 just as Carlos Andrés Pérez was taking office as president for a second time. He had run a populist election campaign, but on taking office he announced a policy which had the full backing of the International Monetary Fund: to minimise state intervention in the economy, to no longer seek to generate employment or engage in e.g., housing projects. Instead, there would be privatisation of state-owned enterprises and an accelerated expansion of the private sector. To attract foreign investment financial rules would be relaxed, and existing price controls were removed beginning with an immediate 100 per cent increase in the cost of petrol.[22]

---

21 Wilpert, G., *The Economics, Culture, and Politics of Oil in Venezuela*, 30 August, 2003, VA.com.

22 Gott, R., *Hugo Chávez and the Bolivarian Revolution*, Verso, London, 2005.

4) THE *CARACAZO*, CHÁVEZ AND THE 1998 PRESIDENTIAL ELECTION

On the morning of Monday 27 February, 1989, those travelling to work by bus found fares had doubled. Students who simultaneously lost their half-price concessions found their fares had quadrupled. Popular demonstrations began in Guarenas, near the capital and then spread nationally. This was a spontaneous rising of the masses. The fare rises ignited the bonfire of injustices accumulated over years. This expression of the rage felt by the poor and downtrodden became known as the *Caracazo*, a misnomer, since the uprising was not confined to Caracas but was nationwide. Protests escalated: first the burning of buses, and then widespread rioting and looting. The government and its intelligence agencies were taken by surprise, but so too were all the political parties, including the PCV, MAS and LCR. With no leadership and no clear aims, the *Caracazo* dissipated in anarchy and chaos.

However, the *Caracazo* taught the popular masses of Venezuela a severe lesson in the realities of bourgeois democracy. On 28 February, Pérez declared a state of emergency, but both the police and the National Guard baulked at the mass shooting of civilian protesters. The army was called in. The killings went on for a fortnight in a calculated warning to the *barrios* of what they could expect in any further attempt at rebellion. Even though the army had carried out its murderous orders, a group of politically motivated officers (co-ordinated through the Bolivarian Revolutionary Movement – 200 [*Movimiento Bolivariano Revolucionario – 200*, MBR-200]), one of whose leaders was Major Hugo Chávez, became convinced of the need to overthrow the regime.[23]

These young officers did not keep their secret very well and, in December, Chávez and several others were arrested, charged with plotting against the government and planning to assassinate the president. Nothing was proved, the accused were allowed to take leave of absence, after which they were again appointed to responsible posts – Chávez, for example, now a lieutenant-colonel, was given command of a paratrooper battalion.

Chávez and his associates continued with their plans and launched their 'military-civilian' uprising on 4 February, 1992. However, Pérez managed to rally the rest of the military against the plotters. Chávez and a small group of rebels were soon isolated in the Military Museum in Caracas, without any means of contacting their collaborators. Chávez gave himself up to the government and was allowed to appear on national television – for seventy-two seconds – to call for all remaining rebel detachments in Venezuela to cease hostilities. When he did so, Chávez famously quipped that he had only

---

23 Martin, J., 'Chávez and his government's policies', 2004, www.marxist.com

failed "*por ahora*" ("for now"). This was taken by many that Chávez' project to overthrow the government was only suspended, and he would return. Chávez was catapulted into the national spotlight as a man of action, with many poor Venezuelans seeing him as an admirable figure who had stood up against government corruption, and a hope for the future.[24]

Together with his fellow officers, Chávez was tried under military regulations, and imprisoned at the San Carlos military stockade, but pro-Chávez demonstrations outside led to his transfer to the more secure Yare Prison. Conditions in Venezuelan prisons were appalling, inmates were left to their own devices and it was only by the rebels keeping together as a group that they were able to survive. On the other hand, Chávez was able to give radio interviews, to receive visitors – including representatives of MAS and LCR – and to write his manifesto: *How to escape the labyrinth* (*Cómo salir del laberinto*).[25]

While Chávez was being held in prison, on 27 November, 1992, a second short-lived attempt to overthrow the government was launched by a group of young officers loyal to MBR-200. By mid-day it was over, with the leading conspirators having fled. Unlike in February, government agents now took advantage of the situation to kill surrendered rebels and oppositionists, arbitrarily arresting and assaulting hundreds, including entirely innocent student leaders. Pérez was now seen as a threat to the regime by the old guard of AD and the opposition in Congress, who ganged up to impeach him, placed him under house arrest, and removed him from office.

Caldera, now eighty-six years old, was unacceptable to COPEI as its presidential candidate, and he was forced to found a brand-new political movement, *Convergencia*, which contained seventeen smaller political parties including the PCV, MAS and URD. Caldera ran a campaign that had two clear planks: to stand up to the IMF, and to release Hugo Chávez. When the returns were in, Caldera had won by a slim margin but with abstentions at a record forty per cent.

Caldera's presidency began with popular decisions. Chávez and others were pardoned, and their political rights reinstated. Founding members of the MAS: Petkoff and Márquez were appointed as Ministers of Planning, and Frontiers, respectively. But the honeymoon was short-lived. Financial deregulation allowed banks to aggressively compete for deposits, with many banks paying higher interest rates than they could afford. With little banking supervision the market was full of speculative bubbles. It only needed a weakening of the oil price to trigger a banking crisis.

24 Canache, D., *The Emergence of Popular Support for Hugo Chávez*, Latin American Politics and Society, 2002, 44(1)69-90.

25 Marcano, C., and Tyszka, A., *Hugo Chávez*, Random House, 2007.

Between January 1994 and August 1995, seventeen of the country's forty-nine commercial banks, representing just over half of the system's assets, failed. Caldera guaranteed the safety of deposits at a total cost of US$12 billion.[26] The falling oil price simultaneously led to a collapse in government revenues, so Caldera attempted to raise the moneys required using neo-liberal methods, including (in 1997), selling a majority share in the giant state-owned steel corporation SIDOR to private investors. It was workers who shouldered the cost of saving the banks, SIDOR cut its workforce by a third (18,000 to 12,000), and then replaced half the remaining permanent employees with non-union labour hired via sub-contractors and often paid below the official minimum wage.[27]

Caldera pursued a policy known as *Apertura* – opening the state sector to privatisation. The steel industry was the most extreme example, but the state oil companies investment plan expected one third of new investment to be from such companies as Shell or BP. Between 1994 and 1998 the world price of oil fell from about US$26 to under US$18 a barrel, and combined with neo-liberal economic policies, this meant that, in Venezuela, real wages fell, on average, by a quarter, with additional cuts in healthcare (thirty-seven per cent), in education (forty per cent) and in housing (seventy per cent). By 1998, one third of Venezuelans lived in extreme poverty and another third lived in poverty. Yet, over the same period the share of the national income pocketed by the top ten per cent rose from 21.8 per cent to 32.8 per cent.[28]

Caldera and the traditional parties, offering no real solution to the crisis, became increasingly unpopular, with the masses looking for alternative ways out of their poverty. The MAS lost credibility when Petkoff actively supported even the most conservative and reactionary of Caldera's policies, ignoring the rank and file opposition within MAS.

After his release from prison in March 1994, Chávez travelled around Venezuela, reaching out to the politically-excluded, establishing links with the existing informal networks, primarily those campaigning for clean water, drainage, sewage disposal, electricity, education, and health provision. These were, in their great majority, women. In Venezuela, as in so many other under-developed countries, poverty had been feminised and, in reaching out to the poor, Chávez was reaching out to women. The majority of his support from

---

26 De Krivoy, R, *The Venezuelan Banking Crisis of '94*, Group of Thirty, 2000.
27 Cornejo, C., and Koppel, M., *Steelworkers end strike in Venezuela*, Militant, 31 May, 2004.
28 Wilpert, G., *Collision in Venezuela*, New Left Review, 2003, May-June pp 101-116.

then until his death was the women of the *barrios*[29] In discussion with MAS and LCR leaders, he concluded he should stand for president in the 1998 elections. In January 1997 the MBR-200 held its first congress, and agreed it should field candidates in the elections for president, congress, senate, state governors, and local mayors to be held on 6 December, 1998.

Chávez' decision to run for election caused the LCR to split in February 1997, with the majority of the rank and file forming Homeland for Everyone (*Patria Para Todos*, PPT) to support Chávez in his bid for the presidency, a small rump containing most of the leaders continuing as *La Causa Radical*. Chávez launched the Movement for a Fifth Republic (*Movimiento Quinta Republica*, MVR), in July 1997, to act as his political party and organise his electoral campaign. The MVR itself was very small, and would gain the great majority of its members from mergers with other parties. In parallel, and largely independently, groups of *barrio* activists mobilised in his support.[30]

Almost in its entirety, the MAS chose to align itself with Chávez, though some big names such as Petkoff remained with Caldera. Noting which way the wind was blowing – Chávez had by far the highest rating of any of the candidates – the PCV and a host of tiny groups declared for Chávez who won handsomely with just over fifty-six per cent of the vote. His nearest rival, formally representing Project Venezuela, but with the whole of the establishment lined up behind him, got forty per cent.

This was the first time for a generation that an election had delivered a candidate with genuine majority support, and it gave Chávez unprecedented authority as president. However, in both the Senate and Chamber of Deputies, AD and COPEI had the majority of seats. Chávez had become president without any real party apparatus behind him; this gave the MAS and PPT a head start in, for example, drafting a new Bolivarian Constitution, but it also meant that Chávez relied very heavily on bourgeois figures such as the businessman and industrialist Luís Miquilena who had joined him in founding the MVR and would be appointed Minister of the Interior and Justice. It would later become clear that many such people had joined Chávez in the hope of re-legitimising bourgeois democracy in Venezuela while limiting any changes introduced.

The politics of the MVR in 1998 were radical, but neither socialist nor revolutionary. Its programme, the so-called 'Plan Bolívar 2000', was essentially limited to: (i) changing the name, Republic of Venezuela to the Bolivarian Republic of Venezuela (*República Bolivariana de Venezuela*), (ii) a

29 Motta, S., *The Feminization of Resistance in Venezuela*, Latin American Perspectives, 2013, 40(4)35-54.

30 Roberts, K., *Populism, Political Conflict and Grass-roots Organization in Latin America*, Comparative Politics, 2006, 38(2)127-148.

new Bolivarian Constitution, which would require a national referendum to endorse the creation of a National Constituent Assembly (*Asamblea Nacional Constituyente*, ANC) to draft it, and (iii) the goal of integrating the armed forces into the economic and social life of the country. The groups supporting Chávez projected the constitutional reform under the slogan, 'All power to the people'. This may have been more an expression of their own hopes than reality, but it sparked an explosion of self-activity by the masses, including many who had taken to the streets during the *Caracazo*.

Even a section of the Venezuelan ruling class backed Chávez' campaign, hoping to use him as a pressure washer to clean the façade of Venezuelan politics and give bourgeois democracy a new lease of life. However, his campaign reached out to the people who had risen up in February 1989, those in fundamental conflict with the interests of the landlords, capitalists, bankers, media owners and wealthy parasites who formed the Venezuelan oligarchy. Speaking the colloquial language of the people, Hugo Chávez travelled the length and breadth of the country engaging in a dialogue with the poorest and most oppressed. His message was simple, clear and appealing: against the old order. For the first time in decades the masses were drawn into political activity, as they saw a candidate with whom they could identify, and who reflected their interests and aspirations. Spontaneous, and with no central plan, the upsurge was chaotic, but it demonstrated how eager the Venezuelan masses were to have some control over their own lives and this, of course, terrified the oligarchy.

The referendum to approve a Constituent Assembly took place on 19 April, 1999, voters being asked two questions: (i) should the ANC be convened? (ii) do you agree with the President's suggestion of how the ANC should be elected? Both measures were overwhelmingly approved. Two months later (25 July), the elections for the ANC took place and 125 seats out of a total of 131 were Chávez supporters. On 3 August, the ANC met to begin drafting the new constitution.

President Chávez then undertook a series of presidential visits to Japan, China, Malaysia, Spain and France, intended to boost trade. While he was away, the MAS, PPT and others on the left had a field day drawing up the most democratic and libertarian of bourgeois constitutions; it still guaranteed the right for individuals to own the means of production (Article 115 of the Constitution). The rights of the Venezuelan people now included the right to healthcare and the right to employment providing an adequate salary. The indigenous population (twenty-six ethnic groups comprising less than 1.5 per cent of the total) were given specific rights, including education in their own languages, their own territories, and a guaranteed three seats in the

National Assembly. The ANC gave the people the right of recall over their representatives. It also ended state funding of political parties, a means by which the party tops in AD and COPEI had been assured luxurious lifestyles. The legislature changed from a bicameral system, similar to the US, to a unicameral one where a National Assembly would be the only legislative body.

With the masses, these measures were hugely popular even if many were only statements of intent. But the constitution was also popular because the left groups and ANC members took the discussion on the constitution into the localities, calling public meetings at which the population could have its say. In the Bolivarian Circles (*Círculos Bolivarianos*) of the *barrios* it was a subject of much discussion and debate, one result being that the country's poor in particular supported the new constitution with genuine intensity. The constitution was, and is, widely available as a little blue book that was enthusiastically waved at demonstrations and rallies by pro-government supporters. It pulled together the heterogeneous, dispersed and fragmented support of Chávez by reflecting the democratic goals of the masses. The fear amongst the oligarchs was that the masses would strive to make it a reality. The task for revolutionaries was to make this Bolivarian Constitution a call for mass action, the logic of which would lead the popular masses to overthrow the oligarchy.

The ANC gave itself seniority over all the existing state institutions, a move vigorously opposed by the existing lower and higher chambers of Congress. The matter was both important and urgent because the ANC had determined to investigate the judiciary – it being universally acknowledged except by those who benefited that the court system in Venezuela was totally corrupt. A nine-member commission was appointed by the president with powers to dismiss even the Supreme Court (*Tribunal Supremo de Justicia*, TSJ). Congress, itself deeply mired in the corruption, attempted to engineer a confrontation with the ANC, and decided to review the resignation of the president of the TSJ who had quit in protest at the investigation. Across the country there were demonstrations for and against the ANC's actions, and the first street battles of the Chávez presidency took place. Faced with inciting events that could only make things worse for themselves, the opposition backed down.

When Chávez arrived home, he found his pet project to rename the country as the Bolivarian Republic of Venezuela had been dropped because the Assembly considered it too costly to change all the government's letterheads, official seals, etc. Chávez had it re-instated. The Assembly had also decided that Venezuela's citizens not only had the right to information, but information that was "timely, true, and impartial". The opposition read this as the state having the right to censor newspapers and TV stations for providing information it did not consider "true." The final version declared that information was to be provided "without censorship, in accordance with the principles of this constitution".[31] This unbecoming compromise freed the media to launch a virtual war, based on lies, slander and provocations against all the progressive content of government policies.

In Grenada, the short-lived Workers' and Peasants' Government (1979-83) had faced similar hostility and misreporting in the bourgeois press. The action taken there was to 'democratise' the newspapers by passing a law restricting ownership to citizens of Grenada and limiting any one person to no more than four per cent of the shares.

In early 1999, the US ambassador, John Maisto, appreciating the radical nature of the upcoming ANC, hurried the government to sign the treaty the US administration had forced on all other Latin American countries (save Cuba), guaranteeing protection of foreign investments. Chávez made no objection and the treaty was duly signed in the October. At much the same time, the ANC was inserting into the new constitution a clause forbidding the presence of foreign troops on Venezuelan soil which, given the history of Latin America, was clearly aimed at the US. Maisto, an astute man, appraised the situation with his comment: "Watch what Chávez does, don't listen to what he says".[32]

Probably the most indicative issue that had been a litmus test for the regimes in Cuba and Nicaragua, was a woman's right to choose. The ANC was on the verge of having the draft constitution approving the right to abortion, but, as Gott explains, this was unacceptable to Chávez so while many progressive principles were included in the constitution with respect to women's rights, "motherhood" was to be protected from the point of conception. This was a political statement that put the Venezuelan state alongside the Catholic Church hierarchy against a woman's right to choose.[33] This is not to say the new constitution did not represent a big step forward for women's rights. Article 21 stated: "No discrimination based on race, sex, creed or social standing shall be permitted, nor... any discrimination... nullifying or impairing the recognition, enjoyment or exercise, on equal terms, of the rights and liberties of every individual". This denial of abortion rights was a bad omen for the future.

The ANC's commission on judicial restructuring threatened the privileges enjoyed by corrupt bankers and politicians. It was judges who ensured charges were dropped on the flimsiest grounds, guaranteed errors in court procedures

31 Wilpert, G., *Constitutional Reform*, 2003, VA.com.
32 Jones, B., *Hugo*, Bodley Head, 2008.
33 Gott, op cit.

as would lead to acquittals, or simply postponed proceedings *sine die*. On the other hand, over half of Venezuela's prison population, many incarcerated for years in dreadful conditions, had never been brought to trial.

The commission's report claimed most of the country's judges were so corrupt and/or incompetent that they should be summarily dismissed, and by 2000, over three-quarters had been removed, a process of repair and rectification of a bourgeois system. To keep the courts operating, the commission quickly appointed a large number of new judges. There were no people's courts, no involvement of the masses, no election of judges, and no revolutionary code for the courts. Instead, a raft of provisional judges were put in place, most of whom were lawyers, products of the same corrupt system that was meant to be eliminated. Many were openly hostile to the cleansing process.

On taking office, Chávez had been faced with the lowest oil prices (in real terms) since before WWII and an industry that, left to its own devices, put its own interests and the needs of the USA first, even if that meant the impoverishment of millions of Venezuelans. The Chávez government took immediate action under the guidance of Ali Rodríguez Araque, an ex-guerrilla fighter and member of the PPT. Araque transformed Venezuela from quota avoider into OPEC's most enthusiastic quota-enforcer. A major success of Chávez' government in its first year was that oil prices rallied, and by the year 2000 would have doubled. This inevitably brought Venezuela into conflict with the big oil companies and US imperialism.

Chávez had no defined economic policy. In his first speech as president (2 February, 1999) he defined his perspective: "as much state as necessary, and as much market as possible".[34] However, just by attempting to impose a rational system (even in bourgeois) terms on the PDVSA inspired hatred of the new government. Yes, Venezuela did have huge oil revenues, but the entire system had grown and developed so that the richest ten per cent acquired over half the national income. There had been some face-saving social expenditure, but any suggestion that the system would be re-organised and open to inspection threatened to rob the oligarchs of their plunder.

At the same time, Chávez attempted to affect one of his pre-election promises and put 70,000 of Venezuela's 120,000 soldiers to useful social work. Military personnel (about 200 active duty officers) appeared in responsible posts in important ministries. But this was not a smooth process; too many of these officers were university graduates with working-class backgrounds who thought 'Plan Bolivar 2000' was a good idea, and were looking for ways

---

34 Quoted in Gott, op cit.

to implement it. Voices began to be raised in the bourgeois media asking whether Chávez was the right man to revitalise Venezuela.

The PDVSA had been formally nationalised in 1976 but was run almost independently of the government, for the benefit of the top executives who not only pocketed exorbitant salaries but had in place all kinds of schemes for transferring company monies into the pockets of themselves, and their families and friends. For example: PDVSA oil was carried in a fleet of oil tankers owned by the company president; the computer services used by the PDVSA were supplied by a company owned by a member of the board of directors; the company employed two to three times the number of administrators and managers as its rivals but far fewer employees in total, meaning a substantial amount of field work was outsourced to private companies, many of which were owned by friends and family, or gave large kickbacks for their contracts.

Naturally, the PDVSA tops were bitterly opposed to paying increased royalties to the Venezuelan state. They had in place a highly developed strategy for keeping profits out of the hands of government. Refineries had been purchased in the US and Europe and then, using an in-house mechanism not open to government scrutiny, oil was sold substantially below the market price to its own subsidiaries who kept their huge profits in overseas trusts. This scheme for siphoning off national resources was wildly successful. Between 1981 and 2000, the royalties paid to the state fell from seventy-one cents per $1 of gross earnings to thirty-one cents.[35] Araque was determined to end these practices; the PDVSA managers were equally determined that he would not.

5) THE 'MEGA-ELECTION' OF 30 JULY, 2000, AND THE FORTY-NINE ENABLING LAWS

The changes in the constitution meant every holder of an elected office, from president to local council had to stand for re-election. In the 'mega-election' of 30 July, 2000, 33,000 candidates stood for over 6,000 posts. In the presidential race Chávez obtained 59.8 per cent of the votes cast, Francisco Arias Cárdenas (officially representing the rump of Radical Cause, but with the backing of AD and COPEI) obtained 37.5 per cent. In the elections for the National Assembly the Chavistas won 104 out of 165 seats, marking a transformation of political power. Chávez and his supporters held the presidency and, effectively, a two-thirds majority in the Assembly. The election results made Chávez even less acceptable to the oligarchs.

Chávez' political platform now included: a fight against corruption, a fairer distribution of incomes, greater support by the state for local self-help

---

35 Wilpert, op cit, Aug. 30, 2003.

initiatives, greater accountability of the lower levels of government and greater grassroots participation in community improvement. The programme caught the imagination of those at the bottom of Venezuelan society struggling to make ends meet. This activation of the masses was not welcomed by the oligarchs who had previously kept political power firmly in their hands and excluded the popular masses from effective participation.

For those who had siphoned state revenues into their pockets, the Chávez government was a nightmare and a disaster rolled into one. This ultra-conservative layer had, in the space of months, been faced with the loss of their political hegemony with the defeat of AD and COPEI; the courts which had protected them from prosecution for their corrupt practices were to be made responsible to a democratically-elected government; anti-discriminatory legislation had given those they despised and feared (women, the people of the *barrios* and the indigenous peoples) protection from their discriminatory practices; and – worst of all – the government was now threatening to re-organise the PDVSA to remove from them a major source of income. They determined to use their hold over the mass media to block any further moves.

In October 2000, Chávez announced the appointment of General Guaicaipuro Lameda, Head of the Central Planning Bureau of the Venezuelan army, as President of PDVSA. In February 2001, a series of public announcements by dissident officers in the armed forces were choreographed by the media to give the impression that opposition was gathering momentum and that Chávez could no longer rely on the backing of the military. The so-called Democratic Co-ordination, which included most anti-Communist elements in Venezuela, attacked government polices as 'Castro-Communism' while actively sabotaging the economy (some US$50 billion of Venezuelan capital had been sent abroad by the summer of 2002).

Under a new bilateral agreement, Venezuela supplied Cuba with up to 53,000 barrels of oil a day in exchange for Cuban teachers, doctors, and nurses serving in Venezuela and assisting in a range of social projects. The Cuban teachers were a special target of the Democratic Co-ordination, as government "endorsement of Cuba's education system and policies". By the summer of 2001, with extensive media support, 'concerned mothers' had organised a movement against the 'revolutionary propaganda' being imported into Venezuelan schools. Many, perhaps most, of the leaders of this campaign were from the wealthy middle classes, whose children had never met a Cuban exchange teacher. The result was a stand-off; the government would provide free education for the masses, and guarantee no interference in the private education of the better off.

One aim was to change the traditional pattern of healthcare in Venezuela to be more like the Cuban model of community and family care based on preventative medicine. As in Nicaragua, this sparked strike action led by the Medical Federation, demanding an end to the hiring of Cuban doctors. In the face of this opposition, the government again sought a compromise. It would not interfere with private practices, but would provide a parallel system of free healthcare for the poorest in society.

Before Chávez came to office, Venezuela's hospital and medical system was a shambles. Insufficient hospital beds and provisions meant that patients had to bribe doctors and bring their own medical supplies if they wanted treatment. *Barrio Adentro I* (Into the Neighbourhood I) was a programme of healthcare based on the construction of over 3,000, two-storey medical centres (*consultorios*) in the *barrios* delivering universal healthcare, from cradle-to-grave, free at the point of delivery. This project would grow until, at its height, over 31,000 Cuban healthcare workers were serving in Venezuela.[36] This scheme would be followed by *Barrio Adentro II* and *III*, to overhaul the hospital system and open military hospitals to the public so that all hospital care is free.[37]

Oppositionists, who had previously ignored the healthcare of the poor, now voiced a range of criticisms: Cuban doctors lack proper training; the Ministry of Health should be training and recruiting Venezuelan doctors; the deal was an intolerable way of supporting the communist regime in Cuba, and so on. One reason for the attack on the *consultorios* was that they were (and are) a major reason why the *barrios* support the Bolivarian Revolution so strongly. The opposition, on the other hand, promised (and promises) that if it ever takes power the Cuban doctors will be forced to leave.[38] But the *consultorios* again revealed a systemic weakness: instead of purging from the state machine those functionaries who actively opposed the new health system, Chávez compromised and created a parallel system to accommodate them. Protests notwithstanding, Chávez' government would progressively strengthen diplomatic and economic ties with Cuba, leading to Venezuela becoming Cuba's biggest trading partner.

The employers' anti-Chávez campaign was openly racist, describing Chávez supporters as *lumpen* or *negros* or *pata en el suelo* (barefoot). Chávez himself was *zambo* – a mix of both Amerindian and Black African – which the *barrios* love, and the white, wealthy middle-class suburbs hate. TV news

36 Arsenault, C., *Cuban doctors prescribe hope in Venezuela*, Al Jazeera, 31 December, 2012.

37 Wilpert G., *Venezuela to Completely Overhaul Its Healthcare System*, VA.com, Aug. 29, 2005.

38 Rodríguez, A., *Cuban doctors in eye of...* Associated Press 16 April, 2014.

reports show pro-Chávez demonstrations in Venezuela as mostly *pardos* or black people, the opposition mostly whites. The ongoing virulent racist campaign in the press, TV and radio, was intended to, and succeeded in, polarising Venezuelan society by whipping up every prejudice of the middle classes.[39]

Officially, as part of Plan Bolívar 2000, but also to structure his base in society, Chávez campaigned for the Bolivarian Circles to organise grassroots movements around local priorities in shanty towns, neighbourhoods and villages across Venezuela. For example, in *Barrio La Palomera*, community leaders, mostly women, organised a badly-needed medical supply dispensary. The initiative gave rise to more than 5,000 Health Committees (*Comités de Salud*) staffed almost entirely by women and these became the support organisations on which the health service relied. Bolivarian Circles, supported by hundreds of ad-hoc groups organised on the basis of a single issue, began extensive social and political activities across Venezuela to, for example, provide school after-care for poor children, etc.

In a move that very much caught the mood of the times, a Women's Development Bank was set up with Professor Nora Castañeda, an economist and university professor, a woman of African and Indigenous descent and the daughter of a low-income single mother, as Head. Since the bank's formation, thousands of women have been able to start their own businesses thanks to low or no interest loans and advice and assistance.[40] Women activists entered the public arena as leaders who were largely responsible for the distribution of the funds and resources provided by the government to the localities. The collectivisation of private tasks, food kitchens, food banks and child care gave many women the opportunity to transform their lives. This new layer of community activists, while not linked organisationally to the MVR, were invariably dedicated Chavistas.[41]

Seeing the poor self-organise sent a shiver of fear through the middle and upper classes and, immediately, stories appeared in the media presenting the circles as armed bands funded by the government out to terrorise society. To make things worse, the serving officers in the ministries were taking Plan Bolívar 2000 seriously, and co-operating with the Bolivarian Circles to, for example, provide construction equipment to help build the *consultorios* and schools where they were most needed, in *barrios* throughout Venezuela.

Chávez' social programme was tremendously progressive, and it was the duty of all revolutionaries and democrats to defend it. Chávez was an honest

39 Cannon, B., *Class/Race in Venezuela*, Third World Quarterly, 2008, 29(4)731-748.

40 Sanchez, *Bolivarian Circles: A Grassroots Movement*, VA.com, 30 September, 2003.

41 Fernandes, op cit., 2007.

and able man, who genuinely wanted to act in the interests of his country, and the poor and dispossessed who make up the vast majority of its people. But he was no Marxist, had no perspective of establishing a workers' state, which, in the era of imperialism, was the only means of attaining his declared goals. Instead, Chávez called for an increase in the number of Bolivarian Circles believing that a loose network of socially-heterogeneous groups was sufficient for the tasks he had in mind. Not so. What was necessary was to establish a co-ordinated network of action committees in every *barrio*, army barracks, oil refinery, factory and landed estate, with a clear and common political perspective. This was the only way to defend the new constitution and to deter a counter-revolution.

Matters came to a head when, in November 2001, the Assembly passed an enabling law empowering Chávez to unilaterally enact forty-nine decrees. These did not go beyond the democratic tasks of the Venezuelan revolution but two, the 'Organic Law of Hydrocarbons' and land reform touched the opposition where it hurt – in their pockets and their inalienable right to their properties. The Venezuelan oligarchy raised a massive outcry in a clear demonstration of their particularly parasitical and reactionary character.

The first sign of the coming crisis between the PDVSA and the government occurred during the temporary fall in oil prices in 2001. The government refused to cut back its spending on public housing and healthcare and passed a new law in November 2001 doubling the fixed royalties that had to be paid, and limiting foreign companies to a maximum of fifty per cent share of new ventures. Worse, in the small print was the requirement that the murky finances of the PDVSA be opened up, restructured and rationalised to allow effective government inspection and a greater degree of government control. The executives and managers of PDSVA, in the words of Wilpert, "went ballistic".

Also, in November 2001, the first ever direct elections within the official union were held. The new government had held a national referendum on the need for democratic elections in the CTV and as a result, had passed a law requiring the CTV to hold elections. This was the direct intervention of a bourgeois state in trade union affairs implemented under the slogan of democratising the union movement. It earned the Chavistas the undying hatred of the CTV bureaucrats. The elections were marked by widespread and blatant fraud in which tens of thousands of votes (the records for 9,000 polling stations) went 'missing'. The results were announced when fewer than half the votes had arrived to be counted, and the old trade union bureaucrats declared themselves the winners.

Under pressure from PDVSA managers, *Fedecámaras*, the largest and most effective of the employers' organisations, decided to test the mettle of the government and, after discussions with the CTV, a joint call for a one-day general strike on 10 December, 2001 was issued. The privately-owned media hailed the "success" of the "strike" when, in fact, it was a lock-out that achieved little. In many working-class neighbourhoods, street demonstrations by government supporters took place on the day of the stoppage, including one march to the headquarters of *Fedecámaras* to protest the lock-out. In a show of defiance, on the day of the 'strike', Chávez told a crowd of 7,000 in central Caracas that he would speedily implement the forty-nine decrees.[42]

Chávez' economic and social programmes were certainly not meant to challenge the capitalist nature of Venezuela, but he was doing something the US Administration saw as very dangerous and a serious threat to the interests of US imperialism. He was raising the expectations of the Venezuelan popular masses, and the US had learned its lesson in Cuba: such expectations were a danger to capitalism. The bourgeois press in the USA was increasingly hostile. On 7 December, 2001, Mary O'Grady, editor of the *Wall Street Journal's* Americas section supported the 'strike' and voiced her own fears in an article entitled, 'Opposition builds to Castroite tactics of Hugo Chávez'. Behind the scenes, the US actively encouraged the employers' lock-out.

By the end of 2001, the US Congress was intervening directly in Venezuelan politics through the National Endowment for Democracy (NED), which provided as much as US$3 million to opposition parties that supported the coming April coup. All available records show that the NED provided not a cent to any party of the left, nor for women's groups, nor for any of the multitude of groups and organisations attempting to involve the masses in politics. NED exclusively promoted those political organisations which endorsed the violent overthrow of Chávez and opposed mass participation in politics.[43]

An independent audit of the PDVSA in January 2002, found that under Lameda, Chávez' appointee to the presidency, numerous dubious contracts had been entered into which appeared to personally benefit managers at the expense of serious losses for the company. Chávez fired Lameda.[44]

The style of Chávez, while popular in the *barrios*, was shocking for the middle and upper classes. He fired five (of the seven) directors of the PDVSA board live on his 7 April TV talk show *Aló Presidente*, broadcast

42 Wiley, J., *Venezuelan bosses strike against Chávez government*, *Militant*, 24 December, 2001 Vol.65/No.49.

43 Golinger, E., *The CIA Was Involved In the Coup Against Venezuela's Chávez*, 22 November, 2004 VenezuelaFOIA.info.

44 Wilpert, op cit., 30 August, 2003.

weekly on Sundays, reading out their names, showing a red card with 'You're out' as though they were being sent off in a baseball match.[45] In the same programme, Chávez announced that the national minimum wage would be increased by twenty per cent from 1 May. He then appointed five new PDVSA board members from outside, breaking with the tradition of jobs for the boys. This struck a serious blow at management perks, underhand payments and corrupt practices. Lameda, and the PDVSA's top managers, charged Chávez with politicising the PDVSA on the grounds that the new appointments were for political loyalty rather than merit. Unarticulated, but overshadowing these events, was the fear that these appointees would enforce the new oil law, which meant that monies previously diverted into the pockets of friends and families would now be paid to the government.

Top management pondered, discussed with *Fedecámaras* and the CTV, and issued an ultimatum to Chávez to dismiss the newly-appointed directors, otherwise managers throughout PDVSA would strike indefinitely. On 4 April, all administrative offices, several petrol distribution centres and the El Palito refinery were shut down. Two days into the shut-down, the CTV leader Carlos Ortega called his members to join the strike for twenty-four hours from 9 April, and told them to be prepared for indefinite action. His call was welcomed by Pedro Carmona, head of *Fedecámaras*.

The ongoing and vitriolic media campaign against Chávez was all-encompassing. Polls conducted on behalf of the capitalist media showed Chávez' popularity fell from sixty-five per cent in June 2001 to less than forty per cent in January 2002. The opposition became convinced it could oust Chávez from the Presidency in the short term and not have to wait until the next elections. Their next action, with the support of CTV officials, was to hold a demonstration of some 70,000 people in Caracas on 23 January, 2002, the anniversary of Pérez' overthrow by a combination of military actions and mass demonstrations. This, undoubtedly, was the model the opposition wished to emulate. The relatively low turnout at the pro-government rally on the same day confirmed in their eyes the declining support for the Chávez government and boosted their self-confidence.[46]

The PDVSA managers were defending the indefensible: their right to rob the government through corrupt practices. The Land Law, however, could be presented as stealing the land that families had owned for generations. This allowed those opposing the law to claim right was on their side, which every commercial newspaper, magazine and TV station did on an hourly

45 Wilpert, G., *The 47-Hour Coup That Changed Everything*, VA.com, 14 April, 2012.

46 Calero, R., *Bosses seek to topple Chávez government, Militant*, 11 February, 2002, Vol.66/No.6.

basis, with commercial breaks trumpeting the *latifundistas'* case. The Land
Law and the promised agrarian reform was the most emotive issue in the new
legislation, because it could be presented as attacking the principle of private
ownership of property. The background was much the same as had existed
some forty years before, when Betancourt made similar proposals: one per
cent of farms incorporated over half the arable land while seventy-five per
cent of proprietors owned a mere six per cent of the land, and of these, about
two-thirds farmed with no title to the land they worked. The land reform law
called for a government review of the holdings of wealthy land-owners and
the expropriation of unproductive or unused land, with compensation paid
at market value. The big difference, however, from the situation in the 1960s
was that the US administration now opposed the proposals, fearing them as
a potential step towards a revolution, and threw its support behind the anti-
Chavistas.

Less than one tenth of Venezuelans lived in the countryside, so the
importance of these proposals lay in their symbolic value – that it was possible
for the Bolivarian Revolution to break the power of the oligarchy. In terms
of the numbers affected, land reform in the cities was much more significant.
Over half of Venezuelans lived in the slums that are the *barrios* – squatter
encampments of tin and breezeblock huts perched on the sides of the hills
surrounding Caracas, in perpetual danger of being washed away in heavy
rain. Of course, few, if any, of the *barrios* dwellers had title to land. During
the 1998 election, voices in the *barrios* had called for the new government
to legitimise their home ownership. Chávez now adopted this call as his
own, and on 4 February, 2002, he dramatically announced the Decree on
Regularisation of Urban Land: the government would give the people of
the *barrios* the legal ownership of the land on which their houses stood.[47]
By March 2005, over 4,000 Urban Land Committees (*Comités de Tierras
Urbanas*, CTUs) had distributed more than 170,000 property titles.

6) THE ATTEMPTED COUP OF APRIL 2002

Carlos Ortega, the head of the pro-capitalist CTV, announced plans to hold
a nationwide work stoppage as part of the efforts to weaken and destabilise
the government. *Fedecámaras* encouraged employers to give workers paid
time off to join anti-government protests and simultaneously raised the
demand for a re-call referendum on Chávez' presidency, as provided in the
new constitution.

A planned coup was being put into operation, but Chávez was due to
attend a meeting in Costa Rica when it was scheduled to occur and the

---

47 Wilpert, op cit., May-June 2003.

plotters needed him to be in the country so he could be arrested and forced to resign, giving a form of legitimacy to their plan. Napoleón Bravo, host of Venevisión's *24 Horas*, broadcast on Wednesday 10 April, a message by Brigadier General Néstor González (then under investigation for corruption) announcing he no longer recognised President Chávez as his Commander in Chief, demanding Chávez resign, and declaring there was significant opposition within the military to Chávez continuing in office.[48] Chávez duly cancelled his visit. This was the first of a series of incidents, each giving the lie to all those who claimed the attempted coup was a spontaneous reaction to what happened on the streets of Caracas.

On Thursday 11 April, an opposition demonstration in Caracas, was re-routed by the organisers in order to clash with a much smaller pro-government rally being held in front of the presidential palace. Depending on one's source of information this, demonstration numbered one million (opposition newspapers and TV stations), 150,000 (BBC News) or 50,000 (Press Agency and government sources). Gunshots were fired, people were killed and wounded. It was immediately claimed that armed thugs from the Bolivarian Circles had mowed down defenceless defenders of democracy. Footage of Chávez supporters firing in self-defence at snipers was manipulated to look like Chávez supporters firing indiscriminately on the opposition demonstration. In fact, seven Chávez supporters, seven oppositionists and five by-standers were shot dead.[49]

To justify the coup that allegedly resulted from these events, but which, in reality, had been long-planned and was now underway, the privately-owned media declared that law and order had broken down. All the private TV stations broadcast scenes from the streets, commentators continually repeating, that Chavistas were shooting at unarmed opposition demonstrators. This lie would be the key element in justifying the coup.

Shortly after the first demonstrators were killed, at 3:45 pm, Chávez took over the airwaves in a national broadcast (a *cadena* in which the government broadcast simultaneously on all TV stations), asking people to remain calm, and severely criticising the opposition. A few minutes into the broadcast, however, the TV stations, in a co-ordinated action, split their screens and showed Chávez on one half, and biased footage of the street shootings on the other. Chávez responded by issuing an order, to take all private TV stations off the air. This was a well-planned *coup d'etat*, and Chávez' move had been anticipated. The TV stations immediately switched to cable and satellite.

48 Wilpert, op cit., 14 April, 2012.
49 Fischer-Hoffman, C., *Victims of 2002 Venezuelan Coup Denounce Double Standards*, VA.com, 22 September, 2014.

At 7 pm, Vice-Admiral Hector Ramírez called on 'the people' to no longer recognise the authority of President Chávez or the government. The deaths and woundings in the city centre, Ramirez claimed, obligated 'us' to stop further bloodshed and justified forcing the departure of the president, and his substitution by the High Command.

The four major television channels (all private, still broadcasting via cable and satellite), constantly repeated the images of Chavistas shooting at off-screen targets, and commentators claiming that they were firing at unarmed opposition demonstrators. This footage was now intermingled with the pronouncements of a parade of politicians and military officers declaring their opposition to Chávez and demanding a return to the 'status quo': Inspector General of the National Guard, Carlos Alfonso Martinez, backed by a group of high-ranking officers, condemned the Bolivarian Circles for firing on civilians; Vice-Minister for State Security, General Luis Alberto Camacho Kairuz called for Chávez' resignation, announced the defection of various regiments throughout the country, and suggested a provisional junta be installed to govern the country.

At 8 pm, the head of the army, General Efraín Vásquez Velasco and General Manuel Rosendo, head of the military high command, declared for the coup. The mayor of Greater Caracas Alfredo Pena, accused government snipers of firing on the opposition demonstration, claiming: "Chávez has shown his true face". Luís Miquilena, Minister of the Interior until earlier in the year, denounced the "repression".[50]

Meanwhile, the state television channel (VTV), broadcasting live from the Miraflores Palace, where ministers and pro-Chávez National Assembly deputies were assembled, flatly contradicted the private TV stations' claims that only opposition demonstrators had been shot. VTV announced that Chávez was meeting with both his ministers and the military high command, to decide how to deal with the crisis. Then, suddenly, at 9.30 pm, VTV went off the air, by 10 pm cell phones were no longer effective, isolating the occupants of the palace. Simultaneously, the private TV channels came back on air over the regular airwaves spreading the rumour that Chávez had resigned and had asked to be taken to Cuba.

The private media refused to give air time to pro-government officials and, when protests broke out following news of Chávez' detention, declined to give any coverage to them. Attempts to disclose that Chávez had not resigned, and was being held prisoner, were cut off. Attempts by military units to publicise their rejection of the coup were ignored.

---

50 Wilpert, op cit., 14 April, 2012.

By 9 pm, members of the military High Command had arrived at the palace to meet with Chávez and demand his resignation. Chávez, shocked by the desertion of so many top military officers, concluded that he and his cabinet could not get out of the palace alive, and surrendered.

At 3:30 am, General Lucas Rincón Romero took to the airwaves to announce in a brief statement that the "President of the Republic was asked to resign, which he accepted". This was a lie. Chávez had not agreed to resign. Rincón added that the military high command would be at the service of the "new authorities". About half an hour later, Chávez, was escorted to the military base on the island of La Orchila, via Fort Tiuna (*Fuerte Tiuna*). The officer in command of Fort Tiuna, General García Carneiro, was sympathetic to Chávez and informed the international media that Chávez had not resigned but had been arrested, and notified them of his location.

At 4:50 am, wealthy businessman Pedro Carmona, head of *Fedecámaras* appeared on television, as interim president, to announce, the transitional cabinet, and to dissolve the constitution and National Assembly in one fell swoop. He ably demonstrated that the corrupt and rotten Venezuelan bourgeoisie was (and remains) incapable of playing a progressive role.

BBC News, Saturday 13 April, described how Mr Chávez (note 'Mr', not 'President', a simple demonstration of where the BBC's loyalties lay) was being held at the Fuerte Tiuna military base in the capital, Caracas. It reported that Mr Carmona had:

- Declared himself President of the Republic of Venezuela.
- Dissolved the National Assembly, promising elections by December.
- Annulled the Land Law.
- Pledged presidential elections – in which he would not stand – within one year.
- Declared the 1999 constitution introduced under 'Mr' Chávez void.
- Promised a return to the pre-1999 bicameral parliamentary system.
- Repealed the decrees that gave the government greater control of the economy.[51]

The announcements were made to applause and cheering from the 300 or so present – the heart of the Venezuelan oligarchy, the coup organisers and participants; bank owners, army officers, media moguls and churchmen. So arrogant were they, so sure of success that they flaunted themselves before the TV cameras and signed an attendance list (available in *Los Documentos del Golpe, 2009, Fundacion Editorial El Perro y la rana*). The Bolivarian

51 The full list of announcements can be seen on: https://www.aporrea.org/actualidad/n155077.html

Revolution would have been completely justified in arresting every one of them, expropriating their property and, in so doing, would have broken the back of capitalism in Venezuela.

Nothing revealed the class interests behind the coup so clearly as the plans to put the country and its oil wealth firmly in the grasp of US imperialism: the PDVSA would suspend oil exports to Cuba immediately, and expand production by more than 300,000 barrels per day above its OPEC quota to bring down world oil prices.

During 11 and 12 April, the police were attempting to physically crush any public displays of support for Chávez. The "return to democracy" in Venezuela was marked by an aggressive "disarmament plan". With the excuse of searching for illegal weapons, oppositionists went on a rampage, raiding the homes and work places of known Chavistas. Chávez' supporters were hunted down and arrested wholesale, taken to police stations and National Guard barracks where many were severely beaten. Police and National Guards used shotguns, rubber bullets, tear gas and clubs with abandon. Agency reports claimed that at least sixty people were killed and hundreds wounded by police gunfire.[52]

However, by the night of 12 April, the international media carried reports that Chávez had not resigned and signs of opposition to the coup were beginning to appear. By the Saturday morning, the people of the *barrios* were beginning to congregate across Caracas in huge crowds of such numbers that the police were simply pushed aside (though not before using water cannon and firing on the people). In the front ranks were Chávez' most loyal supporters: the women of the *barrios*. Elizabeth, an activist who had campaigned for water and health provision, explained:

> We marched to Miraflores and refused to leave until they returned Chávez to us. We elected him, and we would not let them take our elected president away from us. It was like what they always did to us, denying us our rights… Well this time we weren't going to let that happen.[53]

By 1 pm on 13 April, Miraflores was besieged by a crowd of many tens of thousands of Chávez supporters, and hundreds of thousands of people occupied roads and squares throughout the country. The overwhelming majority was from the *barrios* and a large number of them were waving the blue book containing the constitution. This mass outpouring strengthened the resolve of pro-Chávez units in the military. In 2002, the army was no longer monolithic, it had been 'infected': many young officers had genuinely

---

52 Bellow, A., 'Chávez rises from very peculiar coup', *The Guardian*, 15 April, 2002.
53 Motta, op cit.

bought into the Plan Bolívar 2000, they had gone into communities and built bridges, roads and medical centres. They had been welcomed and feted by the local people, and liked it. Demonstrators fraternised with rank and file soldiers, many of whom remembered Chávez as a leader and heroic figure.

The Forty-Two Parachute Regiment in Maracay, besieged by tens of thousands protesting the coup, declared for Chávez. Without these mass actions, these military units would have been isolated and not felt able to come out in opposition to the generals. For the plotters, reports were arriving from around the country that important army units were preparing to resist the coup. The high command was divided and paralysed; it feared an uncontrollable response from the people and clashes between military units. It had lost its grip. In Miraflores, the conspirators, after furtively peeping through the curtains and weighing up the situation, and with TV crews recording their actions, ran for it. When faced with a serious challenge, the quality of leadership is a key element, and the counter-revolution collapsed.

Bizarrely, none of this was reported on Venezuelan TV or in the Venezuelan press. On 12 April, all private TV channels broadcast interviews with exulting opposition leaders. On 13 April, an almost complete news blackout was in place. Venezuelan television media failed to broadcast news of Chávez supporters retaking Miraflores Palace; the four major television networks stopped providing news reports altogether.[54] The largest television station RCTV (Radio Caracas Television) showed Walt Disney cartoons. Venevisión ran Hollywood movies, Televen treated its viewers to baseball and soap operas. Globovisión, supposedly the top twenty-four-hour news station, re-broadcast old footage of Chávez' removal. Two of the three major newspapers, *El Universal* and *El Nacional*, cancelled their Sunday editions rather than report Chávez' return. The third major newspaper, *Últimas Noticias*, printed a limited Sunday edition accurately reflecting events; some regional television stations began to cover the events that were taking place. Channel 8, the state television channel remained off the air all day on 12 April and for most of the day on 13 April.

It was as though nothing newsworthy was happening. But anyone who received cable television, or who was in some way connected to the network of Chávez supporters, or had sight of a *barrio*, knew that something big was indeed happening. The masses of Venezuela were on the move. Such a thing had never crossed the minds of the conspirators.

The events of the coup were recorded by an Irish camera crew as a documentary and can be seen on YouTube under the title *Hugo Chávez – The Revolution will not be Televised*. Chávez and his cabinet were meeting,

---

54 Dinges, J., *Soul Search*, Columbia Journalism Review, 2005, 44(2) pp 52-8.

the High Command arrive to deliver an ultimatum: "surrender or we bomb the palace". Chávez surrenders five minutes before the ultimatum ran out, is led away, but refuses to resign. The cabinet, now without Chávez, was paralysed. There was no attempt to rally support or to organise against the coup. Instead, they said things like "the game is up", "they were too strong for us"; the best that was recorded was "the people are with the president they'll defend him – you'll see". There was no concept that they, themselves, should lead a fight back against the coup, the words 'headless' and 'chicken' spring to mind. But this lack of leadership was no accident; these ministers had governed under the illusion that they controlled the bourgeois state. The Bolivarian government failed to recognise the class nature of the state, even after three years in power. There was no party organisation, no team of leaders educated and trained to think and act for themselves, no network of cadres to give the mass upsurge an organised character and direction.

By the afternoon of 13 April, crowds had gathered not only in front of Miraflores, but also RCTV and Venevisión, Globovisión and Televen and the offices of El Universal and El Nacional, throwing stones and compelling reporters to broadcast a message reporting Chávez had been restored. This was later presented as an intolerable attack on press freedom.[55]

The popular movement played a profoundly revolutionary role on 12 and 13 April, 2002, the masses mobilised and defeated the coup. This included the working class, but it did not play an independent role with its own working-class methods and objectives, it intervened as part of the spontaneous and disorganised movement of the masses comprised in their majority of the unemployed and the self-employed (e.g. street vendors). These sectors have an immense capacity for struggle and their participation was decisive. But, because of their class nature, a movement based in these sectors always tends to be explosive and disorganised. Such a movement finds it difficult to form stable organisational structures that can develop a worked-out programme, provide the movement with a clear leadership and generate organs of dual power to serve as an embryo of a new revolutionary state capable of replacing the old bourgeois one.

In the months and years after the coup, it became fashionable to argue that its defeat was down to the coup plotters' internal wrangling. Not so. It was the spontaneous revolutionary movement of the masses that caused hesitation and divisions amongst the coup plotters. Let nobody be fooled by this historical revisionism: the coup was well prepared, carefully orchestrated and all the actors played their given roles. This was not the first oligarchic

---

55 Lemoine, M., *Venezuela's Press Power*, *Le Monde Diplomatique*, August 2002.

imperialist coup in Latin America and in fact, the script closely followed that of the coup against Allende in Chile in 1973, but with a very different result.

In *My Life*, Fidel Castro revealed that his advice to Chávez, during the coup was "trying to meet with the people in order to trigger national resistance... had virtually no possibility of success"! This blind spot to the power of mass action flowed from his view of the masses as an auxiliary to guerrilla action, rather than the dynamo of the revolution.

6.1) US INVOLVEMENT IN THE COUP ATTEMPT

Diligent reporters using the Freedom of Information Act obtained CIA documents showing that weeks prior to the coup the CIA had detailed plans in their possession of the events about to occur. A 6 April, 2002 intelligence briefing headlined 'Venezuela: Conditions Ripening for Coup Attempt', stated:

> Dissident military factions... are stepping up efforts to organise a coup against President Chávez, possibly as early as this month... To provoke military action the plotters may try to exploit unrest stemming from opposition demonstrations slated for later this month...[56]

A vast amount of evidence has surfaced showing the coup attempt was pre-planned in conjunction with the US administration. The earliest, and one of the most revealing, was a news programme on Saturday morning, 12 April, when Napoleon Bravo interviewed Vice-Admiral Carlos Molina Tamayo, a self-professed coup leader who gave a detailed account of the events leading up to the coup, claiming it had been in preparation for over a year, naming key individuals, and praising the private television stations for their complicity and assistance. The interview provided positive proof that the overthrow of Chávez was a premeditated event. This was later confirmed by The New York Times:

> [D]iscontented military officers had been meeting among themselves and with business leaders for almost a year to discuss ways to oust Mr. Chávez.[57]

The *Observer* newspaper on Sunday, 21 April, reported that visits to the White House by Venezuelans plotting the coup, including Carmona himself, began several months prior, and continued until just weeks before the coup attempt. The visitors were received at the White House by President George Bush's key policy-maker for Latin America, Otto Reich, previously heavily

56 In Golinger, E., *The CIA Was Involved In the Coup Against Venezuela's Chávez*, 22, 2004 VenezuelaFOIA.info.
57 Rohter, L., *Venezuela's 2 Fateful Days*, *The New York Times*, 20 April, 2002.

involved in destabilising the Nicaraguan government. The CIA knew that a coup attempt was being planned for the near future, that the plan was to exploit violence in an opposition march, and to use that as the excuse for deposing Chávez. This begs the question: how could the plotters have been sure sufficient violence would erupt to justify a coup? The answer is only too obvious, they would ensure it happened: on 3 April, 2009, Ivan Simonovis, former Security Secretary of the Metropolitan Mayor of Caracas with former Police Commissioners Henry Vivas and Lázaro Forero were sentenced to thirty years in prison after being found guilty of playing leading roles in the massacre. The violence of 11 April was organised and orchestrated by opposition leaders using Metropolitan Police personnel.[58]

Not having foreseen the mass actions that overturned the coup was not just a failure in intelligence gathering and analysis. The mass upsurge was outside the comprehension of the CIA analysts and their political masters: indeed, it was exactly what they feared, the aspirations of the masses expressed in action. Just as Trotsky had organised the October 1917 Russian Revolution as defence of the Soviets against reaction, so the *barrios* had shown their preparedness to act to defend what they believed to be 'their' government. And let us confirm the truly remarkable character of that intervention, it was unprecedented – for the first time in the history of Latin America, mass action had defeated a military coup. The question was: how would Chávez, the undoubted leader, react.

Venezuela was an example of the economic and social disaster that capitalism offers the workers and peasants of semi-colonial nations. Despite the country's vast oil wealth, two-thirds of the population lived below the official poverty line, while imperialist investors and domestic capitalists raked in massive profits. The prospect of losing control of 'their' state to the popular masses, had inflamed the oligarchs more than the reforms actually proposed. The coup attempt showed just how much the oligarchs valued democracy and how far they were willing to go to get rid of the country's democratically-elected president and its democratically-elected National Assembly. The self-mobilisations of the popular masses against the coup simultaneously showed the effectiveness of workers and *campesinos* when defending their class interests, and their potential to make a revolution that would take power out of the hands of the capitalist minority.

The counter-revolution was defeated by a spontaneous uprising of the masses; with no party, no leadership, no programme and no clear idea of where they were going, women and men, largely from the *barrios*, rose up

---

58 Wilpert, G., *Two More Arrests and one More Death in the Case of Venezuelan Prosecutor's Assassination*, VA.com, 28 November, 2004.

and attempted to take their destinies into their own hands. The collapse of the coup created extraordinarily favourable conditions for going onto the offensive and dealing a decisive blow against the counter-revolution. There should have been a determined effort to smash the resistance of the bosses and their cronies under a call to protect the government – the crowds that had besieged the private TV and radio stations should have been called on to go one step further and take over those stations, placing them under workers' control. There can be absolutely no doubt that if Chávez had given the lead, capitalism in Venezuela could have been overthrown that April, and it could have been achieved relatively painlessly. Unfortunately, Chávez had no such perspective. Instead of calling on the masses to take decisive action, he temporised and attempted to appease the counter-revolutionaries.

A key factor was missing, the lack of understanding of the class nature of the divisions in Venezuelan society. This was epitomised by the actions of Chávez, a deeply-religious man, immediately following the coup. Chávez appeared on the balcony of the Miraflores Palace, in one hand he held the small blue book containing the constitution and in the other a crucifix.[59] A middle-aged woman, a practising Catholic, who had been in the crowd told one of the authors (JM) that her heart sank when she saw the crucifix, "I knew that meant bad news, he should have held the sword of Bolivar". Chávez explained that he was "in shock", he was still assimilating events, but had "no thirst for revenge", that he was willing to listen to the grievances of the opposition. He invited the plotters to join him in a round-table discussion, and to show good faith he had those plotters arrested, including Carmona, released from custody. The masses gathered in front of the Miraflores Palace were thanked for their support and told to go home quietly! This was a serious mistake; it allowed the plotters to think they could have another bite of the cherry and emboldened them to believe that they could do so with impunity. Instead of arresting those who had fired on the masses during the coup attempt, the regime hesitated and backed off, limiting itself to transferring responsibility for the police organisation for central Caracas (*Distrito Metropolitano*) from the local mayor to the Commission for Citizen Security (*Comisión de Seguridad Ciudadana*).

The forces of reaction, under the tutelage of the USA, immediately prepared a new challenge to the regime in the form of defence of the democratic rights of the plotters. Military action on the streets is not the only way to defeat the masses. With the opposition's real face revealed, rank and file Chavistas understood – probably better than Chávez himself – they were facing greater threats than they had previously imagined.

---

59 Bellos, A., 'Chávez rises from very peculiar coup', *The Guardian*, 15 April, 2002.

Chávez used every occasion possible to insist that anyone wishing to support the Bolivarian process should not remain on the side-lines. The Bolivarian Circles expanded rapidly and by the end of 2003 the government would claim as many as 2 million Venezuelans were members of about 200,000 circles. This was an extensive grassroots organisation. Bolivarian women, youth and workers organised food distribution, medical centres, and education provision. The great majority of these activities, while enacting government policies, were separate from the MVR, and did not consider themselves party organs.[60] Chávez saw these grassroots organisations as a counterweight to the oligarchy and key to deepening social reforms. The weakness was that, dispersed, and without a political understanding of the class nature of the state, these organisations posed no existential threat to the oligarchy.

The mass mobilisation and class action against the coup had shown that the overthrow of the old ruling class was possible, but had failed because the necessary political understanding and organisation were lacking. There was no party to develop the necessary revolutionary class consciousness and guide the strategy during the revolutionary upsurge. Such a political organisation can grow very rapidly during a revolutionary upsurge, but it cannot arise spontaneously. Rather, it must be continuously, consistently and consciously built. The experience of the coup incontestably demonstrated that a nonchalant or lackadaisical attitude in this vital area would mean disorientation and defeat of the Bolivarian Revolution, whether from another coup or degeneration at the top.

The failed coup also showed the weakness of the Venezuelan capitalists. The opposition had lacked a decisive leader but nothing was settled. The same opposing class forces remained in sharp conflict, Washington had not surrendered its goal of overthrowing the Chávez government. The coup had been defeated in time for many in Venezuela to celebrate the 19 April anniversary of Cuba's crushing victory over a US-organised mercenary invasion at the Bay of Pigs – a victory that underlined how, by taking power and ending capitalist rule, Cuban workers and farmers were able to defeat imperialist assaults and defend their sovereignty and social gains. Yet, economically, technologically, in terms of infrastructure and urbanisation, Venezuela was far more developed than Cuba had been in 1959.

A number of generals closely associated with the coup were removed from their posts, sufficient for the opposition (including the US) to give up, temporarily, hope of a military coup. Charges were brought against only the most senior officers who participated in the coup and remained in Venezuela.

---

60 Roberts, Op cit. 2006.

But on three occasions between the end of July and 14 August, Venezuela's full TSJ by eleven votes to eight dismissed the charges against them, claiming that what had occurred was not a military coup, but a 'power vacuum'. The TSJ decisions revealed the cost of not eradicating the corruption of the old regime. By voting to acquit, the TSJ cast doubt on the legitimacy of the government. The legal establishment, reflecting its social origins, its interests and the pressure of the bourgeoisie and imperialism, took the side of the *golpistas* against the democratically-elected government.[61] To assure itself of the continuing support of the armed forces, the regime should have launched rank and file committees in the military of Bolivarians, revolutionaries, and patriots and so isolated the reactionaries.

The TSJ did not stop there. In November 2002, it rescinded Article Eighty-Nine of the constitution, the legal basis on which peasants could begin to cultivate idle land before they acquired formal title to it. Without Article Eighty-Nine, land-owners could successfully challenge land redistribution. Article Ninety was also rescinded. This stated that, if lands had been occupied illegally, then the government did not have to recompense the occupier for investments in infrastructure, such as buildings or watering systems. Rescinding these two Articles meant, in effect, the end of government seizures of private land.

7) THE BOSSES LOCK-OUT, PDVSA AND WORKER'S CONTROL IN ACTION

The oligarchy still believed it had the whip hand in the all-important oil industry, and, through that, control of the economy. *Fedecámaras* and the leadership of the CTV, jointly called an "indefinite general strike" to start on 2 December, 2002, with the goal of toppling the government by stopping oil production. This was a coup attempt by non-military means. As in the April coup, the privately-owned media launched a campaign of disinformation in support of the strike, TV stations went so far as to suspend normal programmes to broadcast reports of the 'successes' of the strike, reports which were repeated in the bourgeois media all round the world. However, to any experienced observer it was clear almost from the start that the strike, outside of the PDVSA, never really got off the ground but, nevertheless, because of its dominance in the economy, shutting down the PDVSA would give the counter-revolution victory.

In the state of Carabobo, a key manufacturing centre, workers in the most important factories (including Ford, General Motors, Chrysler, Pirelli, Good Year and Firestone) declared their opposition to the strike. In some

---

61 Wilpert, G., *Constitutional Reform*, VA.com, 2003.

factories the bosses locked out their workers, in others the workers threatened to occupy if the factories were closed and they remained open. The workers of closed factories demanded to be paid their wages since they had gone to work, and in most cases, they were. The same was true in some sections of the food and beverages industry, controlled almost in its entirety by *Grupo Polar*, owned by the opposition leader, Lorenzo Mendoza.

On 11 December, eye-witnesses reported the airport to be working normally, as was public transport (buses, coaches and the Caracas Metro), and most shops, restaurants and bars. The state-owned basic industries (iron, steel, and aluminium), continued working at 100 per cent capacity because the workers and their local unions opposed the strike. It was soon clear that, apart from the oil industry, in those enterprises that were closed the workers were not on strike but were locked out. This was not a strike at all, but a bosses' lock-out with the active support of the executive of the CTV.

In the PDVSA, an alliance of directors, managers, supervisors and senior technicians sabotaged production and almost brought the industry to a halt. Having fixed the computerised systems to continue delivering their salaries, they withdrew key passwords and codes in an attempt to halt production. Slowly, sometimes having to battle through police lines, but progressively, the oil workers took control of the refineries and oil fields and started to revive production. By 10 January, PDVSA was working at fifty per cent capacity.[62]

In refineries like Puerto la Cruz and El Palito, and the Yagua distribution centre, most workers turned up for work and in an organised way re-established normal functioning under their direct control. The lock-out was defeated by a revolutionary alliance of oil workers and people from the poor communities. It was a measure of the enhanced class-consciousness of the popular masses at this time that the communities surrounding the oil installations came out onto the streets in mass demonstrations, supporting and encouraging the workers. It can be said without fear of exaggeration that it was the oil workers supported by the poor, who saved the Chávez government in a marvellous example of the capacity of the working class to organise production.

The picture was repeated in the massive iron and steel industry, SIDOR. At a time when SIDOR's management was supporting the conspiracy to overthrow Chávez, thousands of SIDOR workers requisitioned company buses and travelled to the Anaco PDVSA gas plant, breaking through police lines on the way, to re-establish gas supplies to keep SIDOR and other Guayanan companies producing.

---

62 Smith, M., *Venezuela, Oil and Chávez*, CNBC, 11 January, 2013.

The media, both nationally and internationally, reported opposition demonstrations demanding the resignation of the government, claiming that these mobilisations of mainly the rich and middle classes brought 100,000, 200,000 or even 300,000 people onto the streets. The media carrying the reports were owned by the same people organising the demonstrations and, given the quality of their reporting of the April coup, we can be confident that these figures were generous estimates. On 7 December, a Bolivarian demonstration of more than 2 million people took to the streets of Caracas against the 'strike' and to defend the democratically-elected government. Strange to say, there was virtually no reporting of this demonstration in the capitalist press in Venezuela or worldwide.

Facing the failure of their 'strike', the opposition upped the stakes and announced the closure of banks, and that schools and universities would not re-open after the Christmas holiday. Some banks did close, but only for forty-eight hours. All over the country, communities ensured that the schools did open. In the universities, a strong movement by the students demanded resumption of lectures, which forced the opening of most universities, strengthening the influence of the left-wing students and increasing their base in the universities and colleges. It was in this framework that the giant Chavista mobilisation of 23 January took place. Again, about 2 million people took part in an impressive show of strength against the 'strike', and in defence of the government. That demonstration was the last nail in the coffin: the opposition had no other option but to admit defeat, announce its 'easing of the strike', and then call it off altogether.

From the beginning of the lock-out on 2 December, every action of the counter-revolutionary forces had the effect of increasing revolutionary support for the Bolivarian process and raising the level of consciousness and organisation of the people generally, and the workers in particular. Low paid workers did what had previously been thought impossible, they took the place of the well-heeled elite and production had reached seventy per cent capacity.[63] There was a discussion in parliament of introducing a new law of social responsibility of the media which had played a crucial role in organising both coup conspiracies and had lied outrageously when doing so. Alas, nothing came of that. Chávez' position was extremely legalistic, faithfully remaining within the constraints of bourgeois legality.

The fightback of the workers and the people, while marvellous, was much less effective than it should have been. There were tens of thousands of rank and file organisations all over the country, but there was no nation-wide coordinating body, no national leadership to organise their efforts and

---

63 Jones, op cit.

realise the revolutionary potential of the struggle to overthrow capitalism. A major factor in this was Chávez' lack of understanding of the fundamental antagonism between the class forces at work, and his refusal to support workers' control of PDVSA other than as an emergency measure. During the lock-out, if the state-owned industries had led the way for the social transformation of society through implementation of workers' control, it would have been only a short time before the sabotage of the economy by the mass media, the banks and the private companies was halted.

The attempted coup of April 2002 and the lock-out of 2002/2003 meant a sharp contraction in production. The 'strike' caused losses to the national economy of more than US$7 billion with GDP falling by twenty-seven per cent in the first quarter of 2003. The proportion of people in formal employment fell sharply. When Chávez was first elected, the unemployment rate was about fourteen per cent. As a result of the lock-out, unemployment reached 20.7 per cent. Naturally, the opposition blamed government policy. The government attempted to borrow its way out of the problem in the expectation of future oil revenues, ignoring the abject failure of this policy under previous governments when the cure had proved worse than the disease.

The defeat of the lock-out, following the failure of the April coup had plunged the reactionary forces into a state of deep demoralisation, and it would take some time for them to recover their ability to mobilise. The opposition's hope of dealing a serious blow to the revolutionary process was now aided by the new constitution. Having bitterly opposed it, they now determined it would be an integral part of their war against the Chávez regime through the recall referendum.

The Chavista victory march to celebrate the defeat of the lock-out was on 13 April, timed also to celebrate the popular uprising that defeated the attempted military coup. In a mood of jubilation and celebration, the revolutionary masses were perfectly aware of the significance of having defeated reaction twice. This was summed up in the marchers' victory chant "every 11th has its 13th".

Given the extent and depth of their defeats, the oligarchy and imperialism hunkered down and adopted the policy that had been so successful in Nicaragua, a war of attrition and economic sabotage; making the lives of Venezuelans progressively less bearable economically and socially until, using the provisions of the constitution, they could remove Chávez legally. Integral to this strategy of disruption were unwarranted price increases, artificial shortages of food and other necessities, inflation accompanied by refusal to pay wage increases, forced unpaid holidays and unpaid wages, and more and more bankruptcies of small enterprises. In a whole series of factories across the country, the workers took the initiative and fought back. They organised democratic unions to replace the hated CTV, and occupied factories to force bosses to resume production and pay unpaid wages. These were important precedents and government support through, for example, freezing of rents to the levels before the bosses' lock-out were very welcome, but without a plan for the economy as a whole, these individual measures would, sooner or later, fail.

The advances of the revolutionary process had been concentrated in the extension of formal democracy, but had left the economic base of the country largely untouched. Still at the disposal of the Venezuelan ruling class were the economic levers necessary to sabotage and destroy the revolutionary process. To have left the banks, the means of production, processing and distribution of food, and the mass media, in private hands meant leaving high-powered weapons in the hands of an enemy that had already shown its willingness to use them against the revolution.

Indicative of the bourgeois thinking that remained rampant in the legal system was the suspension, by the Attorney General in 2003, of the Law on 'Violence Against Women and the Family', removing protection for abused women and children. This ruling was upheld by the Supreme Court. It was not until 25 November, 2006, that the Organic Law on the 'Right for Women to a Life Free From Violence' was passed.[64]

7.1) PDVSA AND WORKERS' CONTROL IN ACTION

During the lock-out, the oil workers destroyed the myth that the managerial layers of the PDVSA were the only ones who could organise production. In doing this, they saved the Chavista government. Ordinary oil workers, supported by local communities, and some who had been kicked out of the industry because of their political and trade union activities, responded by taking over the industry, overcoming sabotage and keeping it running. This was a clear demonstration that workers' control was an effective way to defeat reaction and its corruption and cronyism.

The bureaucratic leadership of the official, oil workers' union supported the CTV. Their total alienation from the workers became obvious when they told the rank and file not to collect their wages during the shut-down, losing the official leaders and CTV any remaining credibility amongst rank and file workers, and clearing the way for militant action. The state bureaucracy, the civil servants in the various ministries, were largely inherited from the Fourth Republic and, in their majority, especially at the tops, were ideologically

---

64 Espina, G., *Beyond polarization: organised Venezuelan women promote their 'minimum agenda'*, NACLA Report on the Americas, 2007, 40(2)20-24.

committed to a particularly reactionary and backward form of capitalism. These people were not on the side of the Chavista government during the lock-out and became increasingly hostile as it took actions in the interests of the poor. As a body, the state bureaucracy firmly believed that the popular masses could never run a factory, an industry or the state, and acted to undermine and sabotage all and any progress towards workers' control.

This experience of workers' control occurred not in a small bankrupt company, but in the main industry in the country, and one of the fifty largest companies in the world. The lock-out meant that the working class, for the first time, participated in the revolutionary process as a class. However, this immense collective effort, during which the workers elected those to carry out the most responsible tasks, was maintained only during the lock-out.

On 12 December, the government fired the four PDVSA executives leading the strike, and sacked a further 300 in early January. Eventually, nearly 12,000 from the upper echelons of the company were sacked. The PDVSA could have been the launch pad for workers' control in all state-owned companies – the directors of many of which had declared themselves to be 'in rebellion' and with the opposition. That was the only way to guarantee that 'PDVSA belongs to the people' and that state-owned industries were run for the benefit of all. But there was no organisation with an understanding of the class forces at work, capable of generalising the experiences of the workers and giving voice to their demands.

Rejecting the wishes of a large swathe of oil workers for democratic management, the state bureaucracy and conservative elements within the government re-instated the old management structure of the PDVSA, the very system which had given rise to the conflict. To absorb the pressure for workers' control, a substantial number of workers were promoted to replace sacked managers. This gave the appearance of democratising PDVSA, but this new layer of managers was neither answerable to the workers, nor subject to their recall. Instead, honest workers were absorbed into a capitalist business, which was structured to prevent democratic control. An indication of the attitude of the new senior managers (appointed by the ministry) was their hiring of many middle-managers who had been sacked for actively supporting the lock-out. Of course, some high-profile changes were made: i.e., many of the operations and services, which had been previously outsourced, were brought in-house, giving an additional 20,000 workers the same working conditions and benefits as PDVSA workers.

Once normal production was resumed, the oil workers' participation in the control and running of their industry rapidly declined. A new technocratic bureaucracy, supported from the very pinnacles of government, soon asserted control on the grounds that the company was strategically important to the economy, an argument that flew in the face of the history of the lock-out. With oil prices high and rising, the PDVSA was soon generating enough income to allow public spending to expand and the tops of the MVR were euphoric.

The events at the PDVSA were a focus of discussion amongst trade union activists. Although it was not clear at the time, the failure to maintain control by the workers over an enterprise that generated nearly eighty per cent of the wealth of the country would fatally undermine the campaign for workers' control that would soon erupt across Venezuela. An example of the attitude of top Bolivarians to oil workers took place in July 2009. Rafael Ramírez, Minister of Energy and, simultaneously, PDVSA president (a post he held to 2014) intervened in the elections for the national leadership of the United Federation of Venezuelan Oil Workers (FUTPV) which represented more than half the workers in the company. This union had been formed in 2007 under government pressure, when Jose Ramón Rivero, Minister of Labour, had appointed a provisional, and malleable, national leadership committee but the promised democratic elections had never taken place. Given the example of leadership elections, even in the CTV, a number of activists demanded democratic elections in the FUTPV. In an attempt to retain control, Ramírez categorised the activists as 'Adecos' – supporters of the counter-revolutionary AD Party. Ironically, one of those accused, Gregorio Rodríguez, had been decorated with the 'Order of the Liberator' for defending the oil industry during the lock-out. Ramírez, the longest serving cabinet minister under President Chávez would, in early 2018, be subject to an international arrest warrant on grounds of embezzlement and money laundering while at the top of the PDVSA.

8) THE FOUNDING OF THE NATIONAL WORKERS' UNION, CO-OPERATIVES AND THE RECALL REFERENDUM

The recklessness of the bosses' actions meant many smaller factories faced two months loss of income and were genuinely bankrupted. The great majority of private companies attempted to make workers pay the cost to the bosses of their own lock-out: many workers were not paid for the time they were locked out, some companies declared the lock-out an unpaid holiday, others told their workers they would have to wait weeks or months for their pay, and so on. In other cases, 'bankruptcy' was a tool of economic sabotage, so that assets could be sold off and the capital realised was transferred out of the country. Where they could, the employers organised the closure so that the workers were left unpaid.

The CTV, had openly sided with the oligarchs against the government in both the coup and the lock-out and, as expected, it made no attempt to support the workers in their fight backs. In many factories, workers attempted to organise democratic unions and fought for recognition. The bosses replied by making union organisers redundant, which led to strike action and factory occupations. In several cases, the bosses, faced with a militant workforce, declared bankruptcy and abandoned the premises; to get wages due and to defend their jobs, the workers often occupied the enterprise, seizing stock and machines. For example, the workers at the Convencaucho rubber works in Barquisimeto had to simultaneously occupy the factory, change their union and defend themselves from attacks from thugs, before the employer agreed to pay the wages owed and keep the factory open.[65]

The Chavista government moved to replace the CTV with a friendly trade union confederation. The proposal originated from established trade union leaders close to the government, but who appeared to believe that the best way to launch a new national union was from above without any real involvement of, or even consultation with, the rank and file; that it was sufficient to set a date for the founding conference and have leadership and programme settled by horse-trading behind the scenes. These were bureaucratic and arbitrary methods. A real re-founding of the trade union movement would have meant a serious campaign of explanation, discussion and struggle to win the rank and file in the existing unions, and to bring the unorganised into union membership. Such a campaign based on the principles of democratic and militant trade unionism would have given the class struggle a massive push forward.

The process by which the National Workers' Union (UNT), a trade union umbrella organisation, was founded received strong criticism from rank and file activists as undemocratic; the *pro-tem* leadership had been self-selected with support of government functionaries, too many had been closely associated with the CTV and were more concerned with their own interests than those of the workers they were supposed to serve.

A proclamation at the Caracas National Theatre on 5 April, 2003 launched the UNT, and the founding congress took place in Caracas on 1 and 2 August, 2003. More than 1,500 delegates from all over the country, representing over 120 local unions participated. The Congress passed a radical programme calling for: a thirty-six-hour working week; closed factories to be occupied and placed under workers' control; nationalisation of the banks, and abrogation of the foreign debt. In its statement of principles, the UNT declared itself an internationalist, class-struggle movement based on the

---

65 *Venezuelan Trade Unionists Shot At*, www.marxist.com, 29 January, 2003.

equality of men and women and for emancipation from class exploitation, oppression, discrimination and exclusion.

The CTV was rapidly shown to be a hollow shell supported more by employers than by workers. On May Day 2004, the UNT demonstration had tens of thousands of workers, but there was hardly a sign of the CTV. In Carabobo, a state which concentrates a large proportion of the country's private industry, dozens of factories were soon organised in UNT-affiliated unions. An important example was at the Daimler-Chrysler assembly plant where, after twenty-five years of CTV mafia-type trade unionism, 400 workers set up an independent class-struggle union affiliated to the UNT.

The leadership of the UNT had been agreed with government bureaucrats without reference to the rank and file. Consequently, in its first two years it ignored the policies of class struggle agreed at the founding congress, and stayed well away from any issue that might be opposed by Ministers or their civil servants, such as factory occupations and workers' control. Of course, some leaders were more militant than others and made serious attempts to build the UNT, but even these did not prove capable of leading and organising on the central issues of the day: factory expropriations, and workers' control in the nationalised industries. The lack of either a united or a class-struggle leadership in the UNT meant the workers' battles actually taking place at a time of heightened class struggle were uncoordinated, often isolated, and rarely supported.

From July 2005, the government gave special attention to closed businesses, because the closures resulting from the lock-out had poured many thousands of redundant and angry workers onto the streets. There followed a succession of expropriations, usually of factories that had been deliberately run down and, subsequently, occupied by protesting workers: Industrial de Perfumes, a perfume-making company in Caracas; Sanitarios Maracay, a factory for sanitary facilities in Maracay; Sidororca, a pipe manufacturer for the oil industry; Fribasa an industrial slaughterhouse; a tomato-processing plant of the U.S. multinational Heinz; the cornflour processing plant Promabasa; and several other plants occupied or previously occupied by employees. The owners received compensation equivalent to the market value. This was often generous for the larger companies, but many smaller companies left dilapidated buildings, out-of-date machinery that had been run into the ground, and huge debts (workers' back pay, gas, electricity and phone bills, unpaid taxes, etc.): these owners received little, if any, payment.

At the other end of the scale, according to a parliamentary commission of inquiry, was Polar, which had bought Promabasa years before, in order to eliminate competition and achieve a monopoly position. Polar closed down production at the site and relocated a number of machines to Colombia, re-exporting the processed corn products to Venezuela to be sold through Polar's distribution network. In September 2005, the governor of Barinas state in Venezuela (Chávez' father), signed a decree stating that the abandoned Promabasa corn processing plant was of public interest, and it was expropriated and handed over to the co-operative, *Maiceros de la Revolución*, created by former workers in the context of *cogestión*.

Cogestión (a form of co-management), was to be a feature of the government's industrial strategy, but was understood differently by the groups affected. As expressed by the Ministry of Light Industry and Commerce, and Ministry for the Popular Economy, *cogestión* was worker participation, possibly even on the board of directors, owning shares in the company through a co-operative. Workers on the other hand had a somewhat different view. Joaquín Osorio, a leader of the electrical workers' union, declared *cogestión* should have nothing to do with workers owning shares, as this would transform workers into owner-bosses and reproduce capitalist antagonisms. Freteco (*Frente Revolucionario de Trabajadores de Empresas Cogestiónadas y Ocupadas*) saw *cogestión* as a form of workers' control, and argued for the creation of workers councils along the lines of those that existed in revolutionary Russia.[66]

It was right and proper for revolutionaries to take a leading role in these occupations to both deepen and extend them. In this Freteco was giving effect to Trotsky's analysis:

> The various capitalist enterprises, national and foreign, will inevitably enter into a conspiracy with the state institutions to put obstacles in the way of the workers' management of nationalised industry. On the other hand, the workers' organisations that are in the management of the various branches of nationalised industry must join together to exchange their experiences, must give each other economic support, must act with their joint forces on the government on the conditions of credit, etc. Of course such a central bureau of the workers' management of nationalised branches of industry must be in closest contact with the trade unions.[67]

Workers' control could have been a big step forward, and was strongly encouraged by the revolutionary left. It challenges the 'sacred right' of the capitalists to own, and the bureaucrats to manage industry, it gives the workers priceless experience in administration and control that could be put to good use in a socialist planned economy, and it gives direct contact on a common platform to the most politically-advanced workers and Marxists.

66 *El Freteco y la Empresa Socialista*. Fundación Federico Engels de Venezuela, Los Teques 2007.
67 Trotsky, L., *Nationalised Industry and Workers' Management*, www.marxists.org.

Attempts to introduce *cogestión* into enterprises invariably brought the workers into confrontation with an amalgam of: those whose who had been robbing the state for years and whose activities would be brought to light; managers, who were used to running a company and saw their authority being challenged; those who believed the popular masses were quite incapable of running their own lives let alone a factory; and all those who were fed crumbs from the oligarch's table, particularly trade union bureaucrats.

8.1) 2004: CO-OPERATIVES, THE RECALL REFERENDUM AND REGIONAL ELECTIONS

After the lock-out, there was a desperate need to create jobs. From about 2004 to 2006/7, the government promoted co-operatives. In the expectation they would create hundreds of thousands of jobs, the movement received massive injections of state credit.[68] At the turn of the century, fewer than 800 co-operatives were officially registered, mostly due to the initiatives of young Catholic activists. Legal hurdles to their creation were removed and a series of incentives were offered, including: approved co-operatives exempt from income tax, and small co-operatives getting interest-free loans.

Such favourable conditions meant a boom in co-operatives. At the end of 2008 according to the national co-operative supervisory institute, Sunacoop, there were over a quarter of a million officially registered.[69] Subsequent evaluation showed that only about a third were viable and operating as intended, with the majority of these being family businesses from the most marginal sectors of society. The process was greatly hindered by the private financial institutions administering it, which demonstrated an alarming lack of commitment, taking many months to deliver promised funds. Where the co-operatives were peasants this meant the loss of a year, or borrowing at commercial rates. Government departments were no better, taking months to deliver technical equipment and/or assistance.[70]

All too often, the co-operatives were created as capitalist enterprises, with members pushed into reproducing the same exploitative working conditions as in traditional capital-labour relations, resulting in workers concentrating on maximising their own earnings. This was particularly true in co-operatives where the state was a co-owner; government bureaucrats pressured the co-operative to become a small capitalist enterprise, competing for business.[71]

---

68 Wilpert, G., *Co-operatives are the businesses of the future*, VA.com, 17 September, 2003.

69 *Management Achievements*, Sunacoop 2008.

70 Piñeiro, C., *Main Challenges for Co-operatives in Venezuela*, Critical Sociology, 2009, 35(6):841-862.

71 Ibid.

Nevertheless, there was job creation and, generally, greater job security, better working conditions and an improvement in the quality of life of the employees, despite the co-operatives being encouraged to compete one with another for the work outsourced by larger companies. The government rated the experience with co-operatives as a worthwhile investment, successfully increasing national production and import substitution.

The opposition now adopted a course of action intended to rally its base and sow confusion in the Chavista ranks. The constitution contained a recall clause, symbolising the commitment to making public officials accountable. Any elected official, whether President or local councillor, could be subject to a recall referendum once that person had completed half their term in office, and a petition containing the signatures of at least twenty per cent of the registered electors submitted to the National Electoral Commission (CNE). The CNE checked the legitimacy of the signatures and, if verified, organised the referendum.

In August, the opposition presented their petition calling for a presidential recall referendum, but the CNE annulled many signatures as fraudulent, the most common ground being that the signee was dead. The number of legitimate signatures fell to below the number required, and the opposition had to restart the recall process.

The opposition collected a second set of signatures and submitted them on Friday, 28 November. Nearly half of these were rejected by the CNE, but an appeal to the TSJ reinstated sufficient to take the number of legitimate signatures above the 2.4 million required. Rank and file Chavistas responded by collecting signatures to recall dozens of opposition members of parliament, many of whom had been elected on a Chavista ticket, but later joined the opposition without relinquishing their seats. Surprisingly, this initiative was not welcomed, and soon died a death, an early indication that many party and government tops felt more comfortable with oppositionists than rank and file Chavistas.

Only the most short-sighted of the oppositionists could have believed the recall referendum would unseat Chávez. No restrictions were placed on freedom of speech during the recall referendum and known coup-plotters appeared on television to talk, more or less openly, of how best to overthrow the democratically-elected head of state. In this respect, the cynicism of the Bush administration in the US was shameless: it claimed the Venezuelan government was anti-democratic because it was closing down the private TV channel Globovisión. This was completely untrue. The only media outlet closed down was a community-based TV station called Catia TV and this was done by opposition leader, Alfredo Peña, because it was openly in favour

PERMANENT REVOLUTION IN LATIN AMERICA

of the revolutionary process. Catia TV had been founded largely due to the efforts of Bianca Eekhout, and was a focal point for breaking down gender barriers in TV reporting.[72] The barrage of lies had one main objective: to create a massive web of confusion so that the workers of the world were unable to follow what was really going on in Venezuela.

During the campaign, to support their allegations that Chávez was ruining the country, the oppositionists stepped up their economic sabotage: closing factories, firing workers, creating shortages of goods, and so on. It was the government's economic response that was, and remains, its weakest point. In the fields of health, housing and education the government had achieved great things, but the fate of a revolution ultimately depends on its ability to raise the living standards of its supporters – and key factors in that are quality of life, food, and employment.

By 2004, the regime had established over 4,000 food banks and/or soup kitchens across the country at which children and needy mothers could get one square meal a day. These were often sited in the houses of Chavistas, and almost entirely staffed by women. In the recall referendum, *barrio* women played a major role in motivating people to register and getting the votes out, activities that were key to Chávez' victory.[73]

Chávez had also launched a number of educational initiatives specifically aimed at women in the *barrios*: from basic literacy programmes to Misión Ribas, a college level work-study programme leading to university courses. These were advertised, for example, on billboards and were unlike anything previously seen in Venezuela. First, there was the presence of black and *mestiza* women – in contrast to the pictures of young, fair-skinned, blonde-haired, bikini-clad women with European features that dominated advertising in Venezuela, and distorted and belittled the expectations and self-esteem of young women. Second, the campaign showed black and indigenous women taking control of their lives, achieving their aspirations, moving from domestic worker to business administrator, social worker or doctor, challenging the racism and prejudice so prevalent amongst the oligarchs.

On the morning of 16 August, 2004, the CNE announced the result of the recall referendum: on an electoral turnout of over ninety per cent, the opposition obtained 40.74 per cent of the votes cast while Chávez obtained 59.25 per cent. Before the official announcement was made, there was a separate announcement by CNE board members Sobella Mejias and Ezequiel Zamora, questioning the result. It was an open secret that both were aligned with the opposition. By such tricks the opposition sought to discredit the

72 Schiller, N., *Gender, Power and Community Television*, 2008, Taylor & Francis.
73 Fernandes, op cit., 2007.

referendum and, as expected, the opposition immediately and 'categorically' refused to recognise their defeat, claiming it was based on electoral fraud. The internal and external enemies of the Bolivarian Revolution will never be bound by elections, referendums or negotiations. They will be satisfied only when the revolution is defeated. Not to recognise that was, and is, irresponsible wishful thinking, but the Bolivarian leaders saw themselves as liberalising social democrats, not revolutionary socialists, and argued for 'moderation'. The inevitable result would be a new offensive of the counter-revolution.

The recall referendum was the eighth victory in a row for the Bolivarians. Jimmy Carter, ex-president of the USA, had acted as observer and declared the presidential referendum results fair and transparent. Later, at a very swanky restaurant in Caracas, he was booed and spat on by upper-class opposition supporters, demonstrating their democratic credentials.

It was at this time that Trotskyist groups, while supporting Chávez in the face of US imperialism, and praising his progressive measures, began publicly, to draw attention to the bureaucratic behaviour of his government; that those who called for unity, even with known coup-plotters, were the same people who attempted to block every progressive measure. These compromisers had a solid base of support in the civil servants and top state officials inherited from the Fourth Republic, and eventually joined with them to accumulate and consolidate substantial wealth.

Warning that a revolution that stopped half way would be defeated (i.e., Chile and Nicaragua), the Trotskyists proposed a series of transitional demands to weld together the popular masses by offering solutions to their immediate problems, giving them confidence in their own strength and ability to carry the revolution through to completion. At that time, the core economic demands were: nationalisation under workers' control of the big food and transport companies and the mass media; non-payment of the foreign debt; workers' control and management of the PDVSA and basic industries; nationalisation of the banking system; and state control over foreign trade. Other important demands were: setting up self-defence brigades; a workers' and people's militia in every neighbourhood, workplace, town and village, to protect the people, to maintain order, and to defend the revolution from any internal or external aggression.

Chávez' social policies were radical and aroused colossal enthusiasm. There was no mistaking the intense loyalty and extraordinary devotion felt for him by the masses. It was Chávez who, for the first time in modern history, gave the great majority of Venezuelans hope for a better future. For the popular masses, Chávez and the Revolution were one and the same thing.

But it was not until after the failed coup of April 2002, after the bosses' lock-out of December 2002-January 2003, and after his victory in the recall referendum of 2004, that Chávez' economic policies were radicalised with the call to re-nationalise those enterprises privatised under the neo-liberal policies of previous governments. The call was soon extended to include companies of 'strategic importance' or those occupied by their workers as part of an industrial dispute. These measures were meant to transform the social basis of production from production for profit to production for need, with the added goal of overcoming the social divisions within the enterprise. The economic balance of many small companies and co-operatives was transformed, but state subsidies using monies obtained from the PDVSA became essential to keep them operating.

Regional elections throughout Venezuela had been postponed to 31 October, 2004, due to the recall referendum. Oppositionists won only two of the twenty-two governorships and lost the post of metropolitan mayor in both Caracas and the capital district. Former opposition strongholds were won by Bolivarian candidates, confirming the support for Chávez shown in the recall referendum. This was the ninth consecutive election victory for the Bolivarian movement.

During the election campaign, Chávez raised the need to proceed with the land reform against the *latifundia*. He very publicly directed a number of candidates for state governor to tackle this issue immediately after being elected. First, they were to attempt to persuade *caudillos* to give up land they did not really need. Only if that failed was the expropriations law to be used to purchase and distribute the land. Later, at a rally on 10 January, 2005, Chávez announced a new decree aimed at accelerating land reform. The December 2001 Land Act, had been half-hearted and largely thwarted by the TSJ decision of August 2002. True, since the Land Act, the National Land Institute *(Instituto Nacional de Tierras*, INTI) had distributed 2.2 million hectares of land to peasant co-operatives, but this had been state-owned. There were few, if any, expropriations, though there had been spontaneous peasant occupations. Generally, the *latifundia* had been left well alone.

The proposed new decree, *Decreto Zamorano* was cautious and offered no existential threat to the *caudillos*. A special land commission investigated whether the *latifundia* had proper land titles. In Venezuela, over the years, it was common practice for *caudillos* to occupy land that belonged to the state, *de facto* appropriating it. A second issue was whether the land was sufficiently productive as only underused land could be expropriated (with compensation at market rates) and distributed to, for example, peasant co-operatives. The corollary was that the peasants received the least productive land to farm.

While insisting that he preferred reaching agreement with the land owners, Chávez claimed that he would go as far as using the army to enforce expropriation of the land if needed. This, of course, was no more than Betancourt had done, only with much more militant language. The hopes of thousands of peasant communities were again lifted. Vice-President Jose Vicente Rangel, rushed to reassure the opposition that the measures did not threaten private property; those with their titles in order and their lands productive had "nothing to fear". Such assurances did little to calm the fears of the numerous *caudillos* who had stolen state land.

On 5 and 6 February, 2005, the 'Peasant Conference in Defence of National Sovereignty and for the Agrarian Revolution' sponsored by the *Frente Nacional Campesino Ezequiel Zamora* (FNCEZ) severely criticised the realities of the Agrarian Reform Law. Land needed to be uncultivated not just underutilised to be expropriated. The process was so slow and bureaucratic that the land could be stripped of entire forests while a decision was being made. The peasants expressed "universal support for President Hugo Chávez", and welcomed the *Decreto Zamorano*, but simultaneously observed that it did not go far enough: far too little land would be taken and re-distributed. It was also pointed out that over 100 peasant leaders and activists had been killed in disputes over land in the previous four years but little or nothing had been done to bring the culprits to justice. The Conference agreed that the best way to help the government's land programme was to step up actions from below and it wanted the means to do this – armed peasant militias, noting that despite Chávez' many calls, very little had been done to establish them. This should surprise few people; a bourgeois state bureaucracy can never be an instrument for revolutionary change, in particular the arming of the masses.

In April 2005, the new Land Law was passed, reversing the 2002 TSJ decision and introducing 'agrarian letters' (*cartas agrarias*), which provided farmers with government permission to develop land even if ownership had not been resolved by the courts. Chávez stressed that *Decreto Zamorano* would mean more redistribution of privately-held land. Six months into this plan, the INTI had identified some 5.2 million hectares for redistribution. Six years later, at the end of 2011, only half had been 'rescued' and turned over to landless peasants. A more important part of the land reform programme was the 'regularisation' of land tenancies, meaning the verification of existing land-ownership claims. Between 2003 and 2011 the government would regularise 5.9 million hectares. These changes were more substantial than the change of land-ownership implied, the previous agrarian economy had been built on cattle, coffee and cacao but never foodstuffs. Now the aim was for Venezuela to feed itself.

Every genuine revolutionary and democrat is duty-bound to support the agrarian revolution. But whatever laws were passed, the land-owners would not give up their power, land and privileges without a fight. In order to succeed against the oligarchs, the most energetic and revolutionary measures were necessary. The mobilisation of the peasants was the only guarantee that the agrarian reform of the Bolivarian Revolution would be carried through, and not remain a dead letter, a scrap of paper in the drawer of some bureaucrat.

The optimal way to effect a peaceful and orderly transfer of land to the *campesinos* was, as the FNCEZ had demanded, for the *campesinos* to be armed, able to defend themselves against the counter-revolution, and to establish a network of peasant defence committees linking with workers in the urban centres. But land reform could only succeed if the *campesinos* received cheap credit, cheap fertilisers, tractors and combine harvesters, lorries for transportation, and guaranteed markets for their products. That could only be achieved if they were integrated in a national plan of food production.

9) 'RECOVERED' COMPANIES (*EMPRESAS RECUPERADAS*)

The government's policies had, from the end of 2005, permitted smaller firms faced with laying off workers, to access government subsidies and cheap loans through the programme *Fábrica adentro*. To obtain these funds, owners had to agree to (i) some form of co-management, (ii) a share of the profits to go to the workers, (iii) at least ten per cent of any gains made to be donated to a fund for industrial transformation, and (iv) the creation of new jobs, and no person could be sacked. The government hoped to generate 100,000 jobs this way. Small firms, about 1,500 in the first year flocked to join. With this venture, it was clear that civil servants, and many private enterprises, were seeing co-management and social partnership as drawing workers into taking partial responsibility for increasing production and profitability, and as a means to avoid industrial conflicts. Many of the more militant workers, conversely, saw co-management as a possible step towards workers' control and a socialist society.

The quality and type of co-management in different factories reflected these differences. In some companies, co-management gave the employees shares in the company, or transferred twenty-five per cent of the ownership to a co-operative of employees. This enmeshed the workers into the drive for profitability, but without giving them any real say in decision-making. The state bureaucracy was, of course, always on the look-out for any progress towards real democratisation and, as soon as it was discerned, the relevant Ministry moved in to behead it, usually by replacing the leaders with persons more complaint, even outright reactionary.

However, against the wishes of many of his own party tops, and in the face of the opposition of the state bureaucracy Chávez unexpectedly launched a number of initiatives. The first was *Empresas Recuperadas*, companies 'recovered' from their private capitalist owners and operated under some form of co-management by employees, the state and local community. In particular, factories shut down by bankrupt owners could be subject to a state take-over in the national interest. Included was the re-nationalisation of companies privatised under the neo-liberal policies of previous governments, which included the electricity sector and the national telephone company, *CA Nacional Telefonos de Venezuela* (CANTV), both in February 2007, and SIDOR, in April 2008.

The response of the authorities was less then half-hearted. There were a few interventions to stop workers being forcibly ejected by employers' goons, but government bureaucrats refused to nationalise companies as the workers demanded, on the grounds that no law had been enacted. In fact, it had been legal to expropriate since 2000, under Articles 115 and 117 of the Constitution, and in 2001 a closed sugar processing plant, Pío Tamayo Sugar Mill, had been re-opened as a co-governed enterprise, though it soon lapsed into 100 per cent government ownership. The bureaucrats preferred the economic stranglehold of the employers to a workers' fight back, especially if it risked deepening the Bolivarian Revolution by placing factories under workers' control. To take some heat out of the struggle, a law preventing arbitrary redundancies was passed, but only as a lesser evil.

However, there was opposition to workers' control by many managers in state-owned enterprises, who held to the old ways, even with revolutionary changes happening around them. In the state-owned electricity company (*Cadafe*), the workers demanded participation in the decision-making processes and were met with determined resistance from the management. The trade union *Fetraelec* (Federation of the Electric Industry of Venezuela) had long campaigned for worker participation and in 2001 signed a collective contract with *Cadafe* which included the right of workers to participate in managing the industry. After the defeat of the bosses' lock-out at the end of 2002, workers began to organise committees across the industry to implement the agreement. They encountered fierce resistance from company managers, who succeeded, by 2005, in smothering any meaningful workers' participation.[74] It was highly significant that the managers and bureaucrats were able to successfully subvert the president's declared policy.

Because of the opposition to workers' control within the government itself, the civil service and the state governors, there was no clear or systematic

---

74 Cerceau, G., *Experiencia de Cogestión en CADAFE*, 2007, ILDIS, Caracas.

policy either for nationalisation of companies or the introduction of *cogestión*. The most publicised cases of successfully-completed expropriations were the paper factory *Venepal* (later Invepal) in January 2005 and, at the end of April 2005, *Constructora Nacional de Válvulas* (CNV, now Inveval), a factory producing industrial valves.

Workers' control at Invepal was effected by a militant occupation, but the experiment was short-lived due to a destructive dispute between full-time and temporary workers. This gave the state bureaucracy the excuse to intervene and end workers' control. In April 2006, a board of directors was appointed with Minister María Cristina Iglesias the president of the factory.

9.1) INVEVAL – 28 APRIL, 2005

Constructora Nacional de Valvulas (CNV) in Los Teques, near Caracas, had been producing high-pressure valves for PDVSA for more than thirty years. Andrés Sosa Pietri, owner of CNV, a member of one of the traditional families of the Venezuelan oligarchy, and director of the PDVSA in the 1990s, had wholeheartedly supported the failed coup in 2002, and on 9 December, 2002, as part of the lock-out, he closed CNV, after which he refused to pay wages to the workers for time lost.

After months of negotiations, in May 2003 a group of workers placed a picket line across the entrance to the factory to prevent finished products or machinery leaving the premises. The owner replied by closing the factory. Inspired by the nationalisation of Venepal, a group of sixty-three CNV workers decided to take over their factory and, on 17 February, 2005, occupied the premises and campaigned for CNV to be nationalised, pointing to its strategic importance to the PDVSA. On 28 April, 2005, Chávez announced the expropriation of CNV, saying it would be run under a system of worker-state co-management with fifty-one per cent state and forty-nine per cent employee ownership in a joint co-operative.[75] Unfortunately, the expropriation did not include Pietri's foundry at nearby Acerven, which produced the outer casings of the valves, and, without which, production soon came to a halt.

Initially, the Ministry of Popular Economy proposed co-management with all five directors named by the Minister, which reneged on Chávez' promise that the majority of directors would be elected by and from the workers. The proposal was rejected, the workers demanded the Ministry honour Chávez' promise.

On 4 August, 2005, a deal was signed in which the factory became a co-managed co-operative with day-to-day management in the hands of the

75 Gindin, J., *Venezuela Expropriates… Valve Factory*, 28 April, 2005, VA.com.

workers' assembly. The legal administration was a five-member executive board, including the factory president. Two members of the boards were elected directly by the workers, and two members represented the Ministry. The fifth member, the president, was appointed by the state, but at Chávez' insistence, this person was a worker at the factory, chosen by the workers. All the important decisions affecting the factory were to be ratified by the weekly factory assembly. One of the first actions of the workers' assembly was a wage increase and a seven-hour working day. Such measures would become common practice at the first meetings of workers' assemblies. The two board members chosen by the Ministry showed their appreciation of the importance of this initiative by never turning up for any meetings.

Inveval restarted partially in mid-2006, but was largely limited to carrying out maintenance and repairs. Without the Acerven foundry, essential valve components were made at another, private, foundry, which placed all kinds of obstacles in the way of the Inveval workers, sometimes refusing orders, sometimes imposing unscheduled delays, but most often delivering substandard or deficient parts. Inveval workers continued to press the government to either buy or expropriate the Acerven foundry, but their efforts were in vain.[76] Meanwhile, PDVSA was importing valves, an arrangement that simultaneously satisfied the prejudices of state functionaries while generously lining the pockets the private sector.

The workers of Inveval, supported by Freteco, took up a proposal by Chávez made in January 2007, to deepen the revolution through the formation of workers' councils, and decided with immediate effect to elect a factory council with thirty-two members. The workers themselves, from their own experiences, had concluded that co-operative-state joint ownership with co-management in a mixed economy was not suited to building socialism. "What a co-operative does is to feed capitalism because it is created as part of the capitalist system and that's what we don't want here. We didn't kick out one capitalist to have the sixty capitalist instead," explained one Inveval worker.[77] In only a short time, by mid-2008, the Inveval workers had dissolved the co-operative arrangement so they were no longer owners of the means of production, turning the factory into state property.

The workers had found that Inveval, rather than moving towards socialism, was moving in the reverse direction, with the workers' co-operative being forced to adopt a capitalist-commercial logic; that co-management as it had been applied was at best a moderate reform of capitalism. The workers

---

76 Kiraz Janicke, K., *Venezuela's Co-Managed Inveval*, 27 July. 2007, VA.com.
77 Ness, I., and Azzellini, D., *Ours to master and to own*, Haymarket Books, 2011.

remained keen to have workers' control and pushed strongly for its adoption, but in a form that gave them real authority.

For years, the Inveval workers had to struggle against the top managers of the PDVSA to make the state-owned oil company honour existing contracts, let alone sign new ones This was sabotage by state and PDVSA bureaucrats, who waged a consistent campaign of slanders and lies against workers' control in general and Inveval in particular. At a meeting at which Jorge Paredes, president of the democratically-elected workers' council at Inveval, was present, President Chávez asked why Inveval was no longer producing valves. Paredes replied that, despite production difficulties, they were ready to supply the PDVSA. This exchange resulted in an agreement for Inveval to supply valves, but then the PDVSA bureaucrats demanded a new style of valve, which they knew would incur development costs for Inveval and production delays. The workers responded with a determined campaign to acquire their own foundry. Chávez was persuaded to order the expropriation of Acerven which would allow Inveval to manufacture the new valves in-house. But it took until 2010 before the National Assembly declared the Acerven foundry to be of public interest, and February 2011 before it was nationalised.[78]

Ministry bureaucrats, certain Ministers and some PDVSA tops had, as part of their campaign against workers' control, actively sabotaged the process. Sabotage would begin by the Ministry demanding the workers accept a form of management structure, in the full knowledge it would be unacceptable. The to-and-fro arguments were stretched as long as possible to dampen the workers' enthusiasm. Start-up funds were mysteriously delayed, for months, possibly years. Payments for work done and subsidies failed to arrive. Requests for technical support were mislaid, and then the necessary staff occupied elsewhere. At the local level the opposition could be open and blatant. A regional governor, Didalco Bolivar, a member of *Podemos*, a party in the government coalition, met one peaceful delegation of workers from Sanitarios Maracay with National Guard units firing tear gas and bullets.[79]

By 2009, a thirty-two-strong council, answerable to regular mass meetings, was the supreme authority within the company. Jobs inside the factory were rotated in an attempt to overcome the social divisions of labour (e.g., intellectual and manual), and all positions were recallable by the workers' assembly. In addition, salaries were the same for everybody, truck drivers, line workers, or the company president.

---

78 Ness, and Azzellini, op cit.
79 Hise, M., *Workers Control... under Attack*, VA.com, 18 August, 2007.

Inveval maintained a significant degree of workers' control (despite the sabotage of the bureaucracy) until early 2015 when Jorge Paredes was removed as president, and a military officer, Vice-admiral Alcibiades Paz, appointed in his place. This changed the character of the administration. As the state bureaucracy regained full control, the PDVSA ordered valves again, payments were made on time, government funds arrived and bureaucratic sabotage largely ceased.

However, Paredes was a thorn in the side of the new administration. He knew too much about the company, its dealings with suppliers, with other companies, etc., and remained a focus for the forces opposing the change in character of the factory. He was arrested in 2016, accused of domestic violence by his ex-wife from whom he had been separated for four years. He was jailed immediately and held there. His trial has been postponed numerous times with different excuses, and militants in the factory believe the case was fabricated with the aim of removing Paredes permanently from the company. Since then the factory council has been disbanded, and workers' control smothered by the state bureaucracy.

9.2) THE STRUGGLE AT ALCASA ALUMINIUM FOR WORKERS' CONTROL

Strictly, Alcasa, as a nationalised company, was not 'recovered', but the introduction of co-management occurred at the same time as at Invepal and Inveval. In 2005, Alcasa in Ciudad, Guayana, in the state of Bolívar, was the second largest aluminium smelter in Venezuela, employing around 3,000 workers. It is part of the state-owned industrial conglomerate Corporacion Venezolana de Guayana (CVG). The Minister responsible in 2005 was Víctor Álvarez, who was strongly in favour of co-management[80] and Álvarez wanted a form of production that integrated an enterprise with its local communities. *Cogestión* at Alcasa was expected to have a model character and, indeed, its achievements appear to have been amongst the most advanced.

In the previous seventeen years, largely due to an inefficient and corrupt system, Alcasa had acquired huge debts. Attempts to privatise the company had sunk in a swamp of corruption and embezzlement. At the beginning of 2005, on Álvarez' recommendation, Chávez appointed Carlos Lanz as President of Alcasa. Lanz was tasked by Álvarez to introduce a *cogestión* scheme whose end goal would be workers' control of the company; giving the workers complete authority over distribution, production and product development. The aim was to help meet the need for cheap, good quality

---

80 Álvarez, V.*¿Hacia donde va el modelo productivo?* 2009, CIM, Caracas.

housing. The company soon became a political symbol of workers holding real power.[81]

The immediate goals were: democratisation of the plant, making it productive and profitable, and reducing corruption. Some fifteen days after Lanz arrived, all heads of department were replaced and new ones elected by a workers' assembly with the new heads receiving the same wages as the workers. All posts could be revoked by the workers' assembly. Department meetings were established and representatives elected. To help win the support of the workers, an initial decision of the workers' assembly was to increase wages by fifteen per cent.

In November 2005, a new five-member executive board was selected: of these, three, including Lanz, were employees of Alcasa. In July 2006, Lanz stood for election as president of the factory and obtained 1,800 votes from the 1,920 employees who voted. His plan for co-management began with restructuring the board, adding two workers from Alcasa. Production levels rose by eleven per cent.[82] At the end of 2006, Alcasa had paid all salaries and pensions owed to workers and former employees, and signed a new collective agreement with the union, Sintralcasa, confirming that a workers' council would select the management model to be adopted for Alcasa.[83]

However, within Alcasa powerful forces were pushing hard to get rid of Lanz. The previous managers, in alliance with the leaders of the FSBT union (*Fuerza Socialista Bolivariana de Trabajadores* or Bolivarian Socialist Workers' Front), were undermining the departmental meetings, ensuring they met less frequently and, in some departments, managed to stop the meetings completely. The multinationals hit by new arrangements responded with a barrage of adverse publicity. Ministry officials, who opposed co-management, erected bureaucratic barriers and made public statements detrimental to Lanz. In the January 2006 union elections, those opposing *cogestión* ran a campaign demanding a big increase in wages, Lanz' supporters, who campaigned almost exclusively on the issue of *cogestión*, got less than ten per cent of the vote. Then in June 2006, the workers voted to restructure the management system, and elected many of the same managers whom they had removed in the previous elections.

In May 2007, Lanz left Alcasa for health reasons. The state bureaucracy, holding fifty-one per cent of Alcasa stock, appointed a new president with little interest in co-management, and active engagement by the workers fell rapidly. A hangover from Lanz was that employees of co-operatives associated

81 Thomas, F., *"Co-management" in Venezuela's Alcasa*, VA.com, 25 October, 2005.
82 news.bbc.co.uk/hi/spanish/latin_america, 19 August, 2005.
83 Azzellini, D., and O. Ressler, 2006, *5-Factories: Workers control in Venezuela*, Film, trailer on YouTube.

with Alcasa were scheduled to join the fixed payroll. There were about sixty such people, but 600 new workers were taken on, most of the excess were friends and families of management.[84] Production and productivity suffered immediately, and by the end of 2007 Alcasa was again reporting enormous losses. So catastrophic was the decline that, in April 2008, a replacement president, Carlos Aguilar, was installed. Aguilar was even more undemocratic than his predecessor. The new president started selling the company's huge aluminium stocks at below market prices in exchange for cash payments; he went further and tried to pull Alcasa out of the social projects which it had agreed to support. The number of workers who favoured *cogestión* expanded rapidly under Aguilar's presidency.

In February 2009, Sintralcasa organised a referendum in the factory for a vote of no confidence in Aguilar. Given the public fiction that the company was co-managed, it would have been difficult for the state-appointed directors to ignore a clear workers' vote. In May 2009, Chávez met some of these workers and agreed with their call for the election of managers from below. The workers seized on this speech and, basing themselves on it, made a series of demands, one being the democratic election of the company president. The Ministry bureaucrats had little choice but to give in, though with considerable ill-will, and active opposition from Jose Khan, the minister directly involved, Cristina Iglesias, Minister of Labour, Nicolas Maduro, Foreign Minister, and Jorge Giordani, Minister of Planning and Finance. Elio Sayago, long time trade union activist and well know leftist was elected president with an overwhelming majority, and personally approved by Chávez on 15 May, 2010.[85]

Merely by showing it was possible to challenge the forces of reaction, and setting an example for workers in other industries (particularly the workers in SIDOR), the Alcasa workers made important enemies. The supposedly pro-Chávez, but reactionary, Governor of the Bolívar state, General Francisco Rangel Gómez, bitterly opposed the links formed with workers from other factories, teachers' unions, communal councils, students' organisations and co-operatives. Behind the scenes, Rangel threw his weight against the Alcasa workers. The state bureaucracy, the right-wing within government and the FSBT tops joined forces to launch a sustained and aggressive campaign against co-management in general, and Sayago in particular.

Over his period as president, Aguilar, had signed deals with international companies that were seriously disadvantageous to Alcasa, but very profitable for others. The workers' assembly decided to abrogate them and to concentrate

84 Azzellini, D., *Communes and Workers' Control in Venezuela*, Haymarket, 2018.
85 Interview with Elio Sayago, *Lucha de Clases*, 25 October, 2011.

instead on supplying domestic customers as required by Alcasa's designation as a Social Production Enterprise. These moves were opposed by the FSBT union, which was closely allied with Aguilar. Early on the morning of 9 November, 2010, about twenty FSBT members entered the factory before the first shift, chained the gates shut, as though executing a *coup d'etat.* Sayago swiftly organised the mass of workers and an estimated six hundred from the first shift accompanied him into the factory to make it perfectly evident who had their support.[86]

The FSBT now raised questions of back-pay dating from when Aguilar was president, which had not been raised at the time but now were posed as most urgent. The FSBT leader in Alcasa was José Gil who was determined to see workers' control fail in Alcasa and, in January-February, 2011, led a group of armed supporters of the FSBT to blockade the gates. The action stopped workers entering the factory for over a month. When Sayago, backed by workers who supported workers' control, attempted to access the installation, he was brutally beaten up. The day after, two women members of the FSBT accused Sayago of assaulting them, videos of the attack, however, clearly showed Sayago as the victim. Here, the FSBT was acting as a front for an unholy amalgam of corrupt politicians, company managers and multinational interests. It is widely believed that the same ministers who opposed Sayago's election – Khan, Iglesias, Maduro and Jaua – did more than a little to assist this adventure. The lock-out did enormous financial damage, deliberately exacerbated by the state machine, which punished the workers by holding back funds promised for modernising plant and equipment.

Allegedly taking advantage of Chávez' ill-health and weakened condition, governor Rangel is supposed to have pressurised him into signing an order to remove Sayago as president. On 25 February, Vice-President Elias Jaua formally announced that, by order of President Chávez, Elio Sayago was to be replaced by one of Rangel's cronies, Ángel Marcano (a government deputy in the National Assembly for 2005-2010, and member of the FSBT), as president of Alcasa. Jaua himself had drafted the order and the major reason given for Sayago's dismissal was that he had been responsible for trade union conflicts in the company – the very conflicts which those sacking him had instigated! Sayago later pointed out that, given Marcano had been one of the leaders of the thirty-four-day lock-out the previous year, his appointment was a "contradiction in terms".[87]

In a packed press conference on 29 February, 2012, Yasmín Chaurán, a CVG worker herself, reported that Ángel Marcano had already begun

---

86 Ness, and Azzellini, op cit.
87 Robertson, E., *Revolutionary Democracy in the Economy?* VA.com, 3 August, 2012.

undermining the structures of workers' control in the factory, by refusing to attend factory working group meetings and setting up a 'parallel apparatus' of six vice-presidents who were making appointments '*a dedo*' (arbitrarily). She argued that the 'sin' that cost Sayago his post was the ending of corrupt practices that had put a lot of money into private pockets. The press conference was followed by a centre-spread in *Tribuna Popular*, the PCV's paper, publicly criticising the "internal right-wing" within the revolution in Bolivar state. It warned that "harmful bureaucratic actions" emanating from the Bolivar state governance were "grinding down the revolutionary process" and working with transnational corporations to regain control of state industries in the region.

The matter was sufficiently serious for Chávez, despite being in Cuba for medical attention, to respond on 2 March: "I carried out changes there (Alcasa) in the directors' board, and I ask for support, unity and patriotic consciousness of the whole of the working class in the factories in Guayana". Chávez gave no reason for removing Sayago, but simply used his personal authority to get the workers to accept the decision. On 8 March, a spokesperson for the political team governing Bolivar state made great play of Chávez' endorsement of the decision to replace Sayago with Marcano. The spokesperson was José Ramón Rivero. No attempt was made to defend the indefensible, instead Rivero used the age-old trick of diverting attention by attacking the 'unacceptable behaviour' of those National Assembly members who had dared to criticise governor Rangel.

Workers' control at Alcasa was threatening long-standing and very profitable arrangements between international and local interests. To make matters worse, Alcasa was entering talks with other companies to persuade them do the same. What was clear was that the interests of the 'Bolivarian' bureaucrats at different levels of the state and national apparatus and the trade union movement coincided, in the last instance, with the interests of the oligarchs and multinational companies, and any form of workers' control threatened those interests.[88] Under Marcano, production at Alcasa steadily decreased, the unions within the plant were soon at each other's throats with no common policy and, despite five attempts to restart it, the main extrusion plant still lies idle. Alcasa was a prime example of how workers' control in a bourgeois state is a transitional phenomenon, it either leads on to the overthrow of capitalism or it will, itself, be overthrown.

---

88 Martín. J., 'Workers' Control vs Bureaucrats, Mafia and Multinationals in Bolivar', VA.com, 10 July, 2011.

10) SOCIALISM FOR THE TWENTY-FIRST CENTURY (FEBRUARY 2005)

Worker activists and socialists were beginning to see flaws in the revolutionary process. The state bureaucracy contained layers of people, especially at the top, who, although publicly endorsing Chávez' actions, privately did not believe in the revolutionary capacity of the masses; self-activity by the workers was perceived as something dangerous, a threat to privileges and perks. This pressure from below, combined with the intransigent opposition to even the meekest of reforms, had pushed Chávez to become more radical in his calls for workers to occupy factories, to make "the revolution within the revolution" by struggling against bureaucracy and, for the first time, to speak openly about socialism.

The language of Chávez both reflected and stimulated the growing consciousness of the masses. Attempts by the masses to take the revolution forward, to enact Chávez' calls and proposals, clashed with the reality that there were no channels by which these actions could be organised. Despite popular involvement in Bolivarian Circles, community projects, health centres, education, housing, etc. there were still no organisational structures in which the masses could discuss and organise how to overcome the resistance of governmental and regional bureaucracies, or to hold their leaders to account. This contradiction was because the capitalist mode of production and bourgeois state had both been left intact.

On the sixteenth anniversary of the *Caracazo*, in his *Aló Presidente* programme, Chávez made an appeal for the opening of a discussion on socialism within the MVR and the Bolivarian movement: "I am convinced… that the path to a new, better and possible world is not capitalism, the path is socialism". However, Chávez was not ready to define his concept of socialism: "…we will have to invent it, this is why this debate is so important, we must invent twenty-first century socialism". That Chávez deliberately differentiated his proposal from previous socialisms was significant.

It is true that every revolution has its own character, personality and historical antecedents and it is essential to recognise national specificity. But if Socialism for the Twenty-First Century was to be the Venezuelan road to socialism it had to, of necessity, include the lessons of the past. In particular, the need for a participatory democracy in which decisions made are binding on the leaders. Certainly, the Venezuelan masses, in common with previous revolutions, had demonstrated a colossal capacity for creativity and inventiveness, but that had highlighted the main weakness of the Bolivarian movement. There was no national structure that enabled the movement to generalise its experiences, to decide policy, to elect the leadership that would co-ordinate the revolutionary upsurge. Instead, the heterogeneous and largely arbitrary nature of the leadership meant there was ongoing confusion and conflict regarding both the aims and the means of the Bolivarian Revolution.

It was three years since the attempted coup and President Chávez, for all his radical social programme and fighting courage, his challenges to the power and privileges of the ruling class, and his resistance to the pressure of the imperialists, had never previously posed the question of socialism. To solve the structural problems of Venezuelan society and to protect the gains made, it was necessary for the government to introduce economic planning – to draw up a national plan based on the needs of the majority, not the profits of the minority. But the government could not plan what it did not control: key economic levers such as the banks remained in the hands of the rich and the state machine remained structured to serve the oligarchy, with many of the tops in the nationalised industries part of the problem, not the solution.

When he came to power in 1998, Chávez believed he could solve the problems of inequality, poverty, and misery within the limits of capitalism. His government went out of its way not to violate the private property rights of big land-owners, bankers and businessmen, but any attempt to seriously address the problems faced by the masses clashed head-on with an ultra-reactionary oligarchy which, en bloc, was quite prepared to overthrow a democratically-elected government by an armed insurrection. Chávez and many in the Bolivarian movement had been pushed into the conclusion: "Within the framework of capitalism it is impossible to solve the challenges of fighting against poverty, misery, exploitation, inequality". The revolutionary appeals of Chávez did not fall on deaf ears. They were eagerly listened to by millions of dispossessed workers and peasants in Bolivia, Ecuador, Peru, Argentina and Brazil. But would Chávez carry that analysis forward into action?

The hope and expectation on the political left was that the dynamic of the Bolivarian Revolution would now parallel the first years of the Cuban Revolution; and opening a debate about socialism was seen as representing an important point in the Venezuelan revolution with worldwide implications. For the first time in many years, the leader of a mass revolutionary movement had drawn the conclusion from his own experience that capitalism cannot solve the problems of the masses and that socialism is the only way forward. Now Chávez had to convert his words into deeds!

On 17 July, 2005 President Chávez, during his weekly television programme *Aló Presidente*, announced that nationalised companies would become Social Production Enterprises (*Empresas de Producción Social*, EPS); in all of which, solidarity, co-operation, complementarity, and equity would be more important than producing a profit, and which would help bring about Socialism of the Twenty-First Century. The President urged all co-operatives to become one of three types of EPS: communal production, communal distribution or communal services. Jointly, these would form the Communal Economic System (*Sistema Económico Comunal*, CES).

A major part of his speech was that if a factory was closed down by the employers "(it) will probably have to be expropriated... the workers should occupy, try to start production, and discuss the legal aspects later".[89] Workers in Venezuela were being encouraged to take the initiative and not wait for the government to give them the green light. Labour Minister, María Cristina Iglesias, urged unions, workers, and former employees to 'recover' their companies, arguing that such moves could help overcome Venezuela's dependence on imports. The UNT declared its support, and announced in mid-September, it would call on its members to occupy over 800 closed-down businesses.

In fact, only about forty of the 800 enterprises were occupied and even fewer were expropriated. It was immediately obvious that there was no government policy of any kind for expropriation. Occupying workers calling for expropriation were hindered by government bureaucrats and actively opposed by local authorities who, on many occasions, sent in the police and National Guard to eject them. A major factor was the failure of the UNT to deliver on its own statement. It can rightly be said that inactivity, and in some cases even hostility, to factory occupations was the mark of the UNT over this period. Chávez' call for action was effectively smothered by the bureaucratic apparatus, which justified its lack of promotion of, or support for, occupations on the grounds that it could respond only to processes self-initiated by the rank and file.

The oligarchs, ever sensitive to any threat to their authority or property were up in arms. An intense media campaign claimed the expropriations were illegal, arbitrary and confrontational. *Fedecámaras* demanded "an immediate end to arbitrary and illegal actions against private property... (and)... respect of the right to work for workers and employees of the companies affected". The petty bourgeoisie were whipped up by being told their homes could be taken from them. In upper-middle-class neighbourhoods in the main cities (Caracas, Valencia, etc.), rallies were called against expropriations, but the live coverage of these events revealed a poor attendance.

The media campaign of the oligarchy was to protect their sacred right to retain property filched from the state, pretending to defend the national interest while exporting their money and investing it abroad, defending their

---

89 www.rebelion.org., 22 July, 2005.

right to keep factories and land idle in order to undermine the government. These would be enduring themes in the private media and would rise to a crescendo every time the government took a significant step forward in the interests of the peasants and workers.

Venezuela could not advance towards social equality while the *latifundia*, factories and banks remained in the hands of the oligarchs. Chávez' call, while enormously positive and raising the question of who held the power, was still constrained within a capitalist framework and, as such, was doomed to fail. Solving the problems of the Venezuelan people was only possible on the basis of common ownership of the means of production and the democratic planning of the economy. That was the only way of overcoming economic sabotage and achieving real economic development. It was also the only way to build any kind of effective Socialism for the Twenty-First Century. But it was at just this point that the Bolivarian Revolution drew back.

The EPSs were soon central to the government's strategy for stimulating internal production and exchange through the investment of oil money in previously neglected sectors of society; for Venezuela to stop importing what could be produced nationally.[90] In theory, EPSs were to be a central element of the "economic turnaround in the direction of Socialism for the Twenty-First Century". However, Yaffe has accurately described this initiative as the Bolivarian government attempting to avoid a head-on confrontation with the oligarchs:

> Instead of dismantling the old apparatus and infrastructure of capitalism, it has attempted to build a parallel apparatus to create an alternative system of social relations, production, distribution and political power.[91]

In April 2006 the government passed the Communal Council Law for the creation of communal councils throughout Venezuela, formalising the shift in emphasis from co-operatives to communal activities. A state-owned company had to become an EPS, and any goods or services it needed had to be acquired from an EPS. The EPSs were expected to spread like a red tide across Venezuela, gradually engulfing all economic enterprises until the country woke up one morning as socialist. This was a re-presentation of the failed ideas of the utopian socialists of the nineteenth century, now to be funded by oil revenues.

By early 2007, many hundreds of communal ventures had been opened. These EPSs were to be based on equality, fairness and social needs;

90 Purcell, T., *The Political Economy of Social Production Companies in Venezuela*, Latin American Perspectives, 2013, 40(3)146-168.

91 Yaffe, H., *Venezuela: Building a Socialist Communal Economy?*, International Critical Thought, 2015, 5(1) 23–41.

work responsibilities would be decided democratically, no employee's position was meant to give him or her any privilege. EPSs were expected to invest at least ten per cent of any surplus in local social projects and infrastructure, integrating themselves into the local communities. The priority for an EPS was social benefit (termed 'social profit') and production had to be directed toward fulfilling Venezuela's social needs rather than monetary profitability and capital accumulation. In line with this communalistic approach, in October 2005, the president signed a decree by which all EPSs were required to undertake work in the communities where they were located, such as maintenance of schools and, for this reason, representatives of the local community had a right to be present at EPS management meetings.

Yaffe has described the heroic efforts, hard work, ingenuity and innovation of the workers in their attempts to get the EPSs running efficiently and profitably. She also describes the numerous challenges and obstacles they face: no mechanism for the rational allocation of resources, no mechanism for the sharing of information, not even a central inventory of machines and equipment. Because the EPSs are invariably small, lacking experience and separate, the very same problems have to be solved again and again, wasting time and resources. A major government initiative was the building of millions of new homes. Because the state does not own the full chain of production, the door is opened for the private sector to make huge profits by, for example, transporting materials at exorbitant prices from one EPS to another. Estimates suggest that the final cost to the state is approximately three times the production cost. But this lack of coherence also allows private sector sabotage. For example, delivering necessary nails a week late costs the private supplier little or nothing, but it can paralyse an entire housing project. Yaffe reports that the private sector disrupts production on a grand scale, with the clear political objective of sabotaging the Bolivarian Revolution.

Social ownership came in two quite different types. The 'indirect', enterprises managed by the state (e.g. PDVSA) which, despite all the hype, are left largely alone. Chávez, shortly before his death, declared that PDVSA was abjectly failing in its progress towards an EPS, but took no action, Rafael Ramírez remained head of the PDVSA, no call was directed to the workers of the PDVSA to take control of the company; with a metaphorical shrug of his shoulders Chávez classified the problem as "cultural" and moved on.[92] The 'direct' type, the more than 200 'socialist factories' funded by the state would, it was said, strengthen Venezuelan independence and sovereignty, by establishing a national production network to reduce imports and foreign dependence. These direct EPSs, were the supposed embryos of the new

---

92 Chávez, H., *Strike at the Helm*, 20 October, 2012, Monthly Review.

socialist economy, but most were too small to compete even with private companies in Venezuela, let alone internationally. Only about ten per cent of ESPs make a surplus, the remainder fail to fill their production targets most often because of over-charging by private sub-contractors and obstruction of production by bourgeois elements, usually in the state machine.[93]

Nevertheless, co-operatives and communal activities remain a major factor in the lives of poor Venezuelans, because the government has periodically extended their powers by, for example, providing them with the materials and means for house construction, and giving them responsibility for delivering the state-sponsored, house-to-house food distribution.[94]

10.1) *LATIFUNDIA* AND PARLIAMENTARY ELECTIONS

On Wednesday, 21 September, 2005, during a ceremony for aerospace technicians, Chávez stated: "The *latifundio* is one of the most powerful obstacles for the development of the country and as long as it exists, it is impossible to begin the foundations of progress".[95] This is, of course, the classic argument of the bourgeois revolution but in the era of imperialism, in semi-colonial countries, it threatened the entire rotten system.

Four days later Chávez renewed the offensive in his television programme, *Aló Presidente*, from *La Marqueseña*, a large landed estate of about 8,500 hectares (21,000 acres) which the INTI had recently declared to be state property. According to the President, the Azpurua family had held the land illegally for decades and now had to return it to the state, to use for the government's land reform programme. The land seized was eventually given to eighty peasant families and the sixty workers at the ranch. Many land-owners had been found to have no property titles, or deeds, for the land they occupied; they had simply extended the boundaries of their estates arbitrarily, illegally appropriating land that belonged to the state or to poor peasants. The INTI had plans to assess land titles in 317 *latifundia* up and down the country. Genaro Mendez, president of *Fedenaga*, the association of cattle ranchers and *latifundia* owners responded, "the land that is threatened is the whole of Venezuela…"

Chávez replied in a speech on 16 October:

> The capitalist economic system is a system of domination imposed on our people so that a wealthy minority dominates an impoverished majority. This is economic tyranny. And this economic tyranny is still intact. We are going

93 Yaffe, op cit.
94 Ellner, S., *Social Programs in Venezuela…* VA.com, 7 November, 2017.
95 Wilpert, G., *Chávez Highlights Venezuela's Land Reform*, 26 September, 2005, VA.com

to break it up once and for all through a revolutionary process of economic and social liberation.

He again demanded: "wherever there is a factory that is closed it must be handed over to the workers, wherever there is a plot of land that is idle it must be given to the peasants... we must break with the capitalist model". The masses of workers and peasants at the heart of the Bolivarian movement whole-heartedly supported these appeals, but also wanted organised action. Certainly, the conditions were favourable, the Bolivarian Revolution had brought the masses to their feet but the lack of political understanding, the absence of a party with such a perspective meant the strength of the movement was nowhere fully utilised. Venezuelan Marxists strove to make the masses conscious of the real meaning of their actions, to understand the objective necessity of a break with capitalism, but were unable to make good the main weakness of the Bolivarian movement, which was (and is) its lack of a revolutionary party.

In 2008, the government launched a Food Sovereignty initiative to radically transform agriculture. The new effort was to be a means to solve the problem of rural poverty and energise food production. Any head of household or young person could apply to become a leader of a co-operative, regardless of whether s/he had any experience of working the land. By the end of 2008, the INTI claimed to have redistributed more than 4.38 million hectares of 'recovered' land to over one hundred thousand families and co-operative-owned farms.

The bureaucracy and complexity of state aid meant that many of these initiatives received investment and advice too little and too late. For example, credit was provided by the Agricultural Bank of Venezuela; infrastructure – provision of water and rural roads – was provided by the National Institute of Rural Development; technical assistance and training was provided by the Foundation for Capacity Building and Innovation to Support the Agrarian Revolution; assistance in bringing products to the market was provided by the Venezuelan Food Corporation; advice on how to develop as an agro-ecological enterprise was given by the National Institute of Agricultural Investigation; and finally the provision of the land itself, of deeds etc., was the responsibility of the INTI. This vast array of institutions was (and is), of course, grossly inefficient, confusing and offered golden opportunities for corrupt practices. Wilpert reports that the INTI had retained in its files about 30,000 cartas agrarias. No-one could say why, but in July 2016, a director at the INTI was arrested for demanding millions of Bolívars in bribes to finalise the transfer of land deeds. It was no wonder that many co-operatives were soon struggling, failing to achieve necessary levels of production, to gain access to internal markets, and to repay loans. The most harmful pressure on the peasants was the inefficiency and corruption of the state institutions.[96]

The peasants were, in their majority, expected to participate in co-operatives which were attached to, or were themselves EPSs intended to transform the agricultural sector from a capitalist to a socialist model of production with the constraint that all food-production had to supply domestic demand first. However, these were operating within a capitalist system which functions according to its own laws, so that, even with the government attempting to empower small agrarian producers, the reality meant that, in the end, the peasants faced the same inequalities as the *campesinos* always had.

Pre-election polls for the 4 December, 2005, parliamentary election for the National Assembly showed the opposition would struggle to gain even a third of the votes cast and would lose over fifty of the seventy-six seats they held. Rather than face such public humiliation, the opposition decided to hide their weakness by boycotting the election. The Chavistas gained 116 of the deputies and their allies, the PCV, Podemos and PPT another thirty-five. The Bolivarian Revolution had total control of the National Assembly, enough to legally abolish capitalism if it so decided.

However, the Bolivarian leaders had no perspective of ending capitalism in Venezuela; they had set themselves the task of managing a 'mixed economy'. Not prepared to take decisive action against the oligarchs, they prevaricated, retreated and then attempted a compromise, which naturally exposed them to pressure, bullying and blackmail by the oligarchy and imperialism. For too many of these Bolivarians, 'defence of democracy' meant freedom for private ownership, with revolutionaries constrained to act within the existing bourgeois law. One of the arguments heard was classical social democratic: "The economy is in a mess, we have to fix the problems before we can introduce socialism". This was, of course, the cart before the horse, the economic problems could be solved only by introducing socialist measures.

Marxists have long argued that it is impossible for the working class to carry out the socialist transformation of society using the existing bourgeois state, because the bourgeois state was created by capitalists to serve their needs. Attempts by the masses to advance 'towards socialism' within the existing Venezuelan state inevitably lead to clashes with a bureaucracy that serves the state, does not believe in socialism, or in the ability of the masses to consciously participate in the leadership of the country. How could state functionaries, bureaucrats and others left over from the old, discredited Fourth Republic be relied upon to progress the interests of the masses? Such a question answers itself. The corollary is also true, how could the Bolivarian

---

96 Wilpert, G., *Chávez' Legacy of Land Reform*, Review of Agrarian Studies, 3(2).

Revolution progress towards socialism if it did not recognise the class nature of the state?

The vast majority of Venezuelans sided firmly with Chávez and wanted to push the revolution forward. The main and immediate task of Marxists was to organise the advanced layer and educate them as cadres with a correct programme and method, so that they could provide an alternative leadership to the reformists in the Bolivarian movement and win the Bolivarian masses to the ideas of Marxism. This would have to be done as part of the Bolivarian movement because there was no other possibility of melding with the revolutionary mass movement. Any attempt to do otherwise would have separated the revolutionary layer from the popular masses.

11) LAUNCH OF PSUV AND THE CONSTITUTIONAL REFERENDUM

During 2006 the oligarchy significantly advanced its strategy of economic sabotage, particularly in the food sector where wholesale distribution was largely in the lorries of *Grupo Polar*. The model had been successfully tested in Chile and again in Nicaragua, and was now the agreed strategy in Venezuela. The measures would be stepped up before every election and/or referendum.

This was the context in which the UNT held its Second Congress. However, the UNT leadership was more intent on jockeying for positions than solving the problems of the workers. The Congress was scheduled to begin on Thursday, 25 May, 2006, but the 2,000+ delegates had to wait until the following day due to arguments over delegate accreditation, always a sign of hard-fought battles on the floor of the Congress. This Congress was all the more relevant because, on 3 December, there would be a presidential election. Any rational observer would have expected the union to agree to take a leading role in the election campaign and used it to publicise its solutions to the grave problems from which the workers (and the vast majority of the population) continued to suffer. Far from it, the entire congress centred on the issue of the leadership elections. Instead of addressing economic and political questions the elections emphasised personalities, with the inevitable mud-slinging that served only to smother discussions on policy and programme. The congress ended in chaos, fist fights, walkouts and the splintering of the UNT, marking its end as a united force for some years.

The FSBT had only about one third the Congress delegates, but was the current within the UNT that was closest to the MVR tops. In January 2007, Chávez appointed Jose Ramón Rivero, a leader of the FSBT faction, as Labour Minister. He then used his position to intervene in industrial disputes to advance the FSBT at the expense of other currents within the

UNT, even to the extent of siding with the bosses in specific disputes. The FSBT allied itself increasingly closer with the government and, in April 2008, it was Labour Minister Rivero who announced the formation of a new national union federation and called on unions to disaffiliate from the UNT. The FSBT then cuddled up with the more reactionary elements within the government, increasingly acting as a brake on the Bolivarian Revolution.

It was obvious that, in the run-up to the December 2006 Presidential election, many people were noticing a heightened scarcity of basic foodstuffs. Supermarkets and markets, both in the private sector and the public distribution network, were short of milk powder, chicken, cooking oil, cheese, sardines, refined sugar, and black beans – a staple in Venezuela. The bourgeois media carried hysterical campaigns aimed at inducing panic buying in order to exacerbate the shortages and, more importantly, to create dissatisfaction amongst the social base of the revolution. The oligarchs were attempting to grab the revolution by its throat. Now the private media did something it had never done before: it championed the health of the poor, of children, and the elderly.

The government attempted price controls, but food producers avoided these by selling their products on the black market, selling to foreign companies and re-importing, or by diverting production to products that were not regulated. For example, milk was regulated but cheese was not, plain rice was regulated but flavoured rice was not (with Polar foods, for example, ninety per cent of rice produced was flavoured). The bosses blamed the government for causing the food shortages, saying price controls meant it was no longer profitable to produce items such as milk, so the population would have to go without.

The bosses' organisations demanded the government remove all controls saying they would then respond by producing more goods. In fact, the situation pleaded for the opposite course – nationalisation of food production and distribution under the democratic control of workers, peasants, and communal councils. FNCEZ, the peasant organisation, was right when it responded to the refusal of processing plants to buy their crops, especially sugar cane, by saying to the bosses: "If you refuse to feed us we will take over your factories". This should have been the practice nationwide.

One factor not mentioned in the bourgeois media was that some shortages were due to the improved diet and nutrition of the most downtrodden layers of the population. The actions of the Chavista government had given them increased purchasing power, and, as revealed by the Venezuelan-American Chamber of Commerce and Industry, between 2004 and 2006, the poorest sections of the population had their real incomes doubled. By organising artificial scarcity, the opposition was ensuring the creation of a parallel black market with high-priced goods, which it hoped would neutralise the effect of increased purchasing power and controlled prices. It aimed to demoralise those layers of the population who were hardest hit and who constituted the social base of the revolution. 'What is the point of a revolution if you cannot buy milk anymore?' was the feeling the counter-revolution wanted to induce among the poorest sections of the population.

The reaction of the government was a combination of appeals to business to increase production, massive imports of goods and their distribution through the state-run company, Mercal (*Mercados de Alimentos, C.A.*), to provide subsidised food and basic goods through a nationwide chain of stores. Despite the enormous barrage of propaganda to the contrary, there were few expropriations of abandoned companies in the food production chain and only mild measures against the most blatant examples of hoarding, corruption and speculation.

However, because Mercal was not under democratic workers' control, it was riddled with corruption. Large amounts of produce were leaking onto the black market, not through petty pilfering, though there was plenty of that, but because of crooked bureaucrats diverting whole containers of food. The economy was, and remains, the Achilles heel of the revolution, half-hearted measures weakly applied have failed to end the reality of economic sabotage. The reformists in the government shrug their shoulders and call for more public money, borrowed against future oil revenues, to spend on imports and so avoid confrontation with the oligarchy and its agents.

Chávez declared the existence of a social (but not socialist) state and called on the masses to struggle for socialism while accepting that Venezuela would have a 'mixed economy'. He carried out expropriations, but continued to support MPs, governors and mayors discredited for their anti-worker practices. Such contradictions reflected the different class pressures that bore down on him. His programme of democratic and national reforms inevitably came into conflict with a parasitic capitalist system and this pushed him to the left time and time again. Chávez increasingly used language that was critical of capitalism but, while a revolutionary leader, he was not a Marxist intervening in events with a clear, revolutionary programme.

The prevailing mood among the masses continued to be one of waiting for the proposals of President Chávez to be implemented, but with a growing sense of unease. Class contradictions were growing and intensifying within the Bolivarian movement, different tendencies were beginning to crystallise, revealing that not everyone was fighting for the same aims and ideas.

The presidential elections held on 3 December, 2006, were won by Chávez with the widest margin in the history of Venezuela: 62.8 per cent of votes cast to his opponent's 36.9 per cent. Chávez won in all twenty-four states, but the MVR was not a democratic party and its leaders had exercised a tight grip over the election campaign. The major slogan was: '10 million votes!', with '*por amor*' (for love) and '*Chávez, victoria de Venezuela*' (Chávez, Venezuela's victory) the slogans preferred by the party bureaucrats. Standing in contradiction was Chávez' own pledge to "nationalise everything that was privatised" by previous administrations, focusing on the "strategic industries" of oil, cement, steel and telecommunications.

This was the first election campaign after Chávez declared socialism as the aim of the revolution. As the campaign progressed, he spoke at mass rallies in increasingly radical language, receiving an enthusiastic reception. Simultaneously, the opposition campaign and the bourgeois media chose to run a campaign based on Chávez' 'communism': they will take away your house, your children, etc., and managed to get as many as 300,000 at their main rallies. This was a factor in radicalising both the masses and Chávez himself. He increasingly posed the choice between the Bolivarian Revolution and imperialism in terms of: if you vote for me, you vote for socialism. In his victory speech on election night Chávez said "Long live the socialist revolution". And added:

> I said that 3 December was not a point of arrival, but a point of departure… Today, a new epoch begins, that we can sum up in four points. The central idea is the deepening, widening and extending of the socialist revolution. More than sixty per cent of the people has not voted for Chávez but for a project that has a name: Venezuelan Socialism.[97]

On 15 December, 2006, almost two weeks after his massive electoral victory, Chávez made a speech, broadcast on national TV, in which he made clear his belief that a new stage had opened up for the Bolivarian Revolution: "we are going towards socialism", though "I haven't got a blueprint, we must build it from below, from within, our own socialist model". Of course, the reformists and moderates within the Bolivarian movement also talked about socialism, but only to ensure it was a watered-down socialism with no anti-capitalist content. Importantly, Chávez' speech contained the call to form a new party: The United Socialist Party of Venezuela (*Partido Socialista Unido de Venezuela*, PSUV).

This speech was a conscious attempt to give the Bolivarian movement an organised democratic structure, built from the bottom up. If successful, this

---

97 Fox, M., *Chávez Inaugurates Blitzkrieg of Projects* VA.com, 29 November, 2006.

would have remedied the key weaknesses of the revolutionary movement in Venezuela: the lack of a mass revolutionary organisation to give the Bolivarian movement an organised expression. However, this was quite a different method of party building from Lenin's, with consequences that would be apparent all too soon. The Chavistas had absolute control of parliament and the presidential vote showed Chávez retained massive support among the population. It appeared that the balance of forces remained ripe for snuffing capitalism out in Venezuela once and for all, and quite easily. Would the new PSUV be the means of doing that?

At the swearing in of his new government, Hugo Chávez gave a fiery speech in which he proposed a series of radical changes to the constitution, declaring it was necessary to "dismantle the bourgeois state". In that he was absolutely right. Not only was the Venezuelan state riddled with active supporters of the old regime, but its very structure was inimical to socialism. The proposed changes to the constitution would be subject to a referendum on 2 December, 2007.

11.1) THE CONSTITUTIONAL REFERENDUM DEFEAT

The recent nationalisations of CANTV and EDC (with compensation), the promise to re-nationalise steel maker SIDOR, and the call to set up the PSUV were, for the oligarchy, clear signs that Chávez was moving in a dangerously leftward direction. The oligarchs were, as ever, anxious to present a scenario to the world in which Chávez would be seen as a 'dictator'. The private cable TV station RCTV was due to have its licence renewed at the end of May 2007, but the government awarded the licence to Venezuela Social Television instead. The counter-revolution prepared to test its strength on the streets using 'free speech' as a mobilising issue. The irony was that the group of which RCTV was the hub, was an empire that controlled sixty-six per cent of transmitting capacity and eighty per cent of the production of all media content in the country: 'defence of free speech' was the slogan of precisely those who proposed to monopolise it.[98]

The oligarchs were reluctant to attempt mass demonstrations; instead, gangs of thugs erected burning barricades during the night and terrorised neighbourhoods. During the day there were 'peaceful demonstrations', mainly of students from private, and some elite state universities. Active in these demonstrations was the organised counter-revolution (the CIA and its paid agents) throwing bricks and Molotov cocktails.

These noisy adventures could not hide the fact that the balance of forces remained extremely favourable to the revolution, as confirmed by the more

---

98 Ciccariello-Maher, G., *Zero Hour for Venezuela's RCTV*, VA.com, 29 May, 2007.

than 5 million that registered to join the PSUV, enough to brush aside the counter-revolutionary gangs occupying the streets in the East of Caracas. However, it is not enough for a revolutionary movement to have the support of the majority of the population; the initiative cannot be in the hands of the counter-revolution.

In November 2007, Chávez made a personal appeal for workers in every workplace to set up Socialist Workers' Councils (SWCs). Workers responded enthusiastically. Thousands of existing workers' councils adopted the new designation and, throughout the country, many new councils were launched, usually on the initiative of a new generation of young workers, who had only recently woken to political activity, and who threw themselves into the struggle to establish SWCs.

The SWCs were launched with no legal provisions or regulations covering their activities or responsibilities, so workers improvised. The majority of these councils took on the improvement of workers' rights and conditions, but they also assumed responsibility for implementing some sort of *cogestión*. As part of the latter, the more militant demanded access to the financial dealings of the company and a say in all the main decisions. Though they were attempting to implement an appeal by the President himself, the workers faced hostility and harassment at all levels. Often the SWCs were ignored, but sometimes workers were accused of counter-revolutionary activities and sacked for attempting to set up SWCs. This occurred in both the private and public sectors.[99]

Fourth Republic bureaucrats allied themselves with new 'Bolivarian' bureaucrats in their common fear of workers. One scandalous case was the harassment of the promoters of the SWCs at *Fundacomunal*, an institution whose purpose was creating communal councils such as *Misión Madres del Barrio* (a social programme for mothers in poor neighbourhoods). That an institution, whose purpose is to help establish organisations through which communities can run their own affairs democratically, used repression against its own staff for wanting to have a democratic say in the running of their own institution is Kafkaesque. A more recent example of such repression was in 2016 when Tromerca, the state-run tram system in Mérida State, fired workers quite illegally for attempting to organise a SWC.[100]

The FSBT came out in opposition to SWCs, particularly in the basic industries in the Guayana region. Here there were (and are) particularly close links between the local FSBT tops, the local PSUV leadership including the state governor, and top managers in the CVG. Azzellini

99 Pearson, T., *First National Meeting of SWCs*, VA.com, 24 May, 2011.
100 Dobson, P., *Venezuelan Constituent Assembly Approves Workers' Councils Law*, VA.com, 3 February, 2018.

suggests this is a hang-over from the days of the Fourth Republic, when the AD and COPEI ran the unions with "a corporate structure for private appropriation of public goods and funds... creating a culture of theft that in many places has remained in effect".[101] As *cogestión* became more of a threat to the activities of these crooks, so the resistance and active opposition of the PSUV tops and the state machine increased. *Cogestión* was an immediate threat to the material benefits of state, party and company bureaucrats, and so came under direct and continuous attack until, during Chávez' terminal illness, a coup would be carried out to remove the most radical worker-presidents.

The PCV sponsored a 'Special Law on Workers' Councils' empowering and giving legal protection to the SWCs. This was put before the National Assembly in 2007, but no decision was reached. This happened on several subsequent occasions, indicating the political strength of the interests opposing this move. The question is: why didn't Chávez support the PCV proposal? A law on SWCs is still promised, at some unspecified time in the future.

Chávez' proposed amendments to the constitution were formally announced in July; sixty-nine articles of the Venezuelan constitution were to be amended for the country to begin the transition to 'Socialism for the Twenty-First Century'. The Episcopal Conference of Catholic bishops declared the proposed reforms "morally unacceptable" and paid for a two-page advertisement in *Ultimas Noticias*, claiming that the State would take people's children away from them and that freedom of religion would be abolished. Every Sunday, the Church preached from its pulpits against Chávez and 'godless communism' and was supported in its crusade by the privately-owned newspapers, TV and radio stations. These latter were able to carry this hysterical campaign of lies and slander against Chávez, the Revolution and socialism only because the Revolution had been far too generous, far too tolerant, far too patient, and far too soft. Despite the media's open collaboration in the coup attempt, the Revolution had made no attempts to limit 'press freedom', it left this weapon in the hands of the oligarchs with which to sabotage the Revolution, with the goal of ultimately destroying it.

Opposition students played a crucial role. They had received vast amounts of publicity when challenging the non-renewal of the RCTV broadcast license, gaining support within the student body by claiming they were 'standing up for free speech' and denying affiliation to any political party. Their largest demonstration numbered 50,000 and attracted much publicity, but more for the accompanying violence than the number of demonstrators. After the

---

101 Azzellini, D., *Communes and Workers' Control in Venezuela*, Haymarket, 2018.

referendum, the Cato Institute, located in Washington, DC, reported it had awarded the Venezuelan student movement $500,000 for acting as the storm troops of the opposition during the referendum. But the Chavista students had over 200,000 on their rallies. In the ideological struggle for the youth, the Revolution attracted far greater numbers than the counter-revolution. But to take the movement forward there needed to be a programme of action that would enable the students to unite in common cause with the workers. Some students did this by support work around the factory occupations, but what the campaign made clear was the need for a youth organisation of the PSUV.

Regarding the referendum itself, the bureaucrats within the government and the Bolivarian movement again showed their complete inability to organise a serious mass campaign. How could they, when they themselves were opposed to the proposed changes? Many 'Chavista' governors and mayors actively sabotaged the 'Yes' campaign because they correctly saw that democratisation of the state would mean the end of their perks. It was both significant and disappointing that while there was a clause stipulating non-discrimination on the basis of sexual orientation there was no parallel proposal to decriminalise abortion, access to which was, and remains, severely restricted. These false 'Chavistas' failed to answer the lies of the opposition. They failed to publicise the many points in the reformed constitution that would have benefited the working class, such as the thirty-six-hour week.

For all the talk about Socialism for the Twenty-First Century, the oligarchy was still firmly entrenched and using its wealth and power to sabotage, undermine and roll-back the gains of the Revolution. The right-wing media was free to spew out lies and slanders, peasant activists were murdered and nothing was done about it. Despite the reforms of the government, which undoubtedly had greatly helped the poor and disadvantaged, the majority still lived in poverty. The *caudillos* and capitalists got away with open economic sabotage, substantially worsening the living conditions of the popular masses. All this had a cumulative effect.

The masses wanted decisive action against landlords and capitalists, action against corrupt governors and officials. There was a growing weariness of going to the polls every year being promised changes, followed by a lack of concrete action. Furthermore, the referendum was not an election in which to clearly vote for Chávez or an opposition candidate. The referendum took place on 2 December, 2007, and gave Chávez the first election defeat of his nine-year presidency (50.65 per cent to 49.35 per cent). The result, as expected, was greeted with jubilation by the opposition. For the first time in a decade they had secured a victory. Chávez went on television accepting the results, saying that he would continue to struggle to build socialism. However, the joy of the reactionaries was exaggerated. They had won only because a large number of Chavistas had not voted.

Despite the referendum result, the real balance of class forces was shown by the rallies at the end of the campaign. The opposition moved heaven and earth to mobilise its mass base and succeeded in assembling a large crowd. However, the next day the streets of central Caracas were flooded by a sea of red shirts and banners. The two rallies revealed that the active base of the Chavistas was five to eight times bigger than that of the opposition. The decisive force, the working class, in its overwhelming majority, was on the side of the Revolution.

The Bolivarian Revolution was still holding its ground and, in certain areas, making progress, but in a piecemeal, ad-hoc manner that reflected the lack of any commonly agreed idea on just where the Revolution was going. Its great weakness remained the lack of a subjective factor in the sense of a revolutionary party. But it was the very dynamism of the Revolution that made it so hard for the development of a Marxist party, in particular the role played by Chávez, who made one radical announcement after another in support of the struggles of the workers and peasants but, no matter how militant they sounded, they always remained within the bounds of the bourgeois state. The majority of Bolivarians who voiced criticisms still believed that building a revolutionary tendency, with a clear strategy of how the working class could take power, was secondary to the practical work of building Socialism for the Twenty-First Century. Activism substituted for analysis.

A key element in the workers' movement had been the factory occupations, nationalisations under *cogestión*. In Inveval a small group of Marxists was leading the struggle for workers' control and having to fight battles they could never have foreseen: for new sources of parts and materials, against sabotage by the state bureaucracy, and against the tops of the state oil company the PDVSA. Though successfully recruiting workers to their organisation, they had the central problem that an isolated Inveval could not survive amid a capitalist economy. Efforts were made to link up with other occupied factories and factories threatened with closure by establishing Freteco to co-ordinate common struggles across the country. Such co-ordination was anathema for the bureaucracy, which had put considerable effort into isolating the different factories, asphyxiating the movement, starting with the more advanced forms of workers' control. First, they starved them of cash and resources, and then, when the workers were worn down, they replaced the elected leader with their own appointee.

Ultimately, the economic question is decisive. As Trotsky had said, the masses can sacrifice their today for their tomorrow only up to a certain point. For the masses, the question of socialism and revolution are not abstract questions, but very concrete ones. They had shown a high degree of revolutionary maturity and willingness to fight. But the oligarchs and their CIA analysts had rolled with the punches and countered by planning to have the situation drag on until the masses tired. They planned to generate a mood of apathy and scepticism in the most backward layers, leaving the most advanced elements isolated. When that moment arrived, the counter-revolution would strike. Those who argued that the Revolution had gone too far too fast, that it was necessary to reach a compromise to save the Revolution, were playing into the hands of the oligarchs.

Food shortages throughout 2007 and 2008 were part of everyday life for millions of Venezuelans and reached major proportions during the run-up to the constitutional reform referendum. It was certainly a factor in the collapse in Bolivarian votes in working-class areas. It was not the food scarcity itself that was the reason why 3 million abstained in the referendum. Most of them knew from their own experience that food scarcity was created by a deliberate campaign of sabotage by the oligarchy. The crucial factor was that the government was seen not to be doing anything about it.

For example, in March 2007 the government had passed the 'Law against Sabotage, Hoarding and Speculation', which allowed for the seizure of food stocks and the expropriation of those involved. However, as with so many things that adversely affected the oligarchs, this law had not been implemented in any serious way. Chávez himself became frustrated by the lack of action and tasked the Minister of Agriculture, Elias Jaua, to produce a list of those companies involved in sabotaging food distribution and production in order to expropriate them. Do something or resign, was Chávez' demand, but still no serious action was taken. However, the defeat of the constitutional reforms made it impossible to continue with merely face-saving measures. In *Aló Presidente* on 22 January, 2008, Chávez announced his personal intervention against "the monopolies and rackets". In two weeks more than 13,000 tons of food was seized. This figure gives an indication of the scale of the sabotage, but it was only the tip of an iceberg. Elias Jaua was promoted to be both Minister of Agriculture and Vice-President in January 2010.

The National Guard targeted Polar group's food distribution chain and confirmed that food scarcity was largely a deliberate campaign organised by the oligarchy against the Bolivarian Revolution. The biggest seizures were in the regions bordering Colombia, where convoys of trucks were smuggling produce to Colombia. On 24 January, twenty-seven lorries belonging to

Alimentos Polar were seized, containing 165 tonnes of maize flour and 350 tonnes of basic foodstuffs including many which had been scarce in Venezuelan shops for many months (i.e., sugar, rice, pasta and milk). The goods seized by the National Guard were then sold at regulated prices.

Food was not the most valuable commodity smuggled across the border into Colombia. State-subsidised gasoline was sold in Venezuela at about one tenth a Bolivar per litre, whilst in neighbouring Colombia and Brazil the price was over 200 Bolívars per litre. This created a massive black market in Venezuelan gasoline. It was more profitable than smuggling narcotics and was a major business for the bourgeois and paramilitaries. Fuel subsidies amounted to nearly one quarter of government expenditure in 2015, and estimates showed that smuggling using heavy freight vehicles accounted for an annual loss of over US$5 billion to Venezuela. Food smuggling gave a much lower profit and was undertaken for political, not financial, reasons. In 2016, the price of petrol would be increased to one Bolivar per litre.

In January 2008, as part of the Food Sovereignty Plan, the PDVAL – a subsidiary of the PDVSA – was launched. It was expected to expand rapidly to purchase food on the international market and distribute it throughout Venezuela, with the aim of ensuring basic foodstuffs for all Venezuelans.[102] In the same month, while inaugurating the first Socialist Dairy Plant in Machiques, Zulia, Chávez declared that companies that sold their milk directly to foreign multinationals above the regulated price would be expropriated, along with the dairy plants involved. He repeated the same message when he announced the nationalisation of the *Lacteos Los Andes* milk processing plant and a chain of slaughterhouses, which gave the state control over forty per cent of milk processing and seventy per cent of the meat processing sectors.

But food production remained within a mixed economy and was controlled by bureaucrats whose loyalty lay with the capitalists. The only guarantee of food sovereignty was to nationalise the whole of the food and agricultural industry and run it under democratic workers' control. This would include not only processing plants and distribution, but also the *latifundia*. The workers, the real producers, needed to be brought together as employees of a national food producing company, publicly owned and managed by themselves. This would have allowed the planning, co-ordination and control of everything related to food, from production of the raw materials to the processing and distribution of the final products.

Instead, in late summer of 2008, the government again offered the hand of compromise to the oligarchs. Prices of around 400 products were raised,

---

102 PDVSA, *Venezuelan Government Launches New State Food Company*, VA.com, 22 January, 2008.

with the price of milk increased by a third. The ranchers saw this as weakness on the government's part, claiming it was too little, too late, and demanded a 100 per cent increase. No amount of concessions would satisfy the oligarchy, short of ending the revolution. Economic sabotage was intensified, hoarding of basic foodstuffs increased, as was making small changes to production lines so that the end product was not on the regulated list. The end result was even greater scarcity on the supermarket shelves.

On 28 February, 2009, Chávez decreed state intervention in Polar's rice processing plant in Guárico. The workers at the plant supported this measure and turned production to wholly unmodified rice with enthusiasm. Outraged at Polar's tricks to avoid price control, Chávez on *Aló Presidente*, on 1 March threatened: "we will expropriate all of their plants, and convert them from private property into social property". The government then decreed compulsory production quotas from 3 March, for all companies producing white rice, sugar, flour, cooking oil and foodstuffs, to ensure companies produced these items at the controlled price rather than divert production to non-regulated products.

Then, on Wednesday, 4 March, 2009, Chávez announced the expropriation of the rice plants owned by Cargill, a US-owned multinational food company. This rice-processing plant in Portuguesa was refusing to produce rice at the regulated market price, using the dodge of adding artificial flavouring; 2,400 tons of this presentation rice was found. Documentation recovered at the plant showed that massive quantities of rice had been smuggled to Colombia to be sold at unregulated prices.

Two days later Chávez signed an official decree expropriating the Polar rice plants, warning: "my hand will not shake when it comes to expropriating the whole of the Polar group if they are found to be breaking the law". In what was a very radical speech, President Chávez dismissed the need to conciliate with the ruling class: "There cannot be any agreement with the oligarchy or agreements at the top with anybody; I will make sure that we put our foot down on the accelerator of the Revolution". He went further stating it was time to "dismantle the old bourgeois state, before it dismantles us". A striking feature of the actions against Polar was the response of workers. Once the ice was broken with the state intervention, workers from the food industry all over Venezuela began to call for action against the sabotage by 'their' capitalists. Wherever officials of the INDEPABIS (National Institute in Defence of People's Access to Goods and Services) went, they were welcomed by the workers. Juan Crespo, the national leader of *Fetraharina* (Trade-union federation of flour workers, which organises more than 25,000 workers nationally) explained; "It is the workers who are going to open up the companies and say, here there is speculation, here there is hoarding…"

On 7 March, the Minister of Agriculture and Land, Elías Jaua called on the "people to come out and occupy the means of production", explaining that this was "a fight between the people and the oligarchy which creates hunger, exploits the people, and hoards produce". Calls from 'on high' from Jaua or even Chávez, for radical action were welcome, but the Bolivarian movement contained no structure or mechanism for transforming those calls into action. In a few small factories that were closing down, workers did occupy, but these were the rare exception, not the rule. The UNT gave little or no support, while the FSBT opposed such actions.

Shortages were accompanied by soaring inflation. Soon, the prices of many vegetables were higher than in most European countries (where wages were much higher than in Venezuela). The combination of food shortages and inflation created a very dangerous situation from the viewpoint of the Revolution because, as intended, it hit the poorest layers of society hardest and undermined support for the government. The land reforms of the government, intended to increase home production in order to be less dependent on imports, did help slightly, but the measures taken fell well short of what was required to fulfil the most elementary needs of the national democratic revolution: at the end of 2008, some eighty per cent of farmland was still controlled by fewer than five per cent of land-owners.

Government attempts to create alternative supermarket chains, such as Mercal and the PDVAL, providing cheap food products, had proved inadequate. There were relatively few of these stores, often many basic food products were missing and even if they had the required goods, customers had to queue for hours. Corruption by bureaucrats was widespread, underlining how the bourgeois character of the Venezuelan state meant it could not be used as an instrument to carry out even social-democratic measures, let alone a revolution. As long as the old state inherited from the Fourth Republic remained in place, the cancer of corruption and bureaucratism would continue to undermine the progressive reforms that Chávez proposed.

Neither price regulation nor partial nationalisations were solving the food crisis. Capitalists produce with the aim of making profits. If they consider that regulated prices do not allow them a sufficient rate of profit, they stop producing, even breaking the law if necessary. The obvious and correct conclusion was that there is a fundamental contradiction between the needs and interests of the majority of the population and the private ownership of the means of production. But the government would not countenance the nationalisation of the food monopolies under workers and community control. The shortage of food and lack of leadership were two sides of the same coin and the defeat in the reform referendum had been a warning.

The food crisis in Venezuela contained very important lessons. The continued existence of private ownership of the means of production, processing, distribution and sale of food was in direct contradiction with the needs of the population and provided the basis for the effective undermining of all government measures.

Concessions were the natural response of the state apparatus, confirming that it could not be relied upon to carry out revolutionary policies in favour of the masses. Concessions to the capitalists only made the crisis worse. They strengthened the hand of the oligarchy because they could present them as the government recognising it had been wrong and the capitalists right, it led to an increase in confidence amongst the oligarchs and greater determination on their part to intensify their offensive against the revolution. Worse, they introduced demoralisation and apathy amongst the ranks of the revolutionary masses.

12) THE PSUV FOUNDING CONGRESS (JANUARY 2008)

The declaration of the decision to launch a mass socialist party threw the parties of the left into confusion and even crises. The PCV suffered an important split when half of its central committee left to join the PSUV. The PPT and Podemos opposed joining the PSUV, but a large proportion of their leading militants defected to the PSUV.

The expectation was that the PSUV would be the arena in which the struggle between the revolutionary and reformist tendencies in the Bolivarian movement would unfold. This was expected to begin immediately with the selection of candidates for the coming regional elections for governors, scheduled for November, 2008. Chávez' call to form the PSUV was in the wake of his overwhelming victory in the presidential elections but when, on Saturday, 12 January, 2008, the new socialist party opened its First (two-month long) Congress it was after a referendum defeat that reflected a tiredness amongst layers of the masses due to lack of effective action by the government.

Chávez had proposed the PSUV as "the most democratic party in the history of Venezuela… genuine leaders will rise from the rank and file… enough of appointments from above". That the PSUV would hold both government and state to account, that it would be a tool to eliminate bureaucracy and complete the revolution, gripped the minds of the masses – and in just two months, April-May, 5.6 million registered for membership. Present at the Congress were almost 1,700 delegates from all over the country.

A *vocero* (spokesperson) had been elected from each of the over 20,000 Socialist Battalions, the base units of the PSUV. Groups of ten *voceros* met to elect one delegate. At battalion level, 1.4 million people showed up for the elections.

This party was supposed to represent the next step forward for popular participatory democracy. By 12 January, the congress had two plenary sessions. Between these, the delegates returned to their home regions and met and discussed with the rank and file, reporting on the Congress and its debates. The draft of the 'Declaration of Principles' and Party Programme had been circulated for discussion by a committee, led by former Vice-President Jorge Rodríguez. Both texts reflected the contradictions seen in the speeches of Chávez and the policies of the Venezuelan government.[103]

The draft programme was long on what should be done: Section 4, on the 'Planned Economy and Communal State', stated that the PSUV wanted a "democratically planned and controlled economy... capable of ending alienated labour and satisfying all the necessities of the masses". To accomplish this, two measures were proposed: the end of monopolies and the *latifundios*. These were measures that Marxists would whole-heartedly support, and would have supported even more keenly had the programme included any concrete steps for their implementation. Instead, the programme contained formulations that were ambiguous, but open to interpretation, and party tops and Ministry bureaucrats did the interpreting.

Delegates from Caracas proposed that 'anti-capitalism' be included in the Declaration of Principles. Party tops, supported by the PCV, argued against, but during the final session, the rank and file heckled the platform until the issue was brought before Congress, approved, and included in the text.

Most members had joined the PSUV to end economic sabotage (particularly of basic food products), abolish unemployment, poverty and homelessness, and end corruption in the state apparatus. But to do so effectively, meant the overthrow of capitalism, just what the party tops and state bureaucracy were committed not to do. Regarding the forthcoming regional elections, Chávez in, *Aló Presidente*, on 20 January, called on PSUV members to de-select those Bolivarian governors who swore loyalty to the revolution and socialism, but carried out pro-capitalist policies in practice, working with the opposition and opposing all initiatives by workers, peasants and youth to change society. A glaring example was Podemos member, Didalco Bolívar, Governor of Aragua State, who was elected as a supporter of

---

103 *Draft Program and Principles of the PSUV*, January 2008, www.handsoffvenezuela. org.

the revolution, but advocated a 'No' in the referendum and who had sent in the police against the occupying workers of Sanitarios Maracay.

In a dynamic situation where the masses were becoming involved in 'party politics' for the first time, and were joining the PSUV en masse, with the expectation of creating a genuine revolutionary party with a real anti-bureaucratic, socialist programme, it would have been criminal for Marxists to have allowed the reformists and bureaucrats a clear path to take over the PSUV. The expectation was they could join forces with the tens of thousands of revolutionary workers, youth, poor peasants and small shopkeepers and help lead a definitive struggle against the oligarchs, and bureaucrats, and for socialism.

However, the right wing inside the Bolivarian movement (all who wished to reach a compromise with the oligarchs and imperialism) managed to put their stamp on the congress. These people were (and remain) installed in key positions within the PSUV, state apparatus and nationalised industries, and from these positions they effectively control the party from above. Their major ideological thrust at this congress was to promote a reformist concept of socialism that allowed different forms of property. Behind this concept they would oppose nationalisations and defend private ownership of the means of production.

The major clash between the left and the right occurred on the decisive issue of how the national leadership would be chosen. The demand was that the party be controlled democratically by the rank and file in line with Chávez' repeated statements, and that meant, amongst other things, that the leaders should be elected and subject to recall. The right fought back; this was a key question for them because it threatened their whole way of operating. The congress could not reach agreement on the method of electing the leadership. In the end, Jorge Rodríguez took everyone by surprise by suddenly declaring that each delegate should write three names on a sheet of paper and then all the ballots would be taken to Miraflores Palace where Chávez, taking the wishes of the delegates into account, would name sixty-nine candidates who would stand for election – fifteen full members and fifteen alternate members to be the national leadership. Then Rodríguez dropped the bombshell, the three names could only be 'recognised leaders'.

On the last weekend in February, Chávez had been elected President of the party; now he used his enormous personal authority to impose the proposed election method. The role of Chávez in these manoeuvres was, at best, ambiguous and contradictory. He attacked the "splitting elements" and called for "unity and discipline", using his authority to get the Congress to accept a fundamentally flawed leadership election procedure, objectively, supporting the bureaucracy. These actions reflected the limits on his perspective of how to advance the revolution. Chávez' military background helped explain his emphasis on party unity and discipline but, of course, during a revolutionary period it is quite impossible have unity between reformism and revolution. By not defending democracy, by remaining tied to individuals who were clearly integral to the party bureaucracy, he was undermining the very revolution that he had done so much to initiate and progress. No matter how honest a man Chávez was, his balancing between the forces of reformism and the revolution was acting as a brake on the revolution.

Taking the ballots to Miraflores prevented the delegates from knowing either who the candidates were, or how many nominations each candidate had received. Forcing the delegates to name three candidates there and then prevented consultation with the rank and file and also stopped prospective candidates from presenting themselves and their ideas to the delegates. Limiting the proposals to 'recognised leaders' biased the election in favour of established leaders who were, in their majority, reformists.

The right wing got away with imposing an election process that was rigged in their favour from start to finish. In the final list of the sixty-nine candidates, which Chávez presented for election, there were a large number of people who were seen by the masses as useless and discredited bureaucrats. The vote took place on 9 March and, as would be expected, the resulting PSUV leadership came predominantly from the right wing of the party. Prominent right wingers, who failed to make the 'first fifteen' were either elected as alternates or found jobs elsewhere. Significantly, there was only one trade unionist on the list and he topped the poll.

The left had put its mark on the congress, most notably on the Declaration of Principles, but the national leadership which would enact the Declaration was firmly under bureaucratic control. This set the scene for an ongoing fight between the rank and file members of the PSUV and the bureaucrats, but without a party structure that was democratic, the likely outcome of that struggle was obvious.

13) NATIONALISATION OF STEEL (SIDOR) AND WORKERS' CONTROL

The giant steel producer, SIDOR, was founded as a state-owned company during the 1950s and then privatised and sold to the Argentinian company Techint in 1997. From 1997 to 2008, when SIDOR was re-nationalised, the workers went through what they describe as a 'living nightmare'. Thus, when Chávez made his call in January 2007 to "nationalise all that was privatised",

SIDOR erupted in jubilant celebrations with spontaneous walk-outs and the Venezuelan flag was raised over the installations.

After oil, the SIDOR steel mills are the most important industries in the country, with the largest concentration of industrial proletariat. Prior to re-nationalisation, the negotiation of a new collective contract had escalated into strike action. SIDOR's management were supported by the Minister of Labour, Jose Ramón Rivero, and the governor of Bolivar state, retired General Francisco Rangel Gómez. Rivero slandered the workers, falsely claiming they had supported the boss's lock-out in 2002-2003, when in fact, it was their actions which had kept the plant open. Next, Rivero threatened the workers: if they continued their action the government would consider forcing them back to work. He then accused members of the union negotiating committee of being agents of the oligarchy, intent only on disruption.[104]

The situation intensified in 2008, when Rivero tried to bypass the elected union leaders and impose a referendum on the company's pay offer. On 14 March, 2008, the local National Guard, allegedly acting under the orders of the governor, attacked SUTISS (the steel workers' union) members using tear gas and rubber bullets, arresting about fifty and hospitalising three. They then began a hunt to arrest the leaders of SUTISS. The workers in the region responded with a clear class instinct, organising solidarity meetings and pickets, and threatening strikes in other plants.[105]

This was an intolerable situation and Chávez had no alternative but to sack Rivero as Minister when he announced that SIDOR would soon be re-nationalised. A compromise between the Argentinian owners and the Venezuelan government meant the company was not 're-nationalised', but instead sold its shares at preferential prices on the open market, with the only buyer prepared to pay the enhanced price of US$1.9 billion being the Bolivarian government. This was doubly generous given how cheaply Techint had bought the plant. It was also a contradiction: one of the reasons Chávez gave for re-nationalising companies privatised under the neo-liberal policies of previous governments was that they were practically given away, now his government paid over full market price when re-nationalising.

The question raised on the shop floor was, would a re-nationalised SIDOR be run to suit the oligarchs, to suit the bureaucrats, or would it be run in the interests of the Venezuelan masses? Although Chávez had sacked Rivero and nationalised SIDOR, the whole episode showed the government's contradictory approach. Chávez was supporting the workers but the PSUV

---

104 Kiraz J., SIDOR workers reject arbitration, VA.com, 27 February, 2008.
105 Fuentes, F., *Venezuela: Class Struggle Heats Up*, 26 July, 2009, Green Left Weekly.

right wing was hand-in-glove with the oligarchs. Rivero was gone, but Gómez and the bureaucracies remained.

The nationalisation of the steel industry followed on the heels of important nationalisations in another sector of the economy. On 3 April, Chávez announced the compulsory purchase sixty per cent of each of the three major cement producers in Venezuela. These three overseas-owned companies (Mexican Cemex, French Lafargue, and Swiss Holcim) controlled over three-quarters of the industry. Producing primarily for the international market, these companies sold their products in Venezuela at the same price as their exports, the result being that Venezuela suffered both high prices and severe shortages. Chávez assured these foreign companies that they would be fairly compensated, but Venezuela was determined to solve its housing shortage – then standing at about 2.7 million dwellings.[106]

These particular nationalisations followed that of a much smaller enterprise, *Cementos Andinos*, the previous year, when all 4,600 workers were put on full-time contracts, ending the casualisation of labour. How such nationalisations were viewed by the workers was articulated by Alexander Santos, a leading member of the union at *Cementos Andinos* and spokesperson of its newly-formed Socialist Factory Council: "This measure will put the industry at the service of the people, to develop a state policy of house building without allowing a multinational to put its own interest above the interests of the people". However, management of these companies was assigned to ex-military officers who completely opposed *cogestión* in any form. Soon they were mired in mismanagement, corruption and theft with the result that output fell catastrophically.

The re-nationalisation of SIDOR, was largely due to the heroic determination of the SIDOR workers, despite the ferocious opposition of Rivero, despite sabotage by many bureaucrats in both the state apparatus and SIDOR, and despite opposition within SUTISS. It was thanks to the determination of the workers in action not words, that the strategic goal of re-nationalising SIDOR was achieved. With a clear revolutionary and class instinct, the workers immediately acted to protect the plants to defend the equipment, materials and technical and administrative information necessary for normal working.

The day after the announcement, the Automatic Production System (the control centre for all aspects of production) ceased to function. A group of workers, suspecting sabotage, confronted the managers. After a heated exchange, normal operations were resumed. In another incident workers discovered a TV crew pretending to be a team from the state-owned TV

---

106 Sugget, J., *Venezuela To Nationalize Cement Industry*, VA.com, 5 April, 2008.

station VTV. The workers confronted them and seized the tapes: it appeared that a group of hired thugs was to destroy company property, that this would be recorded and broadcast in order to accuse the workers of hooliganism. It was the workers, not the managers, who spontaneously defended the plant, implementing a basic form of workers' militia to protect plant and equipment from wilful destruction and prevent the theft of equipment, instruments and computer systems, not only for their resale value but in order to sabotage the nationalisation.

SIDOR was formally re-nationalised on 30 April, 2008, accompanied by wide-spread discussion on the future of state industries, with the idea of putting all Guayanan heavy industries under workers' control rapidly gaining momentum. Re-nationalisation was a giant step forward but carried out reluctantly by bureaucrats from several Ministries. With extensive mismanagement and corruption at the top, many acute problems remained unsolved and the re-nationalised SIDOR experienced a veritable battle between workers, who wanted to implement an effective system of workers' control, and those elements in management, the trade union and state bureaucracies, who were doing all they could to make the attempts to build a 'socialist enterprise' fail. Having control of the local union in any company gives the bureaucrats power, access to key information about contracts, suppliers, etc., and with these comes the possibility to steal and demand bribes. It was widely believed this was the reason behind the concerted campaign organised by the FSBT, that used mafia type methods, in the various companies of the Guayanan heavy industry complex against worker-directors and workers' control.

The question of the election of supervisory staff arose very concretely due to the experience of workers in the Maintenance Department who demanded their manager, an individual closely linked to the Argentinean multinational and in a position to cause serious damage, be replaced by a safe pair of hands elected from the shop floor. Faced with a campaign by the workers, the company permitted an election for the post, which a well-known Socialist and member of the Revolutionary Front of Steelworkers (FRTS), won easily. Workers in other departments now demanded the right to elect managers. As in the case of PDVSA at the time of the lock-out in 2002, all conditions were present in SIDOR for the rapid and full implementation of workers' control. This did not happen because of the combined resistance of managers, government bureaucrats, corrupt trade union officials and local PSUV tops.

SIDOR generated massive resources but had inherited from the totally corrupt neo-liberal practices of previous regimes, widespread *mafioso* networks; e.g., repairs and maintenance awarded to friends and family, or for kick-backs. After the leftist, Carlos d'Oliveira, had been sworn in as president it was discovered that top managers were involved with the theft of materials for sale on the black market.[107] A huge scandal erupted on 9 June, 2011, with the arrest of Luís Velasquez, SIDOR's Commercial Director. Velasquez, it emerged, was head of a so-called '*cabilla mafia*', guilty of the wholesale theft of *cabillas,* the steel bars used in construction. In November 2010 alone, twelve lorries loaded with 336 tonnes of *cabillas*, worth US$373,000 went missing. Velasquez was a Bolivarian top. He was the former finance director of the PSUV and a member of the management boards of the recently-nationalised Cemex and Lafargue. Apparently, Velasquez was, amongst other things, diverting *cabillas* to private companies with which he was involved. These would then sell the *cabillas* on the black market at three or four times the official price. Other materials were diverted to Colombia and Brazil where there are no regulated prices and where Velasquez also had business interests.

Jesús Pino, a leading member of the FRTS at SIDOR insisted these crimes were revealed only because the worker-directors of SIDOR noticed irregularities in the financial records that had previously been 'overlooked', found proof of misdeeds and alerted the authorities. Velasquez was the tip of an iceberg of a large-scale operation. The FRTS pointed out publicly and loudly that he was a personal friend of 'Bolivarian' Governor Rangel and that top people in the region and the national government were exerting strong political pressure to prevent the investigation of the thefts from going any further, i.e., workers who provided evidence against Velasquez were threatened with dismissal.[108]

With Velasquez holding such powerful positions and having such influential connections, the only effective way to combat the corruption was through the democratic participation of the workers at all levels of management in the companies. After robbing hundreds of poor families of a decent home, and the state of millions of dollars, Velasquez was released from prison in 2013, the short length of his internment a further demonstration that he still had powerful friends in high places in a corrupt system.

The Velasquez episode again confirmed that with a mixed economy, especially one in which capitalists are put in charge of the nationalised industries, wholesale corruption is only to be expected with the nationalised industries being blamed as inherently inefficient. Either the means of production are taken over and integrated into a democratic plan of production, or the anarchy of the profit motive will sabotage any attempts at regulation. The New Democracy in China was a period of mixed economy.

107 Larsen, P., *Chávez Appoints Workers to Lead Factories...* VA.com, 2 June, 2010.
108 Martín, op cit., 10 July, 2011.

For historic reasons the capitalists produced only a minute proportion of the GDP but their corrosive effect, particularly the corruption of the Chinese Communist Party, was out of all proportion to either their numbers or their economic strength.[109] In Venezuela the mixed economy was dominated by the capitalists, so it was only to be expected that there would be powerful interests within the Bolivarian movement opposing workers' control because it threatened their corrupt practices.

Behind Velasquez were those who had opposed the introduction of workers' control: the state bureaucracy, top managers at SIDOR, the 'Chavista' trade union leaders of the FSBT, the governor of Bolivar state and the former Minister of Labour, Rivero, who had progressed to be an alternate member of the National Assembly, a Member of the Bolivar state Bureau of the PSUV, and aide to Governor Rangel.[110] This powerful alignment of reactionary forces was one more manifestation of the impossibility of running Venezuela in the interests of the popular masses without expropriating the means of production and putting them under workers' control, as part of a democratic plan for the economy.

In early 2011, Chávez was openly favouring Nicolás Maduro as his successor. This worried many trade union activists as Maduro had been a leading member of the FSBT, had actively opposed workers' control, possibly even supporting the strong-arm tactics at Alcasa, and was feared to have kept his links with former colleagues. All this boded ill for workers, certainly in the nationalised industries.

The workers faced powerful enemies, but the SIDOR workers had shown their mettle during the bosses' lock-out in 2002-2003, when their actions in keeping the Anaco gas plant open had ensured continued production in all Guayana. Following the assault on Sayago at Alcasa, workers across the region responded by organising the first National Meeting for Workers' Control in May 2011 on the SIDOR site. More than 900 representatives of workers' councils, occupied factories, trade unions and revolutionary workers' organisations met for two days to discuss the challenges facing workers' control and to develop a plan of action. The meeting passed a very sharp and clear manifesto entitled 'Neither capitalists nor bureaucrats – all power to the workers'.

While the Meeting was largely upbeat and projected that the "conjuncture of forces is still favourable to the workers" the delegates expressed concern with the de-politicisation, apathy and scepticism of many workers, which had been seen in the September 2010 National

109 Roberts, J., *China: From Permanent Revolution to Counter-Revolution*, Wellred Books, 2016.

110 Martín, J., op cit., 10 July, 2011.

Assembly elections, where the PSUV gained the majority of seats, but with only a slim majority of votes over the joint opposition coalition (MUD) – 5,451,422 votes against 5,334,309. The leftist PTT, which refused to join the Chavista alliance garnered 354,677.

In 2012, the workers' control movement in Venezuela, and in Bolivar state in particular, was at a crossroads. The many achievements of the workers in forcing nationalisations, of driving toward workers' control of the state-owned heavy industries, threatened the interests, not only of the US-backed political opposition, transnational companies and private bosses, but also of those who supported the Bolivarian Revolution only for personal gain. After all, there is little need for state managers if workers eliminate management hierarchies and operate factories themselves in a participatory democratic manner, and open democratic control of finances brings to a sudden halt the schemes for filching monies from the state.

Workers' control also gave the lie to those who argued that workers are 'not ready' to operate factories themselves and showed that it was active sabotage by the reactionary forces that was undermining the Bolivarian Revolution. This had been particularly evident in Alcasa, which had been considered by many as the most advanced of the Guayanan factories in implementing workers' control. In August 2012, some six months after successfully removing Sayago, the Ministry dismissed the elected worker president of SIDOR, Carlos d'Oliveira, a leading member of the Revolutionary Front of Steelworkers.

The process by which d'Oliveira was removed was very similar to that of Sayago. The FSBT trade union (under the name 'Union Alliance') organised a conflict, this time regarding the outsourcing of work. This was done in order to disrupt production, and caused damage to plant and equipment estimated at US$431 million. President Chávez explained that the events and protests were "a management error" by Oliveira and he had to go. Rafael Gil Barrios, a member of the FSBT, president of the CVG, and an ally of Governor Rangel was named as d'Oliveira's successor by the government. To stop any fight-back in SIDOR, a story was put about that d'Oliveira had been arrested for embezzlement.

14) THE FINANCIAL CRASH OF 2008

2008 was the year of the financial crash. Starting in March, the world's banking system tottered on the brink of collapse. Around the world dozens of banks were saved only because their governments stepped in and forced their citizens to foot the bill for the greed of the bankers. Santander sought a local bank to take Banco de Venezuela (BdV) off its hands. Chávez offered to have the government buy the bank. To his amazement, Santander refused. It appeared to prefer BdV going bust than being state-owned.

Chávez often said that the nationalised industries had almost been given away and that the Banco de Venezuela was one such. BdV had been nationalised in 1994 after the massive banking crisis, only to be privatised in 1996 and bought by the Spanish multinational banking group Grupo Santander for US$300 million. It made US$325.3 million profit in 2007 alone and in the first half of 2008 a further US$170 million. This is just one example of how big foreign multinationals plunder the resources of Latin America.[111]

In his TV programme on 31 July, 2008, Chávez announced the government was going ahead with the nationalisation of BdV; assuring both employees and account holders their jobs and savings would be protected. He added that the bank's profits "will not go to one private group, they will be invested in socialist social development". Reuters later reported[112] that Chávez paid $1 billion for BdV. Marxists, certainly, welcomed every forward step in nationalisation in Venezuela while pointing out that nationalising in an ad-hoc, partial manner would not solve the fundamental problems of the Venezuelan economy. The Bolivarian Revolution still did not understand that nationalisation of the entire banking and financial sector was necessary to establish a planned economy. Socialism is only possible when the working class holds state power, takes the productive forces into its hands and runs society for the benefit of the popular masses. There had been extensive state ownership in Venezuela before Chávez but, as part of a capitalist rentier state, this had generated a thick layer of bloated bureaucrats interested only in their own inflated salaries, while over a third of the population went hungry, living in shacks without running water.

At every decisive juncture, young people had energetically mobilised demonstrations of hundreds of thousands in support of the Revolution. The need for a Bolivarian youth organisation was obvious, and the PSUV called the four-day founding congress of the J-PSUV (PSUV Youth) to begin 11 September, 2008. The process of electing delegates was the same as for the PSUV, and around 1,300 young people from all over Venezuela arrived at Puerto Ordáz in the eastern state of Bolívar. The Congress revealed a well-organised bureaucracy around Héctor Rodríguez, Minister of the Office of the Presidency, intent on stifling genuine debate, but it also showed the revolutionary qualities of the youth, who managed to block all attempts to impose undemocratic statutes on the organisation.

---

111 Woods, A., *Nationalisation of the Banco de Venezuela*, VA.com, 18 August, 2008.
112 8 October, 2012

Distribution of the statutes and accompanying documents was deliberately delayed until the Congress, so delegates would have no chance to collaborate to submit amendments or make alternative proposals. The cause was the grossly undemocratic structure proposed: the national leadership of the J-PSUV was to be fifteen members directly elected by the rank and file and ten appointed by the PSUV national leadership. This was flatly rejected by the delegates. During the morning of 12 September, there was so much dissent that the plenary session to discuss the proposed statutes was cancelled. Instead, Rodríguez gave a very short speech in which he stated that: "ninety per cent of the proposals received would be incorporated into new statutes".

The J-PSUV Congress served to bring many genuine young revolutionaries together to discuss how to defeat the bureaucracy. It successfully opposed attempts to turn it into a bureaucratic apparatus, fought for internal democracy, and forced the leaders to change the statutes from top to bottom. There were no appointments to the J-PSUV National leadership, all positions being filled by national elections. A paragraph was also introduced stressing that the leaders were open to recall. The paragraphs directed at curtailing internal oppositions were deleted. But it was a pyrrhic victory. The leadership of the PSUV saw the first J-PSUV congress as a warning, and successfully resisted having a second until 2014. The Second Congress was tightly controlled by the party bureaucracy and the new leaders of the J-PSUV were appointed. Today the J-PSUV is, largely, an empty shell, an electoral machine for bringing out the youth vote.

In the November 2008 regional elections for local councils and state governors, the PSUV won about 5.8 million votes and the opposition about 4.6 million. Compared to the referendum defeat, the Chavistas had recouped about 1 million votes while the opposition had lost nearly half a million. But compared to the 2004 regional elections, the PSUV lost Miranda, Carabobo and the Metropolitan District of Caracas, all of them extremely important from the point of view of politics, industry, and population. However, the important losses of Carabobo and Miranda were explained as due to special circumstances.

In industrial Carabobo the sitting 'Bolivarian' governor, Luis Acosta Carlez, was typical of the corrupt breed of politicians occupying many of the top positions of the Chavista movement. He was deselected and expelled from the PSUV because of corruption and financial irregularities. In revenge, he stood as an independent and took enough votes to prevent the election of PSUV candidate, Mario Silva from the left-wing of the party.

In Miranda state (surrounding and including parts of the capital city), Diosdado Cabello the sitting Bolivarian governor, and the most outspoken representative of the right wing of the Bolivarian movement, lost his seat to Capriles Radonski. Having also lost his position as a full member of the national committee his influence appeared to be waning, but Chávez stepped in to rescue him. He was appointed Minister of Public Works and Housing, then in 2009 as Head of the National Commission of Telecom. On 11 December, 2011, Cabello was installed as Vice-President of the PSUV, becoming the second most powerful figure in the party after Chávez. In 2012, he was sworn in as President of the National Assembly.[113]

There may have been specific reasons for the loss of Miranda and Carabobo, but generally the level of abstentions was a warning to be added to the defeat of the constitutional referendum. The popular masses were learning that when they attempted direct action, the first opposition they faced was from a corrupt PSUV bureaucracy. No wonder that the abstention rate in the traditional Chavista areas was typically over forty per cent, whereas in opposition areas it was much lower, between twenty and thirty per cent.

Within a couple of weeks of the elections, oppositionists launched a series of assaults against the grassroots of the revolutionary movement. In Carabobo, Miranda, and the Caracas Metropolitan area, groups of reactionary thugs with police protection, attacked and closed down Radio Voz de Guaicaipuro, a revolutionary radio station in Los Teques, and Avila TV, run by young revolutionary activists. The western media was silent concerning these attacks on free speech. Next, the thugs targeted social programmes involving Cubans; forcibly closing down educational programmes and *consultorios*, shouting: "Now we rule Miranda". However, local people soon rallied and attempts to evict the *misiones* from their buildings were defeated. These actions were a real eye-opener for many young Venezuelans who had little previous memory of the rule of the oligarchs.

On the morning of Thursday 27, three UNT activists Richard Gallardo, Luis Hernandez, and Carlos Requena arrived at the Alpina processing plant in Aragua, to give support to the 400 workers occupying the plant against closure. Police arrived, entered the premises and brutally kicked out the workers. The three trade unionists immediately rallied support from UNT branches in the area and soon the processing plant was surrounded. The police, outnumbered, allowed the workers to re-occupy the building. That evening, the three trade union leaders were assassinated on their way home.

On learning of the killings, the Aragua UNT immediately called for a day of protest action with mass meetings in all the factories and workplaces. Thousands of workers downed tools and came out on the streets the

---

113 *Venezuela National Assembly chief: Diosdado Cabello*, BBC News, 5 January, 2012.

following afternoon. Thousands attended the funeral, and the Aragua UNT in an emergency meeting agreed a plan of action, holding mass meetings in all the region's workplaces, a regional strike on Tuesday 2 December, and a national day of action the following day. The leader of the left within the UNT, Orlando Chirino, called on workers to respond to any threats by the bosses by "occupying the factories and demanding expropriation by the government". The Aragua UNT now raised the need for workers' defence.

The killings and wave of provocations on the part of reactionary gangs in the states and local municipalities where the opposition had won seats, was an indication of what would happen on a national scale if these counter-revolutionaries ever took power again. In an angry speech on Sunday 30, Chávez gave numerous well-documented examples of such attacks. The international media, in a concerted effort, despite all the evidence to the contrary, chose to dismiss these reports. The mass demonstrations by workers, students, and poor people who marched in defence of the *misiones* and against the counter-revolutionary attacks were never mentioned. The role of the 'liberal' press, in particular, was especially vile, accepting the smokescreen of lies erected by the opposition as good coin.

14.1) THE FEBRUARY 2009 REFERENDUM AND PLAN SOCIALIST GUAYANA

On Thursday, 12 February, 1 million people marched in favour of a 'Yes' vote in the constitutional amendment to abolish the limit on the number of times the President, state governors, mayors and National Assembly deputies could stand for office. The amendment was passed with 54.4 per cent in favour and 45.6 per cent against, a clear victory for the Bolivarian Revolution. The masses saw a 'Yes' vote as defence of the gains of the revolution against the attacks by the semi-fascists on health and educational centres.

The bureaucrats, however, perceived it as approval of their policy of compromise and moderation. But the international crisis of capitalism during 2008 and subsequently, caused a collapse in the price of oil, with the PDVSA announcing a forty per cent cut-back in the year's budget which seriously undercut the country's economy. Prices of other raw materials, such as aluminium, cement and steel, which Venezuela exports, also dropped dramatically. The Venezuelan economy was capitalist, and therefore obeyed the basic laws of the market, meaning the gains of the revolution were seriously threatened. Inflation soared, and food prices in Caracas rose by fifty per cent in a single year. To escape the oscillations in oil prices it was necessary to break the power of the oligarchy and activate the country's productive capacity, particularly in food. But in revolutionary struggles, what is needed to win over hesitating elements is decisive action. The slower the pace of the revolution, the more difficult it is to convince doubters that socialism will be the final victor.

After the nationalisation of SIDOR it was natural for the leading militants from across the CVG factories to discuss common problems and try to hammer out a common approach and policy on the future development of state industries. Chávez gave form to this by establishing the Guayana Presidential Commission with representatives from the PSUV National Executive Committee and some 400 workers from across CVG factories. On 21 May, 2009, all 400 workers, met with Chávez at a 'Workshop of Socialist Transformation' to loudly demand Guayana's basic industries be placed under workers' control. The President responded with his now famous cry "I unconditionally support the workers!" and announced the launch of Plan Socialist Guayana (PGS).

Chávez began his report to the Workshop by announcing that the state would retake control of a gas bottling plant in the eastern state of Monagas, and five steel and iron briquette companies that had been sold off to foreign multinationals under Caldera. These were to be integrated into the planned Iron-Steel and Aluminium Socialist Corporations as a sign of the government's commitment to the PGS. Chávez declared: "these companies must be under workers' control. That's how it must be". He continued, "What is happening here today is very important, since it is an example of the consciousness of the need for unity through debate", the problem was that the Bolivarian Revolution was suffering from too much 'debate' and too little action. To the cheers of the workers Chávez announced ratification of a hard-fought collective bargaining agreement at Ferromineran (CVG), with, and here the applause rose to a crescendo, a ten to twenty per cent reduction in the salaries of the company managers.

The major outcome of the Workshop was the launch of the PGS with Labour Minister Maria Cristina Iglesia, and Planning and Development Minister Jorge Giordani appointed to lead working parties to flesh out the plan into a final form and provide a scheme for assimilating the country's heavy industry into the government's strategic development plan. The president emphasised the need for this new industrial complex to break with the old structures, he appealed for a "struggle against the mafias, corruption, bad management, against the deviations and vices of the Fourth Republic" as these were a "threat to the socialist revolution".

Chávez went further and declared to the enthusiasm of the workers, the need for *cogestión* in the industrial sector in general: "The plan is an integrated plan. And we want you to carry it out, of course! We must raise all of these companies' productivity, efficiency, and transparency... The entire productive process... needs to be under workers' control". How many times previously had the president outlined similar plans and given direct orders to his ministers, only to have them ignored and buried. To go from words to deeds is, in the first place, the responsibility of the revolutionary leaders, to project a course of action that would motivate the industrial proletariat of Guayana, particularly the iron and steel workers.

For all the hype, concretely, the proposals outlined by Chávez amounted to little more than the participation of the workers in the election of the management in a company that operated within a capitalist economy. It was true that many managers holding senior positions in re-nationalised companies were counter-revolutionaries and often worked hard to ensure the failure of those companies, as was the case with Inveval and Alcasa. However, even if all reactionary managers were replaced with revolutionaries, the bourgeois character of the system would remain unchanged.

Guayana covers nearly half of Venezuela's land area, it comprises the three eastern states: Bolivar – population 1.4 million, Amazonas – 140,000, and Delta Amacuro – 170,000. This region is home to extraction and manufacturing industries: iron, steel, aluminium, gold and more. The CVG is a state-holding company comprising seventeen basic industries, directly employing over 30,000 workers. Azzellini describes the situation in Guayana as an open conspiracy by which an association of imperialist interests, the oligarchy, the state governors, bureaucrats left over from the Fourth Republic and still holding top jobs in the various Ministries, local entrepreneurs, the managers of the CVG industries, and an elite of privileged workers and trade union bureaucrats "operating something like a paradise of 'free theft'", filching billions of dollars a year from the state.[114] After 1998, the Chavista government showed little interest in intervening, not least because the elected governor of Bolivar, the dominant state, in 2004, 2008 and 2012, was retired General Francisco Rangel Gómez, a high-ranking member of the ruling Chavista party and fellow graduate of Chávez from the Venezuelan Military Academy.

The report from Iglesia and Giordani was presented to Chávez on 9 June, 2009, as *Plan Socialist Guayana 2009-2019*, the blueprint for the future development of state-owned industries in Guayana. The PGS had serious implications for power relations in the Guayana industries, even if in a limited form of co-management. Robertson describes how these basic industries would become the key battleground between those wishing

---

114 Azzellini, D., *Communes and Workers' Control in Venezuela*, Haymarket, 2018.

to advance workers' control and vested interests within the Bolivarian movement, who would fight bitterly to oppose it.[115]

The introduction of *Plan Socialist Guayana 2009-2019* states "the aluminium, iron and steel workers of Guayana, alongside the Bolivarian government, have decided to take a step forward in the construction of socialism, by assuming direct control of the production of the region's heavy industries". To this end, the PGS presented nine goals, with detailed plans for their achievement. Seven were unobjectionable and ranged from integration of all CVG industries into two mega companies, one iron and steel production, the other aluminium processing, democratisation of management, promotion of health and safety in the work environment, to the provision of educational opportunities for workers.

However, two of the goals were for every worker to participate in formulating projects for implementation, which had to be costed by the work force as a collective, and to establish codes for public accountability of the management of the CVG factories. These sent shivers down the spines of those who had made rich livings for many years by robbing the state in one form or another.

The PGS recognised that the Venezuelan economy was still overwhelmingly based on bourgeois social relations. These took the form of private ownership of production, but included state ownership even when fulfilling a social need such as housing, because state ownership in itself did not necessarily challenge either hierarchical capitalist power relations or the bourgeois nature of the state.

The general argument behind the PGS was that participatory decision-making in both public and economic life was emancipatory, and therefore a step towards socialism. The call was for active participation of the popular masses in all areas of public and economic life as an important mechanism to stop the formation of elite groups which could lead to the bureaucratisation of the revolutionary processes. Marxists pointed out the impossibility of attaining equality in decision-making in societies where large-scale private ownership of, for example, newspapers and television exists. To realise meaningful democracy, the mass media must be under democratic control through, for example, workers' control and soviets.

The PGS proposed a 'worker council' model for running the factories, with each work section electing one or more representatives to a General Management Council (with any sub-committees deemed necessary) responsible for the day-to-day running of the enterprise. Proposals of a substantive nature had to be approved by an assembly of all the workers.

---

115 Robertson, op cit.

Representatives of the local community or co-operatives with which the company was linked could be seated on the Council or invited to attend as and when required. In a typical nationalised company or joint enterprise where the state held a fifty-one per cent share, the executive committee or board of directors would have equal numbers of workers and state representatives, but the president, would be determined by the state. This gave ultimate control to the Minister and the PSUV bureaucracy.

Class-conscious workers made every effort to advance the workers' council as a step towards workers' control, hoping to lay the basis for radical social transformation by introducing mechanisms of democratic decision-making 'from below'. Revolutionaries naturally supported these efforts and pushed for the most democratic and complete form of workers' control in all enterprises. However, they simultaneously explained that without a social transformation of society the gains being made would, sooner or later, be in danger of being lost to the counter-revolution.

The PGS moved into a new phase on 15 May, 2010, when, after pressure from the rank and file, worker-presidents were sworn-in at each of the CVG companies. These included Elio Sayago in Alcasa, and Carlos d'Oliveira in SIDOR. Chávez warned against reluctance on the part of managers and administrators to accept these appointments, declaring that "it's necessary to defeat such resistance to change". and that some management positions were occupied by "enemies of the revolutionary process". The question was, where would the PSUV tops and Chávez, stand in such disputes?

On 6 October, Elio Sayago found himself barred from entering a PGS Sub-Committee meeting attended by government ministers Khan, Iglesias, Maduro, and Giordani who had opposed his appointment as worker president. Jose Khan, had been appointed Minister at the Ministry of Basic Industries and Mines (MIBAM) in April, 2010. By December, he had stopped meeting with PGS working groups, side-lining them. The US$403 million approved for Alcasa by President Chávez earlier in 2010 failed to materialise, frozen between the bureaucracies of the CVG and MIBAM. Very powerful people were actively sabotaging workers' control in CVG companies. Pro-PGS activists claimed this informal alliance included PSUV Governor Rangel (himself a former CVG president) and the FSBT.

In October 2011, trade union elections were scheduled in the SIDOR steel plant. The Revolutionary Marxist Current, a group within the PSUV, accused Khan, Iglesias and Vice-President Elias Jaua, of attempting to influence the vote to get a candidate less committed to the PGS elected. After a period in which the workers' control movement had made many advances, often due to the direct intervention of President Chávez, Freteco warned that counter-revolutionaries were organising to intervene, using the disruption of production that they themselves were causing, to 'prove' workers' inability to administer companies. A similar warning was expressed by the Alcasa Socialist Workers Front in January 2012: that the "internal right-wing" faction around Rangel and the FSBT union was engaged in a campaign to gain control of the CVG companies. According to the statement, the aims of this faction were to make the PGS "unworkable", in order to achieve "the elimination of workers' control (and) the removal of Sayago". In the view of the Alcasa union, if the Rangel faction were to achieve these goals "all the achievements of the Bolivarian Revolution in the basic industries would be brought down".[116]

An orchestrated crusade against co-management and workers' control in Venezuela, and the PGS in particular, was being voiced by conservatives of all stripes, from the tops of the state bureaucracy to the most backward layers of workers. The CVG industries had become the site of an intense political conflict over the future of the Bolivarian Revolution. This conflict over *cogestión* between different groups, each identifying itself as Bolivarian, revealed one of the sharpest contradictions in the revolution. The struggle within the PGS intensified in 2012, reflecting the intensification of the fight within the Bolivarian Revolution between the bureaucracy and reactionary political sectors, and those forces genuinely committed to further radical transformation.

The course of the struggle for workers' control highlighted important characteristics of the Bolivarian Revolution. In particular, the on-going, and growing, internal contradiction between the bureaucracy and their reformist and reactionary allies and the more radical Chavistas committed to a deeper process of revolutionary change. The reactionary elements had one major advantage: they were not concerned with the efficiency with which the nationalised companies operated; their concern was to protect their personal interests. For example, after the dismissal of Sayago, production at Alcasa steadily declined and the latest figures (2015) show a production level of one-quarter that achieved under Sayago's leadership.

The bureaucracy appears to have successfully blunted the struggle for workers' control which, in many ways, was the spearhead of the Bolivarian Revolution. Not only by economic sabotage but going so far as to organise physical attacks on workers leaders who threatened their under-the-counter deals with the oligarchs.

---

116 Ibid.

14.2) FIRST EXTRAORDINARY CONGRESS OF THE PSUV

The year 2009 began with a politically-motivated and illegal lock-out at the Mitsubishi plant, intended to crush the trade union. An initial occupation by the workers was ended on 29 January, when police broke into the plant, shooting and killing two workers, but the workers stood firm and their militant action won a temporary victory on what, initially, appeared to be generous terms but which contained the condition that production was raised to a new high. This target proved impossible to achieve and, in August, Mitsubishi closed the plant 'indefinitely'. The Ministry of Labour intervened and the plant re-opened when Minister, Maria Cristina Iglesias, agreed to 150 workers, including eleven union leaders, being fired.[117]

In early May, Argenis Vasquez, general secretary of the workers' union at the Toyota assembly plant in Cumana, who had led a four-week strike in March was shot dead, triggering an occupation of the factory. In June, General Motors, which supplies Venezuela with forty per cent of all its vehicles, closed its production plants for three months, alleging a lack of dollars with which to buy parts, and thousands of workers were laid off. At the end of August, the government agreed to provide additional support despite a fall of almost half in oil revenues that year, and production re-started.[118]

The First Extraordinary PSUV Congress (also referred to as the PSUV Second Congress), commenced on Saturday 21 November, 2009, with a five-hour speech by Chávez that contained the now legendary call for a 'Fifth International'. Holding aloft a copy of Lenin's *State and Revolution*, he stressed the necessity of destroying the bourgeois state and replacing it with a revolutionary one. The speech reflected the enormous pressure of the masses who were demanding real progress towards genuine change. The PSUV bureaucracy, supported by the Stalinists, argued that this was an uncalled-for provocation, the regime should not adopt an openly anti-capitalist stance. The call for the Fifth International faded away.

Chávez admitted that Venezuela remained a capitalist state and this was the central problem of the revolution. He, once again, repeated his call for the establishment of a people's militia, that every worker, peasant, student, man and woman, should receive military training, and that this must not remain on paper but be put into practice. Chávez had called several times for the formation of workers' militias but almost nothing had been done. The previous May, he had said: "in every factory there must be a workers'

---

117 Suggett, J., *Venezuelan Auto Workers Decry Possible Firings of Union Leaders as Mitsubishi Plant Reopens*, VA.com, 24 September, 2009.

118 Suggett, J., *Venezuela Invests Surplus Oil Dollars in Education, Housing, and Industry*, VA.com, 3 September, 2009.

battalion… with the weapons kept there". Not surprisingly, no-one in the leadership of the PSUV nor the UNT and certainly not the FSBT, took the call into the factories or the *barrios*.

Chávez used his speech and the Congress to attempt to breathe new life into the revolution, to overcome the general feeling that the leadership of the PSUV was out of touch, not listening to the masses and not concerned with their problems. For example, he announced that seven medium-sized banks were to be taken over. His speech was enthusiastically received by the 772 red-shirted delegates, but seven years after defeating the attempted coup there were clear signs that the masses were frustrated with the slow pace of the revolution. The state sector was dominated by bureaucracy and corruption, and workers' control, which had shown so much promise, was being strangled. The communal forms of property did not represent more than ten per cent of GDP, the *latifundia* remained relatively untouched, and Socialism of the Twenty-First Century had sunk in a swamp of endless debates.

The banks referred to were merged into a new state sector bank, *Banco Bicentenario*, holding about one-third of all personal deposits. These nationalisations were a government bail-out to protect the banks concerned from insolvency. In June 2010, the government would take control of *Banco Federal* (which held less than three per cent of total deposits in the banking system), for failing to maintain minimum reserve levels. However, Venezuela's financial sector remained largely free to suck enormous wealth out of the country. An article in the bourgeois financial journal *Reporte Diario de la Economía* from 5 February, 2010 revealed that the banks had made US$2.6 billion in profits in 2009, of which eighty-three per cent came from fees charged. This was a grotesque figure when it is remembered that millions of Venezuelans lived in shanty towns and survived on US$5-10 a day. The amazing thing here is that much of the profit came from the state. Even today, oil money passes not through the nationalised banks but bourgeois financial institutions. Using *Banco Bicentenario* for these transactions would not only save the state huge sums of money but would be a body blow against the oligarchy.

The PSUV primaries for selecting candidates for the Assembly elections were held on 2 May with 3,527 registered candidates in eighty-seven constituencies. During the Congress Chávez had warned party officials, especially those who served in powerful government posts such as Ministers and state governors, to refrain from campaigning for or against candidates at the local level: "The party base should be the ones who decide". National Executive member Freddy Bernal came forward to argue that the election of candidates should be open to the entire membership, rather than just the

2.5 million active members registered in 'patrols'. He suggested that this would counter the influence of governors and mayors. Those with experience of elections within a mass political party know full-well that moves to get the 'entire membership' (i.e. the non-active members) voting is invariably a manoeuvre to retain the *status quo*.

The party apparatus ('*la maquinaria*') did everything possible to ensure its candidates would be selected in the primaries, and no left-wing candidate would win. In this they were aided by the officials of the CNE. Favoured candidates were assisted in the production and distribution of posters and leaflets. Full-page adverts in newspapers, spot adverts on sports programmes, promotional openings of *misións*, trucks and cars used to bring supporters to voting booths, the picture was everywhere the same – the apparatus used every possible trick to crush the left.

The result was an outright victory for the apparatus. True, the masses did get some 'popular' figures onto the final list, such as Andreina Tarazón of the M-28 student movement and the J-PSUV. But nationally, the picture was bleak. The rank and file protested the rigging manoeuvres of the bureaucracy, and the dissent was of sufficient weight that, on Thursday, 7 May, PSUV Vice-President Cilia Flores, announced that the national leadership was "investigating the claims of inequality in the campaigns". As though nothing untoward had occurred, President Chávez gave a very radical speech to the 110 winners of the primaries: "You must put yourself at the service of the people, not of yourselves, nor of a governor or a mayor, but of the people who are still suffering". His audience were those who had just rigged the primaries so that no such things would happen!

The state machine and most governmental ministers were intent on paralysing any advance of the Revolution; sabotaging progressive legislation, cancelling out the initiatives of the president and stubbornly opposing nationalisation under workers' control. Nowhere was this clearer than in the food sector, as demonstrated by the scandal in PDVAL, the state-owned food company, which delivered more than 1,000 tons of food on a daily basis. The Venezuelan intelligence service found that twelve top managers had organised a network which systematically hoarded containers and hid them until the contents were beyond their sell-by dates, classified as inedible, and then sold on the black market. Anyone who dared oppose them was immediately dismissed and silenced by death threats. A hoard of 2,334 containers of food goods was found. This case shows how impossible it is to build a new, socialist society for the Twenty-First Century, or any other century, with the old bourgeois state still in place. Without the democratic control of the working class, it is impossible to root out corruption and bureaucracy. *Últimas Noticias*, 9 June, 2010, reported it was the workers of PDVAL who blew the whistle on how the organised crime syndicate operated within the company.

As time went on the actions of the bureaucracy against the left wing became ever bolder, even ministers were sidelined or removed. The most scandalous case was the sudden removal on 10 February, of Professor Eduardo Samán, Minister of Trade, the most popular minister in the government. According to Samán it was Chávez' decision: "the capitalists in the food sector... asked for my head as a guarantee and then in turn they promised not to generate food scarcity in this year of elections. ...I was the obstacle that they wanted to remove".[119] The man who replaced Samán, Richard Canán, immediately increased the price of a whole series of basic food products, and lifted the price controls on basic products which Samán had kept in place. For whose benefit did he do this? The question was particularly relevant in an election year.

It was noticeable that trends seen in Nicaragua were making an appearance – companies subsidised by the government were making fortunes by currency speculation, while producing practically nothing. In the decade up to 2012 the state had ploughed US$317 billion into subsidising the private sector instead of investing in productive machinery.[120] Much of this became capital exported to American banks. Increasingly, the nationalisations that took place were dubious; the bureaucracy was learning its lessons, and now nationalisation was used not to support but to smother the struggle for workers' control in a factory; in other cases, the old owners continued to run the companies but with government subsidies so that all that changed were the labels on the tins. What these obvious social injustices reflected was that, nearly a decade after the start of the Bolivarian Revolution, the Venezuelan economy was clearly still a market economy in which private manufacturing provided three out of every four jobs. The capitalist element clearly dominated the mixed economy.

Nicaragua had demonstrated that, within a market economy, there is no way of solving the most pressing problems of the masses. In Venezuela, partial nationalisation as a launch pad for socialism was daily being shown not to work. The failure of the President to put his words into practice was allowing demagogic calls from the opposition to penetrate layers of the urban poor who were desperate to reverse the now continuous decline in their living standards. Demonstrations, even mass demonstrations, were now being seen by many militants as drawing attention away from the problems that really

119 Lucha de Clases, *Venezuela: Interview with... Eduardo Samán*, VA.com, 15 October, 2010.

120 Yaffe, op cit.

concerned ordinary people. One Chavista activist commented bitterly: "In the past, people used to fight to get on the buses to go to our rallies. Now nobody wants to go. Some even say: 'I will go if you pay me.' They say: 'there is plenty of money in this country – for some!'"

The opposition had learned its lesson from its abstention in the 2005 Assembly elections, now they were clearly mobilising for the National Assembly elections that coming September, convinced their economic sabotage was undermining the revolutionary morale of the masses. Its goal was to win a sufficient number of Assembly members to be able to wage an effective propaganda campaign of pointing the finger of blame at the government, in particular for the food shortages. After ten years of unfulfilled revolution, the economic situation was worsening not improving. Within the Chavista camp, those who would abstain were growing in number, but simultaneously, more radical elements, especially within the J-PSUV, were openly calling for destroying the source of the oligarchy's power, i.e., private ownership of the means of production.

The opposition was ready to complement its ongoing economic sabotage by street actions whenever it could present the unrest as justified. In January, middle-class students demonstrated violently against the alleged closure of RCTV and in defence of 'press freedom'. RCTV's broadcasting licence had not been renewed in 2007, and it was now a cable TV channel. It was closed by its private license owners temporarily, in protest at being judged as subject to the national rules on Social Responsibility in Radio and Television. These protests left one Chavista student dead and several injured.

The opposition was convinced that its well-organised campaign to produce food shortages had helped score a victory in the constitutional referendum. Similar plans were now laid for the coming 26 September, 2010, National Assembly elections. The government tried but failed to make good the food shortages. The problem was four-fold: the majority of the food production and distribution sector remained in private hands; the network of government stores was limited and corrupt; there was no monopoly on foreign trade to control the flow of food out of the country; national food production remained low level because many of the peasants granted land never received the cheap credits and technical assistance they had been promised, and had been forced into subsistence farming.

In the months preceding the National Assembly elections, the counter-revolution was yet again on the offensive, using its control over the media to maximise the effects of the food shortages. An extensive investigation by Professor Pasqualina Curcio of the Universidad Simón Bolívar reported in her book subtitled *Economic Warfare in Venezuela*, a clear and significant correlation between intensity of food shortages and politically important moments, such as the lead-up to elections. She also found that, despite Venezuela being largely self-sufficient in root crops, fruit and vegetables, there were shortages because the food supply chains were largely controlled by a single, private, corporation.

The opposition again opened a campaign of disinformation and destabilisation; doctored opinion polls made it appear as though the PSUV was losing ground and the opposition Coalition for Democratic Unity (MUD) would win the election. *El Universal* published polls showing the MUD miraculously increasing its share of the vote until on the eve of the election it reached fifty-seven per cent. This prepared the ground for undermining the integrity of the elections, calling them rigged, and providing justification for the proto-fascists to take to the streets.

The right wing claimed victory before the votes were counted, the international media reported that Chávez had lost before the election results were announced: "Venezuela has said no to Cuban-style communism". The actual results showed the PSUV with a majority, but no longer a two-thirds majority, dropping from 118 to ninety-six seats, while the MUD went from eighteen to sixty-four seats. Officially, the PSUV won the majority of the seats in sixteen of Venezuela's twenty-three states, but in terms of votes cast in the industrial states, the PSUV won by a whisker in Bolivar, but lost decisively in Carabobo, Miranda, and Zulia.

The role of the reformists at the top of the PSUV was particularly pernicious. In an entirely parliamentary interpretation they tried to present the election victory as a step forward, an endorsement of their class-collaborationist policy. As for the drop in votes they drew all the wrong conclusions: we are too confrontational and that cost us the support of the people, we must draw back and govern on behalf of all the people.

But, for every step back, the MUD would demand ten more, and for every step back the enthusiasm of the masses for the PSUV would fall even further. It was class conciliation that was undermining the Revolution and alienating its base. This was demonstrated by the result in Anzoátegui, where the MUD gained a big victory, reflecting discontent with the scandalous behaviour of the governor, Tarek William Saab and the right-wing Chavista bureaucracy who backed the bosses against the factory occupations in Mitsubishi, Vivex and Macusa, alienating many Chavista voters. The counter-revolutionaries were encouraged and emboldened to go onto the offensive.

The PSUV retained a majority in the National Assembly and was able to control the passage of laws and most other functions of the legislative body. However, the opposition, even though a minority, would now be able to intervene in the parliamentary processes and obstruct the actions of the government, and would be able to use its position in the Assembly to mobilise the masses of enraged petty-bourgeois on the streets to create an atmosphere of chaos and disorder.

In a press conference on Monday night, 27 September, Chávez, putting on a brave front, said the next phase would be to "accelerate the programmes of the new historical, political, social, and technological project". The president concluded: "We must continue strengthening the revolution!" But who would translate these words into action? The emphasis on bourgeois legality and parliamentary politics had divided, weakened and put a block on the Bolivarian Revolution. No matter how many idealistic revolutionaries are employed by the bourgeois state on valuable and worthwhile social projects, the socialist revolution can only be achieved by the destruction of that state.

15) OFFENSIVE AGAINST LANDLORDS AND SPECULATORS

Due to the 2008 crash, for the eighteen months prior to the 2010 election Venezuela had been in recession and, for the workers and poor, the situation was very bleak indeed. The Bolívar was devalued in January 2009 and food prices rose by thirty per cent in a year. Cheap credit to private companies contributed to increasing inflation, but that did not stop business executives from demanding ever more dollars from the government. Carlos Larrazábal, president of *Conindustria* (the industrial employers' federation) demanded that the government "invest in private initiative", conveniently ignoring that Venezuelan capitalists were not investing in their own businesses. They were continuing their strike of capital, amplifying the effects of the crisis. The government was nationalising firms that were at a standstill, putting compensation payments into the pockets of those causing the problems.

After the September election, workers and *campesinos* demanded that the government use the last three months of the old parliament (where it still had the required two-thirds majority) to enact the organic laws it had promised, in particular: legitimisation of workers' and factory councils, and Agrarian Reform to destroy the rule of the *caudillos*. Pressure was also coming from the rank and file of the PSUV, reflecting the widespread anger provoked by the undemocratic nature of the primaries. Activists linked the fall in the overall vote to the lack of decisive measures to advance the revolution. There was a sense of outrage amongst the grassroots that the revolution was now in serious danger of being thrown back.

It was in this context, that Eduardo Samán opened a debate within the PSUV on the balance sheet and the lessons to be drawn from the election results. He stressed the need for profound change within the PSUV and the need to create a Radical Tendency to achieve this. Samán toured the country publicising his proposal. Many PSUV rank and file were attracted by Samán's clear statements on the need to accelerate action against the capitalists and push for what he called 'Socialist definitions'. However, the Tendency faded away after Samán was appointed President of Indepabis at the end of May 2013, a position in which he vigorously fought for a tough new approach against price speculators. Chávez accepted that the Radical Tendency had a place within the PSUV, but only on the condition it was not 'divisive'. Interestingly, no sooner had Radical Tendency appeared than a disciplinary tribunal was established within the PSUV under the control of Ramón Rodríguez, former Minister of Interior.[121]

Chávez repeated his calls for the radicalisation of the revolution, and rejected any possibility of a pact with the bourgeoisie. Amongst others he nationalised Agroislena, owned by the multinational Vestey group, an agricultural supplies company that served seventy per cent of Venezuela's producers, and US-based glassmaker Owens-Illinois, placing sixty per cent of Venezuela's glass bottle industry under government ownership. Many of the firms taken over were badly run, unprofitable or occupied by workers in dispute with the owner. Usually, to make them viable, they required government investment over and above the compensation paid. It was becoming a case of nationalising the losses and privatising the profits. These actions combined the worst evils of capitalist anarchy (falling investment, flight of capital, factory closures, inflation and unemployment) with all the most negative features of bureaucracy (waste, mismanagement, inefficiency and corruption). This was a viable scenario only while the oil money continued to flow.

At the end of November, Venezuela was hit by torrential rain causing widespread flooding and mudslides, killing at least twenty-five people and leaving 130,000 homeless. The *barrios* were particularly hard hit. On Friday 17 December, 2010, the Venezuelan parliament passed an Enabling Law giving Chávez the power to legislate by decree for the next eighteen months in matters concerning human needs generated by the rainstorms, including infrastructure, transport and public services, housing, the use of urban and rural lands, international co-operation and socio-economic systems. The President explained that he would use the Enabling Law not only to tackle the negative consequences of the prolonged period of rainfall, but also some of the structural problems of capitalism which had worsened the crisis. The reaction of the Venezuelan oligarchy was furious. Articles in *El Universal*

---

121 Pearson, T., *United Socialist Party of Venezuela Defines New Strategies for 2011-2012*, VA.com, 24 January, 2011.

compared Chávez to Hitler. Clearly, the bourgeoisie was worried that some of its more scandalous behaviour would be unearthed. Their concerns were well-founded. Chávez would soon act against speculators in the housing sector, nationalising construction firms that were cheating people with empty promises of future homes, and companies which left houses half completed and moved on as soon as payment was received.

Peasant organisations, like the FNCEZ, had been calling for years for an acceleration of the struggle against *latifundia*, both to alleviate Venezuela's dependence on imported foodstuffs and to satisfy the *campesinos*' demand for land. Land reform was enormously popular with Chavistas, its effect on the economy was largely beneficial, and it directed the attention of the masses onto the most parasitic elements of the oligarchy. Chávez now directed that action be taken against forty-seven *caudillos*, who owned huge territories south of Lake Maracaibo in South-western Venezuela.

The new expropriations met with a ferocious media barrage on behalf of the land-owners. Opposition MPs demonstrated the kind of role they expected to play in the new National Assembly. Hermann Escarrá urged people to take to the streets to "show civil and military resistance". Miguel Ángel Rodríguez appealed for "a civilian uprising". Abelardo Díaz urged protesters to block the Pan-American highway, in order to "send a message to the president". There were only a few minor clashes between landowners and the National Guard and soldiers sent by Chávez to protect the newly expropriated land.

By 2011, rural land reform has been in effect for nearly a decade and despite the *caudillos* retaining most of their lands, rural poverty had diminished significantly. The government had 'rescued' 5.8 million hectares of land, regularised 5.9 million hectares, and distributed nearly 180,000 titles or agrarian letters. About half of Venezuela's, rural population had directly benefited from the reform which explained the solid support for the PSUV in rural areas. By giving peasants the means with which to challenge the *latifundios* and to engage in land reform 'from below', the 2005 Land Law had meant, at least for the time being, greater empowerment of poor farmers vis-à-vis the *caudillos*.

Government statistics showed that overall food production had increased by twenty-two per cent in the decade ending in 2009. This increase, welcome though it was, fell far behind the increase in demand. By 2011, Venezuelans were much better fed, with a per capital increase in daily calories consumed of about a third. Over the same time period there had been a population increase of twenty-five per cent, which explains why food imports doubled.

These figures do not record the food produced for home consumption by the recipients of land reform.

In the spring of 2011 a serious political scandal erupted. Colombian political refugee Joaquín Pérez Becerra, a naturalised Swedish national, was arrested on 23 April by Venezuelan security as he arrived at Maiquetía airport. After being held incommunicado for nearly forty-eight hours, Becerra was handed over to the Colombian authorities and taken across the border. This raised deep questions about the direction of the Bolivarian Revolution, especially as Chávez himself assumed full responsibility.

The effect of handing over Becerra was to drive a wedge between Chávez and revolutionary activists, the very backbone of the Bolivarian movement. As demonstrators massed outside the Caracas headquarters of Venezuela's Bolivarian Intelligence Service (SEBIN), to protest Becerra's illegal detention, the Venezuelan government was deporting Becerra to Colombia without granting him access to legal counsel or representatives of the Swedish embassy.[122] Chávez had respected bourgeois legality when it came to actions concerning the oligarchy but now approved the handing over of a revolutionary activist to the reactionary Colombian regime in flagrant disregard of the rights of the accused. This was a serious mistake which did not serve to defend the Venezuelan revolution, quite the contrary.

Becerra was found guilty on terrorist charges by the Columbian Supreme Court on 12 September, 2012, and sentenced to eight years imprisonment. However, on appeal in 2014, the evidence submitted by the prosecution collapsed and Becerra was released.

16) CHÁVEZ' DEATH, AND THE ELECTION OF MADURO

On 30 June, 2011, Chávez revealed in a televised address from Havana, Cuba, that he was recovering from an operation to remove an abscessed tumour with cancerous cells. On 17 July, he returned to Cuba for further cancer treatment. On 28 July, his fifty-seventh birthday, Chávez made a public appearance and gave a short speech in which he stated that his health troubles had led him to radically reorient his life. He went on to call on the middle classes and the private sector to get more involved in the Bolivarian Revolution, something he saw as "vital" to its success. Symbolically, he wore a yellow, rather than his customary red shirt.

Initially, the opposition tried to take advantage of Chávez' stay in Cuba by cynically arguing that there was a 'power vacuum' and that this had to be filled. This backfired badly as it reminded everyone of April 2002 when the

---

122 Rosales, F., *Deportation of Alternative Journalist Becerra...* VA.com, 29 April, 2011.

oligarchy attempted to justify the coup against Chávez by falsely arguing there had been a 'power vacuum' which they had proceeded to fill.

The implications of Chávez' announcements were discussed everywhere. In particular whether he would be able to stand in the 7 October, 2012 presidential elections. For the masses, Chávez personified the revolution, they saw him as quite separate from the inept, corrupt and incompetent layer of managers, directors, regional governors, local mayors, ministers, state apparatchiks, etc., who were regarded as interested only in their personal advancement, and were openly counter-revolutionary. In the eyes of the masses, only Chávez remained as a genuine and honest revolutionary leader.

Despite all the hopes raised by the formation of the PSUV, the organisation's structures were increasingly being emptied of any real democratic content. At the end of 2011, Chávez appointed Diasdado Cabello as First Vice-President and five other vice-presidents: Elias Jaua, Nicolás Maduro, Tarek El Aissami, Adan Chávez (Hugo's elder brother), and Ramón Rodríguez. This was a pretty unsavoury bunch. Jaua, Maduro, and El Aissami had openly and actively opposed workers' control and sabotaged Plan Socialist Guayana. Cabello was a capitalist who had a track record of undermining internal party democracy. El Aissami had also been heavily involved in the arrest and expulsion of Becerra. Ramón Rodríguez was head of the PSUV's disciplinary tribunal.

With Chávez ill, the PSUV tops moved quickly to increase their control over the party, ruling that local leadership structures of the party at parish and municipal level would be appointed rather than elected. This was a giant step in top-down control of the party. 'Cadres' could now be parachuted in to take control of any dissident local organisation.[123]

The campaign by the opposition for the 2012 presidential elections was more of the same: to focus on immediate issues while using economic sabotage to make living conditions as unbearable as possible for the poorest, all the time blaming the government for every problem of daily life; even the recent heavy rain storms. This time, the opposition made crime a critical issue, bombarding the people with alarming figures for homicides, robberies and kidnappings. The government consistently failed to produce an effective response, and for that reason the bourgeoisie made crime their battle cry. The least the government needed to do was accept the level of crime with a 'Yes, it's true' and not equivocate. This would have removed the criticism that the government denied the level of crime to be an issue.

The high level of crime was an evil inherited from the Fourth Republic and greatly exacerbated by the particular contradictions of the Venezuelan capitalist system. The problem was that Socialism for the Twenty-First

123 Martin, J., 'Venezuela: Revolutionary Vignettes', VA.com, 25 September, 2011.

Century offered no solutions. The functioning of a corrupt state apparatus, particularly in the food chain, the wholesale theft that went on in state enterprises, fed both petty and organised crime. But Venezuela did not need more police, more jails, more judges and more attorneys; it needed effective workers' control and peoples' militias united with communal councils and the popular masses to excise the cancer at the heart of the system.

In the last weeks of the campaign the opposition's economic policy was leaked: a classic austerity package, proposing cuts in pensions, social spending and the 'opening up' of the PDVSA and other state-owned companies to private investment. The plan was so scandalous that four smaller parties in the MUD withdrew their support for Capriles and a whole host of opposition figures distanced themselves from him. In response, the opposition attempted to shift the emphasis to Chávez' illness: stressing Chávez' "frailty", in contrast to the good health and energy of his opponent. They highlighted that the Chavistas did not have anyone who could take his place. On this they had a point; it was an undoubted weakness of the Bolivarian Movement that it depended so much on one man.

The bourgeoisie, having spread lies and more lies for twelve years, acted no differently in the 2012 election campaign: the oligarchy's media told of a sure victory for their candidate, of his enormous support among the popular masses and declining popular support for the president. Shamelessly, the polling firm Consultores had Capriles pulling ahead in September with a two per cent lead. Again, these polls were not meant to reflect reality, they were preparation for making trouble when the results were announced.

The election gave Chávez 55.1 per cent of the vote and Capriles 44.3 per cent. The turn-out was a record eighty-one per cent. The opposition had worked hard on its campaign of dirty tricks; from early in the day rumours were spread about so-called 'exit polls' which gave Capriles an advantage over Chávez by as much as ten percentage points. These were intended to create the impression that any official results showing a Chávez victory were dubious. However, the defeat was so definite that the opposition had no choice but to recognise they had been beaten.

In his election victory speech from the 'People's Balcony' of Miraflores Palace, Chávez announced that the march toward democratic Socialism for the Twenty-First Century would continue. It was seven years since he had first declared that the Venezuelan economy and state apparatus was capitalist and dominated by an oligarchy, inextricably linked to foreign imperialism. This speech contained no definite measures on how to bring their rule to an end.

The more intelligent sections of the ruling class understood that they would not win this election. They wanted to capitalise on the 6 million votes they received (their highest result ever) and play the long game of economic sabotage, while hoping that Chávez' illness would prevent him from completing his term of office. They knew there was no-one else in the Bolivarian leadership who commanded the same level of support and authority amongst the masses so they expected to make big gains in any election held after his death.

Immediately after the presidential election, Vice-President of the PSUV, Diosdado Cabello, announced the party's list of candidates for governors in the forthcoming elections on 16 December. This was a substantial increase in the powers of the party tops over the appointment of local PSUV leaders. The response from the grassroots of the party was fast in coming and was essentially the same everywhere: What had happened to party democracy? Where are the militants who enjoy the support of the local PSUV branches and would take the Revolution forward?

The PSUV was no longer for revolutionary change; it had discarded the objectives on which it had been founded and had become an election machine. The lack of democracy in what was supposed to be "the most democratic party in the history of Venezuela" was due, of course, to the intensity of the struggle between the party machine and the masses. The candidates, in their great majority, fitted in with the leadership, and avoided any action that would embarrass the party tops in Caracas. As they were chosen centrally, they were not responsible to the local PSUV and could be expected to carry out policies quite the opposite of what the local rank and file wanted. These were not the kind of people who would support Socialism for the Twenty-First Century or any other century.

To everyone's surprise, the PSUV candidates for governors won twenty out of the country's twenty-three states, including five which had been run by the opposition. The opposition's only consolation was that their defeated presidential candidate, Henrique Capriles Radonski, retained the important Miranda state, beating former Vice-President Elias Jaua. The official PSUV candidates won 56.2 per cent of the votes, the opposition received 43.8 per cent. The reason for these candidates doing so well was rather obvious. Despite assurances to the contrary, as soon as the opposition had won governorships in the 2008 election it had immediately launched a campaign to reverse the gains made under Chávez; it unleashed its supporters against the healthcare and education programmes, attempting to close them down by expelling them from the premises they occupied. Now the MUD was calling the Housing Mission "a fraud and a failure". Clearly, if the MUD had won then not only would health and education suffer but hundreds of thousands of Venezuelans could be transferred from social housing to the private market.

16.1) DEATH OF CHÁVEZ AND ELECTION OF PRESIDENT MADURO

The 23 January remains a national day celebrating the struggle for democracy in Venezuela. The opposition attempted to take advantage of Chávez' illness by calling a demonstration to protest against "the unconstitutional situation", i.e., the postponement of the swearing-in of Chávez due to his illness (he would never be sworn in). The PSUV leaders responded by calling on the masses to take the streets on the same day. Faced with the prospect of being completely surpassed in numbers, the opposition leaders replaced their march with a rally in Parque Miranda, an upper-class area of Caracas. Fewer than 6,000 attended.

Meanwhile, hundreds of thousands of Chavistas marched, with a big contingent from the unions, both the UNT and the CBST (the Bolivarian Socialist Union of Workers, the new name of the FSBT). It was reported that "thousands of militia men and women in green uniforms" also marched. These were not the people's or workers' militia that Chávez had called for numerous times, these were army reservists who had been renamed the Bolivarian National Militia, as opposed to the popular militia of his original proposals. Rank and file Chavistas carrying banners and chanting slogans against any pacts or deals with the right-wing cheered at the news that the government's campaign against hoarding of basic food products had seized thousands of tons of food hidden in secret depots.

On Friday, 8 February, 2013, the President of the Venezuelan Central Bank, Nelson Merentes, announced the devaluation of the Bolivar from 4.3 to the US dollar to 6.3. At the end of the day, devaluation inevitably leads to higher prices for the final consumers – that is, higher prices for working class families. Currency exchange controls had been introduced in 2003 in an attempt to curb the massive flight of capital, the bourgeoisie had responded with a black market with its own dollar exchange rate. Just as had happened in Nicaragua, the state currency administration division gave dollars to capitalist enterprises at the official exchange rate so they could import materials for production or goods for re-sale. The capitalists then sold the dollars on the black market, making profits of over 1,000 per cent without having to produce anything. The trade was so profitable that even though dozens of businessmen and capitalists were arrested the process flourished. No complete figures have been produced, but at one point the government revealed that around US$20 billion of the subsidies given to the private sector in 2013 had been illegally used for speculation against the Bolivar. However, to this day, tens of billions of dollars are still being handed over to capitalists every year from the state coffers.

This was (and remains) a ludicrous situation, the state is pouring money into the pockets of those who are most actively sabotaging the country's economy. The black market in dollar exchange is ever more under the control of a few politically minded individuals who use it to increase the inflation rate. Government tops sit tight and take no action. The obvious solution is the centralisation of foreign trade, the creation of a single State Importation Centre that would co-ordinate all the country's imports that depend on the dollars supplied by the state. This would be a major brake on inflation and stop the draining away of foreign exchange. It would also be an important step forward in combating corruption, particularly in the state institutions; which may be the reason nothing has been done.

The shortage of medicines is a case in point. Between 2004 and 2014, the scarcity of pharmaceutical products increased dramatically, and headlines screamed of extreme shortages due to the cut-back in government dollars given to the pharmaceutical importers. But analysis by Pasqualina Curio has shown that between 2004 and 2014 there had been cuts in neither the monies allocated, nor the amount of pharmaceutical goods imported. Curia concluded that the shortages were due to hoarding and provides additional evidence by demonstrating that despite the claimed lack of medicines, none of the top ten pharmaceutical importers reported any drop in sales or profits.

Hugo Chávez died on 5 March, 2013, before he could be sworn in as president for the fourth time, and before coming anywhere near to completing a socialist revolution in Venezuela. Important reforms had been carried out that had greatly improved the conditions of the poor and given them hope for the future, but Venezuela had remained a mixed economy and no definite measures had been taken to change that. The bourgeoisie hoped that without Chávez in the presidency, a rapid transition back to 'normality' could occur: undoing the gains of the revolution, the social missions, the nationalisations, the remaining elements of workers' control, agrarian reforms, and so on. The goal, of course, would be to return the 'honey pot' that was the PDVSA to the oligarchy through full or partial privatisation.

Revolutions are made by the masses in motion, gripped by revolutionary ideas. No single individual was more effective in setting the Venezuelan masses into motion than Hugo Chávez. As many as 2 million people took part in the procession accompanying the coffin, as it was transported from the Military Hospital to the *Próceres* where it was to be displayed. For the previous fourteen years, the overwhelming majority of the population, workers, the poor, peasants, and many who would describe themselves as middle class, had gained a deep feeling of pride and dignity from participating directly in activities which changed their lives, learning to read and write, building medical centres and schools, taking ownership of a new house, and defending those gains against the repeated assaults of the oligarchy and imperialism.

But because Chávez was the undisputed leader of the Bolivarian Revolution, of the Venezuelan state and PSUV, it is all the more important to examine his most important mistakes. The absence of a party to focus activity, democratically deciding policies, democratically electing its leaders and able to hold them to account, was a serious impediment to the revolutionary process. Chávez repeatedly made radical proposals, but no mechanisms existed for advancing them. They were not party policy, the PSUV tops simply ignored or sabotaged them, safe in the knowledge there was no structure to hold them to account. With no elected collective leadership, Chávez was constrained by the right-wing tops in the PSUV, who were able to curb his more left-wing tendencies. Without Chávez, this central weakness of the Bolivarian movement would be writ large.

The bourgeois media and US imperialism immediately insisted that "the Constitution must be respected". The opposition went further and alleged that a "coup" had taken place, when Vice-President Nicolás Maduro was sworn as President-in-charge by the National Assembly, and boycotted the ceremony. The constitution clearly stated that in the case of "permanent absence" of the president, the vice-president would take over and new elections would be called within thirty days. The Venezuelan ruling class did not really care who took over until the presidential elections on 14 April. What they wanted was a climate of uncertainty, and to tarnish the institution of the presidency with suspicions of illegitimacy.

On Friday 8 March, 2013, the main opposition leader, Capriles, went on the offensive saying that the decision for Maduro to become President-in-charge was a "constitutional fraud". In an arrogant and condescending tone, he opened a campaign attacking Nicolás Maduro for having been a "simple bus driver" and therefore, unsuitable to be a president. Maduro replied to these insults by driving a bus to register as a presidential candidate. In public Capriles described Maduro as "Satan", "bird brain", "great fool", and "liar". These insults exposed the depth of class hatred which inspired the oligarchs, the bankers, *caudillos* and capitalists, but it was also a quite deliberate attempt to lower the tone of the campaign into the gutter, to undermine the authority of the election and the democratic process. Capriles then refused to sign the standard CNE document committing him to recognising the result, saying instead that he would "respect the popular will", preparing the ground for not acknowledging the election outcome.

The election was held on 14 April, 2013. The result was sufficiently close (7.6 million votes [50.6 per cent] against 7.4 million [49.1 per cent]), for Capriles to call his supporters onto the streets banging pots and pans to demand the CNE not proclaim Maduro the winner. Right-wing students hurling chunks of concrete took over squares in Caracas, burning several clinics and attempting to block the main roads. Seven deaths were reported. National Guards were called to disperse the demonstrators.

Capriles refused to concede defeat and raised accusations of fraud, demanding an audit of all votes cast, with detailed examination of voters' signatures and fingerprint records to see if dead people, or foreigners, or duplicates had voted.[124] The CNE rejected this as "impossible" since the process would take up to five years to complete. Capriles responded that, without this audit, the result was "a joke". As late as 30 April, the opposition was still refusing to recognise Maduro as the elected president. On that day opposition legislators prepared to disrupt National Assembly proceedings, arriving with a large "*Golpe al Parlamento*" (Coup in Parliament) banner and interrupting the session with whistles and air horns.

After his narrow victory, Maduro appealed to businessmen to stay away from politics and concentrate on production. He offered the creation of Special Economic Zones modelled on those in China, and to ease foreign exchange controls. There was even talk of reforming some of the articles of the Labour Law. Several prominent radical Bolivarian talk show hosts and presenters were removed from state TV and radio stations. None of that pacified the opposition, of course, but it indicated that Maduro was not intending to move in a socialist or even radical direction. Quite the reverse, it looked as though he was attempting to strike a deal with the MUD at the expense of a deepening crisis for the poorest.

Over the summer and into the autumn, the oligarchy, buoyed up by the election results, escalated its economic sabotage. Inflation soared, reaching fifty-four per cent between January and October, with a record level of shortages. The opposition believed that, having caused so much economic distress for so long, the government would fare badly in the 8 December, municipal elections.

In September, four months before the election, the government was against the ropes, with its level of support falling sharply. Then, in late October and early November, the government launched a massive campaign against the hoarding of goods. Led by Eduardo Samán, the campaign

---

124 Carlson, C., VA.com, 25 April, 2013.

started with Daka, a white goods and electronics chain, warehouses full of goods were seized and the business forced to sell them at 'fair prices'. The government measures had a two-fold impact. On the one hand, they made products available which were previously scarce or too expensive, and on the other, they rekindled the revolutionary expectations of the rank and file. Here was a government clearly identifying the enemy and taking harsh measures against them. This is what the popular masses wanted to see. This offensive enabled the Bolivarian movement not only to win the municipal elections but to increase its lead over the opposition.

The opposition presented these municipal elections as a plebiscite on Maduro's presidency. In the event, the PSUV and its allies in the Great Patriotic Pole received 5.2 million votes with 4.4 million going to the opposition. Celebrating the election results, President Maduro pledged to intensify the offensive against the economic war, the campaign of hoarding, speculation, sabotage and corruption launched by the "parasitic bourgeoisie". Concrete measures were absent.

17) THE OPPOSITION OFFENSIVE AND ELECTORAL GAINS

After the elections, President Maduro met with representatives of the national bourgeoisie. Adopting a conciliatory tone, he offered concessions, such as increasing state credit in the form of US dollars. Thanking the president for his generosity, the opposition left the meeting and immediately ramped up the economic war. The bourgeoisie showed a complete lack of interest in working with the government, intending to continue their campaign of economic sabotage, and with the main means of production in their hands, they had the power to do it.

The conciliatory attitude of the PSUV leaders was taken as weakness and convinced the most extreme of the opposition leaders that they should take their fight onto the streets. Leopoldo Lopez and Maria Corina Machado (an opposition MP) were convinced that action on the streets would bring the government down. This campaign was launched on 23 January, 2014, under the banner of *La Salida* (the way out) with the stated aim of forcing the removal of democratically-elected President Maduro.

A *guarimba* (creation of public disorder and unrest) was launched. In some cases, it could count on the passive support of opposition mayors and regional governors who would do nothing to stop them or to clear the streets of roadblocks. Destruction of buses, fire bomb attacks against public institutions, notably the VTV state TV station in Los Ruices which was besieged for seven nights, followed. Actions took place in different towns, such as Mérida and San Cristobal. In Caracas, the *guarimba* was concentrated in the rich areas of the East. This was akin to rioting in London taking place in Hampstead, Kensington and Chelsea, with the centre of protests in Belgravia. It is also interesting to note that there was no looting, as opposed to what usually happens when people are moved by hunger.

Capriles Radonski, and the main body of the opposition opposed this campaign of street violence because it was obvious that the interests of the ruling class were best served by consolidating their positions in regional governments and municipalities and waiting for a more propitious time when they would win an election and assume power more gently. It is not that they were opposed to the violent overthrow of the government, they simply did not think that the conditions were right and hoped to do it peacefully. The bourgeois press referred to "a brainless mob which wants to destroy everything in its wake", complaining that such actions strengthened the Chavistas and could incite the masses to action.

On 18 February, the opposition called a march which was widely reported in the world's press, and which, according to Associated Press, had 5,000 participants. On the same day, the workers at the PDVSA had their own counter-demonstration in defence of the revolution, with tens of thousands participating. The latter was barely mentioned by the world's media. The oil workers' demonstration marked the beginning of a Bolivarian counter-offensive against the small groups of opposition rioters. On 19 February, a large demonstration of pro-revolution workers from the basic industries in Puerto Ordaz, Bolivar took place. The workers, who had suffered road blockades by a small number of opposition thugs, quickly cleared their barricades. They were then shot at by fascist elements from one of the neighbouring buildings, resulting in nine workers being wounded. In other parts of the country there were mobilisations in defence of the revolution, in many instances with workers playing a leading role. In a televised speech on the night of 19 February, President Maduro appealed to the working class to be united and mobilised and "to strengthen the workers' militias".

President Maduro had talked of workers' militias before, and this was clearly a time to put words into actions. But talk is one thing, action is another. The government action was not to arm its citizens but to appeal to the ruling class and offer even greater access to foreign exchange. Samán, one of the main driving forces behind the campaign against the economic sabotage, was removed from his position without explanation. This constant oscillation between strong words and conciliatory actions was deepening the disillusion, scepticism and cynicism of the Bolivarian masses and encouraging the oppositionists to believe their methods were working.

The bureaucracy simultaneously acted as a brake on workers' struggles. To give just one example: the workers at *ABC Formas y Sistemas*, faced with an illegal lock-out by their bosses, had been occupying their factory for over a year. They had tried all the existing legal avenues for the expropriation of the factories but had come to a dead end, with the Ministry of Labour taking no action (not refusing to act, just taking no notice, leaving the workers in limbo). There were dozens of examples like that throughout the country. The state bureaucracy and the reformist elements within the PSUV and government acted as saboteurs, blocking the initiatives of the masses and giving support to the counter-revolution.

There was increasing and widespread discontent amongst the Bolivarian ranks at the open control of the movement at all levels by the bureaucrats at the top. President Maduro made calls for unity and discipline, but the forthcoming congress of the PSUV, scheduled for the end of July was already getting off to a bad start, it had been announced that the 900 delegates would include the PSUV's national leadership, ninety-six parliamentary deputies, twenty state governors and 242 mayors, some forty per cent of the total.

There were also widespread protests within the PSUV over the number of prominent radical or left-wing Bolivarian journalists who, since the presidential election, had been removed from state TV and radio channels without explanation. Whatever the reason might have been, the result was clear: critical left-wing voices were being silenced or denied access to larger audiences. Whether or not these sackings were part of a backroom deal with the opposition, or just a gesture of good will to them, they did not moderate the opposition, but rather helped demoralise the revolutionary movement.

On the evening of 10 April, 2014, the main political representatives of the Venezuelan opposition met with the government at Miraflores Palace in a 'Dialogue for Peace'. Present at the meeting were international observers from UNASUR (Union of South American Nations, an inter-governmental body). A famous quote from Bolivar seems applicable here:

> Every conspiracy was followed by forgiveness, and every forgiveness was followed by another conspiracy which was in turn forgiven again… Criminal clemency, more than anything else, contributed to the destruction of the structure which we had not yet entirely completed![125]

Much the same sentiments were expressed by French revolutionary Hébert, if in a sharper manner:

> The moderates have buried more victims than those that fell before the steel of our enemies. Nothing is more harmful in a revolution than half measures.

---

125 Simon Bolivar, *Cartagena Manifesto*, 1812.

The national and international media painted a picture of the government of Venezuela as dictatorial, attacking the human rights of unarmed, peaceful and defenceless people. In reality, if the Bolivarian Revolution can be accused of anything, it is of being too soft on its opponents. This was graphically seen at the 'Dialogue for Peace': nearly all the opposition representatives had participated to some degree in the 11 April, 2002, coup. None of them had faced trial. On the contrary, they had been allowed to go free. President Chávez, magnanimously, perhaps naively, called for dialogue and forgiveness. The capitalist class responded by organising a lock-out to bring the government to its knees, followed by an ongoing media war and continuing economic sabotage and the *guarimbas*. Why would it be different now?

The representatives of the bourgeoisie brought to the 'Dialogue for Peace' proposals which included: fiscal discipline (i.e., cuts in social spending); national production with a free market (i.e., lifting price controls); encouraging productivity through the 'flexibilisation' of labour (i.e., abolishing job security and destroying the labour rights contained in the Organic Labour Act); and liberalisation of foreign exchange controls (i.e., free access to oil revenue dollars). These measures, taken together, would have meant a brutal shift in the balance of power in favour of the oligarchy and allowed exploitation of the labour force with little hindrance. The popular masses would face savage cuts, an end to the measures which the revolution had implemented to better their lives.

The opposition also demanded: all talk of socialism and revolution to be stopped ("it's not in the Constitution"), the release of 'political prisoners' (i.e., immunity for those involved in the terrorist *guarimbas*), fairness in public institutions (i.e., the capitalists to regain direct control over the most important levers of the state apparatus), and disarm the *colectivos* (i.e., criminalisation and destruction of the rank and file organisations of the Bolivarian Revolution).

For fifteen years the Bolivarian Revolution had restricted itself to bourgeois legality, while the oligarchy resorted, time and again, to any means at their disposal to try to overthrow it. The bourgeoisie had spared no effort, legal or illegal, to crush the revolution. They had consistently defended their class interests. To each and all of these the Bolivarian tops extended the hand of forgiveness and friendship. Now they were doing the same again. Emboldened by the discussions, *caudillos* were increasingly challenging land occupations, claiming that the INTI had committed legal errors or not properly compensated them for the lands expropriated. The murdering of *campesino* leaders to prevent land occupations went largely unpunished because of the land-owners' control over the local judiciary. At the same time, the MUD campaigned against expropriating unproductive land, despite agricultural production, largely by co-operatives, having increased to a level where it supplied 100 per cent of the demand for basic root vegetables.

On 2 May, 2014, the TSJ ordered the INTI to dispossess a twelve-year-old co-operative known as *Brisas de Masparro* and return the 3,600 hectares of land to Rogelio Peña Aly, an ex-mayor of the region who, according to the peasants, had acquired the land through corruption and intimidation. The ruling was symbolic as Hugo Chávez had personally introduced the Land Law into Barinas state. The ruling was a double strike because the co-operative was producing 30,000 litres a day of much needed milk, had over 25,000 livestock, had built over 230 km of agricultural roadways and fourteen schools. To put the cap on it, Ruben Dario Mendoza, representative of the cattle and agribusiness federation claimed that, on the basis of the decision, ten other plots of land could now be taken back.[126]

On 9 December, 2014, the TSJ made a second important decision when it revoked the property title of the *El Maizal* commune with about 7,500 members. At a time of food shortages this was known as the most productive commune in the nation, with crops of corn, legumes, and vegetables. Chávez had twice broadcast his weekly show *Aló Presidente* from the commune, and commended its progress. *El Maizal* was in the process of building a cornflour factory, to combat the monopoly of the Mendoza family, who had long used the distribution of this staple as a political tool against the government. It may not have been entirely coincidental that the person taking the court action was an associate of Polar. One thing was clear the *caudillos* and forces within the state were again criminalising the struggles of the *campesinos*, the bourgeoisie were feeling strong enough to openly use the judicial power against the popular masses.

Ángel Prado, a spokesperson for *El Maizal* argued that local Chavista leaders and the PSUV were their main enemies, actively attempting to "extinguish the commune… the grassroots sectors that withstood the *guarimba* protests, that withstood the coup d'etat and oil strike, that resisted all of these and neutralised the right wing".[127] In public, Maduro declared the TSJ decision "counter-revolutionary", but there was no suggestion of taking active measures in support of the commune. On the strength of Maduro's response, the opposition prepared the ground for a determined assault on co-operatives, and the state chosen to spearhead that was Barinas, where Chávez' brother Adan was governor.

---

126 Dutka, Z., *Venezuelan Peasants Protest Supreme Court*, VA.com, 29 May, 2014.
127 Ciccariello-Maher, G., *Venezuela: ¡Comuna o Nada!*, VA.com, 22 March, 2016.

On 17 June, 2014, President Maduro announced the removal of Minister of Finance and Planning Jorge Giordani, a key architect of the government's economic policy since 1999. This move towards 'normality' was commended by the US Bank of America in glowing terms:

> [A] strong sign of the waning influence of the radical Marxist wing on economic policy issues... there is evidence of greater willingness by officials to engage the private sector and investors than there was in the past.

Giordani, now publicly describing government policies as inefficient and opening the door to corruption, challenged the very basis on which the government had convened the so-called 'Economic Peace Roundtable', disputing the idea that there could be a *modus vivendi* between the Bolivarian Revolution and big businesses. In response, the Minister of Oil and Vice Minister for the Economy, Rafael Ramirez, embarked on a series of meetings and press conferences with the aim of "re-establishing relations with the financial markets" (while declaring "socialism would be maintained"). The bankers, of course, had no intention of investing in Venezuela unless the demands made at the roundtable were agreed.

Some six weeks later, on 28 July, 2014, the PSUV's Third National Congress began with Vice-President Diosdado Cabello announcing Nicolás Maduro as PSUV candidate for the presidency, to the "acclamation" of the 985 delegates. Maduro's acceptance speech declared that the government's "foremost task in the coming period (was) the advancement and transition towards a socialist economy". When details emerged, they showed the advance would, in practice, be the continuation of the government's perverse and ineffective policy of class conciliation. Maduro sat down with Lorenzo Mendoza and Henrique Capriles, providing them with a political platform and economic concessions, but failing to reduce the economic sabotage.

On 12 February, 2015, a coup attempt was foiled with the arrest of seven Air Force officers. Many in the Bolivarian movement had been convinced that the armed forces were "as red as red can be" and there was no threat from that quarter. But, within the confines of the bourgeois state, military men, as they rise up the ranks and receive higher salaries, perks and privileges, tend to identify more with the bourgeoisie than the dispossessed masses. As long as the military apparatus remained based on a bourgeois state and organised according to the social relations that dominate in a bourgeois society, there will always be pressures pushing the top military officers towards the interests of the ruling class.

For revolutionaries this confirmed the need to consolidate militias in every neighbourhood, workplace, union, school, and university, as an independent armed force and not under the tutelage of the army. It also confirmed the need for rank and file committees within the armed forces, and for political commissars linked to the Bolivarian masses. Without such measures the events of 12 February will surely be repeated. Just as US Imperialism finances sectors of the opposition, so US agents will be working to convince army officers to effect a coup if the bourgeoisie can engineer an appropriate scenario. In this the PSUV tops and state bureaucrats, with their policies of sabotaging workers' initiatives, aid the destabilisation of the country.

In early August 2015, there was a sudden upsurge in attacks on communes. The two main targets were the *comuneros* in *El Maizal* who were still holding out, and a large commune in Barinas state. According to reports, the attack on *El Maizal* was by local National Guard units which had previously been known to act on the orders of big landowners allegedly implementing TSJ rulings.

An attack on the communities of *Orticero, Las Mercedes*, and *Jovito* in Barinas state commune was an even murkier incident. The land had been occupied since 2011 with permission from the INTI. This should have meant that, under the law, the *comuneros* were protected from eviction. In April of 2017, a new co-ordinator for the Barinas INTI took office, Ingrid Gil Guzmán. Under her orders National Guard units removed more than 860 people from their homes in an early morning raid. "When they arrived to evict us, they drove the tractors over to destroy our crops, they poured gasoline on the plantains and poisoned the wells that the campesinos had made for human and animal consumption" testified María Alejandra Tovar from *Las Mercedes*. "They took our animals, burnt our homes, our harvests, they destroyed everything in their path".[128] Communities Minister, Elias Jaua, remained silent.

For more than six months, the *campesinos* in Barinas had been demanding the removal of Guzmán, even to the extent of occupying the local INTI offices on the grounds that she had been 'doing business' with local landowners. An investigation into alleged involvement in illegal expulsions and corruption in the INTI regional authority, arranged a few days after the events, was rapidly discontinued. During the short-lived search, files and documents were found in which INTI officials had allocated themselves land. It was also found that land titles issued by the central authority in Caracas were not delivered, so that the *campesinos* lived and worked without formal

---

128 Boothroyd Rojas, R., *Investigation Launched into Violent Eviction of Rural Families in Venezuela*, VA.com, 14 March, 2017.

legal authority, which meant they could be subject to arbitrary eviction or made to pay a bribe.[129]

17.1) COUNTER-REVOLUTION WINS 2015, NATIONAL ASSEMBLY ELECTION

To help set the tone for the National Assembly elections, to be held on 9 March, 2015, US President Obama issued an Executive Order declaring a "national emergency" affirming that "the situation in Venezuela" posed an "unusual and extraordinary threat to the national security and foreign policy of the United States". This was US imperialism unjustifiably meddling in the internal affairs of a sovereign nation. The threat which Venezuela presented to US imperialism was the threat of inspiring progressive and democratic change in Latin America and beyond. The democratic credentials of the Bolivarian Revolution cannot be questioned by anyone.

The collapse of oil prices, exacerbated by US sanctions, meant the previous three years had seen a sharp deterioration of the economic situation in Venezuela. Oil hovered around $100 a barrel in 2013, but in 2016 it reached its lowest level for over ten years – $24 a barrel. The government decided to prioritise the payment of foreign debt, thereby severely constraining its ability to invest money in social programmes, to import food and other products. To continue paying for the social programmes to which it was committed, the state started to print massive amounts of money, resulting in galloping inflation, which hit working people especially hard. In a year, the price of many basic products rose by over 100 per cent. In real terms state subsidies on most products, including food, fell substantially.

Eggs, one of the main protein sources in the Venezuelan diet, were sold at around 100 Bolívars per carton of thirty eggs at the beginning of 2014. As prices rose, the government stepped in to regulate the price at 420 Bolívars. The result was the immediate and complete disappearance of eggs from the shops, as producers and shopkeepers refused to sell at the official price. By the end of October 2015, the street price was 1,000 Bolívars. Similar examples can be given for every basic product.

The dislocation of normal economic activity led to the collapse of the little private investment that was still taking place. The capitalists made more money exploiting the exchange rate differential than investing in production. Without nationalisation of the banking system, the exchange rate controls, instead of protecting the government's reserves, were becoming a means by which the country's oil revenue was being returned to the pockets of the

---

129 Haule, E., *Forcible Transfer of Farmers in Venezuela, Corruption in Land Authority,* Amerika 21, 18 March, 2017.

oligarchy. The country's hard currency reserves dropped from around US$30 billion in 2012, to less than US$15 billion at the end of 2014.

On 6 December, 2015, the result of the parliamentary election was a decisive victory for the counter-revolutionary opposition, the MUD, which gained 7.7 million votes and 112 seats, to the PSUV's 5.6 million and fifty-five seats. The PSUV tops had believed the path of compromise to be safest, when it was, in fact, the most treacherous. Maduro's policy had backfired spectacularly. The opposition made inroads into what had previously been revolutionary strongholds, even managing to win in the *23 de Enero* parish in Caracas. If this pattern were to be repeated in the presidential elections, the oligarchy would be returned to power.

The never-ending stresses and strains of ordinary life were becoming steadily worse, not better. The realisation that many Bolivarian tops were benefiting massively from the endemic corruption, the weariness brought on by having to battle continuously against layers of corrosive bureaucracy, all of this had an impact on the consciousness of layers of the masses who previously supported the revolution. These were the key reasons for the defeat in the National Assembly elections.

The government's attempts to compromise with the opposition meant there had been no large-scale seizures and distribution of hoarded goods, a situation perceived by the masses as a serious failure of leadership. The public wanted action. Denouncing and threatening to nationalise *Grupo Polar* was seen as weakness when nothing resulted. Nor had the PSUV election campaign projected any sense it would solve these problems. Maduro accepted the election results with the words "it could be said that the economic war has won", but it was his inaction that had handed victory to the oligarchs. With the victory of the right wing, the cries of 'fraud' which had dogged the very same electoral process for seventeen years were noticeable by their absence.

The state and party bureaucracies had refused to support workers in action and deliberately stifled workers' democracy. Their corruption and mismanagement of nationalised factories and enterprises caused even militant workers to doubt whether state control and planning was the way forward. On many fronts the bureaucracy had acted as the vanguard of the capitalists: every time a group of workers moved forward, by setting up a workers' council, by occupying a factory and running it themselves, by taking over idle land, by setting up communes, they were blocked and pushed back by the bureaucracy, often using the police and National Guard.

One example: *Industrias Diana* is a food plant processing oil and margarine, which was expropriated in 2008 and was then run very successfully under workers' self-management. A major success was that eighty per cent of the output was going to Mercal, much of the remainder went to community collectives and only a small proportion to the open market. In July 2013, Minister of Food, Félix Osorio, decided to impose a new manager without consulting the workers. The workers resisted and argued that they had a say in the matter. Osorio was determined to have his way, and the measures he took included subjecting leading members of the union to detention and interrogation by the National Intelligence Service. Finally, after months of struggle, the workers won, the new manager was removed and a former military officer who vowed to continue to the existing self-management was accepted by both sides and appointed.[130]

This example could be replicated many times across the country at all levels, but in most cases the workers did not emerge victorious, and in this context, talk of 'revolution' and 'socialism' became empty rhetoric. The opposition won the election not because of any failure by the Bolivarian masses, but because their reformist leaders had consistently avoided the path of expropriating the capitalist class, and chose instead to appeal to the goodwill of private capitalists.

With 112 seats in the National Assembly the opposition appeared to have a two thirds majority and the wide-ranging powers that went with it. Drunk with victory and seething with revenge, on the night of the election the representatives of the opposition announced the measures they would implement: nothing less than rescinding every progressive law passed by the Bolivarian government. The Law on Fair Prices, the Labour Law and the Health and Safety at Work Act would be made more 'business friendly'. The Land Law would be repealed and all expropriated *latifundia* returned. A law for Activation and Strengthening of National Production was promised for privatisation of all state-owned land. All state-owned enterprises (i.e. PDVSA) and expropriated factories (i.e. SIDOR) would be privatised with their new owners being exempt from all taxes for four years. The opposition also announced its intention to purge all state institutions, including the CNE and the TSJ.

Venezuela now faced the unique situation where the National Assembly was in the hands of the MUD, and the President and Executive in the hands of the PSUV. The MUD needed a two-thirds majority in the National Assembly to change the organic laws and overrule the President, but during the election campaign some of its hotter heads had played fast and loose with the electoral rules. At the end of December 2015, the TSJ ruled that there had been irregularities in the election of deputies in the Amazonas state on

130 Robertson, W., *Venezuela's Diana Industries Workers Claim Victory in Struggle vs. Managerial "Imposition"*, VA.com, 16 August, 2013.

the grounds that the MUD had been involved in vote buying. The election in that state was declared invalid and ordered to be re-run. This affected four deputies, two from the MUD, one from the PSUV and another one elected in the indigenous list (also a MUD supporter). However, the three deputies were essential to give the MUD its two thirds majority.

At first, the National Assembly refused to accept the TSJ ruling and swore in the three MUD deputies for Amazonas on Wednesday 6 January. The TSJ declared that this act threatened to make the entire swearing-in process null and void. The National Assembly temporarily retreated and a week later suspended the members for Amazonas. However, just to show its resolve, on the same day it introduced a bill to privatise state housing but this, and other reactionary measures, were blocked either by the President or the TSJ. In parallel, measures taken by the President were ruled out of order by the Assembly. Government was paralysed.

Throughout January 2016, President Maduro was in a running fight with the National Assembly. He claimed the economic situation amounted to a State of Emergency and introduced special powers for sixty days under an 'Economic Emergency Decree'. These included sweeping powers to deal with, amongst other things, problems of food production and distribution. However, the National Assembly refused to accept the decision and responded by announcing that it would instead concentrate its efforts on removing Maduro as President. The new President of the National Assembly, Henry Ramos Allup (from AD with a long history of actively promoting neo-liberal policies) promised on taking office "to get rid of the Maduro government within six months". The first of the anti-Maduro street demonstrations was scheduled for Saturday 12 March, 2016, in Caracas. In the event, some ten thousand attended, but a rival PSUV march was much larger, with tens of thousands supporting Maduro. It was becoming clear that a layer of people who had voted for the opposition from desperation, and wanting to end the economic impasse were having second thoughts on seeing what the rule of the right wing really entailed.

Maduro now embarked on a two-pronged approach to resolve the problem. In an attempt to assuage the capitalists, he established the National Council for a Productive Economy, a diverse body composed of ministers, private business leaders, governors, mayors, and others, tasked with finding solutions to the country's deepening economic crisis. This was an ideological throwback to the time when Chávez still believed in the third way of Tony Blair. Simultaneously, he announced economic measures to show he was willing to compromise: capitalists would receive even more preferential dollars, soft loans, the passage of imports and exports would be smoothed, prices of goods and services could be increased, there would be devaluation and increased gasoline prices. For the financiers he promised to continue prioritising the payment of foreign debt.

To defuse any backlash from the masses, he announced some face-saving and limited social programmes, a small wage increase and food stamps. At the same time the PSUV bureaucracy called mass demonstrations in support of Maduro which, given the shock of the electoral defeat, were well attended. In a fanfare of publicity, the government also launched the Congress of the Fatherland, with 100 elected delegates with responsibility for drawing up a strategic plan "for the strengthening of the socialist project in Venezuela". Initially well-received, it soon became clear that it would have no effect on government policy. This manoeuvre was totally inadequate to block the counter-revolution and take back political power. It soon faded away. Both the Congress and the demonstrations were intended to act only as safety valves for dissent; instead they increased the cynicism, scepticism, and apathy of the masses.

On 28 March, the TSJ ruled that the National Assembly remained in contempt of court. Seeing his opportunity, Maduro sent a memo to the TSJ asking whether his presidential decisions still needed ratification by the National Assembly. The TSJ replied with its now-famous ruling of 29 March, that since the National Assembly was in contempt of court, the government did not have to send its decisions to it for ratification, that the TSJ was taking over the National Assembly's legislative powers to exercise as it saw fit.

The National Assembly could have easily regained its powers if the MUD had agreed to re-elections in Amazonas. Its refusal to take the obvious and peaceful path to government says much about the character and intentions of the oligarchy. The opposition was not really interested in parliamentary procedures, it was determined to remove Maduro from office as soon as it could. This was not a question of who was right and who was wrong from a legal or procedural viewpoint, but of who held real power, in terms of mass mobilisations and the loyalty of the army.

Following this announcement by the TSJ, the MUD launched a campaign of almost continuous violent street protests with the aim of overthrowing the president. A spokesperson for the most radical wing of the opposition, María Corina Machado, in an opinion article in the Ecuadorean paper *El Comercio*, made clear: "The aim is not to hold elections... The aim is to depose the regime". These protests were extremely violent, leading to over thirty people, mostly Chavistas, being killed. There were violent clashes with small groups of young MUD supporters who used firearms, home-made explosives and rocket launchers against the police, but also against educational institutions, state buildings, housing projects, hospitals and public transport.

On 8 April, MUD supporters ransacked and attempted to set fire to the TSJ building, they then set out to march to the buildings of the CNE. The government called out the National Guard to prevent them reaching their destination. However, these protests were not occurring throughout Venezuela, not even the whole of Caracas. They were concentrated in municipalities ruled by opposition mayors, particularly in Carabobo, Lara, Mérida, Táchira, and eastern Caracas.

To make matters worse, Venezuela was suffering a severe drought bringing problems in energy generation at, for example, the El Guiri hydroelectric dam. This led to regular power outages and, in April, the government decreed a two-day working week in public institutions to reduce electricity consumption. Of course, MUD supporters took advantage of this with bomb attacks against power generating plants, power stations and substations in different parts of the country with the aim of creating additional power outages to spread feelings of chaos and instability.

Despite the popularity of the PSUV being at a low ebb, there was still a hardcore of working class and poor people who came out on May Day. Hundreds of thousands of people marched against MUD's attempts to overthrow the government. The world's media, which had been paying much attention to Venezuela and had correspondents in Caracas at the time, was unanimous in its silence on this demonstration; instead, they painted a picture of an authoritarian regime with no support holding power only by its repression of peaceful protesters.

In May, the TSJ blocked a law for the privatisation of 1.2 million homes built as social housing for families on low incomes. The law as it stood gave 'Deeds of Use', which granted the right to the home, to the family as a whole and the property could not be sold on the open market. Change of residence would be a swap with a family in a suitable home. The new law would give ownership to the (usually male) head of the family who would then have the legal right to sell the property privately.

In July, the MUD decided to ignore the TSJ and again swore in the three Amazonas deputies. This was followed in August by the TSJ declaring that the National Assembly Presiding Council and the MUD deputies were all in contempt of court. In a further escalation of the institutional conflict, in October, the National Assembly voted to initiate proceedings to declare that Maduro had "abandoned his office" based on claims which included Maduro not being a Venezuelan citizen and therefore, unable to be president.

But if Maduro's government regained power, what would it do with it? Since the exit of Giordani from the government in July 2014, there was increasing recognition of the failure of the previous model of using oil revenues to attempt to regulate capitalism and fund social programmes. But the changes proposed were not a move leftwards. Ignoring the lessons of history, the new policy was to make even more concessions to the capitalists, national and international, in the forlorn hope they would collaborate with the government and help to turn the economic situation around. This was expressed in a whole series of measures such as further liberalising of foreign exchange and the establishment of Special Economic Zones, where companies did not have to abide by labour laws or pay any taxes. The majority of those who now continued to support Maduro did so because the alternative, a MUD government, would have made their lives even worse.

These measures were very unpopular amongst the ranks of the Bolivarian movement as representing a betrayal of the legacy of Chávez. But really, they were no more than a continuation and a deepening of the policy which the Maduro government had inherited: making ever more concessions to the capitalists in the economic field while defending itself against the MUD's attacks in the political and institutional arenas. The oligarchy had maintained its economic sabotage and there were now widespread media reports of food scarcity, hunger and looting across Venezuela.

The MUD was attempting to create a situation of such chaos and violence as would justify a coup or foreign intervention to remove President Maduro. Inevitably, the massive expansion of the money supply had caused hyperinflation, a rapid depletion of foreign reserves and a further decrease in government imports of food and other basic products. More people had to buy a greater proportion of their food on the black market, with prices between twenty and seventy times the official price. The government decreed increases in the minimum wage, but nowhere near enough to feed a family.

Scarcity led to massive corruption at all levels; from criminals who hired people to queue for hours to buy whatever subsidised products were available to re-sell on the black market, to the nationwide director of the *Bicentenario* state supermarket chain who diverted entire ship-loads of products. To some extent, the majority of Venezuelans were aware of the despicable role played by private companies, like *Grupo Polar*, in hoarding, racketeering, speculation, etc., and of the government's failure to take the necessary measures to solve the problems.

In the summer of 2016, the government began formally promoting mixed public-private investment in the mining of diamonds, copper, silver and gold. Maduro invited multinational corporations to bid for concessions;

an initiative which authorised open pit mining in 112,000 square kilometres of the mineral-rich south-eastern Amazonian state of Bolivar. These will be environmentally destructive projects; all mining and oil extraction projects are, and there is no exception to this anywhere in the world.

An integral part of this venture is the military. Previously, President Maduro had approved a Socialist Military Economic Zone, allowing initiatives in different economic sectors, from transport, agriculture and communications to construction, finance and hospitality. Now, CAMIMPEG (Military Company for the Oil, Mining, and Gas Industries) was launched to provide a wide range of industrial services as an integral part of a US$580 million deal in mining and gas production in the Orinoco Mining Arc backed by Chinese investment. The Maduro Administration has placed the Arco region under military control, suspended constitutional rights and already begun to expel the residents. CAMIMPEG will administer the resource extraction as an autonomous enterprise and not be subject to public accountability. These ventures are widely seen as attempts by Maduro to tie the military to his regime. The Orinoco Mining Arc project, taking into account only the gold reserves of the area, is estimated to be worth more than US$200 billion.[131]

In a separate multi-million dollar deal, the Venezuelan government will work with Yuankuang and other Chinese companies to jumpstart nickel mining in the central states of Aragua and Miranda.[132]

On Monday, 16 May, Minister of Economic Development, Pérez Abad, in the face of rumours to the contrary, stressed Venezuela's intention to continue to pay its foreign debt obligations in full and on time. He added that this would mean a further reduction in food imports in 2016 and, behind the scenes, sold US$2.8 billion of PDVSA bonds maturing in 2020 to Goldman Sachs for only US$865 million, a give-away price that has been termed absurd.

The government's concessions were accompanied from time to time with threats of expropriation, which were given headlines by the bourgeois press world-wide. In Venezuela the threats were never followed up; the reality was quite the opposite. Workers, who took over factories where production had been suspended by the bosses, were met with either an endless string of bureaucratic obstacles or direct repression by police or National Guards. Even though laws were formally on the side of the workers and did allow for expropriations, the majority of labour inspectors were in the pockets of the

131 Egaña-Prodavinci, C., *Venezuela's Orinoco Mining Belt*, VA.com, 8 September, 2016.

132 Koerner, L., *Venezuela Signs Controversial $1.16 bn Mining Deal*, VA.com, 24 July, 2017.

bosses. Instead of expediting expropriation, the owners were given extension after extension in which to restart production, until the workers were so demoralised they gave up their fight.

The bourgeoisie, however, feared rekindling the revolutionary fervour of the masses; they remembered the extraordinary vitality and strength of the revolutionary mobilisation of the popular masses in 2002 and 2003. The government and PSUV tops also feared the masses, which accounts for the calls to form popular and workers' militias never being carried through. The bureaucracy was organically incapable of activating the revolutionary mobilisation of the masses because they knew they had more to lose from a socialist revolution than from the bourgeoisie.

18) THE RECALL REFERENDUM AND THE CONSTITUENT ASSEMBLY

The MUD was collecting signatures for a recall referendum, but evidence presented to the courts of widespread irregularities meant the process was suspended, effectively ruling out any possibility of a presidential recall referendum being held in 2016. In response, the MUD called the decision "a coup carried out by the government of President Maduro against the Constitution". On Sunday, 23 October, an extraordinary session of the National Assembly, which was still in contempt, adopted a resolution declaring that the government had committed a "breach of the constitutional order", and symbolically appointed new members to the CNE and the TSJ.

The sharpening of the economic war and rampant inflation had meant the impoverishment of vast sectors of the popular masses. One survey by Venebarómetro carried out between February and December 2016 described how, over that time, the percentage of Venezuelans who ate three times per day dropped from 69.5 per cent to 34.3 per cent; and those who ate just once a day rose from 4.8 per cent to 19.8 per cent. There was a parallel resurgence in the number of Venezuelans, predominantly children and young men, who rummaged through garbage in search of food or some other product for use or resale. In these circumstances the opposition was able to mobilise large numbers, but still largely limited to its traditional areas of support. It had failed to break into the army, despite repeated attempts to do so, with public calls for a military coup. The situation appeared to be one of a stalemate.

On May Day 2017, hundreds of thousands of supporters of the Bolivarian Revolution marched from three different gathering points to Bolivar Avenue in Caracas. The whole route was teeming with people from early in the morning. Chavismo still had a core of support, which could be mobilised when faced with the whip of counter-revolution. However, it was noticeable that, for the first time for over a decade, a Bolivarian president did not mention socialism on May Day. During his speech, Maduro, announced the convening of a National Constituent Assembly (ANC), which he described as a workers' and communal assembly. The same process was used by Chávez over a decade previously. The MUD and its international supporters responded with a frenzied campaign: "There's been a coup in Venezuela! Maduro has carried out a power-grab!"

The ANC was to be all-powerful, meaning that once it finished its work, the authority of every elected body would be superseded and required renewal, as in the 'mega-election' of 2000. The MUD denounced the move and immediately called for an escalation of protests: for supporters to march to the TSJ with a second march to the CNE. Given the level of violence unleashed on previous opposition marches to these destinations, it was obvious that the government would deploy police to protect them. The opposition strategy was a provocation aimed at creating a scenario of violence, which would be portrayed in the world's media as police repression, to put the government under more pressure at home and internationally. As expected, opposition protesters clashed violently with the police and National Guard, providing an abundance of images for the bourgeois media.

The MUD's economic programme was released to the press: to privatise state-owned companies, to reduce the fiscal deficit by implementing massive cuts in social spending (particularly on education and health), privatisation of social housing, to sack hundreds of thousands of public sector workers, to liberalise prices, greater access to dollars from oil revenue, and the abolition of labour and trade union rights.

Simultaneously, the MUD rank and file were becoming tired, having been demonstrating for sixty days with no obvious results. In certain parts of the country (San Antonio de los Altos in Miranda, and Socopó in Barinas amongst others) there had been well organised, violent riots, in connivance with the local police. In right-wing municipalities, with MUD mayors, the rioters had taken control of urban centres, sometimes for days, where they destroyed public buildings, imposed a shut-down of commercial establishments and replaced the authority of the state. But increasingly, the *guarimbas* were degenerating into gang warfare, taken over by hooligan and criminal elements: those suspected of being Chavista were set upon, stabbed or shot, and even set alight but, in reality, many victims were attacked simply for being *pardo*. By the end of June, the right-wing offensive had left eighty-five people dead but had failed to achieve any of its aims. Importantly, it had not provoked any public fissures within the Armed Forces.

While bitterly opposed to the MUD, many Chavistas were deeply sceptical of the proposed ANC and believed rank and file participation would be more form than substance. The experience of the Congress of the Fatherland was an all-too-recent memory. The issues for discussion by the ANC were certainly not radical, but more of the same. Venezuela was to build a 'post-oil' economy that worked for all, and with all the different property forms that existed, implying the maintenance of a capitalist economy. Nevertheless, the call for the ANC woke sections of the Chavista vanguard, who wanted to elect deputies to the ANC to represent the rank and file and who would propose a programme of revolutionary demands. The government called the ANC elections for 30 July, in what marked a major test of its popular support.

The practice of the PSUV bureaucracy of appointing candidates, at all levels, without reference to the rank and file members was universally detested. So, the announcement that the ANC elections would not take place on the basis of lists prepared by the party machine was welcomed. In a short space of time a number of Chavista left lists were being circulated. The programmes proposed by these different groupings all reflected a deep-seated hatred of the bureaucracy and reformism, and a desire to move forward, to take power. But there was little co-ordination between them. In addition, their demands shared a common weakness – although containing anti-capitalist and anti-bureaucratic language, there was little clear understanding of the need to expropriate the means of production under democratic workers' control, almost certainly because of the way in which workers' control had been subverted by the PSUV.

At the beginning of the campaign these initiatives were accompanied by large meetings in neighbourhoods and workplaces. But slowly and surely, the bureaucratic machinery of the PSUV imposed itself. The practicalities of the process, such as there being only a very short time to get organised and collect supporting signatures, made it very difficult for anyone outside the apparatus to actually become a candidate.

18.1) OPPOSITION AND THE 'SOVEREIGN CONSULTATION'

In late June, the MUD's more violent activities appeared to have regained some momentum. Their road blocks were proving more effective. There had been severe rioting in Maracay and Aragua, with over sixty shops looted, a number of official buildings, including the PSUV offices, ransacked and one member of the National Guard shot dead. These were not peaceful pro-democracy protests, but terrorist attacks combined with appeals to the army to effect a coup.

On 28 June, opposition politicians, in a 'state of disobedience' called on their supporters to extend the road blocks. What other country in the world would allow protesters to set up and maintain road blocks across its motorways? How would London, Madrid or Washington react to a para-military assault on government buildings? What would be the response of Berlin or Paris if gangs descended on urban areas and stabbed, shot and set light to people?

On Sunday 16 July, 2017, the opposition held a 'sovereign consultation'. Voting booths were placed all over the country so that people could give their opinions on three issues: 1. Was Maduro's call for a National Constituent Assembly legitimate? 2. Should the MUD reject and not recognise the ANC? and 3. Should the armed forces mutiny, remove the government and form a 'government of national unity'? To complement the consultation, the opposition announced that 16 July was "zero hour" after which their supporters would be "stepping up the pressure" and using "even harsher actions", including setting up permanent road blocks until the "fall of the dictatorship".

The parallel with the attempted coup of April 2002 was obvious: especially the suggestion that the armed forces remove the president and establish a 'government of national unity'. This time, however, the opposition was attempting to give its moves a sense of legitimacy. On the day, the MUD was able to mobilise large numbers of people, and there were queues at many of their polling stations. However, the figures issued were questionable. In Catia for instance (Parroquia Sucre of Libertador council), the electoral register contained over 290,000 names, of which thirty-nine per cent (91,000) had previously voted for the MUD. This area had only one polling station. Even if the opposition had only their own supporters voting that would be less than half a second per person per vote! In that half a second every voter had to have their details checked against the electoral register, receive a ballot paper, fill it in and put it in the ballot box. Nor was there any restriction on how many times an individual could vote. Chavistas, on the look-out for multiple voting, were able to produce video evidence of multiple voting in, at least, the right-wing stronghold of Chacao. The ballots and registers were burned after the count to ensure that whatever result was announced it could not be checked.

The *New York Times* of 16 July reported that:

> More than 98% of voters sided with the MUD in answering three yes-or-no questions drafted with the aim of weakening Mr. Maduro's legitimacy days before his constituent assembly is expected to convene.

To their shame, across the political spectrum, the western media almost entirely agreed on the same narrative. So poor was their checking of the facts, that the main photo used to show crowds queuing to vote was, in fact, a photo of Chavistas queuing to vote in support of Maduro's call for the ANC. The declared result of the opposition consultation was that 7,186,170 people had participated, a figure which, even if true, was less than their own candidate had received in the presidential election and fell well short of the 7,587,579 votes for Maduro.

The government decided to have a dry run on that very same Sunday to show Chavista support for the ANC. The two sets of voting were in parallel though, of course, it was possible to vote in both. Almost entirely ignored in the western press, was the massive turn out in support of Maduro. The queues outside the official CNE polling stations were massive throughout the country, even in cities such as Barquisimeto, Valencia, and Mérida where the opposition was very strong, and its thugs had been terrorising the streets for over three months.

The opposition did not expect this and they were unsettled. The consultation had backfired and threw the opposition leaders into a state of indecision on how to proceed. Their rhetoric before 16 July had been fiery, they had planned for a result so positive that the government would not last until the 30 July ANC elections. As the campaign for the ANC elections progressed, PSUV Minister, Pérez Abad, backed by so-called 'patriotic businessmen' such as Oscar Schemel (candidate for the business section of the ANC), appealed to the MUD for peace and dialogue, and advocated the ANC should "strengthen private property rights" by the privatisation of expropriated companies.

On 30 July, the vote for the ANC was held. The opposition abstained. However, the government was worried about the outcome, as all polls were predicting a turnout so low the vote would be a farce. It called on all its employees to make a point of voting and to encourage all their friends, neighbours and colleagues to vote. There may be some truth in claims that workers' jobs would be under threat if they did not vote. The PSUV party machine also applied a great deal of pressure on its Chavista base in order to mobilise it into the voting booths. Party cadres used social benefits such as the CLAP (government provided food parcels), special pensions such as 'mothers of the *barrio*' and the '*chamba juvenil*' plan, to pressurise recipients to go out and vote. The attitude of the party tops was very reminiscent of the old '*Adeco*' style of doing politics, in that the working masses and poor were bought with a mix of food bags and social benefits along with threats of the suspension of those benefits. On the day, the Chavista vote rallied and

8,089,230 voted – not too different from the turnout for the dry run on 16 July. All 545 seats went to the PSUV and its supporters.

The other side of the coin was the deadly violence of opposition supporters aimed at preventing the election. The Public Prosecutor listed ten deaths of Chavistas and National Guard officers, assassinated on the eve of the election or on Election Day. Over the course of the day, 200 voting stations across the country were attacked by opposition militants and "large-scale explosive devices" were exploded near other polling stations.[133]

19) THE 'ADVANCE' OF THE COUNTER-REVOLUTION

On Tuesday 8 August, 2017, Donald Trump warned: "We have many options for Venezuela. And by the way, I am not going to rule out a military option". Trump cares not a jot about "lives being lost" in Venezuela, a situation he could stop tomorrow by ending US support for the opposition and removing trade sanctions. What he is really concerned about is that, for nearly two decades, Venezuela has been an example of how the revolutionary masses could seize their destinies into their own hands; defy imperialism, the oligarchy, and fight to reorganise society along more democratic and participatory lines. In Venezuela, oil revenues have been used to eliminate illiteracy and provide healthcare for all; how different to the USA.

In Venezuela, the response of the ultra-right to the ANC elections was, throughout August, to launch hit-and-run attacks on working-class neighbourhoods killing several people. But the political landscape of the country had changed; the great majority of the opposition had gone home. From the PSUV point of view, things looked good for the regional elections and the government brought them forward to October, in order to take advantage of the temporary demoralisation of the opposition and the mobilisation achieved on 30 July. However, Maduro's government, while attempting to cuddle up to the capitalists, was economically paralysed. Its belief in the possibility of a deal with the opposition had no foundation in reality, but prevented it from tackling economic sabotage, the lack of food, medicine, etc. Continuing this pro-capitalist policy could only estrange important sectors of the proletarian masses, meaning it placed increasing restrictions on internal party democracy, further transforming the PSUV into an instrument of political control.

It was at this time that the Marxists openly classified Maduro and his supporters at the top of the PSUV and government as "the Mensheviks of our time" whose goal was a popular front with the bourgeoisie. The parallel was

133 Koerner, L., *Venezuela: 10 Dead, 200 Voting Centers Attacked*, VA.com, 1 August, 2017.

drawn between Lenin and Trotsky's call for the Bolsheviks to stand shoulder-to-shoulder with Kerensky against the open counter-revolution in the form of General Kornilov, and the need to defend the PSUV government, by describing the MUD as the modern Kornilov at the gates of Caracas. Lenin and Trotsky understood that the masses, no matter how long it took, had to learn from their experiences before progressing to 'All power to the Soviets'. The Bolsheviks, of course, carried on their own propaganda campaigns for 'Bread, Peace and Land' and 'All power to the Soviets!' against Kerensky even while defending his government.

The overwhelming vote on 30 July, was the result of the millions of workers who knew the MUD would worsen their conditions, and hoped that the PSUV would, finally, tackle galloping inflation and chronic shortage of basic necessities. The result had demoralised and demobilised the opposition rank and file, even the most violent groups. Simultaneously, the PSUV leadership took the victory in the ANC election as an endorsement of its policies, with the result that the campaign for the 2017 regional elections lacked any spark of originality, and was devoid of any measures that were capable of solving the pressing problems of the masses. The campaign was social-democratic and demagogic, full of promises that were forgotten once the candidates were elected.

Most of the candidates were either already establishment figures up for re-election or those parachuted in by the PSUV bureaucracy. In the first category were candidates such as Arias Cárdenas [Zulia state] or Vielma Mora [Tachira] who, in their previous terms of office had clearly governed to enrich the local party bureaucracies and benefit their respective bourgeoisie. In the second case, the party 'changed the face' of the local administration by inserting candidates such as Justo Noguera in Bolívar, and Margaud Godoy in Cojedes. These may have been new candidates, but they were establishment figures.

Once again, on time and in tune, the mass media began to issue opinion polls that showed a secure MUD victory. In October, in the run-up to the election, the average poll rating for MUD was fifty-seven per cent and for the government thirty per cent. On the Election Day, Sunday 15 October, 2017, the PSUV achieved a substantial victory with 5.8 million votes against 5 million for the MUD, whose candidates were elected governors in only five states: Anzoátegui, Nueva Esparta and three border states, Zulia, Táchira and Mérida. Following the expected and customary pattern, as soon as the final count was announced, the MUD declared that it did not recognise the results, but this time, two of its leading contenders Carlos Ocariz and Henry

Falcón, refused to go along with the charade and publicly acknowledged the results in their respective states; the matrix of 'fraud' collapsed.

Despite the brutal deterioration in their living conditions, the working masses had rallied to the PSUV. But the ANC failed to take any decisive action, and the economic crisis worsened with each passing week. The major achievement of the ANC was not any concrete measure it took. It was, as expected, a talking shop, but it served to legitimise Maduro's government and allowed him to bypass the National Assembly. Gradually, the ANC came to dominate the parliamentary processes, accruing for itself powers that were not initially specified.

The regional election victory was a defeat for the forces of counter-revolution but, by itself, did not change the prospect of economic desolation facing the working masses. The atmosphere of triumphalism amongst the Bolivarian leaders did not suggest much likelihood of significant changes in government economic policies over the coming months. Quite the opposite, the bureaucrats again saw the election victory as endorsement of the government's reformist, social-democratic policy of class conciliation.

With the results of the elections announced, President Maduro boasted that Chavismo had "obliterated" the opposition, and loudly declared he would not accept *guarimba* rioters and coup plotters as governors. In the next breath he declared that he was prepared to sign a "dialogue agreement". It turned out that representatives of the government and the MUD had already met in the Dominican Republic for round-table discussions on Venezuela's economic and political problems. Subterfuges of this kind showed that the government was quite incapable of implementing even the most basic measures associated with the bourgeois-democratic revolution: agrarian reform, social justice, and national independence.

The opposition, after much internal discussion, decided to boycott the municipal elections of 10 December, 2017. The official reason given was that elected mayors would have to be sworn in before the ANC, which the MUD considered illegitimate. A much more likely reason was the opposition's deep demoralisation and fear of a landslide defeat, further legitimising the government.

The Bolivarian movement had closed ranks for the regional elections, but the withdrawal of the main opposition parties from the municipal elections opened the door for candidates representing the revolutionary wing of the Bolivarian movement to stand against the official, hand-picked candidates. The tension between the rank and file, revolutionary left of Chavismo and the bureaucrats and reformists who dominated the PSUV party machine and state apparatus burst into the open. The bureaucracy and the state responded by using all sorts of tricks to prevent the local PSUV from endorsing leftists, and to stop candidates from socialist groups and/or parties from standing.

In a number of municipalities, mainly rural, alternative Bolivarian candidates did stand against the PSUV, some standing under the banner of the PCV, or the PPT or the Tupamaros, but all having in common the fact that they represented areas where the communal movement had taken real roots and developed. These were areas where the struggle against the reactionary offensive earlier in the year had a more militant character, with the organisation of self-defence committees and occupation of land belonging to *caudillos*. Some of these areas included occupied factories linked to agricultural production and communes with a history of fighting against the capitalists and landowners, and also against sabotage by local bureaucrats, regional governors as well as government institutions.

The bureaucracy was furious. The CNE was used, quite improperly, to 'weed out' left candidates who might have been successful. In the Simon Planas council in Lara, Ángel Prado, a member of the ANC was told by the CNE that he needed permission to stand. Other high-profile members of the ANC, chosen by the PSUV leadership, were standing as candidates and no obstacles had been put in their way. On 28 November, in an outrageous decision, the ANC denied him permission, the real reason being that, if he had been allowed to stand, he would certainly have won the election. The bureaucracy was mortally afraid of the challenge posed by a candidate who genuinely represented the rank and file of the movement and who stood for revolutionary democracy and no compromise with the capitalist class. Basing himself on the support of the local *campesinos*, Prado insisted he would stand on the PPT ticket. The CNE printed ballot papers in which the PPT was presented as supporting the official PSUV candidate. Despite these manipulations, fifty-seven per cent of the vote went to Prado and only thirty-four per cent for the PSUV. Since Prado's name was not on the ballot paper, the CNE insisted that the winner was the PSUV candidate, Jean Ortiz.

The highest profile case was that of Eduardo Samán, both because of his history and the office for which he was standing – the mayor of Libertador Council, which covers most of the centre of Caracas, and the western working-class and poor districts. Samán was standing against the official PSUV candidate, Erika Farias, who had initially been elected to the PSUV leadership as a left candidate, but was now Chief of Staff for President Maduro. Initially, Samán, known for his fierce opposition to the capitalists, his struggle against racketeering and his defence of workers' control, won the support of the Communist Party, the PPT and the MEP. Under pressure, the MEP later withdrew its support but the PCV and PPT stood firm. The CNE attempted to block Samán's registration, but public pressure finally got his candidature allowed. The CNE then resorted to another trick. As both the PPT and the PCV had already pre-emptively registered their candidates, the CNE argued that the names on the ballot box next to those party logos could not be changed. Therefore, Samán's name would not appear on the ballot paper. This was a complete scandal because there was no real reason why his name could not appear next to the PCV and PPT logos; it was a stratagem to create confusion.

From the bureaucratic perspective, there was more danger in Samán winning than the MUD, because he would be in a position to promote an alternative, socialist policy for government. Samán represented the struggle against the black market, the speculators, the capitalists and multinational companies, the struggle for accountability within the movement, for revolutionary democracy and workers' control. It was right and proper under the specific circumstances of there being no opposition candidate, for Marxists and revolutionaries to support his candidature. With voters having to write in his name, Samán received 6.6 per cent of the vote against sixty-six per cent for the official Chavista candidate. Nevertheless, his campaign managed to pull together into a joint effort, most of the revolutionary left of Chavismo in Caracas.

Samán later denounced a boycott of his candidature in the state media during the election campaign. On 30 November, he was invited to a TV interview in the state-owned ViveTV and interviewed for half an hour in a morning talk show. The channel's director, press officer and co-ordinator were fired as a direct result of this interview.

The PSUV won 308 out of 335 local councils and twenty-three out twenty-five state capitals. The opposition largely boycotted the election, but did stand for, and win, two significant local councils – San Cristobal, the capital of Táchira, and Libertador, the capital of Mérida. After the defeat of their violent attempt to overthrow the government in the first half of the year, their strategic defeat with the ANC, and their electoral defeats at the end of the year, the opposition ended 2017 fractured, with their ranks demoralised and without a clear strategy.

Open conflicts and tensions within Chavismo, though limited to a minority of municipalities, revealed the lengths to which the PSUV and state bureaucracy would go to squash potential challengers from the left of the movement. The methods used against these candidates were very similar to those used during the Fourth Republic: bureaucratic manoeuvres, political patronage, intimidation and threats, media blackout, the use of state resources to cajole people to vote for the 'right' candidate, and so on.

It also showed a widespread mood of discontent amongst the Bolivarian rank and file against the reformists leading the party and the state bureaucracies. This was compounded by the severe economic crisis and the sight of the government making all sorts of concessions to the capitalists. The leftist movement was embryonic, disorganised and scattered, but the campaign for leftist candidates in the municipal elections and then the struggle to defend their victories provided a focal point around which the left Chavismo could organise.

20) PRESIDENTIAL ELECTIONS AND ECONOMIC CRISES

At the end of 2017, the severe economic crisis forced the government to renegotiate its foreign debt to avoid default. Maduro still appeared to believe that his policies were capable of controlling and containing the opposition. But he also needed to be seen to respond, in some ways, to the criticisms raised by his own rank and file. An offensive against corruption in the PDVSA saw dozens of high-ranking officials arrested and charged including Rafael Ramirez, oil minister from 2002 to 2014, head of the PDVSA between 2004 and 2014. The public prosecutor talked of US$4.8 billion lost from the public purse.

The Central Bank had been printing money so that the government could pay staff Christmas bonuses ahead of the 10 December municipal elections. This added substantially to a doubling of the money supply in the two months starting with October. Such irresponsible moves made to retain power, undermined the remaining gains of the revolution. The policies of the Maduro government continued to do little other than prepare the way for the return of the oligarchy.

Events in 2017 showed that, despite everything the masses had endured, there remained a healthy class instinct of rejecting the right-wing opposition's attempts to overthrow the government. This instinct is cynically used by the bureaucracy to keep itself in power.

In such a situation, any challenge from the left must take place within the framework of the Bolivarian Revolution. Anything else would be a sectarian mistake that would allow the bureaucracy to depict the leftists as part of the opposition, discrediting them in the eyes of the masses. A revolutionary opposition coming from within the rank and file could have as its central theme reclaiming the revolutionary content of Chavismo by putting meat on the bones of Chávez' calls to action: for rank and file democratic participation, accountability of the leadership, radical land reform and against capitalism.

Since Maduro came to office, three themes can be discerned in the government's apparently haphazard and chaotic actions: the transformation of the PSUV into an instrument of political control, attempts to revive foreign investment in extractive industries, and increased use of authoritarian measures.

When Chávez announced the PSUV, the party was supposed to represent a substantial step towards popular participatory democracy as enshrined in the 2003 constitution. Chávez intended the PSUV to be an open, democratic party that would hold both government and state accountable. What emerged, however, was the very opposite: a top-down, authoritarian structure that rigidly controlled dissent and debate. The degree of control exerted over the *barrios* and other poor communities increased as the economic sabotage of the oligarchs bit deeper. For example, the government developed a programme to bring food parcels to poor homes at guaranteed official prices, but the PSUV took over the distribution and used the programme to ensure political loyalty at election times. The system, despite good intentions, was under the control of the party machine and riddled with corruption. Since then, a so-called Fatherland Card (*carnet de la patria*) has been introduced. This is state-issued and gives access to pensions, disability benefits, etc., and its use has been similarly exploited.

Maduro's solution to the massive hole in the state budget is opening up to foreign investment of the Arco Minero, Venezuela's Amazon region, which holds a cornucopia of minerals, oil, and gas and, incidentally, is also the country's principal source of freshwater. This is a development rejected by Chávez due to environmental concerns, and in recognition of indigenous communities' human and territorial rights.

The Venezuelan Presidential elections on 20 May 2018 were yet one more episode in a long saga of imperialist aggression, economic crisis and the deterioration of living conditions for the working class and poor. Re-elected, Maduro continued his policy of making concessions and appeals to the capitalists. The mood of the Chavista rank and file is increasingly angry and critical of the PSUV leadership. Without the subsidised food parcels, and migration to surrounding countries, the situation would have already generated to a social explosion.

Washington and Brussels have been joined by the Organisation of American States, in declaring that the elections were not 'legitimate'. Maduro was re-elected with 6,248,864 votes on a 46.07 per cent turnout. His nearest rival, opposition candidate Henri Falcón, received 1,927,958 votes. The MUD, in its majority, called for abstention and so, in opposition strongholds, Falcón received far fewer votes than he expected. The working class and *campesinos* voted overwhelmingly for Maduro, but the votes cast show that a section of those who traditionally voted for Chávez and supported Maduro in

2013, stayed home because of the perception that the government is unable or unwilling to take the necessary measures to deal with the economic crisis.

The imperialists, under the fig-leaf of 'concern for democracy' and the 'humanitarian crisis' increased their diplomatic pressure, added more sanctions and called for a coup. The Trump administration was quick to tighten the sanctions against Venezuela, even before the final results of the election had been announced. Existing sanctions, decreed by Trump in August 2017 on the basis of an Obama-signed Executive Order, as well as targeting high-ranking officials in the Venezuelan state, make it illegal to renegotiate Venezuelan-issued debt. The new sanctions, announced on 21 May, will bar US companies or citizens "from buying debt or accounts receivable" from the Venezuelan government, including the PDVSA. These sanctions are intended to make it increasingly difficult for Venezuela to access the world's financial system. The hope is that tightening the economic screws will lead to a section of the army deciding it should remove the Maduro government.

Meanwhile, the economic crisis in Venezuela continues its course, aggravated by a serious deterioration of all infrastructure as a result of years of bureaucratic mismanagement and corruption, the lack of funds for investment, maintenance and repairs, and now the exodus of workers migrating to other countries, fleeing the collapse in the purchasing power of wages, and the regular electricity outages and water cut-offs, which now affect millions of people on a regular basis. As a result, areas of the capital go without water for days or weeks. People have to resort to all sorts of tricks to wash themselves and their clothes and to get water for drinking and cooking.

Inflation, for which there are no official figures, has become hyperinflation, pulverising the purchasing power of wages. In the first four months of 2018 the price of chicken increased by over 500 per cent, and by mid-summer the increase was 1,500 per cent. Meanwhile, the integral wage (minimum wage plus food tickets) increased by just 220 per cent in the same period. At the beginning of the year the minimum wage would buy 4.4 kg of chicken, by mid-summer it bought just over half a kilo.

The only reason the economic crisis has not precipitated a social explosion is its alleviation by factors such as the system of subsidised food parcels provided by the government's Local Provision and Production Committees (CLAPs), which, at least in the capital region, reach a large proportion of the population; and regular bonuses granted by the government to different groups of the population (workers in general, families, mothers, the youth). There have been eleven such bonuses between January and July in 2018.

Neither CLAPs nor bonuses are a real solution, but they provide a welcome relief from the brutal impact of the crisis. The problem is that what these measures amount to is the government printing money in order to provide subsidies. This only adds to the massive fiscal deficit, which amounts to between fifteen and twenty per cent of GDP (again, no official figures are available). There is no way this can continue in the long term, because many of the products making up the CLAP parcels are imported, and thus are vulnerable to sanctions. But the importance of these parcels and bonuses should not be underrated, it is these which secure the turn out for the PSUV because the MUD is pledged to end them.

Another escape valve is migration. This is a hotly-contested issue and it is clear that hundreds-of-thousands of Venezuelans, mainly youth, have left the country in search of jobs abroad, and are maintaining their families through remittances. A few years ago, this was a phenomenon affecting mainly middle-and-upper-class families, and the destination was Europe and the USA. Now there are growing numbers of youth from working-class families who leave for Bolivia, Colombia, Ecuador, Mexico and Peru, where they are brutally exploited. Considering the minimum wage in Venezuela is the equivalent (on the black market) to US$1.25, the money these migrants send back enables their families to survive.

This is not to say that everyone in Venezuela is suffering from the impact of the economic crisis, some are actually benefiting. There are those who receive hard currency to pay for imports. They and the government officials in charge of the system, have made massive fortunes via the black market. Despite government attempts, the dollar black market continues to exist and is run by a small number of increasingly wealthy people.

The government's response to the growing crisis has been to resume its policy of concessions and appeals to both the opposition and the capitalists. Soon after the presidential election, Maduro held a high-profile meeting with bankers at which he agreed, amongst other things, to delay the introduction of a new currency, which gave black marketeers and speculators time to launder their ill-gotten gains. This meeting enraged the Chavista rank and file. It was not only the fact that, once again, the government was prepared to do deals with those it accuses of being responsible for the economic war, but also the arrogant way in which the president of the Banking Association demanded concessions from Maduro, on live TV, and the way Maduro acquiesced.

To add insult to injury, the TSJ decided to release a number of those jailed for their involvement in the opposition's violent offensives of 2014 and 2017. These unrepentant thugs were responsible for the deaths of many loyal Chavistas. A number of directors of Venezuela's leading private bank, Banesco, were released separately. They had been arrested just prior to the elections, accused of being part of the economic war against the Venezuelan economy. The question asked was: were they arrested and jailed as a stunt to give the appearance that the government was being tough on capitalists?

Meanwhile, the conflict in the countryside continues between *comuneros* fighting the *latifundia* and a coalition of state officials, local judges, and police officials who have launched a broad offensive to reverse the gains of agrarian reform. Increasingly, peasant communes were expelled from land they were occupying legally, and at least two leading *campesinos* were executed on orders from landowners. A few days after the election, the spokesperson of the *El Maizal* commune, Angel Prado, and two other *comunero* leaders were illegally detained by police officers, accused of purchasing products they need for sowing from illegal sources on the black market. They replied that the official state-owned company, Agropatria, was refusing to sell the products to them legally and that, in fact, it was the managers at this company (expropriated under Chávez) who were the black market! The peasant leaders were eventually released, but the countryside is quickly becoming a battlefield between revolution and counter-revolution, and in most cases the state apparatus is, either by action or omission, on the side of counter-revolution.

The re-election of Maduro on 20 May, has not solved anything; it may have postponed the oligarchy's return to power, but the government's policies prepare the conditions for defeat. However, events in 2017/18 showed that, despite everything they had endured, there remains a healthy class instinct of rejecting the opposition's attempts to overthrow the PSUV government and the remaining gains of the Revolution.

A small but significant indication of a growing mood amongst Chavista activists, a video containing extracts from a speech by Chávez during his first swearing-in, in February 1999, has gone viral. In a hard-hitting statement, which fits the situation today like a glove, he says: "to look for consensus with those who oppose the changes that are necessary is betrayal". He could be responding to Maduro's public statements made after 20 May. At the beginning of August, there was a terrorist attempt on Maduro's life while he was presiding at a military parade in the centre of Caracas. This confirmed that, within the military, oligarchy and state apparatus there still exists a current that is prepared to overthrow the elected government through a coup.

On 17 August, 2018, Maduro announced an economic plan to deal with the economic crisis, including launching a new currency,[134] recognising the fact that some government policies have played a role in exacerbating hyperinflation.

---

134 Dobson, P., *Venezuela Rolls out New Currency amid General Economic Overhaul,* VA.com 20 August, 2018.

The government *de facto* adopted the black-market exchange rate for the dollar (6 million *Bolívar Fuerte*) as the basis for the new currency, *Bolívar Soberano* (BsS), which will eliminate five zeros from prices. Turkey did much the same thing in 2005, when it reduced the value of the lira by a factor of one million. For Venezuelans, this has meant a devaluation of 95.85 per cent from the previous official exchange rate. Maduro said the BsS would be anchored to the Petro, the Venezuelan state-backed crypto-currency. In turn, the price of the Petro is linked to the price of a barrel of oil, which stands at US$60. Maduro also recognised that inorganic money had been issued by the government in order to pay for the budget deficit and that this would have to end. He announced that, from now on, there would be zero fiscal deficit. Value Added Tax would increase from twelve per cent to sixteen per cent. Subsidies on fuel phased out over time.

In essence, these measures amount to an adjustment programme aimed at recovering confidence in the currency and stopping its precipitous devaluation. However, these measures are accompanied by others aimed at easing the pain they will inflict on working people and the poor. The minimum wage, which was around US$1 at black market exchange rates, will be increased to 1,800 BsS, the equivalent to US$30 in the new exchange rate. However, while wages are to be paid in BsS, the minimum wage will be set at half a Petro (US$30). The idea is that, even if the BsS devalues, the wages will keep their purchasing power. Increasing the minimum wage from US$1 to US$30 appears a massive enhancement, but does little to recover the purchasing power of wages if we remember that, on Maduro's election in 2013, the minimum wage was US$325 at the official exchange rate (US$100 at the black-market rate).

Maduro also announced that the state will cover the differential in wages with the new rate for all private sector small- and medium-size companies for ninety days; and pay around 10 million people a bonus of 600 BsS. The state is promising to pay for all this, and, at the same time, to balance its books by increasing taxes on the wealthy and introducing a new system for paying income tax on a weekly basis as opposed to fortnightly. The proposed lifting of subsidies on fuel is aimed at decreasing government expenditure and saving the huge amounts of money lost through the smuggling of heavily-subsidised Venezuelan fuel into Colombia, where it is sold at market price. The universal fuel subsidy is to be replaced by targeted subsidies to prevent contraband. In addition, regulated prices have been introduced for twenty-five basic food products, as agreed with the main private sector suppliers. The increased cost of public transport already represents a substantial increase in the cost of living: in the case of the Caracas Metro, the new fare will be 0.5

BsS (it had been free for over a year), while bus fares will go up tenfold from 0.1 BsS to one BsS.

The programme seems to be modelled on the 1994 *Plan Real* applied in Brazil to stabilise the economy. However, in Brazil the plan 'worked' (from the point of view of the ruling class) because of increasing fiscal revenues obtained by the wholesale privatisation of public assets plus a steep hike in interest rates to attract foreign investment. Neither of these measures has been proposed in Venezuela. It is thus difficult to see how the Venezuelan state can achieve both its aims simultaneously: 'fiscal discipline' and higher real wages, particularly when oil production was only 1.28 million barrels per day in July (down from a peak of 3 million).

The plan cannot solve any of the basic and acute problems facing the Venezuelan economy – a crisis with only two possible outcomes. One is the implementation of a capitalist, monetarist adjustment programme, lifting all controls and restrictions on the normal functioning of the 'free market', and ending any regulation of the prices of basic products and foreign exchange controls. That would be accompanied by a brutal programme of cuts in public spending (including an end to all subsidies and social programmes), privatisation of state assets and severe economic contraction. In order to create a 'business-friendly' environment, trade union and labour protection laws would be scrapped. On such a basis there could be a certain stabilisation of the economy with the workers and poor made to pay the price of the crisis.

In the current political climate in Venezuela, the implementation of these measures would meet fierce resistance by sections of the workers, peasants and poor, and so it would require restricting democratic rights and the repression of social movements and their organisations. If the government attempted to fully implement such a programme, the Bolivarian movement would split down the middle, with a clear break between its openly capitalist wing, and all those defending, to one degree or another, the revolutionary legacy of Chavismo.

The other solution to the crisis is a revolutionary one: taking over the means of production under democratic workers' control to resolve the crisis in the interests of working people. From the standpoint of the workers and the poor, the enactment of a genuine revolutionary programme is the only acceptable solution. Such a programme must be compiled by those on the spot, but would likely include:

- State monopoly on foreign trade, so that no more dollars are handed over to the bourgeoisie.

- A worker's audit of preferential dollar allocations over the last fifteen years. Confiscation of properties and jail for all those involved in theft and mismanagement (capitalists and bureaucrats).

- Nationalisation and centralisation of banking and finance companies so that all their resources are put to the service of a rational plan of production, under democratic workers' control.

- The creation of socialist workers' councils in every factory and workplace, expropriation of large industries, under workers' control.

- Nationalisation under workers' control of all companies involved in hoarding, speculation and the black market.

- Expropriation of the *latifundios* under *campesino* control organised in communes. Peasant communes to be given credit for the purchase of seeds, fertilisers, machinery and so forth.

- Nationalisation of all food production, processing and distribution under the democratic control of peasant communes, workers, and consumers.

- Revolutionary provisioning committees in every neighbourhood with powers to control and organise the distribution of food.

- Suspension of all payments of the foreign debt. Imports of basic food and medicines to be prioritised.

- Internationalist appeal to the workers and peasants of Latin America and the world to come to the aid and defence of the Venezuelan revolution against imperialist intervention.

A revolutionary solution to the crisis is also one which recognises the basic fact that capitalism cannot be persuaded to act 'patriotically' or for the 'general good'. The Venezuelan national bourgeoisie have no interest in advancing those national democratic tasks still outstanding; rather, they remain tied to US imperialism and demand the reversal of the remaining gains of the Bolivarian Revolution. In this, they confirm a basic premise of the theory of permanent revolution.

The reformists and bureaucrats will argue that such a programme is utopian and cannot be implemented. They will say that the Venezuelan working class is not strong enough or has too low a level of consciousness. The truth is that the programme of the reformists in the leadership of the Bolivarian movement is the one which has proven to be completely utopian. Venezuela has seen huge amounts of money spent on social programs, and there have been countless attempts to regulate a capitalist 'mixed economy' in order to protect the interests of working people. They have led directly to the present economic collapse (a fall in GDP of nearly fifty per cent since 2013). As for the consciousness and strength of the working class, this could not have been higher. At all decisive junctures the working class and the poor have responded, showing a fine class instinct and a consciousness much higher than that of any of the bureaucrats which dominate the ministries and the leading echelons of the Bolivarian movement.

In April 2002 it was the poorest of the poor who came down from the *barrios* and defeated the US-backed military coup. From December 2002-January 2003 it was the workers, particularly those in the oil industry, who defeated the bosses lock-out by implementing workers' control. Later they developed the workers' control movement, taking over abandoned factories and running state-owned enterprises under one form or another of workers' management. When Chávez made a call to struggle for socialism they responded in their millions by joining the PSUV. Whenever there has been a threat by imperialism and reaction, the workers and the poor have come out in their hundreds of thousands, in the streets and on the barricades. The Venezuelan working class cannot be faulted if the revolution has ended in a cul-de-sac.

What has been missing is a clear revolutionary leadership, which could have led to victory by expropriating the oligarchy and smashing the capitalist state. Unfortunately, the self-styled Trotskyists in leadership positions in the UNT have wasted opportunity after opportunity for the last twenty years. Their political position has been simultaneously opportunist and sectarian: opportunist in the support they gave some employers against striking workers, and sectarian in holding back UNT support for the wave of factory occupations that took place in response to the calls from Chávez.

President Chávez himself started from a position where he honestly wanted to cleanse Venezuelan politics and use the oil revenue for the benefit of the majority. He gradually came to understand that this could only be done through the struggle for socialism. However, he was not a Marxist and had no clear idea of how to implement this. Many times, he talked about socialism, but his speeches were mostly left at the level of words. He consistently failed to take action against those reformists and bureaucrats in the PSUV, the state machine or the nationalised industries who openly sabotaged his proposals. By his end he was painfully aware of this, and in his last speeches he stressed the idea, in a confused way, that the revolution had to move towards a socialist economy and the smashing of the bourgeois state.

The key task for revolutionaries in Venezuela today is precisely the preparation of that one factor, which was missing all of these years: a revolutionary leadership with a clear socialist programme. Amongst the revolutionary elements of Chavismo there is a growing critical mood and realisation that the obstacles to be overcome are not only the oligarchy and imperialism but also the reformists and bureaucrats who have led the movement to a disastrous dead end. It is from these forces and through a process of political clarification, that a new and necessary leadership can emerge.

INDEX

LIST OF TITLES BY
WELLRED BOOKS

Wellred Books is a UK-based international publishing house and bookshop, specialising in works of Marxist theory. A sister publisher and bookseller is based in the USA.

Among the titles published by Wellred Books are:

Anti-Dühring, Friedrich Engels
Bolshevism: The Road to Revolution, Alan Woods
China: From Permanent Revolution to Counter-Revolution, John Roberts
Dialectics of Nature, Frederick Engels
Germany: From Revolution to Counter-Revolution, Rob Sewell
Germany 1918-1933: Socialism or Barbarism, Rob Sewell
History of British Trotskyism, Ted Grant
In Defence of Marxism, Leon Trotsky
In the Cause of Labour, Rob Sewell
Lenin and Trotsky: What They Really Stood For, Alan Woods and Ted Grant
Lenin, Trotsky and the Theory of the Permanent Revolution, John Roberts
Marxism and Anarchism, Various authors
Marxism and the USA, Alan Woods
My Life, Leon Trotsky
Not Guilty, Dewey Commission Report
Permanent Revolution in Latin America, John Roberts and Jorge Martin
Reason in Revolt, Alan Woods and Ted Grant
Reformism or Revolution, Alan Woods
Revolution and Counter-Revolution in Spain, Felix Morrow
Russia: From Revolution to Counter-Revolution, Ted Grant
Stalin, Leon Trotsky
Ted Grant: The Permanent Revolutionary, Alan Woods
Ted Grant Writings: Volumes One and Two, Ted Grant

Thawra hatta'l nasr! - Revolution until Victory! Alan Woods and others
The Classics of Marxism: Volume One and Two, by various authors
The History of the Russian Revolution: Volumes One to Three, Leon Trotsky
The History of the Russian Revolution to Brest-Litovsk, Leon Trotsky
The Ideas of Karl Marx, Alan Woods
The Permanent Revolution and Results & Prospects, Leon Trotsky
The Revolution Betrayed, Leon Trotsky
What Is Marxism?, Rob Sewell and Alan Woods
What is to be done?, Vladimir Lenin

To order any of these titles or for more information about Wellred Books, visit wellredbooks.net, email books@wellredbooks.net or write to Wellred Books, PO Box 50525, London E14 6WG, United Kingdom.

Lightning Source UK Ltd.
Milton Keynes UK
UKHW020640280820
368978UK00009B/399